1534
Five Books of Moses
By
William Tyndale

Copyright 2009
ISBN
978-1-61898-029-8
Reformed Church Publications
P.O Box 171
Zeeland, MI 49464

Table of Contents

Title Page	1
To the Reader	2
Aprologe	7
Genesis	15
Aprologe to Exodus	159
Exodus	171
Aprologe to Leuiticus	287
Leuiticus	299
Aprologe to Numeri	383
Numeri	399
Aprologe Deuteronomye	515
Deuteronomye	523

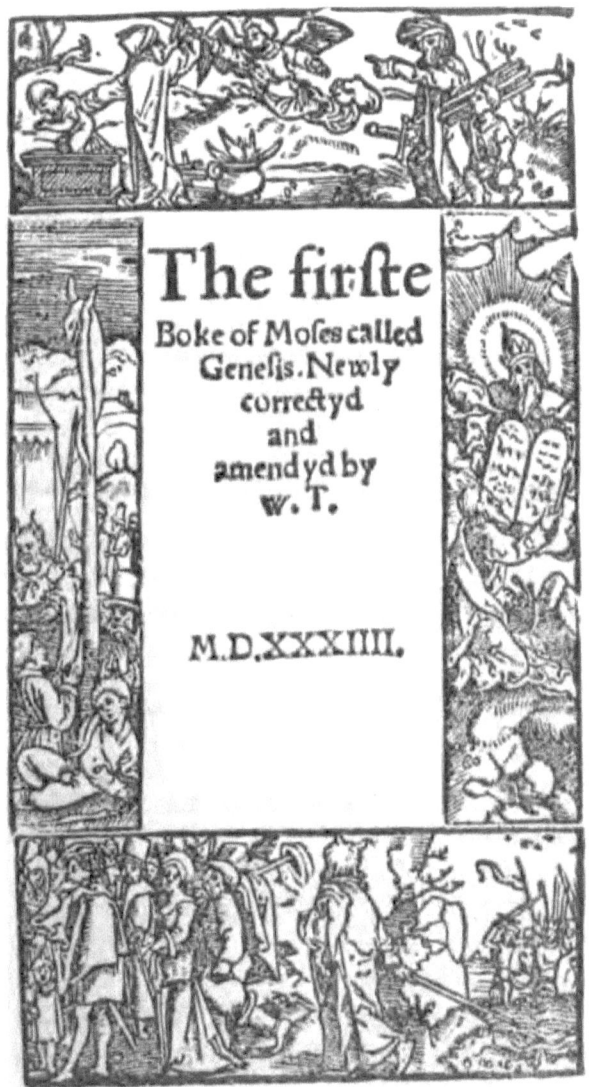

The firste

Boke of Moses called
Genesis. Newly
correctyd
and
amendyd by
W. T.

M.D.XXXIIII.

ABBREVIATIONS.

ON THE SIDE MARGIN.

𝔐. ℭ. 𝔖. denotes the Chapter Summaries in *Matthew's Bible*

IN THE LOWER MARGIN.

𝔐. denotes the Text, 𝔐. 𝔐. N. the Marginal Notes, in *Matthew's Bible*, 1537.

𝔏. denotes the Text, 𝔏. 𝔐. N. the Marginal Notes, in Luther's *Das Alte Teſtament*, 1523.

𝔙. denotes the Text of the Vulgate in the *Biblia* of Stephanus, 1528.

The beginning of the *recto* of Tyndale's folio is indicated thus: [Fo. I.], the beginning of the *verso* by the mark .𝔓.

A dash over a vowel denotes that *n* or *m* should be supplied; *e. g.*, ī, is the contraction of *in*, ād, of *and*, Adā, of *Adam*, &c.; ẙ denotes *the*, and ẙ, that.

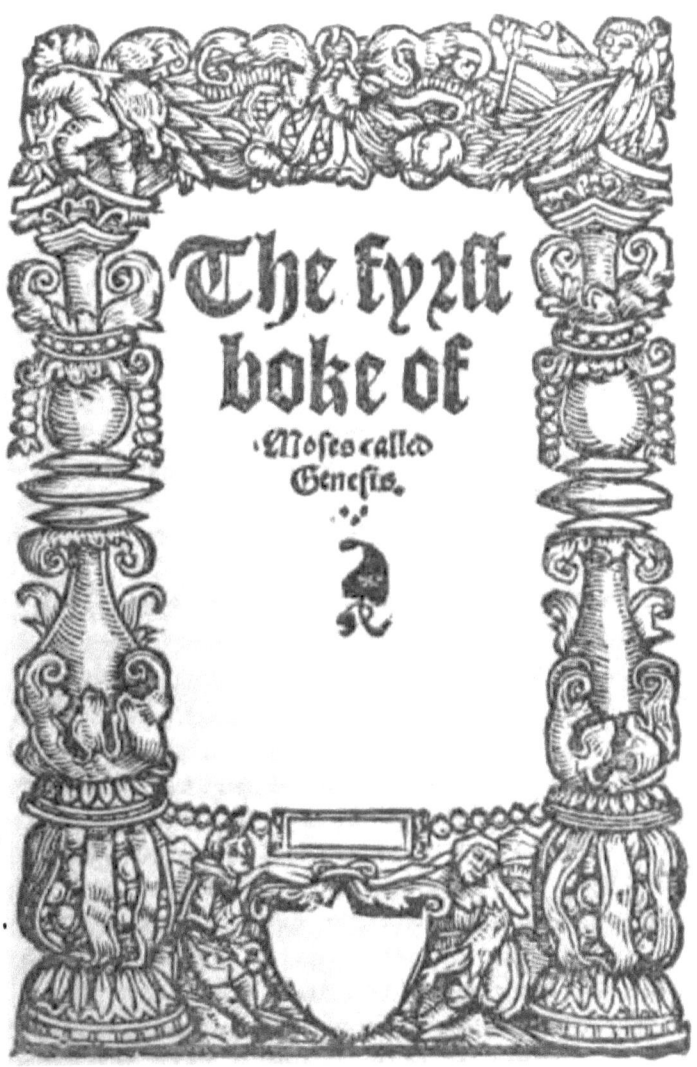

The fyrst boke of Moses called Genesis.

*W. T. To the Reader.

WHEN I had tranflated the newe teftament, I added a piftle vnto the latter ende, In which I defyred them ẏ were learned to amend if ought were founde amyffe. But
5 oure malicious and wylye hypocrytes which are fo ftubburne and hard herted in their weked abhominaciōs that it is not poffible for them to amend any thinge atall (as we fee by dayly experience, when their both lyvinges and doinges are rebuked with the
10 trouth) faye, fome of them that it is impoffible to tranflate the fcripture In to Englifh, fome that it is not lawfull for the laye people to haue it in their mother tonge, fome, that it wold make them all heretykes, as it wold no doute from many thinges which
15 they of longe tyme haue falfly taught, ād that is the whole caufe wherfore they forbyd it, though they other clokes pretende. And fome or rather every one, faye that it wold make them ryfe ageynft the kinge, whom they them felves (vnto their damnatyō) never yet obeyed.
20 And lefte the temporall rulars fhuld fee their falfehod, if the fcripture cam to light, caufeth them fo to lye.

And as for my tranflatiō in which they afferme vnto the laye people (as I haue hearde faye .P. to be I wotte not how many thoufande herefyes, fo that it cā
25 not be mēded or correcte, they haue yet taken fo greate payne to examyne it, & to compare it vnto that they wold fayne haue it and to their awne imaginations and iugglinge termes, and to haue fome what to rayle at, and vnder that cloke to blafpheme

---

* This entire prologe "W. T. To the Reader," is not in the Bristol copy of the edition of 1534.

the treuth, that they myght with as litle laboure (as
I fuppofe) haue tranflated the mofte parte of the bible.
For they which in tymes pafte were wont to loke on
no more fcripture then they founde in their duns or
foch like develyfh doctryne, haue yet now fo narowlye
loked on my tranflatyon, that there is not fo moch as
one I therin if it lacke a tytle over his hed, but they
haue noted it, and nombre it vnto the ignorant people
for an herefy. Finallye in this they be all agreed, to
dryve you from the knowlege of the fcripture, & that
ye fhall not haue the texte therof in the mother tonge,
and to kepe the world ftyll in darkeneffe, to thentent
they might fitt in the confciences of the people, thorow
vayne fuperftition and falfe doctrine, to fatiffye their
fylthy luftes, their proude ambition, and vnfatiable
covetuoufnes, and to exalte their awne honoure aboue
kinge & emperoure, yee & aboue god him filfe

⁋ A thoufand bokes had they lever to be put forth
agenfte their abhominable doynges and doctrine, then
that the fcripture fhulde come to light. For as longe
as they maye kepe that doune, they will fo darken the
ryght way with the .P. mifte of their fophiftrye, and fo
tangle the that ether rebuke or defpyfe their abhomin-
ations with argumentes of philofophye & with wordly
fymylitudes and apparent reafons of naturall wifdom.
And with wreftinge the fcripture unto their awne pur-
pofe clene contrarye unto ỹ proceffe, order and meaninge of the texte, and fo delude them in defcantynge
vppon it with alligoryes, and amafe the expoundinge
it in manye fenfes before the vnlerned laye people,
(when it hath but one fymple litterall fenfe whofe
light the owles cā not abyde) that though thou feale
in thyne harte and arte fure how that all is falfe ỹ they
faye, yet coudefte thou not folve their fotle rydles.

⁋ Which thinge onlye moved me to tranflate the
new teftament. Becaufe I had perceaved by expery-
ence, how that it was impoffible to ftablyfh the laye
people in any truth, excepte ỹ fcripture were playnly
layde before their eyes in their mother tonge, that they
might fe the proceffe, ordre and meaninge of the texte:
for els what fo ever truth is taught them, thefe ennymyes

of all truth qwench it ageyne, partly with the smoke of
their bottomlesse pytte wherof thou readest apocalipsis
ix. that is, with apparent reasons of sophistrye & tradi-
tions of their awne makynge, founded with out grounde
of scripture, and partely in iugglinge with the texte, expoundinge it in soch a sense as is impossi- .P. ble to
gether of the texte, if thou see the processe ordre and
meaninge therof.

⁋ And even in the bisshope of londons house I en-
tended to have done it. For when I was so turmoyled
in the contre where I was that I coude no lenger there
dwell (the processe wherof were to longe here to re-
herce) I this wyse thought in my silfe, this I suffre because the prestes of the contre be vnlerned, as god it
knoweth there are a full ignorant sorte which haue
sene no more latyn then that they read in their por-
tesses and missales which yet many of them can scacely
read, (excepte it be Albertus de secretis mulierū in
which yet, though they be never so soryly lerned,
they pore day and night and make notes therin and
all to teach the mydwyves as they say, and linwod a
boke of constitutions to gether tithes, mortuaryes,
offeringes, customs, and other pillage, which they
calle, not theirs, but godes parte and the deuty of
holye chirch, to discharge their consciences with all:
for they are bound that they shall not dimynysh, but
encreace all thinge vnto the vttmost of their powers)
and therfore (becaufe they are thus vnlerned thought
I) when they come to gedder to the ale house, which
is their preachinge place, they afferme that my sa-
inges are heresy. And besydes ẏ they adde to of thir
awne heddes which I never spake, as the maner is to
prolonge the tale to shorte .P. the tyme with all, and
accuse me secretly to the chauncelare and other the
bishopes officers, And in deade, when I cam before
the chauncelare, he thretened me grevously, and re-
vyled me and rated me as though I had bene a dogge,
and layd to my charge wherof there coude be none
accuser brought forth, (as their maner is not to bringe
forth the accuser) and yet all the prestes of ẏ contre
were ẏ same daye there. As I this thought the

bishope of london came to my remembrance whom
Erasmus (whose tonge maketh of litle gnattes greate
elephãtes and lifteth upp aboue the starres whosoever
geveth him a litle exhibition) prayseth excedingly
amonge other in his annotatyons on the new testament for his great learninge. Then thought I, if I
might come to this mannes service, I were happye.
And so I gate me to london, & thorow the accoynt-
aunce of my master came to sir harry gilford the
kinges graces countroller, ãd brought him an oration
of Isocrates which I had translated out of greke in to
English, and desyred him to speake vnto my lorde of
london for me, which he also did as he shewed me, ãd
willed me to write a pistle to my lorde, and to goo to
him my silf which I also did, and delivered my pistle
to a servaunt of his awne, one wyllyam hebilthwayte,
a mã of myne old accoyntaũce. But god which knoweth what is within hypocrites, sawe that I was begyled,
ãd that that councell was not the nexte way vnto .P. my
purpose. And therfore he gate me no favoure in my
lordes sight ⁋ Wheruppõ my lorde answered me, his
house was full, he had mo thẽ he coude well finde, and
advised me to seke in london, wher he sayd I coude
not lacke a service, And so in london I abode almoste
an yere, and marked the course of the worlde, and herde
oure pratars, I wold say oure preachers how they bosted
them selves and their hye authorite, and beheld the
pompe of oure prelates and how besyed they were as
they yet are, to set peace and vnite in the worlde
(though it be not possible for them that walke in
darkenesse to cõtinue longe in peace, for they can not
but ether stõble or dash them selves at one thinge or
a nother that shall cleane vnquyet all togedder) & sawe
thinges wherof I deferre to speake at this tyme and un-
derstode at the laste not only that there was no rowme
in my lorde of londons palace to translate the new testament, but also that there was no place to do it in all
englonde, as experience doth now openly declare.

⁋ Vnder what maner therfore shuld I now sub-
mitte this boke to be corrected and amended of them,
which can suffer nothinge to be well? Or what pro-

testacyon shuld I make in soch a matter vnto oure prelates those stubburne Nimrothes which so mightely fight agenste god and resiste his holy spirite, enforceynge with all crafte and sotelte to qwench the light of the everlastinge testament, promyses, and a-. P. poyntemente made betwene god & vs: and heapinge the firce wrath of god vppon all princes and rulars, mockinge thē with false sayned names of hypocrysye, and servinge their lustes at all poyntes, & dispensinge with thē even of the very lawes of god, of which Christe him silf testifieth Mathew v. ẏ not so moch as one tittle therof maye perish, or be brokē. And of which the prophete sayth Psalme .cxviii. Thou haste cōmaunded thy lawes to be kepte **meod,** ẏ is in hebrew excedingly, with all diligēce, might & power, and haue made thē so mad with their iugglinge charmes and crafty persuasiōs that they thinke it full satissfaction for all their weked lyvinge, to tormēt soch as tell thē trouth, & to borne the worde of their soules helth, & sle whosoever beleve theron.

⁋ Not withstōdinge yet I submytte this boke and all other that I haue other made or trāslated, or shall in tyme to come, (if it be goddes will that I shall further laboure in his hervest) unto all them that submytte thē selves vnto the worde of god, to be corrected of thē, yee and moreover to be disalowed & also burnte, if it seme worthy when they have examyned it wyth the hebrue, so that they first put forth of their awne translatinge a nother that is correcte.

.P. ¶ *Aprologe

shewinge the vse of the scripture

THOUGH a man had a precious iuell and a rich, yet if he wiste not the value therof nor wherfore it serued, he were nother the better nor rycher of a straw. Even so
5 though we read the scripture & bable of it never so moch, yet if we know not the use of it, and wherfore it was geven, and what is therin to be sought, it profiteth vs nothinge at all. It is not ynough therfore to read and talke of it only, but we must also desyre god daye
10 and night instantly to open oure eyes, ãd to make vs vnderstond and seale wherfore the scripture was geuen, that we maye applye the medicyne of the scripture, every mã to his awne sores, inlesse then we entend to be ydle disputers, and braulers aboute vayne wordes,
15 ever gnawenge vppon the bitter barcke with out and never attayninge vnto the swete pith with in, and persequutinge one an other for defendinge of lewde imaginacions and phantasyes of oure awne invencyon

** ¶ Paule, in ỹ thyrde of ỹ secõde epistle to Tymothe

---

* The Bristol copy of the edition of 1534 gives instead of the title "Aprologe shewinge," etc., the title:

Vnto the reader W. T.

** Lines 19 *sqq.* above stand in the Bristol copy thus: Page Signature Aij.

Paule in the third of the seconde epistle to Timothe saith, that the scripture is good to teache (for that ought men to teache) and not dreames of their awne makinge, as the pope doth,) and also to improue, for that scripture is the twichstone that tryeth al doctrines, and by that we know the false from the true. And in the .vi. to the Ephesians he calleth in the swerde of the spirite by cause it killeth hypocrites and vttereth and improueth their false inuentions

The scripture wherfore it is good.

fayth, ẙ the fcripture is good to teache (for ẙ ought mē to teach & not dreames of their awne makīge, as ẙ pope doth) & alfo to improve, for ẙ fcripture is ẙ twichftone ẙ tryeth all doctrynes, ād by ẙ we know the falfe from ẙ true. ¶. And in the .vi. to the ephefians he calleth it the fwerd of the fpirite, by caufe it killeth hyppocrites, and vttereth ād improveth their falfe inventyons. And in the .xv. to the Romayns he fayth all that are wryten, are wryten for oure learninge, that we thorow pacyence and cōforte of the fcripture myght have hope. That is, the enfamples that are in the fcripture comforte vs in all oure tribulacyons, and make vs to put oure trufte in god, and pacyently to abyde his leyfure.

And in the .x. of the firfte to the Corinthyans he bringeth in examples of the fcripture to feare vs and to bridle the flefhe, that we cafte not the yoke of the lawe of god from of oure neckes, and fall to luftynge and doinge of evill.

¶ So now the fcripture is a light and fheweth vs the true waye, both what to do, and what to hope. And a defence from all erroure, and a comforte in adverfyte that we defpayre not. and feareth vs in profperyte that we fynne not *Seke therfore in the fcripture

---

* The passage "Seke therfore" to "world a new." is not in the Briftol copy of the edition of 1534, which has inftead:

Seke therfore in the fcripture as thou readeft it, chefely and aboue all, the conuenaūtes made betwene god and vs. That is to faye; the lawe and cōma]undementes which God commaūdeth vs to do. And then the mercie promyfed vnto all them that fubmite them felues vnto the lawe. For all the promyfes thorow out the hole fcripture do include a couenaūt. That is: god byndeth him felfe to fulfil that mercie vnto the, onlye if thou wilt endeuoure thy felfe to kepe his lawes: fo that no man hath his parte in the mercie of god, faue he onlye that loueth his lawe and confenteth that it is righteous and good, & fayne wolde do it, ād euer mourneth becaufe he now and then breaketh it thorow infirmite, or dothe it not fo perfectly as his harte wolde

And let loue interprete the lawe: that thou vnderftōde this to be the finall ende of

as thou readeſt it firſt the law, what god cōmaundeth vs to doo. And ſecundarylye the promyſes, which god promyſeth us ageyne, namely in Chriſte Ieſu oure lorde. Then ſeke enſamples, firſte of comforte, how god purgeth all them that ſubmitte them ſelves to walke in his wayes, in the purgatorye of tribulatyon, delyveringe them yet at the latter ende, and never ſoferinge any of them to peryſh, that cleave faſte to his promyſes.

---

the lawe, and the hole cauſe why the lawe was geuen: euen to bringe the to the knoledge of god, how that he hath done all thinge for the, that thou mighteſt loue hym agayne with al thine harte and thy neyboure for his ſake as thy ſilfe and as Chriſt loued the. Becauſe thy neyboure is the ſonne of god alſo and created vnto his lykenes as thou arte, and bought with as dere bloude as arte thou. Whoſoeuer ſeleth in his herte that euery man ought to loue his neyboure as Chriſt loued him, and conſenteth therto, and enforſeth to come therto: the ſame onlye vnderſtondeth the lawe aryght and can interprete it. And he that ſubmyt-

A iij.]

teth not hī ſelfe in the degre he is in, to ſeke his neyboures proffite as Chriſt did his, cā neuer vnderſtonde the lawe, though it be interprete to him. For that loue is the light of the lawe, to vnderſtonde it bye.

And beholde how righteous, howe honeſt and howe due a thinge it is by nature, that euery man loue his brother vnſaynedly euē as him ſelfe, for his fathers ſake. For it is the fathers great ſhame and his hie diſpleaſure, if one brother hurte another, Yf one brother be hurte of another, he maye not aduēge him ſelfe, but muſt complayne to his father or to them that haue auctorite of his father to rule in his abſence. Euen ſo if any of godes children be hurt by any of his brethren, he maye not aduenge him ſelfe with hande or herte. God muſt aduenge. And the gouerners and miniſters of the lawe that God hath ordeyned to rule vs by concerninge oure outwarde conuerſacion of one with another, they muſt aduenge. If they will not auenge, but rather maynte ne wronge, and be oppreſſers them ſelues, then muſt we tarye paciently tyll God come which is euer readie to reape tirauntes from of the face of the erth, aſſone as theyr ſinnes are rype.

Conſidre alſo what wrath, vengeaunce

And fynallye, note the enſamples which are w- .P.
riten to feare the fleſh that we ſynne not. That is, how
god ſuffereth the vngodlye and weked ſynners that reſiſte god and refuſe to folow him, to contynue in their
wekedneſſe, ever waxinge worſe and worſe vntyll their
ſynne be ſo ſore encreaſed and ſo abhomynable, that if
they ſhuld longer endure they wold corrupte the very
electe. But for the electes ſake god ſendeth thē preachers. Nevertheleſſe they harden their hartes agenſte
and plages god threateneth to them that ar rebellious and diſobedient.]
Thē go to & reade the ſtoryes of the byble for thy lerninge & comforte, & ſe euery thinge practyſed before thyne eyes: for accordinge to thoſe enſamples ſhall it goo with the & all mē vntill the worldes ende. So that into whatſoeuer caſe or ſtate a mā be brought, accordīge to whatſoeuer ēſāple of the bible it be, his ende ſhalbe accordige as he there ſeith and readeth. As god there warneth yer he ſmyte, & ſoffreth lōge yer he take extreme vēgeaūce, ſo ſhall he do with vs. As they that turne, are there receaued to mercie, & they that maliciouſly reſiſt, periſſhe vtterlye, ſo ſhall it be with vs. As they that refuſe the coūſel of God periſſhe thorow their awne coūcel, ſo ſhall it be with vs vntill the worldes ende. As it wēt with their kinges & rulers, ſo ſhall it go with oures As it was with their comē people, ſo ſhall it be with oures. As it was with theyrſpirituall officers, ſo ſhall it be with oures. As it was wyth theyr true prophetes, ſo ſhall it be with oures vntill the worldes ēde. As they had euer amōge thē falſe prophetes & true: & as their falſe*perſecuted the true, & moued the prynces to ſle thē, ſo ſhall it be with vs vntyll the ende of the worlde. As there was amōge thē but a ſewe true herted to god, ſo ſhall it be amōge vs: & as their ydolatry was ſo ſhall ours be vntyll the ende of the worlde. All mercy that was ſhewed there, is a*pro-]
myſe vnto the, if thou turne to god. And all vengeaunce and wrath ſhewed there, is threatened to the, if thou be ſtoubourne ād reſiſte &c.

Then follows:

And this lerninge and comforte ſhalt th ou euermore finde, etc.

* *per* and *pro*, instead of abbreviated letters not in our fonts.

the truth, and god deftroyeth thē vtterlye and begynneth the world a new.

⁋ This comforte fhalt thou evermore finde in the
playne texte and literall fenfe. Nether is there any
5 ftorye fo homely, fo rude, yee or fo vyle (as it femeth
outwarde) wherin is not exceadinge greate comforte.
And when fome which feme to them felves great
clarkes faye: they wott not what moare profite is in
many geftes of the fcripture if they be read with out
10 an allegorye, then in a tale of robenhode, faye thou:
that they were wryten for oure confolacyon and
comforte, that we defpayre not, if foch like happen
vnto vs. We be not holyer then Noe, though he were
once dronke. Nether better beloved then Iacob, though
15 his awne fonne defyled his bedde. We be not holyer
than lot, though his doughters thorow ignorance deceaved him, nor peradventure holyer then thofe doughters. Nether are we holyer then David, though he
brake wedlocke and uppon the fame commytted ab-
20 homynable murther. All thofe men have witne- .P. ffe
of the fcripture that they pleafed god and ware good
men both before that thofe thinges chaunfed them
and alfo after. Neverthelefſe foch thinges happened
them for oure enfample: not that we fhuld contrafayte
25 their evill, but if whyle we fight with oure felves
enforfynge to walke in the law of god (as they
did) we yet fall likewife, that we defpayre not, but
come agayne to the lawes of god and take better
holde

30 ⁋ We read fens the tyme of Chriftes deeth of
virgins that have bene brought vnto the comē ftues,
and there defyled, and of martyrs that haue bene
bounde and hores haue abvfed their bodyes. Why?
The iudgemētes of god are bottōleffe. Soch thinges
35 chaunced partely for enfamples, partely God thorow
fynne healeth fynne Pryde can nether be healed nor
yet appere but thorow foch horrible deades. Parad-
uenture they were of ẏ popes fecte ād reioyfed flefhly,
thinkinge that heaven came by deades and not by
40 Chrift, and that the outwarde dead iuftyfyed them &
made them holy and not the inward fpirite receaved

by fayth and the confent of the harte vnto the law
of god.

⁋ As thou readefte therfore thinke that every
fillable pertayneth to thyne awne filf, and fucke out
the pithe of the fcripture, and arm thy filf ageynft all
affaultes. Firfte note with ftronge faith the power of
god in creatinge all of nought Then marke the
grevous fall of Adam and of vs all in him, thorow
the lightregardige of the .℣. commaundement of god.
In the .iiii. Chapitre god turneth him vnto Abel and
then to his offeringe, but not to Cain and his offeringe.
Where thou feeft that though the deades of the evel
apere outwardly as gloryous as the deades of the good:
yet in the fight of god which loketh on the harte, the
deade is good becaufe of the man, and not the man
good becaufe of his deade. In the .vi. God fendeth
Noe to preach to the weked and geveth them fpace to
repent: they wax hard herted, God bringeth them to
nought And yet faveth Noe: even by the fame water
by which he deftroyed them. Marke alfo what folowed
the pryde of the buyldinge of the toure of Babel

Confydre how God fendeth forth Abrahā out of his
awne countre in to a ftrange lande full of weked people,
and gave him but a bare promeffe with him that he
wold bleffe him and defende him. Abraham beleved:
and that worde faued and delyuered him in all parelles:
fo that we fe, how that mannes life is not mayntayned
by bred onlye (as Chrifte fayeth) but moch rather by
belevinge the promyfes of god. Behold how foberly and
how circũfpectly both Abraham and alfo Ifaac behaue
them felves amõge the infideles. Abraham byeth that
which might have ben geven him for nought, to cutte
of occafions. Ifaac when his welles which he had digged
were taken from him, geveth rowme and refifteth not.
More over they ere and fo- .℣. we and fede their catell,
and make confederacyons, ād take perpetuall truce, and
do all outward thinges: Even as they do which have
no faith, for god hath not made vs to be ydle in this
world. Every man muft worke godly and truly to
the vttmofte of the power that god hath geven him:
and yet not trufte therin: but in goddes worde or

shewinge the vſe of the ſcripture 13

promeſſe: and god will worke with vs and bringe that
we do to good effecte. And thē when oure power will
extend no further, goddes promeſſes wyll worke all
alone

5 ⁋ How many thinges alſo reſiſted the promeſſes of
god to Iacob? And yet Iacob coniureth god with his
awne promeſſes ſayenge? O god of my father Abraham:
and god of my father Iſaac, O Lorde which ſaydeſte
vnto me returne vnto thyne awne contre, and vnto
10 the place were thou waſte borne and I wil do the good
I am not worthy of the leſte of thoſe mercyes, nor of
that trouth which thou haſte done to thy ſeruant I
went out but with a ſtaffe, and come home with .ii
droves, delyver me out of the handes of my brother
15 Eſau, for I feare him greatly &c. And god delyvered
him, and will likewyſe all that call unto his promeſſes
with a repentinge herte, were they never ſo great
ſynners. Marke alſo the weake infirmites of the mā
He loveth one wife more than a nother, one ſonne
20 more than a nother. And ſe how god purgeth him.
Eſau threteneth him: Laban begyleth him. The beloued wife is longe baren: his .P. doughter is ravyſhed:
his wife is defyled, and that of his awne ſonne. Rahel
dieth, Ioſeph is taken a way, yee and as he ſuppoſed
25 rent of wild beaſtes And yet how gloryous was hys
ende? Note the wekeneſſe of his Children, yee and
the ſynne of them, and how god thorow their awne
wekednes ſaved them. Theſe enſamples teach vs that
a man is not attonce parfecte the firſte daye he be-
30 ginneth to lyve wel They that be ſtronge therfore
muſte ſuffre with the weake, and helpe to kepe them in
vnite & peace one with a nother vntill they beſtrōger
Note what the brothren ſayde when they were tached
in Egipte, we haue verelye ſynned (ſayde they) ageynſte
35 oure brother in ẏ we ſawe the anguyſh of his ſoule when
he beſought vs, and wold not heare him: ād therfore is
this tribulation come vppon vs. By which enſample
thou ſeiſte, how that conſcience of evyll doenges findeth
men out at the laſte. But namely in tribulacyon and
40 adverſyte: there temptacyon and alſo deſperacyon:
yee and the verye paynes of hell find vs out: there

the ſoule feleth the ſerſe wrath of god and wyſſheth mountaynes to falle on her and to hyde her (yf it were poſſible) frō the angrye face of god.

Marke alſo how greate evelles folow of how litle an occaſion Dinah goeth but forth alone to ſe the doughters of the contre, and how greate myſcheve and troble folowed? Iacob loved but one ſonne more then a nother, ād how grevous .P̃. murther folowed in their hartes? Theſe are enſamples for oure learninge to teach us to walke warely and circūſpectlye in the worlde of weake people, that we geve no mā occaſions of evyll

⁋ Finally, ſe what god promyſed Ioſeph in his dreames. Thoſe promeſſes accōpanyed him all ways, and went doune wyth him even in to the depe dongeon, And brought him vppe agayne, And never for ſoke him till all that was promyſed was fulfilled. Theſe are enſamples wrytē for oure learnīge (as paule ſayth) to teach vs to truſte in god in ẙ ſtrōge fyre of tribulation and purgatorye of oure fleſh. And that they which ſubmytte them ſelves to folow god ſhuld note and marke ſoch thinges, for theyr lerninge and comforte, is the frute of the ſcripture and cauſe why it was wryten: And with ſoch a purpoſe to read it, is the waye to everlaſtynge life, and to thoſe ioyfull blyſſinges that are promyſed vnto all nacyons in the ſeade of Abraham, which ſeade is Ieſus Chriſte oure lorde, to whom be honoure and prayſe for ever and unto god oure father thorow him.

A M E N .

1. Chapter.

THE FYRST BOKE

OF MOSES CALLED GENESIS

1. 1–9.   The fyrſt Chapiter.

1 IN the begynnynge God created
2 heaven and erth. The erth was voyde and emptie, ād darckneſſe was vpon the depe, and the ſpirite of god moved vpon the water
3 Than God ſayd: let there be lyghte and
4 there was lyghte. And God ſawe the lyghte that it was good: & devyded
5 the lyghte from the darckneſſe, and called the lyghte daye, and the darckneſſe nyghte: and ſo of the evenynge and mornynge was made the fyrſt daye

M.C.S. How heauen & erth, the lyght, the fyrmament, the ſonne, the mone, the ſterres, and all beaſtes, foules & fyſſhes in the ſee were made by the worde of God. And how man alſo was creat.

6 And God ſayd: let there be a fyrmament betwene
7 the waters, ād let it devyde the waters a ſonder. Than God made the fyrmament and parted the waters which were vnder the fyrmament, from the waters that were
8 above the fyrmament: And it was ſo. And God called the fyrmament heaven, And ſo of the evenynge and morninge was made the ſeconde daye
9 And God ſayd, let the waters that are vnder heaven gether them ſelves vnto one place, that the drye londe

M. 1·beginnyng. God, throughout with capital G. 3 ſayde, and ſo throughout the chapter. lyght, *bis* 4 lyght, nyght, and often. 5 the day, the night. 7 mornyng 9 lande
V. 2 ferebatur 5 tenebris. appellauitque. factumque eſt veſpere· & mane dies vnus (cf. vv. 8, 13, 19, 24, 31) 7 et factum eſt ita (ſo vv. 9, 15, 24, 30).
L. 2 tieffe. auf dem Waſſer 3 es ward liecht 5 da ward aus abend und morgen der erſte tag.
M. M. N. 2 *moued.* brethed or ſtyred 7 *fyrmamēt,* or heauen, Ps. cxxxv a. v. b. It is an Hebrew worde and ſygnyfyeth thruſting forth or ſpredynge abrode.

10 may appere: And it came ſo to paſſe. And god called the drye lande the erth and the gatheringe togyther of waters called he the ſee, And God ſawe that it was good

11 .P. And God ſayd: let the erth bringe forth herbe and graſſe that ſowe ſeed, and frutefull trees that bere frute every one in his kynde, havynge their ſeed in them ſelves vpon the erth. And it came ſo to paſſe:
12 ād the erth brought forth herbe and graſſe ſowenge ſeed every one in his kynde & trees berynge frute & havynge their ſeed in thē ſelves, every one in his kynde.
13 And God ſawe that it was good: and thē of the evenynge and mornynge was made the thyrde daye.

14 Than ſayd God: let there be lyghtes in ẏ firmament of heaven to devyde the daye frō the nyghte, that they
15 may be vnto ſygnes, ſeaſons, days & yeares. And let them be lyghtes in the fyrmament of heavē, to ſhyne
16 vpon the erth. & ſo it was. And God made two great lyghtes A greater lyghte to rule the daye, & a leſſe
17 lyghte to rule the nyghte, and he made ſterres alſo. And God put them in the fyrmament of heaven to ſhyne
18 vpon the erth, and to rule the daye & the nyghte,
19 ād to devyde the lyghte from darckneſſe. And God ſawe ẏ it was good: and ſo of the evenynge ād mornynge was made the fourth daye.

20 And God ſayd, let the water bryng forth creatures that move & have lyfe, & ſoules for to flee over the
21 erth vnder the fyrmament of heaven. And God created greate whalles and all maner of creatures that lyve and moue, which the waters brought forth in their kindes, ād all maner of federed ſoules in their kyndes.
22 And [Fo. II] God ſawe that it was good: and God bleſſed them ſaynge. Growe and multiplye ād fyll the

M. 14 lightes 22 ſayinge
V. 10 maria 12 habens vnumquodque ſementem 14 et diuidant diem ac noctem 16 vt præeſſet. nocti: & ſtellas. & poſuit 21 omne volatile 22 benedixitque eis
L. 10 Meere 12 vnd yhren eygen ſamen bey ſich ſelbs hatten 16 furſtunde 21 allerley gefidderts geuogel
M. M. N. 22 *Bleſſed*, here is bleſſynge takē for encreaſynge & multiplyenge.

waters of the fees, & let the foules multiplye vpõ the
23 erth. And fo of the evenynge & morninge was made
the fyfth daye.

24 And God fayd: let the erth bring forth lyvynge
creatures in thir kyndes: catell & wormes & beaftes
25 of the erth in their kyndes, & fo it came to paffe. And
god made the beaftes of the erth in their kyndes, &
catell in their kyndes, ãd all maner wormes of the erth
in their kyndes: and God fawe that it was good.

26 And God fayd: let vs make man in oure fymilitude
ãd after oure lyckneffe: that he may have rule over
the fyfh of the fee, and over the foules of the ayre,
and over catell, and over all the erth, and over all
27 wormes that crepe on the erth. And God created man
after hys lyckneffe, after the lyckneffe of god created
he him: male & female created he them.

28 And God bleffed them, and God fayd vnto them.
Growe and multiplye and fyll the erth and fubdue it,
and have domynyon over the fyfh of the fee, and over
the foules of the ayre, and over all the beaftes that
move on the erth.

29 And God fayd: fe, I have geven yow all herbes that
fowe feed which are on all the erth, and all maner
trees that haue frute in them and fowe feed: to be
30 meate for yow & for all .P. beaftes of the erth, and
vnto all foules of the ayre, and vnto all that crepeth
on the erth where in is lyfe, that they may haue all
maner herbes and graffe for to eate, and even fo it
31 was. And God behelde all that he had made, ãd loo
they were exceadynge good: and fo of the evenynge
and mornynge was made the fyxth daye

𝔐. 26 domynion. fyfhes 29 fee. whyche. 31 fyxte.
𝒱. 24 reptilia 25 omnique reptili 26 ad imaginem et fimilitudinem 29 Ecce. in efcam.
𝕷. 24 gewurm 26 eyn bild das uns gleych sey 29 fehet da.
zu ewr fpeyfe.
𝔐. 𝔐. N. 26 *Lyckneffe of God*, that is after the fhape and
ymage whyche was before appoynted for the fonne of God: The
chefepart of man alfo, whyche is the foule is made lyke vnto God
in a certen proporcyon of nature, of power workynge, fo that in
that we are made lyke vnto God.

The Seconde Chapter.

1,2 THUS was heavē & erth fynifhed wyth all their apparell: ād i ẏ feuēth daye god ended hys worke which he had made & refted in ẏ feventh daye frō all his workes
3 which he had made. And God bleffed ẏ feventh daye, and fanctyfyed it, for in it he refted from all his workes which he had created and made.

4 ¶ Thefe are the generations of heaven & erth when they were created, in the tyme when the LORde God created heaven and erth and all the fhrubbes of the felde
5 be fore they were in the erthe. And all the herbes of the felde before they fprange: for the LORde God had yet fent no rayne vpon the erth, nether was there yet any
6 man to tylle the erth. But there arofe a myfte out of the ground and watered all the face of
7 the erth: Then the LORde God fhope man, even of the moulde of the erth and brethed into his face the breth of lyfe. So man was made a lyvynge foule.

8 ¶ The LORde God alfo planted a garden in Eden from the begynnynge, and there he fette [Fo. III.] man
9 whom he had formed. And the LORde God made to fprynge out of the erth, all maner trees bewtyfull to

M.C.S. The Chapter that went before is here repeted agayne: the halowing of the Saboth daye: the foure floudes of paradyfe: The fettynge in of man in paradyfe: the tree of knowledge is forbydden hym: how Adam named all creatures: the creacyon of Eua: the inftitutyon of maryage.
apparell, *the heavenly bodies*
fhope, *created*
moulde, *earth*

V. 1 perfecti 5 non enim pluerat dominus deus 6 fed fons afcendebat e terra 7 de limo terræ, & infpirauit in faciem eius 8 paradifum voluptatis a principio

L. 4 Gepurt 7 vnd blies ynn feyn angeficht eyn lebendigen odem, vnd alfo wart der menfch eyn lebendige feele. 8 Eden, gegen dem morgen

M. M. N. 1 *apparell,* The apparell of heauē is the fterres and planettes, etc., 3 *bleffed,* Bleffe here is taken for magnifyenge and prayfynge, as it is in Ps. xxxiii, a. *fanctyfyed,* Sanctifyēg in this place is as moche to faye as to dedicate & ordayne a thing to his awne ufe as Ex. xiii, a and .xx, b. 7 *moulde,* Slyme: duft or claye.

the fyghte and pleafant to eate, and the tree of lyfe in the middes of the garden: and alfo the tree of knowledge of good and euell.

10 ⁋ And there fpronge a rever out of Eden to water the garden, and thence devided it felfe, and grewe in to 11 foure principall waters. The name of the one is Phifon, he it is that compaffeth all the lande of heuila, where 12 gold groweth. And the gold of that contre ys precious, 13 there is found bedellion and a ftone called Onix. The name of the feconde ryver is Gihon, which compaffyth 14 all the lande of Inde. And the name of the thyrde river is Hidekell, which runneth on the eafte fyde of the affyryans. And the fourth river is Euphrates.

15 ⁋ And the LORde God toke Adam and put him in 16 the garden of Eden, to dreffe it and to kepe it: and the LORde God cōmaunded Adā faynge: of all the 17 trees of the gardē fe thou eate. But of the tre of knowlege of good and badd fe that thou eate not: for even ÿ fame daye thou eateft of it, thou fhalt furely dye.

18 ⁋ And the LORde God fayd: it is not good that man fhulde be alone, I will make hym an helper to 19 beare him company: And after ÿ the LORde God had make of the erth all maner beaftes of the felde, and all maner foules of the ayre, he brought them vnto Adam to fee what .℈. he wold call them. And as Adā called all maner livynge beaftes: evē fo are their names.

20 And Adam gave names vnto all maner catell, and vnto the foules of the ayre, and vnto all maner beaftes

𝕸. 10 fprange 16 fayinge 17 dye the dethe. 19 made
𝖁. 13 omnem terram Æthiopiæ 14 Tigris 17 morte morieris. 18 faciamus
𝕷. 10 es gieng aus ... teylet fich dafelbs ynn vier hewbtwaffer 12 koftlich 17 wirftu des tods fterben.
𝕸.𝕸.𝕹. 10 *Eden;* Eden fygnifieth pleafures 17 *dye the dethe;* Soche reherfalls of wordes dothe fygnifye fomtyme an haftynes or vehemēce, fomtyme an affewrance that the thinge fhalbe performed that is promyfed, as it is Ps. cxvii, c.
𝕷.𝕸.𝕹. 11 *Pifon* ift das groffe waffer ynn India, das man Ganges heyft, denn *Heuila* ift Indienland, *Gihon* ift das waffer ynn Egypten das man Nilus heyft, *Hydekel* ift das waffer in Affyria das man Tygris heyft. *Phrato* aber ift das nehift waffer ynn Syria das man Euphrates heyft.

of the felde. But there was no helpe founde vnto Adam to beare him companye

21 Then the LORde God caſt a ſlomber on Adam, and he ſlepte. And then he toke out one of his rybbes, and in ſtede ther of he fylled vp the place with fleſh.
22 And the LORde God made of the rybbe which he toke out of Adam, a womã and brought her vnto Adam.
23 Then ſayd Adã this is once bone of my boones, and fleſh of my fleſh. This ſhall be called woman: becauſe ſhe was take of the man. *once, now (a Saxon idiom).*
24 For this cauſe ſhall a man leve father and mother &
25 cleve vnto his wyfe, & they ſhall be one fleſh. And they were ether of them naked, both Adam and hys wyfe, ãd were not aſhamed:

The .III. Chapter.

1 BUT the ſerpent was ſotyller than all the beaſtes of the felde which ẏ LORde God had made, and ſayd vnto the woman. Ah ſyr, that God hath ſayd, ye ſhall not eate of all maner trees in the
2 garden. And the woman ſayd vnto the ſerpent, of the frute of the trees in the gar-
3 den we may eate, but of the frute of the tree ẏ is in the myddes of the garden (ſayd God) ſe that ye eate not, and ſe that ye touch it not: leſt ye dye.

M. C. S. The ſerpent deceaueth the woman. The ſerpẽt the woman & the man are curſed, and dryuen out of Paradiſe. Chriſt oure ſauyour is promyſed.
Ah ſyr, ah ſurely

4 [Fo. IIII.] Then ſayd the ſerpent vnto the woman:
5 tuſh ye ſhall not dye: But God doth knowe, that whenſoever ye ſhulde eate of it, youre eyes ſhuld be

M. 1 ye, hath God ſayd in dede
V. 1 callidior. Cur præcepit 4 nequaquam morte moriemini.
L. 21 ein tieffen ſchlaff fallen 23 das were eynmal beyn
iii. 1 Ja, ſollt Gott geſagt haben 4 yhr werdet mit nicht des tods ſterben 5 ſo werden ewer augen wacker

opened and ye fhulde be as, God and knowe both good
6 and evell. And the woman fawe that it was a good
tree to eate of and luftie unto the eyes and luftie, *afford-*
a pleafant tre for to make wyfe. And *ing pleafure*
toke of the frute of it and ate, and gaue vnto hir huf-
7 band alfo with her, and he ate. And the eyes of both
of them were opened, that they vnderftode how that
they were naked. Than they fowed fygge leves togedder and made them apurns.

8 And they herd the voyce of the LORde God as
he walked in the gardē in the coole of the daye.
And Adam hyd hymfelfe and his wyfe alfo from the
face of the LORde God, amonge the trees of the
9 garden. And the LORde God called Adam and fayd
10 vnto him where art thou? And he anfwered. Thy
voyce I harde in the garden, but I was afrayd becaufe
11 I was naked, and therfore hyd myfelfe. And he fayd:
who told the that thou waft naked? haft thou eaten
of the tree, of which I bade the that thou fhuldeft not
12 eate? And Adam anfwered. The woman which thou
gaveft to bere me company fhe toke me of the tree, ād
13 I ate. And the LORde God fayd vnto the woman:
wherfore dideft thou fo? And the woman anfwered,
the ferpent deceaved me and I ate.

14 ⁋ .P. And the LORde God fayd vnto the ferpēt
becaufe thou hafte fo done mofte curfed be thou of
all catell and of all beaftes of the feld: vppō thy
bely fhalt thou goo: and erth fhalt thou eate all dayes
15 of thy lyfe. Morover I will put hatred betwene.the
and the woman, and betwene thy feed and hyr feed.

𝔐. 6 for to geue vnderftondynge
𝔙. 8 ad auram poft meridiem
𝔏. 7 wurden yhr beyder augen wacker
𝔐. 𝔐. N. 6 *eyes fhulde be opened*, To haue their eyes opened
is to knowe or vnderftonde 8 *from the face*, That is from hys
prefence
𝔏 𝔐. N. 8 *Adam verfteckt*, Adam heyft auff Ebreifch, Menfch,
darumb mag man menfch fagen, wo Adam fteht vnd widderumb.
tag kuele war, Das war vmb den abent, wenn die hitze vergangen
ift, bedeut, das nach gethaner fund, das gewiffen angft leydet,
bis das Gottis gnedige ftym kome vnd wider kule vn erquicke
das hertz, wie wol fich auch die blode natur entfetzt vnd fleucht
fur dem Euangelio, weyl es das creutz vnd fterben leret.

And that feed fhall tread the on the heed, ād thou
fhalt tread hit on the hele.

16 And vnto the woman he fayd: I will fuerly encreafe
thy forow ād make the oft with child, and with payne
fhalt thou be deleverd: And thy luftes fhall pertayne
vnto thy hufbond and he fhall rule the.

17 And vnto Adā he fayd: for as moch as thou haft
obeyed the voyce of thy wyfe, and haft eaten of the
tree of which I commaunded the faynge: fe thou eate
not therof: curfed be the erth for thy fake. In forow
18 fhalt thou eate therof all dayes of thy life, And
it fhall beare thornes ād thyftels vnto the. And thou
19 fhalt eate the herbes of ẏ feld: In the fwete of thy
face fhalt thou eate brede, vntill thou returne vnto the
erth whēce thou waft takē: for erth thou art, ād vnto
erth fhalt thou returne.

20 And Adam called his wyfe Heua, becaufe fhe was
21 the mother of all that lyveth   And the LORde God
made Adam and hys wyfe garmentes of fkynnes, and
22 put them on them. And the LORde God fayd: loo,
Adam is become as it were one of vs, in knowlege of
good and evell. But now left he ftrech forth his hand
[Fo. V.] and take alfo of the tree of lyfe and eate and
lyve ever.

23 And the LORde God caft him out of the garden of
24 Eden, to tylle the erth whēce he was taken. And he

𝔐. 15 treade it on the hele
𝒱. 15 ipfa conteret 16 erūnas tuas—in dolore paries filios, &
fub viri poteftate eris & ipfe dominabitur tui 17 maledicta terra
in opere tuo 19 puluis. puluerem
𝓛. 15 ynn die verfen beyffen
𝔐. 𝔐. 𝔑. 15 *on thy heed*, The heed of the ferpent fygnifyeth
the power and tyranny of the deuell whych Chrift the feede of the
womā ouercame. The hele is Chriftes māhod which was tēpted
wyth oure fynnes. 22 *Loo*. Here thys worde *lo* is taken as a mocke
as it is in iii Regu. xviii, c.
𝓛. 𝔐. 𝔑. 15 *Derfelb*, Dis ift das erft Euangelion vnd verheyf-
fung von Chrifto gefchehen auff erden, Das er folt, fund, tod vnd
helle vber winden, vnd vns von der fchlangē gewalt felig machen.
Daran Adam glawbt mit allen feynen nach komē, dauon er
Chriften vnd felig worden ift von feynem fall. 20 *Heua*, Hai heyft
lebē, Daher kompt Heua oder Haua, Leben oder lebendige.

cast Adā out, and sette at ẏ enteringe of the garden Eden, Cherubin with a naked swerde swerd, *sword* movinge in and out, to kepe the way to the tree of lyfe.

⁋ The .IIII. Chapter.

1 AND Adam lay wyth Heua ys wyfe, which conceaved and bare Cain, and sayd: I haue gotten a mā of the LORde.
2 And she proceded forth and bare hys brother Abell: And Abell became a sheperde, and Cain became a ploweman.
3 And it fortuned in processe of tyme, that Cain brought of the frute of the erth:
4 an offerynge vnto the LORde. And Abell, he brought also of the fyrstlynges of hys shepe and of the satt of them. And the LORde loked vnto Abell and to his
5 offrynge: but vnto Cain and vnto hys offrynge, looked he not. And Cain was wroth exceadingly,
6 and loured. And the LORde sayd vnto Cain: why art thou angry, and why
7 loureste thou? Wotest thou not yf thou dost well thou shalt receave it? But & yf thou dost evell, by & by thy synne lyeth open in the dore. Not withston-.P.dyng let it be subdued vnto the, ād see thou
8 rule it. And Cain talked with Abell his brother.

M.C.S. Cayn kylleth hys ryghteous brother Abell. Cayn dispayreth & is cursed. The generacyō of Enoch, Mathusael, Tuball, Lamech, Seth and Enos.

loured, lourest, looked sullen

𝒱. 24 flammeum gladium atque versatilem. iiii. 5 et concidit vultus eius 8 Dixitque Cain ad Abel fratrē suū, Egrediamur foras

ℒ. 24 vnd eyn glentzendes fewrigs schwerd. iiii. 1 ich hab vberkomen den man des Herren

M.M.N. 4 *loked vnto Abell,* The Lorde looked vnto Abel & to hys offerynge: that is he was pleased with Abell & his offeringe, but with Cayn nor his offering was he not pleased: & therfore he saith that he loked not therto, the same vse of spekynge is also in the .ii. of kynges in the .xvi. Chapter.c. Ps. xxx. b.

ℒ.M.N. 1 *vberkomen,* Kain heyst, das man kriegt odder vberkompt, Heua aber meynet, er solt der same seyn, da der herr võ gesagt hatte, das er der schlangen kopff zutretten wurde.

And as foone as they were in the feldes, Cain fell
9 vppon Abell his brother and flewe hym. And ẏ LORde
fayd vnto Cain: where is Abell thy brother? And he
10 fayd: I cannot tell, am I my brothers keper? And
he fayd: What haſt thou done? the voyce of thy
11 brothers bloud cryeth vnto me out of the erth. And
now curfed be thou as pertaynyng to the erth, which
opened hyr mouth to receaue thy brothers bloud of
12 thyne hande. For when thou tylleſt the grounde fhe
fhall hẽceforth not geve hyr power vnto *rennagate, re-*
the. A vagabunde and a rennagate fhalt *negade, i. e.*
wanderer, fu-
thou be vpon the erth. *gitive.*
13 And Cain fayd vnto the LORde: my fynne is greater,
14 than that it may be forgeven. Beholde thou caſteſt
me out thys day from of the face of the erth, and frõ thy
fyghte muſt I hyde myfelfe ãd I muſt be wandrynge
and a vagabunde vpon the erth: Morover whofoever
15 fyndeth me, wyll kyll me. And the LORde fayd vnto
hĩ Not so, but who fo ever fleyth Cain fhalbe punyfhed
vii. folde. And the LORde put * a marke   * *Of this*
vpõ Cain that no mã ẏ founde hym fhulde *place no doute*
ẏ pope which
16 kyll hym. [Fo. VI.] And Cain went out *in all thinges*
frõ the face of the LORde and dwelt in *maketh hifelf*
equal with
the lande Nod, on the eaſt fyde of Eden. *god, toke an*
17 And Cain laye wyth hys wyfe, which *occafion to*
conceaved and bare Henoch. And he *marke all his*
creatures: and
was buyldinge a cyte and called the *to forbid vn-*
the name of it after the name of hys *der payne of*
excõmunicatiõ
18 fonne, Henoch. And Henoch begat Irad. *ẏ no mã (whe-*
And Irad begat Mahuiael. And Mahuiael *ther he were*
kige or em-
begat Mathufael. And Mathufael begat *peroure) be fo*
Lamech. *hardy to pun-*
ifhe them for
19 And Lamech toke hym two wyves, *what fo ever*

    𝔐. 10 bloud cryed vnto me
    𝔙. 13 quam ut ueniam merear 16 habitauit profugus in terra
ad orientalem plagam Eden
    𝔏. 12 Soll'er dyr fort feyn vermugen nicht geben 16 jenfyd Eden
gegen den morgen.
    𝔐. 𝔐. N. 10 *cryed,* Cryeth: that is afketh vengeaunce, as ye
haue Genefis xix. c.

the one was called Ada, and the other *myſchef they doo.*
20 Zilla. And Ada bare Iabal, of whome *The crowne is to*
came they that dwell in tentes ād poſſeſſe *thē a licence*
21 catell. And hys brothers name was Iubal: *to do what they liſte a*
of hym came all that exercyſe them ſelves *protectiō &· a*
22 on the harpe and on the organs. And *ſure ſentu-*
Zilla ſhe alſo bare Tubalcain a worker in *arye.* =ſentu-
metall and a father of all that grave in braſſe and *ary,protection*
yeron. And Tubalcains ſyſter was called Naema.
23 Then ſayd Lamech vnto hys wyves Ada ād Zilla: heare my voyce ye wyves of Lamech and herken vnto my wordes, for I haue ſlayne a man and wounded my ſelfe, and have ſlayn a yongman, and gotte my ſelfe
24 ſtrypes: .P. For Cain ſhall be avenged ſtrypes,*wounds* ſevenfolde: but Lamech ſeventie tymes ſevenfolde.
25 ☙ Adam alſo laye with hys wyfe yet agayne, and ſhe bare a ſonne ād called hys name Seth for god (ſayd ſhe) hath geven me a nother ſonne for Abell
26 whom Cain ſlewe. And Seth begat a ſonne and called hys name Enos. And in that tyme began men to call on the name of the LORde.

The .V. Chapter.

1 **T**HYS is the boke of the gener- *M. C. S. The*
acion of man, In the daye *genealogye of Adam vnto*
when God created man and *Noe.*
made hym after the ſymilytude of god.
2 Male and female made he thē and called their names
3 man, in the daye when they were created. And when Adam was an hundred and thirty yere old, he begat a ſonne after his lyckneſſe and ſymilytude: and called

V. 21 cithara & organo 25 ſemen aliud 26 Enos. iſte cœpit in-uocare nomen domini .v, 1 Adam. hominem

M.M.N. 26 *To call on the name of the Lorde* is to requyer all thynges of hym and to truſt in him, geuing hym the honour and worſhyp that belongeth to hym, as in Gen. xii b.

4 hys name Seth. And the dayes of Adam after he begat Seth, were eyght hundred yere, and begat
5 sonnes and doughters, and all the dayes of Adam which he lyved, were .ix. hundred and .xxx. yere, and then he dyed.
6 And Seth lyved an hundred and .v. yeres, and
7 begat Enos. And after he had begot Enos he lyved viii. hundred and .vii. yere, and begat sonnes and
8 doughters. And all the dayes of Seth were .ix. hundred and .xii. yeres and dyed.
9 And Enos lyved .Lxxxx. yere and begat [Fo. VII.]
10 kenan. And Enos after he begat kenan, lyved .viii hundred and .xv. yere, and begat sonnes and dough-
11 ters: and all the dayes of Enos were .ix. hundred and v. yere, and than he dyed.
12 And kenan lyved .Lxx. yere and begat Mahalaliel.
13 And kenan after he had begot Mahalaliel, lyved .viii hundred and .xl. yere and begat sonnes and doughters:
14 and al the dayes of kenan were .ix. hundred and .x yere, and than he dyed.
15 And Mahalaliel lyued .Lxv. yere, and begat Iared.
16 And Mahalaliel after he had begot Iared lyved .viii hundred and .xxx. yere and begat sonnes and dough-
17 ters: and all the dayes of Mahalalyell were .viii. hun-
18 dred nynetye and .v. yeare, and than he dyed And Iared lyved an hundred and .Lxii. yere and begat He-
19 noch: and Iared lyved after he begat Henoch, .viii
20 hundred yere and begat sonnes and doughters. And all the dayes of Iared were .ix. hundred and .Lxii yere, and than he dyed.
21 And Henoch lyved .Lxv. yere ãd begat Mathusala.
22 And Henoch walked wyth god after he had begot Mathusalah .iii. hundred yere, and begat sonnes and
23 doughters. And all the dayes of Henoch were .iii
24 hundred and .Lxv. yere. and than Henoch lyved a

M. 4 daughters
V. 9 Enos nonaginta annis 22 Et ambulauit Enoch cũ deo
M. M. N. 22 *And Henoch walked with God*, To walke wyth God, is to do hys will & leade a lyfe accordynge to hys worde.

godly lyfe, and was no more fene, for God toke him away.

25 And Mathufala lyved an hundred and .Lxxxvii.
26 yere and begat Lamech: and Mathufala .P. after he had begot Lamech, lyved .vii. hundred and .Lxxxii.
27 yere: ãd begat fonnes and doughters. And all the dayes of Methufala were .ix. hundred .Lxix. yere, and than he dyed.
28 And Lamech lyved an hundred .Lxxxii. yere and
29 begat a fonne and called hym Noe sayng. This fame fhall comforte vs: as concernynge oure worke and forowe of oure handes which we haue aboute the erthe
30 that the LORde hath curfed. And Lamech lyved after he had begot Noe .v. hundred, nynetie and .v
31 yere, and begat fonnes and doughters. And all the dayes of Lamech were .vii. hundred .Lxxvii. yere,
32 and than he dyed. And when Noe was .v. hundred yere olde, he begat Sem, Ham and Iaphet.

⁋ The .VI. Chapter.

1 AND it came to paffe whã men begã to multiplye apõ the erth ãd had begot them doughters,
2 the fonnes of God fawe the doughters of men that they were fayre, and toke vnto them wyves, which they
3 beft liked amõge thẽ all. And the LORd fayd: My fpirite fhall not all waye ftryve withe man, for they are

M. C. S. The caufe of the floude. God warneth Noe of the cõmyng of the floud: The preparing of the arcke.

V. 24 ambulavitque cũ deo, & nõ apparuit: quia tulit eũ deus.
vi. 3 non permanebit fpiritus meus in homine
L. 2 Kinder Gottis
M. M. N. 2 *The fonnes of God* are the fonnes of Seth which had inftruct & norifhed thẽ in the feare of God. The fonnes of men are the fonnes of Cayn inftruct of him to all wyckednes.
L. M. N. 2 *kinder Gottis*, Das waren der heyligen vetter kinder, Die ynn Gottiffurcht auferzogen, darnach erger, den die ander worden, vnter dem namen Gottis, wie altzeyt die geyft-lichen, die ergiften tyrannen vnd verkeritiften zu letzt worden find.

fleſh. Nevertheles I wyll geue them yet ſpace, and hundred and .xx. yeres

4 There were tirantes in the world in thos dayes. For after that the children of God had gone in vnto the doughters of men and had begotten them childern, the ſame childern were the mightieſt of the world and men of renowne. [Fo. VIII. miſplaced in the original]

5 And whan the LORde ſawe ẏ the wekedneſſe of man was encreaſed apon the erth, and that all the ymaginacion and toughtes of his hert was
6 only evell continually, he repented that he had made man apon the erth and
7 ſorowed in his hert. And ſayd: I wyll deſtroy mankynde which I haue made, frō of the face of the erth: both man, beaſt, worme and foule of the ayre, for it
8 repēteth me that I haue made them. But yet Noe found grace in the ſyghte of the LORde.

toughtes, ſhould be, thoughtes

9 Theſe are the generatiōs of Noe. Noe was a righteous man and vncorrupte in his tyme, &
10 walked wyth god. And Noe begat .iii. ſonnes: Sem,
11 Ham and Iapheth. And the erth was corrupte in the
12 ſyghte of god, and was full of miſchefe. And God loked vpon the erth, ād loo it was corrupte: for all fleſh had corrupte his way vppon the erth.
13 Than ſayd God to Noe: the end of all fleſh is come before me, for the erth is full of there myſchefe. And
14 loo, I wyll deſtroy them with the erth. Make the an arcke of pyne tree, and make chaumbers in the arcke, and pytch it wythin and wythout wyth pytch.
15 And of this facion ſhalt thou make it.

The lenth of the arcke ſhall be .iii. hundred cubytes, ād the bredth of it .L. cubytes, and the heyth of it
16 xxx. cubytes. A wyndow ſhalt thou make aboue in

M. 5 thoughtes
V. 4 gigantes autem 9 Noe vir iuſtus atque perfectus fuit 14 arca de lignis leuigatis
L. 4 tyrannen 12 alles fleyſch hatte ſeyn weg verterbet auff erden 14 thennen holtz
M.M.N. 12 *All fleſh*. All fleſſhe that is all men that lyue fleſhly, as in the .viii. of the Roma. 13 *The ende of all fleſh*. The ende of all fleſſhe: that is, the ende of all men is come before me.

the arcke. And wythin a cubyte compaſſe ſhalt thou finyſh it. .P. And the dore of the arcke ſhalt thou ſette in ẙ ſyde of it: and thou ſhalt make it with .iii. loftes
17 one aboue an other. For behold I will bringe in a floud of water apon the erth to deſtroy all fleſh from vnder heaven, wherin breth of life is ſo that all that
18 is in the erth ſhall periſh. But I will make myne apoyntement with the, that both thou ſhalt come in to ẙ arcke and thy ſonnes, thy wyfe and thy ſonnes wyves with the. *apoyntement, covenant*
19 And of all that lyveth what ſoever fleſh it be, ſhalt thou brynge in to the arcke, of every thynge a payre, to kepe them a lyve wyth the. And male
20 and female ſe that they be, of byrdes in their kynde, and of beaſtes in their kynde, and of all maner of wormes of the erth in their kinde: a payre of every thinge ſhall come vnto the to kepe them a lyve.
21 And take vnto the of all maner of meate ẙ may be eaten & laye it vp in ſtoore by the, that it may be
22 meate both for ẙ and for thē: and Noe dyd acordynge to all that God commaunded hym.

The .VII. Chapter.

1 AND the LORde ſayd vnto Noe: goo into the arcke both thou and all thy houſſold. For the haue I ſene rightuous before *M. C. S. The entraunce of Noe & them that were with him into the arcke.*
2 me in thys generacion. Of all clene beaſtes *The ryſynge*

M. 16 aboue a nother
V. 18 ponamque fœdus meū tecum 20 ut poſſint viuere vii. 1 dominus ad eum
L. 18 bund auffrichten .vii. 1 rechtfertig erſehen fur myr zu diſer zeit
M. M. N. 1 *For the haue I ſene ryghteous*, They are ryghteous before God that loue their neybours for gods ſake, vnfaynedly: hauynge the ſpirite of god whych maketh thē the ſonnes of God & therfore are accepted of God as iuſt and ryghteous as it is in Gen. xviii. c. 2 *and of clene beaſtes*, cleane beaſtes is ſoche as they mught lefully eate, and the vncleane are thoſe that they might not eate, as it apereth in Leuit. ii. a & Deut. xiiii.

take vnto the .vii. of every kynde the male *of the floude wherwith all thynges dyd peryshe.* and hys female [Fo. IX.] And of vnclene beaftes a payre, the male and hys female:

3 lykewyfe of the byrdes of the ayre .vii. of every kynde,
4 male and female to fave feed vppon all the erth. For vii. days hence wyll I fend rayne vppō the erth .XL. dayes. & .XL. nyghtes and wyll dyftroy all maner of thynges that I haue made, from of the face of the erth.
5 And Noe dyd acordynge to all ẏ the lorde cō-
6 maunded hym: and Noe was .vi. hundred yere olde, when
7 the floud of water came vppon the erth: and Noe went and his fonnes and his wyfe and his fonnes wyves wyth
8 hym, in to the arke from the waters of the floud. And of clene beaftes and of beaftes that ware vnclene and
9 of byrdes and of all that crepeth vppō the erth, came in by coopfes of every kynde vnto Noe in to the arke: a male and a female: even as God commaunded Noe.
10 And the feventh daye the waters of the floud came vppon the erth.
11 In the .vi. hundred yere of Noes lyfe, in the fecōde moneth, in the .xvii. daye of the moneth, ẏ fame daye were all the founteynes of the grete depe broken vp,
12 & the wyndowes of heavē were opened, ād there fell a rayne vpon the erth .XL. dayes and .XL. nyghtes.
13 And the felfe fame daye went Noe, Sem, Ham and Iapheth, Noes fonnes, and Noes wyfe and the .iii. wyves
14 of his fonnes wyth them in to the arke: both they and all maner of beaftes in their kīde, & all maner of catell in their kynde & all maner of wormes that crepe vppon .P. the erth in their kynde, and all maner of byrdes in there kynde. and all maner off foules what

𝒱. 11 omnes fontes abyffi magnæ & cataractæ cæli 13 In articulo diei illius
𝑳. 11 da auff brachen alle brunne der groffen tieffen, vnd theten fich auff die fenfter des hymels
𝕸. 𝕸. 𝕹. 11 *Founteynes,* The fountaynes of the great depe etc. that is, all the waters that were on the erth fprāge vp, encreafed & multyplyed. *Wyndowes of heaven,* The wyndowes of heuē opened &c. that is, all waters aboue the erth defcendea and increafed the floude.

15 foever had feders. And they came vnto Noe in to the arke by cooples, of all flefh ẏ had breth of lyfe in it.
16 And they that came, came male ād female of every flefh accordīge as God cōmaunded hym: & ẏ LORde fhytt the dore vppō him
17 And the floud came .XL. dayes & .XL. nyghtes vppon the erth, & the water increafed and bare vp
18 the arcke ād it was lifte up from of the erth   And the water prevayled and increafed exceadingly vppon the erth: and the arke went vppō the toppe of the waters.
19 And the waters prevayled excedingly above mefure vppō the erth, fo that all the hye hylles which are vnder
20 all the partes of heaven, were covered: evē .xv. cubytes hye prevayled the waters, fo that the hylles were covered.
21 And all flefhe that moved on the erth, bothe birdes catell and beaftes periffhed, with al that crepte on the
22 erth and all men: fo that all that had the breth of liffe in the noftrels of it thorow out all that was on drye lond dyed.
23 Thus was deftroyed all that was vppō the erth, both man, beaftes, wormes and foules of the ayre: fo that they were deftroyed from the erth: fave Noe was referved only and they that were wyth hym in the
24 arke. And the waters prevayled vppon the erth, an hundred and fyftye dayes.

L. 22 Alles was eyn lebendigen oden hatte ym trocken, das ftarb.

The .VIII. Chapter.

The .VIII. Chapter. [Fo. X.]

1 AND god remēbred Noe & all ẙ beaſtes & all ẙ catell ẙ were with hī in ẙ arke And god made a wynde to blow vppō 2 ẙ erth, & ẙ waters ceaſed: ād ẙ fountaynes of the depe ād the wyndowes of heavē were ſtopte and the rayne of heaven was 3 forbiddē, and the waters returned from of ẙ erth ād abated after the ende of an hundred and .L. dayes.

M.C.S. After the sendyng forth of the rauē & the doue Noe went forth of the arcke. He offreth sacrifice. The malyce of mannes heart.

4 And the arke reſted vppō the mountayns of Ararat, 5 the .xvii. daye of the .vii. moneth. And the waters went away ād decreaſed vntyll the .x. moneth. And the fyrſt daye of the tenth moneth, the toppes of the mounteyns appered.

6 And after the ende of .XL. dayes. Noe opened the 7 wyndow of the arke which he had made, ād ſent forth a raven, which went out, ever goinge and cominge agayne, vntyll the waters were dreyed vpp vppon the erth

8 Then ſent he forth a doue from hym, to wete whether the waters were fallen 9 from of the erth. And when the doue coude fynde no reſtinge place for hyr ſote, ſhe returned to him agayne vnto the arke, for the waters were vppon the face of all the erth. And he put out hys honde and toke her and pulled hyr to hym in to the arke

wete, know

10 And he abode yet .vii. dayes mo, and ſent out the 11 doue agayne out of the arke, And the doue came to hym agayne aboute eventyde, and beholde: There

M. 10 more
V. 1 adduxit ſpiritum ſuper terram 2 & prohibitæ ſunt 4 viceſimoſeptimo die—montes Armeniæ 7 et non reuertebatur
L. 1 waſſer fielen 2 ward gewehret
L. M. N. 7 *vnd kam widder*, Das iſt, er machts ſo lange mit ſeym widder komen bis das alles trocken wart, das iſt ſo viel geſagt, Er ſoll noch widder komē.

was in hyr mouth a lefe of an olyve tre which fhe had plucked. ℙ. wherby Noe perceaved that the waters were
12 abated vppon the erth. And he taried yet .vii. other dayes, and fent forth the doue, which from thence forth came no more agayne to him.

13 And it came to paffe, the fyxte hundred and one yere and the fyrft daye of the fyrft moneth, that the waters were dryed vpp apon the erth. And Noe toke off the hatches of the arke and loked: And beholde,
14 the face of the erth was drye. So by the .xxvii. daye of the feconde moneth the erth was drye.

15, 16 And God fpake vnto Noe faynge: come out of the arcke, both thou and thy wyfe ād thy fonnes and
17 thy fonnes wyues with the. And all the beaftes that are with the whatfoever flefh it be, both foule and catell and all manner wormes that crepe on the erth, brynge out with the, and let them moue, growe ād multiplye
18 vppon the erth. And Noe came out, ād his fonnes
19 and his wyfe and his fonnes wyues with hym. And all the beaftes, and all the wormes, and all the foules, and all that moved vppon the erth, came alfo out of the arke, all of one kynde together.

20 And Noe made an aulter vnto the LORDE, and toke of all maner of clene beaftes and all maner of clene foules, and offred facrifyce vppon the aulter.
21 And the LORDE fmellyd a fwete favoure and fayd in his hert: I wyll henceforth no more curfe the erth for mannes fake, for the imagynacion of mannes hert is [Fo. XI.] evell even from the very youth of hym. Moreouer I wyll not deftroy from henceforth all that
22 lyveth as I haue done. Nether fhall fowynge tyme and harveft, colde, and hete, fomere & wynter, daye and nyghte ceaffe, as longe as the erth endureth.

V. 11 ramum oliuæ virentibus foliis 20 Ædificauit .. obtulit holocaufta

L. 11 eyn oleblat 13 Ym fechs hunderften und eynem iar 19 eyn iglichs zu feyns gleychen 20 bawet .. brandopffer 21 hinfurt nicht mehr fchlahen

M. M. N. 21 The Lordes fmellynge of fauoure: is the alowāce of the workes of the faythfull, as in Ex. xxix. Lev. i. iii. iv.

L. M. N. 11 *oleblat;* Das Blat bedeut das Euangelion, dz der heylig geyft ynn die Chriftenheyt hat predigen laffen, Denn ole bedeutt barmherzickeyt vnnd fride, dauon das Evangelion leret

¶ The .IX. Chapter.

1 AND God bleſſed Noe and his ſonnes, and ſayd vnto them: Increaſe and multiplye and fyll the erth.
2 The feare alſo and drede of yow be vppon all beaſts of the erth, and vppon all foules of the ayre, ād vppon all that crepeth on the erth, and vppon all fyſhes of the ſee, which are geuen vnto youre
3 handes   And all that moveth vppon the erth havynge lyfe, ſhall be youre meate: Euen as ẙ grene herbes, ſo geue I yow all thynge.
4 Only the fleſh with his life which is his bloud, ſe that ye eate not.
5 * For verely the bloude of yow wherein youre lyves are wyll I requyre. Euē of the hande of all beaſtes wyll I require it, And of the hande of man and of the hand off euery mannes brother, wyll I requyre the
6 lyfe of man: ſo ẙ he which ſhedeth mannes bloude, ſhall haue hys bloud ſhed by man agayne: for God made man after hys awne
7 lyckneſſe. See that ye encreaſe, and waxe, and be occupyde vppon the erth, & multiplye therein.
8 Farthermore God ſpake vnto Noe &
9 to hys ſonnes with hym ſaynge: ſee,

M.C.S. God bleſſeth Noe and hys ſonnes. He forbyddeth to eate the bloude of beaſtes and forbyddeth the ſhedinge of mānes bloude. The lawe of the ſwerde. He maketh a couenaunt that he wyll deſtroye the world no more by water, and geueth the raynebowe as a token & confirmacyon of the ſame. Noe is droncken, and Ham vncouereth hym, and getteth his curſe.

5 * *This lawe and ſoch like to exequute, were kinges and rulars ordeyned of God wherfore they ought not to ſuffre the popes Caimes thus to ſhede bloud theirs not ſhed ageyne, nether yet to ſett vpp their abhominable ſetuaryes & necke verſes cleane agenſte the ordinaunce of*

V. 5 Sanguinem enim animarum veſtrarum 7 et ingredimini
L. 2 vnd alle fiſch ym meer ſeyen ynn ewer hend geben 4 Alleyne .. darynn die ſeele iſt 8 vnd reget euch auff erden
M. M. N. 5 *the bloude of you;* Here is all cruelnes forbydden mā: ſo that he will not let it be vnauēged in beſtes, moche leſſe in oure neybour.
L. M. N. 6 *durch menſchen;* Hie iſt das welltlich ſchwerd eyngeſetzt, das man die morder todten ſal.

	god, but vnto	I make my bŏd .P. wyth you
10	*their dāna-*	and youre feed after you, and
	cyon.	wyth all lyvynge thinge that is wyth you:

bond, covenant

both foule and catell, and all maner befte of the erth that is wyth yow, of all that commeth out of the arke what foeuer befte of the erth it be.

11 I make my bonde wyth yow, that henceforth all flefh fhall not be deftroyed wyth ẙ waters of any floud, ād ẙ henceforth there fhall not be a floud to deftroy the erth.

12 And God fayd. This is the token of my bŏde which I make betwene me and yow, ād betwene all
13 lyvynge thyng that is with yow for ever: I wyll fette my bowe in the cloudes, and it fhall be a fygne of the appoyntment made betwene me and
14 the erth: So that when I brynge in cloudes vpō ẙ erth, the bowe fhall appere in ẙ cloudes.

appoyntment covenant

15 And than wyll I thynke vppon my teftament which I haue made betwene me and yow, and all that lyveth what foeuer flefh it be. So that henceforth there fhall be no more waters to make a floud to deftroy all flefh.

teftament, couenant

16 The bowe fhalbe in the cloudes, and I wyll loke vpon it, to remembre the euerlaftynge teftament be-twene God and all that lyveth vppon the erth, what
17 foeuer flefh it be. And God fayd vnto Noe: This is the fygne of the teftament which I have made betwene me and all flefh ẙ is on the erth.

18 The fonnes of Noe that came out of the arcke were: Sem, Ham, and Iapheth. And Ham [Fo. XII.] he is
19 the father of Canaā. Thefe are the .iii. fonnes of Noe, and of thefe was all the world overfpred.

20 And Noe beynge an hufbād man, went furth and

𝔐. 10 all maner beftes 20 forth
𝒱. 9 Statuam pactum meum 12 hoc eft fignum fœderis 14 nubibus cælum 15 anima viuente quæ carnem vegetat 20 cœpitque Noe
𝑳. 9 Sihe ich richte mit euch eyn bund auff 14 foll das zeychen feyn meyns bunds—wolken vber die erden fure 16 Darumb foll meyn bogen ... allem lebendigen thier ynn allem fleyfch, das auff erden ift 19 alle land befetzt 20 Noah aber fieng an

21 planted a vyneyarde and drancke of the wyne and was
droncke, and laye vncouered in the myddeſt of his
22 tēt. And Ham the father of Canaan ſawe his fathers
prevytees, & tolde his .ii. brethren that were wythout.
23 And Sem and Iapheth toke a mantell and put it on
both there ſhulders ād went backward, ād covered there
fathers ſecrets, but there faces were backward So
24 that they ſawe not there fathers nakydnes. As ſoone
as Noe was awaked frō his wyne and wyſt what his
25 yongeſt ſonne had done vnto hym, he ſayd: curſed be
Canaan, ād a ſeruante of all ſeruantes be he to his
26 brethren. An he ſayd: Bleſſed be the LORde God of
27 Sē, and Canaan be his ſeruante. God increaſe Iapheth
that he may dwelle in the tentes of Sem. And Canaan
be their ſeruante.
28 And Noe lyved after the floude .iii. hundred and .L
29 yere: So that all the dayes of Noe were .IX. hundred
and .L. yere, ād than he dyed.

The .X. Chapter.

1 THESE are the generations of the ſonnes of Noe: of Sem, Ham and Iapheth, which be-
2 gat them children after the floude. .P. The ſonnes of Iapheth were: Gomyr, Magog, Madai, Iauan,
3 Tuball, Meſech and Thyras. And the ſonnes of Gomyr
4 were: Aſcenas Riphat and Togarma. And the ſonnes

M.C.S. The genealogye of Iaphet, Sem and Ham.

M. 21 wus 23 their
M. M. N. 27 *God increaſe;* To encreaſe, that is: to reioyſe or to be in peace & of good comfort, as it is in Gen. xxvi. c & Ps. iiii. a.
L. M. N. 22 *Vatters ſcham*, Dis geſchicht deuten viel dahyn. man ſolle der prælatō laſter nit ſtraffen wilchs doch Chriſtus vnd alle Apoſtel thatten, Aber deute du es recht, das Noe ſey Chriſtus vnd alle glewbigen, die trunckenheyt ſey die lieb vnd glawbe ym heyligen geyſt die bloſſe ſey das creutz vnd leyden fur der wellt Ham ſey, die falſchen werck beylegen vnd gleyſſener, die Chriſtum vnd die ſeynen verſpotten vnd luſt haben ynn yhrem leyden. Sem vnd Iaphet ſeyen die fromen Chriſten die ſolch leyden preyſen vn ehren.

of Iauan were: Elifa, Tharfis, Cithim, and Dodanim.
5 Of thefe came the Iles of the gentylls in there contres, every man in his fpeach, kynred and nation.
6 The fonnes of Ham were: Chus Misraim Phut and
7 Canaan. The fonnes of Chus: were Seba, Heuila, Sabta, Rayma and Sabtema. And the fones of Rayma
8 were: Sheba, & Dedan. Chus also begot Nemrod,
9 which begā to be myghtye in the erth. He was a myghtie hunter in the fyghte of the LORde: Where of came the proverbe: he is as Nemrod that myghtie
10 hunter in the fyghte of the LORde. And the begynnynge of hys kyngdome was Babell, Erech, Achad
11 and Chalne in the lande of Synear: Out of that lande came Affur and buylded Ninyue, and the cyte reho
12 both, and Calah. And Reffen betwene Ninyue ād
13 Chalah That is a grete cyte. And Mizraim begat
14 ludim, Enanum, Leabim, Naphtuhim, Pathrufim & Cafluhim: from whence came the Philyftyns, and the Capththerynes.
15 Canaan alfo begat zidon his eldeft fonne & Heth,
16, 17, 18 Iebufi, Emori, Girgofi, Hiui, Arki, Sini, Aruadi, Zemari and hamati. And afterward fprange the
19 kynreds of the Canaanytes And the coftes of the Canaanytes were frō Sy- [Fo. XIII.] don tyll thou come to Gerera & to Afa, & tyll thou come to Sodoma,
20 Gomorra, Adama Zeboim: evē vnto Lafa. Thefe were the chyldrē of Ham in there kynreddes, tonges, landes and nations.
21 And Sem the father of all ẏ childrē of Eber and the
22 eldeft brother of Iapheth, begat children also. And his fonnes were: Elam Affur, Arphachfad, Lud ād
23 Aram. And ẏ children of Aram were: Vz, Hul,
24 Gether & Mas And Arphachfad begat Sala, and
25 Sala begat Eber. And Eber begat. ii. fonnes. The

M. 13 Mizrim 18 Harmati
L. 5 fecundum linguam fuam & familias in nationibus fuis. 11 Niniuen, & plateas ciuitatis 18 per hos difseminati funt populi chananæorum 20 filii cham in cognationibus (cf. v 31.)
V. 5 fprach gefchlecht vnd leuten 11 Niniue vnd der ftat gaffen 18 daher find aufgebreyt

name of the one was Peleg, for in his tyme the erth was devyded. And the name of his brother was Iaketan.

26 Iaketan begat Almodad, Saleph, Hyzarmoneth, 27, 28 Iarah, Hadoram, Vſal, Dikela, Obal, Abimael, Seba, 29 Ophir, Heuila & Iobab. All theſe are the ſonnes of 30 Iaketan. And the dwellynge of them was from Meſa vntill thou come vnto Sephara a mountayne of the 31 eaſte lande. Theſe are the ſonnes of Sem in their kynreddes, languages, contrees and nations.

32 Theſe are the kynreddes of the ſonnes of Noe, in their generations and nations. And of theſe came the people that were in the world after the floude.

⁋ The .XI. Chapter.

1. AND all the world was of one
2. tonge and one language. And as they came from the eaſt, they founde a play-.P.ne in the lande of Synear, and there they dwelled.
3. And they ſayd one to a nother: come on, let us make brycke ād burne it wyth fyre. So brycke was there ſtone and ſlyme was there morter And they ſayd: Come on,
4. let vs buylde us a cyte and a toure, that the toppe may reach vnto heauen. And let vs make us a name, for perauenture we ſhall be ſcatered abrode over all the erth.

M.C.S. The buylding of the tower of Babel. The confuſyon of tonges. The generacyon of Sem the ſonne of Noe vntyll Abrā which goeth with Lot vnto Haran.

V. 30 Sephar montem orientalem 32 Hæ familiæ Noe. xv. 1 ſermonum eorundem 4 antequam diuidamur in vniuerſas terras

L. 30 gen Sephara, an den berg gegen dem morgen. xi. 2 eyn plan ym land Sinear 4 denn wyr werden villeicht zurſtrewet ynn alle lender

L. M. N. 25 *Peleg;* auff deutſch, Eyn zuteylung.

5 And the LORde came downe to see the cyte and the toure which the childern of Adā had buylded.
6 And the LORde fayd: See, the people is one and haue one tonge amonge them all. And thys haue they begon to do, and wyll not leaue of from all that they haue purpofed to do.
7 Come on, let vs defcende and myngell theire tonge even there, that one vnderftonde not what a nother fayeth.
8 Thus ỹ LORde fkatered them from thence vppon all the erth. And they left of to buylde the cyte.
9 Wherfore the name of it is called Babell, becaufe that the LORDE there confounded the tonge of all the world. And becaufe that the LORde from thence, fkatered them abrode vppon all the erth.
10 Thefe are the generations of Sem: Sē was an hundred yere olde and begat Arphachfad .ii. yere after the floude.
11 And Sē lyved after he had begot Arphachfad v. hundred yere and begat fonnes and doughters
12 And Arphachfad lyued .xxxv. yere and be- [Fo. XIIII.] gat Sala,
13 and lyved after he had begot Sala .iiii. hūdred yere & .iii. & begat fonnes and doughters.
14 And Sala was .xxx. yere old and begat Eber,
15 ād lyved after he had begot Eber .iiii. hūdred and thre yere, ād begat fonnes and doughters.
16 When Eber was .xxxiiii. yere olde, he begat Peleg,
17 and lyued after he had begot Peleg, foure hundred and .xxx. yere, and begat fonnes and doughters.
18 And Peleg when he was .xxx. yere olde begat

V. 7 vnusquifque vocem proximi fui
L. 7 dafelbs verwyrren
M. M. N. 5 *came downe;* God is counted to come downe, whē he dothe any thing in the erthe amōge men that is not accuftomed to be done: in maner fhewynge hymfelfe prefent amonge men by his wonderfull worke, as it is in Ps. xvii. b. and .cxliii. a. *To fe the cyte;* not that god feeth not at all tymes, but only that he maketh hym felfe both to be fene and knowen in his wonderfull workes amōge vs. 12 *Arphachfad;* Here the feuentie Interpreters leaue oute the generacion of Caynan, the which after the reconynge of the Ebrues begat Sala, when he was .xxx. yere of age. Luke .iii. g.
L. M. N. 9 *Babel;* auff deutfch Eyn vermiffchung oder verwyrrung

19 Regu, and lyued after he had begot Regu .ii. hundred and .ix. yere, and begat sonnes and doughters.
20 And Regu when he had lyued .xxxii. yere begat
21 Serug, and lyued after he had begot Serug .ii. hundred and .vii. yere, and begat sonnes and doughters.
22 And when Serug was .xxx. yere olde, he begat
23 Nahor, and lyued after he had begot Nahor .ii. hundred yere, and begat sonnes & doughters.
24 And Nahor when he was .xxix. yere olde, begat
25 Terah, and lyved after he had begot Terah, an hundred and .xix. yere, .P. and begat sonnes and doughters.
26 And when Terah was .Lxx. yere olde, he begat Abram, Nahor and Haran.
27 And these are the generations of Terah. Terah begat Abram, Nahor and Haran. And Haran begat
28 Lot. And Haran dyed before Terah his father in the
29 londe where he was borne, at Vr in Chaldea. And Abram and Nahor toke them wyves. Abrās wyfe was called Sarai. And Nahors wyfe Mylca the doughter
30 of Haran which was father of Milca ād of Iisca. But Sarai was baren and had no childe.
31 Then toke Terah Abram his sonne and Lot his sonne Harans sonne, & Sarai his doughter in lawe his sone Abrams wyfe. And they went wyth hym from Vr in Chaldea, to go in to the lāde of Chanaan. And
32 they came to Haran and dwelled there. And when Terah was .ii. hundred yere old and .v. he dyed in Haran.

⁋ The .XII. Chapter.

1 THEN the LORde sayd vnto Abrā Gett the out of thy contre and from thy kynred, and out of thy fathers house, into a londe which I wyll shewe the.

M.C.S. Abram is blessed of God, and goeth with Lot into a straunge lande that apered

M. 29 Iesca.

2 And I wyll make of the a myghtie people, and wyll bleffe the, and make thy name grete, that thou mayft be a bleff-
3 inge. And I wyll bleffe thē that bleffe the, ād curfe thē that curfe the. And in the fhall be bleffed all the generations of the erth.

to hym in Canaan. And God promyfeth to geue the fame lande to hym and to his fede. And afterwarde goeth Abram into Egypt & caufeth Sarai his wyfe to faye that fhe is his fifter. And fhe was rauyfhed of Pharao, for whyche the Lorde plageth hym.

4 And Abram wēt as the LORde badd hym, [Fo. XV.] and Lot went wyth him. Abram was .Lxxv. yere olde, when he
5 went out of Haran. And Abram toke Sarai his wyfe ād Lot his brothers fonne, wyth all their goodes which they had goten and foulles which they had begoten in Haran. And they departed to goo in to the lāde of Chanaan. And when they were come in
6 to the lande of Chanaan, Abram went furth in to the lāde tyll he came vnto a place called Sychem, and vnto the oke of More. And the Canaanytes dwelled then in the lande.
7 Then the LORde apeared vnto Abram ād fayd: vnto thy feed wyll I geue thys lāde. And he buylded an aultere there vnto the LORDE which apeared to
8 hym. Then departed he thence vnto a mountayne that lyeth on the eaft fyde of BETHEL and pytched hys tente: BETHEL beynge on the weft fyde, and Ay on the eaft: And he buylded there an aulter vnto the LORde & called on the name of y̌ LORde.
9 And than Abram departed and toke his iourney fouthwarde
10 After thys there came a derth in the lande. And Abram went doune in to Egipte to foiourne there, for

℔. 6 forth
V. 6 pertranfiuit . . Sichem, & vfque ad conuallem illuftrem 10 fames
L. 6 Zoch er durch . . an den hayn More 10 eyn tewere zeyt
℔. ℔. N. 2 *Bleffe the;* To bleffe, is here to be made happye and fortunate. And to make great his name, is to aduaunce and extolle hym and aboue other people. 5 *Soules;* Soules here are taken for his feruauntes and maydens, which were very many as ye maye fe in Gen. xiv, c.

11 the derth was fore in the lande. And when he was come nye for to entre in to Egipte, he fayd vnto Sarai his wife. Beholde, I knowe that thou art a
12 fayre woman to loke apō. It wyll come to paffe therfore whē the Egiptians fee the, that they wyll fay: fhe is his wyfe. And fo fhall they fley me and
13 fave the. .P. Saye I praye the therfore that thou art my fifter, that I maye fare the better by reafon of the and that my foule maye lyue for thy fake.
14 As foon as he came in to Egipte, the Egiptiās fawe
15 the woman that fhe was very fayre. And Pharaos lordes fawe hir alfo, and prayfed hir vnto Pharao: So
16 that fhe was taken in to Pharaos houfe, which entreated Abram well for hir fake, fo that he had fhepe, oxfen ād he affes, men feruantes, mayde feruātes, fhe affes and camels.
17 But God plaged Pharao and his houfe wyth grete
18 plages, becaufe of Sarai Abrams wyfe. Then Pharao called Abram and fayd: why haft thou thus dealt with me? Wherfore toldeft thou me not that fhe was thy
19 wife? Why faydeft thou that fhe was thy fifter, and caufedeft me to take hyr to my wyfe? But now loo,
20 there is the wife, take hir ād be walkynge. Pharao alfo gaue a charge vnto his men over Abram, to leade hym out, wyth his wyfe and all that he had.

𝔐. 19 there is thy wyfe
𝔙. 12 et te referuabunt 15 principes Pharaoni 16 Abram vero bene vfi funt 17 Flagellauit autem dominus 19 vt tollerem eam mihi in uxorem
𝔏. 12 vnd dich behalten 14 das fie faft fchon war 15 und die furften des Pharao 17 Aber der Herr 19 derhalben ich fie myr zum weybe nam

¶ The .XIII. Chapter.

1 HAN Abram departed out of Egipte, both he and his wyfe and all that he had, and Lot wyth hym vnto the [Fo. XVI.]
2 fouth. Abram was very rich in catell,
3 fyluer & gold. And he went on his iourney frō the fouth even vnto BETHEL, ād vnto the place where his tente was at the fyrft tyme betwene BETHEL and
4 Ay, and vnto the place of the aulter which he made before. And there called Abram vpon the name of the LORde.
5 Lot alfo which went wyth him had fhepe, catell
6 and tentes: fo that the londe was not abill to receaue them that they myght dwell to gether, for the fubftance of their riches was fo greate, that they coude
7 not dwell to gether And there fell a ftryfe betwene the herdmen of Abrams catell, and the herdmen of Lots catell. Moreouer the Cananytes and the Pheryfites dwelled at that tyme in the lande.
8 Than fayd Abram vnto Lot: let there be no ftryfe I praye the betwene the and me and betwene my
9 herdmen and thyne, for we be brethren. Ys not all the hole lande before the? Departe I praye the frō me. Yf thou wylt take the lefte hande, I wyll take the right: Or yf thou take the right hande I wyll take
10 the left. And Lot lyft vp his eyes and beheld all the contre aboute Iordane, which was a plenteous contre of water every where, before the LORde deftroyed Sodoma and Gomorra. .P. Even as the garden of the

M.C.S. Abram & Loth departe oute of Egypt. And Abram deuyded his lande & catell with his brother Lot. Here agayne is promysed to Abram the lande of Canaan.

M. 3 to the place
V. 1 Afcendit . . . auftralem plagam 3 Reuerfufque 4 quod feceret prius 6 habitarent fimul . . communiter
L. 7 vnd war ymer zank
M. M. N. 8 *brethren;* The Hebrues vnderftonde by this worde brother al nevews, coffyns & neyboures, & all that be of one ftocke. Rom. ix, a; Ino. vii, a.

LORde, & as the lande of Egipte tyll thou come to
Zoar.

11 Than Lot chofe all the coftes of Iordane ãd toke
hys iourney from the eaft. And fo departed the one
brother from the other.

12 Abram dwelled in the lande of Canaan. And lot
in the cytes of the playne, & tented tyll he came to
13 Sodome. But the men of fodome were wyked and
fynned exceadyngly agenft the LORde.

14 And the LORde fayed vnto Abram, after that Lot
was departed from hym: lyfte vp thyne eyes & loke
from ỹ place where thou art, northward, fouthward,
15 eaftward and weftward, for all the lande which thou
feifte wyll I gyue vnto the & to thy feed for ever.

16 And I wyll make thy feed, as the duft of the erth;
fo that yf a mã can nombre the duft of the erth, than
17 fhall thy feed alfo be nombred. Aryfe and walke
aboute in the lande, in the length of it ãd in the
bredth for I wyll geue it vnto the.

18 Than Abrã toke downe hys tente, & went and
dwelled in the okegrove of Mamre which is in Ebron
and buylded there an altar to the LORde.

The .XIIII. Chapter.

1 AND it chaunfed within a while, *M.T.S. Lot
that Amraphel kynge of Sy- is takcn pryf-
near, Arioch kynge of Ellafar, victory of Ab-
Kedorlaomer kynge of Elam rã of the Sodomytes. Lot
2 and Thydeall kynge of the nations: made is delyuered
warre wyth Bera kynge of Sodõe and by Abram.*

M. 1 Kedorlaomor cf. vv. 4. 9
V. 18 iuxta conuallem
L. 14 heb deyn augen auff
M. M. N. 15 *for ever;* Euer is not here taken for tyme wythoute ende; but for a longe ceafon that hath not his ende apoynted.
18 *Ebron* is the name of a citie where Adam Abraham and his
wyfe with Ifaac etc. were buryed, as in Gen. xxiii, d.

with Birsa kynge of Gomorra. And wyt- *Melchisedech*
[Fo. XVII.] he Sineab kynge of Adama, *offreth gyftes*
& with Semeaber kynge of Zeboim, and *Abram payeth*
wyth the kynge of Bela Which Bela is *tythes vnto*
Melchisedech.
3 called Zoar. All thefe came together *Abram hold-*
vnto the vale of fiddim which is now the *eth nothynge*
of the kynge
4 falt fee Twelve yere were they fubiecte *of Sodomes*
to kinge kedorlaomer, and in the .xiii *goodes.*
yere rebelled.

5 Therefore in the .xiiii. yere came kedorlaomer and the kynges that were wyth hym, and fmote the Raphayms in Aftarath Karnaim, and the Sufims in
6 Ham, ād the Emyms in Sabe Kariathaim, and the Horyms in their awne mounte Seir vnto the playne
7 of Pharan, which bordreth vpon the wyldernesse. And then turned they and came to the well of iugmente which is Cades, and fmote all the contre of the Amalechites, and alfo the amorytes that dwell in Hazezon Thamar.

8 Than went out the kynge of Sodome, and the kynge of Gomorra, and the kynge of Adama and the kynge of Zeboijm, and the kynge of Bela now called Zoar. And fette their men in aray to fyghte wyth
9 them in the vale of fiddim, that is to fay, wyth kedorlaomer the kynge of Elam and with Thydeall kynge of the Nations, and wyth Amraphel kynge of Synear. And with Arioch kynge of Ellafar: foure
10 kynges agenfte v. And that vale of fiddim was full of flyme pyttes.

And the kynges of Sodome and Gomorra fled, and fell there. And the refydue fled to the moun-
11 taynes. And they toke all the goodes .P. of Sodome and Gomorra and all their vitalles, ād went

𝕸. 2 Semeabar
𝖁. 3 conuenerunt in vallem fylueftrem 6 campeftria Pharan quæ eft in folitudine
𝕷. 3 das breytte tall cf. vv. 8, 10 5 die Ryfen zu Aftaroth 6 bis an die breyte Pharan, wilch an die wuften ftoft 7 an den Rechtborn
𝕸. 𝕸. N. 2 *kynge of Bela;* Bela is the citie that Lot defyred for his refuge when he came oute of Sodome as in Gen. xix, c. 5 *Raphaim*, are counted in the fcripture for gyauntes as in .ii Reg. v, b. Es. xvii. which lyued by theft and robberye.

12 their waye. And they toke Lot alſo Abrams brothers ſonne and his good (for he dwelled at Sodome) and departed.

13 Than came one that had eſcaped, and tolde Abram the hebrue which dwelt in the okegrove of Mamre the Amoryte brother of Eſchol and Aner: which were
14 confederate wyth Abram. When Abram herde that his brother was taken, he harneſſed his *harneſſed,* ſeruantes borne in his owne houſe .iii *armed* hundred & .xviii. ãd folowed tyll they came at Dan.
15 And ſette hymſelfe ãd his ſeruantes in aray, & fell vpon them by nyght, & ſmote them, & chaſed them awaye vnto Hoba: which lyeth on the lefte hande of
16 Damaſcos, and broughte agayne all the goodes & alſo his brother Lot, ãd his goodes, the wemē alſo and the people.

17 And as he retourned agayne from the ſlaughter of kedorlaomer and of the kynges that were with hym, than came the kynge of Sodome agaynſt hym vnto the vale of Saue which now is called kynges dale.
18 Than Melchiſedech kinge of Salem brought forth breed and wyne. And he beynge the preſt of the
19 moſt hygheſt God, bleſſed hym ſaynge. Bleſſed be Abram vnto the moſt hygheſt God, poſſeſſor of heaven
20 and erth. And bleſſed be God the moſt hygheſt, which hath delyvered thyne enimies in to thy handes. And Abrã gaue hym tythes of all.
21 [Fo. XVIII.] Than ſayd the kynge of Sodome vnto

𝔐. 13 Abram the Hebrew 16 women alſo 17 returned .. Sodome to mete him in the vale of Saue 18 Preſte.

𝒱. 15 Et diuiſis ſociis, irruet ſuper eos nocte: 17 a cæde Chodorlaomor 18 proferens panem et vinum 20 quo protegente

𝑳 12 und ſeyn habe 13 dem Auſländer 15 vnd teylet ſich 17 von der ſchlacht des Kedorlaomor 18 trug brot vnd weyn erfur

𝔐. 𝔐. N. 18 *Melchiſedech;* The Jewes ſuppoſed Mechiſedek to be Sem the ſonne of Noe becauſe he lyued after the floude .v hũdred yere, & after the death of Abraham (by godes prouidence) was kynge of Salem 19 *Bleſſed* be Abram, that is prayſed be Abrã. And prayſed be the mooſt hygheſt God as it is in Genes. xlvii, b.

𝑳. 𝔐. N. 18 *Trug brod;* Nicht das ers opferte, ſondern das er die geſte ſpeyſet vnd ehret da durch Chriſtus bedeut iſt, der die wellt mit dem Euangelio ſpeyſet.

Abram: gyue me the foulles, and take the goodes
22 to thy felfe. And Abram anfwered the Kynge of
Sodome: I lyfte vpp my hande vnto the LORde God
23 moft hygh poffeffor of heaven ād erth, that I will not
take of all ẏ is thyne, fo moch as a thred or a
fhoulachet, left thou fhuldeft faye I haue made Abrā
24 ryche. Saue only that which the yonge men haue
eaten ād the partes of the men which went wyth me.
Aner, Efcholl & Mamre. Let them take their partes.

XV. Chapter.

1 AFTER thefe deades, ẏ worde of God came vnto Abram in a vifion faynge feare not Abram, I am thy fhilde, and thy re- 2 warde fhalbe exceadynge greate. And Abram anfwered: LORde Iehouah what wilt thou geue me: I goo childleffe, and the cater of myne houffe, this Eleafar 3 of Damafco hath a fonne. And Abram fayd: fe, to me haft thou geven no feed: lo, a lad borne in my houffe fhal be myne heyre.

M.C.S. The lande of Canaan is yet agayne promyfed to Abram. God promyfeth hym feed. He beleueth & is iuftifyed. The prophecye of the bondage wherin the chyldren of Ifrael fhuld be vnder Pharao, & of their delyuerance from the fame.

4 And beholde, the worde of the LORde fpake vnto Abram fayenge: He fhall not be thyne heyre, but one that fhall come out of thyne 5 awne bodye fhalbe thyne heyre. .T. And he brought him out at the doores ād fayde. Loke vpp vnto

---

M. 1 faying 5 out of the dores
V. 21 animas 22 poffefforem. xv, 2 filius procuratoris domus meæ
L. 21 die feelen 22 befitzt. xv, 1 fchilt 2 Herr Herr cf. v. 8.
4 der von deynem leyb komen wirt
M. M. N. 21 *Gyue me the foules;* Soules are men & women, as Gen. xlvi, c & Deut. x, b. xv, 1 *The worde of God;* The word of the Lorde cometh when he fheweth any thynge vnto vs by reuelacyon as it is vfed in diuers places of the Scripture, and fpecially in the Prophetes & is a maner of fpeache of the Hebrewes.

heaven and tell the ſtarres, yf thou be able to nōbre them. And ſayde vnto him Even ſo ſhall thy ſeed be.
6 And Abram beleved the LORde, and it was counted
7 to hym for rightweſnes. And he ſayde vnto hym: I am the LORde that brought the out of Vr in Chaldea to geue the this lande to poſſeſſe it.
8 And he ſayde: LORde God, whereby ſhall I knowe
9 that I ſhall poſſeſſe it? And he ſayd vnto him: take an heyfer of .iii. yere olde, and a ſhe gotte of thre yeres olde, and a thre yere olde ram, a turtill doue and a
10 yonge pigeon. And he toke all theſe and devyded them in the myddes, and layde euery pece, one over
11 agenſt a nother. But the ſoules devyded he not. And the byrdes fell on the carcaſes, but Abrā droue thē
12 awaye. And when the ſonne was doune, there fell a ſlomber apon Abram. And loo, feare and greate darkneſſe came apon hym.
13 And he ſayde vnto Abram: knowe this of a ſuertie, that thi ſeed ſhalbe a ſtraunger in a lande that perteyneth not vnto thē. And they ſhall make bondmen of them
14 and entreate them evell .iiii. hundred yeares. But the nation whom they ſhall ſerue, wyll I iudge. And afterwarde ſhall they come out wyth greate ſubſtāce.
15 Neuertheleſſe thou ſhalt goo vnto thi fathers in peace,
16 ād ſhalt be buried when thou art of a good age: ād in the fourth generation they ſhall come hyther [Fo.

М. 10 pece, one agaynſt another 12 vpon- vpon
V. 10 diuiſit ea per medium 12 horror magnus & tenebroſus inuaſit eum 13 Scito praenoſcens
L. 5 zele die ſterne .. kanſtu ſic zelen 10 zuteylet es mitten von ander 11 das gevogel fiel 12 ſchrecken vnd groſſe finſternifs
M.M.N. 6 *And Abram beleued;* To beleue is to haue a ſure truſt & confydence to obtayne the thing promyſed and not to haue any doute in hym that promyſeth as Rom. iiii, a, Gal. iii, a .ii, d. 14 *ſerue wyll I iudge;* To iudge is here to take vēgeaunce, Pſ. xxxiiii, a. 16 *Fourth generation,* a generacyō or an age is here taken for an hundred yere, as Gen. vi, d.
L. M. N. 11 *Gevogel fiel;* Das gevogel vnd der rauchend offen vnd der feuriger brand, bedeuten die Egypter, die Abrahams Kinder verfolgen ſolltent Aber Abraham ſcheucht ſie davon, das iſt, Got erloſet ſie vmb der verheyſſung willen Abraham verſprochen, Das aber er nach der ſonnen vntergang erſchrickt, bedeut, das Got ſeyn Samen eyn zeyt verlaſſen wollt, das ſie verfolget wurden, wie der herr ſelbs hie deut. Alſo gehet es auch allen glewbigen, das ſie verlaſſen vnd doch erloſet werden.

XIX.] agayne, for the wekedneffe of the Amorites ys not yet full.

17 When the fonne was doune and it was waxed darcke: beholde, there was a fmokynge furneffe and a fyre brand that went betwene the fayde peces.

18 And that fame daye the LORde made a covenaunte with Abram faynge: vnto thy feed wyll I geue thys londe, frō the ryver of Egypte, even vnto the greate ryver euphrates: the kenytes, the kenizites, the Cad-
19
20 monites, the Hethites, the Pherezites, the Raphaims,
21 the Amorytes, the Canaanites, the Gergefites and the Iebufites.

The .XVI. Chapter.

1 SARAI Abrams wyfe bare him no childerne. But fhe had an hand mayde an Egiptian, whofe
2 name was Hagar. Wherfore fhe fayde vnto Abram. Beholde the LORde hath clofed me, that I cannot bere. I praye thee goo in vnto my mayde, peraduēture I fhall be multiplyed by meanes of her. And Abram herde the voyce of Sarai.

3 Than Sarai Abrams wife toke Hagar hyr mayde the Egiptian (after Abram had dwelled .x. yere in the lande of Canaan)

M.C.S. Sarai geueth Abram leaue to take Agar hyr mayde to wyfe. Agar defpyfed hyr mayftres: for which fhe was euyll intreated of Sarai, and therfore runneth awaye. The angell metynge hyr commaundeth hyr to turne agayne and doth

---

M. 1 chyldren 3 Hagar
V. 17 & lampas ignis xvi, 2 conclufit 3 ancillam fuam poft annos decem quam habitare cœperant
L. 17 und eyn fewriger brand. xvi, 2 verfchloffen .. Lieber leg dich .. aus yhr mich bawen muge mehr denn aus mir 3 nachdem fie—gewonet hatten
M.M.N. 17 *That went betwene:* This worde went betwene: is taken for burning or confumynge. xvi, 2 To go in vnto hyr mayde is to haue carnall copulacion with hyr as thefe wordes knowe & flepe do alfo fignifye as Gen. iiii. a and .xxix. c.

and gaue her to hyr huſbonde Abram, to *promyſe hyr*
be his wyfe. *ſede. And*
nameth hyr
4 And he wente in vnto Hagar, & ſhe *fyrſt chylde*
conceaued. And when ſhe ſawe that ſhe *Iſmael.*
had conceyved .P. hyr maſtreſſe was deſpiſed in hyr
ſyghte.
5 Than ſayd Sarai vnto Abram: Thou doſt
me vnrighte, for I haue geuen my mayde vnrighte,*wrong*
in to thy boſome: & now becauſe ſhe ſeyth that ſhe hath
cōceaved, I am deſpyſed in her ſyghte: the LORde iudge
6 betwene the and me. Than ſayd Abrā to Sarai: beholde,
thy mayde is in thy hande, do with hyr as it pleaſeth the.
And becauſe Sarai fared ſoule with her, ſhe fled from
7 her. And the angell of the Lorde founde her beſyde
a fountayne of water in the wyldernes: euen by a well
8 in the way to Sur. And he ſayde: Hagar Sarais
mayde, whence comeſt thou and whether wylt thou
goo? And ſhe anſwered: I flee from my maſtreſſe
9 Sarai. And the angell of the LORde ſayde vnto
her: returne to thy maſtreſſe agayne, & ſubmytte thy
ſelfe vnder her handes.
10 And the angell of ẏ LORde ſayde vnto her: I will
ſo encreaſe thy ſeed, that it ſhall not be numbred for
11 multitude. And the LORdes angell ſayd further
vnto her: ſe, thou art wyth childe and ſhalt bere a
ſonne, and ſhalt call his name Iſmael: becauſe the
12 LORDE hath herde thy tribulation. He will be a
wylde man, and his hande will be agenſt wylde, *not*
every man, & euery mans hande agenſt *domeſticated*
him. And yet ſhall he dwell faſte by all his brothren.
13 [Fo. XX.] And ſhe called the name of the LORde
that ſpake vnto her: thou art the God that lokeſt

🕮. 4 Agar 5 ſeeth 12 brethren
V̄. 9 humiliare ſub manu illius. 12 ferus homo .. et eregione
vniverſorum fratrum ſuorum figet tabernacula.
L. 5 ich muſs vnrecht leyden .. vnter deyner gewallt 6 Da ſie
nu Sarai wolt demutigen 9 vnd demutige dich 11 armſelickeyt
12 ein wilder Menſch.
🕮. 🕮. N. 5 *Boſome:* Boſome after the maner of the Hebrewes
is taken for companyeng wyth a woman, & is alſo takē for ſayth
as in Luc. xvi. f. of Lazarus.
L. 🕮. N. 11 Iſmael, heyſt Gott erhoret.

on me, for she fayde: I haue of a fuertie fene here
14 the backe parties of him that feith me. Wherfore
she called the well, the well of the lyuynge that feith·
me which well is betwene Cades & Bared.
15 And Hagar bare Abram a fonne, and Abram called
16 his fons name which Hagar bare Ifmaell. And Abram
was .lxxxvi. yere olde, when Hagar bare him Ifmael.

⁌ The .XVII. Chapter.

1 WHEN Abram was nynetye yere old & .ix. the LORde apeared to hym fayenge: I am the almyghtie God: walke before
2 me ād be vncorrupte. And I wyll make
bonde, *coue-* my bonde betwene the and
nant me, and wyll multiplye the excedyngly.

M.C.S. Abram is called Abrahā, & Sarai is named Sara. The lande of Canaan is here the fourth tyme promyfed. Circumfyfion is here inftitute. Ifaac is promyfed. Abraham prayeth for Ifmael.

3 And Abrā fell on his face. And God
4 talked moreover with hym faynge: I am,
teftament, beholde my teftamēt is with
couenant the, that thou fhalt be a fa-
5 ther of many natiōs. Therfore fhalt thou no more be
called Abram, but thy name fhalbe Abraham: for a
6 father of many nations haue I made the, and I will
multiplye the excedyngly, and wyll make nations of
the: yee and kynges fhall fprynge out of the.
7 Moreover I will make my bonde betwene me and
the, and thy feed after the, in their tymes .P. to be an
everlaftynge teftament, So that I wyll be God vnto
8 the and to thy feed after the. And I will geue vnto

M. 13 partes
V. 13 pofteriora videntis me. xvii, 3 Cecidit Abram pronus in facie.
L. 1 vnd fey on wandel 2 faft feer mehren 4 Sihe ich byns 6 faft feer fruchtbar machen
M. M. N. 13 They fe the backe partes of God that by reuelaciō or any other wyfe haue perfeuerāce or knowledge of God.
L. M. N. 5 *Abram* heyft hoher vatter, *Abraham* aber der haufen vater, wie wol die felben hauffen nur mit eynen buchftaben antzeygt werden yn feynem namen, nicht on vrfach.

the ād to thy feed after the, the lande where in thou arte a ſtraunger: Euen all the lande of Canaan, for an everlaſtynge poſſeſſion, and will be their God.

9 And God ſayde vnto Abrahā: Se thou kepe my teſtamente, both thou & thy feed after the in their
10 tymes: This is my teſtamente which ye ſhall kepe betwene me and you and thy feed after the, that ye
11 circūſyſe all youre men childern Ye ſhall circumcyſe the foreſkynne of youre fleſh, ād it ſhal be a token of
12 the bond betwixte me and you. And euery man-childe when it is .viii. dayes olde, ſhall be circūſyſed amonge you in youre generations, and all ſervauntes alſo borne at home or boughte with money though they
13 be ſtraungers and not of thy feed. The ſeruaunte borne in thy houſſe, ād he alſo that is bought with money, muſt needes be circumcyſed, that my teſtament may be in youre fleſh, for an everlaſtinge bonde.
14 Yf there be any vncircuncyſed manchilde, that hath not the forſkynne of his fleſh cutt of, his ſoule ſhall periſh from his people: becauſe he hath brokē my teſtamēt

15 And God ſayde vnto Abraham. Sarai thy wyfe ſhall nomore be called Sarai: but Sara ſhall hir name
16 be. For I will bleſſe her & geue the a ſonne of her and will bleſſe her: ſo that people, ye and kynges
17 of people ſhall ſpringe of her. And Abraham fell vpon his face ād [Fo. XXI.] laughte, and ſayde in his harte: ſhall a childe be borne vnto hym that is an hundred yere olde, ād ſhall Sara that is nynetie yere old, bere?
18 And Abrahā ſayde vnto God. O þat Iſmaell myghte lyve in thy ſyghte.
19 Thē ſayde God: na, Sara thy wife ſhall bere the a

𝔐. 19 God: Sarah thy wife . . a ſonne in dede
𝔙. 8 terrā peregrinationis tuæ 14 pactum meum irritū fecit. 19 Sara vxor tua pariet tibi filium . . . & conſtituam pactum meum illi in fœdus ſempiternum
𝔏. 19 ia, Sara deyn weyb ſoll dyr eynen ſon geperen
𝔐. 𝔐. N. 13 *Böde:* The ſcripture vſeth to call the ſigne of a thynge by the name of the thīge it ſelfe only to kepe the thynge ſygniſyed, the better in memory as here he calleth circumciſyon his bonde which is but a token therof, and as Peter calleth baptyme Chriſt. 1 Pet. iii d.

sonne, ād thou shalt call his name Isaac. And I will make my bonde with him, that it shall be an ever-
20 lastynge bonde vnto his seed after him. And as concernynge Ismaell also, I haue herde thy request: loo, I will blesse him and encrease him, and multiplye him excedyngly. Twelve prynces shall he begete, and I
21 will make a great nation of him. But my bonde will I make with Isaac, which Sara shall bere vnto the: euen this tyme twelue moneth.
22 And God left of talkyng with him, and departed vp
23 from Abraham. And Abraham toke Ismaell his sonne & all the servauntes borne in his housse and all that was bought with money as many as were men children amonge the mē of Abrahās housse, and circumcysed the foreskynne of their flesh, even the selfe same daye,
24 as God had sayde vnto him. Abraham was nynetie yere olde and .ix. when he cutt of the foreskynne of
25 his flesh. And Ismaell his sonne was .xiii. yere olde, when the foreskynne of hys flesh was circumcysed.
26 The selfe same daye was Abrahā circūcised & Ismael
27 his sonne. And all the men in his housse, whether thy were borne in his housse or bought wyth .P. money (though they were straungers) were circumcysed with him.

⁌ The .XVIII. Chapter.

1 AND the LORde apeared vnto him in the okegrove of Mamre as he sat in his tent dore in the heate of the daye. And he
2 lyfte vp his eyes and looked: ād lo, thre men stode not farr from hym. And whē

𝔐.𝕰.𝖘. *There apered thre men vnto Abraham. Isaac is promysed to hym agayne, at whych Sara*

𝒱. 1 conualle
𝕷. 1 hayn Mamre 2 drey menner gegen yhm
𝔐. 𝔐. 𝔑. 1 *The heate of the daye* is taken for none.

he fawe them, he ran agenſt them from *laughed. The destruccion of the Sodomites is declared vnto Abraham. Abraham prayeth for them.*
the tent dore, and fell to the grounde
3 and fayde: LORde yf I haue founde
fauoure in thy fyght, goo not by thi
4 feruaunte. Let a litle water be fett,
& waſh youre fete, and reſt youre felues
5 vnder the tree: And I will fett a morfell *fett, fetch*
of breed, to comforte youre harts wythall. And thã
goo youre wayes, for even therfore ar ye come to youre
feruaunte. And they anfwered: Do even fo as thou
haft fayde.

6 And Abrahã went a pace in to his tent vnto Sara
ãd fayde: make redy att once thre peckes of fyne meale,
7 kneade it, and make cakes. And Abraham ran vnto
his beaſtes and fett a calfe that was tendre and good,
and gaue it vn to a yonge man which made it redy
8 attonce. And he toke butter & mylcke and the calfe
which he had prepared, and fett it before them, and
ſtode hymfelfe by them vnder the tre: and they ate.

9 [Fo. XXII.] And they fayde vnto him: Where is
10 Sara thy wife? And he fayde: in the tent. And he
fayde: I will come agayne vnto the as soone as the
frute can lyue. And loo: Sara thy wife frute, *either the child, or the feafon of the year.*
ſhall haue a fonne. That herde Sara,
out of the tent doore which was behind
11 his backe. Abraham and Sara were both olde and
well ſtryken in age, and it ceafed to be with Sara after
12 the maner as it is wyth wyves. And Sara wyves, *women*
laughed in hir felfe faynge: Now I am waxed olde,
ſhall I geue my felfe to luſt, and my lorde olde alfo?

M. 2 ran to mete them
V. 2 cucurrit in occurfum eorum de oſtio .. et adorauit in terra 5 Ponamque buccellam panis 6 tria fata fimilæ .. fubcinericios panes 7 vitulum tenerrimum & optimum 10 vita comite 12 voluptati operam dabo
L. 6 drey mas femel meel 8 vnd von dem kalbe 10 nach der zeyt die frucht leben kan 12 mit wolluſt vmbgehen
M. M. N. 5 *Brede:* By Brede in the fcripture is vnderſtonde all maner of fode, mete for mãnes eatynge as in 1 Regũ. xxviii, d.
L. M. N. 2 *fur yhm nydder:* fur eynem fellt er nydder vnd redet auch als mit evnem vnd mit dreyen, da iſt die drevfelltickeyt ynn Gott antzeyget.

13 Than fayde the LORde vnto Abrahā: wherfore doth Sara laughe faynge: fhall I of a fuertie bere a childe,
14 now when I am olde? is the thinge to harde for the LORde to do? In the tyme appoynted will I returne vnto the, as foone as the frute can haue lyfe, And Sara
15 fhall haue a fonne. Than Sara denyed it faynge: I laughed not, for fhe was afrayde. But he fayde: yes thou laughteft.
16 Than the men ftode vp from thence ād loked towarde Sodome. And Abraham went with them
17 to brynge them on the waye. And the LORde fayde: Can I hyde from Abraham that thinge which I am
18 aboute to do, feynge that Abraham fhall be a great ād a myghtie people, and all the nations of the erth fhalbe
19 bleffed in him? For I knowe him that he will commaunde his childern and .P. his houfholde after him, ў they kepe the waye of the LORde, to do after righte and confcyence, that the LORde may brynge vppon Abraham that he hath promyfed him.
20 And the LORde fayde: The crie of Sodome and Gomorra is great, and there fynne is excedynge
21 grevous. I will go downe and fee whether they haue done all to gedder acordynge to that crye which is
22 come vnto me or not, that I may knowe. And the mē departed thēce and went to Sodomeward. But
23 Abraham ftode yet before ў LORde, and drewe nere & fayde Wylt thou deftroy the rightwes with the
24 wyked? Yf there be .L. rightwes within the cyte, wilt thou deftroy it and not fpare the place for the fake of
25 L. rightwes that are therin? That be farre from the, that thou fhuldeſt do after thys maner, to fley the rightwes with the weked, ād that the rightwes fhulde be as the weked: that be farre from the. Shulde not
26 the iudge of all ў worlde do acordynge to righte? And

Ӎ. 21 together
Ṽ. 14 vita comite 19 & faciant iudicium & iuſtitiam; vt adducat 21 venit ad me, opere compleuerint 25 Abſit a te .. fiatque iuſtus ficut impius .. nequaquam facias iudicium hoc.
Ł. 14 nach der zeyt die frucht leben kan 19 was recht vnd redlich ift 24 dem ort nicht vergeben

the LORde fayde: Yf I fynde in Sodome .L. rightwes within the cyte, I will fpare all the place for their fakes.

27 And Abraham anfwered and fayde: beholde I haue taken vppon me to fpeake vnto ỹ LORde, ãd yet am
28 but duft ãd afhes. What though there lacke .v. of L. rightwes, wylt thou deftroy all the cyte for lacke of .v.? And he fayde: Yf I fynde there .xl. and .v I will not deftroy them.
29 And he fpake vnto him yet agayne and fay-[Fo. XXIII.] de: what yf there be .xl. foũde there: And he
30 fayde: I wyll not do it for forties fake. And he fayde: O let not my LORde be angrye, that I fpeake. What yf there he foũde .xxx. there? And he fayde: I will
31 not do it, yf I finde .xxx. there. And he fayde: Oh, fe, I haue begonne to fpeak vnto my LORde, what yf there be .xx. founde there? And he fayde: I will not
32 diftroy thẽ for twẽties fake. And he fayde: O let not my LORde be angrye, that I fpeake yet, but euẽ once more only. What yf ten be founde there? And he fayde: I will not deftroy thẽ for .x. fake.
33 And the LORde wēt his waye as foone as he had lefte comenynge with Abrahã. And   *comenynge,* Abraham returned vnto his place   *communing*

ℂ The .XIX. Chapter.

1 AND there came .ii. angells to   𝔐.𝔈.𝔖. *Lot* Sodome at euen. And Lot *receaued two Angelles into* fatt at the gate of the cyte. *hys houfe.* And Lot fawe thẽ, and rofe *The fylthy luftes of the* vp agaynft them, and he bowed hym felfe *Sodomytes.*
2 to the grounde with his face. And he *Lot is delyuer-*

𝔐. 1 vp to mete them
𝔙. 26 in medio ciuitatıs, dimittam, omni loco propter eos. 31 Quia femel, ait cœpi 32 Obfecro, inquit, ne irafcaris
𝔏. 26 alle den ortten. xix, 1 buckt fich mit feym angeficht auff die erden

XIX. 3–11. *called Genesis.* 57

fayde: Se lordes, turne in I praye you in *ed & defyreth*
to youre feruauntes houfe and tary all *to dwell in the cytie Zoar.*
nyghte & wafh youre fete, & ryfe up *Lottes wyfe is*
early and go on youre wayes. And they *torned into a pyler of falt,*
fayde: nay, but we will byde in the *Sodome is de-*
3 ftreates all nyghte. And he cōpelled *ftroyed. Lot is dronken &*
them excedyngly. And they turned in *lyeth with his*
vnto hym and entred in to his houfe, and *daughters*
he made them a feafte and dyd bake *whych con-ceaued chyl-*
fwete cakes, and they ate. *dren by hym.*

4 But before they went to reft, the men of the cyte
of Sodome compaffed the houfe rownde .Ṗ. aboute
both olde and yonge, all the people from all quarters.
5 And they called vnto Lot and fayde vnto him: where
are the men which came in to thy houfe to nyghte?
brynge thē out vnto vs that we may do oure luft with
them.
6 And Lot went out at doores vnto them and fhote
7 the dore after him and fayde: nay for goddes fake
8 brethren, do not fo wekedly. Beholde I have two
doughters which haue knowne no man, thē will I
brynge out vnto you: do with them as it femeth you
good: Only vnto thefe men do nothynge, for therfore
9 came they vnder the fhadow of my rofe. And they
fayde: come hither. And they fayde: cameft thou
not in to fogeorne, and wilt thou be now a iudge? we
will fuerly deale worfe with the than with them

And as they preafed fore vppon Lot and *preafed, pref-*
10 beganne to breake vp the doore, the men *fed*
put forth their handes and pulled Lot in to the houfe
to them and fhott to the doore. And the men that
11 were at the doore of the houfe, they fmote with

V. 2 & manete ibi .. in platea manebimus 3 Compulit illos
oppido vt diuerterent ad eum .. azyma 7 Nolite-nolite 8 et abu-
timini eis ... fub vmbra culminis mei 9 Recede illuc 13 coram
domino, qui mifit nos
L. 2 Sihe, meyne Herr, keret eyn .. bleybt vbernacht .. vber
nacht auff der gaffen bleyben 3 buch vngefeurt kuchen 4 aus allen
enden 8 difen mennern Gottis
M. M. N. 5 *Nyght:* The nyght is here taken for the euen-
yng which is the begynnyng of the nyght as in the Prou. vii, b.

blyndneſſe both ſmall and greate: ſo that they coude not fynde the doore.

12 And the men ſayde moreover vnto Lot: Yf thou have yet here any ſonne in lawe or ſonnes or doughters or what ſo euer thou haſt in the cyte, brynge it
13 out of this place: for we muſt deſtroy this place, becauſe the crye of thē is great before the LORde. Wherfore he hath ſent vs to deſtroy it.
14 And Lot went out and ſpake vnto his ſonnes [Fo. XXIIII.) in lawe which ſhulde have maried his doughters, and ſayde: ſtonde vpp and get yow out of this place, for the LORde will deſtroy the cite. But he ſemed as though he had mocked, vnto his ſonnes in law.
15 And as the mornynge aroſe the angells cauſed Lot to ſpede him ſaynge. Stonde vp, take thy wyfe and thy two doughters and that that is at hande, left thou
16 periſh in the ſynne of the cyte. And as he prolonged the tyme, the men caught both him, his wife ād his two doughters by the handes, becauſe the LORde was mercyfull vnto him, ād they brought him forth and ſette him without the cyte.
17 When they had brought them out, they ſayde: Saue thy lyfe and loke not behynde the nether tary thou in any place of the contre, but ſaue thy ſelfe in the
18 mountayne, left thou periſſhe. Than ſayde Lot vnto
19 them: Oh nay my lorde: beholde, in as moch as thy ſeruaunte hath ſownde grace in thy ſyghte, now make thi mercy great which thou ſheweſt vnto me in ſavinge my lyfe. For I can not ſaue my ſelfe in the mountayns, left ſome miſfortune fall vpon me and I dye.
20 Beholde, here is a cyte by, to flee vnto, and it is a

V. 15 vxorem tuam & duas filias quas habes: 16 Diſſimulante illo ... parceret dominus illi 17 Salua animam tuam .. ne & tu ſimul pereas. 19 ſaluares animam meam
L. 13 verderben 14 Aber es war yhn lecherlich. 15 deyn weyb vnd deyn zwoo tochter, die fur handen find, 17 Erredte deyn ſeele 19 meyn ſeel bey dem leben erhielteſt
M. M. N. 15 Synne: The ſynne is taken for the ſynner, as malyce is for the wicked, & righteouſnes for ryghteous, as Paul to Tytus the fyrſt .c.

lytle one, let me faue my felfe therein: is it not a litle one, that my foule may lyve?

21 And he faydè to him: fe I haue receaved thy requeſt as concernynge this thynge, that I will nott overthrowe this cytie for the .ꝑ. which thou haſt ſpoken.
22 Haſte the, ād faue thy felfe there, for I can do nothynge tyll thou be come in thyder. And therfore
23 the name of the cyte is called Zoar. And the ſone was vppon the erth when Lot was entred into Zoar.
24 Than the LORde rayned vpon Sodome and Gomorra, brymſtone and fyre from the LORde out of
25 heaven, and overthrewe thoſe cyteis and all the region, and all that dwelled in the cytes, and that that grewe
26 vpon the erth. And lots wyfe loked behynde her, ād was turned in to a pillare of falte.
27 Abraham rofe vp early and got him to the place
28 where he ſtode before the LORde, and loked toward Sodome and Gomorra and toward all the londe of that contre. And as he loked: beholde, the ſmoke of the contre arofe as it had bene the ſmoke of a fornace.
29 But yet whē God deſtroyed the cities of ẏ region, he thought apon Abrahā: and ſent Lot out from the dāger of the overthrowenge, when he overthrewe the cyties where Lot dwelled.
30 And Lot departed out of Zoar and dwelled in the mountayns ād his .ii. doughters with him for he feared to tary in Zoar: he dwelled therefore in a caue, both he and his .ii. doughters alfo.
31 Than fayde the elder vnto the yonger oure father is olde, and there are no moo men in the erth to come
32 in vnto vs after the maner of all the world. Come therfore, let vs geue oure father wyne to dryncke, and let vs lye with him [Fo. XXV.] that we may faue feed

𝔐. 22 thither
𝒱. 20 Eſt ciuitas hæc iuxta 21 fubuertam 22 Idcirco 25 & cuncta terræ virētia 28 fauillam de terra quaſi fornacis fumum 29 vrbium, in quibus 31 iuxta morem vniuerſæ terræ.
𝑳. 25 vnd was auff dem land gewachſen war 31 nach aller welt weyſe 32 trincken geben, vnd mit yhm truncken werden
𝑳. 𝔐. 𝔑. 20 *kleyn:* Zoar heyſt kleyn.

33 of oure father. And they gaue their father wyne to drynke that fame nyghte. And the elder doughter went and laye with her father. And he perceaued it not, nether when fhe laye downe, nether when fhe rofe vp.

34 And on the morowe the elder fayde vnto the yonger: beholde, yefternyghte lay I with my father. Let us geue hym wyne to drinke this nyghte alfo, and goo thou and lye with him, and let us faue feed of

35 oure father. And they gaue their father wyne to drincke that nyghte alfo. And the yonger arofe and laye with him. And he perceaved it not: nether when fhe laye down, nether when fhe rofe vp.

36 Thus were both the doughters of lot with childe by their father

37 And the elder bare a fone and called hym Moab, which is the father of the Moabytes vnto this daye.

38 And the yonger bare a fonne and called hym Ben Ammi, which is the father of the childern of Ammon vnto this daye.

The .XX. Chapter.

1 AND Abraham departed thence towarde the fouthcontre and dwelled betwene Cades and Sur ād fogeorned in Gerar. *M.C.S. Abraham went as a ſtranger into the lande of Gerar. The kynge of Gerar taketh awaye his wyfe.*

2 And Abraham fayde of Sara his wyfe, that she was his fifter. Than Abimelech kynge of Gerar fent and fett Sara awaye.

3 And God came to Abimelech by nyghte in a dreame and fayde to him: Se, thou art but a .P. deed man for the womās fake which thou haft taken awaye,

V. 33 dormiuitque .. accubuit filia 34 nocte, & dormies cum eo 38 Ammon (marg. Heb. Ben ammi.) id eft filius populi mei xx. 3 En morieris
L. 3 Sihe da

4 for she is a mans wyfe. But Abimelech had not yet come nye her, and therfore fayde: lorde wilt thou fley
5 rightewes people? fayde not he vnto me, that she was hys fifter? yee and fayde not she herfelf that he was hir brother? wyth a pure herte and innocent handes haue I done this.

6 And God fayde vnto him in a dreame. I wot it well that thou dydeft it in pureneffe of thi herte: And therfore I kepte ẏ that thou fhuldeft not fynne agenft
7 me, nether fuffred I the to come nygh her. Now therfore delyuer the mā his wyfe ageyne, for he is a prophete. And let him praye for the that thou mayft lyue. But and yf thou delyuer her not agayne, be fure that thou fhalt dye the deth, with all that thou haft.

8 Than Abimelech rofe vp be tymes in the mornynge and called all his fervauntes, and tolde all thefe thinges
9 in their eares, and the men were fore a frayde. And Abimelech called Abraham and fayde vnto him: What haft thou done vnto vs, & what haue I offended the, that thou fhuldeft brynge on me and on my kyngdome fo greate a fynne? thou haft done dedes vnto me that
10 ought not to be done. And Abimelech fayde morouer vnto Abraham: What faweft thou that moved the to do this thinge?

11 And Abraham Anfwered. I thought that peradvēture the feare of God was not in this [Fo. XXVI.] place, and that they fhulde fley me for my wyfes fake;
12 yet in very dede fhe is my fifter, the doughter of my father, but not of my mother: and became my wyfe.
13 And after God caufed me to wandre out of my fathers houfe, I fayde vnto her: This kyndneffe fhalt thou fhewe vnto me in all places where we come, that thou faye of me, how that I am thy brother.

V. 4 gentem ignorantem & iuftam 7 redde viro fuo vxorem 8 Statimque de nocte .. in auribus eorum 9 quæ non debuifti facere 10 Quid vidifti
L. 4 eyn gerecht volck 7 des tods fterben 8 fur yhr oren
𝔐. 𝔐. 𝔑. 11 *The feare of God* amōge the Hebrewes is princypally takē for the honour and faith that we owe vnto god, & that wyth foche a loue as the childe hathe to the father.

14 Than toke Abimelech ſhepe and oxen, menſervauntes and wemenſeruauntes and gaue them vnto Abraham, and delyvered him Sara his wyfe agayne.
15 And Abimelech ſayde: beholde the lande lyeth be fore
16 the, dwell where it pleaſeth ẏ beſt. And vnto Sara he ſayde: Se I haue geuen thy brother a thouſande peeces of ſyluer, beholde he ſhall be a couerynge to thyne eyes vnto all that ar with the and vnto all men and an excuſe.
17 And ſo Abraham prayde vnto God, and God healed Abimelech and his wyfe
18 and hys maydens, ſo that they bare. For the LORde had cloſed to, all the matryces of the houſe of Abimelech, becauſe of Sara Abrahams wyfe.

couerynge, ſcreening from obſervation; excuſe, a doubtful rendering

---

The .XXI. Chapter.

1 THE lorde viſyted Sara as he had ſayde and dyd vnto her acordynge as he had ſpoken.
2 And Sara was with childe and bare Abrahā a ſonne in his olde age .ꝑ euen the ſame ſeaſon which the LORde
3 had appoynted. And Abraham called his ſonnes name that was borne vnto him
4 which Sara bare him Iſaac: & Abrā circūcyſed Iſaac his ſōne whē he was .viii. dayes olde, as
5 God commaunded him And Abrahā was an hundred yere olde, when his ſonne Iſaac was borne vnto him.

ℳ.C.S. Iſaac is borne. Agar is caſt oute wyth hyr younge ſonne Iſmael. The Angell comforteth Agar. The couenaunt betwene Abimelech andAbraham.

ℳ. 16 beholde this thinge ſhall be .. all men an excuſe 17 maydēs .. ſo that they bare chyldrē. xxi, 1 promyſed
V. 14 reddiditque illi Saram vxorem ſuam 16 & quoc. . perrexeris, memento te deprehenſam. xxi, 5 hac quippe ætate patris, natus eſt Iſaac.
L. 16 Sihe da, ich hab .. vnd allenthalben, vnd eyn verantwortter 17 das ſie kinder geporen 18 zuuor hart verſchloſſen xxi, 1 vnd thet mit yhr
ℳ.ℳ.N. 16 Couerynge & excuſe is all one.

6 And Sara fayde: God hath made me a laughinge
7 ſtocke: for all ẏ heare, will laugh at me She fayde
alſo: who wolde haue fayde vnto Abraham, that Sara
ſhulde haue geuen childern fucke, or ẏ I ſhulde haue
8 borne him a fonne in his old age: The childe grewe
and was wened, and Abraham made a great feaſt, the
fame daye that Iſaac was wened.
9 Sara fawe the fonne of Hagar the Egiptian which
10 ſhe had borne vnto Abraham, a mockynge. Then ſhe
fayde vnto Abraham: put awaye this bondemayde and
hyr fonne: for the fonne of this bondwoman ſhall not
11 be heyre with my fonne Iſaac: But the wordes femed
verey greavous in Abrahams fyghte, becauſe of his
12 fonne. Than the LORde fayde vnto Abraham: let it
not be greavous vnto the, becauſe of the ladd and of
thy bondmayde: But in all that Sara hath faide vnto
the, heare hir voyce, for in Iſaac ſhall thy feed be
13 called. Moreouer of the fonne of the Bondwoman will
I make a nation, becauſe he is thy feed.
14 And Abraham roſe vp early in the mornyng and
toke brede and a bottell with water, and ga- [Fo.
XXVII.] ue it vnto Hagar, puttynge it on hir ſhulders
wyth the lad alſo, and fent her awaye. And ſhe departed and wādred vpp and doune in the wyldernes
15 of Berſeba. When the water was ſpent that was in
16 the botell, ſhe caſt the lad vnder a buſh and went &
fatt her out of fyghte a great waye, as it were a bow-
ſhote off: For ſhe fayde: I will not fe the lad dye.
And ſhe fatt doune out of fyghte, and lyfte vp hyr
17 voyce and wepte. And God herde the voyce of the
childe. And the angell of God called Hagar out of

𝓥. 9 ludentem cum Iſaac 11 Dure accepit 12 Non tibi videatur
aſperum . . in Iſaac vocabitur tibi femen 14 fcapulæ eius, tradi-
ditque puerum . . errabat in ſolitudine Berſabee 15 abiecit puerum
𝕷. 7 das Sara kinder feuget 9 das er eyn ſpotter war 10 treybe
. . . aus 12 dyr der fame genennet werden 14 auff yre ſhulder, vnd
den knaben mit, vnd lies ſie aus . . vnd gieng ynn der wüſten yrre
bey Berſaba 15 warff ſie den knaben 16 eyn ambruſt fchos weit
𝕷. 𝔐. 𝔑. 9 *Hagar*, Merck hie auff Hagar, wie die des Geſetzs vnd glaubloſer werck figur iſt, Gal. iiii. vnd dennoch ſie Gott
zeitlich belonet vnd grofs macht auff erden.

heaven and fayde vnto her: What ayleth the Hagar? Feare not, for God hath herde the voyce of the childe 18 where he lyeth. Aryfe and lyfte vp the lad, and take hym in thy hande, for I will make off him a greate 19 people. And God opened hir eyes and fhe fawe a well of water. And fhe went and fylled the bottell with 20 water, and gaue the boye drynke. And God was 21 wyth the lad, and he grewe and dweld in the wildernefſe, and became an archer. And he dweld in the wyldernefſe of Pharan. And hys mother gott him a wyfe out of the land of Egypte.

22 And it chaunced the fame feafon, that Abimelech and Phicoll his chefe captayne fpake vnto Abraham 23 faynge: God is wyth the in all that thou doift. Now therfore fwere vnto me even here by God, that thou wylt not hurt me nor my childern, nor my childerns childern .℟. But that thou fhalt deale with me and the contre where thou art a ftraunger, acordynge vnto 24 the kyndnefſe that I haue fhewed the. Then fayde Abraham: I wyll fwere.

25 And Abraham rebuked Abimelech for a well of water, which Abimelech fervauntes had taken awaye. 26 And Abimelech anfwered I wyft not who dyd it: Alfo thou toldeft me not, nether herde I of it, but this daye.

27 And Abraham toke fhepe and oxen and gaue them vnto Abimelech. And they made both of them a 28 bonde together. And Abraham fett .vii. lambes by 29 them felues. And Abimelech fayde vnto Abraham: what meane thefe .vii. lambes which thou haft fett by 30 them felues. And he anfwered: vii. lambes fhalt thou take of my hande, that it maye be a wytnefſe vnto 31 me, that I haue dygged this well: Wherfore the place

℣. 25 Abimelechs feruauntes
℣. 18 tolle puerum, et tene manum illius 20 folitudine, lactusque eft iuuenis fagittarius 25 quem vi abftulerant 27 percufſeruntque ambo fœdus.
𝕷. 17 des knabens da, er ligt 18 füre ynn an deyner hand 25 hatten mit gewalt genomen 27 machte beide einen bund mit einander

is called Berſeba, becauſe they ſware both of them.
32 Thus made they a bonde to gether at Berſeba.

Than Abimelech and Phicoll his chefe captayne
roſe vp and turned agayne vnto the lande of the
33 Philiſtines. And Abraham planted a wodd in Berſeba, and called there, on the name of the LORde the
34 everlaſtynge God: and dwelt in the Pheliſtinlāde a
longe ſeaſon

❡ The .XXII. Chapter.

[Fo. XXVIII.] The .XXII. Chapter.

1　AFTER theſe dedes, God dyd *M.C.Z. The fayth of Abraham is proued in offrynge hys ſonne Iſaac. Chriſt our ſauyour is promyſed. The generacyon of Nachor Abrahams brother.*
2　proue Abraham & ſayde vnto him: Abraham. And he anſwered: here am I. And he
ſayde: take thy only ſonne Iſaac whome
thou loueſt, & get the vnto the lande of
Moria, and ſacrifyce him there for a ſacrifyce vpon one of the mountayns which I
3 will ſhewe the Than Abraham roſe vp
early in the mornynge and ſadled his
aſſe, and toke two of his meyny wyth him, and Iſaac
his ſonne: ād cloue wod for the ſacrifyce, and roſe vp
and gott him to the place which God had appoynted
4 him. The thirde daye Abraham lyfte vp his eyes
5 and ſawe the place a farr of, and ſayde vnto his yong
men: byde here with the aſſe. I and the lad will goo

M.　34 Philiſtin lande. xxii, 2 lāde Moria
V.　32 pro puteo iuramēti 33 inuocauit ibi nomen 34 colonus terræ Paleſt. xxii, 2 in terram Viſionis .. holocauſtum 3 ſtrauit aſinum
L.　33 Berſaba, vnnd predigt daſelbſt von den namen 34 im lang zeit. xxii, 2 brand opffer 3 gürtet 5 ich vnnd du knabe
M. M. N.　2 *Only ſonne* for only beloued or mooſt chefly beloued aboue other, after the Ebrew phraſe as in the Prouer. iiii, a.
L. M. N.　31 *Berſaba*, heiſt auff deudſch ſchweer brun, oder erdbrun, möcht auch wol ſieben brun heiſſen. xxii, 2 *Moria* heiſt ſchauung, vnnd iſt der berg, da Salomon hernac zu Ieruſalem den Tempel auff bowet, vnnd heiſt der ſchawen berg, das Gott da ſilbſt hinſchawd.

yonder and worſhippe and come agayne vnto you
6 And Abraham toke the wodd of the ſacrifyce and
layde it vpon Iſaac his ſonne, and toke fyre in his
hande and a knyfe. And they went both of them
together.
7 Than ſpake Iſaac vnto Abraham his father & ſayde:
My father? And he anſwered here am I my ſonne.
And he ſayde: Se here is fyre and wodd, but where is
8 the ſhepe for ſacrifyce? And Abraham ſayde: my
ſonne, God wyll prouyde him a ſhepe for ſacrifyce. So
went they both together.
9 And when they came vnto the place which God
ſhewed him, Abrahã made an aulter there and dreſſed
the wodd, ãd bownde Iſaac his . ͣ. ſonne and layde him
10 on the aulter, aboue apon the wodd. And Abraham
ſtretched forth his hande, and toke the knyfe to haue
kylled his ſonne.
11 Than the angell of the LORde called vnto him
from heauen ſaynge: Abraham, Abraham. And he
12 anſwered: here am I. And he ſayde: laye not thy
handes apon the childe nether do any thinge at all
vnto him, for now I knowe that thou feareſt God, in
13 ẏ thou haſte not kepte thine only ſonne frõ me. And
Abraham lyfted vp his eyes and loked aboute: and
beholde, there was a ram caught by the hornes in a
thykette. And he went and toke the ram and offred
14 him vp for a ſacrifyce in the ſteade of his ſonne And
Abraham called the name of the place, the LORde
will ſee: wherfore it is a comẽ ſaynge this daye: in the
mounte will the LORde be ſene.
15 And the Angell of the LORde cryed vnto Abra-
16 ham from heaven the ſeconde tyme ſaynge: by my
ſelfe haue I ſworne (ſayth the LORde) becauſe thou

𝔙. 7 victima holocauſti 9 in altare ſuper ſtruem lignorum
10 vt immolaret 12 nunc cognoui 14 Dominus videt ... In monte
Dominus videbit

𝔏. 7 Sihe hie iſt .. ſchaff zum brandopffer 9 oben auff das
holtz 10 ſchlachtet 12 Denn nu weis ich 14 Der Herrn ſchawet ..
der Herr geſchawet wird

𝔐. 𝔐. 𝔑. 5 *To worſhyp* is here to do ſacryfyce. 12 *I knowe;*
that is, I haue experiẽce that thou feareſt God, as in Philippẽ. iiii, c.

haſt done this thinge and haſt not ſpared thy only
17 ſonne, that I will bleſſe the and multiplye thy ſeed as
the ſtarres of heaven and as the ſonde vpō the ſee ſyde
And thy ſeed ſhall poſſeſſe the gates of hys enymies.
18 And in thy ſeed ſhall all the nations of the erth be
bleſſed, becauſe thou haſt obeyed my voyce
19   So turned Abraham agayne vnto his yonge men,
and they roſe vp and wēt to gether to Ber- [Fo.
XXIX.] ſeba. And Abraham dwelt at Berſeba
20   And it chaūſed after theſe thiges, that one tolde
Abraham ſaynge: Behold, Milcha ſhe hath alſo borne
21 childern vnto thy brother Nachor: Hus his eldeſt ſonne
and Bus his brother, and Kemuell the father of the
22 Sirians, and Ceſed, and Haſo, and Pildas, and Iedlaph,
23 and Bethuel. And Bethuel begat Rebecca. Theſe
viii. dyd Milcha bere to Nachor Abrahams brother.
24 And his concubyne called Rheuma ſhe bare alſo Tebah,
Gaham, Thahas and Maacha.

⁋ The .XXIII. Chapter.

1 ARA was an hundred and .xxvii
yere olde (for ſo longe lyued
2 ſhe) and than dyed in a heade
cyte called Hebron in the
londe of Canaan. Than Abraham came
3 to morne Sara and to wepe for her. And
Abraham ſtode vp from the coorſe and
talked with the ſonnes of heth ſaynge:
4 I am a ſtraunger ād a foryner amonge
yow, geue me a poſſeſſion to bury in with you, that I
may bury my dead oute of my ſighte.

M.C.S. Sa-rah dyeth & is buried in the felde that Ab-raham bought of Ephron the Hethite.

heade cyte, chief cyte, ca-pital
coorſe, *corpſe, body*

V. 17 inimicorum ſuorum 18 quia obediſti voci meæ. xxiii, 2 in ciuitate Arbee 3 ab officio funeris 4 date mihi ius ſepulchri
   L. 18 vnnd durch deinen ſamen. xxiii, 2 heubſtad 3 von ſeyner leych 4 eyn erb begrebnis . . . der fur myr liegt
   L. M. N. 2 *Hebron* iſt Kiriath Arba (ſpricht Moſe) das iſt, die vierſtad, denn die hohen heubt ſtede, waren vertzeytten alle Arba, das iſt, ynn vier teyl geteylet, wie Rom, Jeruſalem vnd Babylon auch Gen. x.

5 And the children of heth anfwered Abraham faynge
6 vnto him: heare vs lorde, thou arte a prynce of God amonge vs. In the chefeſt of our fepulchres bury thy dead: None of vs ſhall forbydd ẙ his fepulchre, ẙ thou
7 ſhuldeſt not bury thy deade therein. Abrahā ſtode vp & bowed hī ſelfe before ẙ people of ẙ lāde ẙ childrē of
8 heth. And he comoned with them faynge: *comoned, com-*
Yf it . P. be youre myndes ẙ I ſhall bury my *muned*
deade oute of my fighte, heare me ād ſpeke for me tc
9 Ephron the fonne of Zoar: and let him geue me the dubill caue which he hath in the end of his felde, for as moch money as it is worth, let him geue it me in
10 the prefence of you, for a poſſeſſion to bury in. For Hephron dwelled amōge ẙ childern of heth.

Than Ephron the Hethite anfwered Abraham in the audyēce of the childern of Heth and of all that went in at
11 the gates of his cyte, faynge: Not ſo, my lorde, but heare me: The felde geue I the, and the caue that therein is, geue I the alſo, And even in the prefence of the fonnes of my people geve I it the to bnry thy deede in.
12 Than Abraham bowed himſelfe before the people of
13 the lāde and ſpake vnto Ephrō in the audyence of the people of the contre faynge: I praye the heare me, I will geue fylver for the felde, take it of me, ād ſo will I bury my deed there.
14, 15 Ephron anfwered Abrahā faynge vnto him My lorde, harken vnto me. The lande is worth .iiii. hundreth fycles of fylver: But what is that betwixte the
16 and me? bury thy deede. And Abraham harkened vnto Ephron and weyde him the fylver which he had

ℳ. 10 Ephron.
V. 6 in electis fepulchris noſtris fepeli 7 Heth: 8 dixitque ad eos: Si placet animæ veſtræ 9 fpeluncam duplicem 10 cunctis audientibus qui ingrediebantur portam 12 Adorauit Abraham coram domino & populo terræ 13 Dabo pecuniam pro agro 15 iſtud eſt pretium inter me et te, fed quantum eſt hoc?
ℒ. 6 ynn vnſern koſtlichen grebern 8 Iſts ewr gemuete ... todten fur myr begrabe 12 nym von myr des ackers gellt 15 was iſt das aber zwifchen myr vnd dyr
ℒ. ℳ. N. 15 *Sekel* iſt eyn gewichte, an der muntze, eyn orttis gulden, Denn vertzeytten man das gellt ſo wug, wie man itzt mit gollt thut.

ſayde in the audyence of the ſonnes of Heth. Euen iiii. hūdred ſyluer ſycles of currant money amonge marchauntes

17 Thus was the felde of Ephron where in the dubbill caue is before Mamre: euen the felde & [Fo. XXIIII.] the caue that is therein and all the trees of the felde which growe in all the borders rounde aboute, made
18 ſure vnto Abraham for a poſſeſſion, in the ſyghte of the childern of Heth and of all that went in at the gates of the cyte.
19 And then Abraham buried Sara his wyfe in the double caue of the felde that lyeth before Māre, otherwiſe
20 called Ebron in the lande of Canaan. And ſo both the felde ād the caue that is therein, was made vnto Abraham, a ſure poſſeſſion to bury in, of the ſonnes of Heth.

❡ The .XXIIII. Chapter.

1 ABRAHAM was olde and ſtryken in dayes, and the LORde had
2 bleſſed him in all thinges. And he ſayde vnto his eldeſt ſervaunte of his houſe which had the rule over all that he had: Put thy hande vnder
3 my thye that I maye make the ſwere by the LORde that is God of heauen and God of the erth, that thou ſhalt not take a wyfe vnto my ſonne, of the doughters
4 of the canaanytes, amonge which I dwell. But ſhalt goo vnto my contre and to my kynred, and there take a wyfe vnto my ſonne Iſaac.
5 Thā ſayde the ſeruaunte vnto him: what ād yf

M.C.S. Abraham maketh hys ſeruant to ſwere, & ſendeth him to ſeke a wyfe for Iſaac his ſonne. The ſeruaunt was faythfull and broughˀt Rebecca, whych Iſaac toke to his wyfe.

V. 16 probatæ monetæ publicæ 20 ager & antrum quod erat in eo. xxiv, 2 præerat omnibus
L. 16 Sekel ſylbers das ym kauff geng vnd gebe war. xxiv, 4 ynn meyn vatterland
M. M. N. 2 *Put thy hande:* To put the hand under the thyghe was an othe which the Hebreues vſed in ſoch thīges as perteyned to the teſtament & promeſſe of god as in Gen. xlvii, g.

the womā wyll not agree to come with me vnto
this lāde, fhall I brynge thy fonne agayne vnto
6 the land which thou cameſt out of? And Abrahā
fayde vnto him: bewarre of that, that thou brīge
7 not my fonne thither. The LORde God of heauen
which toke me from my fathers .P. houfe and from
the lande where I was borne, and which fpake vnto
me and fware vnto me faynge: vnto thy feed wyll I
geue this lande, he fhall fende his angell before the,
ȳ thou mayſt take a wife vnto my fonne from thence.
8 Neuertheleffe yf the womā will not agree to come
with the than fhalt thou be without daun- without danger of this ooth. But aboue all thinge ger of this
bringe not my fonne thyther agayne. ooth, *i. e. ab-*
folved from
9 And the feruaunte put his hand vnder *its obligation*
the thye of Abraham and fware to him as concernynge that matter.
10 And the feruaunte toke .x. camels of the camels of
his maſter and departed, and had of all maner goodes
of his maſter with him, and ſtode vp and went to
11 Mefopotamia, vnto the cytie of Nahor. And made
his camels to lye doune without the cytie by a wels
fyde of water, at euen: aboute the tyme that women
come out to drawe water, and he fayde.
12 LORde God of my maſter Abrahā, fend me good fpede
13 this daye, & fhewe mercy vnto my maſter Abraham. Lo
I ſtonde here by the well of water and the doughters of
14 the men of this citie will come out to drawe water: Now
the damfell to whom I faye, ſtoupe doune thy pytcher
and let me drynke. Yf fhe faye, drynke, and I will geue
thy camels drynke alfo, ȳ fame is fhe that thou haſt ordened for thy feruaunte Ifaac: yee & therby fhall I
knowe that thou haſt fhewed mercy on my maſter.
15 And it came to paffe yer he had leeft fpakyn- [Fo.
XXXI.] ge, that Rebecca came out, the doughter of
Bethuell, fonne to Melcha the wife of Nahor Abrahams
16 brother, and hir pytcher apon hir fhulder: The damfell

V. 8 non teneberis iuramento
L. 7 von dem land meyner freuntfchafft 10 vnd macht fich
auff vnd zoch

was very fayre to loke apon, and yet a mayde and vnknowen of man.

And fhe went doune to the well and fylled hyr
17 pytcher and came vp agayne. Then the feruaunte ranne vnto her and fayde: let me fyppe a litle water
18 of thi pither. And fhe fayde: drynke my lorde.

And fhe hafted and late downe her pytcher apon
19 hyr arme and gaue him drinke. And whē fhe had geven hym drynke, fhe fayde: I will drawe water for
20 thy camels alfo, vntill they haue dronke ynough. And fhe poured out hyr pitcher in to the trough haftely and ranne agayne vnto the well, to fett water: and drewe for all his camels.

21 And the felowe wondred at her. But ^{felowe, man} helde his peace, to wete whether the LORde had made
22 his iourney profperous or not. And as the camels had lefte drynckynge, he toke an earynge of halfe a ficle weght and .ii. golden bracelettes for hyr hādes,
23 of .x. fycles weyght of gold and fayde vnto her: whofe doughter art thou? tell me: ys there, rowme in thy
24 fathers houfe, for vs to lodge in? And fhe fayde vnto him: I am the doughter of Bethuell the fonne of Milcha
25 which fhe bare vnto Nahor: and fayde moreouer vnto him: we haue litter and prauonder ynough and alfo
26 rowme to lodge in. ℙ. And the man bowed himfelfe
27 and worfhipped the LORde and fayde: bleffed be the LORde God of my mafter Abraham which ceaffeth not to deale mercyfulle and truly with my mafter, And hath brought me the waye to my mafters brothers houfe.
28 And the damfell ranne & tolde them of her mothers
29 houfe thefe thinges. And Rebecca had a brother called Laban.

𝔐. 17 fuppe 22 a golden earyng
𝒱. 17 mihi ad forbendum præbe .. Celeriterque depofuit hydriam fuper vlnam fuam 22 inaures aureas 23 Cuius es filia
𝓛. 17 aus deynem krug trincken 18 vnnd eylent lies fie den krug ernydder uaff yhre hand 22 eyn gulden ftyrnfpangel 23 Meyn tochter, wen gehorftu an?
𝔐. 𝔐. N. 22 *Earyng;* Earynges are deckynges, ether to apparell the face & forhed of the woman, or the eares. And bracelettes is to decke the armes or hādes. 23 *Worfhypped;* To worfhyp is here to geue thankes, as in the .xxiii. afore at this letter B.

And Laban ranne out vnto the man, to the well:
30 for as foone as he had fene the earynges and the bracelettes apon his fifters handes, ād herde the words of
Rebecca his fifter faynge thus fayde the man vnto me,
than he went out vnto the man. And loo, he ftode
31 yet with the camels by the well fyde. And Laban
fayde: come in thou bleffed of the LORde. Wherfore
ftondeft thou without? I haue dreffed the houfe and
32 made rowme for the camels. And than the mā came in
to the houfe. And he vnbrydeld the camels: and
brought litter and prauonder for the camels, and
water to wefhe his fete and their fete that were
33 with him, and there was meate fett before him to
eate.

But he fayde: I will not eate, vntill I haue fayde
34 myne earēde: And he fayde, faye on, And he
35 fayde: I am Abrahās fervaunte, & the LORDE hath
*bleffed my mafter out of meafure that he * *God blef-*
is become greate and hath geven him fhepe *feth vs whē*
oxen, fyluer and golde, menfervauntes, *he geveth vs*
[Fo. XXXI.] maydefervauntes, camels ād *and curfeth*
36 affes. And Sara my mafters wyfe bare *vs, when he*
him a fonne, whē fhe was olde: and vnto *awaye.*
him hath he geven all that he hath.

37 And my mafter made me fwere faynge: Thou fhalt
not take a wyfe to my fonne, amonge the doughters of
38 the cananytes in whofe lāde I dwell. But thou fhalt
goo vnto my fathers houfe and to my kynred, and
39 there take a wyfe vnto my fonne. And I fayde vnto
my mafter. What yf the wyfe will not folowe me?
40 And he fayde vnto me: The LORde before whom I
walke, wyll fende his angell with the and profper
thy iourney that thou fhalt take a wyfe for my
fonne, of my kynred and of my fathers houfe. But
and yf (when thou comeft vnto my kynred) they will

𝒱. 32 aquam ad lauandos pedes camelorum, & virorum 33
donec loquar fermones meos .. Loquere.
𝑳. 33 bis das ich zuuor meyn fach geworben habe .. fage
her 38 vatters haus vnd zu meynem gefchlecht
𝕸. 𝕸. N. 33 The fame note as in Tyndale.

41 not geue the one, thã fhalt thou bere no perell of myne oothe.

42 And I came this daye vnto the well and fayed: O LORde, the God of my mafter Abrahã, yf it be fo that
43 thou makeft my iourney which I go, profperous: beholde, I ftöde by this well of water, And when a virgyn cometh forth to drawe water, and I faye to her: geue
44 me a litle water of thi pitcher to drynke, and fhe faye agayne to me: dryncke thou, and I will alfo drawe water for thy camels: that fame is the wife, whom the LORde hath prepared for my mafters fonne .P.

45 And before I had made an ende of fpeakynge in myne harte: beholde Rebecca came forth, and hir pitcher on hir fhulder, and fhe went doune vnto the well and drewe.
46 And I fayde vnto her geue me dryncke. And fhe made haft and toke doune hir pitcher from of hir, ãd fayd: drinke, and I will geue thy camels drynke alfo. And I dranke, and fhe gaue the camels drynke alfo. And
47 I afked her faynge: whofe doughter art thou? And fhe anfwered: the doughter of Bathuell Nahors fonne whome Milca bare vnto him.

And I put the earynge vpon hir face and the brace-
48 lettes apon hir hondes. And I bowed my felfe and worfhepped the LORde and bleffed the LORde God of my mafter Abrahã which had brought me the right waye, to take my mafters brothers doughter vnto his
49 fonne. Now therfore yf ye will deall mercyfully and truly with my mafter, tell me. And yf not, tell me alfo: that I maye turne me to the right hande or to the left.

50 Than anfwered Laban and Bathuel faynge: The thinge is proceded even out of the lorde, we can not

V. 41 Innocens eris a maledictione mea 49 vt vadam ad dexterã, fiue ad finiftrã 50 A domino egreffus eft fermo

L. 41 fo biftu meyns eydes quyd. 44 das der Herr meyns herrn fon befcheret hat 49 das ich mich wende zur rechten odder zur lincken. 50 von dem Herrn aufzgangen

M. M. N. 49 *Mercyfully and truly* is as moche to faye in this place as to fhewe pleafure, gētlynes or kyndnes, as .iiii Reg. xx, d. 49 *The ryght hãd or the left* is no more to faye, but tel me one thing or a nother, that I may knowe wherevnto to ftycke, and is a phrafe of the Hebrew.

51 therfore faye vnto the, ether good or bad: Beholde
Rebecca before thy face, take her and goo, and let
her be thy mafters fonnes wife, euen as the LORde
52 hath fayde. And whē Abrahams feruaunte herde their
wordes, he bowed him felfe vnto the LORde, flatt vpon
53 the erth. And the feruaunte toke forth iewells [Fo.
XXXIII. *fic.*] of fyluer and iewelles of gold and rayment,
and gaue them to Rebecca: But vnto hir brother &
54 to hir mother, he gaue fpyces. And then they ate and
dranke, both he and the men that were with him, and
taried all nyghte and rofe vp in the mornynge.
55 And he fayde: let me departe vnto my mafter. But
hir brother and hir mother fayde: let the damfell abyde
with vs a while, ād it be but even .x. dayes, and than
56 goo thy wayes. And he fayde vnto them, hinder me
not: for the lorde hath profpered my iourney. Sende
57 me awaye ẏ I maye goo vnto my mafter. And they
fayde: let vs call the damfell, and witt what fhe fayth
58 to the matter. And they called forth Rebecca ād
fayde vnto her: wilt thou goo with this mā? And
59 fhe fayde: Yee. Than they broughte Rebecca their
fifter on the waye and her norfe and Abrahās fer-
60 vaunte, and the men that were wyth him. And they
* bleffed Rebecca & fayde vnto her: Thou
art oure fifter, growe in to thoufande thoufandes, & thy feed poffeffe ẏ gates of
61 their enimies. And Rebecca arofe & hir
damfels, & fatt thē vp apō the camels &
went their waye after the man. And ẏ
feruaunte toke Rebecca & went his waye
62 And Ifaac was a comīge from the well of
ẏ lyvynge & feynge, for he dwelt in the
63 fouth cōtre, & was gone out to walke in his
meditatiōs before ẏ euē tyde. And he lyfte vp his eyes

* *To bleffe a mās neyboure is to praye for hi̅, ād to wiffh him good: and not to wagge ii figers ouer him.* =wagge ii. fingers ouer him, *allufion to facerdotal bleffing in the Church of Rome*

𝕸. 59 So they let Rebecca their fyfter go with her norfe
𝕍. 53 vafis argenteis.. matri dona obtulit 55 faltem decem dies
58 Vadam 61 funt virum: qui feftinus reuertebatur
𝕷. 55 eyn tag odder zehen 58 Ya, ich will mit yhm. 61 nam Rebecca an
𝕸. 𝕸. 𝕹. 60 *And they bleffed Rebecca.* The fame note as in Tyndale. 63 *Meditacyons* is the exercife of the fpirite and lyftynge vp the mynde to God.

64 & loked, & beholde ỹ camels were cominge. And.P. Rebecca lyfte vp hir eyes, & whē she sawe Isaac, she lyghted
65 of the camel ād sayde vnto the servaunte: what mā is this ỹ cometh agenst vs in the feld? And the servaūte sayde: it is my master. And then she toke hir mantell
66 ād put it aboute her. And the servaūte tolde Isaac all
67 that he had done. Thē Isaac broughte her in to his mother Saras tente, ād toke Rebecca & she became his wife, & he loved her: & so was Isaac cōforted over his mother.

The .XXV. Chapter.

1 ABRAHĀ toke hī another wyfe
2 cald Ketura, which bare hī Simram, Iacksam, Medan,
3 Midiā Iesback & Suah. And Iacksan begat Seba & Dedan. And the sonnes of Dedan were Assurim, Letusim
4 & Leumim. And the sonnes of Midian were Epha, Epher, Hanoch, Abida & Elda. All these were the childern of
5 Kethura. But Abrahā gaue all that he
6 had vnto Isaac. And vnto the sonnes of his concubines he gaue giftes, and sent them awaye from Isaac his sonne (while he yet lyved) east ward, vnto the east contre.
7 These are the dayes of the life of Abrahā which he
8 lyved: an hūdred & .Lxxv. yere and than fell seke ād dyed, in a lustie age (whē he had lvved lustie, *good*

M.C.S. Abraham taketh Kethura to his wyfe & begetteth many chyldren. Abrahā dyeth & geueth all his goodes to Isaac. The genealogie of Ismael. The byrth of Iacob and Esau. Esau selleth his byrthright for a messe of potage.

M. 2 Iecksan 4 Ketura
V. 65 pallium suum, operuit se. xxv, 6 separauit eos .. ad plagam orientalem 8 Et deficiens mortuus est
L. 65 den schleyer vnd verhullet sich. xxv, 6 vnd lies sie ... zihen 8 vnd ward krank vnd starb, ynn eynem rugigem allter, da er allt vnd lebens satt war .. zu seynem volck gesamlet,
M. M. N. 6 *Concubynes* in the scripture are not harlottes, but wyues: yet bare they no rule in the house, but were subiectes as seruauntes. As Agar was vnto Sara. Genesis vi, a. Bylha Gen. xxx, a.

9 ynough) ād was put vnto his people. And his sonnes Isaac ād Ismael buried hī in the duble caue in the feld of Ephrō sōne of Zoar the Hethite before Mamre.
10 Which felde abrahā boughte of the sonnes of Heth:
11 There was Abrahā buried and Sara hys wyfe. And after ẏ deeth of Abrahā god blessed Isaac his sonne [Fo. XXXIIII.] which dweld by the well of the lyvīge & seīge
12 These are the generatiōs of Ismael Abrahās sonne, which Hagar the Egiptiā Saras handmayde bare vnto
13 Abraham. And these are the names of the sōnes of Ismaell, with their names in their kīreddes. The eldest sōne of Ismael Neuaioth, thē Kedar, Abdeel, Mib-
14, 15 sā, Misma, Duma, Masa, Hadar, Thema, Ietur,
16 Naphis & Kedma. These are the sōnes of Ismael, and these are their names, in their townes and castels .xii
17 princes of natiōs. And these are the yeres of the lyfe of Ismael: an hūdred and .xxxvii. yere, & than he fell
18 seke & dyed & was layde vnto his people. And he dweld from Euila vnto Sur ẏ is before Egypte, as men go toward the Assiriās. And he dyed in the presence of all his brethren.

19 And these are the generatiōs of Isaac Abrahās
20 sonne: Abrahā begat Isaac. And Isaac was .XL. yere olde whē he toke Rebecca to wyfe the doughter of Bethuel the Sirian of Mesopotamia & sister to Laban the Sirien.
21 And Isaac made intercessiō vnto ẏ LORde for his wife: because she was barē: and ẏ LORde was ītreated
22 of hī, & Rebecca his wife cōceaued: and ẏ childern stroue together withī her. thē she sayde: yf it shulde goo so to passe, what helpeth it ẏ I am with childe?

ℳ. 13 Cedar
𝒱. 16 & hæc nomina per castella & oppida eorū, . . . tribuum suarum. 18 introeuntibus Assyrios. 20 sororem Laban. 21 Deprecatusque 22 Sed collidebantur
ℒ. 9 zwiffachen hole 16 ynn yhren hoffen vnd stedten 18 Assyrian gehet, Vnd vberfiel alle seyne bruder. 22 Kinder stiessen sich miteynander . . da myrs also sollt gehen
ℳ. ℳ. 𝒩. 8 *And was put unto his people;* To be put amōge hys people, is not only to be put in a goodly place of buryall, but to be put with the cōpany of the auncyent fathers that dyed in the same fayth that he dyd.

23 And she went & axed ý LORde. And ý LORde sayde vnto her there are .ii. maner of people in thi wombe and .ii. nations shall springe out of thy bowels, P. and the one nation shalbe myghtier than the other, and the eldest shalbe servaunte vnto the yonger.
24 And whē hir tyme was come to be delyuered be-
25 holde: there were .ii. twyns in hir wōbe. And he that came out first, was redde & rough ouer all as it were
26 an hyde: and they called his name Esau. And after ward his brother came out & his hande holdynge Esau by the hele. Wherfore his name was called Iacob And Isaac was .LX. yere olde whē she bare
27 thē: and the boyes grewe, and Esau became a conynge hunter & a tyllman. But Iacob was a tyllman, *farmer*
28 simple man & dwelled in the tentes. Isaac loved Esau becaufe he dyd eate of his venysō, but Rebecca loued
29 Iacob. Iacob sod potage & Esau came from the feld
30 & was faitie, & sayd to Iacob: let me syppe of ý redde potage, for I am fayntie. And therfore was his name
31 called Edom. And Iacob sayde: sell me this daye thy
32 byrthrighte. And Esau answered: Loo I am at the poynte to dye, & what profit shall this byrthrighte do
33 me? And Iacob sayde, swere to me then this daye. And he swore to him & sold his byrthrighte vnto Iacob.
34 Than Iacob gaue Esau brede and potage of redde ryse. And he ate & dronke & rose vp and went his waye. And so Esau regarded not his byrthrighte.

M. 29, 30 fayntye . fuppe
V. 23 ex vētre tuo diuidentur 25 & totus in morem pellis hispidus .. plantam fratris tenebat manu 27 vir fimplex 28 Ifaac amabat .. Rebecca diligebat 29 Coxit ... pulmētum 30 quia oppido laffus fum 34 Et fic accepto pane & lentis edulio comedit, & bibit, & abijt, paruipendens quod primogenita vendidiffet.
L. 23 werden fich fcheyden 25 gantz rauch wie eyn fell 27 eyn bydder man 31 verkauff myr heutte 33 fchwere myr heut 34 linfen gericht ... vnd ftund auff vnd gieng dauon vnd alfo verachtet Efau
M. M. N. 23 *Two maner of people;* By this .ii. people is fignifyed vnto vs the lawe & the gofpell as ye maye rede in Gal. iii, d. 27 *A symple;* He is fimple that is without craft & decept & contynueth in beleuyng & executynge of godes wyll.

The .XXVI. Chapter.

M.C.S. The iorneye of Isaac toward Abimelech. The promes made vnto Isaac & his seede. Isaac is rebuked of Abimelech for callyng his wyfe his syster. The chydyng of the shepardes for the welles. Isaac is comforted. The atonemēt betwene Abimelech & Isaac.

1 AND there fell a derth in ẏ lande, paſſinge the firſt derth ẏ fell in the dayes of Abraham. Wherfore Iſaac [Fo. XXXV.] went vnto Abimelech kinge of ẏ Phil-
2 iſtiās vnto Gerar. Thē the LORde apeared vnto him & ſayde: goo not doune in to Egipte, but byde in ẏ land which I
3 ſaye vnto ẏ: Sogeorne in this lāde, & I wyll be with ẏ & wyll bleſſe ẏ: for vnto the & vnto thy ſede I wyll geue all theſe cōtreis And I will performe the oothe which I ſwore vnto Abrahā thy father,
4 & will multiplye thy ſeed as ẏ ſtarres of heavē, & will geue vnto thy ſeed all theſe contreis. And thorow thy ſeed ſhall all the natiōs of
5 the erth be bleſſed, becauſe ẏ Abrahā harkened vnto mi voyce & kepte mine ordinaūces, cōmaundmētes, ſtatutes & lawes

6, 7 And Iſaac dwelled in Gerar. And ẏ mē of the place aſked hī of his wife, & he ſayde ẏ ſhe was his ſiſter: for he feared to calle her his wife leſt the mē of the place ſhulde haue kylled him for hir ſake, becauſe
8 ſhe was bewtyfull to ẏ eye. And it happened after he had bene there longe tyme, ẏ Abimelech kinge of ẏ Philiſtiās loked out at a wyndow & ſawe Iſaac ſport-
9 inge with Rebecca his wife. And Abimelech ſende for Iſaac & ſayde: ſe, ſhe is of a ſuertie thi wife, and why ſaydeſt thou ẏ ſhe was thi ſiſter? And Iſaac ſaide vnto hī: I thoughte ẏ I mighte peradventure haue
10 dyed for hir ſake. Thē ſayde Abimelech: whi haſt

V. 1 poſt eam ſterilitatem 3 Et peregrinare 4 benedicentur in ſemine 7 propter illius pulchritudinem. 8 iocantem c. Reb. 9 cur mentitus es eam ſororem
L. 3 dis land geben 4 dis land geben .. vnd durch deynen ſamen. 8 Yſaac ſchertzet mit ſeynem weyb Rẹbeca.

thou done this vnto vs? one of ẙ people myght lightely haue lyne by thy wife & so shuldest thou haue
11 broughte synne vpon vs Thā Abimelech charged all his people saynge: he ẙ toucheth this man or his wife, shall surely dye for it.
12 .P. And Isaac sowed in ẙ lāde, & founde in ẙ same
13 yere an hūdred bushels: for ẙ LORde blessed hī, & the man waxed mightye, & wēt forth & grewe till he was
14 exceadinge great, ẙ he had possessiō of shepe, of oxē & a myghtie housholde: so ẙ the Philestians had envy
15 at him: In so moch ẙ they stopped & fylled vp with erth, all the welles which his fathers servauntes
16 dygged in his father Abrahams tyme. Than sayde Abimelech vnto Isaac: gett the frō me, for thou art myghtier then we a greate deale.
17 Than Isaac departed thenfe & pitched his tente in
18 the valey Gerar & dwelt there. And Isaac digged agayne, the welles of water which they dygged in the dayes of Abrahā his father which the Philestiās had stoppe after ẙ deth of Abrahā & gaue thē the same
19 names which hys father gaue thē. As Isaacs seruaūtes dygged in the valey, they founde a well of springynge
20 water. And the herdmē of Gerar dyd stryue with Isaacs herdmē saynge: the water is oures Than called he the well Eseck becaufe they stroue with hym.
21 Than dygged they another well, & they stroue for
22 ẙ also. Therfore called he it Sitena. And than he departed thēse & dygged a nother well for the which they stroue not: therfore called he it Rehoboth saige: ẙ LORde hath now made vs rowme & we are en-

ℳ. 12 sowed in that lande 19 lyuyng water 20 Eseck
𝒱. 11 morte morietur 12 in ipso anno centuplum 14 Ob hoc inuidentes 16 in tantum vt ipse Abim. 17 torrentem Gerarӕ 18 quos foderant serui patris sui Abraham, & quos illo mortuo olim obstruxerāt Philisthijm: 19 repererunt aquam viuam. 20 ex eo quod acciderat, vocauit Calumniam. 21 appellauitque eum Inimicitias. 22 Latitudo:
𝐋. 11 des tods sterben 12 hundert scheffel 20 das sie yhn da verhonet hatten
𝐋. ℳ. 𝐍. 20 *Esek* heyst, Hon, wenn man yemannt gewallt vnd vnrecht thut. 21 *Sitena*, heyst widderstand, daher der teuffel Satan heyst eyn widder wertiger. 22 *Rehoboth* heyst, raum odder breytte, das nicht enge ist.

23 creafed vpō the erth. Afterward departed he thēce & came to Berfeba

24 And the LORde apered vnto hī the fame nyghte & fayde. I am the God of Abrahā thy father, feare not for I am with the & will bleffe [Fo. .XXXVI.] the & multiplye thy fede for my feruaūte Abrahams fake.

25 And than he buylded an aulter there and called vpō the name of the LORde, & there pitched his tente. And there Ifaacs fervauntes dygged a well.

26 Than came Abimelech to him frō Gerar & Ahufath
27 his frende and Phicol his chefe captayne. And Ifaac fayde vnto thē: wherefore come ye to me, feīge ye
28 hate me & haue put me awaye frō you? Than fayde they: we fawe that the LORde was with the, and therfore we fayde that there fhulde be an oothe betwixte vs ād the, & that we wolde make a bonde with
29 the: ỹ thou fhuldefte do vs no hurte, as we haue not touched the and haue done vnto the nothinge but good, and fēd the away in peace: for thou art now
30 the bleffed of the LORde. And he made thē a feaſt,
31 and they ate ād drōke. And they rofe vp by tymes in the mornynge and fware one to another. And Ifaac fent thē awaye. And they departed from him in peace.
32 And ỹ fame daye came Ifaacs fervaūtes & tolde hī of a well which they had dygged: & fayde vnto hī, that
33 thei had founde water. And he called it Seba, wherfore the name of the cyte is called Berfeba vnto this daye.

𝔐.. 32 that fame daye
𝒱. 29 nec fecimus quod te læderet 33 Vnde appellauit eum Abundantiam:
𝔏. 28 Wyr fehen mit fehenden augen 29 vnd wie wyr dyr nichts denn alles gutt than haben.
𝔐. 𝔐. N. 22 *Encreafed:* as yf he fhulde faye, after fo great paynes & laboures, God hath geuen vs peace & quyetnes. For quyetnes doth open & increafe the hert, & fadnes reftrayneth it: as in Gen. ix, d. Ps. iiii, a.
𝔏. 𝔐. N. 33 *Seba* heyſt eyn, Eyd, oder fchwur *Ber* aber heyſt eyn brun.

The .XXVII. Chapter.

34 WHEN Esau was .XL. yere olde, he toke to wyfe Iudith the doughter of Bery an Hethite, and Basmath the doughter of Elon an Hethite also, which were dishobedient vnto
35 Isaac and Rebecca.

M.C.S. Iacob stealeth the blessynge from Esau by his mothers council. Isaac is sad. Esau is comforted. The hatred of Esau toward Iacob.

1 .¶. And it came to passe that Isaac wexed olde & his eyes were dymme, so that he coude nat see. Thã called he Esau his eldest sonne & sayde vnto him: mi sonne. And he sayde vnto hym: heare
2 am I. And he sayde: beholde, I am olde
3 ãd knowe not the daye of mi deth: Now therfore take thi weapēs, thy quiver & thi bowe, & gett the to the feldes & take me
4 some venyson & make me meate such as I loue, & brynge it me & let me eat that my soull may blesse the before that I dye:
5 But Rebecca hard whē Isaac spoke to Esau his sonne. And as soone as Esau was gone to the felde
6 to catche venyson & to brīge it, she spake vnto Iacob hir sonne sainge? Behold I haue herde thi father talk-
7 inge with Esau thy brother & saynge: bringe me venyson & make me meate that I maye eate & blesse
8 the before the LORde yer I dye. Now therfore my sonne heare my voyce in that which I cõmaunde the:
9 gett the to the flocke, & bringe me thēce .ii. good kiddes, & I will make meate of thē for thi father, soch
10 as he loueth. And thou shalt brīge it to thi father & he shal eate, ỹ he maye blysse the before his deth
11 Than sayde Iacob to Rebecca his mother. Beholde
12 Esau mi brother is rugh & I am smooth. Mi father shal peraduēture fele me, ãd I shal seme vnto hĩ as though

V. 4 pulmentum, sicut velle me nosti 8 escas .. quibus libenter vescitur
L. 4 wie ichs gern hab
M. M. N. 4 *Blesse;* that is that my soule may wyshe the good and praye to God for the.

I wet aboute to begyle hi, & so shall he brige a curse
13 vpō me & not a blessīge: & his mother saide vnto him.
Vppō me be thi curse my sonne, only heare my voyce,
14 & goo and fetch me them. And Iacob went ād [Fo. XXXIX.] fett them and brought them to his mother.
And his mother made meate of them accordinge as
15 his father loued. And she went and fett *sett, fetched.*
goodly rayment of hir eldest sonne Esau which she had in the house with hir, and put them vpon Iacob hir yong-
16 est sonne, ād she put the skynnes vpon his hādes & apon
17 the smooth of his necke. And she put ẏ meate & brede which she had made in the hōde of hir sonne Iacob
18 And he went in to his father saynge: my father, And he āswered: here am I, who art thou my sonne?
19 And Iacob sayde vnto his father: I am Esau thy eldest sonne, I haue done acordinge as thou baddest me, vp and sytt and eate of my venyson, that thi soule maye
20 blesse me. But Isaac sayde vnto his sonne. How cōmeth it that thou hast sownde it so quicly my sonne? He answered: The LORde thy god brought
21 it to my hande. Than sayde Isaac vnto Iacob: come nere and let me sele the my sonne, whether thou be
22 my sonne Esau or not. Than went Iacob to Isaac his father, & he felt him & sayde the voyce is Iacobs
23 voyce, but the hādes ar ẏ hādes of Esau. And he knewe him not, becaufe his handes were rough as his brother Esaus handes? And so he blessed him.
24 And he axed him, art thou my sonne Esau? And
25 he sayde: that I am. Than sayde he: brynge me and let me eate of my sonnes venyson, that my soule maye blesse the. And he broughte him, & he ate. And he
26 broughte him wyne .P. also, and he dranke. And his father Isaac sayde vnto him: come nere and kysse me
27 my sonne. And he wēt to him & kissed him. And

𝒱. 20 Voluntas dei fuit vt cito occurreret mihi quod volebā
𝑳. 20 der Herr deyn Gott bescheret myrs
𝓜. 𝓜. N. 13 *Curse:* There are two maner of curses vsed in the scripture. The one is in the soule, that pertayneth to the soule, & synne & wyckednes. And the other to the bodye, as all tēporall misery and wretchednes, as in Gen. iii, c. & Deut. xxiii, a.

he smelled ẏ sauoure of his raymēt & blessed hī & sayde See, ẏ smell of my sōne is as ẏ smell of a feld
28 which the lorde hath blessed. God geue the of ẏ dewe of heavē & of the fatnesse of the erth and plētie of
29 corne & wyne. People be thy servauntes & natiōs bowe vnto the. Be lorde ouer thy brethrē, and thy mothers children stoupe vnto the. Cursed be he ẏ curseth the, & blessed be he that blesseth the.
30 As soone as Isaac had made an end of blessīg, Iacob & Iacob was scace gone out frō the preasence of Isaac his father: then came Esau his brother frō his
31 huntynge: And had made also meate, and brought it in vnto his father & sayde vnto him: Aryse my father & eate of thy sonnes venyson, that thy soule maye
32 blesse me. Thā his father Isaac sayde vnto him. Who art thou? he answered I am thy eldest sonne Esau.
33 And Isaac was greatly astoyned out of mesure and sayde: Where is he then that hath hūted venyson and broughte it me, *astoyned, amased, struck with amazement.* and I haue eaten of all before thou cameft, and haue
34 blessed him, ād he shall be blessed styll. Whē Esau herde the wordes of his father, he cryed out greatly & bitterly aboue mesure, and sayde vnto his father:
35 blesse me also my father. And he sayde thy brother came with subtilte, ād hath takē awaye thy blessynge.
36 Than sayde he: He maye [Fo. XXXX.] well be called Iacob, for he hath vndermyned me now .ii. tymes, fyrst

𝔐. 30 blessyng, Iacob was 31 brought it vnto hys
𝔙. 27 sensit vestimentorum illius fragrantiam 33 Expauit Isaac stupore vehementi: & vltra quam credi potest admirans
𝔏. 29 Sey eyn herr vber deyne bruder, vnd deiner mutter kinder 33 Da entsatzt sich Ysaac vber die mas seer.... Wer? wo ist denn der ieger

𝔐. 𝔐. 𝔑. 28 *Dewe;* By this worde dewe is vnderstond of the Hebrews al that is in the fyrmament, that cōforteth the erth, as the sonne, the mone, rayne, & temperatnes of wether, as by the fatnes of the erth they vnderstonde all that is brought forthe benethe in the erth, as Ex. xvi, d, and Numeri xi, b. *Corne;* By corne and wyne is vnderstonde aboundance of all tēporall thynges.

𝔏. 𝔐. 𝔑. 36 *Vntertretten;* Ekeb heysst eyn susz soll, da her kompt Iakob oder Iacob eyn vntertreter odder der mit sussen tritt, vnd bedeut alle gleubigen, die durch das Euangelion die wellt vnd das fleysch vnd den teuffel mit sund und todt vnter sich tretten.

he toke awaye my byrthrighte: and ſe, now hath he taken awaye my bleſſynge alſo. And he ſayde, haſt thou kepte neuer a bleſſynge for me?

37 Iſaac anſwered and ſayde vnto Eſau: beholde I haue made him thi LORde & all his mothers childern haue I made his ſeruantes. Moreouer wyth corne ãd wyne haue I ſtableſſhed him, what cã I do vnto the
38 now my ſonne? And Eſau ſayde vnto his father: haſt thou but ẏ one bleſſynge my father? bleſſe me alſo my
39 father: ſo lyſted vp Eſau his voyce & wepte Thã Iſaac his father anſwered & ſayde vnto him

Beholde thy dwellynge place ſhall haue of the fat-
40 neſſe of the erth, & of the dewe of heauen frõ aboue. And wyth thy ſwerde ſhalt thou lyue and ſhalt be thy brothers ſeruaunte But the tyme will come, when thou ſhalt gett the maſtrye, and lowſe his yocke from of thy necke.
41 And Eſau hated Iacob becauſe of the bleſſynge ẏ his father bleſſed him with all, & ſayde in his harte: The dayes of my fathers ſorowe are at hãde, for I will
42 ſley my brother Iacob. And theſe wordes of Eſau hir eldeſt ſonne, were told to Rebecca. And ſhe ſente ãd called Iacob hir yongeſt ſonne, and ſayde vnto hĩ: be-
43 holde thy brother Eſau threatneth to kyll the: Now therfore my ſõne heare my voyce, make the redie &
44 flee to Labã my brother at Haran. And tarie with him a while, vntill thy .℘. brothers fearſnes be ſwaged,
45 and vntill thy brothers wrath turne awaye from the, and he forgett that which thou haſt done to him. Thã will I ſende and fett the awaye from thence. Why ſhulde I loſe you both in one daye.
46 And Rebecca ſpake to Iſaac: I am wery of my life, for feare of the doughters of Heth. Yf Iacob take a wife of the doughters of Heth, ſoch one as theſe are, or of the doughters of the lande, what luſt ſhuld I haue to lyue.

V. 37 et omnes fratres eius 38 Cumque eiulato magno fleret, 39 motus Iſaac dixit .. In ping. terræ, & in rore cæli deſuper erit benedictio tua 40 eum excutias et foluas ... de ceruicibus tuis 41 dies luctus 46 nolo viuere.
L. 40 Vnd es wirt geſchehen daſs du ſeyn ioch ablegiſt vnd von deynem halſze reyſſiſt. 41 das mein vater leyde tragen mus 45 ſeyn zorn wydder dich von dyr wende 46 waſſol myr das leben?

⁋ The .XXVIII. Chapter.

1 THAN Isaac called Iacob his sonne and blessed him, ād charged him and sayde vnto him: se thou take not a wife
2 of the doughters of Canaan, but aryse ād gett the to Mesopotamia to the house of Bethuel thy mothers father: and there take the a wife of the doughters of Laban
3 thi mothers brother. And God allmightie blesse the, increase the and multiplie the that thou
4 mayst be a nombre of people, and geue the the blessynge of Abraham: both to the and to thy seed with the that thou mayst possesse the lāde (wherein thou art
5 a strangere) which God gaue vnto Abraham. Thus Isaac sent forth Iacob, to goo to Mesopotamia vnto Laban, sonne of Bethuel the Sirien, and brother to Rebecca Iacobs & Esaus mother.

M.C.S. Iacob is sent into Mesopotamia to Laban for a wyfe. Esau marieth an Ismaelyte. Iacob dreameth a dreame. Christ is promysed. Iacob maketh a vowe.

6 When Esau sawe that Isaac had blessed Iacob, and sent him to Mesopotamia, to sett him a wife thence, and that, as he blessed him [Fo. XLI.] he gaue him a charge saynge: se thou take not a wife of the
7 doughters of Canaan: and that Iacob had obeyed his father and mother, & was gone vnto Mesopo-
8 tomia: and seynge also that the doughters of Canaan
9 pleased not Isaac his father: Then went he vnto Ismael, and toke vnto the wiues which he had, Mahala the doughter of Ismael Abrahams sonne, the sister of Nabaioth to be his wife.

10 Iacob departed from Berseba and went toward
11 Haran, and came vnto a place and taried there all nyghte, because the sonne was downe. And toke a stone of the place, and put it vnder his heade, and

V. 2 Laban auunculi tui 4 terram peregrinationis tuæ, quam pollicitus est auo tuo. 6 quod post benedictionem præcep. 11 tulit de lapidibus qui iacebant

L. 2 deyner mutter bruder 3 eyn hauffen volcker 5 seyner vnd Esau mutter 6 ynn dem er yhn segenet, yhm gepot 9 nam vber die weyber, die er zuuor hatte 11 eynen steyn des orts

12 layde him down in the same place to slepe. And he dreamed: and beholde there stode a ladder apon the erth, and the topp of it reached vpp to heauē. And se, the angells of God went vpp and downe apon
13 it, yee ād the LORde stode apon it and sayde.

I am the LORde God of Abraham thi father and the God of Isaac: The londe which thou slepest apon
14 will I geue the and thy seed. And thy seed shalbe as the dust of the erth: And thou shalt spreade abrode: west, east, north and south. And thorow the and thy seed shall all the kynreddes of the erth be blessed.
15 And se I am with the, and wylbe thy keper in all places whother thou goost, and will brynge ỹ agayne in to this lande: Nether will I leaue the vntill I haue made good, all that I haue promysed the .P.
16 When Iacob was awaked out of his slepe, he sayde: surely the LORde is in this place, ād I was not aware.
17 And he was afrayde & sayde how fearfull is this place? it is none other, but euen the house of God and the
18 gate of heauē. And Iacob stode vp early in the mornynge and toke the stone that he had layde vnder his heade, and pitched it vp an ende and vp an ende,
19 poured oyle on the topp of it. And he *upright* called the name of the place Bethell, for in dede the name of the citie was called Lus before tyme.
20 And Iacob vowed a vowe saynge: Yf God will be with me and wyl kepe me in this iourney which I goo and will geue me bread to eate and cloothes to put on,

---

M. 15 whether
V. 13 dominum innixum scalæ 14 quasi puluis terræ: dilataberis 18 & erexit in titulum, fundens
L. 14 auszbreyttet werden .. Vnd durch dich 16 gewißlich ist der herr 18 vnd richtet yhn auff
M. M. N. 17 *House of God;* He calleth it the house of god becuse of the housholde of angells that he there sawe: we in lyke maner call the church of lyme and stone the house of God, becuse the people come thether, whych are the church of God. As saynt Paul teacheth 1 Cor. iii. 2 Cor. vi. Eph. xii. (?). 19 *Bethel* sygnifyeth the house of God
L. M. N. 14 *Deynen Samen;* Hie wirt dem dritten Patriarchen, Christus verheyssen der heyland aller wellt, vnd das kunfftige Euangelion von Christo ynn allen landen zu predigen durch die engel auff der leytter fürgebildet.

21 so that I come agayne vnto my fathers house in saftie:
22 then shall the LORde be my God, and this stone which I haue sett vp an ende, shalbe godes house, And of all that thou shalt geue me, will I geue the tenth vnto the.

⁌ The .XXIX. Chapter.

1 THEN Iacob lyfte vp his fete & wēt toward the east countre.
2 And as he loked aboute, beholde there was a well in the feld, and .iii. flockes of shepe laye therby (for at that well were the flockes watered) & there laye a great stone at the well
3 mouth And the maner was to brynge the flockes thyther, & to roull the stone frō the welles mouth and to water the shepe, and to put the stone a- [Fo. XLII.] gayne vppon the wells mouth vnto his place.

M.C.S. Iacob cometh to Laban & serueth seuē yere for Rachel. Lea was brought to his bed in stede of Rachel. He maryeth them bothe, and serueth yet .vii yere more for Rachel. Lea conceaueth.

4 And Iacob sayde vnto thē: brethern, whēce be ye?
5 and they sayde: of Haran ar we. And he sayde vnto thē: Knowe ye Laban the sonne of Nahor. And they
6 sayde: We knowe him. And he sayde vnto thē: is he in good health? And they sayde: he is in good health: and boholde, his doughter Rahel cometh with ẏ shepe.
7 And he sayde: lo, it is yet a great whyle to nyghte, nether is it tyme ẏ the catell shulde be gathered together: water the shepe and goo and fede thē.

V. 3 Morisque erat ... deuoluerent lapidem, & refectis 7 vt reducantur ad caulas greges ... & sic eas ad pastum reducite
L. 3 vnd sie pflegten .. an seyne stett 7 es ist noch viel tages (corrected into: hoch tag)
M. M. N. 22 *Tythes:* By tythes the auncyent fathers meāt all great rewardes as in Gen. xiiii, d.
L. M. N. 21 *Mein Gott seyn;* Nicht das er vorhyn nicht seyn Got gewesen sey, sondern er gelobd eyn gottis dienst auff zu richten, do man predigen vnd betten sollt, Da will er den zehenden zugeben, den predigern, wie Abraham dem Melchisedek den zehenden gab.

8 And they fayde: we may not, vntill all ẏ flockes be brought together & the ftone be roulled frō the wells mouth, and fo we water oure fhepe.

9 Whyle he yet talked with thē, Rahel came with
10 hir fathers fhepe, for fhe kepte them. As foone As Iacob fawe Rahel, the doughter of Laban his mothers brother, and the fhepe of Laban his mothers brother, he went and rowled the ftone frō the wells mouth, and
11 watered the fhepe of Labā his mothers brother And Iacob kyffed Rahel, and lyfte vp his voyce and wepte:
12 and tolde her alfo ẏ he was hir fathers brother and Rebeccas fonne. Thē Rahel ranne and tolde hir
13 father. When Laban herd tell of Iacob his fifters fonne, he ranne agaynft him and embraced hī & kyffed him ād broughte him in to his houfe. And thē Iacob
14 told Laban all ẏ matter. And thē Labā fayde: well, thou art my bone & my flefh .¶. Abyde with me the
15 fpace of a moneth. And afterward Laban fayd vnto Iacob: though thou be my brother, fhuldeft thou therfore ferue me for nought? tell me what fhall thi wages
16 be? And Laban had .ii. doughters, the eldeft called
17 Lea and the yongeft Rahel. Lea was tender eyed:
18 But Rahel was bewtifull ād well fauored. And Iacob loued her well, and fayde: I will ferue the .vii. yere for
19 Rahel thy yongeft doughter. And Laban anfwered: it is better ẏ I geue her the, than to another man? byde therfore with me.

20 And Iacob ferued .vii. yeres for Rahel, and they femed vnto him but a fewe dayes, for the loue he had
21 to her. And Iacob fayde vnto Laban, geue me my wife, that I maye lye with hir For the tyme appoynted me is come.

𝔐. 9 for fhe kepte thē 13 he rāne to mete him ... brought him to his houfe.
𝒱. 10 Quam cum vid. Iac. & fciret confobrinam fuam 13 Auditis autem caufis itineris 17 Lia, lippis erat oculis: Rachel decora facie & venufto afpectu. 18 præ amoris magnitudine
𝑳. 8 zu fammen bracht werden .. vnd alfzo die fchaff 10 die fchaff .. feyner muter bruder. 13 all dis gefchicht 14 Wolan du bift 17 eyn blode geficht 20 vnd dauchten yhn als werens eyntzele tage 21 denn die zeyt ift hie, das ich bei lige

22 Than Laban bade all the men of that place, and
23 made a feaſt. And when euē was come, he toke Lea
his doughter and broughte her to him and he went in
24 vnto her. And Laban gaue vnto his doughter Lea,
Zilpha his mayde, to be hir feruaunte.
25 And when the mornynge was come, beholde it was
Lea. Than fayde he to Laban: wherfore haſt thou
played thus with me? dyd not I ferue the for. Rahel,
26 wherfore than haſt thou begyled me? Laban anſwered:
it is not the maner of this place, to marie the yongeſt
27 before the eldeſt. Paſſe out this weke, & thā ſhall this
alſo be geven the for ẏ feruyce which thou ſhalt [Fo.
28 XLI.] ferue me yet .vii. yeres more. And Iacob dyd
euē fo, and paſſed out that weke, & than he gaue hī
29 Rahel his doughter to wyfe alſo. And Laban gaue to
Rahel his doughter, Bilha his handmayde to be hir
30 ſervaūte. So laye he by Rahel alſo, and loved Rahel
more than Lea, and ferued him yet .vii. yeres more.
31 When the LORde fawe that Lea was deſpiſed, he
32 made her frutefull: but Rahel was baren. And Lea
conceaued and bare a ſonne, ād called his name Rubē,
for ſhe fayde :: the LORde hath loked apon my tribula-
33 tion. And now my huſbonde will loue me. And ſhe
conceaued agayne and bare a ſonne, and fayde: the
LORde hath herde that I am deſpiſed, ād hath therfore
geuen me this ſonne alſo, and ſhe called him Simeon.
34 And ſhe conceaued yet and bare a ſonne, ād fayde: now
this once will my huſbonde kepe me company, becauſe
I haue borne him .iii. ſonnes: and therfore ſhe called
35 his name Levi. And ſhe conceaued yet agayne, and
bare a ſonne faynge: Now will I prayſe the LORde:
therfore ſhe called his name Iuda, and left bearynge.

𝑉. 24 Ad quam cum ex more, Iac. f. ingreſſus 27 Imple hebdo-
madam dierum huius copulæ 30 Tandemque potitus optatis nup-
tijs, amorem fequentis priori prætulit 32 humilitatem meam

𝐋. 25 denn betrogen 26 die iungſt aufgebe 27 hallt diſe woch-
en aus 27 Rahel feyne tochter zum weybe 30 lag er auch bey mit
R. 31 macht er . . . vnd R. vnfruchtbar 33 hat gehoret, das ich
gehaſſet 34 nu . . . . widder zu myr thun

𝐋. 𝔐. N. 32 *Ruben* heyſt eyn fehefon. 33 *Simeon* heyſt eyn
horer. 34 *Leui* heyſt zuthat. 35 *Iuda* heyſt eyn bekenner odder
danck fager. *Dan* heyſt eyn richter. [xxx, 6]

ℭ The .XXX. Chapter.

1 WHEN Rahel fawe that fhe bare Iacob no childern, fhe enuied hir fifter & fayde vnto Iacob: geue me childern, or ells I am 2 but deed. Than was Iacob wrooth with Rahel faynge: Am I in godes fteade which 3 kepeth frō the the frute of thi wōbe? Then fhe fayde: here is my mayde Bilha: go in vnto .P. her, that fhe maye beare vpō my lappe, that I maye be encreafed by her. 4 And fhe gaue him Bilha hir hādmayde to 5 wife. And Iacob wēt in vnto her, And 6 Bilha conceaued and bare Iacob a fonne. Than fayde Rahel. God hath geuen fentēce on my fyde, and hath alfo herde my voyce, and hath geuen me a fonne. 7 Therfore called fhe him Dan. And Bilha Rahels mayde cōceaued agayne and bare Iacob a nother 8 fonne. And Rahel fayde. God is turned, and I haue made a chaunge with my fifter, & haue gotē ỹ vpper hāde. And fhe called his nam: Nepthali.

9 Whē Lea fawe that fhe had left bearinge, fhe toke 10 Silpha hir mayde and gaue her Iacob to wiffe. And 11 Silpha Leas made bare Iacob a fonne. Than fayde 12 Lea: good lucke: and called his name Gad. And 13 Silpha Leas mayde bare Iacob an other fonne. Thā fayd Lea: happy am I, for the doughters will call me bleffed. And called his name Affer.

14 And Rubē wēt out in the wheatharueft & foūde

M.C.S. Rachel and Lea being bothe baren geue their maydēs vnto their hufbande & they bare him chyldren. Iacob deceaueth Laban in the conceyuinge of the fhepe and kyddes. Iacobs rewarde for hys ferues.

V. 2 qui priuauit te fructu ventris 3 fuper genua mea 6 Iudicauit mihi dom. 13 Hoc pro beatudine mea
L. 1 nichts gepar 3 auff meynen fchos .. durch fie erbawet werde.
L. M. N. 8 *Naphthali* heyft verwechfelt, vmbgewand, vmbgekert, wenn man dz widderfpiel thut. Ps. 17. mit dem verkere. en verkeriftu dich. 11 *Gad*, heyft ruftig zum ftreyt 13 *Affer* heyft felig.

mandragoras in the feldes, and brought thē vnto his mother Lea. Than fayde Rahel to Lea geue me of
15 thy fonnes mãdragoras. And Lea anfwered: is it not ynough, ӳ thou haſt takē awaye my houſbōde, but woldeſt take awaye my fons mandragoras alſo? Than fayde Rahel well, let him ſlepe with the this nyghte,
16 for thy fonnes mandragoras And whē Iacob came from the feldes at euen, Lea went out to mete him, & fayde: come in to me, for I haue bought [Fo. XLII.] the with my fonnes mandragoras.
17 And he ſlepte with her that nyghte. And God herde Lea, ӳ ſhe cōceaued and bare vnto Iacob ӳ .v
18 ſonne. Than fayde Lea. God hath geuē me my rewarde, becaufe I gaue my maydē to my houſbōd, and
19 ſhe called him Iſachar. And Lea cōceaued yet agayne
20 and bare Iacob the fexte fonne. Than fayde ſhe: God hath endewed me with a good dowry. *dowry, gift* Now will my houſbond dwell with me, becaufe I haue borne him .vi. fonnes: and called his name Zabulō.
21 After that ſhe bare a doughter and called her Dina.
22 And God remēbred Rahel, herde her, and made
23 her frutefull: fo that ſhe cōceaued and bare a fonne
24 and fayde God hath takē awaye my rebuke. And ſhe called his name Iofeph faynge The lorde geue me
25 yet a nother fonne. As foone as Rahel had borne Iofeph, Iacob fayde to Laban: Sēde me awaye ӳ I
26 may goo vnto myne awne place and cūtre, geue me my wives and my chiḷdern for whom I haue ferued the, and let me goo: for thou knoweſt what feruyce I

ℳ. 15 houſband (alſo vv. 19, 20.)
V. 15 quod præripueris 16 mercede cōduxi te pro mandragoris 20 Dotauit me deus dote bona 25 Nato autem Iofeph
V. 14 der alrun deyns fons eyn teyl 15 wohlan, laſs yhn
ℳ. ℳ. N. 14 *Mandragoras;* The Hebrews call it an erbe or rather a rote that beareth the fimylitude of mānes bodye. Other call it an apple whych being eatē wyth meate caufeth concepciō. Saynt Auften thynketh that it pleafeth women becaufe it hath a pleafant fauoure, or rather for dayntines, becaufe there was not many of them to get.
L. ℳ. N. 18 *Ifachar* heyſt Iohn. 20 *Sebulon*, heyſt beywonung 21 *Dina* heyſt eyn fach oder gericht 24 *Iofeph* heyſt, zuthun, odder fort mehr thun.

27 haue done the. Than fayde Laban vnto hī: If I haue fownde fauoure in thy fyghte (for I fuppofe ẏ the
28 LORde hath bleffed me for thy fake) appoynte what
29 thy rewarde fhalbe and I will geue it ẏ. But he fayde vnto hym, thou knoweft what feruyce I haue done ẏ & in what takynge thy catell haue bene vnder me:
30 For it was but litle that thou haddeft before I came, and now it is encreafed in to a multitude, and the LORDE hath bleffed the for my fake .P. But now when fhall I make provyfion for myne awne houfe
31 alfo? And he fayde: what fhall I geue the? And Iacob anfwerd: thou fhalt geue me nothinge at all, yf thou wilt do this one thinge for me: And then will I turne agayne & fede thy fhepe and kepe them.
32 I will go aboute all thy fhepe this daye, and feparate frō thē all the fhepe that are fpotted and of dyverfe coloures, and all blacke fhepe amonge the lambes
33 and the partie and fpotted amonge the kyddes: And then fuch fhalbe my rewarde. So fhall my rightwesnes anfwere for me: when the tyme commeth that I fhall receaue my rewarde of the: So that what foeuer is not fpeckeld and partie amonge the gootes

M. 31 fhal I then geue the? 32 and the fpotted 33 & the fame fhalbe

V. 27 experimēto didici quia bened. 30 nūc diues effectus es .. deus ad introitū meū 33 Refpondebitque mihi cras iuftitia mea .. furti me argues

L. 29 was fur eynen dienft ich dyr gethan habe

M. M. N. 33 Ryghteoufnes fygnifyeth here true and faythfull feruyce.

L. M. N. 32 *Zigen.* Du muft hie dich nicht yrren, das Mofes, das kleyne viech, itzt zigē, itzt lemmer, itzt bocke heyft, wie difer fprach art ift, Denn er will fo viel fagen, dz Iacob hab alles weys einferbig viehe behalten vnnd alles bundte vnd fchwartz Laban gethan, was nu bund von dem einferbigen viech keme, das follte feyn lohn feyn, des wart Laban froh, vnd hatte die natur fur fich, das vō eynferbigen nicht viel bundte naturlich komen, Aber Iacob halff der natur mit kunft, das die eynferbigen viel bundte trugen.

Durch dis gefchichte ift bedeut, das durchs Euangelion werdē die feelē von den gefetz treybern vnd werck heyligen abgefurt, darynnen fie bund, fprincklicht vnd flecket, dz ift, mit mancherley gaben des geyft getziert werden Rom. 12. vnd 1 Cor. 12. das vnter dem gefetz vnd wercken nur die vntuchtigen bleyben, denn Laban heyft, weys odder gleyfend, vnd bedeut, der gleyffener hauffen ynn den fchonen wercken auch gottlichs gefetzs.

and blacke amonge the lambes, let that be theft with me.

34 Than fayde Laban: loo, I am contēte, that it be
35 acordinge as thou haft fayde. And he toke out that fame daye the he gootes that were partie & of dyuerfe coloures, & all the gootes that were fpotted and partie coloured, & all that had whyte in thē, & all the blacke amonge the lambes: ād put thē in the kepinge of his
36 fonnes, & fett thre dayes iourney betwixte hīfelfe & Iacob. And fo Iacob kepte ẏ reft of Labās fhepe.

37 Iacob toke roddes of grene popular, hafell, & of cheftnottrees, & pilled whyte ftrakes in thē & made
38 the white apere in the ftaues: And he put the ftaues which he had pilled, euē before ẏ fhe- [Fo. XLIII.] pe, in the gutters & watrynge troughes, whē the fhepe came to drynke: ẏ they fhulde cōceaue whē they came
39 to drynke. And the fhepe cōceaued before the ftaues
40 & brought forth ftraked, fpotted & partie. Thē Iacob parted the lābes, & turned the faces of the fhepe toward fpotted thinges, & toward all maner of blacke thinges thorow out the flockes of Labā. And he made him flockes of his owne by thē felfe, which he
41 put not vnto the flockes of Labā. And allwaye in the firft buckinge tyme of the fhepe, Iacob put the ftaues before the fhepe in the gutters, ẏ they myghte
42 conceaue before the ftaues, But in the latter buckynge tyme, he put them not there: fo the laft brode
43 was Labās and the firft Iacobs. And the man became excedynge ryche & had many fhepe, maydeferuauntes, menferuauntes, camels & affes.

V. 37 ex parte decorticauit eas: detractifque corticibus in his quæ fpoliata fuerant, cādor apparuit: illa vero quæ integra fuerant viridia permanferunt: atque in hunc modum color effectus eft varius. 42 Quādo vero ferotina admifura erat, & cōceptus extremus

L. 33 das fey eyn diebftal bey myr. 36 vnd macht rawm

❡ The .XXXI. Chapter.

1 AND Iacob herde the wordes of Labās sonnes how they sayde: Iacob hath takē awaye all that was oure fathers, and of oure fathers goodes, hath he gotē all this
2 honoure. And Iacob behelde the countenaūce of Laban, that it was not toward him as it was in tymes past.
3 And the LORde sayde vnto Iacob: turne agayne in to the lāde of thy fathers
4 & to thy kynred, & I wilbe with ȳ. Thā Iacob sent & called Rahel & Lea to the
5 felde vnto his shepe & sayde vnto thē: I se youre fathers countenaūce ȳ it is not toward me as in tymes past. Morouer .P. ȳ God of my father hath bene with
6 me. And ye knowe how that I haue serued youre
7 father with all my myghte. And youre father hath disceaued me & chaunged my wages .x. tymes: But
8 God suffred him not to hurte me. When he sayde the spotted shalbe thy wages, thā all the shepe bare spotted. Yf he sayde the straked shalbe thi rewarde,
9 thā bare all the shepe straked: thus hath God takē
10 awaye youre fathers catell & geuē thē me. For in buckynge tyme, I lifted vp myne eyes and sawe in a dreame: and beholde, the rammes that bucked the
11 shepe were straked, spotted and partie. And the angell of God spake vnto me in a dreame saynge:
12 Iacob. And I answered: here am I. And he sayde: lyfte vp thyne eyes ād see how all the rāmes that leape vpon the shepe are straked, spotted and partie:
13 for I haue sene all that Laban doth vnto ȳ. I am ȳ god of Bethell where thou anoynteddest the stone ād where thou vowdest a vowe vnto me. Now aryse and

M.C.S. At the cōmaundement of God, Iacob departed frō Laban, & toke hys goodes with hym. Rachel stealeth hyr fathers ymages. Laban foloweth Iacob. The couenaunt betwene Laban and Iacob.

V. 1 ditatus, factus est inclytus 2 heri & nudiustertius [so v. 5]. 6 totis viribus meis
L. 2 wie gistern and ehigstern (and v. 5).

gett the out of this countre, ād returne vnto the lāde
14 where thou waſt borne. Than anſwered Rahel & Lea
& ſayde vnto him: we haue no parte nor enheritaunce
15 in oure fathers houſe he cownteth vs euē as ſtraungers,
for he hath ſolde vs, and hath euen eaten vp the price
16 of vs. Moreouer all the riches which God hath takē
from oure father, that is oures and oure childerns.
Now therfore what ſoeuer God hath ſayde vnto the,
17 that doo. Thā Iacob roſe vp & ſett his ſōnes and wiues
18 vp vpon camels, & caried away all [Fo. XLIIII.] his
catell & all his ſubſtāce which he had gottē in Meſopotamia, for to goo to Iſaac his father vnto the lāde
19 of Canaan. Labā was gone to ſhere his ſhepe, &
20 Rahel had ſtollē hir fathers ymages. And Iacob went
awaye vnknowynge to Laban the Sirië, & tolde him
21 not ẙ he fled. So fled he & all ẙ he had, & made him
ſelf redy, & paſſed ouer the ryuers, and ſett his face
ſtreyght towarde the mounte Gilead.

22 Apō the thirde day after, was it tolde Labā ẙ Iacob
23 was fled. Thā he toke his brethrē with him and folowed after him .vii. dayes iourney and ouer toke him
at the mounte Gilead.

24 And God came to Labā the Siriā in a dreame by
nyghte, and ſayde unto him: take hede to thi ſelfe,
that thou ſpeake not to Iacob oughte ſave good.
25 And Labā ouer toke Iacob: and Iacob had pitched
his tēte in ẙ mounte. And Laban with his brethern
26 pitched their tēte alſo apon the mounte Gilead. Than
ſayde Labā to Iacob: why haſt thou this done vnknowynge to me? and haſt caried awaye my doughters

𝔐. 20 And Iacod ſtale awaye the hert of Laban the Syrien,
in ẙ he tolde hym 22 ẙ Iacob fled 25 tēte in ẙ moūte. 26 done to
ſteale awaye my hert, and carye awaye .. the ſwerde?

𝒱. 14 in facultatibus & haereditate 15 & vendidit, comeditque
pretium noſtrum 21 amne tranſmiſſo pergeret 24 contra Iacob.
25 Iamque Iacob extenderat 26 clam me abigeres

𝑳. 13 zeuch widder ynn das landt deyner fruntſchafft 15 vnſer
lohn vertzehret 20 alſo ſtal Iacob dem Laban zu Syrien das hertz
(v. 28) 21 fur vber das waſſer 23 erwiſſcht yhn

𝑳. 𝔐. N. 20 *Stal das hertz;* hertz ſtelen iſt Ebreiſch geredt,
ſo viel, als etwas thun hynder eyns andern wiſſen, bedeut aber,
das die gleubigen den rechten kern Gottis wort faſſen, des die
werck heyligen nymer gewar worden.

as though they had bene takē captyue with fwerde?
27 Wherfore wenteſt thou awaye fecretly vnknowne to me & dideſt not tell me, ẏ I myghte haue broughte ẏ on the waye with myrth, fyngynge, tymrells and
28 harppes, and haſt not fuffred me to kyſſe my childern
29 & my doughters. Thou waſt a fole to do it, for I am ablé to do you evell. But the God of youre father fpake vnto me yeſterdaye faynge take hede that .P.
30 thou fpeake not to Iacob oughte faue goode. And now though thou wēteſt thi waye becauſe thou lōgeſt after thi fathers houfe, yet wherfore haſt thou ſtollen my goddes?

31 Iacob anfwered & fayde to Labā: becaufe I was afrayed, & thought that thou woldeſt haue takē awaye
32 thy doughters frō me. But with whome foeuer thou fyndeſt thy goddes, let him dye here before oure brethrē. Seke that thine is by me, & take it to the:
33 for Iacob wiſt not that Rahel had ſtollē thē. Thā wēt Labā in to Iacob's tēte, & in to Leas tēte, & in to .ii. maydens tentes: but fownde thē not. Thā wēt
34 he out of Leas tēte, & entred in to Rahels tēte. And Rahel toke the ymages, & put them in the camels ſtrawe & fate doune apō thē. And Labā ferched all
35 the tēte: but fownde thē not. Thā fayde ſhe to hir father: my lorde, be not angrye ẏ I cā not ryfe vp before the, for the difeafe of wemē is come apon me. So fearched he, but foūde thē not.

36 Iacob was wrooth & chode with Labā: Iacob alfo anfwered and fayde to him: what haue I trefpaced or what haue I offended, that thou foloweddeſt after me?
37 Thou haſt fearched all my ſtuffe, and what haſt thou founde of all thy houſholde ſtuffe? put it here before thi brethern & myne, & let thē iudge betwyxte vs
38 both. This .xx. yere ẏ I haue bene wyth the, thy ſhepe and thy gootes haue not bene baren, and the

V. 28 ſtulte operatus es 31 Quod infcio te profectus fum 32 Quod autem furti me arguis 33 Cumque intraſſet t. Rachelis 35 fic delufa folicitudo quærentis eſt. 37 fuppellectilem
L. 29 vnd ich hette, gottlob, woll fo viel macht das ich euch kund vbels thun 35 vnd fand die bilder nicht

39 rammes of thi flocke haue I not eatē. What foeuer was torne of beaftes I broughte it not vnto ẙ, [Fo. XLV.] but made it good my filf: of my hãde dydeſt thou requyre it, whether it was ſtollen by daye or
40 nyghte Moreóuer by daye the hete confumed me, and the colde by nyghte, and my flepe departed frõ
41 myne eyes. Thus haue I bene .xx. yere in thi houfe, and ferued the .xiiii. yeres for thy .ii. doughters, and vi. yere for thi fhepe, and thou haft changed my re-
42 warde .x. tymes. And excepte the God of my father, the God of Abrahã and the God whome Ifaac feareth, had bene with me: furely thou haddeft fent me awaye now all emptie. But God behelde my tribulation, and the laboure of my handes: and rebuked the yefter daye.
43 Laban anfwered ãd fayde vnto Iacob: the doughters are my doughters, and the childern are my childern, and the fhepe are my fhepe, ãd all that thou feift is myne. And what can I do this daye vnto thefe my doughters, or vnto their childern which they
44 haue borne? Now therfore come on, let us make a bonde, I and thou together, and let it be a wytneffe be-
45 twene the & me. Than toke Iacob a ftone and fett it vp
46 an ende, ãd fayde vnto his brethern, gather   vp an ende, ftoones And they toke ftoones ãd made *upright*
47 an heape, and they ate there, vpõ the heape. And Labã called it Zegar Sahadutha, but Jacob called it Gylead.
48 Than fayde Laban: this heape be witneffe betwene the and me this daye (therefore is it called Gylead)
49 and this totehill which the lorde .P. feeth   totehill, (fayde he) be wytneffe betwene me and *watch tower or beacon* the when we are departed one from a

V. 40 fugiebatque fomnus ab oculis meis 42 Abraham & timor Ifaac 45 erexit illum in titulum 47 Laban Tumulum teftis: & Iacob Aceruum teftimonii, vterque iuxta proprietatem linguæ fuæ .. 48 Galaad, id eft tumulus teftis. 49 Intueatur & iudicet

L. 42 meyn elend vnd erbeyt angefehen 45 zu eynem mal 49 vnd fey eyn wartte

M. M. N. 42 Feare is taken for honoure as a fore in Gen. xx, c.

L. M. N. 42 *Furcht;* Iacob nennet hie Gott, Ifaac furcht darumb das Ifaac Gott furchtig war and Gottis diener. 48 *Gilead;* Gilead heyft eyn zeuge hauffe, vnnd bedeut die fchrifft, da viel zeugnis von Gott heuffig ynnen find.

50 nother: that thou shalt not vexe my doughters nether shalt take other wyves vnto them. Here is no man with vs: beholde, God is wytnesse betwixte the
51 and me. And Laban sayde moreouer to Iacob: beholde, this heape & this marke which I haue sett
52 here, betwyxte me and the: this heape be wytnesse and also this marcke, that I will not come ouer this heape to the, ād thou shalt not come ouer this heape
53 ād this marke, to do any harme. The God of Abraham, the God of Nahor and the God of theyr fathers, be iudge betwixte vs.

And Iacob sware by him that his father Isaac feared.
54 Then Iacob dyd sacrifyce vpon the mounte, and called his brethern to eate breed. And they ate breed and
55 taried all nyghte in the hyll. And early in the mornynge Laban rose vp and kyssed his childern and his doughters, and blessed thē and departed and wēt vnto
XXXII, 1 his place agayne. But Iacob went forth on his iourney. And the angells of God came & mett
2 him. And when Iacob sawe them, he sayde: this is godes hooft: and called the name of that same place Mahanaim.

⁋ The .XXXII. Chapter.

3 IACOB sente messengers before him to Esau his brother, vnto the lande of Seir and the felde
4 of Edom. And he cōmaunded them saynge: se that ye speake after [Fo. XLVI.] this maner to my lorde Esau: thy seruaunte Iacob sayth thus. I haue

M.C.S. The vision of the Angells. Iacob sendeth presents vnto hys brother Esau. How he wrestled with the angell which

V. 52 aut ego transiero illum pergens ad te: aut tu præterieris, malum mihi cogitans. 53 per timorem patris sui Isaac. 55 in locum suum. xxxii, 3 Misit autem & nuntios 4 domino meo (v. 5, 18)
L. 50 Es ist hie keyn mensch mit uns 51, 52 das mal .xxxii, 2 heer lager, corrected into Mahanaim.

sogerned ād bene a ftraunger with La- *chaunged his name and cal-*
5 ban vnto this tyme: & haue gotten oxen, *led him Ifrael.*
aſſes and ſhepe, menſervauntes & wemanſeruauntes,
& haue ſent to ſhewe it mi lorde, that I may fynde
grace in thy ſyghte.

6 And the meſſengers came agayne to Iacob ſainge:
we came vnto thi brother Eſau, and he cometh ageynſt
7 the and .iiii. hundred men with hī. Than was Iacob
greatlye afrayde, and wiſt not which waye to turne
him ſelfe, and devyded the people that was with him
& the ſhepe, oxen and camels, in to .ii. companies,
8 and ſayde: yf Eſau come to the one parte and ſmyte it,
the other may ſaue it ſelfe.

9 * And Iacob ſayde: O god of my fa- ** Prayer is*
ther Abraham, and God of my father *to cleave vnto the promyſes*
Iſaac: LORde which ſaydeſt vnto me, re- *of god with a*
turne vnto thy cuntre and to thy kynrede, *ſtröge fayth and to beſech*
10 and I will de all wel with the. I am *god with a*
not worthy of the leaſte of all the mercyes *fervent de-*
and treuth which thou haſt ſhewed vnto *ſyre that he will fulfyll*
thy ſeruaunte. For with my ſtaf came I *them for his*
over this Iordane, and now haue I goten *mercye & truth onlye.*
11 ii. droves Delyver me from the handes *As Iacob here*
of my brother Eſau, for I feare him: leſt *doth.*
he will come and ſmyte the mother with the childern.
12 Thou ſaydeſt that thou woldeſt ſurely do me good, and
woldeſt make mi ſeed as the ſonde of the ſee which
can not be nombred for multitude.

13 And he taried there that ſame nyghte, & toke of
that which came to hande, a preaſent, .℔. vnto Eſau his
14 brother: .ii. hundred ſhe gootes ād .xx. he gootes: .ii
15 hundred ſhepe and .xx. rammes: thyrtye mylch camels
with their coltes: .xl. kyne ād .x. bulles: .xx. ſhe aſſes

𝔐. 9 do all well
𝒱. 6 properat in occurſum tibi 7 & perterritus 8 et percuſſerit
10 minor ſum 11 percutiat matrem cum filiis 12 dilatares ſemen
meum 15 camelos fœtas
𝔏. 6 zeucht dyr auch entgegen 10 ich byn zu geringe
𝔐. 𝔐. N. 10 To go with a ſtaffe is a maner of ſpeakīg of the
Hebrews which ſygnifyeth nothing els but to go ſymply, barely
and without any riches or ſtrēght as in Marc .vi, b.

16 ād .x. foles and delyuered them vnto his feruauntes, euery drooue by them felues, ād fayde vnto them: goo forth before me and put a fpace betwyxte euery drooue.
17 And he cōmaunded the formeſt faynge Whē Efau my brother meteth the ād axeth the faynge: whofe feruaūte art thou & whither gooſt thou, & whofe ar thefe that
18 goo before ỳ: thou ſhalt fay, they be thy feruaunte Iacobs, & ar a prefent fent vnto my lorde Efau, and
19 beholde, he him felfe cometh after vs. And fo cōmaunded he the feconde, ād euen fo the thirde, and lykewyfe all that folowed the drooues fainge, of this maner fe that ye fpeake vnto Efau whē ye mete him,
20 ād faye more ouer. Beholde thy feruaunte Iacob cometh after vs, for he fayde. I will peafe his wrath with the prefent ỳ goth before me and afterward I will fee him myfelf, fo peradventure he will receaue me to grace.
21 So went the prefēt before him ād he taried all that
22 nyghte in the tente, ād rofe vp the fame nyghte ād toke his .ii. wyves and his .ii. maydens & his .xi. fonnes,
23 & went ouer the foorde Iabok. And he toke them ād
24 fent thē ouer the ryuer, ād fent ouer that he had ād taried behinde him felfe alone.

And there wraſtled a man with him vnto the [Fo.
25 XLVII.] breakynge of the daye. And when he fawe that he coude not prevayle agaynſt him, he fmote hī vnder the thye, and the fenowe of Iacobs thy ſhranke
26 as he wraſtled with him. And he fayde: let me goo, for the daye breaketh. And he fayde: I will not lett
27 the goo, excepte thou bleſſe me. And he fayde vnto
28 him: what is thy name? He anfwered: Iacob. And he fayde: thou ſhalt be called Iacob nomore, but Ifraell.

V. 17 iſta quæ fequeris? 20 forfitan propitiabitur mihi 23 Transductifque omnibus quæ ad fe pertinebāt, manfit 25 tetigit neruum femoris . . . emarcuit. 26 afcendit aurora.

L. 20 Ich will yhn verfunen mit dem gefchenck . . . villeicht wirt er mich annehmen. 21 ym lager 25 ruret er das gelenck feyner hufft an

L. M. N. 28 *Ifrael* kompt von Sara, das heyſt kempffen oder vber weldigen, da her auch Sar eyn fürſt oder herr, vnd Sara eyn fürſtyn oder fraw heyſt, vnd Ifrael eyn fürſt oder kempffer Gottis, das iſt, der mit Gott ringet vnd angewynnet, wilchs gefchicht durch den glauben, der fo feſt an Gottis wort helt bis Gottis zorn vber windet vnd Gott zu eygen erlanget zum gnedigen vatter.

For thou haſt wraſtled with God and with men ād haſt preuayled.

29 And Iacob aſked him fainge, tell me thi name. And he fayde, wherfore doſt thou aſke after my name?
30 and he bleſſed him there. And Iacob called the name of the place Peniel, for I haue ſene God face to face,
31 and yet is my lyfe reſerved. And as he went ouer Peniel, the ſonne roſe vpon him, and he halted vpon
32 his thye: wherefore the childern of Iſraell eate not of the ſenow that ſhrancke vnder the thye, vnto this daye: becauſe that he ſmote Iacob vnder the thye in the ſenow that ſhroncke.

The .XXXIII. Chapter.

1 IACOB lyfte vp his eyes and ſawe his brother Eſau come, & with him .iiii. hundred men. And he deuyded the childern vnto Lea and vnto Rahel and vnto ẏ .ii. maydens. *M.C.S. Eſau & Iacob are agreed, & Iacob came into Sichē.*
2 And he put the maydens ād their childern formeſt, ād Lea and hir childern after, and Rahel ād Joſeph
3 hindermoſt. And he went before them and fell on the grownde .vii. .ꝑ. tymes, vntill he came vnto his brother.
4 Eſau ranne agaynſt him and enbraced hym and fell on
5 his necke and kyſſed him, and they wepte. And he lifte vp his eyes and ſawe the wyves and their childern,

M. 28 haſt wraſtled wyth God & haſt preuayled. 30 Pheniel (v. 31). xxxiii, 4 Eſau ranne to mete him
V. 28 quoniam ſi contra deum fortis fuiſti, quanto magis cōtra homines præualebis? 29 nomen meū—quod eſt mirabile? .. in eodem loco. 30 & ſalua facta eſt anima mea. 31 claudicabat pede. 32 femoris eius, & obſtupuerit. xxxiii, 1 Rachel, ambarumque 3 donec appropinquaret frater eius. 4 & oſculans fleuit.
L. 28 mit Gott vnd mit menſchen 30 vnd meyn ſeel iſt geneſen 32 hoh ader auff dem gelenck der hufft. xxxiii, 3 vnd buckt ſich .. auff die erden (and v. 7)
M. M. N. 30 To ſe God face to face is to haue a certē and ſure knowledge of him as in Ex .xxxiii, b.
L. M. N. 30, 31 *Pniel* oder *Pnuel* heyſt Gottis angeſicht odder erkentnis, denn durch den glauben ym ſtreyt des creutzs lernt man Gott recht erkennen, vnd erfaren, ſo hats denn keyn nott mehr, ſo geht die Sonne auff.

and fayde: what are thefe which thou there haft? And
he fayde: they are the childern which God hath geuen
6 thy feruaunte. Than came the maydens forth, ād dyd
7 their obayfaunce. Lea alfo and hir childern came and
dyd their obayfaunce. And laft of all came Iofeph
and Rahel and dyd theyr obayfaunce.

8 And he fayde: what meanyft thou with all ỹ drooues
which I mett. And he anfwered: to fynde grace in the
9 fyghte of my lorde. And Efau fayde: I haue ynough
10 my brother, kepe that thou haft vnto thy filf. Iacob
anfwered: oh nay but yf I haue founde grace in thy
fyghte, receaue my preafēt of my hāde: for I haue fene
thy face as though I had fene ỹ face of God: wherfore
11 receaue me to grace and take my bleffynge that I haue
brought the, for God hath geuen it me frely. And I
haue ynough of all thynges. And fo he compelled
him to take it.

12 And he fayde: let vs take our iourney and goo, and
13 I will goo in thy cōpany. And he fayde vnto him: my
lorde knoweth that I haue tendre childern, ewes and
kyne with yonge vnder myne hande, which yf men
fhulde ouerdryue but euen one daye, the hole flocke
wolde dye. [Fo. XLVIII.].

14 Let my lorde therfore goo before his fervaunte and
I will dryue fayre and foftly, accordynge   *foftly, at a*
as the catell that goth before me and the *gentle pace*
childern, be able to endure: vntil I come to mi lorde
vnto Seir.

15 And Efau fayde: let me yet leaue fome of my folke
with the. And he fayde: what neadeth it? let me

𝔐. 11 geuē it me. And
𝒱. 6 incuruati 7 adoraffent . . adorauerunt. 8 Dixitque Efau . .
domino 9 At ille 10 Noli ita obfecro . . munufculū 11 & quā do-
nauit . . tribuēs omnia. Vix fratre 13 domine . . paruulos te-
neros 14 dominus 15 Non eft . neceffe: hoc vno tantum indigeo,
vt inueniam
𝔏. 11 Nym den fegen an, den ich dyr zubracht hab 13 zarte
kinder . . vbertryben 14 meylich hynnach treyben
𝔏. 𝔐. 𝔑. 14 *Meylich;* Merck, das rechtgleubigen vnd werck
heyligen nicht konnen mit eynander wandeln, denn die gleubigen
faren feuberlich mit ftyllem geyft, aber die werckheyligen faren
ftarck mit vermeffenheyt yhrer werck ynn gottis gefetzen.

16 fynde grace in the fyghte of my lorde So Efau went his waye agayne ý fame day vnto Seir.

17 And Iacob toke his iourney toward Sucoth, and bylt him an houfe, and made boothes for his catell: wherof the name of the place is called Sucoth.

18 And Iacob went to Salem to ý citie of Sichem in the lande of Canaâ, after that he was come from Mef-
19 opotamia, and pitched before the cyte, and bought a parcell of ground where he pitched his tent, of the childern of Hemor Sichems father, for an hundred
20 lambes. And he made there an aulter, and there called vpon the myghtie God of Ifraell.

The .XXXIIII. Chapter.

1 DINA the doughter of Lea which fhe bare vnto Iacob, went out to fee the doughters of the
2 lande. And Sichē the fonne of Hemor the Heuite lorde of the countre, fawe her, & toke her, and laye with
3 her, and forced her: & his harte laye vnto Dina ý doughter of Iacob. And
4 he loued ý damfell & fpake kīdly vnto her, & fpake vnto his father Hemor faynge, gett me this maydē vnto my wyfe.

M.C.S. The raueffhyng of Dyna Iacobs daughter by the men of Sychē. And of the gret bloude fhedynge done by the fonnes of Iacob.

𝔐. 18 And Iacob came peafably in to the cite of Sichem. xxxiv, 3 laye vn Dina

𝔙. 17 Socoth, id eft tabernacula 20 inuocauit fuper illud fortiffimum deum Ifrael. xxxiv, 1 Dina filia Liæ, vt videret 2 adamauit eam: & rapuit... vi opprimēs virginem. 3 Et conglutinata eft anima eius cum ea, triftemque deliniuit blanditiis.

𝔏. 19 Sichem, vmb hundert groffchen, Da felb richtet er feyne hutten auff, 20 vnd richtet daffelbs eyn alltar zu. xxxiv, 2 fchwecht fie, 3 vnd feyn hertz hieng an yhr, vnd hatte die dyrne lieb, vnd redet freuntlich mit yhr

𝔐. 𝔐. N. 2 To lye with hyr, looke in Gen. xix, g.

𝔏. 𝔐. N. 1 *Tochter des lands;* was man auffer Gottis wort, bey der vernunfft vnd menfchlicher weyfheyt fucht, das verterbet gewiflich den geyft and glauben, darumb foll keyn zufatz menfchlicher lere vnd werck zu Gottis wort gethan werden.

5 .¶. And Iacob herde that he had defyled Dina his doughter, but his fonnes were with the catell in the felde, and therfore he helde his peace, vntill they
6 were come. Then Hemor the father of Sichem went
7 out vnto Iacob, to come with him. And the fonnes of Iacob came out of the felde as foone as they herde it, for it greued them, and they were not a litle wrooth, becaufe he had wrought folie in Ifraell, in that he had lyen with Iacobs doughter, which thinge oughte not to be done.

8 And Hemor comened with thē fainge? the foule of my fonne Sichē lōgeth for youre doughter geue her
9 him to wyfe, and make mariages with vs: geue youre doughters vnto vs, ād take oure doughters vnto you,
10 and dwell with vs, & the lande fhall be at your pleafure, dwell and do youre bufynes, and haue youre
11 poffeffions there in. And Sichem fayde vnto hyr father and hir brethern: let me fynde grace in youre eyes, and what foeuer ye apoynte me,   apoynte,
12 that will I geue. Axe frely of me both *name or indicate, tell* the dowry & gyftes, and I will geue dowry, *the* acordynge as ye faye vnto me, and geue *prefent made by Shechem* me the damfell to wyfe.

13 Then the fonnes of Iacob anfwered to Sichem ād Hemor his father deceytefully, becaufe he had defyled
14 Dina their fyfter. And they fayde vnto them, we can not do this thinge, ẏ we fhulde geue oure fyfter to one that is vncircumcyfed, for that were a fhame vnto vs.
15 Only in this will we confent unto you? Yf ye will [Fo. XLIX.] be as we be, that all the men childern
16 amonge you be circumcyfed, thā will we geue oure doughter to you and take youres to vs, and will dwell
17 with you and be one people. But and yf ye will not harken vnto vs to be circumcyfed, than will we take oure doughter and goo oure wayes.

    V. 7 fœdam rem operatus ... rem illicitam perpetraffet. 11 dabo: 12 augete dotē 13 fæuientes ob ftuprum fororis, 14 Non poffumus ... quod illicitum & nepharium
    L. 7 das er eyn narreyt ynn Ifrael begangen 10 wonet vnd werbet vnd erbet drynnen 12 foddert nur getroft yon mvr morgengab vnd gefchenck

18 And their wordes pleafed Hemor and Sichem his
19 fonne. And the yonge man deferde not for to do the thinge, becaufe he had a luft to Iacobs doughter: he was alfo moft fett by of all that were in his fathers houfe.
20 Thã Hemor and Sichem went vnto the gate of their cyte, and comened with the men of their cyte faynge.
21 Thefe men ar peafable with vs, & will dwell in the lãde and do their occupatiõ therin And in the land is rowme ynough for thẽ, let vs take their doughters
22 to wyues and geue them oures: only herin will they confent vnto vs for to dwell with vs and to be one people: yf all the men childern that are amonge
23 vs be circumcyfed as they are. Their goodes & their fubftance and all their catell are oures, only let vs confente vnto them, that they maye dwell with vs.
24 And vnto Hemor and Sichem his fonne harkened all that went out at the gate of his cyte. And all the men childern were circumcyfed what fo euer went out
25 at the gates of his cyte. And the third daye when it was paynefull to them, .ii. of the fonnes of Iacob Simeon & Leui .P. Dinas brethren, toke ether of them his fwerde & went in to the cyte boldly, and flewe
26 all ẏ was male, and flewe alfo Hemor and Sichem his fonne with the edge of the fwerde, ãd toke Dina their fifter out of Sichems houfe, and went their waye.
27 Than came the fonnes of Iacob vpon the deede, and fpoyled the cyte, becaufe they had defyled their
28 fifter: and toke their fhepe, oxen, affes and what fo
29 euer was in the cyte and alfo in ẏ feldes. And all their goodes, all their childern and their wyues toke they captyue, and made havock of all that was in the houfes.

V. 18 Placuit oblatio eorum 19 quin ftatim quod petebatur expleret ... inclytus 21 quæ fpatiofa et lata cultoribus indiget 22 Vnum eft, quo differtur tantum bonum, Si circuncidamus 23 & habitantes fimul, vnum efficiamus populum. 27 in vltionem ftupri. 29 duxerunt captiuas.
L. 21 dife leut find fridfam bey vns 24 zu feiner ftad thor aus vnd eyn giengen (So v. 25)

30 And Iacob fayde to Simeon and Leui: ye haue troubled me ād made me ftyncke vnto the inhabitatours of the lande, both to the Canaanytes and alfo vnto the Pherezites. And I am fewe in nombre. Wherfore they fhall gather them felues together agaynft me & fley me, and fo fhall I and my houfe
31 be dyftroyed. And they anfwered: fhuld they deall with oure fifter as wyth an whoore?

The .XXXV. Chapter.

1 AND God fayd vnto Iacob, aryfe ād get the vp to Bethell, & dwell there. And make there an aulter vnto God that apeared vnto the, when thou fleddeft from
2 Efau thy brother. Than fayd Iacob vnto his [Fo. L.] houfholde & to all ẏ were with him, put away the ftraūge goddes that are amonge you & make youre felues
3 cleane, & chaunge youre garmētes, & let vs aryfe & goo vp to Bethell, ẏ I maye make an aulter there, vnto God which herde me in the daye of my tribulatiō & was wyth me in the waye which I went.

M.C.S. Iacob goeth vp vnto Bethel, & buryeth his ymages vnder an oke. Debora dyeth. Iacob is called Ifrael. The lande of Canaā is promyfed hym. Rachel dyeth in laboure: Ruben laye with his fathers concubyne. The death of Ifaac.

4 And they gaue vnto Iacob all the ftraunge goddes which were vnder their handes, ād all their earynges which were in their eares, and Iacob hyd them vnder an ooke at Sichem.
5 And they departed. And the feare of God fell

V. 30 Quibus perpetratis audacter, Iacob dixit......odiofū.. Nos pauci fumus 31 vt fcorto abuti . forore noftra ? xxxv, 3 Surgite, & afcendamus 4 infodit eas fubter terebinthum .. poft vrbem
L.. 30 das ich ftincke fur den eynwonern 31 mit vnfer fchwefter ... handelln ? xxxv, 2 endert ewr kleyder 4 vergrub fie vnter eyne eyche
M. M. N. 2 *Straunge goddes;* The fcripture calleth all maner of ydolles or ymages ftraunge goddes, becaufe the worfhyppers of them efteme them as goddes.

vpon the cyties that were rounde aboute them, that
6 they durſt not folowe after the fonnes of Iacob. So
came Iacob to Lus in the lande of Canaan, otherwiſe
called Bethell, with all the people that was with him.
7 And he buylded there an aulter, and called the place
Elbethell: becauſe that God appered vnto him there,
when he fled from his brother.
8 Than dyed Debora Rebeccas norſe, and was buryed
benethe Bethell vnder an ooke. And the name of
it was called the ooke of lamentation.
9 And God appeared vnto Iacob agayne after he
10 came out of Meſopotamia, & bleſſed him and ſayde
vnto him: thy name is Iacob. Notwithſtondynge thou
ſhalt be no more called Iacob, but Iſrael ſhalbe thy
name. And ſo was his name called Iſraell.
11 .P. And God ſayde vnto him: I am God allmightie,
growe and multiplye: for people and a multitude of
people ſhall ſprynge of the, yee ād kynges ſhall come
12 out of thy loynes. And the lande which I gaue Abrahā & Iſaac, will I geue vnto the & vnto thi ſeed after
13 the will I geue it alſo. And god departed frō him
14 in the place where he talked with him. And Iacob
ſet vp a marke in the place where he talkẽd with him:
euen a pilloure of ſtone, & powred drynkeoffringe
15 theron & powred alſo oyle theron, and called the
name of the place where God ſpake with him, Bethell.
16 And they departed from Bethel, & when he was
but a feld brede from Ephrath, Rahel began to trauell.
17 And in travelynge ſhe was in perell. And as ſhe was
in paynes of hir laboure, the mydwyſe ſayde vnto her:
18 feare not, for thou ſhalt haue this ſonne alſo. Then
as hir ſoule was a departinge, that ſhe muſt dye: ſhe

M. 7 place Bethell
V. 7 Domus dei 8 ad radices Bethel ſubter quercum 13 Et
receſſit ab eo: 14 titulū lapideum 16 verno tempore 17 pericli-
tari cœpit 18 Egrediente autem anima præ dolore, & imminente
iam morte, . . .
L. 14 eyn ſteynernmal 16 eyn feldwegs 18 Da yhr aber die
ſeel ausgieng, das ſie ſterben muſte
L. M. N. 14 *Tranckopffer;* Das war weyn, wie das ynn den
folgenden buchern gnugſam geſehen wirt.

called his name Ben Oni. But his father called him
19 Ben Iamin. And thus dyed Rahel ād was buryed in
the waye to Ephrath which now is called Bethlehem.
20 And Iacob fett vp a piller apon hir graue, which is
21 called Rahels graue piller vnto this daye. And Ifraell
went thēce and pitched vp his tent beyonde the toure
of Eder.
22 And it chaunced as Ifrael dwelt in that lande, that
Ruben went & laye with Bilha his fathers concubyne,
& it came to Ifraels eare. [Fo. LI.].
The fonnes of Iacob were .xii. in nombre.
23 The fonnes of Lea. Ruben, Iacobs eldeft fonne,
24 & Simeō, Leui, Iuda, Ifachar, & Zabulon. The fonnes
25 of Rahel: Iofeph & Ben Iamin. The fonnes of Bilha
26 Rahels mayde: Dan & Nepthali. The fonnes of Zilpha
Leas mayde Gad & Afer. Thes are the fōnes of Iacob
which were borne him in Mefopotamia.
27 Then Iacob went vnto Ifaac his father to Mamre a
prīcipall cyte, otherwife called Hebron: where Abrahā
28 & Ifaac fogeorned as ftraungers. And the dayes of
29 Ifaac were an hundred & .lxxx. yeres: & than felle
he feke & dyed, ād was put vnto his people: beynge
olde and full of dayes. And his fonnes Efau ād Iacob
buried him.

V. 18 Ben-oni, id eft filius doloris mei . . . Beniamin, id eft filius dextræ. 20 hic eft titulus monumenti Rachel, vfque 21 trans turrem gregis. 22 quod illū minime latuit. 26 Mefopotamia Syriæ. 27 Mambre ciuitatem Arbee 29 Confumptufque ætate . . appofitus

L. 21 richtet eyne hutten auff ienfyddem turn Eder. 27 Mamre ynn die hewbt ftad, 29 ward krank . . . alt vnd des lebens fatt

M. M. N. 18 *Ben Iamin;* that is the fonne of the ryght hād, And right hande is taken for good fortune. 29 To be put vnto his people looke in Gen. xxv, a.

L. M. N. 18 Ben Oni heyft meyns schmertzen fon Ben Iamin heyft, der rechten fon.

The .XXXVI. Chapter.

1 THESE are the generations of Esau which is called Edō. 2 Esau toke his wyues of the doughters of Canaan Ada the doughter of Elon an Hethite, and Ahalibama the doughter of Ana, which Ana 3 was the sonne of Zibeon an heuyte, And 4 Basmath Ismaels doughter & sister of Nebaioth. And Ada bare vnto Esau, Eliphas: and Basmath bare Reguel: 5 And Ahalibama bare Ieus, Iaelam and Korah. These are the sonnes of Esau which were borne him in the lande of Canaan.

M.C.S. The wiues of Esau. Iacob & Esau are ryche. The genealogie of Esau. Esau dwelleth in the hill Seir.

6 And Esau toke his wyues, his sonnes and doughters and all the soules of his house: his .P. goodes and all his catell and all his substance which he had gott in the land of Canaan, ād went in to a countre awaye from his 7 brother Iacob: for their ryches was so moch, that they coude not dwell together, and that the land where in they were straungers, coude not receaue thē: becaufe of their catell.

8 Thus dwelt Esau in moūte Seir, which Esau is called Edō

9 These are the generations of Esau father of the 10 Edomytes in mounte Seir, & these are the names of Esaus sonnes: Eliphas the sonne of Ada the wife of Esau, ād Reguel the sonne of Basmath the wife of Esau 11 also. And the sonnes of Eliphas were. Theman, Omar, 12 Zepho, Gaetham and kenas. And thimna was concubyne to Eliphas Esaus sonne, and bare vnto Eliphas, Amalech. And these be the sonnes of Ada Esaus wyfe. 13 And these are the sonnes of Reguel: Nahath, Serah,

M. 6 catell and all his
V. 6 & cūcta quæ habere poterat .. abiit in alteram regionem, recessitque 8 mōte Seir, ipse est Edom.
L. 2 Ana die neff Zib. 6 ynn eyn land von seynem bruder 7 nicht ertragen fur yhren guttern
M. M. N. 4 *Basmath,* other wyfe called Maheleth and so in other places is there dyuers names geuē to one person.

Samma and Mifa: thefe were the fonnes of Bafmath
14 Efaus wyfe. And thefe were the fonnes of Ahalibama
Efaus wyfe the doughter of Ana fonne of Zebeŏ, which
fhe bare vnto Efau: Ieus, Iealam and Korah.

15 Thefe were dukes of the fonnes of Efau. The childern of Eliphas the firft fōne of Efau were thefe: duke
16 Theman, duke Omar, duke Zepho, duke Kenas, duke
Korah, duke Gaetham & duke Amalech: thefe are ẏ
dukes that came of Eliphas in the lande of Edom, ãd
thefe were the fonnes of Ada. [Fo. LII.]
17 Thefe were the childern of Reguel Efaus fonne: duke
Nahath, duke Serah, duke Samma, duke Mifa. Thefe
are the dukes that came of Reguel in the lande of
Edom, ãd thefe were the fonnes of Bafmath Efaus wyfe.
18 Thefe were the childern of Ahalibama Efaus wife:
duke Ieus, duke Iaelam, duke Korah thefe dukes came
19 of Ahalibama ẏ doughter of Ana Efaus wife. Thefe
are the childern of Efau, and thefe are the dukes of
them: which Efau is called Edom:
20 Thefe are the children of Seir the Horite, the in-
habitoure of the lande: Lothan, Sobal, Zibeon, Ana,
21 Difon, Efer and Difan. Thefe are the dukes of ẏ horites
22 the childern of Seir in the lande of Edom. And the
childern of Lothan were: Hori and Hemam. And
Lothans fifter was called Thimna.
23 The childern of Sobal were thefe: Alvan, Manahath,
24 Ebal, Sepho & Onam. Thefe were the childern of
Zibeŏ. Aia & ana, this was ẏ Ana ẏ foũde ẏ mules in
25 ẏ wildernes, as he fed his father Zibeons affes. The
childern of Ana were thefe. Difon and Ahalibama ẏ
doughter of Ana.
26 Thefe are the childern of Difon. Hemdan Efban,
27 Iethran, & Cherã. The childern of Ezer were thefe,
28 Bilhan, Seavan & Akan. The childern of Difan were:
Vz and Aran.

ℳ. 14 Iealam and Roah 17 Miffa
𝒱. 16 Amalec. hi filii Eliphaz 19 eorũ: ipfe eft Edom. 24 in-
uenit aquas calidas in folitudine, cũ pafceret afinas Sebeon 25
Habuitque filium Difon, & filiam Oolibama.
ℒ. 14 Ana der neffe 15 furften [and fo throughout this
chapter]

29 Thefe are the dukes that came of Hori: duke Lothan,
30 duke Sobal, duke Zibeō, duke Ana .Ƥ. duke Difon, duke
Ezer, duke Difan. Thefe be the dukes that came of
Hory in their dukedōs in the lande of Seir.
31 Thefe are the kynges that reigned in the lande of
Edom before there reigned any kynge amonge the
32 childern of Ifrael. Bela the fonne of Beor reigned in
33 Edomea, and the name of his cyte was Dinhaba. And
when Bela dyed, Iobab the fonne of Serah out of Be-
34 zara, reigned in his fteade. When Iobab was dead,
Hufam of the lande of Themany reigned in his fteade.
35 And after the deth of Hufam, Hadad the fonne of
Bedad which flewe the Madianytes in the feld of the
Moabytes, reigned in his fteade, and the name of his
cyte was Avith.
36 Whē Hadad was dead, Samla of Mafreka reigned in
37 his fteade. Whē Samla was dead, Saul of the ryver
38 Rehoboth reigned in his fteade. When Saul was dead,
Baal hanan the fonne of Achbor reigned in his fteade.
39 And after the deth of Baal Hanan the fonne of Achbor, Hadad reigned in his fteade, and the name of his
cyte was Pagu.

And his wifes name Mehetabeel the doughter of
matred the doughter of Mefaab.
40 Thefe are the names of the dukes that came of Efau,
in their kynredds, places and names: Duke Thimma,
41 duke Alua, duke Ietheth, duke Ahalibama, duke Ela,
42 duke Pinon, duke Kenas, duke Theman, duke Mibzar
43 duke Magdiel, duke Iram. Thefe be the dukes of
[Fo. LIII.] Edomea in their habitations, in the lande
of their poffeffions. This Efau is the father of the
Edomytes.

𝔐. 29 Sabal
𝒱. 30 Horræorum qui imperauerunt in terra 35 Hoc quoque
mortuo.. percuffit Madian in regione Moab 36 Semla de Mafreca.
38 Cumque et hic 39 Ifto quoque mortuo
𝑳. 35 Madianiter.. auff der Moabiter feld 36 Mafrek

⁋ The .XXXVII. Chapter.

1 ND Iacob dwelt in the lande wherein his father was a ſtraunger, ẏ is to ſaye in the lande of Canaan.

2 And theſe are the generations of Iacob: when Ioſeph was .xvii. yere olde, he kepte ſhepe with his brethren, and the lad was with the ſonnes of Bilha & of Zilpha his fathers wyues. And he brought vnto

3 their father an euyll ſaynge ẏ was of them. And Iſrael loued Ioſeph more than all his childern, becauſe he begat hym in his olde age, and he made him a coote of many coloures.

4 When his brothren ſawe that their father loued him more than all his brethern, they hated him and

5 coude not ſpeke one kynde worde vnto him. Moreouer Ioſeph dreamed a dreame and tolde it his breth-

6 ren: wherfore they hated him yet the more. And he ſayde vnto them heare I praye yow this dreame which

7 I haue dreamed: Beholde we were makynge ſheues in the felde: and loo, my ſheſe aroſe and ſtode vp right, and youres ſtode rounde aboute and made obeyſaunce

8 to my ſheſe. Than ſayde his brethren vnto him: what, ſhalt thou be oure kynge or ſhalt thou reigne ouer us? And they hated hĩ yet the more, becauſe

9 of his dreame and of his wordes. ⁋

And he dreamed yet another dreame & told it his brethren ſaynge: behold, I haue had one dreame more: me thought the ſonne and the moone and .xi. ſtarres made

10 obayſaunce to me. And when he had told it vnto his father and his brethren, his father rebuked him and ſayde

M.C.S. Ioſeph accuſeth his brethren. Ioſeph dreameth & is hated of hys brethren & is ſolde to the Iſmaelites. Iacob bewayleth Ioſeph.

V. 2 ſedecim .. ſuis adhuc puer: & erat 3 polymitam 4 quicquam pacifice loqui. 5 maioris odii ſeminarium 8 ſubiiciemur ditioni tuæ? Hæc ergo cauſa ſomniorum atque ſermonum, inuidiæ & odii fomitem miniſtrauit.
L. 4 keyn freuntlich wort zuſprechen
L. M. N. 3 *Der bundte rock* Ioſephs war von mancherley farben faden gewebt, vnd bedeut die mancherley gnade vnd gaben des eynigen geyſts ynn Chriſto vnd ſeynen Chriſten.

vnto him: what meaneth this dreame which thou haſt dreamed: ſhall I and thy mother and thy brethren
11 come and fall on the grounde before the? And his brethern hated him, but his father noted the ſaynge.
12 His brethren went to kepe their fathers ſhepe in Si-
13 chem, and Iſraell ſayde vnto Ioſeph: do not thy brethern kepe in Sichem? come that I may ſend ÿ to thē.
14 And he anſwered here am I And he ſayde vnto him: goo and ſee whether it be well with thy brethren and the ſhepe, and brynge me worde agayne: And ſent him out of the vale of Hebron, for to go to Sichem.
15 And a certayne man founde him wandrynge out of his waye in the felde, ād axed him what he ſoughte.
16 And he anſwered: I ſeke my brethren, tell me I praye
17 the where they kepe ſhepe And the man ſayde, they are departed hēce, for I herde them ſay, let vs goo vnto Dothan. Thus went Ioſeph after his brethren, and founde them in Dothan.
18 And whē they ſawe him a farr of before he came at them, they toke councell agaynſt him, for to ſley
19 him, and ſayde one to another, Beholde this dreamer
20 cometh, come now and let [Fo. LIIII.] us ſley him and caſt him in to ſome pytt, and let vs ſaye that ſome wiked beaſt hath deuoured him, and let us ſee what his dreames wyll come to.
21 When Ruben herde that, he wēt aboute to ryd him out
22 of their handes and ſayde, let vs not kyll him. And Ruben ſayde moreouer vnto them, ſhed not his bloude, but caſt him in to this pytt that is in the wildernes, and laye no handes vpon him: for he wolde haue rydd him out of their handes and delyuered him to his father agayne.
23 And as ſoone as Ioſeph was come vnto his brethren, they ſtrypte him out of his gay coote that was
24 vpon him, and they toke him and caſt him in to a pytt. But the pytt was emptie and had no water

V. 11 Inuidebant ei igitur . . . rem tacitus conyderabat. 14 renuntia mihi quid agatur. 18 antequam accederet ad eos 20 ciſternam veterem 22 animam eius .. manuſque veſtras feruate innoxias. 23 nudauerunt eum tunica talari & polymita 24 ciſternam veterem, quæ non habebat aquam.
L. 11 neydeten yhn 14 ſage mir widder wie fichs hellt

25 therein. And they satt them doune to eate brede. And as they lyft vp their eyes and loked aboute, there came a companye of Ismaelites from Gilead, and their camels ladē with spicery, baulme, and myrre, and were goynge doune in to Egipte.
26 Than sayde Iuda to his brethrē, what avayleth it that we sley oure brother, and kepe his bloude secrett?
27 come on, let vs sell him to the Ismaelites, and let not oure handes be defyled vpon him: for he is oure brother
28 and oure flesh. And his brethren were content. Than as the Madianites marchaunt men passed by, they drewe Ioseph out of the pytt and sold him vnto the Ismaelites for .xx. peces of syluer.

.P. And they brought him into Egipte.

29 And when Ruben came agayne vnto the pytt and
30 founde not Ioseph there, he rent his cloothes and went agayne vnto his brethern saynge: the lad is not yon-
31 der, and whether shall I goo? And they toke Iosephs coote ād kylled a goote, & dypped the coote in the
32 bloud. And they sent that gay coote & caused it to be brought vnto their father and sayd: This haue we
33 founde: se, whether it be thy sōnes coote or no. And he knewe it saynge: it is my sonnes coote a wicked beast hath deuoured him, and Ioseph is rent in peces.
34 And Iacob rent his cloothes, ād put sacke clothe aboute his loynes, and sorowed for his sonne a longe seafon.
35 Than came all his sonnes ād all his doughters to comforte him. And he wold not be comforted, but sayde: I will go doune in to ỹ grave vnto my sonne,
36 mornynge. And thus his father wepte for him. And the Madianytes solde him in Egipte vnto Putiphar a lorde of Pharaos: and his chefe marshall.

V. 30 Puer non cōparet 33 fera pessima .. bestia deuorauit 35 vt lenirent dolorem patris, noluit consolationem accipere .. lugens in infernum. 36 Phutiphari eunucho Pharaonis magistro militum.

L. 33 Eyn boses thier hat yhn fressen, Eyn reyssend thier ... Ioseph zurissen 34 sack vmb seyne lenden .. lange zeyt. 35 ynn die helle, 36 Pharao hoffemeyster.

M. M. N. 34 *Rent hys clothes:* it was specially vsed amonge the hebrewes to rent their clothes whē the glorie of God was cōtēpned as here, where they feared God so lytle as to kyll their awne brother.

L. M. N. 35 *Vatter*, das war Isaac.

❡ The .XXXVIII. Chapter.

1 AND it fortuned at that tyme that Iudas went from his brethren & gatt him to a man called Hira of Odollam,
2 and there he fawe the doughter of a man called Sua a Canaanyte. And he toke
3 her ād went in vnto her. And fhe conceaued and bare a fonne and called his
4 name Er. And fhe conceaued agayne and bare a fonne and called him [Fo.
5 LV.] Onan. And fhe conceaued the thyrde tyme & bare a fonne, whom fhe called Sela: & he was at Chefyb when fhe bare hem.

M.C.S. The maryage of Iuda. The trefpace of her and Onan and the vengeaunce of god that came ther vpō. Iuda laye wyth hys daughter Thamar. The byrthe of Phares and Zarah.

6 And Iudas gaue Er his eldeft fonne, a wife whofe
7 name was Thamar. But this Er Iudas eldeft fonne was wicked in the fyghte of the LORde, wherfore the
8 LORde flewe him. Then fayde Iudas vnto Onan: goo in to thi brothers wyfe and Marie her, and ftyrre vp
9 feed vnto thy brother. And when Onan perceaued that the feed fhulde not be his: therfore when he went in to his brothers wife, he fpylled it on the grounde,
10 becaufe he wold not geue feed vnto his brother. And the thinge whoch he dyd, difpleafed the LORde, wher-
11 fore he flew him alfo. Than fayde Iudas to Thamar his doughter in lawe: remayne a wydow at thi fathers houfe, tyll Sela my fonne be growne: for he feared left he fhulde haue dyed alfo, as his brethren did. Thus went Thamar & dwelt in hir fathers houfe.
12 And in proceffe of tyme, the doughter of Sua Iudas wife dyed. Than Iudas when he had left mornynge, went vnto his fhepe fherers to Thimnath with his

V. 2 & accepta vxore 5 Sela . quo nato, parere vltra ceffauit. 9 non fibi nafci filios 10 et idcirco percuffit eum dominus, eo quod rem deteftabilem faceret. 12 Euolutis autem multis diebus
L. 8 famen erweckift 10 gefiel dem Herrn vbel
M. M. N. 7 *To be wycked in the fight of the lorde*, is to walke in wyckednes: knowinge that the lorde feeth vs and yet we wyll not repēt.

13 frende Hira of Odollam. And one told Thamar faynge: beholde, thy father in lawe goth vp to Thimnath,
14 to ſhere his ſhepe. And ſhe put hyr wydows garmētes
of from her and couered her with a clooke, and dis-
gyſſed herſelf: And ſat her downe at the entrynge of
Enaim which is by the hye- .P. wayes ſyde to Thimnath, for becauſe ſhe ſawe that Sela was growne, and
ſhe was not geūe vnto him to wife.
15 When Iuda ſawe her he thought it had bene an
16 hoore, becauſe ſhe had couered hyr face. And turned
to her vnto the waye and ſayde, come I praye the,
let me lye with the, for he knewe not that it was his
doughter in lawe. And ſhe ſayde what wylt thou
17 gyue me, for to lye with me? Thā ſayde he, I will
ſende the a kydd frō the flocke. She anſwered, Than
18 geue me a pledge till thou ſende it. Than ſayd he,
what pledge ſhall I geue the? And ſhe ſayde: thy
ſygnett, thy necke lace, and thy ſtaffe that is in thy
hande. And he gaue it her and lay by her, and ſhe
19 was with child by him. And ſhe gatt her vp and
went and put her mantell from her, ād put on hir
widowes rayment agayne.
20 And Iudas ſent the kydd by his neybure of Odollam, for to fetch out his pledge agayne from the wifes
21 hande. But he ſownde her not. Than aſked he the
men of the ſame place ſaynge: where is the whoore
that ſatt at Enaim in the waye? And they ſayde:
22 there was no whoore here. And he came to Iuda
agayne ſaynge: I can not fynde her, and alſo the men
of the place ſayde: that there was no whoore there.
23 And Iuda ſayde: let her take it to her, leſt we be
ſhamed: for I ſent the kydd & thou coudeſt not
fynde her.
24 And it came to paſſe that after .iii. mone- [Fo.

𝔐. 18 thy ſygnett, thy bracelet, and
𝒱. 12 Hiras opilio gregis Odollamites 14 aſſumpſit theriſtrum
.. in biuio itineris 15 vultum ſuum ne agnoſceretur. 17 Patiar
quod vis, ſi dederis mihi arabonē 20 per paſtorem ſuum Odoll.
23 certe mendacii arguere nos non poterit
𝐋. 12 mit ſeynem hirtten Hira von Odollam. 14 fur die thur
eraus an dem wege gen Thimn. 18 deyn ſechel 23 Sie habs yhr,
das wyr nicht villeicht zu ſchanden werden

LVI.] thes one tolde Iuda faynge: Thamar thy doughter in lawe hath played the whoore, and with playnge
the whoore is become great with childe. And Iuda
25 fayde: brynge her forth ād and let her be brente. And
when they brought her forth, fhe fent to her father
in lawe faynge: by the mā vnto whome thefe thinges
pertayne, am I with childe. And fayd alfo: loke whofe
26 are this feall necklace, and ftaffe. And Iuda knewe them
faynge: fhe is more rightwes thā I, becaufe I gaue her
not to Sela my fōne. But he laye with her no more.
27 When tyme was come that fhe fhulde be delyuered,
28 beholde there was .ii. twynnes in hyr wōbe. And as fhe
traveled, the one put out his hande and the mydwife toke
and bownde a reed threde aboute it faynge: this wyll
29 come out fyrft. But he plucked his hande backe agayne,
and his brother came out. And fhe fayde: wherfore
haft thou rent a rent vppon the? and called him Pharez.
30 And afterward came out his brother that had the reade
threde about his hāde, which was called Zarah.

⁋ The .XXXIX. Chapter.

1 IOSEPH was broughte vnto
Egipte, ād Putiphar a lorde
of Pharaos: ād his chefe marfhall an Egiptian, bought him
of ẏ Ifmaelites which brought hī thither
2 .P. And the LORde was with Iofeph,
luckie, *prof-* and he was a luckie felowe
perous and continued in the houfe

𝔐.ℭ.𝔖. *God
profpereth
Iofeph. Pha-
raos [fic] wyfe
tempteth hym.
He is accufed
& caft in pryf-
on. God hath
mercye vpon
hym.*

𝔐. 25 feall, bracelet, and ftaffe.
𝔙. 24 vid. vterus illius intumefcere. 26 duceretur ad pœnam 27
ipfa effufione infantium 29 diuifa .. maceria? xxxix, 1 eunuchus
.. princeps exercitus
𝔏. 29 umb deynen willen eyn fach geriffen? xxxix, 2 gluck
feliger man wart, vnd war
𝔏. 𝔐. N. 29 *Perez* eyn zureyfer, Sorah heyft aufgang. Hie
ift bedeut, das die werck heyligen fich euferlich ftellen als wolten
fie erfur vnd die erften feyn, vnd werden die letzten, darvber fich
evn grofs reyffen hebt vnter dem volck Gottis. Aber der rod
faden vmb die hand ift dafz fie fleyfchlich heylickeyt wircken vnd
die rechten heyligē verfolgen.

3 of his master the Egiptian. And his master sawe that the LORde was with him and that the LORde made all
4 that he dyd prosper in his hande: Wherfore he founde grace in his masters syghte, and serued him. And his master made him ruelar of his house, and put all that
5 he had in his hande. And as soone as he had made him ruelar ouer his house ād ouer all that he had, the LORde blessed this Egiptians house for Iosephs sake, and the blessynge of the LORde was vpon all that he
6 had: both in the house and also in the feldes. And therfore he left all that he had in Iosephs hande, and loked vpon nothinge that was with him, saue only on the bread which he ate. And Ioseph was a goodly persone & well favored

7 And it fortuned after this, that his masters wife cast hir eyes vpon Ioseph and sayde come lye with me.
8 But he denyed and sayde to her: Beholde, my master woteth not what he hath in the house with me, but
9 hath commytted all that he hath to my hande He him selfe is not greatter in the house than I, ād hath kepte nothīge frō me, but only the becaufe thou art his wife. How than can I do this great wykydnes,
10 for to synne agaynst God? And after this maner spake she to Ioseph daye by daye: but he harkened not vnto her, to slepe nere her or to be in her com-
11 pany. [Fo. LVII.] And it fortuned aboute the fame feason, that Ioseph entred in to the house, to do his busynes: and there was none of the houshold by, in
12 the house. And she caught him by the garment faynge: come slepe with me. And he left his garment
13 in hir hande ād fled and gott him out When she fawe that he had left his garmēt in hir hande, and
14 was fled out, she called vnto the men of the house, and tolde them faynge: Se, he hath brought in an Hebrewe vnto vs to do vs shame. for he came in to

V. 8 nequaquā acquiescens operi nephario 10 et mulier molesta erat adolescenti... recusabat stuprum. 11 operis quippiam absque arbitris 12 lacinia vestimenti 13 & se esse cōtemptam 14 vt illuderet nobis

L. 9 Vnd hat nichts so gros ynn dem haus 10 das er neben yhr schlieff, noch vmb sie were. 12 erwischt yhn bey seynem kleid 14 das er vns zu schanden mache (v. 17)

me, for to haue ſlept wyth me. But I cried with a
lowde voyce.
15 And when he harde, that I lyſte vp my voyce and
cryed, he left his garment with me and fled awaye and
got him out.
16 And ſhe layed vp his garment by her, vntill hir
17 lorde came home. And ſhe told him acordynge to
theſe wordes ſaynge. This Hebrues ſervaunte which
18 thou haſt brought vnto vs came in to me to do me ſhame.
But as ſoone as I lyſt vp my voyce and cryed, he left
19 his garment with me and fled out. When his maſter
herde the woordes of his wyfe which ſhe told him
ſaynge: after this maner dyd thy ſervaunte to me, he
waxed wrooth.
20 And he toke Ioſeph and put him in pryſon: euen
in the place where the kynges priſoners laye bounde.
21 And there contynued he in preſon. But the LORde
was with Ioſeph ãd ſhewed him mercie, and gott him
22 fauoure in the ſyghte of the keper of y̾ preſon which com- .P. mytted to Ioſephs hãde all the preſoners that
were in the preſon houſſe. And what ſoeuer was done
23 there, y̾ dyd he. And the keper of the preſõ loked
vnto nothinge that was vnder his hande, becauſe the
LORde was with him, & becauſe that what ſoeuer he
dyd, the LORde made it come luckely to paſſe.

The .XL. Chapter.

1 AND it chaunced after this, that *M.C.S. Io-*
the chefe butlar of the kynge *ſeph expoun-*
of Egipte and his chefe baker *deth the drea-*
had offended there lord the *mes of the two*
pryſoners.
2 kynge of Egypte. And Pharao was angrie with them
3 and put thẽ in warde in his chefe marſhals houſe: euen

V. 16 In argumentũ ergo fidei retentum pallium 19 & nimium
credulus verbis coni. 20 cuſtodiebantur 23 & omnia opera eius diri-
gebat. xl. 1 vt peccarent duo eunuchi 2 Pharao (nam alter pincer-
nis præerat, alter piſtoribus)
L. 15 floch vnd lieff hynaus. 17 deyn Ebreiſcher knecht 22 auff
das alles was da geſchach, durch yhn geſchehen muſte 23 gluck-
lich abgehen lies

4 in ẏ preson where Ioseph was bownd. And the chefe marshall gaue Ioseph a charge with them, & he serued them. And they contynued a seafon in warde.

5 And they dreamed ether of them in one nyghte: both the butlar and the baker of the kynge of Egipte which were bownde in the preson house, ether of them his dreame, and eche mānes dreame of a son-
6 drie interpretation When Ioseph came sondrie, *dis-*
in vnto them in the mornynge, and loked *tinct, separate*
7 apon them: beholde, they were sadd. And he asked
8 them saynge, wherfore loke ye so sadly to daye? They answered him, we haue dreamed a dreame, and haue no man to declare it. And Ioseph say- [Fo. LVIII.] de vnto thē. Interpretynge belongeth to God but tel me yet.

9 And the chefe butlar tolde his dreame to Ioseph and sayde vnto him: In my dreame me thought there
10 stode a vyne before me, and in the vyne were .iii. braunches, and it was as though it budded, & her
11 blossōs shott forth: & ẏ grapes there of waxed rype. And I had Pharaos cuppe in my hande, and toke of the grapes and wronge them in to Pharaos cuppe, & delyvered Pharaos cuppe in to his hande.

12 And Ioseph sayde vnto him, this is the interpreta-
13 tion of it. The .iii. braūches ar thre dayes: for within thre dayes shall Pharao lyft vp thine heade, and restore the vnto thyne office agayne, and thou shalt delyuer Pharaos cuppe in to his hāde, after the old maner,
14 even as thou dydest when thou wast his butlar. But thinke on me with the, when thou art in good case, and shewe mercie vnto me. And make mencion of me to Pharao, and helpe to brynge me out of this
15 house: for I was stollen out of the lande of the Hebrues, & here also haue I done nothīge at all wherfore they shulde haue put me in to this dongeon.

V. 5 iuxta interpretationem congruam fibi. 7 tristior .. hodie folito facies 8 referte mihi quid videritis. 13 recordabitur Pharao ministerii tui .. iuxta officium tuum, sicut ante
L. 5 hatte seyne bedeutung 8 Auslegen gehoret Gott zu, ertzelet myrs doch. 11 zudruckt sie ynn den becher 13 deyn heubt erheben .. nach der vorigen weysze 15 das sie mich eyngesetzt haben.

16 When the chefe baker fawe that he had well interpretate it, he fayde vnto Iofeph, me thought alfo in my dreame, ẏ I had .iii. wyker bafkettes on my heade:
17 And in ẏ vppermoſt baſket, of all maner bakemeates for Pharao .P. And the byrdes ate them out of the baſket apon my heade
18 Iofeph anfwered and fayde: this is the interpreta-
19 tion therof. The .iii. bafkettes are .iii. dayes, for this daye .iii. dayes ſhall Pharao take thy heade from the, and ſhall hange the on a tree, and the byrdes ſhall eate thy fleſh from of the.
20 And it came to paſſe the thyrde daye which was Pharaos byrth daye, that he made a feaſt vnto all his ſervauntes. And he lyfted vpp the head of the chefe buttelar and of the chefe baker amonge his ſervauntes.
21 And reſtored the chefe buttelar vnto his buttelarſhipe agayne, and he reched the cuppe in to Pharaos hande,
22 ād hanged the chefe baker: euē as Iofeph had inter-
23 pretated vnto thē. Notwithſtonding the chefe buttelar remembred not Iofeph, but forgat hym.

The .XLI. Chapter.

1 AND it fortuned at .ii. yeres end, that Pharao dreamed, and thought that he ſtode by a ryuers ſyde, and that
2 there came out of the ryuer .vii. goodly kyne and fatt fleſhed, and fedd in a med-
3 owe. And him thought that .vii. other kyne came vp after them out of the ryver evelfauored and leane fleſhed and ſtode

M.E.S. Pharaos dreames are expounded by Iofeph. He is made ruler ouer all Egypt. He hath two ſonnes, Manaſſes and Ephraim. The derth begynneth in Egypt.

V. 16 prudenter fomnium diſſoluiſſet . . . caniſtra farinæ 19 auferet Pharao caput tuū . . in cruce 20 pueris fuis, recordatus eſt inter epulas magiſtri pinc. & piſtor . prin. 22 fufpendit in patibulo, vt coniectoris veritas probaretur. 23 Et tamen ſuccedentibus profperis, præp. pinc. oblitus eſt interpretis fui. xli, 2 & paſcebantur in ipſa amnis ripa in locis virentibus.
L. 19 deynen kopff erheben 20 vnd erhub das hewbt (*bis*). 23 gedacht nicht . . . vergaſs

by the other vpon the brynke [Fo. LIX.] of the ryuer.
4 And the evill favored and leneflefhed kyne ate vp the .vii. welfauored and fatt kyne: and he awoke their with.
5 And he flepte agayne and dreamed the fecond tyme, that .vii. eares of corne grewe apon one ftalke
6 rancke and goodly. And that .vii. thynne eares blafted
7 with the wynde, fpronge vp after them: and that the vii. thynne eares deuowrerd the .vii. rancke and full eares. And then Pharao awaked: and fe, here is his
8 dreame. When the mornynge came, his fprete was troubled And hé fent and called for all the foyth-fayers of Egypte and all the wyfe men there of, and told them his dreame: but there was none of them that coude interpretate it vnto Pharao.
9 Than fpake the chefe buttelar vnto Pharao faynge.
10 I do remember my fawte this daye. Pharao was an-grie with his feruauntes, and put in warde in the chefe
11 marfhals houfe both me and the chefe baker. And we dreamed both of vs in one nyght and ech mannes dreame of a fondrye interpretation.
12 And there was with vs a yonge man, an Hebrue borne, feruaunte vnto the chefe marfhall. And we told him, and he declared oure dreames to vs acord-
13 ynge to ether of oure dreames. And as he declared them vnto vs, euen fo it came to paffe. I was reftored to myne office agayne, and he was hanged.
14 .¶. Than Pharao fent and called Iofeph. And they made him hafte out of prefon. And he fhaued him felf and chaunged his rayment, & went in to Pharao.
15 And Pharao fayde vnto Iofeph: I haue dreamed a dreame and no man câ interpretate it, but I haue herde faye of the ẙ as foone as thou heareft a dreame,
16 thou doft interpretate it. And Iofeph anfwered Pharao

V. 6 percuffæ vredine 7 omnem priorum pulchritudinem. .. poft quietem 8 côiectores 9 Tunc demum reminifcens pincernarũ magifter, ait, Confiteor 11 fomniũ, præfagium futurorũ. 13 audiu. quicquid poftea rei probauit euentus. 14 Iofeph totonderunt
L. 8 der fie... deutten kund. 9 Ich gedencke heut an meyn funde 11 des deuttung yhn betraff 14 vnd lieffen yhn aus dem loch, ... lies fich befcheren

faynge: God fhall geue Pharao an anfwere of peace without me.

17 Pharao fayde vnto Iofeph: in my dreame me thought
18 I ftode by a ryvers fyde, and there came out of the ryver .vii. fatt flefhed ād well fauored kyne, and fedd
19 in the medowe. And then .vii. other kyne came vp after them, poore and very euell fauored ād leane flefhed: fo that I neuer fawe their lyke in all the lande
20 of Egipte in euell fauordneffe. And the .vii. leane and
21 euell fauored kyne ate vpp the firft .vii. fatt kyne And when they had eaten them vp, a man cowde not perceaue that they had eatē them: for they were ftill as evyll fauored as they were at the begynnynge. And I awoke.

22 And I fawe agayne in my dreame .vii. eares fprynge
23 out of one ftalk full and good, and .vii. other eares wytherd, thinne and blafted with wynde, fprynge vp
24 after them. And the thynne eares deuowred the .vii good eares. And I haue tolde it vnto the foth- [Fo. LX.] fayers, but no man can tell me what it meaneth.
25 Then Iofeph fayde vnto Pharao: both Pharaos dreames are one. And god doth fhewe Pharao what
26 he is aboute to do. The .vii. good kyne are .vii yeres: & the .vii. good eares are .vii. yere alfo, and
27 is but one dreame. Lykewyfe, the .vii. thynne and euell fauored kyne that came out after them, are .vii yeares: and the .vii. emptie and blafted eares fhalbe
28 vii. yeares of hunger. This is that which I fayde vnto Pharao, that God doth fhewe Pharao what he is aboute to doo.

29 Beholde there fhall come .vii. yere of great plen-
30 teoufnes through out all the lande of Egypte. And there fhall aryfe after them .vii. yeres of hunger. So

𝔐. 26 and it is 27 are .vii. eares
𝖁. 16 refpondebit profpera 17 Putabā me ftare 21 nullum faturitatis dedere veftigium 25 Somnium regis vnum eft 26 Septem boues pulchræ, & feptem fpicæ plenæ . . feptem vbertatis anni funt, eandemque vim fomnii comprehendunt.
𝕷. 16 gluck fagen laffen 19 Ich hab . . . nicht folch vngeftallte 21 merckt man nicht an yhn, das fie freffen hatten 25 das Got Pharao zeyget was er thut.

that all the plenteousnes shalbe forgeten in the
lande of Egipte. And the hunger shall consume
31 the lande: so that the plenteousnes shal not be once
asene in the land by reason of that hun- asene, *sene,*
ger that shall come after, for it shalbe *i. e. known*
32 exceadinge great And as concernynge that the dreame
was dubled vnto Pharao the second tyme, it betoken-
eth that the thynge is certanly prepared of God, ād
that God will shortly brynge it to passe.

33   Now therfore let Pharao provyde for a man of vnderstondynge and wysdome, and sett him over the
34 lande of Egipte. And let .P. Pharao make officers
ouer the lande, and take vp the fyfte parte of the land
35 of Egipte in the .vii. plenteous yeres and let them
gather all the foode of these good yeres that come,
ād lay vp corne vnder the power of Pharo: that there
may be foode in the cities, and there let them kepte
36 it: that there may be foode in stoore in the lande,
agaynst the .vii. yeres of hunger which shall come in
the lande of Egipte, and that the lande perishe not
thorow hunger.

37   And the saynge pleased Pharao ād all his seruauntes.
38 Than sayde Pharao vnto his servauntes: where shall
we fynde soch a mā as this is, that hath the sprete of
39 God in him? wherfore Pharao sayde vnto Joseph: for
as moch as God hath shewed the all this, there is no
man of vnderstondyng nor of wysdome lyke vnto the
40 Thou therfore shalt be ouer my house, and acordinge
to thy worde shall all my people obey: only in the
41 kynges seate will I be aboue the. And he sayde vnto
Ioseph: beholde, I haue sett the ouer all the lande of
42 Egipte. And he toke off his rynge from his fyngre,
and put it vpon Iosephs fingre, and arayed him in raymēt of bisse, and put a golden cheyne aboute his

---

𝔐. 39 or of wysdome
𝓥. 30 vt obliuioni tractatur 31 & vbertatis magnitudinem
perditura est inopiæ magnitudo. 32 firmitatis indicium .. sermo
dei, & velocius impleatur. 35 sub Phar. potestate condatur 39 sapi-
entiorem & simile tui inuenire potero? 41 rursum 22 stola byssina
𝐋. 32 solch ding von Gott gefertiget .. dasselbs eylend thun

43 necke and fet him vpon the beft charett that he had faue one. And they cryed before him Abrech, ād that Pharao had made him ruelar ouer all the lande of Egipte.
44 And Pharao fayde vnto Iofeph: I am Pharao, without thi will, fhall no man lifte vp e- [Fo. LXI.] ther
45 his hande or fote in all the lande of Egipte. And he called Iofephs name Zaphnath Paenea. And he gaue him to wyfe Afnath the doughter of Potiphara preaft of On. Than went Iofeph abrode in the lāde of Egipte.
46 And he was .xxx. yere olde whē he ftode before Pharao kynge of Egipte. And than Iofeph departed from Pharao, and went thorow out all the lande of Egipte.
47 And in the .vii. plēteous yeres they made fheves
48 and gathered vp all the fode of the .vii. plenteous yeres which were in the lande of Egipte and put it in to the cities. And he put the food of the feldes that grewe rounde aboute euery cyte: euen in the
49 fame. And Iofeph layde vp corne in ftoore, lyke vnto the fande of the fee in multitude out of mefure, vntyll he left nombrynge: For it was with out nombre.
50 And vnto Iofeph were borne .ii. fonnes before the yeres of hunger came, which Afnath the doughter of
51 Potiphara preaft of On, bare vnto him. And he called the name of the firft fonne Manaffe, for God (fayde he) hath made me forgett all my laboure & all my fathers
52 hufholde. The feconde called he Ephraim, for God (fayde he) hath caufed me to growe in the lande of my trouble.

V. 43 currum fuum fecundum . . genu flecterent 44 non mouebit quifquam manu aut ped. 45 & vocauit eum lingua Ægypt. Saluatorem mundi . . . . facerd. Heliopoleos. 47 in manipulos . . . congr. in horrea Ægypti. 49 arenæ maris coæquaretur, & copia menfuram excederet. 52 terra paupertatis

L. 43 auff dem andern wagen faren, . . knye fur yhm beugen 49 alfo das er auffhoret zu zelen, denn man kunds nicht zelen.

M. M. N. 43 *Abrech:* that is tender father or as fome will bowe the knee. 45 *zaphnath paena;* they are wordes of Egypt, and as moch to faye: As a man to whome fecret thynges are opened. 46 *When he ftode before Pharao:* that is whē he was admytted of Pharao into hys office, as in 1 Reg. xvi, d.

L. M. N. 45 *Zaphnath paenea* ift Egyptifch geredt, vnd noch vnbewuft was es fey, on das fo viel man fpuren kan, heyft es wie man auff deutfch fpricht, der heymliche nehifter radt. 51 *Manaffe* heyft vergeffen. 52 *Ephraim* heyft, die gewachfen.

53 And when the .vii. yeres of plenteousnes that
54 was in the lande of Egypte were ended, than came
the .vii. yeres of derth, acordynge as ❡. Ioseph had
fayde. And the derth was in all landes: but in the
55 lāde of Egipte was there yet foode. When now all
the lande of Egipte began to hunger, than cried
the people to Pharao for bread. And Pharao fayde
vnto all Egipte: goo vnto Ioseph, and what he fayth
56 to you that doo And when the derth was thorow
out all the lande, Ioseph opened all that was in the
cities, and folde vnto the Egiptiās And hunger waxed
57 fore in the land of Egipte. And all countrees came
to Egipte to Ioseph for to bye corne: becaufe that the
hunger was fo fore in all landes.

❡ The .XLII. Chapter.

1 WHEN Iacob fawe that there was corne to be folde in Egipte, he fayde vnto his fōnes: why are ye negligent? beholde, I
2 haue hearde that there is corne to be folde in Egipte. Gete you thither and bye vs corne frō thēce, that we maye lyue and not dye. So went Iofephs ten
3 brethern doune to bye corne in Egipte,
4 for Ben Iamin Iofephs brother wold not Iacob fende with his other brethren: for he fayde: fome myffortune myght happen him

M.C.S. Iofephs brethren come into Egypte to bye corne. And he knoweth them and tryeth them. Symeon is put in pryfon, the other retorne to their father to fetche Ben Iamin. His father is lothe to let hym go, but at the laft he graunted it.

5 And the fonnes of Ifraell came to bye
corne amonge other that came, for there was derth
6 alfo in the lande of Canaan. And Io- [Fo. LXII.]
feph was gouerner in the londe, and folde corne to all
the people of the londe. And his brethren came, and

V. 56 vniuerfa horrea & vendeb . . . . nam & illos oppreffera fames. 57 & malum inopiæ temperarent. xlii, 1 Quare negligitis? 2 triticum. . . & non confumamur inopia.

7 fell flatt on the grounde before him. When Ioſeph ſawe his brethern, he knewe them: But made ſtraunge vnto them, and ſpake rughly vnto them ſaynge: Whence come ye? and they ſayde: out of the lande of Canaan,
8 to bye vitayle. Ioſeph knewe his brethern, but they knewe not him.
9 And Ioſeph remembred his dreames which he dreamed of them, and ſayde vnto them: ye are ſpies, and to ſe where the lande is weake is your comynge.
10 And they ſayde vnto him: nay, my lorde: but to bye
11 vitayle thy ſeruauntes are come. We are all one mans ſonnes, and meane truely, and thy ſeruauntes are no ſpies.
12 And he ſayde vnto them: nay verely, but euen to
13 ſe where the land is weake is youre comynge. And they ſayde: we thi ſeruauntes are .xii. brethern, the ſonnes of one man in the lande of Canaan. The youngeſt is yet with oure father, and one no man woteth where he is.
14 Ioſeph ſayde vnto them, that is it that I ſayde vnto
15 you, that ye are ſurelye ſpies. Here by ye ſhall be proued. For by the lyfe of Pharao, ye ſhall not goo hence, vntyll youre yongeſt brother be come hither.
16 Sende therefore one off you and lett him ſette youre .Ᵽ. brother, and ye ſhalbe in preaſon in the meane ſeaſon. And thereby ſhall youre wordes be proued, whether there be any trueth in you: or els by the lyfe
17 of Pharao, ye are but ſpies. And he put them in warde thre dayes.
18 And Ioſeph ſayde vnto thē the thryd daye: This
19 doo and lyue, for I feare God Yf ye meane no hurte, let one of youre brethern be bounde in the preaſon, and goo ye and brynge the neceſſarie foode vnto youre

Ᵽ. 6 atque ad eius nutum 7 durius loquebatur .. victui neceſſaria. 8 infirmiora terræ 11 pacifici venimus, nec quicquam famuli tui machinantur mali. 12 immunita terræ 13 alius non eſt ſuper. 15 per ſalutem Phar. 16 eritis in vinculis 19 Si pacifici eſtis
L. 6 nydder zur erden auff ihr antlitz 7 redet hart 13 nicht mehr furhanden. 16 Bey dem leben Phar. 17 ynn eyn verwarung drey tag lang.

20 houſholdes, and brynge youre yongeſt brother vnto me: that youre wordes maye be beleved, ād that ye dye not. And they did ſo.
21 Than they ſayde one to a nother: we haue verely ſynned agaynſt oure brother, in that we ſawe the anguyſh of his ſoull when he beſought vs, & wold not heare him: therfore is this troubyll come apon vs.
22 Ruben anſwered thĕ ſaynge: ſayde I not vnto you that ye ſhuld not ſynne agaynſt the lad: but ye wolde not heare And now verely ſee, his bloude is requyred.
23 They were not aware that Ioſeph vnderſtode them, for
24 he ſpake vnto them by an interpreter. And he turned from them and wepte, and than turned to them agayne ād comened with them, and toke out Simeon from
25 amonge thĕ and bownde him before their eyes, ād commaunded to fyll their ſackes wyth corne, and to put euery mans money in his ſacke, and to geue them vitayle to ſpende by the waye. And ſo it was done to them.
26 [Fo. LXIII.] And they laded their aſſes with the
27 corne and departed thence. And as one of them opened his ſacke, for to geue his aſſe prauender in the
28 Inne, he ſpied his money in his ſacks mouth· And he ſayde vnto his brethren: my money is reſtored me agayne, & is euĕ in my ſackes mouth Than their hartes fayled them, and were aſtoynyed and ſayde one to a nother: how cometh it that God dealeth thus with vs?
29 And they came vnto Iacob their father vnto the lande of Canaan, and tolde him all that had happened
30 them ſaynge. The lorde of the lāde ſpake rughly to
31 vs, and toke us for ſpyes to ſerche the countre. And we ſayde vnto him: we meane truely and are no ſpies.

𝒱. 20 veſtros probare ſermones et non moriamini. 21 Merito hæc patimur .. anguſtias animæ ... iſta tribulatio. 22 en ſanguis eius exquiritur. 25 ſaccos tritico 31 Pacifici ſumus, nec vllas molimur inſidias.

𝑳. 20 glewben, das yhr nicht ſterben muſſet 21 angſt ſeyner ſeelen 22 blut geſoddert. 28 da entpfiel yhn yhr hertz

𝑴. 𝑴. 𝑵. 22 *To reguyer the bloude of the hāde of another*, is to take vengeaunce of the euell done vnto him, as in Gen. ix, a. Pſal. ix. b, and Ezech iii, c.

32 We be .xii. bretren fones of oure father, one is awaye, and the yongest is now with oure father in the lande of Canaan.

33 And the lorde of the countre fayde vnto us: here by fhall I knowe yf ye meane truely: leaue one of youre brethern here with me, and take foode neceffary

34 for youre houfholdes and get you awaye, and brynge youre yongeft brother vnto me And thereby fhall I knowe that ye are no fpyes, but meane truely: So will I delyuer you youre brother agayne, and ye fhall occupie in the lande.

35 And as they emptied their fackes, beholde: euerymans bundell of money was in his facke And when both they and their father fawe the bundells of money, they were afrayde.

36 .¶. And Iacob their father fayde vnto them: Me haue ye robbed of my childern: Iofeph is away, and Simeon is awaye, and ye will take Ben Iamin awaye.

37 All thefe thinges fall vpon me. Ruben anfwered his father faynge: Slee my two fonnes, yf I bringe him not to the agayne. Delyuer him therfore to my honde,

38 and I will brynge him to the agayne: And he fayde: my fonne fhall not go downe with you. For his brother is dead, and he is left alone Moreouer fome myffortune myght happen vpon him by the waye which ye goo. And fo fhuld ye brynge my gray head with forowe vnto the graue.

V. 32 vnus non eft fuper 34 qui tenetur in vinculis ... emendi habeatis licētiam. 35 His dictis cum frumenta .. ligatas pecunias 36 non eft fuper, Simeon tenetur in vinculis .. in me ... reciderunt. 38 ipfe folus remanfit .. cum dolore ad inferos.

L. 32 ift nicht mehr furhanden 34 im land werben. 36 Iofeph ift nit mehr furhanden 38 alleyn vberblieben .. mit fchmertzen zur helle.

M. M. N. 38 *Brynge me to my graue;* that is, ye fhall brynge me to my death, as in Efa. xxxviii.

❡ The .XLIII. Chapter.

1,2 **A**ND the derth waxed sore in the lande. And when they had eatē vp that corne which they brought out of the lande of Egipte, their father sayde vnto them: goo 3 agayne and by vs a litle food. Than sayde Iuda vnto him: the man dyd testi- fie vnto vs saynge: loke that ye see not my face excepte youre brother be with 4 you. Therfore yf thou wilt sende oure brother with 5 vs, we wyll goo and bye the food. But yf thou wylt not sende him, we wyll not goo: for the man sayde vnto vs: loke that ye see not my face, excepte youre brother be with you.

M.C.S. When Bē Iamin was brought, they retorned with gyftes. Symeon is delyuered out of pryson. Ioseph goeth asyde and wepeth. They feast together.

6 And Israell sayde: wherfore delt ye so cruelly with me, as to tell the man that ye had yet 7 another brother? And they sayde: The man asked vs of oure kynred saynge: is youre father yet alyue? haue ye not another brother? And we tolde him acordynge to these wordes. How cowd we knowe that he wolde 8 byd vs brynge oure brother downe with vs? Than sayde Iuda vnto Israell his father: Send the lad with me, and we wyll ryse and goo, that we maye lyue and not dye: 9 both we, thou and also oure childern. I wilbe suertie for him, and of my handes requyre him. Yf I brynge him not to the and sett him before thine eyes, than let 10 me bere the blame for euer. For excepte we had made this tariēg: by this we had bene there twyse and come agayne.

11 Than their father Israel sayde vnto thē: Yf it must nedes be so now: than do thus, take of the best frutes

V. 2 pauxillum escarum. 3 Denūtiauit nobis... sub attestatione iurisiurandi 4 ememus tibi necessaria. 6 miseriam vt indicaretis 7 per ordinem nostram progeniē.. iuxta id quod fuerat sciscitatus 8 ne moriamur nos et paruuli nostri. 9 suscipio puerum:.. require illum.. ero peccati reus

L. 6 dem man ansaget 8 wir vnd du vnd vnser kindle 9 burge fur yhn seyn

of the lande in youre veſſeles, and brynge the man a
preſent, a curteſie bawlme, and a curteſie *curteſie, a*
of hony, ſpyces and myrre, dates and al- *ſmall quantity*
12 mondes. And take as moch money more with you.
And the money that was brought agayne in youre
ſackes, take it agayne with you in youre handes, peraduenture it was ſome ouerſyghte.

13 Take alſo youre brother with you, and aryſe and
14 goo agayne to the man. And God almightie geue
you mercie in the ſighte of the man and ſend you youre
other brother .P. and alſo Bē Iamin, and I wilbe as a
mā robbed of his childern.

15 Thus toke they the preſent and twiſe ſo much more
money with them, and Ben Iamin. And roſe vp, went
downe to Egipte, and preſented them ſelfe to Ioſeph.
16 When Ioſeph ſawe Ben Iamin with them, he ſayde to
the ruelar of his houſe: brynge theſe men home, and
ſley and make redie: for they ſhall dyne with me at
17 none. And the man dyd as Ioſeph bad, and brought
them in to Ioſephs houſe.

18 When they were brought to Ioſephs houſe, they
were afrayde ād ſayde: becauſe of the money ẏ came
in our ſackes mouthes at the firſt tyme, are we brought,
to pyke a quarell with vs & to laye ſome thinge to
oure charge: to brynge vs in bondage and oure aſſes
19 alſo. Therfore came they to the man that was the
ruelar ouer Ioſephs houſe, and comened with him at
20 the doore and ſayde:

Sir, we came hither at the firſt tyme to bye foode,
21 and as we came to an Inne and opened oure ſackes:
beholde, euery mannes money was in his ſacke with
full weghte: But we haue broght it agene with us,
22 & other mony haue we brought alſo in our handes, to

M. 12 agayne with you, peraduenture
V. 14 vobis eū placabilem: . quē tenet in vinculis, & hunc
Beniamin 16 occide victimas, & inſtrue conuiuium 18 vt deuoluat
in nos calumniā 20 Oramus domine, vt audias nos 21 eodem pondere reportauimus.
L. 14 euch laſſe ewrn andern bruder 18 das ers auff vns brenge
21 mit volligem gewicht
L. M. N. 11 Dieſe namen der fruchten find noch biſzher vn-
gewiſs auch bey den Iuden ſelbs.

bye foode, but we can not tell who put oure money in oure fackes.

23 And he fayde: be of good chere, feare not: Youre God and the God of youre fathers hath put you that treafure in youre fackes, for I had [Fo. LXV.] youre
24 money. And he brought Simeon out to them ād led thē in to Iofephs houfe, & gaue them water to wafhe
25 their fete, and gaue their affes prauender: And they made redie their prefent agaynft Iofeph came at none, for they herde faye that they fhulde dyne there.
26 When Iofeph came home, they brought the prefent in to the houfe to him, which they had in their handes, ād fell flat on the grounde befor him.
27 And he welcomed thē curteoufly fainge: is youre father that old man which ye tolde me of, in good
28 health? and is he yet alyue? they anfwered: thy fervaunte oure father is in good health, ād is yet alyue. And they bowed them felues and fell to the grounde.
29 And he lyfte vp his eyes & behelde his brother Ben Iamin his mothers fonne, & fayde: is this youre yongeft brother of whome ye fayde vnto me? And fayde: God
30 be mercyfull vnto ẏ my fonne. And Iofeph made haft (for his hert dyd melt apon his brother) and foughte for to wepe, & entred in to his chambre, for to wepe there.
31 And he waffhed his face and came out & refrayned him felfe, & bad fett bread on the table
32 And they prepared for him by himfelfe, and for them by them felues, and for the Egiptians which ate with him by them felues, becaufe the Egyptians may not eate bread with the Hebrues, for that is an abhomyna-
33 cyon vnto the Egiptians. And they fatt before him:

𝔐. 30 fought where to wepe
𝒱. 22 in marfupiis noftris. 23 Pax vobifcum .. probatam ego habeo. 25 comefturi effent panem. 26 adorauerunt proni in terram. 27 clementer refalutatis eis 28 Sofpes eft .. incuruati ador. 29 fratrem fuum vterinum 30 commota fuerant vifcera .. et erumpebāt lachrymæ 31 continuit fe 32 prophanum putant
𝐿. 25 das brod effen follten. 27 Er aber gruffet fie freuntlich 30 feyns hertzen grund entbrand yhm 31 hielt fich feft
𝔐. 𝔐. N. 32 *Abhominacion*, that is, it was abhorred of the Egypcians that an Hebrew fhuld eate with thē.

the eldeſt acordynge vnto his .P. age, and the yongeſt acordyng vnto his youth. And the men marveled
34 amonge them ſelves. And they broughte rewardes vnto them from before him: but Ben Iamins parte was fyue tymes ſo moch as any of theirs. And they ate and they dronke, and were dronke wyth him

---

The .XLIIII. Chapter.

1 AND he commaunded the rueler of his houſe ſaynge: fyll the mens ſackes with food, as moch as they can carie, and put euery mans money in his bagge *M.C.S. Ioſeph accuſeth his brother of theft. Iuda becommeth ſurety for Ben Iamin.*
2 mouth, and put my ſyluer cuppe in the ſackes mouth of the yongeſt and his corne money alſo. And he
3 dyd as Ioſeph had ſayde. And in y̑ mornynge as ſoone as it was lighte, the mē were let goo with their aſſes.
4 And when they were out of the cytie and not yet ferre awaye, Ioſeph ſayde vnto the ruelar of his houſe: vp and folowe after the men and ouertake them, and ſaye vnto them: wherefore haue ye rewarded euell for
5 good? is that not the cuppe of which my lorde drynketh, ād doth he not prophefie therin? *prophefie, divine*
ye haue euell done that ye haue done.
6 And he ouertoke them and ſayde the ſame wordes
7 vnto them. And they anſwered him: wherfore ſayth my lorde ſoch wordes? God forbydd that thy ſer-
8 uauntes ſhulde doo ſo. Beholde, the money which we founde in oure ſackes mouthes, we brought agayne vnto the, out of the land of Canaā: how then ſhulde

V. 33 primogenita ſua ... ætatem ſuam. 34 ſumptis partibus quas ab eo acceperant: . et inebriati ſunt cum eo. xliiii, 1 ſummitate ſacci. 2 tritici 5 Scyphus quē furati eſtis 6 apprehenſis per ordinem 8 quomodo conſequens eſt vt furati ſimus
L. 33 gepurt ... iugent 34 vnd wurden truncken mit yhm. xliiii, 1 oben ynn feynen ſack 6 Vnd als er ſie ergreiff

we fteale [Fo. LXVI.] out of my lordes houfe, ether
9 fyluer or golde? with whofoeuer of thy feruauntes it
be founde let him dye, and let vs alfo be my lordes
10 bondmen. And he fayde: Now therfore acordynge
vnto youre woordes, he with whom it is found, fhalbe
my feruaunte: but ye, fhalbe harmleffe.

11 And attonce euery man toke downe his facke to
12 the grounde, ād every man opened his facke. And he
ferched, and began at the eldeft & left at the yongeft.
13 And the cuppe was founde in Ben Iamins facke. Then
they rent their clothes, and laded euery man his affe
14 and went agayne vnto the cytie. And Iuda and his
brethrē came to Iofephs houfe, for he was yet there,
15 ād they fell before him on the grounde. And Iofeph
fayde vnto thē: what dede is this which ye haue done?
wift ye not that foch a man as I can prophefie?

16 Then fayde Iuda: what fhall we faye vnto my lorde,
what fhall we fpeake or what excufe can we make?
God hath founde out ẏ wekedneffe of thy feruauntes.
Beholde, both we and he with whom the cuppe is
17 founde, are thy feruauntes. And he anfwered: God
forbyd ẏ I fhulde do fo, the man with whom the cuppe
is founde, he fhalbe my feruaunte: but goo ye in peace
vn to youre father.

18 Then Iuda went vnto him and fayde: oh my lorde,
let thy feruaunte fpeake a worde in my lordes audyence, and be not wrooth with .P. thi feruaunte: for
19 thou art euen as Pharao. My lorde axed his feruaunte
20 fainge: haue ye a father or a brother? And we anfwered my lord, we haue a father that is old, and a
yonge lad which he begat in his age: ād the brother
of the fayde lad is dead, & he is all that is left of that
mother. And his father loueth him.

𝔐. 18 my lordes eare, and
𝔙. 14 Primufque Iudas cum fratribus . . . omnefque . . . pariter in terram corruerunt. 15 fimilis mei in augur. fcientia? 16 aut
iufte poterimus obtendere? 17 Abfit a me . . . abite liberi 18 propius
Iudas . . tu es enim poft Pharaonem dominus meus. 20 ipfum
folum habet mater fua
𝔏. 15 erradten kunde? 16 fur wenden 17 mit friden 18 fur
deinen oren 20 alleyn vberblieben von feyner mutter

21 Then fayde my lorde vnto his feruauntes brynge him vnto me, that I maye fett myne eyes apon him.
22 And we anfwered my lorde, that the lad coude not goo from his father, for if he fhulde leaue his father, he
23 were but a deed man. Then faydeft thou vnto thy feruauntes: excepte youre yongeft brother come with you, loke that ye fe my face no moare.
24 And when we came vnto thy feruaunt oure father,
25 we fhewed him what my lorde had fayde. And when oure father fayde vnto vs, goo agayne and bye vs a
26 litle fode: we fayd, ỹ we coude not goo. Neverthelefſe if oure yoūgefte brother go with vs then will we goo, for we maye not fee the mannes face, excepte oure
27 yongeft brother be with vs. Then fayde thy feruaunt oure father vnto vs. Ye knowe that my wyfe bare me
28 ii. fonnes. And the one went out from me and it is fayde of a fuertie that he is torne in peaces of wyld
29 beaftes, and I fawe him not fence. Yf ye fhall take this alfo awaye frō me and fome myffortune happen apon him, then fhall ye brynge my gray heed with forow vnto the graue.
30 [Fo. LXVII.] Now therfore whē I come to thy feruaunt my father, yf the lad be not with me: feinge that
31 his lyfe hāgeth by the laddes lyfe, then as foone as he feeth that the lad is not come, he will dye. So fhall we thy feruaūtes brynge the gray hedde of thy fer-
32 vaunt oure father with forow vnto the graue. For I thy feruaunt became fuertie for the lad vnto my father & fayde: yf I bringe him not vnto the agayne. I will
33 bere the blame all my life lōge. Now therfore let me thy feruaunt byde here for ỹ lad, & be my lordes bondman: &
34 let the lad goo home with his brethern. For how can I goo vnto my father, and the lad not wyth me: left I fhulde fee the wretchednes that fhall come on my father.

V. 21 ponam oculos 26 non audemus videre 28 Egreffus eft vnus 29 cum moerore ad inferos. 30 anima illius ex huius anima dependeat 32 recepi fidem, & fpopondi 34 Non enim poffum ... ne calamitatis ... teftis affiftam.
L. 28 Eyner gieng hynaus von myr 29 hynunter in die hell 30 weyl feyn feel an difes feel hanget 32 burge worden 34 iamer fehen, der meynem vatter begegen wurde.

The .XLV. Chapter.

1 AND Ioseph coude no longer refrayne before all them that ſtode aboute him, but commaunded that they ſhuld goo all out from him, and that there ſhuld be no man with him, whyle he vttred him ſelfe vnto his
2 brethern. And he wepte alowde, ſo that the Egip-
3 tians and the houſe of Pharao herde it. And he ſayde vnto his brethern: I am Ioſeph: doth my father yet lyue? But his brethern coude not anſwere him, for they were abaſſhed at his preſence.

M.C.S. Io-ſeph maketh hym ſelfe knowen vnto his brethren, and ſendeth for his father.

4 And Ioſeph ſayde vnto his brethern: come nere to me, and they came nere. And he .P. ſayde: I am
5 Ioſeph youre brother whom ye ſold in to Egipte. And now be not greued therwith, nether let it ſeme a cruel thinge in youre eyes, that ye ſolde me hither. For God
6 dyd ſend me before you to ſaue lyfe. For this is the ſeconde yere of derth in the lande, and fyue moo are behynde in which there ſhall nether be earynge nor herueſt.

7 Wherfore God ſent me before you to make prouiſion, that ye myghte continue in the erth and to ſave youre
8 lyues by a greate delyuerance. So now it was not ye that ſent me hither, but God: and he hath made me father vnto Pharao and lord ouer all his houſe, and
9 rueler in all the land of Egipte. Haſt you ād goo to my father and tell him, this ſayeth thy ſonne Ioſeph: God hath made me lorde ouer all Egipte. Come downe
10 vnto me and tarye not, And thou ſhalt dwell in the londe of Goſan & be by me: both thou and thi chil-

V. 1 intereſſet .. agnitioni mutuæ. 3 nimio terrore perterriti. 5 pro ſalute enim veſtra 6 nec arari .. nec meti 7 & eſcas ad viuêdum habere poſſitis.

L. 1 mit ſeynen brudern bekennete 5 vnd denckt nicht das zorn ſey .. vmb ewers lebens willen 6 pflugen ... erndten 7 durch eyn groſſe errettunge

L. M. N. 4 *su myr:* Das ſind die ſuſſen wort des Euangelii, alſo redet Chriſtus mit der ſeelen im glawben, nach dem ſie durchs geſetz vnd gewiſſen der ſund, woll gedemutiget vnd geengſtet iſt.

dern, and thi childerns childern: and thy ſhepe, and
11 beaſtes and all that thou haſt. There will I make
proviſion for the: for there remayne yet .v. yeres of
derth, leſt thou and thi houſholde and all that thou
haſt periſh.
12 Beholde, youre eyes do ſe, and the eyes alſo of my
brother Ben Iamin, that I ſpeake to you by mouth.
13 Therfore tell my father of all my honoure which I
haue in Egipte and of all that ye haue ſene, ãd make
haſt and brynge mi [Fo. LXVIII.] father hither.
14 ⓒ And he fell on his brother Ben Iamins necke &
15 wepte, & Ben Iamin wepte on his necke. Moreouer
he kyſſed all his brethern and wepte apon them. And
16 after that, his brethern talked with him. And when
the tidynges was come vnto Pharaos houſſe that Ioſephes brethern were come, it pleaſed Pharao well and
all his ſeruauntes.
17 And Pharao ſpake vnto Ioſeph: ſaye vnto thy brethern, this do ye: lade youre beeſtes ãd get you hence,
18 And when ye be come vnto the londe of Canaan, take
youre father and youre houſholdes and come vnto me,
and I will geue you the beſte of the lande of Egipte,
and ye ſhall eate the fatt of the londe.
19 And commaunded alſo. This do ye: take charettes
with you out of the lande of Egipte, for youre childern
and for youre wyues: and brynge youre father and come.
20 Alſo, regarde not youre ſtuff, for the goodes of all the
londe of Egipte ſhalbe youres.
21 And the childern of Iſraell dyd euen ſo, And Ioſeph
gaue them charettes at the commaundment of Pharao,
and gaue them vitayle alſo to ſpende by the waye.
22 And he gaue vnto eche of them chaunge of rayment:
but vnto Ben Iamin he gaue .iii. hundred peces of
23 ſyluer and .v. chaunge of rayment. And vnto his father he ſent after the ſame maner: x. he aſſes laden

𝔐. 23 maner .x. aſſes
𝔙. 11 Ibique te paſcam 16 omnis familia eius. 18 medullam
terræ. 19 ac coniugũ: et dicito, Tollite patrem veſtrum & pro-
perate quantocyus venientes 22 ſtolis optimis 23 tantũdem pe-
cuniæ & veſtium
𝔏. 12 mundlich mit euch rede 20 ſchonet nicht ewrs hauſzradts

with good out of Egipte, and .x. ſhe aſſes laden with corne, bred and meate: to ſerue his .P. father by the
24 waye. So ſent he his brethern awaye, and they departed. And he ſayde vnto them: ſe that ye fall not out by the waye.
25 And they departed from Egipte and came in to the
26 land of Canaan vnto Iacob their father, and told him ſaynge. Ioſeph is yet a lyue and is gouerner ouer all the land of Egipte. And Iacobs hert wauered, for he be-
27 leued the not. And they tolde him all the wordes of Ioſeph which he had ſayde vnto them. But when he ſawe the charettes which Ioſeph had ſent to carie him,
28 then his ſprites reuiued. And Iſrael ſayde. *ſprites, ſpirits* I haue ynough, yf Ioſeph my ſonne be yet alyue: I will goo and ſe him, yer that I dye. *yer, before*

The .XLVI. Chapter.

1 ISRAEL toke his iourney with all that he had, and came vnto Berſeba and offred offrynges vnto the God of his
2 father Iſaac. And God ſayde vnto Iſrael in a viſion by nyghte, and called vnto him: Iacob Iacob. And he anſwered:
3 here am I. And he ſayde; I am that mightie God of thy father, feare not to goo downe in to Egipte. For
4 I will make of the there a great people. I will go downe with ẏ in to Egipte, & I will alſo bringe the vp agayne, & Ioſeph ſhall put his hand apon thine eyes.

M.C.S. Iacob with all his houſholde goeth to Ioſeph in to Egypt. The genealogie of Iacob. Ioſeph meteth hys father.

V. 23 ... addens .. triticum in itinere, paneſque portātes. 24 Ne iraſcamini in via. 26 Quo audito Iacob, quaſi de graui ſomno euigilans 27 reuixit ſpiritus eius, & ait xlvi, 1 puteum iuramenti (v. 5) .. mactatis ibi victimis 2 audiuit eum

L. 24 zancket nicht auff dem wege. 26 ſeyn hertz ſchlugs ynn wind 28 Ich hab gnug. xlvi, 1 opffert er opffer

M. M. N. 3 *I will make the a great people:* that is I wyll multiplye thy ſeede, that many people ſhall come therof 4 *To put hys hande vpon his eyes* is to be preſent at hys death and to burye him, as in Tob. xiiii, d.

5   And Iacob rofe vp from Berfeba. And ẏ fonnes of
Ifrael caried Iacob their father, ād [Fo. LXIX.] their
childern and their wyues in the charettes which Pharao
6   had fent to carie him. And they toke their catell ād
the goodes which they had gotten in the land of Canaan, and came in to Egipte: both Iacob and all his
7   feed with him, his fonnes and his fonnes fonnes with
him: his doughters and his fonnes doughters and all
his feed brought he with him in to Egipte.
8   Thefe are the names of the childern of Ifrael which
came in to Egipte, both Iacob and his fonnes: Rubē
9   Iacobs firft fonne. The childern of Ruben: Hanoch,
10 Pallu, Hezron and Charmi. The childern of Simeon:
Iemuel, Iamin, Ohad, Iachin, Zohar and Saul the fonne
11 of a Cananitifh woman The childern of Leui: Gerfon,
12 Kahath and Merari. The childern of Iuda: Er, Onan,
Sela, Pharez and Zerah, but Er and Onan dyed in the
lande of Canaan. The childern of Pharez, Hezrō, &
13 Hamul. The childern of Ifachar: Tola, Phuva Iob
14 and Semnon. The childern of Sebulon: Sered, Elon
15 and Iaheleel. Thefe be the childern of Lea which fhe
bare vnto Iacob in Mefopotamia with his doughter
Dina. All thefe foulles of his fonnes and doughters
make .xxx. and .vi.
16 The childern of Gad: Ziphion, Haggi, Suni, Ezbon,
17 Eri, Arodi and Areli. The childern of Affer: Iemna,
Iefua, Iefui, Brya and Se- .P. rah their fifter. And
18 the childern of Brya were Heber and Malchiel. Thefe
are the childern of Silpha whom Labā gaue to Lea his
doughter. And thefe fhe bare vnto Iacob in nombre
xvi. foules.
19 The childern of Rahel Iacobs wife: Iofeph and ben
20 Iamin. And vnto Iofeph in the lōde of Egipte were
borne: Manaffes and Ephraim which Afnath the dough-
21 ter of Potiphara preaft of On bare vnto him. The chil-

𝔐. 13 Semfon 15 make .xxx. and .iii.
𝒱. 5 ad portandum fenem [The whole paffage 1–7 is very free.]
15 triginta tres. 20 facerdot. Heliopoleos
𝓛. 6 erworben hatten 11 Gerfon, Cuhuz vnd M., 12 Hezron
vnd Thamul 14 Semron 15 drey vnd dreyzg zeelen 16 Arobi 20
Priefters zu On

dern of Ben Iamin: Bela, Becher, Aſbel, Gera, Nae-
22 man, Ehi Ros Mupim, Hupim and Ard. Theſe are
the childern of Rahel which were borne vnto Iacob:
xiiii. ſoules all to gether.

23, 24 The childern of Dan: Huſim. The childern of
25 Nepthali: Iahezeel, Guni, Iezer and Sillem. Theſe
are the ſonnes of Bilha which Laban gaue vnto Rahel
his doughter, and ſhe bare theſe vnto Iacob, all to-
26 gether .vii. ſoulles   All the ſoulles that came with
Iacob in to Egipte which came out of his loyns (beſyde his ſonnes wifes) were all togither .Lx. and .vi
27 ſoulles. And the ſonnes of Ioſeph, which were borne
him in egipte were: .ii. ſoules. So that all the ſoulles
of the houſe of Iacob which came in to Egipte are .Lxx
28   And he ſent Iuda before him vnto Ioſeph that the
waye myghte be ſhewed him vnto Goſan, and they came
29 in to the lande of Goſan   And Ioſeph made redie his
charett and went agaynſt Iſraell his father vnto Goſan,
ād pre- [Fo. LXX.] ſented him ſelfe vnto him, and fell
on his necke and wepte vpon his necke a goode whyle.
30   And Iſrael ſayd vnto Ioſeph: Now I am cōtēt to dye,
in ſo moch I haue ſene the, that thou art yet alyue.
31   And Ioſeph ſayde vnto his brethrē and vnto his fathers
houſe: I will goo & ſhewe Pharao and tell him: that my
brethern and my fathers houſe which were in the lāde of
32 Canaan are come vnto me, and how they are ſhepardes
(for they were men of catell) and they haue brought their
ſhepe and their oxen and all that they haue with them.
33   Yf Pharao call you and axe you what youre occupa-
34 tion is, ſaye: thi ſeruauntes haue bene occupyed aboute
catell, frō oure chilhode vnto this tyme: both we and oure
fathers, that ye maye dwell in the lande of Goſan. For an
abhominacyon vnto the Egiptians are all that feade ſhepe.

M. 29 and wēt to mete Iſrael 34 For the Egyptiās abhore all
ſheppardes.
V. 27 *in Aegyptum* 28 vt nuntiaret ei, et ille occurreret in
Geſſen. 29 ad eūdem locum ... & inter amplexus fleuit. 32 cu-
ramque habent alendorum gregum: . omnia quae habere pe-
tuerunt 34 reſpondebitis, Viri paſtores ſumus ... Hæc autum
dicetis
L. 26 die aus ſeynen landen komen waren 29 Vnd da er yn
ſahe 32 leute die mit vieh vmbgehen (v. 34) 34 Denn was vieh
hirten ſind, das iſt den Egyptern ein grewel.

ℭ The .XLVII. Chapter.

1 AND Ioseph wēt and told Pharao and fayde: my father and my brethern their fhepe and their beaftes and all that they haue, are come out of the lāde of Canaan and
2 are in the lande of Gofan. And Iofeph toke a parte of his brethern: euen fyue of
3 them, and prefented them vnto Pharao. And Pharao fayde vnto his brethern: what is your occupation? And they fayde vnto Pharao: feaders of fhepe are thi
4 feruauntes, both we ād alfo oure fathers. They fayde moreouer vnto Pha- .P. rao: for to fogeorne in the lande are we come, for thy feruauntes haue no pafture for their fhepe fo fore is the famefhment in the lande of Canaan. Now therefore let thy feruauntes dwell in the lande of Gofan.

M.C.S Iacob cometh before Pharao, & vnto hym is geuē the lande of Gofan. He fwereth his fonne for his buryall.

5 And Pharao fayde vnto Iofeph: thy father and thy
6 brethren are come vnto the. The londe of Egipte is open before the: In the beft place of the lande make both thy father and thy brothren dwell. And euen in the lond of Gofan let them dwell. Moreouer yf thou knowe any men of actiuyte amonge them, make them ruelars ouer my catell. And
7 Iofeph brought in Iacob his father and fett him be-
8 fore Pharao. And Iacob bleffed Pharao. And Pharao
9 axed Iacob, how old art thou? And Iacob fayde vnto Pharao: the dayes of my pilgremage are an hundred and: .xxx. yeres. Few and euell haue the dayes of my lyfe bene, and haue not attayned vnto the yeres of the lyfe of my fathers in the dayes of their pilgrem-
10 ages. And Iacob bleffed Pharao and went out from

men of actiuyte, able men

M. 3 Pharao: fheppardes are
V. 2 Extremos quoque fratrum 6 viros induftrios 7 ftatuit eum coram eo [7–12 is very free with repeated omiffions.]
L. 3 Wes nehret jr euch? 6 offen, las fie . . die tüchtig find 7 ftellet im fur Pharao 9 die zeit meiner walfart (3 times)
M. M. N. 9 *The dayes of hys pilgremage* was all the tyme that he lyued, as in Iob .xiiii, c, and Pfal. cxviii, c. 10 *To bleffe*, is here to prayfe & geue thankes as a fore in the .xiiii. of Gene. d. and 1 Co. x, d.

11 him. And Ioſeph prepared dwellinges for his father and his brethern, and gaue them poſſeſſions in the londe of Egipte, in the beſt of the londe: euē in the
12 lande of Raemſes, as Pharao commaunded. And Ioſeph made prouyſion for his father, his brethern and all his fathers houſholde, as yonge children are ſedd with bread.
13 There was no bread in all the londe, for the derth was exceadīge ſore: ſo ẏ ẏ lōde of Egipte & ẏ lōde of Canaan, were fameſhyd by ẏ reaſon [Fo. LXXI.]
14 of ẏ derth. And Ioſeph brought together all ẏ money ẏ was founde in ẏ lāde of Egipte and of Canaan, for ẏ corne which they boughte: & he layde vp the money in Pharaos houſſe.
15 When money ſayled in the lāde of Egipte & of Canaan, all the Egiptians came vnto Ioſeph and ſayde: geue us ſuſtenaunce: wherfore ſuffreſt thou vs to dye
16 before the, for oure money is ſpent. Then ſayde Ioſeph: brynge youre catell, and I will geue yow for
17 youre catell, yf ye be without money. And they brought their catell vnto Ioſeph. And he gaue them bread for horſes and ſhepe, and oxen and aſſes: ſo he fed them with bread for all their catell that yere.
18 When that yere was ended, they came vnto him the nexte yere and ſayde vnto him: we will not hyde it from my lorde, how that we haue nether money nor catell for my lorde: there is no moare left for my lorde,
19 but euen oure bodies and ourę londes. Wherfore lateſt thou vs dye before thyne eyes, and the londe to goo to noughte? bye vs and oure landes for bread: and let both vs and oure londes be bonde to Pharao. Geue vs ſeed, that we may lyue & not dye, & that the londe goo not to waſt.
20 And Ioſeph boughte all the lande of Egipte for

V. 17 pro commutatione pecorū 19 redigatur terra in ſolitudinem.

L. 12 einem jglichen ſein theil brod, von alten bis auff die jungen kinder. 13 jn allen landen .. verſchmachten 14 bracht alles geld zu zamen 18 vnſern herrn nicht verbergen .. auch alles vieh ... beide vns ſterben vnd vnſer feld.? 19 leibeigen ſeien .. nicht verwüſte.

Pharao. For the Egiptians folde euery man his londe becaufe the derth was fore apō them: and fo the londe
21 became Pharaos. And he appoynted the people vnto the cities, from one fyde of Egipte vnto the other:
22 only the londe of the Preftes bought he not. For there .P. was an ordinaūce made by Pharao for ÿ * preaftes, that they fhulde eate that which was appoynted vnto them: which Pharao had geuen them wherfore they folde not their londes.
23 Then Iofeph fayde vnto the folke: beholde I haue boughte you this daye ād your landes for Pharao. Take there feed
24 and goo fowe the londe. And of the encreafe, ye fhall geue the fyfte parte vnto Pharao, and .iiii. partes fhalbe youre awne, for feed to fowe the feld: and for you, and them of youre houfholdes, and
25 for youre childern, to eate. And they anfwered: Thou haft faued oure lyves Let vs fynde grace in the fyghte of my lorde, and let us be Pharaos fervaūtes.
26 And Iofeph made it a lawe ouer the lāde of Egipte vnto this daye: that men muft geue Pharao the fyfte part, excepte the londe of the preaftes only, which was not bond vnto Pharao.
27 And Ifrael dwelt in Egipte: euen in the countre of Gofan. And they had their poffeffions therein, and they grewe and multi-
28 plyed exceadingly. Moreouer Iacob lyued in the lande of Egipte .xvii. yeres, fo that the hole age of Iacob was an hundred and .xlvii. yere.

The blīde gydes gett previleges frō bearīge with their brethrē contrarye to Chriftes lawe of love. And of thefe preftes of idolles did our cōpaffige yvetrees lerne to crepe vp by litle & litle & to cōpaffe ÿ greate trees of ÿ world with hypocrifye, ād to thruft ÿ rotes of idolatryffe fuperftition in to thē & to fucke out ÿ iuce of thē with their poetrye, till all be feer bowes and no thinge grene fave their awne cōmōwelth.

V. 20 Subiecitque eā Pharaoni 22 quibus & ftatuta cibaria ex horreis publicis præbebantur, & idcirco non funt compulfi vendere poff. fuas. 25 refpiciat nos tantum dom. nofter, et læti feruiemus regi. 26 quæ libera ab hac conditione fuit. 28 vixit in ea

L. 20 tewrung 21 ftedten aus vnd einging 22 was jnen benant war .. durfften .. nicht verkauffen. 23 Sihe, da habt jr famen 25 las vns nur leben 26 nicht eigen Pharao.

M. M. N. 20 This name Pharao was a generall name to all the kynges of Egypte. As abimelech was a cōmen name to all the kynges of the gentiles, as in Exod. xvi.

29 When the tyme drewe nye, that Ifrael muſt dye: he ſent for his ſonne Ioſeph and ſayde vnto him: Yf I haue founde grace in thy ſyghte, put thy hande vnder my thye and deale mercifully ād truely with me, 30 that thou burie me not in Egipte: but let me lye by my fathers, and ca- [Fo. LXXII.] rie me out of Egipte, and burie me in their buryall. And he anſwered: I 31 will do as thou haſt ſayde. And he ſayde: ſwere vnto me: ād he ſware vnto him. And than Ifrael bowed him vnto the beddes head.

The .XLVIII. Chapter.

1 AFTER theſe deades, tydīges were brought vnto Ioſeph, that his father was ſeke. And he toke with him his .ii. ſōnes, Manaſ- 2 ſes and Ephraim. Then was it ſayde vnto Iacob: beholde, thy ſonne Ioſeph commeth vnto the. And Iſrael toke his ſtrength vnto him, and 3 ſatt vp on the bedd, and ſayde vnto Ioſeph: God all mightie appeared vnto me at lus in the lande of Ca- 4 naan, ād bleſſed me, and ſayde vnto me: beholde, I will make the growe and will multiplye the, and will make a great nombre of people of the, and will geue this lande vnto the and vnto thy ſeed after ẏ vnto an 5 euerlaſtinge poſſeſſion. Now therfore thy .ii. ſōnes Manaſſes ād Ephraim which were borne vnto the be- fore I came to the, in to Egipte, ſhalbe myne: euen 6 as Ruben and Simeō ſhall they be vnto me. And the

M.C.S. Ia-cob lyeth ſycke. He de-ſyreth Eph-raim and Ma-naſſes for hys ſonnes and bleſſeth them.

V. 29 cerneret diem .. & facies mihi miſericordiam & verita-tem .. auferas me de terra hac, condaſque in ſepulchro maior. 31 Quo iurante, adorauit Iſr. dom., conuerſus ad lectuli caput. xlviii, 2 Dictumque eſt ſeni .. Qui confortatus ſedit in lectulo.
L. 29 liebe vnd trewe an mir thuſt .. jm jrem begrebnis be-graben 31 jnn dem bette zum heubten. xlviii, 2 vnd Iſrael macht ſich ſtark
M. M. N. 29 To put his hand vnder his thye, loke in Gen. xxiiii, a.
L. M. N. 31 *Nieget:* Er lag im bette kranck, richtet ſich doch auff, nieget ſich zum heubten, vnd bettet, die weil thut Ioſeph den eid.

childern which thou geteſt after them, ſhalbe thyne
awne: but ſhalbe called with the names of their brethern in their enheritaunces.

7 And after I came from Meſopotamia, Rahel dyed
apon my hande in the lande of Canaā, by the waye:
when I had but a feldes bre- .⁊. de to goo vnto Ephrat. And I buried her there in ẏ waye to Ephrat
which is now called Bethlehem.

8 And Iſrael behelde Ioſephes ſonnes & ſayde: what
9 are theſe? And Ioſeph ſayde vnto his father: they
are my ſonnes, which God hath geuen me here. And
he ſayde: brynge them to me, and let me bleſſe them.
10 And the eyes of Iſraell were dymme for age, ſo that he
coude not ſee. And he brought them to him, ād he
11 kyſſed thē and embraced them. And Iſrael ſayde vnto
Ioſeph: I had not thoughte to haue ſene thy face, and
yet loo, God hath ſhewed it me and alſo thy ſeed.
12 And Ioſeph toke them awaye from his lappe, and they
fell on the grounde before him.

13 Than toke Ioſeph them both: Ephraim in his ryghte
hande towarde Iſraels left hande ād Manaſſes in his
left hande, towarde Iſraels ryghte hande, and brought
14 them vnto him. And Iſrael ſtretched out his righte
hande and layde it apon Ephraims head which was
the yonger, and his lyft hāde apon Manaſſes heed,
15 croſſinge his handes, for Manaſſes was the elder. And
he bleſſed Ioſeph ſaynge: God before whome my fathers
Abraham and Iſaac dyd walke, and the God which hath
16 fedd me all my life longe vnto this daye, And the
angell which hath delyuered me frō all euyll, bleſſe
theſe laddes: ẏ they maye be called after my name,

𝒱. 7 ipſo itinere, eratque vernum tempus: & ingred. 12 de
gremio patris, adorauit 14 commutans manus. 15 Benedixitque
Iac. filiis Ios., & ait, Deus ... qui paſcit me 16 et inuocetur ſuper
eos nomen

𝑳. 6 ſollen generet ſein mit jrer brüder namen 7 Ephrath, die
jm Bethelehem heiſt. 8 Wer ſind die? 10 tunkel. für alter .. wol
ſehen .. hertzet ſie, 11 vnd ſprach 12 von ſeinem ſchos, vnd er
nieget ſich 14 Vnd thet wiſſend alſo mit ſeinen henden 15 erneeret
hat .. dieſen tag, 16 das ſie nach meinem

𝔐. 𝔐. N. 14 The puttyng on of hādes was comenly vſed of
the Hebrews, whē they cōmended or offred any thyng to God,
as Leuit. i, b.

and after my father Abraham and Isaac, and that they
maye growe ād multiplie apō [Fo. LXXIII.] the erth.
17 When Ioseph sawe that his father layd his ryghte
hande apon the heade of Ephraim, it displeased him.
And he lifte vpp his fathers hāde, to haue removed it
18 from Ephraims head vnto Manasses head, and sayde
vnto his father: Not so my father, for this is the eldest.
19 Put thy right hand apon his head. And his father
wold not, but sayde: I knowe it well my sonne, I
knowe it well. He shalbe also a people ād shalbe
great. But of a troth his yonger brother shalbe great-
20 ter than he, and his seed shall be full of people. And
he blessed them sainge. At the ensample At the ensam-
of these, the Israelites shall blesse and saye: ple, *according*
God make the as Ephraim and as Manasses. *to*
Thus sett he Ephraim before Manasses.
21 And Israel sayde vnto Ioseph: beholde, I dye. And god
shalbe with you and bringe you agayne vnto the land of
22 youre fathers. Moreouer I geue vnto the, a porcyon of
lande aboue thy brethern, which I gatt out of the handes
of the Amorites wyth my swerde and with my bowe.

The .XLIX. Chapter.

1 AND Iacob called for his sonnes 𝕸.𝕮.𝕾. *Ia-*
ād sayde: come together, that *cob blesseth all*
I maye tell you what shall *his awne son-*
happē you in the last dayes. *nes and shew-*
eth thē what
is to come.
2 Gather you together and heare ye sones *He apoynteth*
of Iacob, and herken vnto Israel youre *where he wyl-*
father. *be buryed:*
and dyeth.

𝖁. 17 Ephraim, grauiter accepit 20 in tempore illo .. In te
benedicentur Israel 22 vnam partem extra fratres
𝕷. 16 .. das sie waschen * 17 gesiel es jm vbel 18 Nicht so
19 Ich weis wol (*bis*) 20 gelegnet er sie des tages .. Nach deiner
weise werde Israel ges... setze dich . setzt.. fur 22 ein stück lands
𝕷. 𝕸. 𝕹. 22 *Stück:* heist im Ebreschen Sichem, vnd die selbe
stat meinet er hie.

* A curious typographical error, *waschen* (to wash) being put
for *wachsen* (to grow).

3 .¶. Ruben, thou art myne eldeſt ſonne, my myghte and the begynnynge of my ſtrength, chefe in receau-
4 ynge and chefe in power. As unſtable as water waſt thou: thou ſhalt therfore not be the chefeſt, for thou wenſt vp vpō thy fathers bedd, and than defyledeſt thou my couche with goynge vppe.
5 The brethern Simeon and Leui, weked inſtrumentes
6 are their wepōs. In to their ſecrettes come not my ſoule, and vnto their congregation be my honoure not coupled: for in their wrath they ſlewe a man, and
7 in their ſelfewill they houghed an oxe. Curſed be their wrath for it was ſtronge, and their fearſnes for it was cruell. I will therfore deuyde them in Iacob, & ſcater them in Iſrael.
8 Iuda, thy brethern ſhall prayſe the, & and thine hande ſhalbe in the necke of thyne enimies, & thy
9 fathers childern ſhall ſtoupe vnto the. Iuda is a lions whelpe. Frō ſpoyle my ſonne thou art come an hye: he layde him downe and couched himſelfe as a lion,
10 and as a lioneſſe. Who dare ſtere him vp? The ſceptre ſhall not departe from Iuda, nor a ruelar from

V. 3 principium doloris mei 4 effuſus es ſicut aqua 6 & in voluntate ſua ſuffoderunt murum 9 quis ſuſcitabit eum

L. 3 öberſt jm opffer . . jm reich 5 Vnrecht haben ſie gehandelt 6 den ochſen verderbt 9 du biſt hoch komen . . widder yhn auff lehnen?

M. M. N. 6 That is, cut the ſenowes on the inſyde the knee, or as ſome call it the hamme, ſo that he coulde not roo. 10 *Sceptre* is here taken for power royall & dignytie. *V*.e is alſo propheſied the cōminge of Chriſt, as in Eſaye. ix, a. *Judge hys people*, that is, he ſhall rule & gouerne them, as Exo. xviii, d.

L. M. N. 3 *Reuben* ſolt der erſte geburte wurde haben, nemlich, das Prieſterthum vnd königreich, Nu aber wirds beides von jm genomē vnd Leui das Prieſterthum, vnd Iuda das königreich gebē, Hie iſt bedeut, die Syund Nagaga, die das bette Iacob, das iſt der Schrifft beſuddelt mit falſche lere darüber ſie verloren hat Prieſterthum & ynn königreich Iſrael. 10 *Scepter;* Hie ſehet an der ſegen von Chriſto, der von Iuda geporn ſollt werden, vnd heyſt yhn Silo, das iſt der gluck ſelig ſeyn vnd friſch durch dringen ſolt, mit geyſt vnnd glauben, das zuuor durch werck ſaur vnd vnſelig ding war, darumb nenn wyr, Silo, eyn helt, denn das vorige teyl dis ſegens betrifft den konig Dauid, vnd iſt ſonſt ynn allen ſegen nichts mehr von Chriſto Sondern alles ander iſt von zeytlichem heyl, das den kindern Iſrael geben iſt, als das *Sebulon* am meer wonen bis gen Sidon, vnd Iſſachar mitten ym land vom meer wonen, vnd doch zinſsbar geweſen iſt den konigen von Aſſyrien,

betwene his legges, vntill Silo come, vnto whome the
11 people ſhall herken. He ſhall bynde his fole vnto the
vine, and his aſſes colt vnto the vyne braunche, ãd
ſhall waſh his garment in wyne and his mantell in the
12 bloud of grapes, his eyes are roudier than   roudier, *rud-*
wyne, ãd his teeth whitter then mylke.   *dier, redder*

13   [Fo. LXXIIII.] Zabulon ſhall dwell in the hauen of the
ſee and in the porte of ſhippes, & ſhall reache vnto Sidon.
14   Iſachar is a ſtronge aſſe, he couched him doune
15 betwene .ii. borders, and ſawe that reſt was good and
the lande that it was pleaſant, and bowed his ſhulder
to beare, and became a ſervaunte vnto trybute.

16   Dan ſhall iudge his people, as one of the trybes of
17 Iſrael. Dan ſhalbe a ſerpent in the waye, and an edder
in the path, and byte the horſe heles, ſo ẏ his ryder
18 ſhall fall backwarde. After thy ſauynge loke I LORde.

19   Gad, men of warre ſhall invade him. And he ſhall
turne them to flyght.

20   Off Aſſer cometh fatt breed, and he ſhall geue pleaſ-
ures for a kynge.

21   Nepthali is a ſwyft hynde, ãd geueth goodly wordes.
22   That floriſhynge childe Ioſeph, that floriſhing childe
and goodly vn to the eye: the doughters come forth

  M. 22 the daughters ran vpon the walle.
  V. 10 qui mittendus eſt, et ipſe erit expectatio gentium. 11 et
ad vitem o fili mi, aſinam 12 Pulchriores ſunt oculi 17 mordens
ungulas equi, vt cadat aſc. eius retro. 18 Salutare tuum expectabo
19 accinctus præliabitur 20 præbebit delicias regibus. 21 dans
eloquia pulchritudinis. 22 filiæ diſcurrerunt ſuper murum.
  L. 10 noch eyn meyſter von ſeynen fuſſen, bis das der Hellt
komme 14 beynern eſel 17 reutter zu ruck falle 18 ich wartte auff
deyn heyl 19 vnd widder erumb furen. 20 konigen niedliche ſpeyſe
22 holdſelige kind . . die tochter tretten eynher im regiment
  M. M. N. 20 Fat brede, is plenteouſnes of the erth: as encreaſe
of corne and other. &c. therwith ſhall fede kinges, & all the mē
of the erth, as .ii. Eſd. ix, c.
  L. M. N. 16 Den Segen *Dan* hat Samp ſon erfullet, Iudic. xii.
19 *Gad* hat ſeyn ſegen aufzgericht, do ſie fur Iſrael her zogë Ios. i.
20 *Aſſer* hat gut getreyde land ynnen gehabt. 21 *Naphthali*
ſegen iſt erfüllet durch Debora vnnd Barac Iud. v. 22 Der ſegen
Ioſeph gehet auff das konigreych Iſrael vnnd iſt ganz von leybli-
chem regiment geſagt, das die tochter (das iſt die ſtedte ym land)
wol regirt worden zeytlich, vnd viel propheten vnd gros leut zu
eckſteyn hatten, vnd wie wol ſie offt angefochtē worden, gewonnen ſie doch, vnd dis konigreich war im geſchlecht *Ephraim*,
alſzo bleybt der geyſtlich ſegen vnd reich auff Iuda, vnd das
leyplich reich auff Ephraim.

23 to bere ruele. The fhoters haue envyed him and chyde
24 with him ād hated him, and yet his bowe bode faft, &
his armes and his handes were ftronge, by the handes
of the myghtye God of Iacob: out of him fhall come
25 an herde mā a ftone in Ifrael. Thi fathers God fhall
helpe the, & the almightie fhall bleffe the with bleffinges
from heaven aboue, and with bleffinges of the water
that lieth vnder, & with bleffinges of the breftes & of
26 the wombes .₽. The bleffinges of thy father were
ftronge: euen as the bleffinges of my elders, after the
defyre of the hieſt in the worlde, and thefe bleffinges
fhall fall on the head of Iofeph, and on the toppe of
the head of him ỹ was feparat from his brethern.
27 Ben Iamin is a rauefhynge wolfe. In the mornynge
he fhall deuoure his praye, ād at nyghte he fhall deuyde his fpoyle.
28 All thefe are the .xii. tribes of Ifrael, & this is that
which their father fpake vnto them whē he bleffed
29 them, euery man with a feverall bleffinge. And he
charged them and fayde vnto them. I fhall be put
vnto my people: fe that ye burye me with my fathers,
in the caue that is in the felde of Ephron the Hethyte,
30 in the double caue that is in the felde before Mamre
in the lande of Canaan. Which felde Abraham boughte
31 of Ephron the Hethite for a poffeffiō to burye in. There
they buryed Abrahā and Sara his wyfe, there they
buryed Ifaac and Rebecca his wyfe. And there I
32 buryed Lea: which felde & the caue that is therin,
was bought of the childern of Heth.

℟. 25 wombe.
𝒱. 24 diffoluta funt vincula brach. & man. illius per .. inde
paftor egreffus eft lapis Ifrael. 26 patris tui confortatæ funt ...
patrum eius: donec ven. defyderium collium ætern., .. et in vertice
Nazaræi 29 ego congregor ad pop. 31 eum, et Saram [v. 32 wanting in Latin]
L. 24 die arm feyner hende .. find komen hirtten vnd fteyn
25 fegen von der tieffe .. an bruften vnd beuchen. 26 nach wundfch
der hohen in der welt .. aus Iofeph follen hewbter werden, vnd
vberfte Naferer 32 ynn dem gut des ackers vnd der hole drynnen
℟. ℟. N. 27 Wolfe is here taken in a good fence, and fignifieth a feruent preacher of godes worde as was Paule in whome
this text is verified.
L. ℟. N. 27 *Ben Iamin* fegen hat S. Paullus erfullet, oder
der Konig Saul vnd die burger zu Gaba. Iudic. xx.

33 When Iacob had commaunded all that he wold vnto his sonnes, he plucked vp his fete apon the bedd
L, 1 and dyed, and was put vnto his people. And Ioseph fell apon his fathers face, and wepte apon him, and kyssed him.

[Fo. LXXV.] The .L. Chapter.

2 AND Ioseph commaunded his seruauntes that were Phisicions, to embawme his father, and the Phisiciōs ēbawmed Israel
3 xl. dayes lōge, for so lōge doth ẏ embawminge last, & the Egiptians bewepte him .Lxx. dayes.

M.C.S. Iacob is buryed. Ioseph forgeueth hys brethrē the Iniury that they dyd to hym. And he dyeth.

4 And when the dayes of wepynge were ended, Ioseph spake vnto ẏ house of Pharao saynge: Yf I haue founde fauoure in youre eyes, speake vnto Pharao and
5 tell him, how that my father made me swere and sayde: loo, I dye, se that thou burye me in my graue which I haue made me in the lande of Canaan. Now therfor let me goo and burye my father, ād thā will I come
6 agayne. And Pharao sayde, goo and burye thy father, acordynge as he made the swere.
7 And Ioseph went vp to burie his father, and with him went all the seruauntes of Pharao that were the
8 elders of his house, ād all ẏ elders of Egipte, and all the house of Ioseph ād his brethern & his fathers house: only their childern & their shepe and their catell leste
9 they behinde them in the lande of Gosan. And there went with him also Charettes and horsemen: so that they were an exceadynge great companye.

V. 33 appositusque est ... 1, 1 quod cernens ... patrem. 2 Quibus iussa 3 explentibus ... cadauerum conditorum 5 in sepulchro meo quod fodi mihi 7 senes domus Phar., cunctique maiores natu terræ 9 turba non modica.
L. 33 bette, nam ab. 1, 2 erzten (*bis*) 5 begrabe ... grabe ... graben hab 10 seer grosse vnd bittere klag

10 And when they came to ẏ felde of Atad beyonde Iordane, there they made great & excea- .P. dinge fore lamentaciō. And he morned for his father .vii. dayes.
11 When the enhabiters of the lande the Cananytes fawe the moornynge in ẏ felde of Atad, they faide: this is a greate moornynge which the Egiptians make. Wherfore ẏ name of the place is called Abel mizraim, which place lyeth beyonde Iordane. And his
12 fonnes dyd vnto him acordynge as he had commaunded them.
13 And his fonnes caried him in to the land of Canaan and buryed him in the double caue which Abrahā had boughte with the felde to be a place to burye in, of
14 Ephron the Hethite before Mamre. And Iofeph returned to Egipte agayne and his brethern, and all that went vp with him to burye his father, affone as he had buryed him.
15 Whē Iofephs brethern fawe that their father was deade, they fayde: Iofeph myght fortune to hate us and rewarde us agayne all the euell which we dyd
16 vnto him. They dyd therfore a commaundment vnto Iofeph faynge: thy father charged before his deth fa-
17 ynge. This wife fay vnto Iofeph, forgeue I praye the the trefpace of thy brethern & their fynne, for they rewarded the euell. Now therfore we praye the, forgeue the trefpace of the fervauntes of thy fathers God. And Iofeph wepte when they fpake vnto him.
18 And his brethern came ād fell before him and fayde:
19 beholde we be thy fervauntes. And [Fo. LXXVI.] Iofeph fayde vnto them: feare not, for am not I vnder
20 god? Ye thoughte euell vnto me: but God turned it vnto good to bringe to paffe, as it is this daye, euen to
21 faue moch people a lyue Feare not therfore, for I will

𝔐. 16 charged vs
𝒱. 11 loci illius, Planctus Ægypti. 15 & mutuo colloquentes 16 mandauerunt ei dicentes .. præcepit nobis 17 Obfecro vt obliuifcaris .. malitiæ quam exercuerūt 19 nū dei poffumus refiftere uoluntati? 20 faluos faceret
𝔏. 11 den ort, der Egypter leyde 14 fie yhn begraben 16 darumb lieffen fie yhm fagen 17 das fie fo vbel an dyr than haben 19 ich byn vnter Gott 20 gedachtet bofes vber mich .. zum gutten gewand

care for you and for youre childern, and he spake kyndly vnto them.

22 Ioseph dwelt in Egipte and his fathers house also,
23 ād lyved an hundred & .x. yere. And Ioseph sawe Ephraims childern, euē vnto the thyrde generation. And vnto Machir the sonne of Manasses were childern borne, and satt on Iosephs knees.
24 And Ioseph sayde vnto his brethern: I die   And God will suerlie vysett you and bringe you out of this lande, vnto the lande which he sware vnto Abraham,
25 Isaac and Iacob. And Ioseph toke an ooth of the childern of Israel ād sayde:

God will not fayle but vysett you, se ther-
26   fore that ye carye my boones hence. And
so Ioseph dyed, when he was an
hundred and .x. yere olde.
And they emba-
wmed him
and
put him in a chest in Egipte. chest. *coffin*

The end of the first boke of Moses.

V. 21 cōsolatusque est eos, & blande ac leniter est locutus. 23 nati sunt in genibus Ioseph. 25 dixisset, Deus visitabit .. de loco isto. 26 repositus est in loculo ..
L. 21 euch versorgen .. vnd er tröstet sie vnd redet freuntlich mit yhn. 23 zeucheten auch kinder auff Ios. schos. 26 eyn lade.
M. M. N. 24 God wyll vyset you, that is, he wyll remember you and delyuer you oute of bōdage that ye shalbe in vnder Pharao.

¶ A table expoundinge certeyne wordes

1   Abrech, tender father, or, as some will, bowe the knee.
   Arcke, a shippe made flatte as it were a chest or a cofer.
5   Bisse: fyne whyte, whether it be silke or linen.
   Blesse: godes blessinges are his giftes, as in the firste chaptre he blessed them, sayng: growe & multiplye & haue dominion &c. And in the .ix. chaptre he blessed Noe and his sonnes, & gaue thē dominiō over all beestes
10 & authoryte to eate thē. And god blessed Abrahā with catell ād other ryches. And Iacob desyred Esau to receaue ẏ blessinge which he brought him, ẏ is, the preasent & gifte. God blessed the .vii. daye, ẏ is, gaue it a prehemynence ẏ men shuld rest therein from
15 bodely laboure & lerne to know the will of god & his lawes & how to worke their workes godly all the weke after. God also blesseth all nations in Abrahams seed, that is, he turneth his loue & favoure unto thē and geveth thē his spirite and knowledge of the true waye,
20 ād lust and power to walke therin, and all for christes sake Abrahams sonne.
   Cain, so it is writen in Hebrue. Notwitstōdinge whether we call him Cain or caim it maketh no matter, so we vnderstond the meaninge. Euery lande hath
25 his maner, that we call Ihonn the welchemen call Evan: the douch hāce. Soch differēce is betwene the Ebrue, greke and laten: and that maketh them that translate out of the ebrue varye in names from them that translate out of laten or greke.
30 Curse: Godes curse is the takynge awaye of his benefytes. As god cursed the erth and made it baren. So now hunger, derth, warre, pestilence and soch like are yet ryght curses and signes of the wrath of God vnto the vnbeleuers: but vnto them that knowe Christ,

they are very bleſſinges and that wholſome croſſe &
true purgatorye of oure fleſh, thorow which all muſt go
that will lyue godly ād be ſaued: as thou readeſt Matt.
v. Bleſſed are they that ſuffre perſecution for right-
ewefnes ſake. &c. And hebrewes .xi. The lorde
chaſtyſeth whom he loveth and ſcorgeth all the
children that he receaveth.

Eden: pleaſure

Firmament: The ſkyes

Fayth is the belevinge of goddes promeſſes & a
ſure truſt in the goodneſſe and truth of god. Which
faith iuſtifyeth Abrahā gen. xv. and was the mother
of all his good workes which he afterward did. For
faith is the goodneſſe of all workes in the ſight of God.
Good workes .P. are thinges of godes commaundemēt,
wrought in faith. And to ſow a ſhowe at the commaundement of god to do thy neyghboure ſervice
withaH, with faith to be ſaved by Chriſt (as god promyſeth vs.) is moch better thē to bild an abbay of thyne
awne imagination, truſtinge to be ſaved by the ſayned
workes of hypocrites. Iacob robbed Laban his vncle:
Moſes robbed the Egiptians: And Abrahā is aboute to
ſlee and burne his awne ſonne: And all are holye
workes, becauſe they were wrought in fayth at goddes
commaundement. To ſtele, robbe and murther are no
holye workes before worldly people: but vnto them
that haue their truſte in god: they are holye when god
commaundeth them. What god commaundeth not
getteth no reward with god. Holy workes of mens
imagination receave their rewarde here, as Chriſt teſ-
tyfyeth Matt. .vi. How be it of fayth & workes I
haue ſpoken abundantly in mammon. Let him that
deſyreth more ſeke there.

Grace: fauoure, As Noe founde grace, that is to
faye favoure and love.

Ham and Cam all one.

Iehovah is goddes name, nether is any creature ſo
called. And it is as moch to ſaye as one that is of
him ſelf, and dependeth of nothinge. Moreouer as oft

as thou feift LORde in gre-.℣.at letters (excepte there be any erroure in the prētinge) it is in hebrewe Iehovah, thou that arte or he that is.

Marſhall, In hebreue he is called Sar tabaim, as thou woldeſt faye, lorde of the flaughtermen   And though that Tabaim be takē for cokes in many places, for the cokes did fle the beaſtes thē felues in thofe dayes: yet it may be taken for them that put men to execution alfo.   And that me thought it ſhould here beſt fignifye in as moch as he had the overfight of the kinges prefon and the kinges prefoners were they neuer fo great mē were vnder his cuſtodye.   And therfore I call him cheffe marſhall an officer as is the lefetenaunte of the toure, or maſter of the marſhalfye.

Slyme was their morter .xi. Chapter, and flyme pittes .xiv. chapter: that flyme was a fatteneſſe that ofed out of the erth lyke vnto tarre, And thou mayſt call it cement, if thou wilt.

Siloh after fome is as moch to faye as fent, & after fome, happie, and after fome it fignifieth Mefias, ẏ is to faye annoynted, and that we call Chriſte after the greke worde.   And it is a prophefie of Chriſt: For after ẏ all ẏ other tribes were in captiuite & their kyngdom deſtroyed, yet the tribe of Iuda had a ruler of the famebloud, even vnto the comynge of Chriſt.

℣. And aboute the comīge of Chriſt the Romayns conquered them, and the Emperoure gaue the kyngdom of tribe Iuda unto Herode which was a ſtraunger, even an Edomite of the generacyon of Efau.

Teſtamēt here, is an appoyntemēt betwene god and mā, and goddes promyfes.   And facramēt is a figne reprefentinge foch an appoyntement and promefes: as the raynebowe reprefenteth the promyfe made to Noe, that god will no more drowne the worlde.   And circumcifion reprefenteth the promyfes of god to Abraham on the one fyde, and that Abrahā and his feed ſhuld circumcyfe and cut off the luſtes of their fleſhe, on the other fyde, to walke in the wayes of the lorde: As baptyme which is come in the roume therof, now fignifieth on the one fyde, how that all that repent and beleve are wafhed in Chriftes bloud: And on the other fyde, how that the fame muft quench ād droune the luftes of the flefh, to folow the fteppes of Chrift.

5 There were tyrantes in the erth in thofe dayes, for the fonnes of god faw the daughters of men. &c. The fonnes of god were the prophetes childerne, which (though they fucceded there fathers) fell yet from the right waye, and thorow falfehod of hypocryfye fubdued 10 the world vnder them, and became tyrantes, As the fuccef- .¶. ours of the apoftles haue played with vs.

Vapor, a dewy mifte, as the fmoke of a fethynge pott.

To walke with god is to lyve godly and to walke 15 in his commaundementes.

Enos walked with god, and was no moare fene: that is, he lyved godly and dyed, God toke him a waye: that is, god hyd his bodye, as he did Mofes ād Aarons: left haplye they fhuld haue made an Idoll of him, for he 20 was a great preacher and an holye man.

Zaphnath paenea, wordes of Egipte are they (as I fuppofe) and as moch to faye: as a man to whom fecrete thinges be opened, or an expounder of fecrete thinges as fome enterprete it.

25 That Iofeph brought the egiptians in to foch fubiection wold feme vnto fome a very cruell deade: how be it it was a very equal waye. For they payde but the fifte part of that that grewe on the grounde. And therwith were they qwytt of all duetyes, both of rent, 30 cuftome, tribute & toll. And the kinge therwith founde them lordes and all miniftres and defended them. We now paye half fo moch vnto the preftes only, befyde their other craftye exactions. Then paye we rent yerely, though there grow never fo litle on the 35 grounde, And yet, when the kinge cal- .¶. leth paye we neuer the leffe. So that if we loke indifferently, their condition was eafyar thē oures, and but even, a very indifferēt waye, both for the comen people and the kynge alfo.

Se therfore that thou loke not on the enſamples
of the ſcripture with worldly eyes: leſt thou pre-
ferre Cain before Abel, Iſmael before Iſaac, Eſau before Iacob, Ruben before Iu
da, Sarah before Pharez, Manaſ
es before Ephraim. And e-
uen the worſt before the
beſt, as the maner
of the worl-
de is.

⁋ Emprented at Malborow in the lan
de of Heſſe, by me Hans Luft,
the yere of oure Lorde, M.
CCCCC.xxx. the xvii.
dayes of Ianu
arij.

A PROLO
GE IN TO THE SECON-
de boke of Mofes called
Exodus.

W T

OF the preface vppō Genesis mayst thou vnderstonde how to behaue thi silf in this boke
also ād i all other bokes of the scripture.
Cleaue vnto the texte and playne storye
and endevoure thi silf to serch out the meaninge of all
that is described therin and the true sense of all maner
of speakynges of the scripture, of proverbes, similitudes
ād borowed speach, wherof I entreated in the ende of
the obedience, and beware of sotle allegoryes. And
note euery thinge ernestly as thinges partayninge
vnto thine awne herte and soule. For as god vsed
hym sylf vnto them of the old testament, even so shall
he vnto the worldes ende vse him silf vnto vs which
haue receaved his holye scripture ād the testimonye of
his sonne Iesus. As god doeth all thinges here for them
that beleve his promises and herken vnto his commaundmentes and with pacience cleaue vnto him and
walke with him: euen' so shall he do for vs, yf we receaue the witnesse of Christ with a stronge faith and
endure paciently folowinge his steppes. And on the
othersyde, as they that fell from the promises of god
thorow vnbeleffe and from his lawe and ordinaunces
thorow impaciencie of their awne lustes, were for saken
of god ād so peryshed: even so shall we as many as do
lykewyse and as.P.manye as mock with the doctrine
of christ and make a cloke of it to lyue fleshlye ād to
folow oure lustes.

Note therto how god is founde true at the last, and
how when all is past remedye ād brought into despera-
cion, he then fulfilleth his promises, and that by an ab-
iecte and a castawaye, a despised and a refused person:
ye and by awaye impossible to beleue.

The cause of all captiuite of goddes people is this.
The worlde ever hateth them for their fayth and trust
which they haue in god: but ī vayne vntill they falle frō
the fayth of the promyses ād love of the lawe ād ordi-

naunces of god, and put their truſt in holy deades of their
awne findinge and live all to gether at their awne luſt
and pleaſure without regard of god or reſpecte of their
neygboure. Then god forſaketh vs and ſendeth vs in to
captiuite for oure diſhonouringe of his name and deſpiſinge
of oure neghboure. But the world perſecuteth vs for oure
faith in chriſt only (as the pope now doeth) ād not for
oure weked livinge For in his kīgdome thou maiſt
quietly ād with licēce ād vnder a protectiō doo what
ſo euer abhominatiō thi herte luſteth: but god perſecuteth us becauſe we abuſe his holye teſtamēt, ād
becauſe that whē we knowe the truth we folowe it
not.

.¶. Note alſo the mightye hand of the Lorde, how
he playeth with his aduerſaries ād provoketh thē ād
ſturreth thē upp a litle ād a litle, ād deliuereth not his
people in an houre: that both the paciēce of his electe
ād alſo the worldly witte ād wilye policye of the weked
wherwith they fight agaynſt god, might appeare.

Marke the longeſoferinge and ſofte paciēce of Moſes and
how he loveth the people ād is euer betwene the wrath of
god ād thē ād is readye to lyue ād dye with thē ād to
be put out of the boke that god had written for their
ſakes (as Paule for his brothren Roma. ix.) and how
he taketh his awne wrōges pacientlie ād never avengeth
him ſilf. And make not Moſes a figure of Chriſt with
Rocheſtre: but an enſample vnto all princes ād to all
that are in authorite, how to rule vnto goddes pleaſure
ād vnto their neyghbours profette. For there is not a
perfecter lyffe in this world both to the honoure of god
and profytte of his neygboure nor yet a greatter croſſe,
thē to rule chriſtenlye. And of Aaron alſo ſe that thou
make no figure of chriſt vntill he come vnto his ſacri-
fiſinge, but an enſample vnto all preachers of goddes
worde, that they adde nothing vnto goddes worde or
take ought therfro.

Note alſo how god ſendeth his promiſſe to .¶.
the people ād Moſes confermeth it with miracles ād
the people beleve. But whē tēptacion cometh they
falle into vnbeleſſe ād few byde ſtōdinge. Where
thou ſeeſt that all be not chriſtē that wilbe ſo called,

ād that the croſſe trieth the true frō the ſayned:
for yf the croſſe were not Chriſt ſhuld haue diſſiples
ynowe. Wherof alſo thou ſeeſt what an excellent gifte
off god true fayth is, ād impoſſible to be had without
5 the ſprete of god. For it is aboue all naturall power
that a man in tyme of tēptation when god ſcorgeth
him ſhuld beleue then ſtedfaſtlye how that god loueth
him ād careth for hī ād hath prepared all good
thinges for him, ād that that ſcorginge is as erneſt that
10 god hath electe and choſe him.

Note how oft Moſes ſturreth thē vpp to beleve ād to
truſt in god, puttinge thē in remembraunce alwaye in
tyme of temptation of the miracles and wonders which
god had wrought before tyme in their eyſight. How
15 diligently alſo forbiddeth he al that might withdrawe
their hartes from god? to put nought to goddes word: to
take nought therfro: to do only that which is right in the
ſyght of the Lorde: that they ſhuld make no maner image
to knele doune before it: ye that they ſhuld make none
20 altar of hewed ſtone for feare off images: .P. to ſlee the
hethen Idolatres vtterly ād to deſtroye their Idolles
ād cutte doune their groves where they worſhupped:
And that they ſhulde not take the doughters of them
vnto their ſonnes, nor geue their doughters to the ſonnes
25 of them. And that whoſoeuer moued any of thē to
worſhuppe falſe goddes, how ſo euer nye of kynne he
were, they muſt accuſe him ād bryng him to deth, ye
and whereſoeuer they hard of mā, womā or citye that
worſhupped falſe goddes, they muſt ſlee thē ād deſtroye
30 the citie for euer ād not bild it agayne. And all becauſe they ſhuld worſhuppe nothinge but God, nor put
confidence in any thinge ſaue in his word Yee and
how warneth he to beware of witchcraft, ſorcery, in-
chauntment, negromātie ād all craftes of the devell,
35 ād of dreamers, ſothſayers and of myracledoers to
deſtroye his worde, and that they ſhulde ſuffer none
ſoch to lyue,

Thou wilt happlye ſaye, They tell a man the truthe.
What then? God will that we care not to knowe what
40 ſhall come. He will haue vs care only to kepe his commaundmētes and to commytte all chaunſes vnto him

He hath promyſed to care for vs and to kepe vs from
all evell. All thinges are in his hande, he can remedye
all thinges and wil for his truthes ſake, yf we praye him.
In his promyſes only will he haue vs truſt ãd there reſt
ãd to ſeke .⁋. no farther.

How alſo doth he prouoke them to loue, euer
reherſynge the benefites of God done to them all-
ready and the godly promyſes that were to come?
And how goodly lawes of loue gevẽth he? to helpe
one another: and that a man ſhuld not hate his
neyghboure in his harte, but loue him as him ſilf,
Leuitici .xix. And what a charge geueth he in euery
place over the poore and neadye: over the ſtraunger
frendleſſe ãd wedowe? And when he deſyreth to ſhew
mercye, he reherſeth with all, the benefites of God done
to them at their neade, that they myght ſe a cauſe at
the left waye in God to ſhew mercye of very loue vnto
their neyghboures at their neade. Alſo there is no
lawe ſo ſimple in apperaunce thorow out all the fiue
bokes of Moſes, but that there is a greate reaſon of the
makynge therof if a man ſerch diligently. As that a
man is forbyd to ſeth a kyd in hys mothers milke, moueth vs unto compaſſyon and to be pytyefull, As doth
alſo that a man ſhall not offer the ſyre or dame and
the yonge both in one daye Leuitici .xxii. For it myght
ſeme a cruell thing in as moch as his mothers milke
is as it were his bloude, wherfore god will not haue him
ſod therin: but will haue a man ſhewe cur-.⁋.teſye vppon
the very beaſtes: As in another place he commaundeth that we moſell not the mouth of the oxe that treadeth oute the corne (which maner of threſſhinge is vſed
in hote contrees) and that becauſe we ſhuld moch rather not grudge to be liberall and kynde vnto mẽ that
do vs ſervice. Or happlye God wold have no ſoch wan-
ton meate vſed among hys people. For the kyd of it
ſelf is noryſhinge and the gotes milke is reſtauretyue,
and both together myght be to rancke and therfore
forbodẽ or ſome other like cauſe therewas.

Of the ceremonies, ſacrifices and tabernacle with all his
glorye ãd pompe vnderſtõde, that they were not per-
mitted only, but alſo commaunded of God to lead the peo-

ple in the fhadowes of Mofes ād night of the old teftamēt, vntyll the light of chrift ād daye of the new teftamēt were come: As childern are ledde in the phantafies of youth, vntyll the difcretiō of mās age become vppon them. And all was done to kepe them from idolatrye. The tabernacle was ordened to the entent they might haue a place appoynted them to do their facrifices openly in the fyght of the people ād namelye of the preaftes which wayted therō: that it might be fene that they dyd all thīge accordīg to gods word, and not after the Idolatrie of their awne .P. imaginacion. And the coftlineffe of the tabernacle ād the bewtye alfo pertayned therevnto, that they fhuld fe nothinge fo bewtifull amonge the hethē, but that they fhuld fe more bewtifull ād wonderfull at home: becaufe they fhuld not be moued to folowe them. And in like maner the diuers facions of the facrifices and ceremonies was to occupye their mindes that they fhuld haue no luft to folow the hethē: ād the multitude of them was, that they fhuld haue fo moch to do in kepinge thē that thei fhuld haue no leyfure to ymagine other of their awne: yee and that gods word might be by in all that they dyd, that they might have their fayth and truft in God, which he can not haue, that ether foloweth his awne invencyons, or tradicyons of mēnes makynge wyth out Gods word.

Finally God hath two teftamentes: the old and the newe. The old teftament is thofe temporall promyfes which God made the childrē of Ifrael of a good londe and that he wolde defende them, and of welth and profperyte ād of temporall bleffynges of whiche thou readeft ouer all the lawe of Mofes, But namelye Leuitici xxvi. And Deuteronomii .xxviii. ād the avoydynge of all threateninges and curfes off which thou readeft lykewyfe everye where, but fpecyallye in the two places aboue reherfed, .P. and the avoydinge of all punyfhmēt ordened for the tranfgreffers of the lawe.

And the old teftamēt was bilt all to gether vppō the kepinge of the lawe ād ceremonyes and was the reward of kepinge of thē in this liffe only, ād reached no further than this liffe and this world, as thou

readeſt leu. xviii. a mā that doth them ſhall live
there in which texte Paule reherſeth Rom. x. and Gala.
iii. · That is, he that kepeth them ſhall haue this liffe
glorioufe accordinge to all the promifes and bleſſinges
of the lawe, and ſhall avoyde both all temporall pun-
iſhment of the lawe, with al the threateninges and curf-
ingesalfo. For nether the lawe, euen of the.x. cōmaundmentes nor yet the ceremonies iuſtifyed in the herte
before god, or purifyed vnto the life to come. Infomoch
that Mofes at his deeth euen. xl. yere after the lawe and
ceremonyes were geuen complayneth fayenge: God hath
not geven you an hart to vnderſtonde, nor eyes to fe,
nor eares to heare vnto this daye. As who ſhuld faye,
god hath geuen you ceremonies, but ye know not the
vfe of them, and hath geuē you a lawe, but hath not
wryten it in youre hartes.

Wherfore ferveth the lawe then, yf it geue vs no
power to do the lawe? Paule anfwereth the, that it
was geuen to vtter fynne onlye and .P. to make it
appere. As a corofye is layde vnto an old fore, not
to heale it, but to ſtere it vp ād to make the difeafe a lyve, that a mā might feale in what ioperdye
he is ād how nye deeth ād not aware, ād to make
awaye vnto the healinge playſter. Euē fo fayth
Paule Gala. iii. The lawe was geven becaufe of tranf-
greſſiō (that is, to make the fynne alyve that it might
be felt and fene) untill the feed came vnto whom it
was promifed: that is to faie, vntil the childern of fayth
came, or vntill Chriſt that feed in whom god promifed
Abrahā that all nations of the worlde ſhuld be bleſſed,
came. That is, the lawe was geuē to vtter fynne,
deeth damnatiō and curfe, ād to dryve vnto Chriſt in
whō forgeueneſſe, life, iuſtifyinge ād bleſſinges were
promifed, that we might fe fo greate love of god to vs
ward in chriſt, that we hēceforth ouercome with kind-
neſſe might love againe ād of love kepe the cōmaūdmētes. So now he that goeth aboute to quiette his
cōfciēce ād to iuſtifye him filf with the lawe, doth but
heale his wondes with freatīge corefyes. And he that
goeth aboute to purchafe grace with ceremonies, doth
but fucke the alepope to qwēch his thirſt, in as moch as

the ceremonies were not gevē to iuſtifie the herte, but
to ſignifie the iuſtifiynge: and forgeueneſſe that is in
chriſtes bloude

.P. Of the ceremonies that they iuſtifie not, thou readeſt. Ebrues .x. It is impoſſible that ſynne ſhuld be done
awaye with the bloud of oxē ād gootes. And of the
law thou readeſt .Gala. iii. Yf there had bene a lawe
geuē that coude haue quykened or geuē liffe, then had
rightuouſneſſe or iuſtifyinge come by the lawe in dede.
Now the lawe not only quyckeneth not the harte, but
alſo woundeth it with conſcience of ſynne and miniſ-
treth deeth ād damnaciō vnto her: ii. Corin. iii. ſo that
ſhe muſt neades dye ād be damned excepte ſhe finde
other remedy, ſo farre it is of that ſhe is iuſtified or
holpe by the lawe.

The newe teſtament is thoſe euerlaſtinge promyſes
which are made vs in chriſt the Lorde thorow out all
the ſcripture. And that teſtamēt is bylt on faith ād
not on workes. For it is not ſayde of that teſtament
he that worketh ſhall lyue: But he that beleveth ſhall
lyue, as thou readeſt .Ioan. iii. God ſo loued the worlde
that he gaue his only begotē ſonne that none which
beleue in hī ſhuld periſh but haue euerlaſtinge lyfe.

And when this teſtament is preached and beleued, the ſprete entreth the hart and quyckeneth
it, and geueth her lyfe and iuſtifieth her. The ſprete
alſo maketh the lawe a lyuely thing .P. in the herte,
ſo that a man bringeth forth good workes of his awne
acord without compulſiō of the lawe, without feare
of threateninges or curſinges: yee and with out all
maner reſpecte or loue vnto any temporal pleaſure,
But of the very power of the ſprete receaued thorow
faith, As thou readeſt .Ioan .i. He gaue them power
to be the ſonnes of God in that they beleued on his
name. And of that power they worke: ſo that he
which hath the ſprete of chriſt is now no moare a
childe: he nether learneth or worketh now any longer
for payne of the rodde or for feare of boogges or pleaſure of apples, But doth althinges of his awne courage
As chriſt ſayeth .Ioan. vii. He that beleueth on me ſhall
haue riuers of lyuinge water flowinge out of his belye.

That is, All good workes ād all giftes of grace fpringe
out of him naturallye and by their awne accorde.
Thou neadeſt not to wreſt good workes out of him
as a mā wold wringe veriuce out of crabbes: Nay thei
flow naturally out of him as fpringes out off hilles or
rockes.

The newe teſtament was euer, euē from the beginning of the world. For there were alwaye promyſes
of Chriſt to come by faith in whiche promyſes the
electe were then iuſtified .P. inwardly before God, as
outwardly before the world by kepynge of the lawe and
ceremonies

And in concluſyon as thou ſeyſt bleſſinges or curſynges folow the kepinge or breakynge of the lawe
of Moſes: euē ſo naturally do bleſſynges or curſynges
folow the breakyng or kepynge of the lawe of nature,
out of which fprīge all oure temporall lawes. So that
whē the people kepe the temporall lawes of their lond
temporall profperite and all maner of ſoch tēporall
bleſſynge as thou readeſt of in Moſes doo accompanye
them and fall vppon them.

And contraryewyſe when they ſynne vnpuniſhed, ād
whē the rulars haue no reſpecte vnto naturall equyte or
honeſtye, thē God ſendeth his curſes amonge thē, as hungre, derth, moren banynge, peſtilēce, warre, oppreſſyon
with ſtraunge ād wonderfull diſeaſes ād newekyndes
of miſſortune ād evell lucke,

Yf any mā axe me, ſeyng that faith iuſtifieth
me why I worke? I anſwere loue cōpelleth me
For as lōge as my ſoule fealeth what loue god hath
ſhewed me in Chriſte, I can not but loue god agayne
ād his will ād cōmaūdmētes and of loue worke them,
nor cā they ſeme hard vnto me. I thinke not my ſelf
better for my workynge, nor ſeke heuē nor an hyer
place in heuē becauſe of it. For a chriſtē worketh to
ma- .P. ke his weake brother perfecter, ād not to ſeke
an hier place in heuē. I cōpare not my ſilf vnto him
that worketh not: No, he that worketh not to daye
ſhall haue grace to turne ād to worke tomorow, ād in
the meane ceaſon I pytye hym ād praye for him. Yf
I had wrought the wil of god theſe thouſande yeres, ād

another had wrought the will of the devell as long ād this daye turne ād be as well willynge to fuffre wyth Chrift as I, he hath this daye ouertakē me ād is as farre come as I, and fhall haue as moche rewarde as I. And I envye him not, but reioyce moft of all as of lofte trefure founde. For yf I be of god, I haue this thoufand yere fofred to wynne him for to come ād prayfe the name of God with me: this .M. yeres I haue prayed forowed, longed, fyghed ād fought for that whiche I haue this daye founde, ād therfore reioyfe with all my myght and prayfe God for hys grace and mercy.

A LBE, a longe garment of white lynen.

Arcke, a cofer or chefte as oure fhrynes faue it was flatte, ād the fample of oure fhrynes was taken thereof.

Boothe, an houffe made of bowes.

Breftlappe or breftflappe, is foche a flappe as thou feift in the breft of a cope.

Confecrate, to apoynte a thinge to holy vfes.

Dedicate, purifie or fanctifie.

.¶. Ephod, is a garment fomwhat like an amyce, faue the armes came thorow ād it was gird to.

Geeras, in weyght as it were an englyfh halffpenye or fomwhat more.

Heveoffringe, becaufe they were hoven vp before the Lorde.

Houfe, he made thē houfes: that is, he made a kynred or a multitude of people to fpringe out of them: as we faye the houfe of Dauid for the kinred of Dauid.

Peaceoffrīge: offerīges of thākesgeuīge of deuotiō, ād not for cōfciēce of finne ād trefpace.

Polute, defyle.

❡ Reconcyle, to make at one and to bringe in grace or fauoure.

Sanctefie, to clēfe ād purifie, to apointe a thinge vnto holie vfes and to feperate frō vnclene ād unholye vfes.

❡ Sanctuarie, a place halowed and dedicate vnto god.

⁌ Tabernacle, an houſe made tentwiſe, or as a pauelion.

Tunicle, moch like the vppermoſt garmēt of the deakē.

⁌ Waueoffringe, becauſe they were wauē in the preaſtes hādes to diuers quarters.

Worſhuppe: by worſhuppinge whether it be in the old teſtamēt or the newe, vnderſtōd the bowenge of a mans ſelf vppon the grounde: As wee oftymes as we knele in oure prayers bowe oure ſelues ād lye on oure armes ād handes with oure face to the grounde.

The fecon
de boke of Mofes, cal=
led Exodus.

[Fo. II.]

¶ THE SECONDE BOKE
OF MOSES CALLED EXODUS.

¶ The firſt Chapter.

1 THESE are the names of the children of Iſrael, which came to Egipte with Iacob, euery man with his houſholde: Ru-
2
3 bē, Simeon, Leui, Iuda, Iſachar, Zabulon,
4 Beniamin, Dan, Neptali, Gad ād Aſer.
5 All the ſoules that came out of the loynes of Iacob, were .Lxx. and Ioſeph was in Egipte all redie.
6 when Ioſeph was dead and all his brethern and all
7 that generation: the children of Iſrael grewe, encreaſed, multiplied and waxed enceadinge myghtie: ſo that the londe was full of them.

M.C.S. The children of Iacob are nō-bred. The new Pharao oppreſſeth thē. The acte of the godly myd-wiues.

8 Then there roſe vp a new kynge in Egipte which
9 knewe not Ioſeph. And he ſayde vnto his folke: be-holde the people of the childrē of Iſrael are moo ād
10 mightier than we. Come on, let vs playe wiſely with them: leſt they multiplie, and then (yf there chaunce any warre) they ioyne them ſelues vnto oure enimies and fyghte ageynſt vs, and ſo gete them out of the lande.
11 .P. And he ſette taſkemaſters ouer them, to kepe them vnder with burthens. And they bylte vnto
12 Pharao treaſurecities: Phiton and Raamſes. But the more they vexed thē, the moare they multiplied and grewe: ſo that they abhorred the childrē of Iſrael.

M. 4 Nephtali 5 All theſe ſoules 6 all his brether 11 Rameſes
V. 7 & quaſi germinātes multiplicati ſunt 10 ſapienter opprimamus eum 11 vrbes tabernaculorum
L. 5 zuuor 7 vnd wymmelten vnd mehrten 10 vnd vns überwinden 11 ſchatzhewſern 12 den kindern Iſrael gram

13 And the Egiptiās helde the childern of Ifrael in bond-
14 age without mercie, and made their lyues bitter vnto them with cruell laboure in claye and bricke, and all maner worke in the feldes, and in all maner of feruice, which they caufed thē to worke cruelly
15 ' And the kynge of Egipte fayde vnto the mydwiues of the Ebruefwomen, of which the ones name was
16 Ziphra ād the other Pua: whē ye mydwiue the women of the Ebrues and fe in the byrth tyme that it is a
17 boye, kyll it. But yf it be a mayde, let it lyue. Notwithftonding the mydwiues feared God, and dyd not as the kinge of Egipte commaūded them: but faued the menchildern.
18 Thē the kinge of Egipte called for the midwiues ād fayde vnto thē: why haue ye delt on this maner and
19 haue faued the menchildern? And the mydwiues anfwered Pharao, that the Ebrues wemen were not as the wemen of Egipte: but were fturdie women, and were delyuered yer the midwyues came at them.
20 And God therfore delt well with the midwyues. [Fo. III.] And the people multiplied and waxed very
21 mightie. And becaufe the mydwiues feared God, he made them houfes.   houfes, *fam-*
22 Than Pharao charged all his pepple *ilies*
fayng All the menchildern that are borne, caft in to the ryuer and faue the maydchildern a lyue.

M. 15 Sephora .. Phua: 16 when ye do ỹ office of a mydwife to the womē 22 people
V. 13 & affligebant illudentes eis & inuidētes. 18 Quibus accerfitis ad fe rex 19 ipfæ enim obftetricandi habent fcientiam 21 ædificauit illis domos. 22 fœminini, referuate.
L. 13 vnbarmhertzickeyt (v. 14) 14 thon vnd zigelln 16 den Ebr. weyb. helfft, vnd auff dem ftuel fehet das 18 die kinder leben 19 hartte weyber 21 machet er jn heufer.
M. M. N. 21 *He made them houfes:* that is, he encreafed and multiplyed them, & made houfholdes of them: geuynge thē both hufbandes and chyldrē, as in Gen. vii, a.

⁋ The Seconde Chapter.

1 AND there wēt a mā of the houſe of Leui ād toke a doughter of Leui. 2 And the wife cōceaued ād bare a ſonne. And whē ſhe ſawe that it was a propre childe, ſhe hyd him thre monethes longe. 3 And whē ſhe coude no longer hyde him, ſhe toke a baſket of bulruſſhes ād dawbed it with ſlyme ād pytche, ād layde the childe therin, ād put it in the flagges by the riuers brynke. 4 And his ſiſter ſtode a ferre of, to wete what wold come of it.

M.C.S. Moſes is borne and caſt into the flagges. He is takē vp of Pharaos daughter. He kylleth the Egypcian. He flyeth & maryeth a wyfe. The Iſraelites crye vnto the Lorde.

wete, *know*

5 And the doughter of Pharao came doune to the riuer to waſhe her ſelfe, and hir maydens walked a longe by the riuers ſyde. And when ſhe ſawe the baſket amōge the flagges, ſhe ſent one of hir maydes 6 and cauſed it to be fet. And whē ſhe had opened it ſhe ſawe the childe, and behold, the babe wepte. And ſhe had cōpaſſiō on it ād ſayde: it is one of the Ebrues childern

7 Then ſayde his ſiſter vnto Pharaos doughter: ſhall I goo and call vnto the a nurſe of the Ebrues wemen, 8 to nurſe the childe? .P. And the mayde ranne and 9 called the childes mother. Thē Pharaos doughter ſaide vnto her, Take this childe awaye ād nurſe it for me, ād I will rewarde the for thi laboure. And the woman toke the childe and nurſed it vp.

10 And whē the childe was growne, ſhe brought it vnto Pharaos doughter, and it was made hir ſonne, and ſhe called it Moſes, becauſe (ſayde ſhe) I toke him out of the water.

V. 1 vxorem ſtirpis ſuæ 3 fiſcellam ſcirpeam .. carecto ripæ fluminis 5 vt lauaretur in flumine ... fiſcellam in papyrione 6 paruulum vagientem 10 adoptauit in locum filii, .. Quia de aqua tuli eum.

L. 3 rhor .. ſchilff 6 das kneblin weynet 10 vnd es ward jr ſon
M. M. N. 10 *Moſes* is an Egipt name & it ſignifieth drawen out of the water.
L. M. N. 10 *Maſa* heyſt zihen daher heyſt Moſe getzogen, nemlich aufs dem waſſer.

11 And it happened in thefe dayes when Mofes was waxte great, that he went out vnto his brethern ād loked on their burthens, and fpied an Egiptian fmyt-
12 ynge one of his brethern an Ebrue. And he loked round aboute: and when he fawe that there was no man by, he flewe the Egiptian and hyd hī in the fonde.
13 And he went out a nother daye: and beholde, two Ebrues ftroue to gether. And he fayde vnto him that dyd the wronge: wherfore fmyteft thou thine neygh-
14 boure? And he anfwered: who hath made the a ruelar or a iudge ouer vs? intendeft thou to kill me, as thou killedft the Egiptian? Then Mofes feared and fayde:
15 of a fuertie the thinge is knowne. And Pharao herde of it and went aboute to flee Mofes: but he fled from Pharao ād dwelt in the lāde of Madian, and he fatt doune by a welles fyde.
16 The preaft of Madian had .vii. doughters [Fo. IIII.] which came ād drew water and fylled the troughes,
17 for to water their fathers fhepe. And the fhepardes came and drove them awaye: But Mofes ftode vp and
18 helped them and waterd their fhepe. And when they came to Raguel their father, he fayde: how happeneth
19 it that ye are come fo foone to daye? And they anfwerede there was an Egiptiā that delyuered vs frō the fhepardes, and alfo drewe vs water & waterd the
20 fhepe. And he fayde vnto his doughters: where is he? why haue ye lefte the man? Goo call him that he maye eate bread.
21 And Mofes was content to dwell with the man.

𝔐. 19 fhepardes, & fo drewe
𝒱. 12 circunfpexiffet huc atque illuc 13 ei qui faciebat iniuriam 14 conftituit te in princ. 15 iuxta puteū. 21 Iurauit ergo Moyfes
𝐋. 13 fprach zu dem gottlofen 14 vbirften odder richter 15 bei eynen brunnen. 20 das jr jn nicht ludet
𝔐. 𝔐. N. 12 *He flew the Egypcyā:* that is, he declared hī felfe to haue fuche loue vnto hys brethrē the Ifraelytes that were the people of god: that he wolde rather flaye or be flayne then that hys brother fhulde fuffer wrōg of the enemy of the lord. In which acte alfo, he fhewed hym felfe to be predeftinate of the lorde, to be a defence and fauer of the Ifraelytes. 17 *Raguel*: This Raguel is not Iethro, but is the father of Iethro and the graundfather of zephora, and was alfo the prefte of Madian. For it was a lyke order with them as it was with the Iewes, that the fonne poffeffed the office of his father.

22 And he gaue Moſes Zipora his doughter which bare a
sonne, ãd he called him Gerſon: for he ſayde. I haue
bene a ſtraunger in a ſtraunge lande. And ſhe bare
yet another ſonne, whom he called Elieſer ſayng: the
God of my father is myne helper, and hath rid me out
of the handes of Pharao.
23 And it chaunced in proceſſe of tyme, that the kinge
of Egipte dyed, and the childern of Iſrael ſyghed by
the reaſon of laboure and cryed. And their complaynt
24 came vp vnto God from the laboure. And God remem-
25 bred his promiſe with Abraham, Iſaac ãd Iacob. And
God loked apon the children of Iſrael and knewe them.

P. ☙ The thyrde Chapter.

1 MOSES kepte the ſhepe of Iethro his father in law preaſt of Madian, and he droue the flocke to the backeſyde of the deſerte, ãd came to the moũtayne of
2 God, Horeb. And the angell of the Lorde apeared vnto hĩ in a flame of fyre out of a buſh. And he perceaued that the buſh burned with fyre and conſumed not.
3 Than Moſes ſayde: I will goo hẽce and ſee this grete ſyghte, howe it cometh that the buſhe burneth not.
4 And whẽ the Lorde ſawe that he came for to ſee, he called vnto him out of the buſh and ſayde: Moſes

M. C. S. Moſes kepeth ſhepe. God appereth vnto hym in a buſh, & ſendeth hym to the chyldren of Iſrael, and to Pharao that tyrant.

M. 22 Zephora
V. 22 Accepitque Sephoram .. *Alterum vero peperit: quem vocauit Eliezer, dicens, Deus enim patris mei adiutor Meus, & eripuit me de manu Pharaonis.* 23 ad deum ab operibus... Et audiuit gemitum .. 24 fœderis quod pepigerat 25 reſpexit ... et cognouit eos. iii, 1 ad interiora deſerti 3 videbo viſionem hanc magn.
L. 22 bewilligete .. vnd er gab 23 Gott erhöret jr wehklagen 24 .. ſeynen bund 25 ſahe ſie an vnd erkennet es. iii, 1 treib .. enhindern 3 beſehen diſz gros geſicht
M. M. N. 25 *Looked vpõ thẽ:* that is he had pitie & compaſſyon ouer their ſoore labours, as Deut. xxvi, d.—iii, 1 *Deſert:* that is in the wyldernes, a place not inhabited.
L. M. N. 22 *Gerſon,* heyſt ein frembder oder auſzlender. *Elieſer,* heyſt Gott meyn hylffe.

5 Moſes   And he anſwered: here am I. And he ſayde: come not hither, but put thy ſhooes off thi fete: for the
6 place whereon thou ſtondeſt is holy grounde. And he ſayde: I am the God of thy father, the God of Abraham, the God of Iſaac and the God of Iacob. And Moſes hyd his face, for he was afrayde to loke vpon God.

7 Than the Lorde ſayde: I haue ſurely ſene the trouble of my people which are in Egipte and haue herde their crye which they haue of their taſkemaſters. For I
8 knowe theire ſorowe and am come downe to delyuer them out of the handes of the Egiptians, and to brynge thē out of that londe vnto a good londe and a lar-[Fo. V.] ge and vnto a londe that floweth with mylke and hony: euen vnto the place of the Canaanites, Hethites, Amorites, Pherezites, Heuites, and of the Iebuſites.
9 Now therfore beholde, the complaynt of the children of Iſrael is come vnto me and I haue alſo ſene the oppreſſion, wherwith the Egiptians oppreſſe them.
10 But come, I will ſende the vnto Pharao, that thou mayſt brynge my people the childern of Iſrael out of Egipte.
11 And Moſes ſayde vnto God: what am I to goo to Pharao and to brynge the childern of Iſraell out of
12 Egipte? And he ſayde: I wilbe with the. And this ſhalbe a token vnto the that I haue ſent the: after that thou haſt broughte the people out of Egipte, ye ſhall
13 ſerue God vppon this mountayne.

Than ſayde Moſes vnto God: when I come vnto the childern of Iſraell and ſaye vnto them, the God of youre fathers hath ſent me vnto you, ãd they ſaye vnto me,
14 what ys his name, what anſwere ſhall I geue them?

ℳ. 11 vnto Pharao
V. 5 ſolue calceamentum .. terra ſancta 6 non enim audebat aſpicere contra 12 immolabis deo
L. 5 zeuch deine ſchuch aus .. ein heylig land 7 die, ſo ſie treyben 9 beſchwerung ... beſchweren. 12 Gotte eyn dienſt thun
ℳ. ℳ. N. 5 The ſcripture vſeth to call that holy whyche ether the Lorde choſeth vnto hym ſelfe: or is dedicate vnto the Lorde as Ex. xxii, d. 8 By *mylcke and hony* is vnderſtonde aboūdaunce & plenteouſnes of all thynges that pertayne to the comfort of mā.

called Exodus.

Then sayde God vnto Moses: I wilbe what I wilbe: ād he sayde, this shalt thou saye vnto the children of Israel: I wilbe dyd send me to you. *Of this vvord, I vvilbe cometh the name of God Iehovah vvhich vve interprete, Lorde, and is as moch to saye as I that am.*

15 And God spake further vnto Moses: thus shalt thou saye vnto the children of Israell: .P. the Lorde God of youre fathers, the God of Abraham, the God of Isaac, and the God of Iacob hath sent me vnto you: this is my name for euer, and this is my memoriall 16 thorow out all generacyons. Goo therfore and gather the elders of Israel to gether and saye vnto them: the Lorde God of youre fathers, the God of Abraham, the God of Isaac and the God of Iacob, appeared vnto me and sayde: I haue bene and sene both you and that 17 whiche is done to you in Egipte. And I haue sayde it, that I will bringe you out of the tribulaciō of Egipte vnto the londe of the Canaanites, Hethites, Amorites, Pherezites, Heuites and Iebusites: euen a londe that floweth wyth mylke ād hony.

18 Yf it come to passe that they heare thy voyce, then goo, both thou ād the elders of Israel vnto the kinge of Egipte and saye vnto him: The Lord God of the Ebrues hath mett with vs: Let vs goo therfore .iii. dayes iourney in to the wildernesse, that we maye sacrifice vnto 19 the Lorde oure God. Notwithstondinge I am sure that the kinge of Egipte will not lett you goo, excepte it be 20 with a mightie hande: ye ād I will therfore stretche out myne honde, and smyte Egipte with all my wōders which I wil do therin. And after that he will let you goo.

𝔐. 14 vnto you
𝔙. 14 Ego sum qui sum . . Qui est, misit me 15 hoc memoriale meum 16 Visitans visitaui 18 vt immolemus 20 in medio eorum
𝔏. 14 Ich werde seyn, der ich seyn werde . . Ich werds seyn, . . . gesandt 16 heymgesucht vnd gesehen 18 das wyr opffern 20 wunder die ich drynnen thun werde
𝔐. 𝔐. N. 14 *I wyll be that I wyll be:* that is I am as some interprete it: which is, I am the begynnyng & endynge: by me haue you all thinges & with out me haue you nothynge that good is, Iohn i, a.
𝔏. 𝔐. N. 14 *Ich werds seyn.* Der name Gottis ich werds seyn zeygt an, wie man mit glawben zu Gott, vnd er zu vns komen musz, denn der glawbe sagt, was God seyn vnd thun wirt mit vns nemlich gnade vnd hulffe.

21 And I will gett this people fauoure in the [Fo. VI.] fyghte of the Egiptians: fo that when ye goo, ye fhall
22 not goo emptie: but euery wife fhall borow of hir neyghbboureffe and of her that fogeorneth in hir houfe, iewels of fyluer ād of gold and rayment. And ye fhall put them on youre fonnes and doughters, and fhall robbe the Egiptians.

❧ The .IIII. Chaptre.

1 MOSES anfwered and fayde: Se, they wil not beleue me nor herkē vnto my voyce: but wil faye, the Lorde hath not
2 apeared vnto the. Then the Lorde faide vnto him: what is that in thine hande?
3 and he fayde, a rodd. And he fayde, caft it on the grounde, and it turned vnto a ferpent. And Mofes rā awaye
4 from it. And the Lorde fayde vnto Mofes: put forth thine hande ād take it by the tayle. And he put forth his hande and caught it, and it became a rodd agayne in his hand,
5 that they may beleue that the Lorde God of their fathers, the God of Abraham, the God of Ifaac ād the God of Iacob hath appeared vnto the.
6 And the Lorde fayde forther more vnto him: thruft thine hande in to thy bofome. And he thruft his hande in to his bofome and toke it out. And beholde, his hand was leporous euen as fnowe. And he

M.C.S. Mofes receaueth fignes of his callynge and was fent into Egypte. His wyfe zephora circumcifeth hir fonne. Aaron meteth with Mofes. Mofes taketh his leaue of his father in lawe.

V. 22 poftulabit mulier a vicina fua & ab hofpita fua vafa .. fpoliabitis. iiii, 4 apprehende caudam eius. 5 Vt credant, inquit
L. 22 foddern filberen vnd gulden gefefz ... entwenden. iiii, 4 erhafche fie bey dem fchwantz.
M. M. N. 22 *Robbe the Egypcians:* here ye maye not note that they ftale and therfore ye maye fteale: but note that it was done at godes cōmaundement & therfore was it a Iuft & a righteous thing to be done. For he is not the auctor of euell &c.

7 faide: put thine hande in .P. to thy bofome agayne. And he put his hande in to his bofome agayne, and plucked it out of his bofome, and beholde, it was
8 turned agayn as his other flefh. Yf they will not beleue the nether heare the voyce of the firft token: yet will they beleue the voyce of the feconde tokē
9 But and yf they will not beleue the two fignes nether herken vnto thy voyce, then take of the water of the riuer and poure it vpon the drye lond. And the water which thou takeft out of the riuer fhall turne to bloude vpon the drie londe.
10 And Mofes fayde vnto the Lorde: oh my Lorde. I am not eloquēt, no not in tymes paft and namely fence thou haft fpoken vnto thy feruaunte: but I am flowe
11 mouthed and flowe tongued. And the Lorde fayde unto hī: who hath made mās mouth, or who hath made the domme or the deaff, the feynge or the blynde? haue
12 not I the Lorde? Go therfore and I wilbe with thy mouth and teach the what thou fhalt faye.
13 And he fayde: oh my Lorde, fend I pray the
14 whome thou wilt. And the Lorde was angrie with Mofes and fayde: I knowe Aarō thy brother the leuite that he can fpeake. And morouer behold, he cometh out agaynft the, ād whē he feyth the, he wilbe glad
15 ī his hert. And thou [Fo. VII.] fhalt fpeake vnto hī and put the wordes in his mouth, ād I wilbe with thy mouth ād with his mouth, ād will teach you what ye
16 fhal do. And he fhalbe thy fpokesmā vnto the people: he fhall be thy mouth, ād thou fhalt be his God.
17 and take this rodd in thy hāde, wherwith thou fhalt do myracles.

M. 14 he cometh to mete the

V. 7 retrahe .. finum tuum .... et erat fimilis 8 audier. fermonem ... credēt verbo 10 obfecro domine, non fum eloquens ab heri & nudiuftertius 12 ero in ore tuo 15 pone verba mea .. quid agere debeatis. 16 tu autem eris in his quæ ad deum pertinent. 17 facturus es figna.

L. 7 vnd er thet fie wieder 8 horen die ftim ... glawben der ftim 10 von giftern vnd ehegiftern her 12 mit deynem mund 14 feer zornig 15 was jr thun folet 16 folet feyn Got feyn 17 zeychen thun folt.

M. M. N. 16 *He fhalbe thy mouth:* that is, he fhall fpeake for the as in Iob xxix, c.

18 And Moſes went ād returned to Iethro his father in lawe agayne ād ſeyde vnto hī: let me goo (I praye the) ād turne agayne vnto my brethern which are in Egipte, that I may ſe whether they be yet alyue.
19 And Iethro ſayde to Moſes: goo in peace. And the Lorde ſayde vnto Moſes in Madiā: returne agayne in to Egipte for they are dead which wēt aboute to kyll
20 the And Moſes toke his wife and his ſonnes and put them on an aſſe, and went agayne to Egipte, and toke the rodd of God in his hande.
21 And the Lorde ſayde vnto Moſes: when thou art come in to Egipte agayne, ſe that thou doo all the wondres before Pharao which I haue put in thy hande: but I will harden his herte, ſo that he ſhall not let the people goo.
22 And tell Pharao, thus ſayth the Lorde: Iſrael is
23 mine eldeſt ſonne, and therfore ſayth vnto the: let my ſonne goo, that he may ſerue me. Yf thou wilt not let hī goo: beholde, I will ſlee thi-.P.ne eldeſt ſonne.
24 And it chaunced by the waye in the ynne, that the
25 Lorde mett him and wolde haue kylled him. Than Zepora toke a ſtone ād circumciſed hyr ſonne, and fell at hys fette, and ſayde: a bloudy huſband art thou
26 vnto me. And he lett him goo. She ſayde a bloudy huſbonde, becauſe of the circumciſion.
27 Than ſayde the Lorde vnto Aaron: go mete Moſes in the wilderneſſe. And he went and mett him in the
28 mounte of God and kiſſed hī And Moſes told Aaron all the wordes of the Lorde which he had ſent by him, ād all the tokens which he had charged him with all.
29 So went Moſes and Aaron and gatherd all the elders
30 of the childern of Iſrael. And Aarō told all the wordes

V. 19 quærebant animam tuam. 25 tetigitque pedes eius 26 poſt-quam dixerat, Sponſus 28 pro quibus miſerat eum 29 & fecit ſigna
L. 19 nach deynem leben ſtunden. 25 ruret jhm ſeyn fuſſe an 28 zeychen .. beſolhen hatte
L. M. N. 25 *Blutbreutgam*, das iſt ſie ward zornig vnd ſprache, Es koſt blut, das du mein man biſt vnd mus mein kind beſchneytten, wilches ſie vngerne thet, als das ein ſchant war vnter dē heydē. Bedeut aber des geſetz volck wilchs gern wollt Got haben, aber es will dz creutz nicht leyden noch den alten Adam beſchneytten laſſen biſz es thun mus.

which the Lorde had fpokē vnto Mofes, and dyd the
31 myracles in the fyght of the people, and the people
beleued. And whē they herde that the Lord had
vifited the children of Ifrael and had loked vpon their
tribulacion, they bowed them felues, and worfhipped

¶ The .V. Chapter.

1 **T**HEN Mofes ād Aarō wēt and *M.C.S. Mo-*
told Pharao, thus fayth the *fes & Aaron*
Lorde God of Ifrael. Let my *goeth vnto*
people goo, that they may *people of If-*
kepe holye [Fo. VIII.] daye vnto me in *preffed more*
2 the wilderneffe. And Pharao anfwered: *and more, and*
what felowe is the Lord, that I fhulde heare *vpon Mofes &*
his voyce for to let Ifrael goo? I knowe *Aaron ther-*
not the Lorde, nether will let Ifrael goo. *fore.*
3 And they fayde: the God of the Ebrues hath mett
with vs: let vs goo (we praye the) .iii. dayes iourney
in to the deferte, that we maye facrifice vnto the
Lorde oure God: left he fmyte vs ether with peftilence
4 or with fwerde. Then fayde the kinge of Egipte vnto
them: wherfore do ye, Mofes and Aaron, let the people frō their worke, gett you vnto youre laboure.
5 And Pharao fayde further more: beholde, there is
moch people in the londe, and ye make them playe
and let their worke ftonde.

V. 2 nefcio dominum 3 Deus Hebr. vocauit nos . . accidat
nobis peftis aut gladius. 5 videtis quod turba fuccreuerit

⁎⁎ NOTE—*The German notes in this Chapter and in Chapters VI., VII., VIII., and IX. were taken from a copy of Luther in the Lenox Library which is made up from different editions; the text of these chapters belongs to later editions. A* PERFECT *copy of the edition of 1523 having come into my use since the notes were prepared and set up in type, they have been carefully compared with that copy and agree with the former text in all particulars except the fpelling, which being materially different from that in the edition of 1523, has been retained as illuftrating the changes intro- duced. The precife date of the later editions I have not been able to verify.*

L. 1 feyre in der wüften 2 weyfz nichts von dem H. 3 der
Ebräer Got hat vns gerufften . . widerfare peftilentz oder fchwerd.

M. M. N. 31 *They bowed thē felues*, that is, gaue thāckes &
prayfed the Lorde. v, 2 *I knowe not the Lorde*, that is: I feare
him not, I beleue not in him: nether haue I any thyng to do with
him. And euen thus faye all hardened hartes that haue not the
feare of the Lorde before their eyes.

6 And Pharao commaunded the fame daye vnto the tafkemafters ouer the people and vnto the officers fa-
7 ynge: fe that ye geue the people no moare ftrawe to make brycke with all as ye dyd in tyme paffed: let
8 them goo and gather them ftrawe them felues, and the nombre of bricke which they were wont to make in tyme paffed, laye vnto their charges alfo, and minyfh nothinge therof. Fôr they be ydill ãd therfore crye faynge: let vs goo and do facrifice vnto oure
9 God. They muft haue more worke layed vpon them, that they maye laboure theryn, and than will they not turne them felues to fal-.P.fe wordes.
10 Than went the tafkemafters of the people and the officers out and tolde the people faynge: thus fayeth
11 Pharao: I will geue you no moare ftrawe, but goo youre felues ãd gather you ftrawe where ye can fynde
12 it, yet fhall none of youre laboure be minyfhed. Than the people fcatered abrode thorowe out all the lande of Egipte for to gather them ftubyll to be in ftead of ftrawe.
13 And the tafkemafters haftied thẽ forward fayng: fulfill youre werke daye by daye, euẽ as when ftrawe
14 was geuen you. And the officers of the childern of Ifrael which Pharaos tafkmafters had fett ouer them, were beaten. And it was fayde vnto them: wherfore haue ye not fulfilled youre tafke in makinge brycke, both yefterdaye and to daye, as well as in tymes paft.
15 Than went the officers of the childern of Ifrael ãd complayned vnto Pharao faynge: wherfore dealeft thou thus with thy fervauntes? there is no ftrawe geuen
16 vnto thy fervauntes, and yet they faye vnto vs: make brycke. And loo, thy fervauntes ar beaten, and thy
17 people is foule intreated. And he anfwered: ydill ar ye ydill and therfore ye faye: let vs goo ãd do fac-

V. 8 imponetis fuper eos, nec minuetis quicquam 9 Opprimantur oper., & expleant ea 12 colligendas paleas. 13 Præfecti 14 Flagellatique funt .. ab exactoribus Pharaonis ... ficut prius, nec heri nec hodie? 16 lateres fimiliter imperantur .. iniufte agitur 17 Vacatis otio

L. 7 famlen vnd geben 8 aufflegen vnd nichts myndern 14 wurden gefchlagen .. heut noch geftern .. wie geftern vnd ehegeftern? 16 man fündiget an deynem volck. 17 Ir feit müffig, müffig feit jr

18 rifice vnto the Lorde. Goo therfore and worke, for [Fo. IX.] there fhall no ftrawe be geuen you, and yet fee that ye delyuer the hole tale of brycke.   *tale, number* cf. German *Zahl*

19 when the officers of the childern of Ifrael fawe them filfe in fhrode cafe (in that he fayde fhrode. *evil* ye fhall minyfh nothinge of youre dalye makīge of
20 brycke) than they mett Mofes and Aarō ftondinge in
21 there waye as they came out frō Pharao, and fayde vnto them: The Lorde loke vnto you and iudge, for ye haue made the fauoure of vs ftincke in the fighte of Pharao and of his feruauntes, and haue put a fwerde in to their handes to flee vs.
22 Mofes returned vnto the Lorde and fayde: Lorde wherfore dealeft thou cruelly with this people: and
23 wherfore haft thou fent me? For fence I came to Pharao to fpeke in thy name, he hath fared foull with this folke, ād yet thou haft not delyuered thy people
VI, 1 at all. Then the Lorde fayde vnto Mofes. Now fhalt thou fee what I will doo vnto Pharao, for with a myghtie hande fhall he let them goo, and with a mightye hande fhall he dryue them out of hys lande.

¶ The .VI. Chapter

2 AND God fpake vnto Mofes fa- yng vnto him: I am the Lorde,
3 and I appeared vnto Abraham Ifaac and Iacob an allmightie God: but in my name Iehouah was I not   *M.C.S. God promyfeth delyueraunce of the Ifraelites, & the lande of Canaan. The genealo-*

V. 19 Videbantque fe ... in malum 20 Occurreruntque Moyfi et Aaron, qui ftabant ex aduerfo 21 coram Pharaone .. ei gladium 23 afflixit populum tuum & non liberafti eos. vi, 1 eiiciet illos 3 in deo omnipotente .. nomen meum Adonai

L. 19 das nicht beſſer ward 20 traten fie dahin, das fie in begegneten 21 vor Pharao. vi, 1 von fich treiben 3 zum almechtigen got ... meinen namē HERRE

M. M. N. 21 *Ye haue made vs ftincke in the fyght of Pharao*, that is, by your wordes & meanes: all the wrath & dyfpleafure of Pharao is brought vpon vs, that he vtterly hateth & abhorreth vs. vi, 3 *Iehouah* is the name of god, wherwith no creature is named, & is as moch to faye as one that is of hym felfe & dependeth of no thing.

4 kno-.P. wne vnto them. Moreouer I made *gie of Ruben,*
appoyntment, an appoyntment with them *Simeon and Leui.*
couenant to geue them the londe of Canaā: the
londe of their pilgremage wherin they were ſtraungers.
5 And I haue alſo herde the gronyng of the childern of
Iſrael, becauſe the Egiptians kepe them in bondage,
ād haue remembred my promyſſe *A promyſe,*
6 wherfore ſaye vnto the childern of *or a teſtamēt*
Iſrael: I am the Lorde, and will brynge you out from
vnder the burdens of the Egiptians, and wyll rydd you
out of their bondage, and wyll delyuer you wyth a
7 ſtretched out arme and wythe great iudgementes. And
I wil take you for my people and wilbe to you a God.
And ye ſhall knowe that I am the Lorde youre God
which bringe you out from vnder the burthens of the
8 Egiptians. And I wyll brynge you vnto the londe
ouer the which I dyd lyfte vpp my hande to geue it
vnto Abraham, Iſaac and Iacob, and will geue it vnto
9 you for a poſſeſſyon: euē I the Lorde, And Moſes
tolde the children of Iſrael euen ſo: But they harkened
not vnto Moſes for anguyſhe of ſprete and *ſprete, ſpirit*
for cruell bondage. *Temptacyon trieth faith.*
10, 11 And the Lorde ſpake vnto Moſes ſaynge Goo and
bydd Pharao kynge of Egipte, that he let the childern
12 of Iſrael goo out of his londe. And Moſes ſpake before
the Lorde ſa-[Fo. X.] ynge: beholde, the childern of
Iſraell herken not vnto me, how than ſhall Pharao
heare me: ſeynge that I haue vncircumciſed lippes.

V. 4 Pepigique fœdus 5 audiui gemitum . . pacti mei. 6 erga-
ſtulo Ægyyt., . . iudiciis magnis. 8 ſuper quam leuaui manum
meā 9 propter anguſtiam ſpiritus, & opus duriſſimum.
L. 4 bund . . auffgericht 5 die wehklage . . bund gedacht. 6 laſten
in Eg. . groſſe gerichte 8 darüber ich habe meine hand gehaben
9 vor keychen des geyſts vnd vor harter arbeyt.
M. M. N. 5 A promyſe or a teſtament. 6 *Iudgemētes* are
taken for the wōderfull dedes of God: as here for his wōderfull
plages as Pſal. xxx, d. & cxviii. 8 *To lyfte vp the hande* is to
promyſe by an othe, as in Gen. xiiii, d. of Abraham.—12 *To be
of vncircumciſed lippes,* is to haue a tonge that lacketh good vt-
terance & lacketh eloquence to ſet out his matter with all.
L. M. N. 3 *Nicht kundt gethan:* Die Patriarchen haben Gott
wol erkand, aber ein ſolche offentliche gemeyne predig war zu
der zeyte von Gott noch nicht auff gangen, wie durch Moſe vnd
Chriſtū geſchehen iſt.

13 And the Lorde fpake vnto Mofes and Aaron and gaue them a charge vnto the childern of Ifrael ãd vnto Pharao kyng of Egipte: to brynge the childern of Ifrael out of the londe of Egipte.
14 Thefe be the heedes of their fathers houffes. The children of Ruben the eldeft fonne of Ifrael are thefe: Hanoh, Pallu, Hezron, Charmi, thefe be the houfholders
15 of Ruben. The childern of Symeon ar thefe: Gemuel, Iamin, Ohad, Iachin. Zohar, and Saul the fonne of a Cananytefh wife: thefe are the kynreddes of Symeon
16 Thefe are the names of the childern of Leui in their generations: Gerfon, Kahath and Merari. And
17 Leui lyued an hundred and .xxxvii. yere. The fonnes of Gerfon: Libni ãd Semei in their kinreddes.
18 The childern of Kahath: Amram, Iefear, Hebron and Vfiel. And Kahath lyued an hundred and .xxxiii. yere.
19 The childern of Merari are thefe: Mahely and Mufi: thefe are the kynreddes of Leui in their generations.
20 And Amram toke Iochebed his nece to wyfe which bare him Aaron and Mofes. And Amram lyued an
21 hundred and .xxxvii. yere. .¶. The childern of Iezear:
22 Korah, Nepheg and Sichri. The childern of Vfiel: Mifael, Elzaphan and Sithri.
23 And Aaron toke Elizaba doughter of Aminadab ãd fifter of Nahafon, to wife: which bare him Nadab,
24 Abehu, Eleazar and Ithamar. The childern of Korah: Affir, Elkana ãd Abiaffaph: thefe are the kynreddes
25 of the Korahites. And Eleazar Aarons fonne toke him one of·the doughters of Putuel to wife: which bare him Pinehas: thefe be the principall fathers of the Leuites in their kynreddes.
26 Thefe are that Aaron and Mofes to whom the Lorde fayde: carie the childern of Ifrael out of the lond of
27 Egipte, with their armyes. Thefe are that Mofes and Aaron whiche fpake to Pharao kynge of Egipte, that they myghte brige the childern of Ifrael out of Egipte.

V. 14 hæ cognationes Ruben. 20 Moyfen *& Mariam* 25 principes familiarum Leuit. 27 Hi funt .. Ifrael de Ægypto: ifte eft Moyfes & Aaron
L. 27 Sie finds

28 And in the daye whē the Lorde ſpake vnto Moſes in
29 the londe of Egipte, he ſpake vnto him ſaynge, I am the Lorde, ſe that thou ſpeake vnto Pharao the kinge
30 of Egipte all that I ſaye vnto the. And Moſes anſwered before the Lorde: I am of vncircumciſed lippes, howe ſhall Pharao than geue me audience?

☞ The .VII. Chaptre.

1 AND the Lorde ſaide vnto Moſes: beholde, I haue made the Pharaos God, and [Fo. XI.] Aaron thy brother ſhal be
2 thy prophete. Thou ſhalt ſpeake all that I commaunde the and Aaron thy brother ſhall ſpeake vnto Pharao: that he ſende the childern of Iſrael out of his londe.
3 But I will harden Pharaos hert, that I may multiplie my myracles and my wondres in the
4 land of Egipte. And yet Pharao ſhall not herken vnto you, that I maye ſett myne honde vpon Egipte and brynge out myne armyes, euē my people the childern of Iſrael out of the lāde of Egipte, with great
5 iudgementes. And the Egiptians ſhall knowe that I am the Lorde when I haue ſtretched forth my hande vpō Egipte, and haue brought out the childern of Iſrael from amonge thē.
6 Moſes and Aaron dyd as the Lorde commaunded
7 them. And Moſes was .Lxxx. yere olde and Aaron
8 Lxxxiii. when they ſpake vnto Pharao. And the

M.C.S. The tokens to knowe God. The rodde of Moſes is torned to a ſerpēt. The ſorcerars do euē the ſame. The waters are tourned into bloude.

V. 28 in die qua locutus eſt dominus... in terra Æg. vii. 1 conſtitui te deum Phar. 3 ſigna & oſtenta 4 exercitum & populum meum... iudicia maxima. 5 de medio eorum.

L. 1 eynen Gott geſetzt vber Phar. 3 zeychen vnd wunder 4 füre meyn heer, meyn volck .. groſſe gerichte 5 mitten auſz ynen

M. M. N. 1 *I haue made the Pharaos God*, that is: I haue made the Pharaos iudge as in Ex. xxii, d.

9 Lorde fpake vnto Mofes and Aaron faynge: when Pharao fpeaketh vnto you and fayth: fhewe a wondre, than fhalt thou faye vnto Aaron, take the rodd and caft it before Pharao, and it fhall turne to a ferpent
10 Than went Mofes and Aarō in vnto Pharao, and dyd euen as the Lorde had commaunded. And Aaron caft forth his rodd before Pharao and before his fer-
11 vauntes, and it turned to a ferpente. Than Pharao called for the .P. wyfe men and enchaunters of Egipte
12 dyd yn lyke maner with there forcery. And they caft doune euery mā his rodd, ād they turned to ferpētes: but Aarons
13 rodd ate vp their roddes: ād yet for all that Pharaos herte was hardened, fo that he herkened not vnto thē, euen as the Lorde had fayde.
14 Than fayde the Lorde vnto Mofes. Pharaos herte is hardened, and he re-
15 fufeth to let the people goo. Get the *Euē fo do ourecharmars novv deceaue all princes vvith theire fophiftrie: ād turnethēclene from repētaūce tovvarde the lavve of god: ād frō the fayth that is in Chrift.* vnto Pharao in the mornynge, for he will come vnto the water, and ftōde thou apon the ryuers brynke agenft he come, and the rodd whiche turned to a
16 ferpente take in thine hande. And faye vnto him: the Lorde God of the Hebrues hath fente me vnto the faynge: let my people goo, that they maye ferue me in the wildernes: but hither to thou woldeft not heare.
17 wherfore thus fayth the Lorde: hereby thou fhalt knowe that I am the Lord. Behold, I will fmyte with the ftaffe that is in myne hand apon the waters that
18 are in the ryuer, and they fhall turne to bloude. And the fifhe that is in the riuer fhall dye, and the riuer fhall ftinke: fo that it fhall greue the Egiptiās to drinke of the water of the ryuer.
19 And the Lorde fpake vnto Mofes, faye vnto Aaron: take thy ftaffe and ftretch out thyne hande ouer the waters of Egipte, ouer the- [Fo. XII.] ir ftreames,

M. 11 Egypte: and they dyd
V. 9 Oftendite figna 12 dracones 14 Ingrauatum 16 vt facrificet mihi in deferto
L. 9 beweyfet ewre wunder 11 fchwarzkünftigen 13 verftockt 16 diene in der wüften.

ryuers, pondes and all pooles off water, that they maye be bloude, and that there may be bloude in all the lande of Egipte: both in veſſells of wodd and alſo of ſtone.

20 And Moſes and Aaron dyd euen as the Lorde commaunded. And he lifte vp the ſtaffe and ſmote the waters that were in the riuer, in the ſyghte of Pharao and in the ſyghte of his ſervauntes, and all the water
21 that was in the ryuer, turned in to bloude. And the fiſh that was in the riuer dyed, and the ryuer ſtanke: ſo that the Egiptians coude not drinke of the water of the ryuer. And there was bloude thorowe out all the lande of Egipte.
22 And the Enchaunters of Egipte dyd lyke wyſe with their enchauntmentes, ſo that Pharaos herte was hardened and dyd not regarde them as the Lorde had ſayde.
23 And Pharao turned him ſelfe and went in to his houſſe,
24 and ſet not his herte there vnto. And the Egiptians dygged round aboute the ryuer for water to drynke, for they coude not drynke of the water of the ryuer.
25 And it continued a weke after that the Lorde had ſmote the ryuer.

The .VIII. Chapter.

.P.

1 THE Lorde ſpake vnto Moſes: Goo vnto Pharao and tell him, thus fayeth the Lorde: let my people goo, that they
2 maye ſerue me. Yf thou wilt not let them goo: beholde I will ſmyte all thy londe with
3 frogges. And the ryuer ſhall ſcrale with frogges, ād they ſhall come vp and goo in to thine houſſe and in to thy chaumbre

M.C.S. The plage of frogges. Moſes prayeth for Pharao. The plage of flyes.

ſcrale, *crawl, creep,* Lev. xi 41, 42.

V. 22 malefici Ægyptiorum 23 nec appoſuit cor etiam hac vice. 27 or viii, 2 terminos tuos 28 or viii, 3 ebulliet fluuius ..
  L. 23 vnd keret ſein hertz noch nit dran 27 or viii, 2 deyne grentzen 28 or viii, 3 wymmeln ..
  M M. N. 23 *He ſet not his heart therō* that is, the danger moued him nothinge, as is declared in Eſ. xlvii, b.

VIII. 4-15. called Exodus. 189

where thou flepeſt ād vppō thy bedd, and in to the houſſes of thy ſervauntes, and vppon thy people, and in to thyne ovens, and vppon thy vitels which thou
4 haſt in ſtore   And the frogges ſhall come vpon the and on thy people and apon all thy ſervauntes.
5   And the Lorde ſpake vnto Moſes, ſaye vnto Aaron: ſtretche forth thine hande with thy rodd ouer the ſtremes, riuers, ād pondes.   And bringe vp frogges
6 apon the londe of Egipte   And Aaron ſtretched his hande ouer the water of Egipte, and the frogges came
7 vp ād couered the londe of Egipte.   And the ſorcerers dyd likewiſe with theire ſorcery, and the frogges came vp apon the lande of Egipte.
8   Then Pharao called for Moſes and Aarō and ſayde, praye ye vnto the Lorde that he may take awaye the frogges from me and from my people, and I will let the people goo, that they maye ſacrifice vnto the
9 Lorde.   And Moſes ſayde vnto Pharao: Appoynte thou the tyme [Fo. XIII.] vnto me, when I ſhall praye for the and thy ſervauntes ād thy people, to dryue awaye the frogges from the and thy houſſe, ſo that they ſhall
10 remayne but in the riuer only.   And he ſayde tomorow. And he ſayde: euen as thou haſt ſayde, that thou may- ſt knowe that there is none like vnto the Lorde oure
11 God.   And the frogges ſhall departe from the ād from thyne houſes, and from thy ſervauntes and from thy people, and ſhall remayne in the riuer only.
12   And Moſes and Aaron went out frō Pharao, and Moſes cryed vnto the Lorde apō the apoyntment of
13 frogges which he had made vnto Pharao.   And the Lorde dyd accordinge to the ſaynge of Moſes.   And the frogges dyed out of the houſſes, courtes and feldes.
14   And they gathred them to gether vppon heppes: ſo that the lande ſtanke of them.
15   But when Pharao ſawe that he had reſt geuen

M. 9 Appoynte thou the tyme
V. 28 or viii, 3 reliquias ciborum tuorum. viii, 9 conſtitue ... a domo tua, *& a ſeruis tuis, & a populo tuo* 12 pro ſponſione ramarum ... quam condixerat
L. 28 or viii, 3, in deyne teyg.   viii, 9 Hab du die ehr für mir, vnd ſtymme mir 12 vmb das gedinge ... zugeſagt 15 das er lufft kriegen hatte

him, he hardened his herte and herkened not vnto
16 them, as the Lorde had fayde. And the Lord fayde
vnto Mofes: Saye vnto Aarō ftretch out thy rodd and
fmyte the duft of the lande that it may turne to lyfe
17 in all the londe of Egipte. And they dyd fo. And
Aaron ftretched out his hande with his rodd and fmote
the duft of the erth. ād it turned to lyfe both in man
and beeft, fo that all the duft of the lande .P. turned
to lyfe, thorowe out all the lande of Egipte.

18 And the enchaunters affayde lykewyfe with their
enchauntmentes to brynge forth lyfe, but they coude
not. And the lyfe were both apon man and beeft.
19 Then fayde the enchaunters vnto Pharao: it is the
fingre of God. Neuerthelater Pharaos herte was hardened and he regarded them not, as the Lorde had fayde.

20 And the Lorde fayde vnto Mofes: ryfe vp early in
the mornynge and ftonde before Pharao, for he will
come vnto the water: and faye vnto him, thus fayth
the Lorde: let my people goo, that they maye ferue
21 me. Yf thou wilt not let my people goo: beholde, I
will fende all maner flies both apon the and thy fervauntes ād thy people and into thy houffes. And the
houffes of the Egiptians fhalbe full of flies, and the
22 grounde where on they are. But I will feperate
the fame daye the londe of Gofan where my people
are, fo that there fhall no flyes be there: that thou
mayft knowe that I am the Lorde vppon the erth.
23 And I will put a deuifion betwene my people and
thine. And euen tomorow fhall this myracle be done.
24 And the Lorde dyd euen fo: and there came noy-
fom flyes in to the houffe of Pharao [Fo. XIIII.] and
in to his fervauntes houffes and in to all the lōde of
Egipte: fo that the londe was marred with flyes.

V. 16 et fint cyniphes 18 vt educerent 21 omne genus mufca-
rum ... mufcis diuerfi generis 22 Faciamque mirabilem in die
illa terram Geffen in qua populus meus eft, vt non fint ibi mufcæ
23 fignum iftud 24 mufca grauiffima .. corruptaque eft terra
   L. 16 das leufe werden 18 erauſz brechten 22 vnd wil des
tages ein fonders thun 23 erlöfung fetzen ... zeichen 24 böſe
würm ... land ward verderbet
   M. M. N. 19 What the fynger of God doth fignifie is expounded in Luke xi, c.

25 Then Pharao sent for Moses and Aaron and sayde:
26 Goo and do sacrifice vnto youre God in the land. And Moses answered: it is not mete so to do. for we must offer vnto the Lorde oure God, that whiche is an abhominatyon vnto the Egiptians: beholde shall we sacrifice that which is an abhominacion vnto the Egiptians before their eyes, and shall they not stone
27 vs? we will therfore goo .iii. dayes yournay in to the deserte and sacrifice vnto the Lorde oure God as he hath comaunded vs.
28 And Pharao sayde: I will late you goo, that ye maye sacrifice vnto the Lorde youre God in the wildernes: only goo not ferre awaye, ād se that ye praye
29 for me. And Moses sayde: beholde, I will goo out from the and praye vnto the Lorde, and the flyes shall departe frō Pharao and from his servauntes and from his people tomorow. But let Pharao from hēce forth desceaue no moare, that he wolde not lett the people goo to sacrifice vnto the Lorde.
30 And Moses went out from Pharao and prayed vnto
31 the Lorde. And the Lorde dyd as Moses had saide: ād toke awaye the flies frō Pharao and from his servauntes ād from hys .P. people, so that there remayned not one. But for all that, Pharao hardened his herte euen then also and wolde not let the people goo,

⁋ 'The .IX. Chaptre.

1 AND the Lorde sayde vnto Moses, goo vnto Pharao and tell him, thus sayeth the Lorde God of the Ebrues: sende out my peo-
2 ple that they maye serue me. Yf thou wilt not let them goo but wilt holde them
3 styll: beholde, the hande of the Lorde

M.C.S. *The moren of bestes. The plage of botches and sores. The horryble hayle, thonder & lyghtenynge.*

M. 29 that he wille not   ix, 1, let my people goo that
V. 25 in terra hac. 28 longius ne abeatis 29 noli vltra fallere 31 non superfuit ne vna quidem
L. 28 nicht ferner zihet 29 alleyne theusche mich nicht mehr

ſhalbe apō thy catell which thou haſt in the feld apon horſes aſſes, camels, oxen, and ſhepe, with a mightye
4 great morrayne. But the Lorde ſhall make a deuyſion betwene the beeſtes of the Iſrahelites, ād the beeſtes of the Egiptiās: ſo that there ſhal nothing dye of all that
5 perteyneth to the children of Iſrael. And the Lorde appoynted a tyme ſaynge: tomorow the Lorde ſhall do this thinge in the londe.

6 And the Lorde dyd the thinge on the morow, and all the catell of Egipte dyed: but of the catell of the
7 childern of Iſrael dyed not one. And Pharao ſent to wete: but ther was not one of the catell wete, *know* of the Iſrahelites dead. Notwithſtondinge the hert of Pharao hardened, and he wolde not let the people goo.

8 And the Lorde ſayde vnto Moſes and Aaron: take youre handes full of aſſhes out of the [Fo. XV.] fornace, and let Moſes ſprynkel it vp into the ayre in
9 the ſyghte of Pharao, and it ſhall turne to duſt in all the londe of Egipte, and ſhal make ſwellynge ſoores with blaynes both on mā and beeſt in all blaynes, *pim-*
10 the londe of Egipte. And they toke *ples, or puſ-tules* aſſhes out of the fornace, and ſtode before Pharao, ād Moſes ſprynkeld it vp into the ayre: And there brake
11 out ſoores with blaynes both in mā and beeſt: ſo that the ſorcerers coude not ſtonde before Moſes, by the reaſon of botches on the enchaunters and *botches, ſwel-*
12 apon all the Egiptians, But the Lorde *lings, blotches* hardened the herte of Pharao, that he herkened not vnto them, as the Lorde had ſayde vnto Moſes.

13 And the Lorde ſayde vnto Moſes: ryſe vp early in the mornynge and ſtonde before Pharao and tell him,

𝔐. 11 before Moſes for there were botches vpon the enchaunters

𝒱. 3 peſtis valde grauis 4 inter poſſeſſiones Iſrael, & poſſeſſiones Ægypt. 7 Miſit Phar. ad vidēdum 8 cineris de camino 9 vlcera, & veſicæ turgētes

𝐋. 3 faſt ſchweren peſtilentz 7 Ph. ſandte darnach, vnd ſihe, 8 ruſz auſz der ſewrmaur 9 ſchweren vnd drüſze

𝔐. 𝔐. N. 6 This word *all:* is not taken here for euery one, but for a great nombre, or of all ſortes of catell ſome, as in 1 Tim. ii, a.

thus fayth the Lorde God of the Ebrues: Let my
14 people goo, that they may ferue me, or els I will
at this tyme fende all my plages apon thine herte and
apon thy fervauntes and on thy people, that thou
mayſt knowe that there is none lyke me in all the erth.
15 For now I will ſtretch out my hande and will ſmyte
the and thy people with peſtilence: ſo that thou ſhalt
16 periſſhe from the erth. Yet in very dede for this caufe
haue I ſterred the vpp, for to ſhewe my power in the,
and to declare my name thorow out all the worlde.
17 P. Yf it be ſo that thou ſtoppeſt my people, that thou
18 wilt not let them goo: beholde, tomorow this tyme I
will fend doune a mightie great hayle: euē foch one as
was not in Egipte fence it was grounded   grounded, .
                                                        eſtabliſhed,
19 vnto this tyme. Sende therfore and fet founded.
home thy beeſtes and al that thou haſt in the felde,
For apon all the men and beeſtes which are founde in
the felde ād not broughte home, ſhall the hayle fall,
20 ād they ſhall dye   And as many as feared the worde
of the Lorde among the fervauntes of Pharao made
21 their fervauntes ād their beeſtes flee to houfe: and they
that regarded not the worde of the Lorde, left their
22 fervauntes and their beeſtes in the felde.

And the Lorde fayde vnto Mofes: ſtretche forth thine
hande vnto heauen, that there may be hayle in all the
lande of Egipte: apō mā ād beeſt, ād apō all the herbes
23 of the felde in the feld of Egipte. And Mofes ſtretched
out his rodd vnto heauen, and the Lorde thondered
and hayled ſo that the fyre ran a longe vppon the
grounde. And the Lorde ſo hayled in the lōde of
24 Egipte, that there was hayle ād fyre mēgled with
the hayle, ſo greuous, that there was none foch in all
the londe of Egipte, fence people inhabited it.
25   And the hayle fmote in the londe of Egip- [Fo.

V. 14 mittam omnes plagas meas 16 Idcirco autem pofui te
18 pluam . . . grandinem 23 discurrentia fulgura fuper terram
24 ignis mifta pariter ferebantur . . ex quo gens illa condita eſt.
L. 14 alle meyne plagen . . fenden 16 Doch darumb hab ich
dich erweckt 18 hagel regen laſſen 23 fewr auff die erden fchoſz.
24 hagel vnd fewr vntereinander furen . . der zeyt leut drynnen
geweſen find.

XVI.] te all that was in the felde: both man and beeſt
And the hayle ſmote all the herbes of the feld and
26 broke all the trees of the felde: only in the lande of
Goſan where the childern of Iſraell were, was there
27 no hayle. And Pharao ſent ãd called for Moſes and
Aaron, and ſayde vnto thē: I haue now ſynned, the
Lorde is rightwes and I and my people are weked.
28 Praye ye vnto the Lorde, that the thonder of God and
hayle maye ceaſe, and I will let you goo, and ye ſhall
tarie no longer.

29 And Moſes ſayde vnto him: aſſoone as I am out of
the citie, I will ſprede abrode my handes vnto the
Lorde, and the thunder ſhall ceaſſe, nether ſhall there
be any moare hayle: that thou mayſt knowe, howe that
30 the erth ys the Lordes, But I knowe that thou and
31 thy ſervauntes yet feare not the Lord God. The flaxe
ãd the barly were ſmyttē, for the barly was ſhott vp
32 ãd the flaxe was boulled: but the whete boulled, *ſwol-*
and the rye were not ſmeten, for they *len, i. e. grown
into buds*
were late ſowne.

33 And Moſes went out of the citie frõ Pharao ãd
ſprede abrode his handes vnto the Lorde, and the
thunder and hayle ceaſed, nether rayned it any moare
34 vppon the erth. whē Pharao ſawe that the rayne and
the hayle and thunder were ceaſed, he ſynned agayn
ãd hardened .P. his herte: both he and his ſervauntes.
35 So was the herte of Pharao hardened, that he wolde
not let the childern of Iſrael goo, as the Lord had
ſayde by Moſes.

   𝖁. 25 lignum regionis 28 vt deſinant tonitrua dei 31 hordeum
eſſet virens
   𝕷. 25 bewm auff dē feld 28 gnug ſey des donnern Gotes
31 gerſten geſchoſſet .. knotten gewunnen
   𝔐. 𝔐. 𝔑. 27 *To be weked*, is: to be without the knowledge
& felynge of the goodnes of God and without hope to receaue any
goodnes at his hande: ſo that we cannot paciently here any of
his truthes nor beleue thē nether ſoffer thē to be taught to other,
as it apereth in all the pſalmes & in Eſa. lvii, d.

⁋ The .X. Chapter.

1 THE Lorde fayde vnto Mofes: goo vnto Pharao, neuertheleffe I haue hardened his harte and the hertes of his feruauntes, that I mighte fhewe thefe my fygnes among- 2 eft thē and that thou tell in the audience of thy fonne and of thy fonnes fonne, the pagiantes which I haue played in Egipte ād the miracles which I haue done amonge them: that ye may knowe how that I am the Lorde.

M.E.S. The heart of Pharao is hardened of God. The grefhoppers. The thicke darcknes.

pagiantes, feats, exploits

3 Than Mofes ād Aaron went in vnto Pharao and fayde vnto him: thus fayth the Lorde God of the Hebrues: how longe fhall it be, or thou wilt fubmyt thy felfe vnto me? Let my people goo that they 4 maye ferue me. Yf thou wilt not let my people goo: beholde, tomorow will I brynge grefhoppers in to thy 5 lande, and they fhall couer the face of the erth that it can not be fene, ād they fhall eate the refidue which remayneth vnto you and efcaped the hayle and they 6 fhall eate all your grene trees vpon the felde, and they fhall fill thy houffes and all thy feruauntes houffes, and the houffes of all the Egiptiās after foch a maner: as nether thy [Fo. *omitted.*] fathers nor thy fathers fathers haue fene, fence the tyme they were apon the erthe vnto thys daye. And he turned him filfe aboute, ād went out from Pharao.

7 And Pharaos feruauntes fayde vnto hym: Howe longe fhall this felowe thus plage vs? Let the men goo that they maye ferue the Lorde their God, or els 8 wilt thou fee Egipte firft deftroyed? And than Mofes and

M. 7 How lōge fhall we be thus euell intreated?... God: wilt thou not yet knowe that Egypt is deftroyed?

V. 2 in auribus .. quoties contriuerim 5 ne quicquam eius appareat .. refiduum fuerit .. ligna, quæ germinant 7 patiemur hoc fcandalum?

L. 2 fur den oren .. getrieben hab 5 land nicht fehen kunde .. vberig vnd erredtet ... grünende bewm 7 das wefen verftricken?

Aaron were brought agayn vnto Pharao, and he fayde vnto them: Goo and ferue the Lorde youre God but
9 who are they that fhall goo? And Mofes anfwered: we muft goo with yonge and olde: ye and with our fonnes and with oure doughters, ãd with our fhepe and oxẽ muft we goo   For we muft holde a feaft vnto the Lorde.
10 And he fayde vnto them: fhall it be foo? The Lorde be with you, fhulde I lett you goo, and youre childern alfo? Take heede, for ye haue fome myfchefe
11 in honde. Nay not fo: but goo ye that are men and ferue the Lorde, for that was youre defyre. And they thruft thẽ out of Pharaos prefence.
12 And the Lorde fayde vnto Mofes: Stretch out thine hande ouer the lande of Egipte for grefhoppers, that they come apon the lande of Egipte and eate all the herbes of the londe, ãd all that the hayle left vn-
13 touched. And Mofes .P. ftretched forth his rodd ouer the londe off Egipte, ãd the Lorde brought an eaft wynde vppõ the lande, all that daye and all nyghte. And in the mornynge the eaft wynde broughte the
14 grefhoppers, ãd the grefhoppers wẽt vp ouer all the lande of Egipte and lighted in all quarters off Egipte verye greuoufly: fo that before them were there no foch
15 grefhoppers, nether after them fhal be. And they couered all the face of the erth, fo that the londe was darke therwith. And they ate all the herbes of the lande and all the frutes of the trees which the hayle had lefte: fo that there was no grene thinge lefte in the trees and herbes of the felde thorow all the lande of Egipte.
16 Then Pharao called for Mofes and Aarõ in hafte and fayde: I haue fynned agaynft the Lorde youre God

M. 9 we wyll go 10 vnto them: let it be fo?
V. 9 eft enim folennitas domini 10 Sic dominus fit .. cui dubium eft quod peffime cogitetis? 13 induxit ventum vrentem 14 innumerabiles 16 Quam ob rem
L. 9 denn wyr haben eyn feft des Herrn. 10 Awe ia, der Herr fey mit euch .... Sehet da, ob yr nicht bofes fur habt? 13 treyb eynen Oftwind 14 fo feer viel 16 Da foddert
L. M. N. 11 Dife hawfchrecken heyffen hie nicht *Hagab* auß Ebreifch, wie an etlichen ortten, fondern *Arbe*, Es find aber vierfuffige fliegende thier vnd reyn zu effen, wie *Hagab* Leuit. xi. aber vnd vnbekand, on dz fie den hewfchrecken glaych find.

17 and agaynſt you. Forgeue me yet my ſynne only this once, and pray vnto the Lorde youre God that he maye
18 take awaye frō me this deth only. And he wēt out
19 frō Pharao ād prayd vnto the Lorde, ād the Lord turned the wynde in to a myghtie ſtronge weſt wynde, and it toke awaye the greſhoppers and caſt thē in to the reed ſee: ſo that there was not one greſhopper left
20 in all the coſtes of Egipte But the Lorde hardened Pharaos herte, ſo that he wold not let the childern off Iſrael goo
21 [Fo. XVII.] And the Lorde ſayde vnto Moſes: Stretch out thy hond vnto heauē ād let there be darckneſſe vppon the londe of Egipte: euē that thei
22 maye ſeale the darckneſſe. And Moſes ſtretched forth his hande vnto heauē, ād there was a darke myſt vppō
23 all the lande off Egipte .iii. dayes longe ſo that no mā ſawe another nether roſe vp frō the place where he was by the ſpace of .iii. dayes, but all the childrē of Iſrael had lighte where they dwelled.
24 Then Pharao called for Moſes and ſayde: goo and ſerue the Lorde, only let youre ſhepe. and youre oxen
25 abyde, but let youre childern go with you. And Moſes anſwered: thou muſt geue vs alſo offringes and burnt-offringes for to ſacrifice vnto the Lord oure God,
26 Oure catell therfore ſhall goo with vs, and there ſhall not one hooffe be left behinde, for therof muſt we take to ſerue the Lorde oure God. Moreouer we cā not knowe wherwith we ſhall ſerue the Lorde, vntyll we come thither.
27 But the Lorde hardened Pharaos herte, ſo that he

M. 19 greſhopper in all the coſtes 22 there was a thicke darcknes vpō
V. 19 flare fecit ventum ab occid., 21 vt palpare queant. 26 præſertim cum ignoremus
L. 19 wendet der Herr eyn ſeer ſtarcken Weſtwind 21 das mans greyffen mag 26 Auch wiſſen wyr nicht
M. M. N. 26 This was an outward ſeruyce, but the true and ryght ſeruyce of god, is to feare him as a father, to loue hym, kepe hys cōmaundementes and to commyt a mānes ſelſe holy to him, truſtynge in hys mercy only: ſetting al thought & care vpō him. And when we haue offended, to repēt and to be ſory, & knowledge oure offence & beleue that he will forgeue it vs, for his truthes ſake as 1 Pet. v, b. & Ps. xxxvi, a.

28 wold not let thē goo. And Pharao fayde vnto him: get the frō me ād take heade to thy felfe that thou fee my face no moare, For whē foeuer thou comeſt in my
29 fyghte, thou fhalt dye. And Mofes faide: let it be as thou haſt fayde: I will fee thy face no moare.

.P. ⁋ The .XI. Chapter.

1 AND the Lorde fayde vnto Mofes: yet wil I brynge one plage moare vppon Pharao and vppon Egipte, and after that he wyll lett you goo hence. And when he letteth you goo, he fhall vtterly dryue
2 you hence. But byd the people that euery man borowe of his neghbour and euery woman of hir neghboureffe: iewels off fyluer and iewels of golde.
3 And the Lorde gatt the people fauoure in the fyghte of the Egiptians. Moreouer Mofes was very great in the lande of Egipte: both in the fyghte of Pharao, and alfo in the fyghte of the people.

M.E.S. The Lorde comaundeth to troble the Egypcyans. The deth of all the fyrſt begotten in Egypt.

4 And Mofes fayde: thus fayth the Lorde. Aboute myd-
5 nyghte will I goo out amonge the Egiptians, and all the firſtborne in the lande of Egipte fhall dye: euen from the firſtborne off Pharao that fitteth on his feate, vnto the firſtborne of the maydefervaunte that is in the mylle,
6 and all the firſtborne of the catell. And there fhall be a great crye thorow out all the lande off Egipte: fo that
7 there was neuer none lyke nor fhall be. And among

V. 28 caue ne vltra videas faciem meam. xi, 1 dimittet vos, et exire compellet. 2 vt poſtulet 3 vir magnus valde 4 egrediar 5 ancillæ .. ad molam
L. 28 hut dich, das du nicht mehr fur meyn augen komſt. xi, 1 laffen von hynnen .. nicht alleyn alles laffen .. von hynnen treyben 2 gefefs foddere . 3 faſt eyn groffer man 4 ausgehen ynn 5 magd die hynder der mul iſt
M. M. N. 5 *To fyt*, is for to beare rule or to mynyſtre any maner of office, as in 1 Reg. ii, b.

all the childern of Israel shall not a dogg move his tongue, nor yet man or beest: that ye may knowe, how the Lorde putteth a difference betwene the Egiptias and Israel. And all these thy servauntes shal come downe vnto me, and fall before me ād saye [Fo. XVIII.] get the out and all the people that are vnder the, and than will I departe. And he went out from Pharao in a great anger.

And the Lorde sayde vnto Moses: Pharao shall not regarde you, that many wondres maye be wrought in the lande of Egipte, And Moses ād Arō dyd all these wondres before Pharao. But the Lorde hardened Pharaos herte, so that he wolde not let the childern of Israel goo out of his londe.

❡ The .XII. Chapter.

AND the Lorde spake vnto Moses and Aaron in the londe of Egipte saynge: This moneth shall be youre chefe moneth: euē the first moneth of the yere shal it be vnto you Speake ye vnto all the felowshipe of Israel saynge: that they take the x. daye of this moneth to euery housholde, a shepe. Yf the housholde be to few for a shepe, then lett him and his neghbour that is nexte vnto his house, take acordinge to the

That I here cal a shepe is in Ebrue a vvorde indifferent to a shepe and a gotte both.

M.C.S. *The passeouer is eaten. The swete brede. They must teache their chyldren what the passeouer signyfyeth. The destruccyō of the fyrst begottē in Egypt. The robbery of the Egypcians. The goynge oute of the Israelytes.*

M. 8 And these thy seruaūtes xii, 2 euen of the fyrst moneth
V. 7 non mutiet canis ab homine vsque ad pecus; ... quanto miraculo diuidat 10 signa et ostenta quæ scripta sunt. xii, 2 principium mensium .. cœtum 3 agnum 4 animarum quæ sufficere possunt ad esum agni
L. 7 hund mit seyner zungen lippern .. wie .. Æg. vnd Israel scheyde xii, 3 eyn schaff 4 vnd rechnets aus, was eyn iglicher essen muge
M. M. N. 8 A soudayne chaunge of speakyng to dyuerse personnes, as in the Psal. xv, a. and thys is referred to the ende of the chapter that goeth before. xii, 3 That is here called a *shepe* is in Ebrew a worde indifferent to be takē ether for shepe or gote.

nombre of foulles, and counte vnto a fhepe acordinge
5 to euery mans eatinge. A fhepe with out fpott and
a male of one yere olde fhall it be, and from amonge
the lambes ād the gootes fhall ye take it.

6 And ye fhall kepe him in warde, vntyll *in ward, in separate confinement*
the .xiiii. daye of the fame moneth. And
euery mā of the multitude of Ifrael fhall
7 kyll him abou- .P. te euē. And they fhall take of the
bloud ād ftrike on the .ii. fyde poftes ād on the vpper
8 dorpoft of the houfes, wher ī they eate hī. And thei
fhall eate the flefh the fame nyght, roft with fyre,
ād with vnleuēded bread, ād with fowre *fowre, bitter*
9 herbes they fhall eate it. Se that ye eate not therof
fodē in water, but roft with fyre: both head fete, ād
10 purtenance together. And fe that ye let nothinge
of it remayne vnto the mornynge: yf oughte remayne
burne it with fyre.

11 Off this maner fhall ye eate it: with youre loines
girded, ād fhoes on youre fete, ād youre ftaves in
youre handes. And ye fhall eate it in hafte, for it
12 is the Lordes *paffeouer, for I will go *The lambe vvas called paffeouer that the very name itſelf ſhuld put thē in remēbrauncevvhat it ſignified, for the ſignes that god ordined*
aboute ī the lāde of Egipte this fame
nyghte, ād will fmyte all the firftborne
in the lande off Egipte: both of mā
ād beeft, ād apō al the goddes off
Egipte will I the Lorde do execution.
13 And the bloude fhall be vnto you a

M̃. 6 fhall kepe hym in, vntyll 9 therof rawe ner foden in water, but roft with fyre: both the head

V̄. 5 Iuxta quem ritum tolletis & hœdum 6 vniuerfa multitudo 8 affas agni, & azymos panes cum lactucis agreftibus 9 crudum quid, nec coctum aqua, fed affum tantum igni: caput cum pedibus eius & inteftinis vorabitis. 11 eft enim phafe, id eft tranfitus domini. 12 faciam iudicia, ego dominus.

L. 5 lemmern vnd zigen 8 mit bitter falzen 9 mit feynen fchenckeln vnd eyngeweyde 12 gerichte vben

M̃. M̃. N. 12 The *lambe* was called the *paſſeouer:* that the very name it felfe fhulde kepe in memorye what was fignyfyed therby, which phrafe & maner of fpeakynge the fcripture vfeth often, callynge the figne by the name of the thynge that it fygnyfieth, as Gen. xvi, b.

L. M̃. N. 6 Was das ofterlamb bedeut, leret gnugfam. S. Paulus. 1 Cor. 5. da er fpricht, vnfer ofterlamb is Chriftus der geopffert ift.

tokē vppon the houses where in ye are, *ether signified*
for whē I see the bloude, I will passe ouer *the benefites*
you, ād the plage shall not be vppō you *myses to come*
to destroye you, when I smyte the londe *ād vvere not*
off Egipte. *dōme as are*
the signes of
14 And this daye shall be vnto you a re- *oure domme*
mēbraunce, ād ye shall kepe it holie vnto *God the Pope.*
the Lorde: euen thorow out youre generacions after you
shall ye kepe it holie daye, that it be a custome for euer
15 vii. dayes shal ye eate vnlevēded bre- [Fo. XIX.] ed, so
that euen the first daye ye shall put awaye leuen out off
youre housses. For whosoeuer eateth leuended bread
from the first daye vntyll the .vii. daye, that soule shall be
16 plucked out frō Israel. The first daye shall be a holie
feast vnto you, and the .vii. also. There shal be no maner
off worke done in thē, saue aboute that only which euery
17 man must eate that only may ye do. And see that ye
kepe you to vnleuēded breed.
 For vppō that same daye I will brynge youre armyes
out off the londe of Egipte, therfore ye shall obserue
this daye and all youre childern after you, that yt be a
custume for euer.
18 The first moneth and the .xiiii. daye off the moneth
at euen, ye shall eate swete brede vnto the .xxi. daye
off the moneth at euen agayne.
19 Seuen dayes se that there be no leuended bred soūde
in youre housses. For whosoeuer eateth leuended bred,
that soule shall be roted out frō the multi- roted, *rooted*
tude of Israel: whether he be a straunger or borne in
20 the londe. Therfore se that ye eate no leuended bred,
but in all youre habitacions eate swete bred.
21 And Moses called for the elders off Israel and sayde
vnto them: chouse out and take to euery housholde a

 𝒱. 14 in monimentum . . cultu sempiterno. 16 sancta atque
solennis . . . . eadem sestiuitate venerabilis: 17 exercitum vestrum
19 de cœtu Israel 21 tollentes animal
 𝕷. 14 zum ewigen brauch 16 on was zur speys gehoret sur
allerley seelen 17 heer
 𝔐. 𝔐. 𝔑. 14 *Euer* is not here takē for a tyme without ende,
but for a longe ceason whose end is not determyned, as in Gen.
xiii, d. and Ex. xxviii, g.

22 ſhepe, ād kyll paſſeouer. And take a bunch of yſope, ād dyppe it in the bloud .P. that is in the baſyn, and ſtryke it vppon the vpperpoſte and on the .ii. ſyde poſtes, and ſe that none of you goo out at the doore
23 of his houſe vntyll the mornynge. For the Lorde will goo aboute and ſmyte Egipte. And when he ſeyth the bloude vppon the vpper doorpoſte ād on the .ii ſyde poſtes, he will paſſe ouer the doore and will not ſuffre the deſtroyer to come in to youre houſſe to plage
24 you. Therfore ſe that thou obſerue this thinge, that it be an ordinaunce to the, and thy ſonnes for euer.
25 And when ye be come in to the land which the Lorde will geue you acordinge as he hath promyſed,
26 ſe that ye kepe this ſeruice.* And when youre childern axe you what maner off
27 ſeruice is this ye doo. Ye ſhall ſaye, it is the ſacrifice of the Lordes paſſeouer which paſſed ouer the houſſes of the childern of Iſrael in Egipte, as he ſmote the Egiptians and ſaued oure houſſes. Than the people
28 bowed them ſelues and worſhipped. And the childern of Iſrael went and dyd as the Lorde had commaūded Moſes and Aaron.
29 And at mydnyghte the Lorde ſmote all the firſtborne in the lōde of Egipte: from the firſt borne of Pharao that ſatt on his ſeat, vnto the firſtborne of the captyue that was in preſone, and all firſt-
30 borne of the catell. Than Pharao [Fo. XX.] aroſe the ſame nyghte and al his ſervauntes ād all the Egiptians, and there was a great crieng thorowe out Egipte, for there was no houſſe where there was not one dead.

Oure ſignes be dōme, vve knovv not the reaſon of oure baptim: ye and vve muſt ſaye oure prayers ād oure beleſſe in a tōge vve vnderſtonde not. And yet yſ vve anſvvere not our prelates vvhen thei be angrie, euen as thei vvolde haue it, vve muſt to the fyre vvithout redemption, or forſvver god

V. 22 in limine ... oſtium domus 23 percuſſorem ... lædere. 25 obſeruabitis ceremonias iſtas 26 iſta religio ?
L. 23 verderber ... zu plagen 25 diſen dienſt 26 fur eyn dienſt?
M. M. N. 23 To paſſe ouer is a maner of ſpeache of the ſcrypture, & ſignyfieth no more, but that as he wolde plage the wycked, as he dyd here the Egypcyās, euē ſo he wold ſhew mercye to the ſaythfull, as he dyd to the Iſraelytes, as in Ex. xxxiii, d.

31 And he called vnto Moses and Aaron by nyghte saynge: Ryse vp and gett you out from amonge my people: both ye and also the children of Israel, and goo
32 and serue the Lorde as ye haue sayde. And take youre shepe and your oxen with you as ye haue sayde,
33 ād departe ād blesse me also. And the Egiptians were serce vppon the people and made haste to send thē out of the lād: for they sayde: we be al deed mē
34 And the people toke the dowe before it was sowered which they had in stoare, and bounde it in clothes
35 ād put it vpō their shulders And the childern of Israel dyd acordinge to the saynge of Moses: ād they borowed of the Egiptians: iewels of syluer, and iewels
36 of gold, and rayment. And the Lorde gat the people fauoure in the syghte of the Egiptians: ād so they bor-
37 owed and robbed the Egiptians.

Thus toke the childern of Israel their yourney frō Ra-
38 emses to suchoth .vi. hundred thousand mē of foote, besyde childern. And moch comon people went also with thē,
39 ād shepe ād oxen ād catell exceadinge moch. And they baked swete cakes of the dowe which they brou- .P. ghte out of Egipte, for it was not sowered: because they were thrust out of Egipte and coude not tarie, nether had they prepared them any other prouision of meate.
40 And the tyme of the dwellinge of the childern of Israel which they dwelled in Egipte, was .iiii. hundred
41 and .xxx. yere. And whē the .iiii. hundred and .xxx yeres were expyred, euē the selfe same daye departed all the hostes of the Lorde out of the lande of Egipte.
42 This is a nyghte to be obserued to the Lorde, becaufe he broughte them out of the lande of Egipte. This is a nyghte of. the Lorde, to be kepte of all the childern of Israel and of their generacions after them.
43 And the Lorde sayde vnto Moses ād Aaron, this is

М. Suchoth, margin: otherwyse Socoth
𝒱. 31 immolate domino 32 vt petieratis 35 vestemque plurimam 36 vt commodarent eis: & spoliauerunt 37 sexcenta sere millia peditum virorum 39 dudum de Æg., consperfam .. & nullam facere sinentibus moram
L. 32 wie yhr gesagt habt (*bis*) 33 versturtzt auff das volck 34 zu yhrer speyse 36 leyheten, vnd entwandtens 39 sonst keyne zehrung zubereyt.

the maner of Paſſeover: there ſhall no ſtraunger eate
44 there of, but all the ſeruauntes that are bought for
money ſhall ye circumciſe, and then let them eat
45 there of. A ſtraūger and a hyerd ſeruaunte ſhall not
46 eate thereof. In one houſſe ſhall it be eatē. Ye ſhall
carie none of the fleſh out at the doores: moreouer, ſe
47 that ye breke not a bone there of. All the multitude
48 of the childern of Iſrael ſhall obſerue it

Yf a ſtraunger dwell amonge you ād wyll holde Paſſeover vnto the Lorde, let him circūciſe all that be males, ād
thē let him come and [Fo.XXI.] obſerue it ād be takē as one
that is borne ī the lōde. No vncircūciſed perſone ſhall
49 eate there of. One maner of lawe ſhalbe vnto thē that
are borne in the lōde, ād vnto the ſtraūgers that dwell
50 amōge you. And all the childern of Iſrael dyd as the
51 Lorde cōmaūded Moſes ād Aarō. And euē the ſelfe
ſame daye dyd the Lorde brynge the childern of Iſrael
out of the londe of Egipte with their armies.

The .XIII. Chapter.

1 AND the Lorde ſpake vnto Moſes ſaynge: ſanctifie vnto me all the *M.C.S. The firſt begotten muſt be ſanctyſyed vnto the Lorde. The memoryall of their delyuer-*
2 firſtborne that opē all maner
matrices amōge the childern
of Iſrael, as well of mē as of beeſtes: for

V. 43 religio phaſe 47 cœtus 48 in veſtram voluerit tranſire colo-
niam 49 colono 51 per turmas ſuas. xiii, 2 Sanctifica . . . mea
ſunt enim omnia
L. 43 die weyſe 45 mietling 48 der beſchneytte 51 mit yhrem
heer.
M. M. N. 49 Thoſe that were borne in the lande, are only
thoſe that were borne amonge thē: not deſcendynge of the ſtocke
or lynage of Iſrael. And the ſtraungers were thoſe that dwelt
amōge the Iſraelites, and were not borne among thē, as aboue in
this ſame chapter at the letter .d. [i. e. v. 15 ſq.] xiii, 2. Sanctifyīg
loke Gene ii, a.
L. M. N. 43 *Paſſah*, heyſt eyn gang, darumb das der herr
ynn Egyptēland des nachts gieng, vnd ſchlug alle erſtegepurt
todt, bedeut aber Chriſtus ſterbē vn aufferſtehen, damit er von
diſer wellt gangen iſt, vnnd ynn dem ſelben ſund, tod, vnd teuffel
geſchlagen vnd vns aus dem rechten Egypten geſurt hat zum
vater, das iſt vnſer Paſſah oder oſtern

3 they are myne. And Moses sayde vnto the people: thinke on thys daye in which ye came out of Egipte and out of the housse of bondage: for with a myghtie hāde the Lorde broughte you out frō thēce. Se therfore that ye eate no leuended bred. *aunce. Why they were caryed thorow the wyldernes. The bones of Ioseph. The pyler of the clowde.*
4 This daye come ye out of Egipte in the moneth of Abib.
5 whē the Lorde hath broughte the ī to the lōde of the Canaanites, Hethites, Amorites, Heuites ād Iebusites, which he sware vnto thi fathers that he wolde geue the: a londe where in milke ād honye floweth, thē se that thou kepe this seruyce in this same moneth.
6 Seuē dayes thou shalte eate swete bred, ād the .vii
7 daye shal be feastfull vnto the Lorde. Therfore thou .P. shalt eate swete bred .vii. dayes, and se that there be no leuended bred sene nor yet leuē amonge you in all youre quarters.
8 And thou shalt shewe thy sonne at that tyme saynge: this is done, becaufe of that which the Lorde dyd vnto me
9 when I came out of Egipte. Therfore it shall be a signe vnto the vppon thine hande and a remembraunce betwene thine eyes, that the Lordes lawe maye be in thy mouth. For with a stronge hāde the Lorde
10 broughte the out of Egipte, se thou kepe therfore this ordinaūce in his seafon from yere to yere. *The fathers novv a dayes maye not be soffred to knovv ought of God them selves, hovv can they then teach their childern vvhat the cermonie meaneth.*

M. 9 hande a remembraūce
V. 4 mense nouarum frugum. 5 hunc morem sacrorum 7 in cunctis finibus tuis. 9 monimentum ante oculos .. semper sit in ore 10 statuto tempore a diebus in dies.
V. 7 an allen deynen ortten 8 son sagen 9 fur deynen augen.
M. M. N. 4 *Abib:* That is the moneth of Apryll. 9 *With a stronge hande:* Looke Psal. cxxxv, b.
L. M. N. 4 *Abib.* Abib ist der mond den wyr April heyssen, denn die Ebreer heben yhr new iar an nach der natur wenn alle ding widder new grunet and wechset vnd sich zichtiget, darumb heysst er auch Mensis nouorum, das denn alles new wirt. 6 *Ungesewrt brod.* So hart wyrt der sawerteyg verpoten, das man ia dz lautter Euangelion vnd Gottis gnade, nicht vnser werck vnd gesetz soll predigen nach der aufferstehung Christi, wie Paulus 1 Cor. v. auch zeygt, vnd ist solch essen nichts anders denn glawben ynn Christo.

11 Moreouer when the Lorde hath broughte the in to the londe of the Canaanytes, as he hath fworne vnto
12 the and to thi fathers, and hath geuen it the, thē thou fhalt appoynte vnto the Lorde all that openeth the matrice, and all the firft- borne among the beeftes which thou haft yf they be *appoynte, afsygn separate*
13 males. And all the firftborne of the affes, thou fhalt redeme with a fhepe: yf thou redeme him not, then breake hys necke. But all the firftborne amonge thi childern fhalt thou bye out.
14 And when thi fonne axeth the in tyme to come faynge: what is this? thou fhalt faye vnto him: with a mightie hande the Lorde broughte us out of Egipte, out of the houffe of bon- *Teach youre chyldern.*
15 [Fo. XXII.] dage. And when Pharao was looth to lete us goo, the Lorde flewe all the firftborne in the lande of Egipte: as well the firftborne of men as of beaftes. And therfore I facrifice vnto the Lorde all the males that open the matrice, but all the firftborne
16 of my childern I muft redeme. And this fhall be as a token in thine hande, and as a thinge hanged vpp be- twene thine eyes: becaufe the Lorde broughte vs out of Egipte with a mightie hande.
17 when Pharao had let the people goo, God caried them not thorow the londe of the Philiftines, though it were a nye waye. For God fayde: the people myghte happly repent when they fe warre, and fo
18 turne agayne to Egipte: therfore God led thē aboute thorow the wyldernesse that bordreth on the redd fee. The childern of Ifrael went harneffed out
19 of the lāde of Egipte. And Mofes toke *harneffed, armed*

ℳ. 12 matryce, all
𝒱. 12 feparabis .. confecrabis domino 13 mutabis oue ... interficies. 14 filius tuus cras 16 appenfum quid, ob recordationem, ante oculos 17 quæ vicina eft 18 & armati afcenderunt
ℒ. 13 lofen mit eynem fchaff ... brich yhm das genick 16 fur deynen augen 17 die am nehiften war 18 vmb, auff die ftraffe 18 gewapnet
ℒ. ℳ. N. 18 *Schilffmeer*. Die kriechen heyffen es, dz rote meer võ dem roten fand vnd boden, aber die Ebreer heyfens fchilffmeer von dem fchilff, vnd bedeut die welt mit yhrem pracht, dadurch die heyligen mit viel leyden gehen muffen.

the bones of Ioseph with him: for he made the childern of Israel swere saynge: God will surely vyset you, take my bones therfore away hence with you,

20 And they toke their iorney from Suchoth: and pitched their tentes in Etham in the edge of the wyl-
21 dernesse. And the Lorde went before them by daye in a piler of a cloude to lede them the waye: and by nyghte in a piler of fyre to geue thē lighte: that they
22 myghte goo both .P. by day ād nyghte. And the piler of the cloude neuer departed by daye nor the piler of fyre by nyghte out of the peoples sighte.

The .XIIII. Chapter.

1 THAN the Lorde spake vnto
2 Moses saynge: byd the chil- dern of Israel that they turne and pytch their tentes before the entrynge of Hiroth betwene Migdole and the se toward Baal zephon: euen before that shall ye pytch apon the see.
3 For Pharao will saye of the childern of Israel: they are tagled in the lōd the
4 wildernesse hath shott thē in. And I will hardē his harte, that he shall folowe after thē, that I maye gett me honoure vppō Pharao ād vppō all his hoste, that the Egiptians maye knowe that I am the Lorde. And they dyd euen so.

M.C.S. Pharaos heart is hardened & soloweth the Israelites with all his hooft & capitaynes and is drowned. The Israelites grudge. They go thorow the red see.

5 And whē it was tolde the kynge of Egipte that the people fled, thā Pharaos harte and all his seruaūtes turned vnto the people ād sayde why haue we this done, that we haue let Israel go out of oure seruyce?

V. 20 in extremis finibus solitudinis. 21 ignis: vt dux esset itineris vtroque tempore. xiiii, 2 eregione Phi-hahiroth .. Magdalum .. mare contra Beel-sephon 3 Coartati 5 immutatumque .. super populum.
L. 20 forn an der wusten 22 die wolckseule vnd fewrs. weych nymer von dem volck. xiiii, 2 gegen dem tall Hiroth 3 wissen nicht wo aus 5 verwandelt ... gegen

6 and he made redie his charettes ād toke his people
7 with hym ād toke .vi. hūdred chosen charettes ād all the charettes of Egipte ād captaynes vppō all his
8 people. For the Lorde hardened the harte of Pharao kynge of Egipte, that he folowed after the childern of Israel which for all that went out thorow an hye hāde,
9 And the Egiptiās folo- [*Fo. XXV.] wed after thē ād ouertoke thē where they pitched by the see, with all the horsses ād charrettes of Pharao ād with his horsse- mē ād his hoste: euē fast by the entrynge
10 of Hiroth before Baal Zephon. And Pharao drewe nye, ād whē the childern of Israel lyft vp their eyes and sawe how the Egiptiās folowed after thē, they were sore a fraide ād cried out vnto the Lorde

* *Folios XXIII, XXIIII are wanting in the original; a typographical error without a break in the text.*

11 Thā sayde they vnto Moses? were there no graues for us in Egipte, but thou must bringe us awaye   *
for to dye in the wyldernesse? wherfore hast thou serued
12 us thus, for to carie us out of Egipte? Dyd we not tell the this in Egipte saynge, let us be in rest and serue the Egiptians? For it had bene better for us to haue serued the Egiptians, than for to dye in the wildernesse.
13 And Moses sayde vnto the people: feare ye not but stonde still and beholde how the Lorde shall saue you this daye: For as ye se the Egiptians this daye, shall ye
14 see them nomore for euer till the worldes ende. The Lorde shall fighte for you and ye shall holde youre peace.
15 The Lorde sayde vnto Moses: wherfore criest thou

V. 6 Iunxit ergo currum 7 duces totius exercitus. 9 vestigia præcedentium 13 Nolite timere: state & videte magnalia domini 14 & vos tacebitis. 15 vt proficiscantur.

L. 6 spannet ... an 8 die doch durch eyn hohe hand 14 yhr werdet styll schweygen.

M. M. N. 9 *An hye hande:* Loke in Psalme. cxxxv, b. 14 *Ye shall holde youre peace:* that is, ye shall be in rest and quyetnes. 15 *To crye vnto the Lorde*, is to praye vnto him wyth full harte & seruēt desyer, as Moses here dyd, & yet spake neuer a worde. And so doth this word cryenge & makynge of noyes sygnifye thorow oute all the Psalmes, as in Psal. v, a. & ix, b &c.

L. M. N. 15 *Was schreyestu:* merck hie eyn treflich exempel, wie der glawbe, kempft zappelt vnd schreyet ynn notten vnd ferlickeyt, vnd wie er sich an Gottis word blos hellt, vnd von Gott trost empfehet vnd vberwindt.

vnto me? fpeake vnto the childern of Ifrael that they
16 goo forwarde. But lifte thou vp thi rodd and ftretch
out thi hande ouer the fee and deuyde it a fondre, that
.¶. the childern of Ifrael may goo on drye groũde
17 thorow the myddeft thereof. And beholde I will
harden the hertes of the Egiptians that they maye
folowe you. And I will gett me honoure vpon Pharao
and vpon all his hofte, vpon his charettes ād vpon his
18 horfe mē. And the Egiptians fhall knowe that I am
the Lord whan I haue gotten me honoure vpō Pharao
vpon his charettes and vpon his horfemen.

19 And the angell of God which went before the hofte
of Ifrael, remoued ād went behinde them. And the
cloudēpiler that was before them remoued ād ftode
20 behinde them ād wēt betwene the hofte of the Egiptians ād the hofte of Ifrael. Yt was a darke clowde,
and gaue lighte by nyghte: fo that all the nyghte long
the one coude not come at the other.

21 when now Mofes ftretched forth his honde ouer the
fee, the Lorde caried awaye the fee with a ftronge eaft
wynde that blewe all nyghte, and made the fee drie
22 londe ād the water deuyded it filfe. And the childern
of Ifrael went in thorow the myddeft of the fee vppon
the drie grounde. And the water was a walle vnto
them, both on their right hande ād on their lefte hande.
23 And the Egiptians folowed ād went in after them to
the myddeft of the fee, with all Pharaos horfes, and
his charettes and [Fo. XXVI.] his horffemen.

24 And in the mornynge watch, the Lorde loked vnto
the hofte of the Egiptiās out of the fyery and clowdie
25 piler, and troubled their hofte and fmote of their charett wheles and caft them doune to the grounde. Than
fayde the Egiptians: Let vs fle from Ifrael, for the
26 Lorde fyghteth for them agaynft vs. Than fayde the
Lorde vnto Mofes: ftretch out thine hand ouer the fee,
that the water maye come agayne vppō the Egiptians

V. 20 ad feinuicem ... accedere non valerent. 21 flante vento
vehementi & vrente 24 interfecit exercitum eorum 25 fereban-
turque in profundum.
L. 24 fchuttert jr getzellte 25 fturtzet fie mit vngeftüm

27 vppon their charettes ād horſemen. Than ſtretched forth Moſes his hande ouer the ſee, and it came agayne to his courſe erly ī the mornīg, ād the Egiptiās fledd agaynſt it. Thus the Lorde ouerthrewe the Egiptians
28 in the middeſt of the ſee, ād the water returned and couered the charettes and the horſemē: ſo that of all the hoſte of Pharao that came in to the ſee after them, there remayned not one.
29 But the children of Iſrael went vpon drie lōde in the myddeſt of the ſee, ād the water was a walle vnto them: both on the righte hand of them and alſo on the lifte.
30 Thus the Lorde delyuered Iſrael the ſelfe ſame daye out of the honde of the Egiptians, and Iſraell ſawe the
31 Egiptians deade vpō the ſee ſyde. And when Iſrael ſawe that myghtye .P. hande which the Lorde had ſhewed vppō the Egiptians, they feared the Lorde: and beleued both the Lorde and alſo his ſervaunte Moſes

¶ The .XV. Chapter.

1 THEN Moſes and the childern off Iſrael ſange this ſonge vnto the Lorde ād ſaide
   Let vs ſynge vnto the Lorde, for he is become glorious, the horſe and him that rode vpon him hath he ouerthrowne in the ſee.

M.C.S. Moſes and the people wyth the wemen ſynge. At the prayer of Moſes, the bytter waters were ſwete. God muſt be heared. They come to Elim.

2 The Lorde is my ſtrength ād my ſonge, ād is become my ſaluation.
   He is my God and I will glorifie him, he is my fathers God and I will lifte him vp an hie
3 The Lorde is a mā off warre, Iehouah ys his name:
4 Pharaos charettes ād his hoſte hath he caſt in to the ſee.

    V. 1 glorioſe enim magnificatus 3 quaſi vir pugnator
    L. 30 Egypter hand, vnd ſie ſahen 31 das volck forchtet xv, 3 rechts kriegsman

His iolye captaynes are drowned in the   iolye, *spir-*
5 red fee, the depe waters haue couered *ited, brave*
them: thei foncke to the botome as a ftone.
6 Thine hande Lorde is glorious in power, thine hād
Lord hath all to dafhed the enemye.   to dafhed,
7 And with thy great glorie thou haft *thruft through*
deftroyed thine aduerfaries, thou fenteft forth thy
wrath ād it confumed them: euē as ftobell.
8 with the breth off thine anger the water gathered
together and the flodes ftode ftyll as a rocke ād the
depe water congeled together in the myddeft off the
fee.
9 [Fo. XXVII.] The enymye fayde, I will folowe and
ouertake thē ād will deuyde the fpoyle: I will fatyffie
my luft apon thē: I will drawe my fwerde and myne
hand fhall deftroye them.
10 Thou blueft with thy breth ād the fee couered thē,
11 and they fanke as leed in the myghtye waters. ❡ who
is like vnto the o Lord amōge goddes: who is like
the fo glorious in holynes, feerfull, laudable ād that
fheweft wondres?
12 Thou ftretchedeft out thy righte hande. ād the erth
fwalowed them.
13 And thou cariedeft with thy mercie this people
which thou deliueredeft, ād broughteft thē with thy
ftrength vnto thy holie habitacion.
14 The nations herde ād were afrayde, pāges came
vpon the Philiftines.
15 Thā the dukes of the Edomites were amafed,
ād trēblinge came apon the myghtieft off the Moabites, and all the inhabiters of Canaā waxed faynte
harted.

V. 4 electi principes 6 magnificata eft in fortitudine: dextera
tua .. percuffit 7 depofuifti 8 fpiritu furoris tui .. ftetit vnda fluens
9 euaginabo gladium 10 Flauit fpiritus tuus .. aquis vehementi-
bus. 11 fimilis tui in fortibus .. terribilis atque laudabilis, faciens
mirabilia? 13 Dux fuifti in mifer. 14 Afcenderunt populi (Heb.
audierunt) 15 conturbati funt principes Edom .. obriguerunt
L. 4 auserwelten hawbtleut 7 deine widderwertigen zuftoffen
8 geyft deyns zorns ... tieffe plumpten ynn eynander 9 mut an
yhn kulen. 11 loblich vnd wunderthettig? 13 geleyttet .. heyligen
haufe. 15 Canaan .. feyg.

16 Let feare and dreade fall apon thē thorow the greatneſſe off thyne arme, and let them be as ſtyll as a ſtone, while thy people paſſe thorow o Lorde while the people paſſe thorowe, which thou haſt goten. goten, ac-
17 Brynge them in and plante them in *quired* the mountayns of thine enherytaūce, the place Lorde whyche thou haſt made for the to dweld in .⁋. the ſanctuarye Lorde which thy handes haue prepared.
18 The Lorde raygne euer and allwaye.
19 For Pharao wēt in an horſebacke wyth his charettes and horſemen in to the ſee, and the Lorde broughte the waters of the ſee apō thē. And the childern of Iſrael went on drie lande thorow the myddeſt of the ſee.
20 And mir Iam a prophetiſſe the ſiſter of Aaron toke a tymbrell in hir hande, and all the wemen came out
21 after her with tymbrells in a daunſe. And mir Iam ſange before them: ſyng ye vnto the Lorde, for he is become glorious in deade: the horſe and his ryder hath he ouerthrowne in the ſee.
22 Moſes broughte Iſrael from the redd ſee, ād they went out in to the wilderneſſe of Sur.

And they went thre dayes longe in the wilderneſſe
23 ād coude finde no water. At the laſt they came to Mara: but they coude not drynke off the waters for bitterneſſe, for they were better. therfore the name of the place
24 was called Mara. Then the people mur-   ⁕
mured agaynſt Moſes ſaynge: what ſhall we drinke?
25 And Moſes cried vnto the Lorde and he ſhewed him a tre: and he caſt it in to the water, and they waxed ſwete.

𝔐. 17 made for to dwell in, 25 waters
V. 16 formido et pauor .. donec pertranſeat 17 plantabis .. ſanctuarium tuum .. firmauerunt 18 in æternum & vltra. 20 Maria prophetiſſa .. tympanis & choris 23 vnde & congruum loco nomen impoſuit, vocans illum Mara, id eſt amaritudinem.
𝔏. 16 erſtarren wie die ſteyne .. erworben haſt. 17 hand bereyt hat. 20 Mir Iam 23 Mararath .. faſt bitter
𝔐. 𝔐. N. 16 *Greatneſſe of thyne arme:* Loke in Iob xl, a. 18 *To raygne euer & all waye* is a maner of ſpeaking of the ebrews, which ſignifieth without ende: becauſe that euer is taken for a lōg tyme whoſe ende is not apoynted, & not for all waye, as in Exod. xii, c.
𝔏. 𝔐. N. 23 *Mara* heyſt bitter Und bedeut leyden vnd anfechtunge, wilche durch das creutz, Chriſti, ym glauben auch ſuſſe werden. Math. xi. Meyn ioch iſt ſufs.

There he made them an ordinaunce and a [Fo. XXVIII.] lawe, and there he tempted them and faide:
26 Yf ye will herken vnto the voyce of the Lord youre God, and will do that which is righte in his fyght and will geue an eare vnto his cōmaūdmentes, and kepe all his ordinaunces: thā will I put none of this difeafes apon the whiche I brought vpon the Egiptiās: for I am the Lorde thy furgione.

furgione, phyſician, healer

Vve muſt do that vvhich is right in gods fight ād as his vvorde teacheth vs and not aftir our avvne imaginacion,

¶ The .XVI. Chapter.

27 AND they came to Elim where were .xii. welles of water and .Lxx. date trees, and they pitched there by the water.
XVI,1 And they toke their yourney frō Elim, and all the hole cōpanye of the childern of Ifraell came to the wildernesse of Sin, which lieth betwene Elim ād Sinai: the .xv. daye of the feconde moneth after that they were come out of the lande of
2 Egipte. And the hole multitude of the childern of Ifrael murmured agaynst Mofes ād Aarō in
3 the wilderneffe and fayde vnto them: wold to God we had dyed by the hande of the Lorde in the lande of Egipte, when we fatt by the flesh pottes and ate bred oure belies full for ye haue broughte vs out in to this wildernesse to kyll this hole multitude for honger.
4 Than fayde the Lorde vnto Mofes: beholde, I will rayne bred frō heauē doune to you, ād let the people

M.C.S. The Ifraelites come into the defert of Sin. It rayneth quaylles & Manna. They grudge.

𝔐. 26 of thefe difeafes
𝒱. 26 cunctum langorem .. fanator tuus. xvi, 3 Vtinam mortui effemus .. ollas carnium .. panem in faturitate .. occider. omnem multitudinem fame ?
𝕷. 26 kranckeyt keyne .. artzt. xvi, 3 Wollt Gott .. bey den fleyfch topffen .. die gantze gemeyne
𝔐. 𝔐. N. 26 We muft *do that whych is right* in gods fyght & as hys worde teacheth vs, & not after our awne ymagynacyon.

goo out ād gather daye by da- .℣. ye, that I maye
proue thē whether they wil walke in my lawe or no.
5 The .vi. daye let thē prepare that which they will
brīge in, ād let it be twife as moch as they gather in
6 dayly. And Mofes ād Aarō fayde vnto all the childerē of Ifrael: at euen ye fhall knowe that it is the
Lorde, which broughte you out of the lāde of Egipte
7 ād in the mornynge ye fhall fe the glorie of the Lorde:
becaufe he hath herde youre grudgynges agaynft the
Lorde: for what are we, that ye fhuld murmure againft
8 vs. And moreouer fpake Mofes. At euē the Lorde
will geue you flefh to eate ād in the mornynge bred
ynough, becaufe the Lord hath herde youre murmur
whiche ye murmur agaynft hī: for what ar we? youre
murmurynge is not agaynft vs, but agaynft the Lorde.
9 And Mofes fpake vnto Aarō: Say vnto all the cōpanye of the childerē of Ifrael, come forth before the
10 Lorde, for he hath herde youre grudgīges. And as
Aarō fpake vnto the hole multitude of the childerē
of Ifrael, they loked toward the wilderneffe: ād beholde, the glorie of the Lord apeared ī a clowde.
11, 12 And the Lorde fpake vnto Mofes fayng: I haue
herde the murmurīg of the childrē of Ifrael, tell thē
therfore ād faye that at euē they fhall eate flefh, ād
ī the morninge they fhall be filled with bred, ād [Fo.
XXIX.] ye fhall knowe that I am the Lorde youre
god
13 And at euē the quayles came ād couered the groūde
where they laye. And in the mornynge the dewe laye
14 rounde aboute the hofte. And whē the dewe was fallē:
behold, it laye apō the grounde in the wilderneffe,
fmall ād roūde ād thyn as the hore froft on the groūde.
15 when the childrē of Ifrael fawe it, they fayde one to

𝔐. 6 at euen ye fhall
℣. 5 parent 8 panes in faturitate 14 minutum, & quafi pilo tufum
𝔏. 5 bereytten 12 zwifchen dem abent 13 bedeckten die getzellte
𝔐. 𝔐. N. 7 *The glory of the Lorde* is here taken for the bryghtnes and lyght that was fene in the clowde. Of whiche glorye the Apoftle maketh mencyon 2 Cor. iii, c. d.

another: what is this? for they wift not what it was
And Mofes fayde: this is the breed which the Lorde
16 hath geuē you to eate. This is the thinge which the
Lorde hath cōmaūded, that ye gather euery mā ynough
for hī to eate: a gomer full for a mā acordīge to the
nōbre off you, ād gather euery mā for thē which are in
his tente.

17 And the childern of Ifrael dyd euen fo, ād gathered
18 fome more fome leffe, and dyd mete it with a gomer.
And vnto him that had gathered moch remayned
nothinge ouer, ād vnto hī that had gathered litle was
there no lacke: but euery mā had gathered fufficiēt for
19 his eatinge. And Mofes fayde vnto them. Se that
no mā let oughte remayne of it tyll the morninge.
20 Notwithftondinge they harkened not vnto Mofes: but
fome of thē lefte of it vntyll the mornynge, and it
waxte full of wormes ād ftāke and Mofes was angrie
wyth them.

21 And they gathered it all morniges: Euery mā .P.
as moch as fuffifed for his eatinge, for as fone as the
22 hete of the fonne came it moulte. And moulte, *melted*
the .vi. daye they gathered twife fo moch bred: .ii
gomers for one mā, ād the ruelars of the multitude
23 came ād tolde Mofes. And he fayde unto thē, this is
that which the Lorde hath fayde tomorow is the Sabbath of the holie reft of the Lord: bake that which ye
will bake ād feth that ye will feth, ād that which
remayneth lay vp for you ād kepe it till the mornynge.
24 And they layde it vp till the mornynge as Mofes bad
ād it ftāke not nether was there any wormes theri.
25 And Mofes fayde: that eate this daye: for todaye it
is the Lordes Sabbath: to daye ye fhal finde none in

𝒱. 15 ad inuicem, Man hu? quod fignificat, Quid eft hoc?
18 habuit amplius... reperit minus 21 incaluiffet fol, liquefiebat.
23 requies fabbathi fanctificata
𝐋. 16 zall der feelen ynn feyner hutten. 18 vbrigs .. feyls
23 der Sabbath der heyligen ruge des Herrn
𝐋. 𝕸. N. 15 *Man* heyft auff Ebreifch eyn gabe odder teyl,
bedeut das vns das Euangelion on vnfer verdienft vnd gedancken,
aus lautter gnaden von hymel geben wirt, wie dis Man auch
geben wart.

26 the feld, Sixte dayes ye fhal gather it, for the .vii. is the fabbath: there fhal be none there in.
27 Notwithftondinge there went out of the people in the feuenth daye for to gather: but they founde none.
28 Thē the Lorde feyde vnto Mofes: how longe fhall it be, yer ye will kepe my cōmaundmētes ād lawes?
29 Se becaufe the Lorde hath geuē you a Sabbath, therfor he geueth you the .vi. daye bred for .ii. dayes. Byde therfore euery mā athome, ād let no mā go out
30 of his place the feuenth daye. And the people refted
31 the feuenth daye. And the houffe of Ifrael called it Man, And it was lyke vnto Coriander [Fo. XXX.] feed and white, and the tafte of it was lyke vnto wafers made with honye.
32 And Mofes fayde: this is that which the Lord commaundeth: fyll a Gomor of it, that it maye be kepte for youre childern after you: that they maye fe the bred wherewith he fedd you in wyldernesse, when he had *Reliques ought to be but a remembraunce only.*
33 broughte you out of the lande of Egipte. And Mofes fpake vnto Aaron: take a crufe and put a Gomer full of man therin, and laye it vppe before the Lorde to be
34 kepte for youre childern after you as the Lorde commaunded Mofes. And Aaron layed it vppe before the teftimonye there to be kepte.
35 And the childern of Ifrael ate man .xl. yere vntill they came vnto a lande inhabited. And fo they ate Man, euen vntill they came vnto the bordres of the
36 lāde of Canaan, And a Gomer is the tenth parte of an Epha.

𝔐. 26 Sixe dayes
𝒱. 28 Vfquequo non vultis 31 fimilæ cū melle. 34 in tabern. referuandum. 35 in terram habitabilem
𝑳. 31 femlen mit honig. 33 kruglin 34 fur dem zeugnis zu behalten.

The .XVII. Chapter.

1 AND all the companye of the childern of Ifrael went on their iourneys from the wilderneffe of Sin at the commaundment of the Lorde, and pitched in Raphidim: where was no water for the people to drynke. And the people 2 * chode with Mofes and fayde: geue us water to drynke. And Mofes fayde vnto them: why chyde ye with me, * and wherfore do .P. ye tempte the Lorde? 3 There the people thyrfted for water, and murmured agenft Mofes ād fayde: wherfore haft thou broughte us out of Egipte, to kyll us and oure childern and oure catell with thyrfte? 4 And Mofes cried vnto the Lorde faynge what fhal I do vnto this people? they be al moft redye to ftone 5 me. And the Lorde fayde vnto Mofes: goo before the people, and take with the of the elders of Ifrael: ād thi rod wherwith thou fmoteft the riuer, take in thine 6 hande and goo. Beholde, I will ftonde there before the vppon a rocke in Horeb: and thou fhalt fmyte the rocke, ād there fhall come water out there of, that the people maye drynke. And Mofes dyd euen fo 7 before the elders of Ifrael   And he called the name of the place: Maffa and Meriba: becaufe of the chidynge of the childern of Ifrael, and becaufe they tempted the Lorde faynge: ys the Lorde amonge us or not? 8 Then came Amalech ād foughte with Ifrael in Ra-

M.C.S. The Ifraelites come into Raphidim. They grudge. Water is geuë them out of the rocke. Mofes holdeth vp his handes & they ouercome the Amelechytes.

M. 4 all moft redye
V. 1 per manfiones fuas 2 iurgatus .. iurgamini 3 præ aquæ penuria: & murmurauit 6 coram te, ibi 7 Tentatio, propter iurgium (Hebr. & iurgium)
L. 1 tage reyfze 2 zanckten 3 murreten 6 dafelbs ftehen 7 Da hies man den ort, Maffa Meriba
M. M. N. 2 *To tempte the Lorde:* is to prouoke the Lorde to be angry with them as Sapiē. 1, a.
L. M. N. 7 *Maffa* heyft verfuchung. *Meriba* heyft zanck.

9 phidim. And Moses sayde vnto Iosua: chose out men and goo fighte with Amelech   Tomorow I will stonde on the toppe of the hyll and the rodd of God in myne
10 hande. And Iosua dyd as Moses bade him, and soughte with the Amalechites. And Moses, Aa- [Fo. XXXI.]
11 ron and Hur went vp to the toppe of the hyll. And when Moses helde vp his hande, Israel had the better. And when he late his hande doune, Amelech had the better.
12 when Moses handes were weery, they toke a stone and put it vnder him, and he satt doune there on. And Aaron and Hur stayed vpp his handes the one on the one syde and the other on the other syde. And his
13 handes were stedie vntill the sonne was doune. And Iosua discomfeted Amalech ād his people with the edge of his swerde.
14 And the Lorde sayde vnto Moses: write this for a remembraunce in a boke and tell it vnto Iosua, for I will put out the remembraunce of Amalech from vnder hea-
15 uen. And Moses made an alter ād called the name of it
16 *Iehouah Nissi, for he sayde: the hande is on the seate of the Lorde, that the Lorde will haue warre with Amalech thorow out all generations.

Iehouah nissi the Lorde is he that exalteth me.

V. 11 vincebat Israel: sin autem paululum remississet, superabat Amal. 12 ex vtraque parte ... non lassarentur 13 Fugauitque 14 trade auribus 15 Dominus exaltatio mea 16 manus solii domini & bellum domini erit

L. 11 lag .. oben 12 schweer .. auff iglicher seytten eyner .. hend gewiss 14 ynn die oren 16 durch eyn hand vnter Gottis schutz

M. M. N. 15 *Iehouah Nissi:* that is, the Lord is he that exalteth.

L. M. N. 12 *Gewiss*, das ist trew, das sie nicht seyleten noch abliesen wie eyn trewloser ablessit, bedeut aber, wie die werck des gesetzs vntreglich vnd vntuchtig find, wo sie nicht durch Christum ym glawben vnterhalten werden. 16 *Nissi*, heyst, mein zeychen, wie eyn panier, wappen odder senlin ym streyt ist, bedeut das Euangelion das auff geworffen wirt zum streyt zeichen, widder sund, fleysch, tod vnd teuffel.

The .XVIII. Chapter.

1 ETHRO the preſt of Madian Moſes father in lawe herde of all that God had done vnto Moſes and to Iſrael his people, how that the Lorde had broughte Iſrael out of Egipte. And he 2 toke Ziphora Moſes wyfe, P. after ſhe was ſente backe, 3 and hir .ii. ſonnes, of which the one was called Gerſon, for he ſayde: I haue bene an alient in a ſtraunge lande. 4 And the other was called Elieſar: for the God of my father was myne helpe ād delyuered me from the ſwerde of Pharao.

M.C.S. Iethros councell is receaued of Moſes.

5 And Iethro Moſes father in lawe came wyth his two ſonnes and his wife vnto Moſes in to the wilderneſſe: where he had pitched his tente by the mounte of God. 6 And he ſent worde to Moſes: I thi father in law Iethro am come to the, and thi wyfe alſo, and hir two ſonnes 7 with her. And Moſes went out to mete his father in lawe and dyd obeyſſaunce and kyſſed him, and they ſaluted etch other ād came in to the tente.

8 And Moſes tolde his father in lawe all that the Lorde had done vnto Pharao and to the Egiptians for Iſraels ſake, and all the trauayle that had happened them by the waye, and how the Lorde had delyuered 9 them. And Iethro reioeſed ouer all the good which the Lorde had done to Iſrael, and becauſe he had de-10 lyuered them out of the hande of the Egiptians. And Iethro ſayde: bleſſed be the Lorde which hath delyuered you out of the hande of the Egiptians ād out of the hande of Pharao, which hath delyuered his people from vnder the power of [Fo. XXXII.] the Egiptians. 11 Now I knowe that the Lorde is greater thē all goddes, 12 for becauſe that they dealte prowdly with them. And

V. 2 quam remiſerat 3 Gerſam, dicente patre 4 Deus enim, ait 7 ſe mutuo verbis pacificis . Cumque intraſſet 8 vniuerſumque laborem 11 eo quod ſuperbe egerint contra illos.

L. 8 Muhe 10 der weys ſeyn volck 11 vermeſſen geweſen ſind an yhn

Iethro Moſes father in lawe offred burntoffrynges and ſacrifyces vnto God. And Aaron and all the elders of Iſrael came to eate bred with Moſes father in lawe before God.

13 And it chaunced on the morow, that Moſes ſatt to iudge the people, and the people ſtode aboute Moſes
14 from mornynge vnto euen. when his father in lawe ſawe all that he dyd vnto the people, he ſayde: what is this that thou doeſt vnto the people? why ſytteſt thou thi ſelf and letteſt all the people ſtonde aboute
15 the frõ mornynge vnto euen? And Moſes ſayde vnto his father in lawe: becauſe the people came vnto me
16 to ſeke councell of God. For whẽ they haue a matter, they come vnto me, and I muſt iudge betwene euery man and his neyboure, and muſt ſhewe them the ordinaũces of God and his lawes.

17 And his father in lawe ſayde vnto him: it is not
18 well that thou doſt. Thou doeſt vnwyſely and alſo this people that is with the: becauſe the thinge is to greuous for the, and thou art not able to do it thi ſelfe
19 alone. But heare my voyce, and I will geue the councell, and God ſhalbe with the. Be thou vnto the people to .P. Godwarde, and brynge the cauſes vnto God
20 and prouyde them ordinaunces and lawes, ãd ſhewe them the waye wherin they muſt walke and the werkes that they muſt doo.

21 Moreouer ſeke out amonge all the people, men of actiuite *which feare God and men that are true ãd hate covetuouſnes: and make them heedes ouer the people, captaynes ouer thouſandes, ouer hundredes, ouer fyf-
22 tie, and ouer ten. And let them iudge

Oure prelates nether feare God,for they preach not his vvorde truely:ner are leſſe covetouſe

𝒱. 13 qui aſſiſtebat 14 cur ſolus ſedes 16 vt iudicem inter eos 18 ſtulto labore cõſumeris .. vltra vires tuas 19 Eſto tu pop. in his quæ ad deum pertinent . 20 oſtendaſque pop. ceremonias & ritum colendi 21 tribunos & centuriones & quinquagenarios & decanos.

𝓛. 13 ſtund vmb 18 du thuſt nerricht .. ſchweer 21 redlichen leuten

𝕸. 𝕸. N. 21 The condicions that Iudges ſhuld haue. 22 To Iudge look in Gen. xlix, c.

the people at all feafons: Yf there beany *thē Iudas: for* greate matter, let them brynge that vnto *they haue re-* *ceaued of the* the, and let them iudge all fmall caufes *deuill the* them felues, and eafe thi felfe, ād let *kyngdomes*
23 them bere with the. Yf thou fhalt doo *of the erth* *and the glo-* this thinge, then thou fhalt be able to *rie thereof* endure that which God chargeth the with *vvhich chrift* *refufedMathe.* all, and all this people fhall goo to their *4.* places quietly.

24 And Mofes herde the voyce of his father in lawe,
25 and dyd all that he had fayde, and chofe actyue men out of all Ifrael and made them heedes ouer the people, captaynes ouer thoufandes, ouer hundreds, ouer
26 fiftie and ouer ten And they iudged the people at all feafons, ād broughte the harde caufes vnto Mofes:
27 and iudged all fmall maters them felues. And thā Mofes let his father in lawe departe, and he went in to his awne londe.

The .XIX. Chapter. [Fo. XXXIII.]

1 THE thyrde moneth after the *ᙏ.C.S. The* childern of Ifrael were gone *chyldren of* *Ifrael come to* out of Egipte: the fame daye *the mounte* they came in to the wilder- *Sinai. The* *people of God*
2 neffe of Sinai. For they were departed *are holy & a* from Raphidim, and were come to the *royall preft-* *hode. He that* deferte of Sinay and had pitched their *toucheth the* tentes in the wilderneffe. And there If- *hill dyeth.* *God appereth*
3 rael pitched before the mounte. And *vnto Mofes* Mofes went vpp vnto God. *vpon the*

V. 22 leuiufque fit tibi, partito in alios onere. 23 implebis imp. dei, & præc. eius poteris fuftentare... ad loca fua cum pace. 24 fuggefferat. 27 reuerfus abiit. xix, 2 in eodem loco.. eregione montis.

L. 23 mit friden an feynen ort. xix, 2 gegen dem berg

L. ᙏ. N. 24 Naturlich vernunft ift ynn weltlichen fachen zu handeln kluger, denn die heiligen leutte, wie Chriftus auch fagt Luc. 16. das die kinder difer wellt kluger find, denn die kinder des liechts. Darumb was vernunfft meyftern kan, da gibt Gott kein gefetz, fondern left die vernunfft, als feyn Creatur (datzu verordnet Gen. i.) hie handeln.

And the Lorde called to him out of *mounte in thonder &* the mountayne faynge: thus faye vnto *lyghtenyng.*
4 the houffe of Iacob and tell the childern of Ifrael, Ye haue fene what I dyd vnto the Egiptians and how I toke you vpp apon Egles wynges and haue broughte
5 you vnto my felfe. Now therfore yf ye will heare my voyce and kepe myne appoyntment: ye fhall be myne
6 awne aboue all nations, for all the erth is myne. Ye fhall be vnto me a kyngdome of preaftes and an holie people: thefe are the wordes which thou fhalt faye vnto the childern of Ifrael.
7 And Mofes came and called for the elders of Ifrael, and layde before them all thefe wordes which the
8 Lorde had commaunded him. And the people anfwered all together and fayde: All that the Lorde hath fayde, we will doo. And Mofes broughte the
9 wordes of the people vnto the Lorde .P. And the Lorde fayde vnto Mofes: Loo, I will come vnto the in a thicke clowde, that the people maye heare when I talke with the and alfo beleue the for euer. And Mofes fhewed the wordes of the people vnto the Lorde
10 And the Lorde fayde vnto Mofes: Go vnto the people and fanctifie them to daye and tomorow, and
11 let them wafh their clothes: that they maye be redie agaynft the thyrde daye.

For the thyrde daye the Lorde will come doune in
12 the fighte of all the people vpon mounte Sinai. And fett markes rounde aboute the people and faye: beware that ye go not vp in to the mounte and that ye twych not the bordres of it, for whofo- twych, twicheuer twicheth the mounte, fhall furely eth, *touch, toucheth*
13 dye There fhall not an hande twych it,

V. 4 portauerim vos .. et affumpferim mihi. 5 in peculium 7 natu populi 12 Conftituefque terminos populo per circumitum .. morte morietur

L. 4 getragen .. zu mir bracht. 5 eygentumb 12 ftecke zeychen vmb das volck her .. feyn ende anruret

𝔐. 𝔐. N. 10 *To fanctyfye* is here to purge & clenfe them from the fylthynes of bothe their body and garmentes, as is in this fame chapter beneth c. d. & xxxi, c.

but that he shall ether be stoned or els shot thorow: whether it be beest or man, it shall not lyue. when the horne bloweth: than let them come vp in to the mounten

14 And Moses went doune from the mounte vnto the people and sanctifyed them, ād they wasshed their
15 clothes: And he sayde vnto the people: be redie agenst the thirde daye, and se that ye come not at
16 youre wiues. And the thirde daye in the mornynge there was thunder, and lightenynge and a thicke clowde apō the mounte, ād the voyce of the horne waxed ex-
[Fo. XXXIII.] ceadynge lowde, and all the people that
17 was in the hoste was afrayde. And Moses brought the people out of the tētes to mete with God. and they stode vnder the hyll.
18 And mounte Sinai was all togither on a smoke: becaufe the Lorde defcended doune vpon it in fyre. And the fmoke therof afcēded vp, as it had bene the fmoke of a kylle, and all the mounte was ex-   *kylle, kiln,*
19 ceadinge fearfull. And the voyce of the *furnace* horne blewe and waxed lowder, ād lowder. Mofes fpake, ād God anfwered hī ād that with a voyce.
20 And the Lord came doune vppon mounte Sinai: euen in the toppe of the hyll, ād called Mofes vp in to the toppe of the hyll. And Mofes went vppe.
21 And the Lorde fayde vnto Mofes: go doune and charge the people that they preafe not vp *preafe, preſſe* vnto the Lorde for to fe hī, ād fo many off thē periffh.
22 And let the preaftes alfo which come to the Lordes prefence, fanctifie them felues: left the Lorde fmyte
23 them, Then Mofes fayde vnto the Lorde: the people can not come vp in to mounte Sinai, for thou charged-

   V. 13 conlodietur iaculis .. buccina 16 & mane inclaruerat... clangorque buc. vehementius perftrepebat 17 ad radices montis. 19 crefcebat in maius, & prolixius tendebatur .. deus refpondebat ei. 20 Defcenditque 22 fanctificentur

   L. 13 mit gefchofz erfchoffen ... horns dohn dehnet, 16 pofaunen 17 vnden an den berg. 18 feer erfchrecklich 19 Gott antwortet yhm laut. 21 nicht erzu brechen 22 nicht zu fcheyttere

   𝔐. 𝔐. Ν. 15 *Come not at youre wyues*, that is, when ye wyll ferue the Lord ye fhall put frō you all luftes and flefhly concupifcenfes, geuing your felfe holy to prayer & abftynence, as Paul teacheth 1 Cor. vii, c. that they that haue wyues fhulde be as though they had none.

eſt vs ſaynge: ſett markes aboute the hyll and ſanctifie it.

24 And the Lorde ſayde vnto him: awaye, and get the doune: and come vp both thou ād Aaron with the. But let not the preaſtes and the .P. people preſume for
25 to come vp vnto the Lorde: leſt he ſmyte them. And Moſes wēt doune vnto the people and tolde them.

❡ The .XX. Chapter.

1 AND God ſpake all theſe wordes *M.C.S. The .x*
2 ād ſaide: I am the Lorde thy *commaundementes are* God, which haue brought the *geuen. The* out of the londe of Egipte ād *altare of erth.*
3 out of the houſe of bondage. Thou ſhalt haue none other goddes in my ſyght.
4 Thou ſhalt make the no grauen ymage, nether any ſymilitude that is in heauen aboue, ether in the erth
5 beneth, or in the water that ys beneth the erth. Se that thou nether bowe thy ſylf vnto them nether ſerue them: for I the Lorde thy God, am a gelouſe God, and viſet the ſynne of the fathers vppon the childern vnto the third and fourth generacion of thē that hate me:
6 and yet ſhewe mercie vnto thouſandes amonge them that loue me and kepe my commaundmentes.
7 Thou ſhalt not take the name of the Lorde thy God in vayne, for the Lord wil not holde him giltleſſe that taketh his name in vayne.
8 Remēbre the Sabbath daye that thou ſanctifie it.
9 Sixe dayes mayſt thou laboure ād do al that thou haſt
10 to doo: but the ſeuenth daye is the Sabbath of the Lorde thy God, in it thou [Fo. XXXV.] ſhalt do no

V. 24 interficiat illos. **xx,** 4 eorum quæ ſunt in aquis 5 deus tuus fortis zelotes

L. 4 des das oben . . des das vnden . . oder des das 5 eyn ſtarcker eyfferer 7 vnſchuldig

M. M. N. 5 *I am gelouſe* that is; I am the Lorde that watcheth and looketh narowly vnto your wekednes, & wyll punyſſhe it ſtraytly. And agayne, that ſeruently loueth youre godlynes & will rewarde it aboundātly.

maner worke: nether thou nor thy fonne, nor thy
doughter, nether thy manfervaunte nor thy maydefervaunte, nether thy catell nether yet the ftraunger
11 that is within thi gates For in fixe dayes the Lorde
made both heauen and erth and the fee and all that
in them is and refted the feuenth daye: wherfore the
Lorde bleffed the Sabbath daye and halowed it.

12   Honoure thy father ād thy mother, that thy dayes
may be lōge in the lōde which the Lorde thy God
geueth the.

13   Thou fhalt not kyll.
14   Thou fhalt not breake wedlocke.
15   Thou fhalt not fteale.
16   Thou fhalt bere no falfe witneffe agēft thy neghboure
17   Thou fhalt not couet thy neghbours houffe: nether
fhalt couet thy neghbours wife, his māfervaunte, his
mayde, his oxe, his affe or aughte that is his.

18   And all the people fawe the thunder *Thelavvecau-*
ād the lyghteninge and the noyfe of the *feth vvrath*
ād maketh a
horne, ād howe the mountayne fmoked. *mā fle from*
And whē the people fawe it, they re- *God: but the*
Gofpelldravv-
19 moued ād ftode a ferre of ād faide vnto *eth ād maketh*
Mofes: talke thou with vs and we wil *a mā bolde to*
come vnto
heare: but let not god talke with vs, left *God.*
20 we dye. And Mofes fayde vnto the people feare not,
for God is come to proue you, and .Ṗ. that his feare
may be amonge you that ye fynne not.
21   And the people ftode aferre of, ād Mofes went in
22 to the thicke clowde where God was And the Lorde
fayde vnto Mofes: thus thou fhalt faye vnto the childern of Ifrael: Ye haue fene how that I haue talked

 Ṽ. 18 videbat voces et lampades ... & perterriti ac pauore
concuffi
 Ľ. 12 geben wirt. 14 nicht ehebrechen. 17 noch alles das deyn
nehifter 18 fahe 19 vnd wancketen vnd tratten von ferne 20 euch fur
augen
 ℳ. ℳ. N. 12 *To honor father and mother* is not only to fhew
obedience to them: but alfo to helpe them in their age yf they be
poore & nedy, as Ephe. vi, a. Col. iii, d. Marc. vii, b. Matt. ix, c.
Rom. xiii, b.

23 with you from out of heauen. Ye ſhal not make therfore with me goddes of ſyluer nor goddes *with, beſide*
24 of golde: in no wyſe ſhall ye do it. An alter of erth thou ſhalt make vnto me ād there on offer thy burntofferinges ād thy peaceoffringes, and thy ſhepe ād thine oxen. And in all places where I ſhall put the remēbraunce of my name, thither I will come vnto the and bleſſe the.
25 But and yf thou wilt make me an alter off ſtone, ſe thou make it not of hewed ſtone, for yf thou lyſte vp thy
26 tole vpon it, thou ſhalt polute it. Moreouer *tole, tool, chiſ-* thou ſhalt not goo vp wyth ſteppes vnto *el or kniſe* myne alter, that thy nakedneſſe be not ſhewed there on

---

The .XXI. Chapter.

1 THESE are the lawes which thou *M.C.S. Tem-*
2 ſhalt ſet before thē. Yf thou *porall and cyuile ordin-* bye a ſervaunte that is an he- *aunces.* brue, ſixte yeres he ſhall ſerue, and the ſeu-
Lawes enth he ſhall goo out fre paynge noth-
3 *Bondemen* inge. Yf he came alone, he ſhall goo out alone: Yf he came maried, his wife ſhall go out with
4 hī. [Fo. XXXVI.] And yf his maſter haue geuen him a wife and ſhe haue borne him ſonnes or doughters: then the wife and hir childern ſhalbe hir maſters ād he
5 ſhall goo out alone. But and yf the ſervaunte ſaye I loue my maſter and my wife and my children, I will
6 not goo out fre. Then let his maſter bringe him vnto the Goddes ād ſet him to the doore or the *Goddes are* dorepoſt, ād bore his eare thorow with a *the iudges vvhich are in* a naule, *an* naule, ād let him be his ſer- *gods ſtede.* *awl* vaunte for euer.

V. 23 Non facietis mecum deos 24 mei: veniam ad te 25 leuaueris cultrum   xxi, 3 Cum quali veſte intrauerit, cum tali exeat. 6 ſubula
 L. 23 neben myr machen 25 deym meſſer 26 fur yhm.   xxi, 3 alleyne komen 6 pfrymen
 M. M. N. 6 Iudges and princes are called in the ſcripture oftentymes *goddes:* becauſe they receaue their office of God, as in Ex. xxii, b. which the apoſtle calleth the myniſters of God. Rom. xiii, a.

7 Yf a man fell his doughter to be a fervaunte: fhe
8 fhall not goo out as the men fervauntes doo. Yf fhe
pleafe not hir mafter, fo that he hath geuen her to no
man to wife, then fhal he let hir goo fre: to fell her
vnto a ftraunge nacion fhal he haue no power, becaufe
9 he defpifed her. Yf he haue promyfed her vnto his
fonne to wife, he fhal deale with her as men do with
10 their doughters. Yf he take him another wife, yet hir
fode, rayment and dutie off mariage fhall he not myn-
11 iffhe. Yf he do not thefe thre vnto her, then fhall fhe
goo out fre and paye no money.

12 He that fmyteth a man that he dye, *Murther*
13 fhalbe flayne for it. Yf a mā laye not awayte but God
delyuer him in to his hande, then I wyll poynte the
14 a place whether he fhall fle. Yf a man *whether, whither*
come prefumptuoufly vppon his neygh- *gile, guile*
boure ād .P. flee him with gile, thou
fhalt take him fro myne alter that he dye. *But the pope faith come to*
15 And he that fmyteth his father or his *myne altare.*
mother, fhall dye for it.

16 He that ftealeth a mā ād felleth him (yf it be
17 proued vppon him) fhall be flayne for it. And he
that curfeth his father or mother, fhall be put to deth
18 for it. Yf men ftryue together and one fmyte another
with a ftone or with his fyfte, fo that he dye not, but
19 lyeth in bedd: yf he ryfe agayne and walke without
vpon his ftaffe then fhall he that fmote hī goo quyte:
faue only he fhal bere his charges while he laye in bed
and paye for his healinge.

20 Yf a man fmite his fervaunte or his mayde with a
ftaffe that they dye vnder his hande, it fhalbe auenged.
21 But ād yf they contynue a daye or two, it fhall not be
auenged for they are his money.
22 when men ftryue and fmyte a woman with childe

V. 7 ficut ancillæ 8 Si difplicuerit oc. dom. fui, cui tradita fuerit, dimittet eam .... fi fpreuerit eam. 10 prouidebit puellæ nupt., & veft., & pretium pudicitiæ non negabit. 12 volens occidere, morte moriatur. 20 criminis reus erit. 22 fed ipfa vixerit

L. 8 verfchmecht 10 futter, decke vnd ehefchuld 12 tods fterben 15 muter fchlegt 20 rach drumb leyden

ſo that hir frute departe from her and yet no myſ-
fortune foloweth: then ſhall he be merſed, acordynge as the womans huſbonde will laye to his charge, and he ſhall paye as the dayeſmen appoynte him. But and yf
23
any myſſortune folowe, then ſhall he paye lyfe for lyfe,
24 eye for eye, toth for toth, hande for hande, ſote for ſote,
25 burnynge for burnynge, wonde for [Fo. XXXVII.] wonde and ſtrype for ſtrype.

merſed, a-merced; dayeſ-*men, judges; appoynte, ad-judge*

26   Yf a man ſmyte his ſervaunte or his mayde in the eye and put it out, he ſhall let thē goo fre for the eyes
27 ſake. Alſo yf he ſmyte out his ſervauntes or his maydes toth, he ſhall let thē go out fre for the tothes ſake.

28   Yf an oxe gore a man or a woman that they dye, then the oxe ſhalbe ſtoned, and hys fleſh ſhall not be eaten: and his maſter ſhall go quyte.
29   Yf the oxe were wont to runne at men in tyme paſt and it hath bene tolde his maſter, and he hath not kepte him, but that he hath kylled a man or a woman: then the oxe ſhalbe ſtoned and hys maſter ſhall dye alſo.

God ſo abhor-reth murther, that the vn-reſonable be-ſtes muſt dye therfore, and there fleſh caſt avvay.

30   Yf he be ſette to a ſumme of money, then he ſhall geue for the delyueraunce off his lyfe, acordynge to all that is put vnto him.

ſette to, fined in

31   And whether he hath gored a ſonne or a doughter,
32 he ſhalbe ſerued after the ſame maner But yf it be a ſervaunt or a mayde that the oxe hath gored, then he ſhall geue vnto their maſter the ſumme of .xxx ſicles, ād the oxe ſhall be ſtoned.

33   Yf a man open a well or dygge a pytt and couer

𝒱. 22 arbitri iudic. 23 Sinautem mors eius fuerit ſubſecuta 26 luſcos eos fecerit 29 bos cornupeta 30 impoſitum .. pro anima ſua .. poſtulatus. 32 inuaſerit 33 ciſternam, & foderit

𝓛. 22 keyn ſchade widerferet .. teydings leut 23 ſeel vmb ſeel 29 vorhyn ſtoſſig geweſen 30 ſeyn ſeel zurloſen 33 gruben .. grube

𝓜. 𝓜. N. 28 God ſo abhorreth *murther,* that the vnreaſonable beaſtes muſt dye therfore. and their fleſh caſt awaye. 32 *Sicle,* after the Ebrewes is an ounce: but after the grekes & Latynes it is but the fourth part of an ounce. And it cōteyneth .xx. geras as in Ex. xxx, b. whych is ten pence ſterlyng or thereaboute.

34 it not, but that an oxe or an aſſe fall theryn, the owner off the pytte ſhall ma- .P. ke it good and geue money vnto their maſter and the dead beeſt ſhalbe his.
35 Yf one mans oxe hurte anothers that he dye: then they ſhall ſell the lyue oxe and deuyde the money,
36 and the deed oxe alſo they ſhall deuyde. But and yf it be knowne that the oxe hath vſed to puſſhe in tymes paſt, then becauſe his maſter hath not kepte hĩ, he ſhall paye oxe for oxe. and the deed ſhalbe his awne.

❡ The .XXII. Chapter

1 YF a man ſteale an oxe or ſhepe ãd kylle it or ſelle it, he ſhall reſtore .v. oxen for an oxe, and .iiii. ſhepe for a ſhepe. *M.C.S. Soche lyke lawes as are in the chapter aboue.*

2 *Thefte* Yf a theſe be founde breakynge vpp ãd be ſmytten that he dye, there ſhall no bloude be ſhed
3 for him: excepte the ſonne be vpp when he is founde, then there ſhalbe bloude ſhed for him,

A theſe ſhall make reſtitucyon: Yf he haue not
4 wherewith, he ſhalbe ſolde for his thefte. Yf the thefte be founde in his hande alyue (whether it be oxe, aſſe or ſhepe) he ſhall reſtore double.

5 Yf a man do hurte felde or vyneyarde, ſo that he put in his beeſt to fede in another mans felde: off the beſt off hys owne felde, [Fo. XXXVII.] and of the beſt of his awne vyneyarde, ſhall he make reſtitucyon.

6 Yf fyre breake out and catch in the thornes, ſo that the ſtoukes of corne or the ſtõdynge corne *ſtoukes, ſtacks* or felde be conſumed therwith: he that kynled the fyre ſhall make reſtitucyon.

7 Yf a man delyuer his neghboure money or ſtuffe to

V. 36 cadauer integrum accipiet. xxii, 2 effringens . . ſiue ſuffodiens 3 homicidium perpetrauit & ipſe morietur. 5 pro damni æſtimatione
L. 36 vnd das aſs haben. xxii, 2 blut gericht (*bis*) 6 die mandel odder getreyde.

kepe, and it be ſtolen out of his houſſe: Yf the theſe
8 be foūde, he ſhal paye double. Yf the theſe be not
founde, then the goodmā of the houſſe *goodman,*
ſhalbe brought vnto the goddes and ſwere, *maſter*
whether he haue put his hande vnto his neghbours good.

9 And in all maner of treſpace, whether it be oxe,
aſſe, ſhepe, rayment or ony maner loſt thynge which
another chalēgeth to be his, the cauſe of both parties
ſhall come before the goddes. And whom *goddes, jud-*
the goddes condēne: the ſame ſhall paye *ges, as xxi, 6*
10 double vnto his neghboure. Yf a man delyuer vnto
his neghboure to kepe, aſſe, oxe, ſhepe or what
ſoeuer beeſt it be and it dye or be hurte or dryu-
11 en awaye and no man ſe it: then ſhall an othe of
the Lorde goo betwene them, whether he haue put
his hande vnto his neghbours good, and the owner
of it ſhall take the othe, and the other ſhall not make
it good:

12 Yf it be ſtollen from him, then he ſhall make reſti-
13 tucion vnto the owner: Yf .P. it be torne with wylde
beeſtes, thē let him bringe recorde of the teerynge:
and he ſhall not make it good.

14 when a man boroweth oughte of his neghbour yf it
be hurte or els dye, and yf the owner therof be not
15 by, he ſhall make it good: Yf the owner there of
be by, he ſhall not make it good namely yf it be an
hyred thinge ād came for hyre.

16 Yf a man begyle a mayde that is not betrouthed
and lye with her, he ſhall endote her and *endote, endow*
17 take her to his wife: Yf hir father refuſe to geue her
vnto him, he ſhall paye money acordynge to the
dowrie of virgens.

V. 8 dominus domus applicabitur ad deos 10 vel captum ab
hoſtibus 13 deferat ad eum quod occiſum 16 dotabit eam
L. 8 hauſswirt fur die Gotter bringen
M. M. N. 11 An othe is the ende of ſtryfe and deuiſyon, the
which is lawfull to be done, when it is ether to the glorie of God
or proffyt of our neyboure or for the comen wealth, or elles not,
as Math. v, f.
L. M. N. 8 *Gotter* heyſſen die richter, darumb dz ſie an Gottis ſtat, nach Gottis geſetz vnd wort, nicht nach eygen dunckel
richten vnd regirn muſten, wie Chriſtus zeugt, Iohan. 10

18 Thou fhalt not·fuffre a witch to lyue, *vvyches*
19 who foeuer lyeth with a beeft, fhalbe flayne for it.
20 He that offreth vnto ony goddes faue vnto the Lorde
21 only, let him dye without redemption vexe not a ftraunger nether oppreffe him for ye were ftraungers in the londe of Egipte.
22 Ye fhall trouble no wedowe nor fa- *Let all op-*
23 therleffe childe: * Yf ye fhall trouble the: *preffars of the pore take hede*
they fhall crye vnto me, ād I wyll *to this texte.*
24 furely heare their crye and then will my wrath waxe hoote and I will kyll you with fwerde, and youre wyues fhalbe wedowes and youre childern fatherleffe. [Fo. XXXVIII.]
25 Yf thou lende money to ani of my *Lend.*
people that is poore by the, thou fhalt not be as an vfurer vnto him, nether fhalt oppreffe him with vferye.
26 Yf thou take thi neghbours raymēt to *Plegge.*
pledge, fe that thou delyuer it vnto him agayne by
27 that the fonne goo doune. For that is his couerlet only: euē the rayment for his fkynne wherin he flepeth: or els he will crye vnto me ād I will heare him, for I am mercyfull.
28 Thou fhalt not rayle vppon the goddes, *Goddes.*
nether curfe the ruelar of thi people.
29 Thy frutes (whether they be drye or moyft) fe thou kepe not backe. Thi firftborne fonne thou fhalt geue
30 me: likewife fhalt thou doo of thine oxen and of thy

M. 24 y̆ fwerde
V. 20 diis, occidetur, præter dom. 25 vrgebis eum quafi exactor, nec vfuris opprimes. 27 indumentum carnis eius nec .. in quo dormiat.
L. 19 der fey verbannet. 26 feyn eynige decke feyner haut, darynn er fchlefft. 29 fulle vnd threnen
M. M. N. 22 Let all oppreffars of the pore take hede to this texte. 29 By tythes & fyrft frutes are vnderftōde geuynge of thākes wher by the heart knowledgeth & confeffeth to haue receaued it of God, as in I Tim. iiii, a.
L. M. N. 29 *Fulle* heyft er alle hartte fruchte als da find, korn, gerftcn, epffel, byrn, da man fpeyfe von macht, *Threnen* heyft er alle weych fruchte, da man fāft vnd tranck von macht, Als da find weyndrauben ole. Bedeut aber das Euangelion dz da fpeyfet vnd trenckt geyftlich.

ſhepe. Seuen dayes it ſhall be with the dame, and the .viii. daye thou ſhalt geue it me.

31 Ye ſhalbe holye people vnto me, and therfore ſhall ye eate no fleſh that is torne of beeſtes in the feld. But ſhall caſt it to dogges.

The .XXIII. Chapter.

1 THOU ſhalt not accept a vayne tale, nether ſhalt put thine hande with the wiked to be an vnrightous witneſſe.

2 *Falſevvitneſſe.* Thou ſhalt not folowe a multitude to do euell: nether anſwere in a mater of plee that thou woldeſt to folow

3 many turne a ſyde .P. from the trueth, nether ſhalt thou paynte a porre mans cauſe.

M.C.S. Here I ſet no ſome: becauſe I wolde all men ſhuld reade the chapter thorow oute, and the two that are next before alſo.

paynte, favor his cauſe, ſee Hebrew.

4 whē thou meteſt thine enimies oxe or aſſe goynge a ſtraye, thou ſhalt brynge thē to him agayne.

5 Yf thou ſe thine enimies aſſe ſynke vnder his burthen, thou ſhalt not paſſe by and let him alone: but ſhalt helpe him to lyfte him vp agayne.

6 Thou ſhalt not hynder the right of the poore that are amonge you in their ſute.

7 Kepe the ferre from a falſe mater, and the Innocent and righteous ſe thou ſley not, for I will not iuſtifye the weked.

8 Thou ſhalt take no giftes, for gyftes *Gyftes.* blinde the ſeynge and peruerte the wordes of the righteous.

    V. 1 non fuſcipies vocem mendacii 2 vt a vero deuies. 3 non miſereberis 5 ſed ſubleuabis cum eo. 6 non declinabis in iud. pauperis. 7 quia averſor impium. 8 ſubuertunt verba
    L. 1 annehmen vnnutzer teydinge 2 vom rechten weycheſt 6 recht .. beugen 7 rechtfertige keynen gotloſen. 8 rechten ſachen.
    M. M. N. 8 By receauyng of gyftes is vnderſtonde all thynge by which one ſeketh hys awne profijt and honoure and not godes, as in Deut. xvi, d. xxvii, d. & Eccli. xx, d.

9 Thou fhalt not oppreffe a ftraunger, *Straunger*. for I knowe the herte of ftraunger, becaufe ye were ftraungers in Egipte.

10 Sixe yeres thou fhalt fowe thi londe ãd gather in the
11 frutes theroff: and the feuenth yere thou fhalt let it reft and lye ftyll, that the poore of thi people maye eate, and what they leaue, the beeftes of the felde fhall eate: In like maner thou fhalt do with thi vyneyarde ãd thine olyue trees.

12 Sixe dayes thou fhalt do thi worke ãd the [Fo. XXXIX.] feuenth daye thou fhalt kepe holie daye, that thyne oxe and thine affe maye reft ãd the fonne of thi mayde and the ftraunger maye be refreffhed.

13 And in all thinges that I haue fayde vnto you be circumfpecte.

And make no reherfall of the names of the ftraunge goddes, nether let any man heare thẽ out of youre mouthes.

14 Thre feaftes thou fhalt holde vnto me in a yere.
15 Thou fhalt kepe the feaft of fwete bred that thou eate vnleuend bred .vii. dayes lõge as I cõmaunded the in the tyme appoynted of the moneth of Abib, for in that moneth thou cameft out of Egipte: ãd fe that noman
16 appeare before me emptie. And the feaft of Herueft, when thou reapeft the firftfrutes of thy laboures which thou haft fowne in the felde. And the feaft of ingaderynge, in the ende of the yere: when thou haft gathered in thy laboures out of the felde.

17 Thre tymes in a yere fhall all thy menchildern appere before the Lorde Iehouah.

18 Thou fhalt not offer the bloude of my facrifyce with

V. 9 fcitis enim ad. animas 12 refrigeretur 13 cuftodite .. non iurabitis neque audietur 15 menfis nouorum 16 menfis primitiuorum

L. 9 yhr wiffet vmb der fremdling herz 17 Herrn des hirfchers

L. M. N. 14 Das ift, das ofterfeft ym april, Pfingften ym brachmond vnd das lauberhutten feft ym weynmond, davon lies am 23. Cap. des dritten buchs. Des iars ausgang heyft er den weynmond, das als denn aus ift mit frucht wachfen vnd famlen. 18 Das blut etc. das ift du folt das ofter lamb nicht opffern ehe denn all gefeurt brod aus deynem haufe kompt, Bedeut das Chriftus blut nicht neben fich leydet eygẽ menfchen leer vnd werck, Matth. 16, hut euch fur dem faurteyg der Pharifeer.

leuended bred: nether fhall the fatt of my feaſt remayne vntill the mornynge.

19 The firſt of the firſtfrutes of thy lode thou .P. ſhalt bringe in to the houſſe of the Lorde thy God thou ſhalt alſo not ſeth a kyde in his mothers mylke.

20 Beholde, I. ſende mine angell before the, to kepe the in the waye, and to brynge the in to the place
21 which I haue prepared Beware of him and heare his voyce and angre him not: for he wyll not ſpare youre
22 myſdedes, yee and my name is in him. But and yf thou ſhalt herken vnto his voyce ād kepe all that I ſhall tell the, thē I wilbe an enimye vnto thyne enimies and an aduerſarie vnto thine aduerſaries.

23 when myne angell goth before the ād hath broughte the in vnto the Amorites, Hethites Pherezites, Canaanites, Heuites and Iebuſites and I ſhall haue de-
24 ſtroyed them: ſe thou worſhippe not their goddes nether ſerue them, nether do after the workes of them: but ouerthrowe them and breake doune the places of them
25 And ſe that ye ſerue the Lorde youre God, ād he ſhall bleſſe thi bred and thy water, ād I will take all ſyckneſſes awaye from amonge you.

26 Moreouer there ſhalbe no woman childleſſe or vnfrutefull in thi londe, and the nombre of thi dayes I
27 will fulfyll. I will ſende my ſeare before the and will kyll all the people whether thou ſhalt goo. And I will make all thine enemies turne their backes vnto
28 the, ād I will [Fo. XL.] ſend hornettes before the, and they ſhall dryue out the Heuites, the Cananites and the Hethites before the.

V. 18 ſuper fermēto 24 confringes ſtatuas eorum. 25 vt benedicam .. auferam infirm. 26 dier. tuor. implebo. 28 emittēs crabrones prius, qui fug.

L. 18 neben dem ſawrteyg 19 an ſeyner mutt. milch 24 gotzen abthun vnd zubrechen 26 eynſame noch vnfruchtbar .. alter vol machen 28 horniſſen .. ausjagen

M. M. N. 19 That is, thou ſhalt not ſethe it ſo longe as it ſoucketh, or as ſome thynke: they ſhuld not kyll bothe the dāme & the kyd. 28 A hornet is lyke a waſpe—ſhe is of a more venemous nature & ſtyngeth moche ſorer, as in Deut. vii. & Ioſu. xxiiii. c.

L. M. N. 19 Das bocklin etc. das iſt die ſchwachglewbigen vnd iunge Chriſten ſolltu nicht ergern noch mit ſtarcker lere vnd wercken beladen.

29 I will not caſt them out in one yere, leſt the lande growe to a wyldernesse: and the beeſtes of the felde multiplye apon the.
30 But a litle and a litle I will dryue them out before the, vntill thou be increaſed that thou mayſt enherett
31 the londe. And I will make thi coſtes frō the red ſee vnto the ſee of the Philiſtenes and from the deſerte vnto the ryuer. I will delyuer the in- *By the ryuer vnderſtonde* habiters of the londe in to thine hande, *the river Eu-* and thou ſhalt dryue them out before the. *phrates,*
32 And thou ſhalt make none appoyntment with them
33 nor wyth their goddes. Nether ſhall they dwell in thi londe, leſt they make the ſynne agaynſt me: for yf thou ſerue their goddes, it will ſurely be thy decaye.

The .XXIIII. Chapter.

1 AND he ſayde vnto Moſes: come vnto the Lorde: both thou and Aaron, Nadab and Abihu, and the .Lxx. elders of Iſrael, *M.C.S. Moſes aſſendeth vp to the mount and wryteth the wordes of the Lorde.*
2 and worſhippe a ferre of. And Moſes went him ſelf alone vnto the Lorde, but they came not nye, nether came the people vp with him. *The bloude of the couenaunt. The elders of Iſrael iudge the people.*
3 And Moſes came ād tolde the people al the .P. wordes of the Lorde and all the lawes. And all the people anſwered with one voyce and ſayde: all the wordes which the Lorde hath ſayde, will wee doo.
4 Then Moſes wrote all the wordes of the Lorde and roſe vp early ād made an alter vnder the hyll, and .xii

V. 31 tradam in man. veſtris 32 inibis ... fœdus 33 quod tibi certe erit in ſcandalum. xxiiii, 1 Aſcēde 3 iudicia 4 ad radices montis
L. 30 meylich 32 bund machen 33 zum ergernis geratten. xxiiii, 1 Steyg erauff 4 vnden am berge
L. M. N. 3 *Eyner ſtym:* Das geſetz zwinget wol euſerlich eynerley zu ſagen oder geloben, aber das hertz iſt nicht da, drumb iſt hie des volcks wol eyne ſtym, aber keyn hertz.

pilers acordynge to the nombre of the .xii. trybes of
5 Ifrael, ãd fent yonge men of the childern of Ifrael to
facrifyce burntoffrynges ãd to offre peaceoffrynges of
oxen vnto the Lorde.
6 And Mofes toke halfe of the bloude and put it in
bafens, and the otherhalfe he fprenkeld on the alter.
7 And he toke the boke of the appoynt- *appoyntment,*
ment and red it in the audience of the *covenant*
people. And they feyde. All that the Lorde hath
8 fayde, we will do and heare. And Mofes toke the
bloude ãd fprinkeld it on the people ãd fayde: beholde, this is the bloude of the appoyntment which
the Lorde hath made with you apon all thefe wordes.
9 Then went Mofes and Aaron, Nadab ãd Abihu and
10 the .Lxx. elders of Ifrael vppe, and fawe the God of
Ifrael, and vnder his fete as it were a brycke worke
of Saphir and as it were the facyon of *facyon, ap-*
pearance, v.
11 heauen when it is cleare, and apõ the *17.*
nobles of the childern of Ifrael he fett not his hande.
And when they had fene God [Fo. XLI.] they ate and
dronke.
12 And the Lorde fayde vnto Mofes: come vpp to me
in to the hyll and be there, ãd I will geue the tables
of ftone and a lawe and commaundmentes, which I
13 haue written to teach them. Then Mofes rofe vppe
ãd his minifter Iofua, and Mofes went vppe in to the
14 hyll of God, ãd feyde vnto the elders: tarye ye here
vntill we come agayne vnto you: And beholde here is
Aaron and Hur with you. Yf any man haue any
maters to doo, let him come to them

V. 5 victimas pacificas 7 volumen fœderis .. erimus obed.
8 fuper cunct. ferm. 10 opus lapidis fapphirini .. cælum cum fe-
renum 11 eos qui procul receff. 12 doceas eos. 14 referetis ad eos.

L. 5 fridopffer 7 buch des bunds .. gehorchen 8 vber allen
dif. wortten 10 zigel von Sapphir werck .. geftalt des hymels, wens
klar ift, 11 furnemiften 14 an die felben gelangen.

M. M. N. 5 *Peace offrynge* is to reconcile God toward mẽ, to
be at peace wyth them & to forgiue thẽ their trefpace: or as
fome men faye for peace obtayned after victorie in batayle, as
afore in the .ix. chapter, d and here after xxxii, b. 10 *They fawe*
God, that is: they knewe certenly thatt he was there prefent, and
they fawe him as in a vifyon, not in his godly maieftie: but as it
were by a certen reuelacion.

15 when Mofes was come vpp in to the mounte, a
16 clowde couered the hyll, and the glorye of the Lorde abode apon mounte Sinai, and the clowde couered it vi. dayes. And the feuenth daye he called vnto Mo-
17 fes out of the clowde. And the facyon of the glorie of the Lorde was like confumynge fyre on the toppe of the hyll in the fyghte of the childern of Ifrael.
18 And Mofes went in to the mountayne And Mofes was in the mounte .xl. dayes and .xl. nyghtes.

The .XXV. Chapter

1 AND the Lorde talked with Mofes *M.C. S. The*
2 faynge: fpeake vnto the chil- *Lord fheweth Mofes the faf-* dern of Ifrael that they geue *fyon of the* me an heueoffrynge, and of *holy place and the thynges* euerey man that geueth it willingly wyth *pertaynynge*
3 his herte, ye fhall take it. And this is *therto.* the heue- .P. offrynge which ye fhall take of them:
4 gold, filuer ãd braffe: and Iacyncte col- iacyncte, *hya-* oure, fcarlet, purpull, byffe and gootes *cinth, blue*
5 here: rams fkynnes that are red, and the fkynnes of
6 taxus and fethimwodd, oyle for lightes and fpices for
7 a noyntynge oyle and for fwete cenfe: Onix ftones and fett ftones for the Ephod and for the *Ephod is a garment lyke* breftlappe. *an amyce.*
8 And they fhall make me a fanctuarye that I maye
9 dwell amonge them. And as I haue fhewed the the facion of the habitaciõ and of all the orna- facion, *pat-* mentes therof, euẽ fo fe that ye make it in *tern v. 40.* all thynges.

M. 9 And I fhall fhewe the
V. 15 op. nubes mont. 16 medio caliginis. 17 ignis ardens 18 Ingreffufque M. medium nebulæ, afcendit in .. xxv, 2 primitias 4 purpuram, coccumque bis tinctum 5 pellefque hyac. 7 ephod ac rationale.
L. 17 vertzehrend fewr. . xxv, 1 Hebopffer 4 gelle feyden, fcharlacken, rofynrodt, 5 dachs fell 7 bruft latzen.
M. M. N. 16 Of this glorie is fpoken before in the .xvi. Chapter, c. xxv, 7 *Ephod* is a garment lyke an amyce.

10 And they shall make an arke of sethim wodd .ii. cubittes and an halfe longe, a cubite ād an halfe brode
11 and a cubitt and an halfe hye. And thou shalt ouerleye it with pure golde: both within and without, and shalt make an hye vppon it a crowne of golde rounde
12 aboute. And thou shalt cast .iiii. rynges of golde for it and put them in the .iiii. corners there of .ii. rynges
13 on the one syde of it and .ii. on the other. And thou shalt make staues of sethim wodd and couer them with
14 golde, and put the staues in the rynges alonge by the
15 sydes of the arke, to bere it with all. And the staues shall abyde in the rynges of the arke, and shall not be
16 taken awaye. [Fo. XLII.] And thou shalt put in the arke, the wytnesse which I shall geue the.

17 And thou shalt make a mercifeate of pure golde .ii. cubytes and an halfe longe and a cubete and an halfe
18 brode. And make .ii. cherubyns off thicke golde on
19 the .ii. endes of the mercyfeate: and sett the one cherub on the one ende and the other on the other ende of the mercyfeate: so se that thou make them on the .ii
20 endes there of. And the cherubyns shall stretch theyr wynges abrode ouer an hye, ād couer the mercy feate with their wynges, and theyr faces shall loke one to another: euē to the mercyfeate warde, shall the faces of
21 the cherubyns be. And thou shalt put the mercyfeate aboue apon the arke, ād in the arke thou shalt put the wytnesse which I will geue the.

22 There I will mete the and will comon comon, *com-mune* with the from apon the mercyfeate from betwene the two cherubyns which are apon the arke of witnesse, of all thynge which I will geue the in commaundment vnto the childern of Israel.

23 Thou shalt also make a table of sethim wod of two

V. 11 supra coronam 16 testificationē 18 productiles facies ex vtraque parte oraculi. 22 Inde præcipiam, & loquar
L. 11 oben vmbher 12 geuss 13 foern holtz 16 zeugnis 17 Gnaden stuel 22 Von dem ort
L. M. N. 22 *Dyr zeugen:* das ist, dabey als bey eym gewissen zeichen vnd zeugnis will ich dich wissen lassen, das ich da bin gegenwertig, das ich daselbs reden werde etc. Bedeut aber Christum ynn der menscheyt. Ro. 3.

cubittes longe and one cubett brode ād a cubett ād an
24 halfe hye. And couer it with pure golde and make
25 there to a crowne of golde rounde aboute. And
make vnto that .¶. an whope of .iiii. fyngers brode,
rounde aboute, And make a goldē crowne alfo to the
26 whope rounde aboute. And make for it .iiii. rynges
of golde and put them in the corners that are on the
27 iiii. fete therof: euē harde vnder the whope *harde vnder,*
fhall the rynges be, to put in ftaues to *immediately under*
28 bere the table with all. And thou fhalt make ftaues
of Sethim wodd and ouerleye thē with golde, that the
29 table maye be borne with them And thou fhalt make
his diffhes, fpones, pottes and flatpeces to poure out
30 withall, of fyne golde. And thou fhalt fett apon the
table, fhewbred before me allwaye. *Shevvbred be-*
31 And thou fhalt make a candelfticke of *caufe it vvas*
pure thicke golde with his fhaft, braunches, *alvvay in the prefence and*
bolles, knoppes ād floures proceadynge *fight of the*
32 there out Syxe braunches fhall procede *Lorde*
out of the fydes of the candelfticke .iii. out of the one
33 fyde and .iii. out of the other. And there fhalbe .iii
cuppes like vnto almondes with knoppes *knoppes, buds*
ād floures vppon euery one of the .vi *of a flower, now fpelled*
braunches that procede out of the cādel- *knob*
34 ftycke: and in the candelfticke felfe .iiii. cuppes like
35 vnto almondes with their knoppes and floures: that
there be a knope vnder eueri .ii. braūches of the fyxe
36 that procede out of the cādelftycke. And the knoppes
and the braunches fhal be altogether, one pece of pure
thicke golde.

[Fo. XLIII.] *Woodcut with the infcription:* ¶ The
forme of the arke of witneffe with his ftaues and two
cherubyns.

.¶. *Verfo of* Fo. XLIII. *Woodcut with the infcrip-*

V. 24 labium aureum 25 coronam interrafilem 29 libamina, ex
auro puriffimo 30 panes propofitionis 36 vniuerfa ductilia de auro
puriff.
L. 29 aus lauter golt 30 fchawbrod 36 alles eyn ticht lautergolt.
M. M. N. 30 *Shewbreed,* becaufe it was alwaye in the prefence
and fyght of the Lorde.

tion: ⁋ The table of fhewbreed with the loves of breed vppon it, and his other veffels.

[Fo. XLIIII.] *Woodcut with the infcription*: ⁋ The facion of the cãdelfticke with his lampes, fnoffers and other neceffaryes. F. S. by H. [*in lower right hand corner*.]

37 .P. *Verfo of folio, but marked* [Fo. XLV.] And thou fhalt make .vii. lampes and put them an hye there on, to geue lighte vnto the other fyde that is ouer agaynft 38, 39 it: with fnoffers and fyre pannes of pure golde. And hundred pounde weyghte of fyne golde fhall make it 40 with all the apparell. And fe that thou make them after the facyon that was fhewed the in the mounte.

The .XXVI. Chapter.

1 AND thou fhalt make an habitatyõ with ten curteynes of twyned byffe, Iacyncte fcarlet and purpull, and fhalt make them with cherubyns of broderd 2 worke. The lenghte of a curtayne fhalbe .xxviii. cubyttes, and the bredth .iiii. and they fhalbe all of one 3 meafure: fyue curtaynes fhalbe coupled together one to a nother: and the other fyue likewife fhalbe coupled together one to another.

M.C.S. This chapter alfo defcrybeth the thynges pertaynynge to the holy place.

4 Then fhalt thou make louppes of Iacyncte coloure, a longe by the edge of the one curtayne even in the felvege of the couplinge courtayne. And likewife fhalt thou make in the edge of the vtmoft curtayne

M. 39 And an hundred
V. 37 vt luceant ex aduerfo. xxvi, 1 opere plumario 2 Vnius menfuræ fient vniuerfa tentoria. 4 anfulas hyac.
L. 1 cherubim folltu dran machen kunftlich.
M. M. N. 1 *Byffe* loke in xxxv. of Exo. 4 *Iacynct* is a floure that we call: a vyolet: & it is alfo a precious ftone or the coloure therof: but here it is taken only for the colore of Iacynct of which colore the curtayns fhuld be of, as afore in the xxv, a.
L. M. N. 4 *Gell feyden:* dife farbe nennen viel, blawbefarb odder hymelfarb. So doch beyde kriechifch vnd latinfch Bibel Hiacinthen farb fagt, Nu ift yhre Hiacinht beyde die blume vnd der fteyn gell oder goltfarb, darumb zu beforgen, das hie aber mal die fprach verfallen vnnd vngewifz fey.

XXVI. 5-16. called *Exodus.* 241

5 that is coupled therwith on the other fyde. Fyftie
louppes fhalt thou make in the one curtayne, ād
fiftie in the edge of the other that is couppled therwith on the other fyde: fo that the louppes be one
6 ouer agenfte a nother. And thou fhalt make fyftie

.¶. *Recto of folio, but without a folio numeral.
Woodcut with the infcription:* ⁋ *The forme of the
ten cortaynes of the tabernacle with their cherubins
and fiftye loupes.* F. S. by H. [*in lower right hand corner*.]

buttons of golde, and couple the curtaynes together
with the buttons: that it maye be an habitacyon.
7 And thou fhalt make .xi. curtaynes of gotes heere,
8 to be a tente to couer the habitacyō The lenght of
a curtayne fhalbe .xxx. cubettes, and the bredth .iiii
9 ād they fhalbe all .xi. of one meafure. And thou fhalt
couple .v. by thē felues, and the other fixe by them
felues, ād fhalt double the fixte in the forefront of the
10 tabernacle, And thou fhalt make fyftie loupes in the
edge of the vtmoft curtayne on the one fyde: euen in
the couplynge courtayne, and as many in the edge
11 of the couplynge curtayne on the other fyde. And
thou fhalt make fyftie buttones off braffe and put them
on the louppes, and couple the tente together with
all: that there maye be one tabernacle.
12 And the remnaunt that refteth in the curtaynes of
the tente: euē the bredeth of halfe a curtayne that
refteth, fhalbe lefte on the backe fydes of the habita-
13 cyon: a cubite on the one fide and a cubite on the
other fyde, of that that remayneth in the length of
the curtaynes off the tabernacle, which fhall remayne
of ether fyde of the habitacion to couer it with all.
14 And thou fhalt make another coueringe for the
tente of rams fkynnes dyed red: ād yet ano- [Fo.
XLVI.] ther aboue all of taxus fkynnes. taxus, *badger,
cf. German*
15 And thou fhalt make bordes for the Dachs
16 habitacion of fethim wod to ftonde vp righte: ten cubettes long fhall euery borde be, ād a cubette and an

𝒱. 6 circulos aureos 7 faga cilicina 11 vnum ex omnib. op-
erimētum fiat. 14 fuper hoc .. de hyac. pellibus 15 tabulas ftantes
𝓛. 7 zigen haar 14 dachs fellen. 15 bretter machen

17 halfe brode. Two fete shall one borde haue to couple them together with all, and so thou shalt make vnto
18 all the bordes of the habitacion. And thou shalt make .xx. bordes for the habitacion on the south syde,
19 and thou shalt make, xl. sokettes of syluer ād put them vnder the .xx. bordes: two sokettes vnder euery borde,
20 for their two fete. In lyke maner in the northsyde of
21 the habitacyon there shalbe .xx. bordes ād .xl. sokettes
22 off syluer: two sokettes vnder eueryborde. And for the west ende off the habitacyon, shalt thou make syxe
23 bordes, ād two bordes moo for the two west corners of
24 the habitaciō: so that these two bordes be coupled to gether beneth and lykewyse aboue with clampes. And
25 so shall it be in both the corners. And so there shalbe viii. bordes in all and .xvi. sokettes of syluer: ii. sokettes vnder euery borde.
26 And thou shalt make barres off sethimwod fiue for
27 the bordes of the one side of the tabernacle, and fyue for the other syde, and fyue for the bordes off the west
28 ende. And the mydle barre shall goo alonge thorow the myddes

.P. *Verso of* Fo. XLVI. *Woodcut with the inscription*: ℭ The facion of the bordes of the tabernacle, with their fete, sockettes and barres,

[Fo. XLVII.] *Woodcut with the insoription*: ℭ The facion of the corner bordes with their fete sockettes and barres.

29 .P. of the bordes and barre them together frō the one ende vnto the other. And thou shalt couer the bordes with golde and make golden rynges for them to
30 put the barres thorow, ād shalt couer the barres with golde also. And rere vp the habitacion acordinge to the facion ther of that was shewed the in the mount.
31 And thou shalt make a vayle off Iacyncte, of scarlett, purpull and twyned bysse, and shalt make it off broderd
32 worke and full of cherubyns. And hange it vppon .iiii

V. 18 latere merid. quod vergit ad austrum. 28 per medias tabulas a summo vsque ad summum 31 & pulchra variet. contextum
L. 24 eynem klammer 26 rigel 31 geller seyden, scharlacken vnd rosinrodt vnd getzw. weysser seyde

pilers of fethim wodd couered with golde ād that their knoppes be coured with golde alfo, and ftonde apon
33 iiii. fokettes of fyluer. And thou fhalt hāge vp the vayle with rynges, and fhall brynge in within the vayle, the arke of wittneffe. And the vayle fhall deuyde the holye from the moft holye.
34 And thou fhalt put the mercyfeate vppon the arcke
35 of witneffe in the holyeft place. And thou fhalt put the table without the vayle and candelfticke ouer agaynft the table: vppon the fouth fyde of the habitacion. And put the table on the north fyde.
36 And thou fhalt make an hangynge for the doore of the tabernacle: of Iacyncte, off fcarlett, off purpull and
37 off twyned byffe, wroughte with nedle worke. And thou fhalt [Fo. XLVIII.] make for the hangynge, fiue pilers off fethim wodd, and couer both them ād their knoppes with golde, and fhalt caft .v. fokettes off braffe for them.

ℭ The .XXVII. Chapter

1 AND thou fhalt make an altare of fethim wodd: fyue cubettes longe ād .v. cubettes brode, that it be fourefquare, and .iii
2 cubettes hye. And make it hornes proceding out in
3 the .iiii. corners of it, and couer it with braffe. And make his affhepannes, fhovels, bafens, flefhhokes, fyre-
4 pannes and all the apparell there of, of braffe after the fafcyon of a net, ād put apon the nette .iiii. rynges:

M.C.S. Yet mo thynges pertaynynge to the holye place.

𝔐. 33 fhalt brynge. xxvii, 4 and thou fhalt make a gredyern alfo lyke a net of-braffe, vpon whofe .iiii. corners fhalbe .iiii. brafen rynges: and the gredyern fhall reache vnto the myddes of the altare. And thou fhalt make
𝒱. 33 quo et fanct. & fanct. fanctuaria diuidentur. xxvii, 2 ex ipfo erunt 4 in modum retis .. annuli aenei.
𝔏. 33 dem Heyligen vnd dem Aller heyligften. 36 tuch machen ... geftrickt von geller feyden, rofinr., fcharl., vnd getzwyrnet weiff. feyden. xxvi, 3 ertz 4 gitter .. ehern netz
𝔐.𝔐.𝔑. 33 *The moft holy place*, was the fecrete and inwarde place of the fanctuary wherī ftode the arcke & the mercyefeate, and into which none but the preftes only might come, and that but once a yere. The figure of which thynge is declared in the Hebrewes ix, a. iii. Reg. vi, c.

5 euen in the .iiii. corners of it, and put it beneth vnder the compaſſe of the altare, and let the net reache vnto
6 the one half of the altare, And make ſtaues for the
7 altare of ſethim wodd, and couer thē wyth braſſe, and let them be put in rynges alonge by the ſydēs off the altare, to bere it with all.
8 And make the altare holowe with bordes: euen as it was ſhewed the in the mount, ſo lett them make it,
9 And thou ſhalt make a courte vnto the habitacion, which ſhall haue in the ſouth ſyde hāgynges of twyned
10 byſſe, beyng an hundred cubettes longe, and .xx pilers thereof with there .xx. ſockettes of braſſe: but the knoppes of the

P. Verſo of Fo. XLVIII. *containing a woodcut with the inſcription:* ⁋ The forme of the alter of the burnt-offrynge with his hornes, ringes ſtaues, gredyernes and other ornamētes.

11 [Fo. XLIX.] pilers and their whopes ſhalbe ſyluer. In like wiſe on the north ſyde there ſhalbe hāgynges of an hundred cubettes longe and .xx. pilers with their
12 ſokettes of braſſe, and the knoppes and the whopes of ſyluer. And in the bredth of the courte weſtwarde, there ſhalbe hangynges of fyſtye cubettes longe, and
13 x. pilers with their .x. fokettes. And in the bredth of the courte eaſtwarde towarde the ryſynge of the ſonne,
14 ſhalbe hangynges of .L. cubyttes. Hāgynges of .xv cubittes in the one ſyde of it with .iii. pilers, and .iii
15 ſokettes: and likewiſe on the other ſyde ſhalbe hangynges of .xv. cubettes with .iii. pilers and .iii. ſokettes.
16 And in the gate of the courte ſhalbe a vayle of .xx cubettes: of Iacyncte, ſcarlet, purpul and twyned byſſe wroughte with nedle worke, and .iiii. pilers with their
17 iiii. ſokettes. All the pilers rounde aboute the courte ſhalbe whoped with ſyluer, and their knoppes of ſyluer,
18 and their ſokettes of braſſe. The length of the courte, ſhall be an hundred cubettes, and the bredth fiftye, and

V. 5 ſubter arulam .. ad alt. medium. 8 Non ſolidū, ſed inane & cauum 10 viginti cum baſibus ... capita cum caelaturis
L. 5 vnden auff vmb 9 hoff
M. M. N. 9 *The cowrte* is that whych we call a church yarde.

the heygth fyue, and the hangynges ſhalbe of twyned
19 byſſe and the ſokettes of braſſe. And all the veſſels of
the habitacion to all maner ſeruyce ād the pynnes there
of: ye and the pynnes alſo of the courte, ſhalbe braſſe.

.¶. *Verſo of* Fo. XLIX. *containing a woodcut with
the inſcription*: ¶ The figure of the orderinge of all
the ornamētes which muſt ſtande in the tabernacle.

20 [Fo. L.] And commaunde the childern of Iſrael that
they geue the pure oyle olyue beaten for the lyghtes
11 to poure all way in to the lampes. In the tabernacle
of witneſſe without the vayle which is before the wytneſſe, ſhall Aaron ād his ſonnes dreſſe it both euen and
mornynge before the Lorde: And it ſhalbe a dewtie
for euer vnto youre generacyons after you: to be geuen
of the childern of Iſrael.

The .XXVIII. Chapter.

1 AND take thou vnto the, Aaron thi brother and his ſonnes with him, from amonge the childern of Iſrael, that he maye minyſtre vnto me: both Aaron, Nadab, Abihu,
2 Eleazar and Ithamar Aarons ſonnes. And thou ſhalt make holye rayment for Aaron thy brother, both honorable and glory-
3 ous Moreouer ſpeake vnto all that are wyſe harted which I haue fylled with the ſprete of wyſdome: that they make Aarons rayment to conſecrate him wyth, that he maye myniſtre vnto me.

ℳ.ℭ.𝔖. Aarons apparell, & hys ſonnes.

Frō hēce vnto the bokes ende ād thorovve out all the nexte boke, thou ſhalt ſe vvhat moued the Pope and vvhence he toke the faſcion of the garmētes and ornamētes that are novveuſed in the chyrche

ℳ. 21 and Aaron and hys ſonnes ſhall dreſſe
𝒱. 19 cuncta vaſa 20 vt ardeat lucerna ſemper 21 collocab.
eam ... vt vſque mane luceat ... cultus per ſucceſſiones eorum.
xxviii, 1 vt ſacerdotio fungantur 2 in gloriam et decorem.
ℒ. 19 negel 21 von morgen bis an den abent. xxviii, 1 meyn
Prieſter ſey 2 zu ehren vnd ſchmuck 3 weyſen hertzen
ℳ. ℳ. N. 21 It is called the *tabernacle of witneſſe:* becauſe
therin was contayned the couenaūt & witneſſe wheruntō god
wold that the chyldren of Iſrael ſhuld truſt, as Leu. iii. c. *Foreuer:* loke in Geneſis xiii, d.

4 These are the garmentes which they shall make: a breſtlappe, Ephod, a tunycle, a ſtrayte cote, a myter and a girdell. And they ſhall make holye garmentes for Aaron thi brother ād his ſōnes, that he maye myniſtre vnto
5 me. And they ſhal take there to, golde, Iacincte, ſcarlet,

⁋. Verſo of Fo. L. *containing a woodcut with the inſcription*: ❡ The forme of Aaron with all his apparell.

* [Fo. LI.] purpull and byſſe.
6 And they ſhall make the Ephod: of golde Iacyncte, ſcarlett, purpull ād white twyned
7 byſſe with broderdworke, The two ſydes ſhall come
8 to gether, cloſſed vppe in the edges thereof And the girdell of the Ephod ſhalbe of the ſame workemanſhippe ād of the ſame ſtuffe: euen of golde, Iacyncte, ſcarlete, purpull ād twyned byſſe,

9 And thou ſhalt take two onyx ſtones and graue
10 in them the names of the childern of Iſrael: ſixe in the one ſtone, and the other ſixe in the other ſtone:
11 acordinge to the order of their birth. After the worke of a ſtonegrauer, euē as ſygnettes are grauen, ſhalt thou graue the .ii. ſtones with the names of the childern of Iſrael, ād ſhalt make thē to be ſet
12 in ouches of golde. And thou ſhalt put the two ſtones apō the two ſhulders of the Ephod, ād they ſhalbe ſtones off remembraunce vnto the childern off Iſrael. And Aaron ſhall bere their names before the Lorde vppon hys two ſhulders for a remembraunce.
13, 14 And thou ſhalt make hokes off golde and two

and the maner of halovvenge off the churck, altare, chalice, fonte, belles, ād ſo forth, ād is become as it vvere a preſt of the olde lavve, ād hath brought vs in to captiuite as it vvere vnder the ceremonies of the old lavve, ſaue theirs ſpak and ours be domme.

ouches, ornaments fit to diſplay jewels or precious ſtones.

V. 4 Rationale & ſuperhumerale, tunicam et lineam ſtrictam 6 byſſo retorta, opere polymito. 7 Duas oras iunctas, 10 iuxta ordinem natiuit. eorum. 11 Opere ſculptoris & cælatura gemmarii 12 memoriale fil. Iſrael, . . . ob recordationē. 13 vncinos ex auro
L. 4 weyhe . . bruſtlatz, leybrock, ſeyden rock, engen rock 10 orden yhrs alters 12 gedechtnis (*bis*)
M. M. N. 4 *Breſtlappe* or breſtflappe is ſoche a flappe as is ī the breſt of a cope.

cheynes off fine golde: lynkeworke and wrethed, and
faften the wrethed cheynes to the hokes.

15 And thou fhalt make the breftlappe of enfample with broderd worke: euē after the worke of
the Ephod fhalt thou make it: of golde, Iacyncte,
fcarlet, purple ād twyned byffe fhalt thou make it.
16 Fourefquare it fhall be ād double, an hande brede
17 longe and an hande brede brode. And thou fhalt fyll
it with .iiii. rowes of ftones. In the firft rowe fhalbe
18 a Sardios, a Topas and Smaragdus. The feconde rowe:
19 a Rubyn, Saphir and a Diamonde. The thyrd: Lygu-
rios an Acatt and Amatift.
20 The fourth: a Turcas, Onix and Iafpis. And they
fhalbe fett in golde in their inclofers.
21 And the ftones fhalbe grauen as fygnettes be grauē:
with the names of the childern of Ifrael euen with
xii. names euery one with his name acordynge to
the .xii. trybes.
22 And thou fhalt make vppon the breftlappe .ii
fafteninge cheynes of pure golde ād wrethen worke.
23 And thou fhalt make likewyfe vppon the breftlappe
ii. rynges of golde and put them on the edges of the
24 breftlappe, and put the .ii. wrethen cheynes of golde in
the .ii. rynges which are in the edges of the breftlappe,
25 And the .ii. endes of the .ii. cheynes thou fhalt faften
in the .ii. rynges, and put them vppon the fhulders
of the Ephod: on the forefyde of it.
26 And thou fhalt yet make .ii. rynges of gol- [Fo.
LII.] de ād put them in the .ii. edges of the breftlappe
euē in the borders there of towarde the infyde of the

𝔐. 15 breftlappe of iudgemēt 19 Rubye
𝒱. 15 rationale quoque iudicii 17 Ponefque in eo .. ordines
lapidum 17 in primo verfu 20 in quarto chryfolitus, onych., et
beryllus 21 cælabuntur 25 quod rationale refpicit.
ℒ. 15 bruftlatz des rechts .. nach der kunft 17 fullen mit vier
rigen 25 ecken am leybrock gegen ander vber.
𝔐. 𝔐. N. 17 *Smaragdus:* Or an emeraude. 18 *Rubye:* Some
rede a carbuncle.
ℒ. 𝔐. N. 15 *Des rechts:* Mit dem wort zeygt er an, was der
bruftlatz bedeut, nemlich, das ynn Chrifto dem hohen priefter die
macht ftehet das gefeze aus zu legen vnnd zu lencken nach ge-
legenheyt der fachen vnnd notturft der gewiffen, wie Chriftus
Matth. 12 mit dem Sabbath thut.

27 Ephod that is ouer agaynſt it. And yet .ii. other rīges of golde thou ſhalt make, ād put thē on the ii. ſydes of the Ephod, beneth ouer agaynſt the breſtlappe, alowe where the ſydes are ioyned together
28 vppō the brodered girdell of the Ephod. And they ſhall bynde the breſtlappe by his ryngates vnto the ryngates of the Ephod with a lace of Iacyncte, that it maye lye cloſſe vnto the brodered girdell of the Ephod, that the breſtlappe be not lowſed from the Ephod.
29 And Aarō ſhall bere the names of the childern of Iſrael in the breſtlappe of enſāple vppō his herte, whē he goth in to the holy place, for a remēbraūce before
30 the Lorde allwaye. And thou ſhalt put ī the breſtlappe of enſāple* lighte and perfectneſſe: that they be euē vpon Aarōs herte whē he goeth ī before the Lorde ād Aarō ſhall bere the enſāple of the childern of Iſrael vpō his herte before the Lorde alwaie

Light ād perfecteneſſe: In Hebrue it is lightes and perfectneſſes: ād I thynke that the one vvere ſtones that did gliſter ādhad light in them and the other clere ſtones

31 And thou ſhalt make the tunycle vnto the Ephod, all to gether of Iacyncte.
32 And ther ſhalbe an hole for the heed in

ℳ. 27. bordered 29 breſtlappe of iudgement, ſo v. 30.   30 Vrim and Thumin
V. 28 vitta hyacinthina, vt maneat iunctura fabrefacta 29 ſuper pectus 30 doctrinam et veritatem 32 capitium, & ora per gyrum eius textilis
L. 30 Liecht vnd vollickeyt
ℳ. ℳ. N. 30 Vrym and Thumin, are Hebrue wordes: Vrim ſignifieth light & Thumin perfectnes: and I thynke that the one were ſtones that dyd glyſter and had light in thē, the other clere ſtones as criſtall. And the lighte betokened the light of Godes worde & the pureneſſe cleane lyuynge acordynge to the ſame, & was therfore called the enſample of the chyldern of Iſrael, becauſe it put them in remembraunce to ſeke Gods worde & to doo therafter.
L. ℳ. N. 30 Liecht etc. Ebreiſch heyſſen diſe wort Urim and Thumim, Urim heyſt liechte odder glentze, Thumim heyſt, vollige vnd on wandel, was ſolchs ſey geweſen leyplich, weyſs man itzt nit mehr, Bedeut aber on zweyffel, das Chriſtus lere iſt vnd wirt behalten lauter, hel vnd on wandel ynn des prediger hertzen, wie paulus. Tito gepeut, das er das wort heylſam, redlich vnd vnſtrefflich furen ſol, vnd Timotheo befilt, eyn gutte beylage zu bewarē, das heyſt auch hie, das recht der kinder Iſrael auff Aarons hertzen tragen.

the myddes of it, ād let there be a bonde
of wouen worke rounde aboute the colore
^{colore of a} of it: as it were the colore
^{partlet, collar}
^{of a ruff, or} of a partlet, that it rent not·
33 ^{neckband.} And beneth .P. vppon the
hem thou fhalt make pomgranates of Iacyncte, of fcarlet, and of purpull rounde
aboute the hem, and belles of golde be-
34 twene them rounde aboute: that there be
euer a golden bell and a pomgranate, a
golden bell and a pomgranate rounde
aboute vppon the hem of the tunicle.
35 And Aaron fhall haue it vppon him
when he minyftreth, that the founde
maye be herde when he goeth in to the holy place
before the Lorde and when he cometh out, that
he dye not.

36 And thou fhalt make a plate of pure golde, and
graue there on (as fignettes are grauen) the ho-
37 lynes of the Lorde, and put it on a lace
of Iacyncte and tye it vnto the mytre,
38 vppon the forefrunt of it, that it be apon
Aarōs foreheed: that Aaron bere the
fynne of the holy thynges which the
childern of Ifrael haue halowed in all their holye
giftes. And it fhalbe alwayes vpon Aarons foreheed,
that they maye be accepted before the Lorde
39 And thou fhalt make an albe of byffe, and thou
fhalt make a mytre of byffe ād a girdell of nedle
worke.
40 And thou fhalt make for Aarons fonnes alfo cotes,

*as cristall.
And the lighte
betokened the
light of Godes
vvorde and
the pureneffe
cleane livinge
acordynge to
the fame and
vvas therefore
called the en-
fample of the
childern of If-
rael, becaufe it
put thē in re-
membraunce
to feke Gods
vvorde ād to
do there after.*

*That he call-
eth the holy-
neffe of the
Lorde I fup-
pofe it be this
name Ieho-
uah.*

V. 35 vt audiatur fonitus 36 Sanctum domino. 38 muneribus
et donariis 40 tunicas lineas

L. 35 an haben wenn er dienet 36 die heylickeyt dem Herrn
38 gaben vnd heylthum . . das er fie verfune

M. M. N. 36 *The holynes of the Lord*, was a name of God
made with .iiii. letters, which the Hebrues durft not name for
honoure wyich they had to God, in ftede wherof they fayd
Adonay. Which we haue interpret in Ex. vi, a. by his name
Iehouah. 38 *The fynne:* for the offryng made for fynne, as
Rom. viii, a.

41 girdels and bonettes honourable and glorious, and thou shalt put them vppon Aaron thy brother ād on his sonnes with him [Fo. LIII.] and shalt anoynte them and fyll theyr handes and confecrate them,
42 that they maye myniftre vnto me. And thou shalt make them lynen breches to couer their preuyties:
43 from the loynes vnto the thyes shall they reach. And they shalbe apon Aaron and his sonnes, whē they goo in to the tabernacle of wytneffe, or when they goo vnto the altare to myniftre in holynes, that they bere no synne and so dye. And it shalbe a lawe for euer vnto Aaron ād his seed after him.

The .XXIX. Chapter.

1 THIS is the thinge that thou shalt doo vnto them when thou haloweft them to be my preaftes. Take one oxe and two
2 rammes that are without blemysh, ād vnleuēded bred and cakes of fwete bred tempered with oyle and wafers of fwete bred anoynted with oyle (of
3 wheten floure shalt thou make them) and put them in a maunde and brynge thē in the maunde with the oyle and the .ii rammes.

M.C.S. The confecracion of Aaron and his sonnes.

maunde, a hand basket.

M. 3 maunde with the oxe
V. 41 cunct. confec. manus 43 vt min. in fanctuario, ne iniq. rei moriantur. xxix, 2 cruftulam abfque fermento .. lagana 3 in caniftro .. vitulū autem
L. 40 zu ehren vnd schmuck. 41 hende fullen 42 nydderkleyd 43 yhr miffethat tragen.
M. M. N. 43 *Tabernacle of witneffe:* Loke in Ex. xxvii, d. *Foreuer:* Loke in Gen. xiii, d.
L. M. N. 41 *Fullen:* Dis fullen ift ein Ebreifch fprach, der man mus gewonen, vnd war das, wie ym folgend capitel fteht, das ynn der weyhe den Prieftern die hende mit opfer gefullet wurden fur dem herrn, Bedeut, das die prediger follen vol gutter werck feyn fur allen, wie Chriftus Math, 5. leret laft ewr gutte werck fur den menfchen leuchten.

4 And brynge Aaron ād his sonnes vnto the doore of the tabernacle of wytnesse, ād 5 wassh them with water, and take the garmentes, and put apon Aaron: the strayte cote, and the tunycle of the Ephod, and the Ephod ād the brestlappe: and gerth thē to him with the brodered girdel of 6 the Ephod. And put the mitre vppō .P. his heed and 7 put the holy crowne vpon the mytre. Then take the anoyntynge oyle and poure it apon his heed and 8 anoynte him. And brynge his sonnes and put albes 9 apon them, ād gerth them with girdels: as well Aaron as his sonnes, And put the bonettes on them that the preastes office maye be theirs for a perpetuall lawe.

Of thys they take the confecratynge of bisshoppes ād annoyntynge of preastes, though they haue altered the maner some vvhat.

And fyll the handes of Aaron and of hys sonnes, 10 and brynge the oxe before the tabernacle of witnesse. 11 And let Aaron ād his sōnes put their hādes apō his heed ād kyll hī before the Lord in the dore of the 12 tabernacle of witnesse And take of the bloud of the oxe ād put it apō the hornes of the alter with thi finger ād poure all the bloude apon the botome of the 13 alter, ād take all the fatt that couereth the inwardes, ād the kall that is on the lyuer, and the .ii. kydneys with the fatt that is apō thē: and burne thē apō the 14 alter. But the flesh of the oxe and his skynne and his donge, shalt thou burne with fyre, without the hoste. For it is a synneofferynge.

15 Then take one of the rammes, ād let Aaron and his sonnes put their hondes apon the heade of the ram, 16 and cause him to be slayne, ād take of his bloude, and 17 sprenkell it rounde aboute apon the alter, and cutt the ram in peces and [Fo. LIIII.] wessh the inwardes of him and his legges, ād put them vnto the peces

M. 17 wash
V. 7 atque hoc ritu confecrabitur. 9 eruntque facerd. mihi religione perpetua . 9 initiaueris manus 12 reliquum autem 13 et offeres incenfum
L. 6 heylige kron an den huet 9 hend fullen 10 hutte des zeugnis 12 alles ander blut 14 fundopffer.

18 ād vnto his heed, ād burne the hole ram apon the alter. For it is a burntofferyng vnto the Lorde, and a ſwete ſauoure of the Lordes ſacrifice.

19 And take the other ram and let Aaron and hys
20 ſonnes, put their hondes apon hys heed and let him than be kylled. And take of his bloude and put it apon the typpe of the righte eare of Aaron and of his ſonnes, and apon the thombe of their righte handes, and apon the great too of their ryghte fete: and ſprenkell the bloude apon the alter rounde aboute.

21 Than take of the bloude that is apon the alter and of the anoyntynge oyle, ād ſprēkell it apon Aaron and his veſtimētes, ād apō his ſonnes ād apō their garmētes alſo. Thā is he ād his clothes holy ād his ſonnes ād their clothes holye alſo

22 Than take the fatt of the ram and hys rompe and the fatt that couereth the inwardes and the kall of the lyuer and the two kydneys, and the fatt that is apon them and the righte ſhulder (for that ram is a
23 fulloffrynge) and a ſymnell of bred ād a cake of oyled bred ād a wafer out of the baſkett of ſwete bred that is before ſymnell, *a kind of cake*, *cf. Germ*. Semmel.
24 .F. the Lorde, and put all apon the handes of Aaron and on the handes of his ſonnes: and waue thē in and
25 out a waueoffrynge vnto the Lorde. Than take it from of their handes and burne it apon the alter: euen apon the burntoffringe, to be a ſauoure of ſwetneſſe before the Lorde. For it is a ſacrifice vnto the Lorde.
26 Then take the breſt of the ram that is Aarons fulloffrynge and waue it a waueoffrynge before the Lorde,
27 ād let that be thy parte. And ſanctifie the breſt of the waueoffrynge and the ſhulder of the heueoffrynge whiche is waued and heued vp of the ram whiche is

V. 18 oblatio eſt domino, odor ſuauiſſimus victimæ domini. 20 ac pedis, dextri 22 aruinā quæ operit vitalia .. aries conſecrationis 24 eleuans coram dom. 25 holocauſtum, odorem ſuauiſſimum 26 in partem tuam.

L. 18 den gantzen wider antzunden ... brandopffer, eyn ſuſſer geruch des opffers dem HERRN. 22 eyn widder der fulle 24 webe es 25 zunde es an .. des HERRN opffer. 27 gewebet vnd gehebet

ℳ. ℳ. N. 18 What a *ſwete ſauoure* is ye ſhall fynd in Leui. i, c. and Ez. xx, f.

28 the full offrynge of Aaron ād of his sonnes. And it shal be Aarons ād his sonnes dutye for euer, of the childrē of Israel: for it is an heueoffrynge. *dutye, due, i. e. that which belongs to him.* And the heueoffrynge shalbe the Lordes dutie of the childern of Israel: euen of the sacrifice of their peaceoffrynges which they heue vnto the Lorde.

29 And the holye garmentes of Aaron shalbe his sonnes after him, to anoynte them therin, and to fyll
30 their handes therin. And that sonne that is preast in his stede after him, shall put them on seuen dayes: that he goo in to the tabernacle of witnesse, to ministre in the holye place.

31 Thā take the ram that is the fullofferyng ād [Fo.
32 LV.] seth his flesh in an holye place. And Aarō and his sonnes shall eate the flesh of hī, ād the bred that is in the basket: euen in the dore of the tabernacle
33 of witnesse. And they shall eat thē, becaufe the attonmēt was made therewith to fyll their handes and to sanctifie thē: but a straunger shal not eate therof, becaufe they are holie

34 Yf oughte of the flesh of the fulloffrynges, or of the bred remayne vnto the mornyng, thou shalt burne it with fyre: for it shall not be eaten, becaufe it is holye.
35 And se thou do vnto Aaron and his sonnes: euen so in all thynges as I haue commaunded the: that thou
36 fyll their handes seuen dayes and offre euery daye an oxe for a synneoffrynge for to recōcyle with all. And thou shalt halowe the alter when thou reconcyleft it,
37 and shalt anoynte it to sanctifie it. Seuē dayes thou shalt reconcyle the alter and sanctifie it, that it maye

V. 26 quo initiatus eft Aaron (and v. 28) 28 quia primitiua funt & initia de victimis eorum pacificis 29°confecrentur manus 33 placabile facrificium et fanct. off. manus. 36 confecrabis manus 36 Mundabifque alt . cum immol. exp. hoftiam

L. 28 todopffern vnd hebungen 36 vmb der willen die verfunet werden

M. M. N. 33 *Sanctifie:* Loke in Genefis .ii, a.

L. M. N. 36 *Entfundigen:* das ift abfoluieren vnd los fprechen wie Ps. 50 *afperges me yfopo,* das ift, entfundige vnd abfoluir mich mit Ifopen.

be an alter moſt holye: ſo that no mā maye twich it
but thei that be conſecrate.

38 This is that which thou ſhalt offre vpō
the alter: ii. lambes of one yere olde daye
39 by daye for euer, the one thou ſhalt offre
in the morninge and the other at euen.
40 And vnto the one lābe take a tenth
deale of floure myngled with the fourth parte of an
hin of beaten oyle, and the fourth parte of an hin of
41 wyne, for a drinc- .P. keoffrynge. And the other
lambe thou ſhalt offer at euen and ſhalt doo thereto
acordynge to the meateoffrynge and drinkeoffrynge
in the mornynge, to be an odoure of a ſwete ſauoure
42 of the ſacrifice of the Lorde. And it ſhalbe a con-
tinuall burntoffrynge amonge youre children after you,
in the doore of the tabernacle of witneſſe before the
Lorde, where I will mete you to ſpake vnto you there.
43 There I will mete wyth the childern of Iſrael, and wilbe
44 ſanctified in myne honoure. And I will ſanctifie the
tabernacle of witneſſe and the alter: and I will ſanctifie alſo both Aaron and his ſonnes to be my preaſtes.
45 And moreouer I will dwell amōge the children of
46 Iſrael and wilbe their God. And they ſhal knowe
that I am the Lorde their God that broughte them out
of the lond of Egipte for to dwell amonge them: euen
I the Lorde their God,

Toch not the chalyce northe altare ſtōne nor holy oyle and holde youre hande out off the fonte.

❡ The .XXX. Chapter.

1 AND thou ſhalt make an alter to
burne cēſe therin, of ſethim
2 wod: a cubet longe, and a
cubet brode, euen foureſquare
ſhall it be and two cubettes hye: with hornes proced-

ℳ.𝔈.𝔖. The altare of incenſe. The braſen lauer. The anoyntynge oyle.

𝒱. 38 iugiter 40 & vinum ad libandum eiuſdem menſuræ 41 et
iuxta ea quæ diximus 42 oblat. perpetua ... vbi cōſtituam 43 Ibique
præcipiam filiis Iſr.,.. altare in gloria mea. xxx, 1 ad adolendum
thymiama
 𝐋. 37 wer.. anruren wil, der ſol geweyhet ſeyn. 39 zwiſſchen
abents (v. 41) 42 betzeugen vnd mit dyr reden

3 yng out of it, ãd thou fhalt ouerlaye it with fyne golde both the roffe ãd the walles round aboute, ãd his hornes alfo, ãd fhalt make vnto it a crowne of gold
4 roũde aboute, ãd .ii. goldẽ ringes

Fo. LVI. *containing a woodcut with the infcription*: ⓒ The forme of the altare of incenfe with all that belongeth vnto it.

₧. on ether fyde, euen vnder the croune, to put ftaues
5 therin for to bere it with all. And thou fhalt make the ftaues of fethim wodd and couer them with golde.
6 And thou fhalt put it before the vayle that hangeth before the arcke of witneffe, and before the mercyfeate that is before the witneffe, where I will mete the.
7 And Aaron fhall burne thereon fwete cenfe euery
8 mornynge when he dreffeth the lampes: and lykewyfe at euen when he fetteth vpp the lampes he fhall burne cenfe perpetually before the Lorde thorow out youre
9 generacions Ye fhall put no ftraunge cenfe thereon, nether burntfacrifice nor meateoffrynge: nether poure
10 any drynkeoffrynge thereon. And Aaron fhall reconcyle his hornes once in a yere, wyth the bloude of the fynneoffrynge of reconcylīge: euen once in the yere fhall he reconcyle it thorow youre generacions. And fo is it moft holye vnto the Lorde.
11,12 And the Lorde fpake vnto Mofes faynge: when thou takeft the fumme of the childern of Ifrael ãd telleft them, they fhall geue euery mã a   telleft, *num-* reconcylinge of his foule vnto the Lorde, *bereft.*
that there be no plage amonge them when thou tel-
13 left them. And thus moch fhall euery man geue that goeth in the nombre: halfe a fycle, after the holye fycle: a fycle is .xx. geeras: [Fo. LVII.] and an halfe
14 fycle fhalbe the heueoffrynge vnto the Lorde. And

ℳ. 10 reconcyle vpon the hornes of it 13 after the fycle of the fanctuarye

𝒱. 3 coronam aureolam per gyrum 6 propitiatorio ... vbi loquar tibi. 8 collocat eas ad vefp. 9 compofitionis alterius 10 deprecabitur ... fuper cornua 12 tuleris fummam .. recenfiti 13 menfuram templi .. obolos

ℒ. 3 feyn dach 6 Gnaden ftuel der auff dem zeugnis ... zeugen. 9 fremd gereuch 10 auff feynen h. verfunen 12 verfunung feyner feel 13 feckel des heyligthums

all that are numbred of thē that are .xx. yere olde
and aboue fhall geue an heueoffrynge vnto the Lorde.
15 The rych fhall not paffe, and the poore fhall not goo
vnder halfe a fycle, when they geue an heueoffrynge
16 vnto the Lorde for the attonemēt of their foules. And
thou fhalt take the reconcylinge money of the children
of Ifrael and fhalt put it vnto the vfe of the tabernacle of witneffe, and it fhall be a memoriall of the
childern of Ifrael before the Lorde, to make attonement for their foules.
17,18 And the Lorde fpake vnto Mofes faynge: thou
fhalt make a lauer of braffe and his fote alfo of braffe
to wafh with all, and fhalt put it betwene the tabernacle of witneffe and the alter and put water there-
19 in: that Aaron and hys fonnes maye wefh both their
20 handes ād theyr fete thereout, whē they go in to the
tabernacle of witneffe, or whē they goo vnto the
altare to miniftre and to burne the Lordes offrynge,
21 left they dye. And it fhalbe an ordinaunce for euer
vnto him and his feed amonge youre children after you.
22,23 And the Lorde fpake vnto Mofes faynge: take
principall fpices: of pure myrre fiue hundred fycles, of
fwete cynamone half fo moch

.P. *Verfo of* Fo. LVII. *containing a woodcut with the inscription*: ⁋ The figure of the lauer of braffe with his fote.

[Fo. LVIII.] two hundred and fyftie ficles: of fwete
24 calamyte, two hundred and .L. Of caffia, two hundred
and .L. after the holye fycle, and of oyle olyue an hin.
25 And make of them holye anoyntynge oyle euen an oyle
26 compounde after the crafte of the apoticarye. And noynt

𝕸. 16 an attonement
𝖁. 14 dabit pretium. 16 monim. eorum 20 offerant... thymiama domino 23 aromata primæ myrrhæ & electæ 24 pondere fanctuarii
𝕷. 18 handfafs 19 draus waffchen 23 fpecerey der beften myrrhen 25 nach der apotecker kunft.
𝕸. 𝕸. 𝕹. 25 *Anoyntynge oyle:* This holy anoynting oyle doth figure the vertue of the holy ghooft declared or fhewed by the worde of god: & defcendynge downe fyrft on the hed of Aarō which is Chrift & confequently vpon the Apoftles & all the faythfull, as in Ps. cxxxii, a.

the tabernacle off wytneſſe therewyth, and the arcke
27 of witneſſe, and the table with all his apparell, and the
candelſticke with all his ordinaunce, and the alter of
28 incenſe, and the alter of burntſacrifice and all his
29 veſſels, and the lauer and his fote. And ſacrifie them
that they maye be moſt holye: ſo that no man twyche
30 them but they that be halowed. And anoynte Aaron
and his ſonnes and conſecrate thē to miniſtre vnto me.
31 And thou ſhalt ſpeake vnto the childrē of Iſrael
ſaynge: this ſhalbe an holye oyntynge oyle vnto me,
32 thorow out youre generacions. No mans fleſh ſhalbe
anoynted therewith: nether ſhall ye make any other
after the makynge of it for it is holye, ſe therfore that
33 ye take it for holye. whoſoeuer maketh like that, or
whoſoeuer putteth any of it apon a ſtraunger, ſhall
peryſh from amonge his people.
34 And the Lord ſayd vnto Moſes: take vnto the ſwete
ſpices: ſtacte, onycha, ſwete galbanū ād pure ſrākē-
35 ſens, of etch like moch: ād make .℣. cens of them cō-
pounde after the crafte of the apoticarye, myngled
36 together, that it maye be made pure and holye. And
beat it to powder and put it before the witneſſe in the
tabernacle of witneſſe, where I will mete the, but let it
37 be vnto you holye. And ſe that ye make none after
the makinge of that, but let it be vnto you holye for
38 the Lorde. And whoſoeuer ſhall make like vnto that,
to ſmell thereto, ſhall periſh from amonge his people.

❡ The .XXXI. Chapter

1 AND the Lorde ſpake vnto Moſes   𝔐.𝕮.𝕾. *The*
2 ſaynge: beholde, I haue called   *callynge of Bezaleel and*
by name, Bezaleel the ſonne   *Ahaliab the*
of Vri ſone to Hur of the   *woorkmen.*
3 tribe of Iuda. And I haue filled hī with   *The Sabboth is commaunded.*

𝔐. 29 ſacrifye
℣. 28 vniuerſam ſupellectilem quæ ad cult. eor. pertinet. 34 thus
lucid. . 35 & ſanctificatione digniſſimum. 36 pones ex eo . . ſanctum .
ſanctorum erit vobis thym. 38 vt od. illius perf., peribit
𝕷. 29 das allerheyligſt ſeyen . . . anruren wil der ſol geweyhet
ſeyn. 33 ausgerottet

the fprete of God, with wifdome, vnder- *The tables of*
ftondinge ād knowlege: euē in all maner *ftone are geuen Mofes.*
4 worke, to finde out fotle faytes, to worke *faytes, fkilful*
5 in golde fyluer ād braffe and with the *workes.*
crafte to graue ftones, to fet ād to carue in tībre, ād
6 to worke in all maner workmāſhipe. And beholde,
I haue geuē him to be his companion Ahaliab the
fonne of Ahifamach of the tribe of Dan, and in the
hertes of all that are wife harted I haue put wifdom
7 to make all that I haue commaunded the: the tabernacle of witneffe, and the arcke of witneffe, and the
mercyfeate that is there vppon, all the ornamentes
8 of the tabernacle and [Fo. LIX.] the table with his
ordinaunce, ād the pure cādlefticke with al his appar-
9 ell, ād the alter of incens, ād the alter of burntoff-
10 rynges with al his veffels, ād the lauer with his fote,
ād the veftimētes to miniftre in, ād the holye garmētes
for Aarō the preaft, ād the garmētes of his fonnes to
11 miniftre in, and the anoyntinge oyle and the fwete
cenfe for the fanctuarye: acordinge to al as I haue
commaunded the ſhall they doo.

12, 13 And the Lorde fpake vnto Mofes fayng: fpeake
ūto the childern of Ifrael ād faye: ī any wyfe fe that
ye kepe my Sabbath, for it ſhalbe a fygne *The fabbath*
betwene me and you in youre generacions *befide that it*
for to knowe, that I the Lorde doo fanctifie *ād heare the*
14 you. Kepe my Sabbath therfore, that *vvorde of god and to feke his*
it be an holye thynge vnto you. He *vvil ād to*
that defileth it, ſhal be ſlayne therfore. *offer ād reconcile thē*
For whofoeuer worketh therein, the fame *felues vnto*
foule ſhalbe roted out from amonge his *god, it vvas a figne vnto*
15 people. Sixe dayes ſhall men worke, but *them alfo ād*

V. 4 ad excogitandum quic. fabrefieri poteft 10 vt fungantur
officio fuo in facris. 14 fanctum eft enim
L. 6 allerley weyfen die weysheyt 14 wer yhn entheyliget..
des tods fterben (v. 15)
M. M. N. 13 *Sabboth:* The Sabboth befyde that it ferued to
come and heare the worde of God and to feke hys wil & to offer
& recōcyle them felues vnto God. It was a fygne vnto thē alfo
& dyd put thē in remembraunce that it was god that fanctyfied
thē with his holye fprete & not they thē felues with their holy
workes.

the feuenth daye is the Sabbath of the holye refte of the Lorde: so that whofoeuer doeth any worke in the Sabbath daye,
16 fhal dye for it. wherfore let the childern of Ifrael kepe the Sabbath, that they obferue it thorowe out their generacions, that
17 it be an appoyntement for euer. For it fhalbe a fygne betwene me, and the childern of Ifrael for euer. For in fixe dayes the Lorde made heauen and erth, and the .P. feuenth daye he refted and was refreffhed.

18 And whē he had made an end of comening with Mofes vppon the mounte Sinai, he gaue him two tables of witneffe: which were of ftone and written with the finger of God.

did put thē in remēbraūce that it vvas god that fanctified thē vvith his holy fprete ād not thei them felues vvith their holy vverkes.

❡ The .XXXII. Chapter

1 AND when the people fawe that it was lōge or Mofes came doune out of the mountayne, they gathered them felues together ād came vnto Aaron and fayde vnto him: Vp ād make vs a god to goo before vs: for of this Mofes the felowe that brought vs out of the londe of Egipte, we wote not what ys become.
2 And Aaron faide vnto them: plucke of the golden earynges which are in the eares of youre wyues, your fonnes ād of youre doughters: and brynge them vnto
3 me. And all the people plucked of the golden earinges that were in their eares,

M.C.S. The Ifraelytes worſhip the golden calffe. Mofes prayeth for them puttynge God in remēmbraunce of his promyfe. He breaketh the tables for anger. He chydeth Aaron. The ydolaters are ſlayne. Mofes prayeth God to forgeue them, or to put him oute of the booke of lyfe.

V. 15 requies fancta domino 16 Pactum eft fempiternum . 17 fignumque perpetuum. xxxii, 1 congregatus aduerfus Aaron . . deos
L. 15 Sabbath, die heylige ruge des HERRN 17 wart erquicket. xxxii, 1 widder Aaron . . Götter
M. M. N. 18 *Wyth the fynger of god*, that is: wyth the fpyrite of God, or with the power of god, as Luc. xi, c.

4 and broughte them vnto Aaron And he receaued them of their handes and facyoned it with a grauer and made it a calfe of molten metall. And they fayde: This is thi god, O Ifrael, whiche brought the out of the londe of Egipte.

5 And when Aaron fawe that, he made an altare before it, and made a proclamacion faing tomor-
6 row fhalbe holy daye vnto the Lorde. And they rofe vp in the mornynge and offred burntoffrynges, and brought offrynges of attonement alfo. And than they fatt them doune to eate and drynke, and rofe vpp agayne to playe.

7 Than the Lorde fayde vnto Mofes: go get the doune, for thi people which thou broughteft out of the lāde
8 of Egipte, haue marred all they are turned at once out of the waye whiche I cōmaunded thē, ād haue made thē a calfe of molten metall, ād haue worfhipped it and haue offred therto and hauę faide: This is thy God thou Ifrael, which hath brought the out of the lande
9 of Egipte. And the Lorde fayde vnto Mofes: beholde,
10 I fee this people, that it is a ftife necked people, and now therfore fuffre me that my wrath maye waxe hote vppō thē, and that I may confume thē: and than will I make of the a mightie people,
11 Than Mofes befoughte the Lorde his God and fayde: O Lord, why fhuld thy wrath waxe hote apō thy people which thou haft brought out of the lande of Egipte with great power and with a
12 mightie hande? wherfore fhuld the Egiptians fpeake and faye: For a mifchefe dyd he

The pope vvolde curfe .xx. hundred thoufande as blacke as coles, and fend thē to hell for to haue foche a profre, and vvolde not haue prayed as Mofes did.

V. 4 opere fuforio .. dii tui 5 præconis voce clam. 9 duræ ceruicis
L. 4 entwarffs mit eym griffel .. gotter 9 halfftarrig 10 fie auff freffe
L. M. N. 4 *Entwarffs:* das ift er malet es yhn fur was fie fur eyn bild machen folten. Das bedeut, das menfchen lere, dem volck fur bilden, was fie fur werck thun follen da mit fie Gott dienen, denn hie fiheftu, das die ynn difem kalb vermeynet haben dem rechten Gott zu dienen, weyl Aaron rufen left. Es fey des Herrn feft vnnd bawet ym eyn altar.

brynge them out: euen for to flee .̃p. them in the mountayns, and to confume them from the face of the erth. Turne from thi fearfe wrath, ād haue com-
13 paffion ouer the wikedneffe of thi people. Remēbre Abrahā, Ifaac ād Ifrael thy fervauntes, to whō thou fworeft by thyne owne felfe ād faideft vnto thē: I wil multiplye youre feed as the ftarres of heauen, ād al this lande which I haue faide, I will geue vnto youre
14 feed: ād they fhall ēheret it for euer. And the Lorde refrayned him felfe from that euell, which he fayde he wolde do vnto his people.

15 And Mofes turned his backe and wente doune frō the hyll, and the .ii. tables of witneffe in his hande: which were wryttē on both the leaues and were the worke
16 of God, ād the writīge was the writinge of God grauē
17 apon the tables. And when Iofua herde the noyfe of the people as they fhouted, he faide vnto Mofes: there
18 is a noyfe of warre in the hofte. And he fayde: it is not the crye of thē that haue the maftrye, nor of thē that haue the worfe: but I doo heare the noyfe of fynginge.

19 And as foone as he came nye vnto the hofte and fawe the calfe and the daunfynge, his wrath waxed hote, and he caft the tables out of his hande, and
20 brake them euen at the hyll fote. And he toke the calfe which they had made [Fo. LXI.] ād burned it with fyre, ād ftampt it vnto powder and ftrowed it in the water, and made the childern of Ifrael drynke.
21 And thā Mofes fayde vnto Aarō: what dyd this people vnto the that thou haft brought fo great a fynne apon them.

22 And Aaron fayde: let not the wrath of my Lorde waxe fearfe, thou knoweft the people that they are

V. 12 callide eduxit .. efto placabilis 13 & poffidebitis 15 ex vtraque parte 16 fculpta in tabulis. 17 Vlulatus pugnæ 18 clamor adhort. ad pugnam .. vociferatio compell. ad fugam .. vocem cant. 19 & choros 20 contriuit vfque ad 22 pronus fit ad malum
L. 13 deyne diener ... deyner knechte 14 gerewet 17, 18 gefchrey (*thrice*) .. fingentantzs. 19 den reygen .. malmetz 22 volck bofe ift

23 euen fett on myfchefe: they fayde vnto me: make vs a god to goo before us, for we wote not what is become of Mofes the felow that brought us out
24 of the lande of Egipte. And I fayde vnto them: let them that haue golde, take and brynge it me: and I keft it in to the fyre, and there of came out this calfe

25 when Mofes fawe that the people were naked (for Aaron had made them naked vnto their fhame when they made infur-
26 rection) he went and ftode in the gate of the hofte ād fayde: Yf any man perteyne vnto the Lorde, lett him come to me. And all the fonnes of Leui gathered them felues together and came
27 vnto him. And he fayde vnto them, thus fayeth the Lorde of Ifrael: put euery man his fwerde by his fyde, and goo in and out from gate to gate thorow out the hofte: and flee euery man his brother, euery man his
28 frende and euery man his neghboure. And the childern of Leui dyd .P. as Mofes had fayde. And there were flayne of the people the fame daye,
29 aboute thre thoufande men. Then Mofes fayde: fyll your handes vnto the Lorde this daye, euery man vppō his fonne and vppon his brother: to brynge vppō you a bleffynge this daye

naked, bareheaded (Luther), more probably unruly (lxx. Onkel. Syriac).

The popis bull fleeth moo thā Aarons calfe, euē an hundred thoufand for one heere of them.

30 And on the morowe, Mofes fayde vnto the people: Ye haue fynned a great fynne. But now I will goo vpp vnto the Lorde, to witt whether I can make an attonement for youre fynne.
31 And Mofes went agayne vnto the Lorde and fayde:

V. 24 Quis .. aurum? 25 nudatus .. propter ignom. fordis & inter hoftes nudū cōftituerat 29 Confecraftis .. vt detur vobis ben.

L. 25 entbloffet .. auffrichtet .. entbloffet zur fchande 29 fullet heutte ... das heutte vber euch

L. M. N. 25 *Entbloffet:* dis bloffen ift, des heubts, wenn das heubt on decke vnnd fchmuck ift, vnd ift die meynung, das Aaron hatte das volck Gotte entzogen, das er nicht mehr vber fie regirt, fondern giengen barheubt ynn eygen wercken, denn dife gefchicht ift eyn exempel, aller die on glauben, ynn eygen wercken wandeln, wilche fchande zu richten die priefter mit menfchen lere, vnd meynen doch die leut damit auff zurichten vnd wol zu helfen.

Oh, this people haue synned a great synne and haue
32 made thē a god of golde: Yet forgeue them their synne
I praye the: Yf not wype me out of thy boke which thou
33 haft written. And the Lorde fayde vnto *O pitiful Mo-*
Mofes: I will put him out of my boke that *fes, ād likewife*
O mercifull
34 hath synned agaynft me. But goo and *Paul Rom. ix.*
brynge the people vnto the lande which *And o abhom-*
inable pope
I fayde vnto the: beholde, myne angell *vvith all his*
fhall goo before the. Neuerthelater in *mercileffe I-*
doles.
the daye when I vyfet, I will vyfett their synne vppon
35 them. And the Lorde plaged the people, because
they made the calfe which Aaron made.

The .XXXIII. Chapter

1 AND the Lorde fayde vnto Mofes: *M.C.S. The*
departe ād goo hence: both *Lord fendeth*
an angell be-
thou ād the [Fo. LXII.] peo- *fore his peo-*
ple which thou haft brought *ple. The Lorde*
denyeth to goo
out of the lād of Egipte, vnto the lande *vp with the*
which I fwore vnto Abrahā, Ifaac ād Ia- *people. The*
people lament
cob, faynge: vnto thi feed I will geue it. *their fynne.*
2 And I will fende an angell before the, *Mofes talketh*
and will caft out the Canaanytes, the *wyth the*
Lorde & de-
Amorites, the Hethites, the Pherezites, *fyreth to fe his*
3 the Heuites and the Iebufites: that thou *face: and is*
commaunded
maft goo in to a lande that floweth with *to ftande vpon*
mylke ād honye. But I will not goo *the rocke.*
among you my felfe, for ye are a ftyfnecked people:
left I confume you by the waye.

𝒱. 31 obfecro, peccauit 32 aut dimitte .. aut 34 iftum quo locutus .. in die vltionis 35 pro reatu. xxxiii, 3 difperdam te in via.
𝐋. 31 Ach, das volck 34 dahyn ich dyr .. heymfuchunge ..
heymfuchen. 35 plaget .. gemacht, .. machet. xxxiii, 3 vnter
wegen auff freffen
𝔐. 𝔐. N. 32 *To wype him oute of the booke,* is to put him
oute of the nombre of the chofen and to caft him cleane oute from
god, as Rom. ix, a. 34 *To vyfet their fynne,* is to haue their
fynne in remēbraunce to ponyfhe it as in Gen. i, d.

4   And when the people heard this euell tydinges, they forowed: ād no mā dyd put on his beft rayment.
5   And the Lorde fpake vnto Mofes, faye vnto the childern of Ifrael: ye are a ftyffnecked people: I muft come ons fodenly apon you, ād make an ende of you. But now put youre goodly raymēt from you, that I maye wete what to do vnto *ons, once, cf.*
  Lat. femel,
  Germ. einmal.
6   you. And the childern of Ifrael layde their goodly raymēt from them euē vnder the mount Horeb.
7   And Mofes toke the tabernacle ād pitched it without the hofte a ferre of frō the hofte, ād called it the tabernacle of wytneffe. And al that wold axe any queftiō of the Lorde, went out vnto the taber-
8   nacle of wytneffe which was without the hofte. And when Mofes wēt out vnto the tabernacle, all the people rofe .P. vp and ftode euery man in his tentdore and loked after Mofes, vntill he was gone in to
9   the tabernacle. And as fone as Mofes was entred in to the tabernacle, the clouden piler defcended and ftode in the dore of the tabernacle, ād he talked with
10 Mofes. And when all the people fawe the clouden piler ftonde in the tabernacle dore, they rofe vp and worfhipped: euery man in his tentdore.
11 And the Lorde fpake vnto Mofes face to face, as a man fpeaketh vnto his frende. And when Mofes turned agayne in to the hofte, the ladd Iofua his feruaunte the fonne of Nun departed not out of the
12 tabernacle. And Mofes fayde vnto the Lorde: fe, thou faydeft vnto me: lede this people forth, but thou fheweft me not whom thou wilt fend with me. And haft fayde moreouer: I knowe the by name and thou haft alfo founde grace in my fyghte:

V. 4 indutus eft cultu fuo. 7 Tabernaculum fœderis .. aliquam quæftionem 8 refpiciebantque tergum Moyfi .. tentorium 11 minifter eius Iofue filius Nun, puer
L. 5 alle machen 7 hutte des zeugnis 10 wolcken feule 11 feyn diener Iofua der fon Nun der iungling
M. M. N. 11 *To fe God or to fpeake to God face to face*, is: to haue a manyfefte & a fure knowledge of him as in Gen. xxxii, g.
L. M. N. 8 Den rucken Mofe fehen alle werck heyligen, die das gefetz nicht verftehen noch vnter augen kennen.

13 Now therfore, yf I haue founde fauoure in thi fyghte, thē fhewe me thy waye ād let me know the: that I maye fynde grace in thi fighte. And loke on this alfo, how that this nacyon is thi people.

14 And he fayde: my prefence fhall goo
15 with the, and I will geue the reft. And he fayde: Yf thi prefence goo not with
16 me, carye us not henfe for how fhall it be knowne now that both [Fo. LXIII.] I and thi people haue founde fauoure in thi fighte, but in that thou goeft with us: that both I and thi people haue a preemynence before all the
17 people that are vpon the face of the erth. And the Lorde fayde vnto Mofes: I will doo this alfo that thou haft fayde, for thou haft founde grace in my fighte, and I knowe the by name.

The popifh faye, my chyrch, mi parefh my diocefe, and the monkes and frires faye all is oures.

18 And he fayde: I befech the, fhewe me thi glorye:
19 And he fayde: I will make all my good goo before the, and I will be called in this name Iehouah before the, ād wil fhewe mercy to whom I fhew mercy, and will haue compaffion on whom I haue compaffion.
20 And he fayde furthermore: thou mayft not fe my face, for there fhall no man fe me and lyue.
21 And the Lorde fayde: beholde, there is a place by

𝒱. 13 vt fciam te .. refpice populū tuum gentē hāc. 14 Facies mea præcedet te .. requiē dabo 16 vt glorificemur ab omnib. pop. 19 oftendam omne bonum tibi .. miferebor .. clemens ero .. mihi placuerit

𝓛. 13 las mich deynen weg wyffen, damit ichs erkenne 14 meyn angeficht wirt gehen 16 etwas befonders werden 19 alle meyn gut ... gnedig ... gnedig ... erbarme ... erbarme 20 kanft .. nicht fehen

𝔐. 𝔐. N. 20 *There fhal no man fe my face and lyue.* Not that the face of God which is the face of lyfe, is the caufe of death to them that fe it, for the fayntes that are in heuen do in dede fe it. But that none that lyueth in the bodye can fe ner cōprehend the maieftye of his face: but muft be fyrft purifyed by death, as Paule declareth. 1 Cor. xv, g.

𝓛. 𝔐. N. 19 Das ift alles gefagt von Chrifto, wie der folt leben, predigen, fterben, vnd aufferftehen vnter dem volck Mofis, vnd fie feyn angeficht nicht fehen fondern yhm hynden nach fehen wurden, das ift, fie folten Chriftum ym glawben feyner menfcheyt vnd noch nicht ynn der gottheyt fehen, vnd das ift der rawm vnnd der fels, darauff alle glewbigen ftehen ynn difem leben. Aber dz ift alles Gottis gabe on vnfer verdienft, drum fpricht er, wem ich gnedig byn dem byn ich gnedig etc.

22 me, and thou ſhalt ſtonde apon a rocke, and while my glorye goeth forth I will put the in a clyſte of the rocke, and will put myne hande apon the while I
23 paſſe by. And then I will take awaye myne hande, and thou ſhalt ſe my backe partes: but my face ſhall not be ſene.

The .XXXIIII. Chapter.

1 AND the Lorde ſayde vnto Moſes: hew the .ii. tables of ſtone like vnto the firſt that I maye write in the the wordes which we-
.P. re in the fyrſt .ii. tables which thou
2 brakeſt. And be redye agaynſt the mornige that thou mayſt come vpp early vnto the mount of Sinai and ſtöde me there apö
3 the toppe of the mount. But let no man come vp with the, nether let any man be ſene thorow out all the mount, nether let ſhepe nor oxen fede before the hyll.
4 And Moſes hewed .ii. tables of ſtone like vnto the firſt ãd roſe vp early in the morn- inge ãd went vp vnto the moūt of Sinai as the Lorde cōmaunded him: ãd toke in his hãde the .ii. tables of
5 ſtone. And the Lorde deſcēded in the cloude, ãd ſtode with him there: ãd he called apõ the name of the Lorde.
6 And whē the Lorde walked before him, he cryed: Lorde Lorde God full of compaſſion ãd mercy, which art not
7 lightly angrye but abundãt in mercy ãd trueth, ãd kepeſt mercy in ſtore for thouſandes, ãd forgeueſt wikedneſſe, treſpace ãd ſynne (for there is no man ynnocēt before the) and viſeteſt the wikydneſſe of the fathers vpõ the

M.C.S. The tables are renued. The mercye of God. To haue felowſhip with the gentyles is forbidden, and their ydolatrie alſo. The feaſt of ſwete breade. The firſt begottē. The Saboth. The feaſt of iii. wekes. The firſt frutes. Moſes faſt, Moſes face glyſtreth.

V. 22 protegam dextera mea 23 poſteriora mea, faciem ... non poteris. xxxiiii, 1 Ac deinceps præcide, ait, tibi duas 2 ſtabiſque mecum 4 Excidit ergo 6 Dominator domine deus 7 apud te per ſe innocens

L. 23 ſol nicht geſehen werden. xxxiiii, 2 zu myr trettiſt 6 HERR HERR GOTT

childern ād apon childerns childern, euen vnto the
8 thryd ād fourth generatiō. And Mofes bowed hymfelf
9 to the erth quykly, ād worfhipped ād fayde: Yf I haue
foūde grace in thi fighte o Lorde, than let my Lorde
goo with us (for it is a ftuburne people) and haue
mercy [Fo. LXIIII.] apō oure wikedneffe ād oure
fynne, and let us be thyne enheritaunce.
10 And he fayde: beholde, I make an appoyntment
before all this people, that I will do maruells: foch as
haue not bene done ī all the worlde, nether amōge
any nacyon. And all the people amonge which thou
art, fhall fe the worke of the Lorde: for it is a terryble
11 thinge that I will doo with the: kepe all that I commaunde the this daye, and beholde: I will caft out
before the: the Amorites, Canaanites, Hethites, Pher-
12 ezites, Heuites and Iebufites. Take hede to thi felfe,
that thou make no compacte with the inhabiters of the
lōde whether thou goeft left it be caufe of ruyne
13 amonge you. But ouerthrowe their alters and breke
14 their pilers, and cutt doune their grooues, for thou
fhalt worfhippe no ftraunge God For the Lorde is
15 called gelous, becaufe he is a gelous God: left yf thou
make any agreament with the inhabiters of the lande,
when they go a whoorynge after their goddes ād do
facrifyce vnto their goddes, they call the and thou eate
16 of their facrifyce: ād thou take of their doughters vnto
thi fonnes, and when their doughters goo a whoorynge
after their goddes, they make thi fonnes goo a whoorynge after their goddes alfo.
17 .¶. Thou fhalt make the no goddes of metall
18 The feft of fwete bred fhalt thou kepe, ād .vii. dayes
thou fhalt eate vnleuended bred (as I commaunded
the) in the tyme apoynted in the moneth of Abib: for
19 in the moneth of Abib thou cameft out of Egipte. All

V. 8 curuatus eft pronus in terrā & adorans 9 & auferas iniq.
... nofque poffideas 10 Ego inibo pactum .. opus dom. terribile quod
facturus fum. 12 ne vnquam ... iungas amicitias, .. in ruinam.
14 Dominus zelotes .. æmulator. 15 ineas pactum .. adorauerint
fimulachra 18 menfis nouorum: menfe enim verni temp.
L. 8 neyget fich eylend .. bettet yhn an .. deyn erbgut feyn.
10 denn fchrecklich fols feyn 14 eyfferer .. eyfferiger Gott

that breaketh vp the matryce ſhalbe mine, and all
that breaketh the matryce amonge thi catell, yf it be
20 male: whether it be oxe or ſhepe. But the firſt of the
aſſe thou ſhalt by out with a ſhepe, or yf thou redeme
him not: ſe thou breake his necke. All *That is a god*
the firſtborne of thi ſonnes thou muſt nedes *texte for the*
pope.
redeme. And ſe that no mā appeare before me emptye.
21 Sixe dayes thou ſhalt worke, and the ſeuēth thou
ſhalt reſt: both from earynge and reap- earynge,
22 ynge. Thou ſhalt obſerue the feaſt of *ploughing, or*
tilling; cf.
wekes with the fyrſt frutes of wheate *Latin* aro.
herueſt, ād the feaſt of ingaderynge at the yeres ende.
23 Thriſe in a yere ſhall all youre men childern appeare
24 before the Lorde Iehouah God of Iſrael: for I will caſt
out the nacyons before the and will enlarge thi coſtes,
ſo that no man ſhall deſyre thi londe, while thou goeſt
vp to appeare before the face of the Lorde thi God,
thryſe in the yere.
25 Thou ſhalt not offre the bloude of my ſacrifyce with
leuended bred: nether ſhall ought [Fo. LXV.] of the
ſacrifyce of the feaſt of Paſſeover, be lefte vnto the
26 morninge. The firſt of the firſtfrutes of thy lōde, thou
ſhalt brynge vnto the houſe of the Lorde thy God.
And ſe, that thou ſeth not a kydd in his mothers mylke.
27 And the Lorde ſayde vnto Moſes: write theſe wordes,
for vppon theſe wordes I haue made a couenaunt with
28 the and with the childern of Iſrael. And he was there
with the Lorde .xl. dayes ād .xl. nyghtes, ād nether
ate bred nor dronke water. And he wrote in the
tables the wordes of the couenaunt: euen ten verſes.
29 And Moſes came doune from mount Sinai and the
ii. tables of witneſſe in his hande, and yet he wyſt not
that the ſkynne of his face ſhone with beames of his

V. 20 dederis, occidetur. 23 omnipotentis domini dei Iſrael.
24 tulero gentes a facie tua 27 quibus . . . pepigi fœdus. 29 cor-
nuta eſſet facies ſua ex conſortio ſermonis domini.
L. 20 brich yhm das genig. 23 dem hirſcher dem Herrn vnd
Gott yſrael. 26 noch an ſeyner mutter milch 28 die zehen wort.
29 die haut ſeyns angeſichts glentzet, dauon, das
M. M. N. 19 *All that breaketh vp the matryce,* that is all
the fyrſt born, as in Gen. xxxviii.

30 comenynge with him. And when Aaron and all the childern of Ifrael loked apon Mofes and fawe that the fkynne of his face fhone with beames, they were a frayde
31 to come nye him. But he called thē to him, and then Aaron and all the chefe of the companye came vnto him, ād Mofes talked with them.
32 And at the laſt all the childern of Ifrael came vnto him, and he commaunded them all that the Lorde had
33 fayde vnto him in mount Sinai. And as foone as he had made an ende of comenynge with them, he put a
34 coueryng .P. apō his face. But whē he went before the Lorde to fpeak with him, he toke the couerīge of vntill he came out. And he came out and fpake vnto the childern of Ifrael that which he was
35 commaunded. And the childern of Ifrael fawe the face of Mofes, that the fkynne of his face fhone with beames: but Mofes put a couerynge vppon his face, vntill he went in, to comen with him.

The Pope fpeaketh that vvhiche he is not commaunded.

The .XXXV. Chapter.

1 AND Mofes gathered all the companye of the childern of Ifrael together, and fayde vnto them: thefe are the thinges which the Lorde hath commaunded to doo:
2 Sixe dayes ye fhall worke, but the feuenth daye fhal be vnto you the holy Sabbath of the Lordes reſt: fo that who-
3 foeuer doth any worke therein, fhall dye. Moreouer ye fhall kyndle no fyre thorow out all youre habitacyons apō the Sabbath daye.

M.C.S. The Saboth. The fyrſt frutes are requyred. The redynes of the people to offer. Bezaleel and Ahaliab are prayfed of Mofes and fett to worke.

    V. 31 principes fynagogæ. 33 velamen. xxxv, 1 Ifrael, dixit ad eos 2 fanctus, fabbathum & requies domini .... occidetur.
    L. 31 vbirſten der gemeyne 33 eyn deck. xxxv. 2 eyn Sabbath der ruge des Herrn
    M. M. N. 30 The fhynynge of Mofes face is expounded in 2 Cor. iii, b.

4 And Moſes ſpake vnto all the multitude of the childern of Iſrael ſainge: this is the thinge which the Lorde
5 cōmaūded ſaynge: Geue frō amōge you an heueoffringe,
vnto the Lorde. All thatt are willynge in their hartes,
ſhall brynge heueoffringes vnto the Lorde: golde, ſyl-
6 uer, braſſe: Iacyncte, ſcarlet, purpull, byſſe ād gootes
7 hare: rams ſkynnes red and taxus ſkyn- [Fo. LXVI.]
8 nes and Sethim wodd: and oyle for lightes ād ſpices
9 for the anoyntynge oyle ād for the ſwete cens: And
Onixſtones and ſtones to be ſett for the Ephod and
for the breſtlappe.
10 And let all them that are wyſeharted amōge you,
come and make all that the Lorde hath commaunded:
11 the habitacion and the tent there of with his couerynge ād his ryngnes, bordes, barres, pilers and ſokettes:
12 the arke and the ſtaues thereof with the mercyſeate
13 ād the vayle that couereth it: the table and his ſtaues
with all that perteyneth thereto ād the ſhewebred:
14 the candelſticke of lighte with his apparell and his
15 lampes ād the oyle for the lyghtes: the cenſalter and
his ſtaues, the anoyntynge oyle and the ſwete cens ād
16 the hangynge before the tabernacle dore: the alter of
burntſacrifyces ād his braſen gredyren that longeth
there to with his ſtaues ād all his ordynaūce ād the
17 lauer and his ſote: the hangynges of the courte with
his pilers and their ſokettes, and the hangynge to the
18 dore of the courte: the pynnes of the habitacion and
19 the pynnes of the courte with their boordes: the myn-
yſtrynge garmentes to mynyſtre with in holyneſſe, and
the holy veſtimentes of Aaron the preaſt and the veſtimentes of his ſonnes to mynyſtre in.
20 .P. And all the companye of the childern of Iſrael
21 departed from the preſence of Moſes. And they went
(as many as their hartes coraged them and as many

V. 12 velum quod ... oppanditur 13 menſam cum vectibus &
vaſis 16 craticulā eius æneā cum vect. & vaſis 18 paxillos tabernaculi atrii 21 mente promptiſſima atque deuota

L. 5 von freyem hertzen 13 tiſch mit .. alle ſeynem geredt
21 hertzen gabe, vnd .. aus freyem willen

M. M. N. 6 *Iacynct* is before in the xxvi, a. *Gotes hearre* is
that which we call chāblet.

as their spirites made them willynge) and broughte heueoffrynges vnto the Lord, to the makynge of the tabernacle of wytnesse and for all his vses and for
22 the holy vestmentes. And the men came with the wemen (euen as manye as were willynge harted) and brought bracelettes, earynges, rynges and girdels and all maner Iewels of golde.
23 And all the men that waued waueoffrynges of golde vnto the Lorde and euery man with whom was founde Iacyncte, scarlet, purpull, bysse or gootes hayre or red skynnes of rammes or taxus skynnes, brought it.
24 And all that houe vpp golde or brasse, brought an heueoffrynge vnto the Lorde. And all men with whom was founde sethim wodd mete for any maner worke or seruyce, broughte it.
25 And all the wemen that were wise herted to worke with their handes, spanne, and brought the sponne worke, both of Iacyncte, scarlet, purpull and bysse.
26 And all the wemen that excelled in wysdome of herte,
27 spāne the gotes hayre. And the lordes brought Onix stones and settstones for the Ephod, and for the brest
28 lappe, and spyce and oyle: both for the lightes [Fo. LXVII.] and for the anoyntyng oyle and for the swete
29 cens. And the childern of Israel brought wyllynge offrynges vnto the Lorde, both men ād women: as many as their hartes made thē wyllynge to brynge, for all maner workes which the Lorde had commaunded to make by the hande of Moses.

V. 22 armillas & inaures, annulos & dextralia . . Omne vas aureū in donaria dom. separatum est. 25 mulieres doctæ . . dederunt 26 sponte propria cuncta tribuentes. 29 mente deuota obtulerunt donaria

L. 22 armspangen, ohr rincken, ringe vnd gurttel vnd allerley gulden geredich 25 spunnen mit yhren henden . . spynwerck 26 spunnen zigen har

M. M. N. 23 *Bysse* is fyne white, whether it be sylke or lynen.

L. M. N. 22 Dise zwey wort, *Heben* vnd *Weben*, müssen wir lernen brauchen vnd verstehen, denn eyn opffer oder gabe zu Gottis dienst heyst darumb eyn Hebe, odder Hebopffer das mans dem herrn stracks empor hub. Webe aber heyst es, das mans hyn vnd her zog ynn vier ortter gegen morgen, abent, mittag vnd mitternacht, Bedeut alles, das Euangelisch wesen, das sich zuerst gegen got hebt mit rechtem glauben, vnd darnach sich ausbreyt ynn alle welt, durch predigen vnd bekentnis des glaubens zu leren auch den nehisten.

30 And Moses sayde vnto the childern of Israel: beholde, the Lorde hath called by name Bezabeel the
31 son of Vri the son of Hur of the trybe of Iuda, and hath fylled him with the sprete of God, with wisdome, vnderstödinge and knowlege, euen in all maner worke,
32 ād to synde out curyous workes, to worke in golde,
33 sylver and brasse: and with grauynge of stones to sett, and with keruynge in wodd, and to worke in all maner
34 of sotle workes. And he hath put in hys harte the grace to teach: both him and Ahaliab the son of
35 Ahisamach of the trybe of Dan hath he fylled with wisdome of herte, to worke all maner of grauen worke: they are also broderers and workers with nedle, In Iacyncte, scarlet, purple and bysse, and are weuers that can make all maner worke, and can deuyse sotle workes.

The .XXXVI. Chapter.

1 AND Bezaleel wrought and Ahaliab ād all wyse harted mē to whom the Lorde .P. had geuen wysdome and vnderstondynge, to knowe how to worke all maner worke for the holye seruice, in all that the Lorde commaunded.

M.C.S. The thynges that Bezaleel and Ahaliab made for the holy place of the Lorde.

2 And Moses called for Bezaleel Ahaliab and all the wife harted men in whose hertes the Lorde had put wysdome, euē as many as their hartes coraged to
3 come vnto the worke to worke it. And they receaued of Moses all the heueoffrynges which the childern of

---

M. 30 by name Bezaleel
V. 31, 32 & omni doctrina ad excogitandū 33 & opere carpentario quicquid fabre adinueniri potest, 34 dedit in corde eius. 35 abietarii, polymitarii, ac plumarii . . & texant omnia, ac noua quæque reperiāt. xxxvi, 1 quæ in vsus sanct. necessaria 2 opus, 3 tradidit eis vniuersa donaria

L. 33 allerley kunstlich erbeyt 34 vnd hat yhm vnterweysung ynn seyn hertz geben 35 machen allerley werck, . . . vnd kunstlich erbeyt erfinden. xxxvi, 1 allerley werck . . . zum dienst des heyligthums

Israel had brought for the worke of the holye fervice
to make it with all. And they brought befyde that
wyllyngeoffringes euery mornyng.

4 And all the wyfe men that wrought all the holye
worke, came euery man from his worke which they
5 made, and fpake vnto Mofes faynge: the people brynge
to moch and aboue that is ynough to ferue for the
werke which the Lorde hath commaunded to make.
6 And then Mofes gaue a commaundment, and they
caufed it to be proclamed thorow out the hofte faynge:
fe that nether man nor woman prepare any moare
worke for the holy heueoffrynge, and fo the people
7 were * forboden to brynge: for the ftuffe
they had, was fufficyent for them vnto all
the worke, to make it and to moch.

8 [Fo. LXVIII.] And all the wyfe harted
men amonge them that wroughte in the
worke of the habytacyon made: euen .x.
corteynes of twyned byffe, Iacyncte, fcarlet and purple, and made them full of
9 cherubyns with broderd worke. The
length of one curtayne was .xxviii. cubettes and the bredth .iiii. and were all
10 off one fyfe. And they coupled fyue cur-
teyns by them felues, and other fyue by them felues.
11 And they made fyftye louppes of Iacincte alonge by the
edge of the vtmoft curtayne, euen in the filvege of the
couplynge courtayne: And likewife they made on the
fyde of the vtmoft couplinge curtayne on the other
12 fyde, fyftye louppes they made in the one curtayne,
and fyftye in the edge of the couplynge curtayne on
the other fyde: fo that the loupes were one oueragenft
13 another. And they made fyftye rynges of golde, and
coupled the curtaynes one to another with the rynges:
and fo was it made a dwellinge place.

when wil the Pope faye hoo, and forbid to offere for the byilding of faint Peters chyrch: and when will our fpiritual-tie faye hoo, and forbid to geue the more londe ad to make moo fu-dacions? neuer verely vntill they haue all.

𝔐. 6 forbidden
𝔙. 3 Qui cum inftarent operi quotidie, mane vota populus
offerebat. 6 præconis voce cantari 7 fufficerent & fuperabūdarent.
8 opere vario & arte polymita 13 qui morderent cortinarum anfas
𝕷. 3 yhr willige fteure zu yhm.

14 And they made .xi. curtaynes of gootes heere to be
15 a tent ouer the tabernacle .xxx. cubettes longe a pece and .iiii. cubettes brode, and they all .xi. of one fyſe.
16 And they coupled .v. by them felues, and .Ṗ. vi. by
17 them felues, and they made fyſtye louppes alonge by the border of the vtmoſt couplinge curtayne on the one ſyde, and fyſtye in the edge of the couplynge cur-
18 tayne on the other ſyde. And they made fyſtye rynges of braſſe to couple the tent together that it
19 myghte be one. And they made a couerynge vnto the tent of rammes ſkynnes red, and yet another of taxus ſkynnes aboue all.
20 And they made bordes for the dwellynge place of
21 ſethim wodd that ſtode vpright euery borde .x. cubetes
22 longe and a cubet ād an halfe brode. And they made ii. fete to euery boorde of the dwellinge place ioyninge
23 one to another. And they made .xx. boordes for the
24 ſouth ſyde of the habytacyon, and .xl. ſokettes of ſyluer vnder the .xx. boordes .ii. ſokettes vnder euery boorde,
25 euen for the .ii. fete of thē. And for the other ſyde of the dwellynge towarde the north, they made other .xx
26 boordes with .xl. ſokettes of ſyluer .ii. ſokettes vnder
27 euery boorde. And behynde in the ende of the taber-
28 nacle towarde the weſt, they made .vi. boordes and .ii
29 other bordes for the corners of the habitacyon behynde, and they were ioyned cloſſe both beneth and alſo aboue with clampes, and thus they dyd to both the corners:
30 ſo they were in all .viii. boordes and .xvi. ſokettes, vn-[Fo. LXIX.] der euery borde two ſokettes.
31 And they made barres of ſethim wodd .v. for the
32 bordes of the one ſyde of the habitacion and .v. for the other, ād fiue for the bordes of the weſt ende of the
33 habitacion. And they madē the myddell barre to ſhote thorowe the bordes: euen from the one ende to
34 the other, and ouerlayde the bordes with golde, and

V. 14 ſaga vndecim 18 quib. necteretur tectū, vt vnum pallium ex omnibus ſagis fieret. 22 Sic fecit in omnibus tabern. tabulis. 27 contra occidentem vero, id eſt, ad eam partē tabernaculi quæ mare reſpicit 29 & in vnam compaginem pariter ferebantur. 32 occidentalem . . . contra mare.
L. 20 ſœrn holtz ſtrack

made thē rynges of golde to thruft the barres thorow,
35 and couered the barres with golde. And they made
an hangynge of Iacincte, of fcarlett purple ād twyned
36 byffe with cherubyns of broderd worke. And made
thervnto .iiii. pilers of fethim wodd and ouerlayde them
with golde. Their knoppes were alfo of gold, ād they
37 caft for them .iiii. fokettes of fyluer. And they made
an hangynge for the tabernacle dore: of Iacincte, fcar-
38 let, purple and twyned byffe of nedle worke, and the
pilers of it were fiue with their knoppes, and ouerlayde
the heades of them and the whooppes with golde, with
their fiue fokettes of braffe.

The .XXXVII. Chapter

1 AND bezaleel made the arcke of fethim wodd two cubettes and an halfe longe and a cubette and a halfe brode, and a cu-
2 bett and a halfe hye: and ouerlayde it with fyne gol- .P. de both within and without, and made a crowne of golde to
3 it rounde aboute, and caft for it .iiii. rynges of golde for the .iiii. corners of it: twoo rynges for the one fyde
4 and two for the other, and made ftaues of Sethim wodd,
5 and couered them wyth golde, and put the ftaues in the rynges alonge by the fyde of the arcke to bere it with all.

6 And he made the mercyfeate of pure golde two cubettes and a halfe longe and one cubette and a
7 halfe brode, and made two cherubyns of thicke golde

M.C.S. The arcke of wit-neſſe. The mercyſeate. The table. The candelſtycke. The lyghtes. The altare and the incenſe.

V. 35 varium atque diftinctum. xxxvii, 2 coronam auream per gyrum 6 propitiatorium, id eft oraculum 7 Duos et. cher. ex auro ductili
L. 35 Vnd machet Cherubim am furhang kunftlich. xxxvii, 7 Cher. von tichtem golt
M. M. N. 6 *Mercyfeate* was the place where God fpake vnto the children of Ifrael, whyche was vpō the arcke of witneffe fygurynge Chriſt, as it is fayde Hebr. ix, b.

8 apon the two endes off the mercyfeate: One cherub on the one ende, and another cherub on the other
9 ende of the mercyfeate. And the cherubyns fpredde out their wynges aboue an hye, and couered the mercyfeate therewith, And their faces were one to another: euen to the mercyfeate warde, were the faces of the cherubins.

mercyfeate warde, i. e. toward the mercy feat

10 And he made the table of fethim wodd two cubettes longe and a cubette brode, and a cu-
11 bette and an halfe hyghe, and ouerlayde it with fine golde, and made thereto a crowne of golde rounde
12 aboute, and made thereto an whope of an hande brede rounde aboute, and made vnto the whope a crowne of

hande brede. the breadth of a hand cf. xxxix, 9.

13 golde rounde aboute, and caft for it .iiii. rynges of golde ād put the rynges in the .iiii. corners by the fete:
14 [Fo. LXX.] euen vnder the whope to put ftaues in to
15 bere the table with all. And he made ftaues of Sethim wodd and couered them with golde to bere the table
16 with all, and made the veffels that were on the table of pure golde, the dyffhes, fpones, flattpeces and pottes to poure with all,

17 And he made the candelfticke of pure thicke golde: both the candelfticke and his fhaft: with braunces,
18 bolles, knoppes ād floures procedynge out of it. Sixe braunches procedinge out of the fydes thereof .iii. out
19 of the one fyde and .iii. out of the other. And on euery braunche were .iii. cuppes like vnto almondes, wyth knoppes and floures thorow out the fixe
20 braunches that proceded out of the candelfticke. And apon the candelfticke felfe, were .iiii. cuppes after the
21 facyon of almondes with knoppes and floures: vnder

V. 8 in fummitate ... duos cherub. 9 feque mutuo & illud refpicientes. 12 coronam aur. interrafilem quatuor digit., & fuper eandem alteram cor. aur. 19 fphærulæque fimul & lilia

L. 13 an feynen fuffen 14 hartt an der leyften 16 aus vnd eyn goffe. 26 feyn dach vnd feyne wende rings vmb her vnd feyne horner

L. M. N. 19 *Wie mandelnuſſe:* das ift dife koppfe oder becher waren aufswendig vmbher bocklicht oder knorricht, als weren gulden nufs fchalen vmbher dreyn gefetzt.

22 eueri two braunches a knoppe. And the knoppes and the braunches proceded out of it, and were all one pece
23 of pure thicke golde. And he made feuen lampes thereto, and the fnoffers thereof, ād fyrepānes of pure
24 golde. An hundred weyghte of pure golde, made both it and all that belonged thereto.
25 And he made the cēsalter of fethī wodd of a cubett lōge ād a cubett brode: euē .iiii. fquare .P. and two cu-
26 bettes hye with hornes procedynge out of it. And he couered it with pure golde both the toppe ād the fydes rounde aboute ād the hornes of it, and made vnto it
27 a crowne of golde rounde aboute. And he made two rynges of golde vnto it, euen vnder the croune apon ether fyde of it, to put ftaues in for to bere it with al:
28 and made ftaues of fethim wodd, ād ouerlayde them
29 with golde. And he made the holy anoyntinge oyle and the fwete pure incēs after the apothecarys crafte.

¶ The .XXXVIII. Chapter

1 AND he made the burntoffrynge-alter of fethim wodd, fiue cubettes longe ād .v. cubettes brode: euen .iiii. fquare, and
2 iii. cubettes hye. And he made hornes in the .iiii. corners of it procedinge out of
3 it, and ouerlayde it with braffe. And he made all the veffels of the alter: the cauldrons, fhovels, bafyns, flefhokes and colepannes all of braffe.

M.C.S. The altare of burntofferynges. The brafen lauer. The fomme of that the people offred to the buyldyng of the habytacyon of the Lorde.

4 And he made a brafen gredyren of networke vnto the alter rounde aboute alowe beneth vnder the compaffe of the alter: fo that it reached vnto half the
5 altare, and caft .iiii. rynges of braffe for the .iiii. endes
6 of the gredyren to put ftaues in. And he made ftaues
7 of fethim wodd and couered them with braffe, and put

V. 26 cum craticula ac parietibus & cornibus.
L. 29 reuchwerck von reyner fpecerey

the ſtaues in the rynges alonge by the alter ſy-[Fo. LXXI.] de to bere it with all, and made the alter holowe with bordes.

8 And he made the lauer of braſſe and the fote of it alſo of braſſe, in the ſyghte of them that dyd watch* before the dore of the tabernacle of witneſſe.

9 And he made the courte with hangynges of twyned byſſe of an hundred cubettes longe vppon the ſouthſyde,
10 ād xx. pilers with .xx. ſokettes of braſſe: but the knoppes
11 of the pilers, ād the whoopes were ſyluer. And on the north ſyde the hanginges were an hundred cubettes longe with .xx. pilers and .xx. ſokettes of braſſe, but the knoppes and the whopes of the pilers were of ſyl-
12 uer. And on the weſt ſyde, were hangynges of .L. cubettes longe, and .x. pilers with their .x. ſokettes, and the knoppes ād the whoopes of the pilers were
13 ſyluer. And on the eaſt ſyde towarde the ſonne ryſynge,
14 were hangynges of .L. cubettes: the hangynges of the one ſyde of the gate were .xv. cubbettes longe, and
15 their pilers .iii. with their .iii. ſokettes. And off the other ſyde of the court gate, were hanginges alſo of xv. cubettes longe, and their pilers .iii. with .iii. ſok-
16 ettes. Now all the hanginges of the courte rounde
17 aboute, were of twyned byſſe, ād the ſokettes of the pilers were braſſe: but the knoppes ād the whoopes of the pilers we-.P. re ſyluer, and the heedes were ouer-

V 7 Ipſum autem altare non erat ſolidum, ſed cauum 8 de ſpeculis mulierū, quæ excubabant
L. 8 auff dem platz der heere die fur der thur der hutten des zeugnis lagen 9 gezwirnter weyſſer ſeyden (and ſo throughout)
L. M. N. Der heere: Diſe heere waren die andechtigen witwynn vnd weyber, die mit faſten vnd beten fur der hutten Gott riterlich dieneten, wie .i. Reg. 2. zeygt, vnd Paulus .i. Tim. 5. beſchreybt, wie auch S. Lucas die heylige prophetyn Hanna rumet Luc. 2. Es reden aber hie die Iuden vnd viel andere, von frawen ſpiegeln, die da ſolten am handfaſs geweſen ſein, die laſſen wyr yhrs ſynnes walden. Es bedeut aber geyſtlich, die hiſtorien des alten teſtamēts die man prediget durchs Euangelion, wilche gar ritterlich ſtreytten den glawben zu beweyſen ynn Chriſto widder die werckheyligen etc.

---

* NOTE.—Tyndale's rendering is suggested by the Latin *excubabant*, while Luther's is an ingenious inferential rendering drawn from the Greek. The Hebrew *marεah* may be rendered *sight*, or *mirror;* the latter is the rendering of the LXX, which, if correct, imports that the laver of brass was made of the brazen mirrors, offered by the women. This meaning is sustained also by the Targums and good critics.

layde wyth fyluer, ād all the pilers of the courte were
18 whoped aboute with fyluer. And the hanginge of the
gate of the courte was nedleworke: of Iacincte, fcarlet, purple, and twyned byffe .xx. cubettes longe and
fiue in the bredth, acordynge to the hangynges of the
19 courte. And the pilers were .iiii. with .iiii. fokettes of
braffe, ād the knoppes of fyluer, ād the heedes ouer-
20 layde with fyluer and whoped aboute with fyluer, ād
all the pynnes of the tabernacle ād of the courte rounde
aboute were braffe.
21 This is the fumme of the habitacyō of witneffe,
whiche was counted at the commaundment of Mofes:
and was the office of the Leuites by the hande
22 of Ithamar fonne to Aaron the preaft. And Bezaleel fonne of Vri fonne to Hur of the trybe of
Iuda, made all that the Lorde commaunded Mofes,
23 and with hī Ahaliab fonne of Ahifamach of the tribe
of Dan, a cōnynge grauer ād a worker of nedle worke
In Iacincte, fcarlett, purple ād byffe.
24 All the golde that was occupyde apon   occupyde,*ufed*
all the worke of the holy place (whiche was the golde
of the waueofferynge) was, .xxix. hundred weyght and
feuen hundred and .xxx. fycles, acordynge to the holy
25 fycle. And the fumme of fyluer that came of the multitude, was .v. [Fo. LXXII.] fcore hundred weyght and
a thoufande feuen hundred and .Lxxv. fycles of the
holye fycle.
26 Euery man offrynge halfe a fycle after the weyght
of the holye fycle amonge them that went to be nombred from .xx. yere olde and aboue, amonge .vi. hundred thoufande ād .iii. thoufande ād .v. hundred ād .L. men.
27 And the .v. fcore hundred weyght of fyluer went to
the caftynge of the fokettes of the sanctuary and the
fokettes of the vayle: an hundred fokettes of the fiue
fcore hundred weigh an hundred weyght to euery
28 fokette. And the thoufande feuen hundred and .Lxxv
fycles, made knoppes to the pilers ād ouerlayde the
heedes and whoped them.

𝒱. 24 ad menfuram fanctuarii
𝑳. 24 nach dem feckel des heyligthums

29 And the braffe of the waueofferynge was .Lxx. hundred weyght and two thoufande, and .iiii. hundred
30 fycles. And therewith he made the fokettes to the doore of the tabernacle of witneffe, and the brafen altare, and the brafen gredyren that longeth thereto,
31 and all the veffels of the alter, and the fokettes of the courte rounde aboute, and the fokettes of the courte gate, and all the pynnes off the habitacyon, and all the pynnes of the courte rounde aboute.

.P. ⁋ The .XXXIX. Chapter.

1 AND of the Iacyncte, fcarlet, purple and twyned byffe, they made the veftimētes of miniftracion to do feruyce in in that holye place, and made the holye garmentes that perteyned to Aaron, as the Lorde commaunded Mofes.

M.C.S. The makynge of Aaron and his fonnes apparell. All that the Lorde commaunded was offred.

2 And they made the Ephod of golde, Iacinte, fcar-
3 let, purple, and twyned byffe. And they dyd beate the golde in to thynne plates, ād cutte it in to wyres: to worke it in the Iacincte, fcarlet, purple,
4 and the byffe, with broderd worke. And they made the fydes come together, and cloofed them vp by the
5 two edges. And the brodrynge of the girdel that was vpon it, was of the fame ftuffe and after the fame worke of golde, Iacincte, fcarlet, purple and twyned byffe, as the Lorde commaunded Mofes.
6 And they wrought onix ftones cloofed in ouches of golde and graued as fygnettes are grauen with the
7 names of the children of Ifrael, and put them on the fhulders of the Ephod that they fhulde be a remembraunce off the childern of Ifrael, as the Lorde commaunded Mofes.
8 And they made the breftlappe of conning worke,

V. 6 duos lap. onychinos, aftrictos & inclufos auro

after the worke of the Ephod: euen of golde, Iacincte,
9 fcarlet, purple ād twyned byſſe [Fo. LXXIII.] And
they made it .iiii. fquare ād double, an hāde bredth
10 longe and an hande bredth brode. And thei filled it
with .iiii. rowes of ſtones (the firſt rowe: Sardios, a
11 Topas ād ſmaragdus. the fecōde rowe: a Rubin, a
12 Saphir ād a Diamōde. The .iii. rowe: Ligurios, an
13 Achat ād a Amatiſt. The fourth rowe: a Turcas,
an Onix ād a Iaſpis) cloſed in ouches of gold in their
14 incloſers. And the .xii. ſtones were gra- incloſers, *fet-*
uē as fygnettes with the names of the *tings*
childern of Iſrael: euery ſtone with his name, acordinge
to the .xii. trybes.
15 And they made apon the breſtlappe, twoo faſten-
16 ynge cheynes of wrethen worke ād pure golde. And
they made two hokes of golde and two golde rynges,
and put the two rynges apō the two corners of the
17 breſtlappe. And they put the two chaynes of golde
in the .ii. rynges, in the corners of the breſtlappe.
18 And the .ii. endes of the two cheynes they faſtened
in the .ii. hokes, ād put them on the ſhulders of the
Ephod apon the forefront of it.
19 And they made two other rynges of golde and put
them on the two other corners of the breſtlappe alonge
apon the edge of it, toward the inſyde of the Ephod
20 that is ouer agaynſt it   And they made yet two other
golde rynges, ād put them on the .ii. ſydes of the
Ephod, beneth .P. on the fore ſyde of it: euē where
the ſydes goo together, aboue apon the brodrynge
21 of the Ephod, ād they ſtrayned the breſt- ſtrayned, *tied,*
lappe by his rīges vnto the ringes of the   *bound*
Ephod, with laces of Iacincte, that it mighte lye faſt
apon the brodrynge of the Ephod, and ſhulde not be
lowſed from of the Ephod: as the Lorde cōmaūded
Moſes.
22 And he made the tunycle vnto the Ephod of wo-

    𝒱. 10 gemmarum ordines quatuor. in primo verſu 11 fapphi-
rus & iafpis 12 amethyſtus 13 chryſolithus
    𝓛. 10 die erſte riege 11 Demant
    𝕸. 𝕸. N. 10 *Smaragdus*, or an Emeraude. 11 *Rubye*, or a
carbuncle.

uen worke and all together of Iacincte, heade, *i. e. the*
23 ād the heade of the tunycle was in the *opening for the head to*
middeſt of it as the color of a partlet, *paſs through,*
with a bonde rounde aboute the color, *ſee xxviii, 32.*
24 that it ſhulde not rent, And they made beneth apon
the hem of the tunycle: pomgranates of Iacincte,
25 ſcarlet, purple, and twyned byſſe, And they made
litle belles of pure golde, ād put them amonge the
pomgranates roūde aboute apō the edge of the tuny-
26 cle a bell ād a pomgranate, a bell ād a pomgranate
rounde aboute the hemmes of the tunycle to myniſtre
in, as the Lorde commaunded Moſes.
27 And they made cotes of byſſe of wouē worke for
28 Aaron and his ſonnes, and a mytre off byſſe, and goodly
bonettes of byſſe, and lynen breches off twyned byſſe,
29 and a gyrdell of twyned byſſe, Iacyncte, ſcarlett and purple: euen of nedle worke, as the Lorde cōmaūded Moſes,
30 [Fo. LXXIIII.] And they made the plate of the
holy croune of fine golde, ād wrote apō it with
31 grauē worke: the holynes of the Lorde. ād tyed it
to a lace of Iacincte to faſten yt an hye apon the
mytre, as the Lorde commaunded Moſes.
32 Thus was all the worke of the habitacyon of the
tabernacle of witneſſe, finyſſhed. And the childern of
Iſrael dyd, acordynge to all that the Lorde had com-
33 maunded Moſes. And they brought the habitacyon
vnto Moſes: the tent and all his apparell thereof: the
34 buttones boordes, barres, pilers and ſokettes: and the
couerynge of rams ſkynnes red, and the couerynge of
35 taxus ſkynnes, and the hanginge vayle, and the arcke
of witneſſe with the ſtaues thereof, and the mercyſeate:
36 the table and all the ordinaunce thereof, and the
37 ſhewbred, and the pure candelſticke, and the lampes

V. 23 capitium in ſuperiori parte contra medium 26 quibus ornatus incedebat pontifex. 30 Sanctum domini 32 Perfectum eſt igitur omne opus tabernac. et tecti teſtimonii. [The references are to the Authorized Version; in the Vulgate see instead vv. 21, 24, 29, 31.]
L. 23 ſevn loch oben mitten ynn 30 Die heylickeyt des HERRN 32 Alſo ward vollendet das gantze werk der wonung der hutten des zeugnis.

prepared therevnto with all the veſſells thereof, and
38 the oyle for lyghtes, and the golden altare and the
anoyntynge oyle and the ſwete cens, and the hang-
39 ynge of the tabernacle doore, ãd the braſen alter, and
the gredyern of braſſe longynge therevnto with his
barres and all hys veſſels, and the lauer with his ſote,
and the hanginges of the courte with his pilers and
40 ſokettes, and the hangynge to the courte gate, hys
boordes and pynnes, ãd all the ordinaunce that .P.
ſerueth to the habitacion of the tabernacle of witneſſe,
41 and the miniſtringe veſtimentes to ſerue in the holy
place, and the holy veſtimentes of Aaron the preaſt
42 and his ſonnes raymētes to miniſtre in: acordyng to
all that the Lorde commaunded Moſes: euen ſo the
43 childern of Iſrael made all the worke. And Moſes
behelde all the worke: and ſe, they had done it
euen as the Lorde commaunded: and thã Moſes
bleſſed them.

❡ The .XL. Chapter

1   AND the Lorde ſpake vnto Moſes *M.C.S. The*
2   ſaynge: In the firſt daye of *tabernacle is*
    the firſt moneth ſhalt thou   *reared vp.*
    ſett vp the habitaciõ of the *The glorye of*
                                  the Lorde ap-
                                  pereth in a
3 tabernacle of witneſſe, ãd put therĩ the *clowde couer-*
arcke of witneſſe, and couer the arcke   *yng the ta-*
                                          bernacle.
with the vayle, ãd bryr.ge in the table and apparell
4 it, and brynge in the candelſticke and put on his
5 lampes, and ſett the cenſalter of golde before the
arcke of witneſſe, and put the hangynge of the dore
6 vnto the habitacion. And ſett the burntoffrynge
alter before the dore of the tabernacle of witneſſe,

V. 43 Quæ poſtq. Moyſes .. benedixit eis. xl, 2 tabernaculum
teſtimonii
L. 43 Und Moſes ſahe an .. vnd ſegnet ſie. xl, 2 die wonung
der hutten des zeugnis 5 das tuch ynn der thur

7 ād sett the lauer betwene the tabernacle of witnesse,
8 ād the alter, ād put water theri, and make the courte roūde aboute, ād set vp the hāgynge of the courte gate.

9 [Fo. LXXV.] And take the anoyntinge oyle and anoynt the habitacion and all that is there in, and halow it and all that belonge there to: that it maye be holye.
10 And anoynte the altar of the burntoffringes and all his vessels, and sanctifye the altar that it maye be most holye.
11 And anoynte also the lauer and his fote, and sanctifye it.
12 Than brynge Aaron and his sonnes vnto the dore of the tabernacle of wit-
13 nesse, and wash them with water. And put apon Aaron the holye vestmentes. and anoynte him and sanctifye him that
14 he maye ministre vnto me, that their *
15 anoyntīge maie be an euerlastinge preasthode vnto thē thorow out their genera-
16 cions. And Moses dyd acordīge to all that the Lorde commaunded him.

Of this texte the scole men dispute that the very smeringe alone maketh the prest now also with out the brestlapp of light and perfectnesse so that they haue all power thereby and what thei saye is done immediatly whether thei send to heuen or hell, and that with out preachynge ether of the lawe of God or of his holy Gospell.

17 Thus was the tabernacle reared vp the first moneth
18 in the secōde yere. And Moses rered vp the tabernacle ād fastened his sokettes, ād set vp the bordes
19 ād put in their barres, ād rered vp the pillers, ād spred abrode the tēt ouer the habitaciō ād put the coueringe of the tent an hye aboue it: as the Lorde commaunded Moses.

20 And he toke ād put the testimonye in the arke ād sett the staues to the arcke and put the merciseate an
21 hye apon the arcke, and brough- .₧. te the arcke in to

M. 17 reared vp the fyrst daye in the fyrst
V. 7 quod implebis aqua. 19 sicut dom. imperauerat. 20 Posuit & testimonium .. subditis infra vectib. 21 vt expleret dom. iussionem.
L. 7 wasser dreyn thun 13 priester sey, 14 Vnd seyne sone auch ertzu furen vnd yhn die enge rocke antzihen vnd sie salben wie du yhren vater gesalbet hast 16 wie yhm der Herr gepotten hatte. [and so throughout the chapter, viz. vv. 19, 21, 23 etc.] 20 vnd nam das zeugnis

the habitaciō and hanged vp the vayle ād couered the arcke of witneſſe, as the Lorde commaunded Moſes.

22 And he put the table in the tabernacle off witneſſe in the north ſyde of the habitaciō with out the vayle, 23 and ſet the bred in ordre before the Lorde, euē as the Lorde had commaunded Moſes.

24 And he put the candelſticke in the tabernacle of witneſſe ouer agaynſt the table in the ſouth ſyde 25 of the habitacion, and ſet vp the lampes before the 26 Lorde: as the Lorde commaunded Moſes. And he put the golden alter in the tabernacle of witneſſe be-27 fore the vayle, ād brent ſwete cens there on as the 28 Lorde commaunded Moſes. And ſet vp the hangynge 29 in the dore of the habitacion, and ſet the burntoffringe alter before the dore of the tabernacle of witneſſe, and offred burntoffringes and meatofferinges there on as the Lorde commaunded Moſes.

30 And he ſet the lauer betwene the tabernacle of witneſſe and the alter, and poured water there in to 31 waſh with all. And both Moſes Aaron and his ſonnes 32 waſhed their hādes and their ſete there at: both when they went in to the tabernacle of witneſſe, or whē they went to the alter, as the Lorde cōmaunded Moſes.

33 [Fo. LXXVI.] And he rered vp the courte rounde aboute the habitacion and the alter, and ſet vp the hanginge of the courte gate: and ſo Moſes ſyniſhed the worke.

34 And the clowde couered the tabernacle of witneſſe, 35 and the glorye of the Lorde fylled the habitacion: ſo that Moſes coude not entre in to the tabernacle of witneſſe, becauſe the clowde abode there in, and the glorye of the Lorde fylled the habitacion.

V. 25 lucernis, iuxta præceptum domini. 27 aromatum. ſicut iuſſerat dominus Moyſi. 29 ſacrificia, vt dom. imperauerat. 30 implens illud aqua 32 ad altare, ſicut præceperat dominus Moyſi. 33 Poſtquam omnia perfecta 35 nube operiēte omnia, & maieſt. dom. coruſcante [The references are to A. V., in the Vulgate, see instead vv. 17, 18, 19, 23, 25, 27, 28, 31, 33, 34, 35, 37.]

L. 24 leuchter auch hyneyn 30 vnd thet waſſer dreyn zu waſſchen 31 draus, 32 denn ſie muſſen ſich wachen 34 Da bedeckt eyn wolcke 35 die wolck drauff bleyb

36 When the clowde was taken vp from of the habitacyō, the childern of Ifrael toke their iornayes as oft as
37 they iornayed. And yf the clowde departed not, they
38 iornayed nott till it departed: for the clowde of the Lorde was apon the habitacion by daye, and fyre by nyghte: in the fighte of all the houfe of Ifrael in all their iornayes.

The ende of the feconde boke of Mofes:

𝔐. 36 had iorneyed
𝒱. 36 per turmas fuas 37 fi pēdebat defuper 38 Nubes . . . incubabat . . cunctas manfiones fuas.
𝑳. 38 denn die wolcke des HERRN war des tags auff der wonung, vnd des nachts war fewr drynnen . . . fo lang fie reyfeten.

A PRO‑
LOGE IN TO THE
thirde boke of Moses
called Leuiticus.

.T.   **W T**

¶ A prologe in to the thirde boke of Moses, called Leuiticus.

THE ceremonies which are defcribed in the boke folowinge, were cheflye ordined off God (as I fayde in the ende of the prologe vppon Exodi) to occupye the mindes of
5 that people the Ifraelites, and to kepe them from fervinge of God after the imaginacyon of their blinde zele and good entent: that their confciences might be ftablifhed and they fure that they pleafed God therein, which were impoffible, yf a man did of his awne
10 heed that which was not commaunded of God nor depēded of any appoyntement made betwene him and God.

Soch ceremonies were vnto them as an A. B. C. to lerne to fpelle and read, and as a nurce to fede them with milke and pappe, and to fpeake vnto them after
15 their awne capacyte and to lifpe the wordes vnto them acording as the babes and childern of that age might founde them agayne. For all that were before Chrift were in the infancye and childhod of the worlde and fawe that fonne which we fe openlye, but thorowe a
20 cloude and had but feble and .T. weake imaginacions of Chrift, as childern haue of mennes deades, a fewe prophetes excepte, whiche yet defcribed him vnto other in facrifices and ceremonies, likeneffes, rydles, prouerbes, and darke and ftraunge fpeakinge vntyll the full
25 age were come that God wold fhewe him openlye vnto the whole worlde and delyuer them from their fhadowes and cloudelight and the hethen out of their dead flepe of ftarcke blinde ignorancye. And as the fhadowe vanifheth awaye at the comynge of the light, euen fo
30 doo the ceremonyes and facrifices at the comynge of Chrift, and are henceforth no moare neceffarye then a

token left in remembraunce of a bargayne is neceffary
whē the bargayne is fulfilled. And though they feme
playne childifh, yet they be not altogither fruteleffe: as
the popettes and .xx. maner of tryfles which mothers
permitte vnto their yonge childern be not all in vayne.
For all be it that foch phantafyes be permytted to
fatiffie the childers luftes, yet in that they are the
mothers gifte and be done in place and tyme at hir
cōmaundement, they kepe the childern in awe and
make them knowe the mother and alfo make them
more apte agenfte a more ftronger age to obaye in
thinges of greater ernefte.

.P. And moraouer though facrifices and ceremonies can
be no ground or fundacion to bild apon: that is, though
we can proue noughte with them: yet when we haue
once found oute Chrift and his mifteries, then we maye
borow figures, that is to faye allegoryes, fimilitudes or
examples to open Chrift and the fecrettes off God hyd
in Chrift euen vnto the quycke, and to declare them
more lyuely and fenfebly with them than with all the
wordes of the worlde. For fimilitudes haue more vertue and power with them than bare wordes, and lead
a mans wittes further in to the pithe and marye and
fpirituall vnderftondinge of the thinge, than all the
wordes that can be imagined. And though alfo that
all the ceremonies and facrifices haue as it were a
fterrelyght of Chrift, yet fome there be that haue as
it were the lighte of the brode daye a litle before the
fonne rifinge, and expreffe him, and the circumftaunces
and vertue of his deth fo playnly as if we fhulde playe
his paffyon on a fcaffold or in a ftage play opēlye before
the eyes of the people. As the fcape gote, the brafen
ferpent, the oxe burnt without the hofte, the paffeouer-
lambe &c. In fo moch that I am fully perfuaded and
can not but beleue that God had fhewed Mofes the
fecrettes of Chrift and the verey maner of his deth
be- .P. fore hande, and commaunded him to ordene
them for the confirmacion of oure faythes whiche are
now in the cleare daye lighte. And I beleue alfo that
the prophetes whiche folowed Mofes to confirme his
prophefyes and to mayntayne his doctrine vnto Chriftes

cominge, were moued by foch thinges to ferche further
of Chriftes fecrettes. And though God wold not haue
the fecrettes of Chrift generallye knowne, faue vnto a
few familier frendes which in that infancye he made
of mans witte to helpe the other babes: yet as they
had a generall promyffe that one of the feed of Abrahā
fhuld come and bleffe them, euen fo they had a generall fayth that God wold by the fame man faue them,
though they wift not by what meanes as the very
apoftles when it was oft told them yet they coude
neuer comprehend it, till it was fulfilled in deade.

And beyonde all this their facrifices ād ceremonies
as farforth as the promyfes annexed vnto them ex-
tende, fo farforth they faued thē and iuftified them
and ftode them in the fame fteade as oure facramentes
doo vs: not by the power of the facrifice or deade it felfe,
but by the vertue of the faith in the promyffe whiche
the facrifice or ceremonye preached and wherof it was
a token or fygne. For the ceremonies .ꝑ. and facrifices were lefte with them and commaunded them to
kepe the promyffe in remēbraunce and to wake vpp
their fayth. As it is not ynough to fende manye on
errandes and to tell them what they fhall doo: but
they muft haue a remembraunce with them, and it be
but a ringe of a rufh aboute one of their fingers. And
as it is not ynough to make a bargayne with wordes
onlye, but we muft put thereto an oth and geue erneft
to confirme the faithe off the perfon with whom it is
made. And in like maner yf a man promyffe, what
foeuer trifull it be, it is not beleued excepte he hold
vppe his finger alfo, foch is the wekeneffe of the world.
And therfore chrift him filf vfed oftymes diuerfe ceremonyes in curynge the feke, to fturre vpp their faith
with all. As for an enfample it was not the bloud of
the lambe that faued thē in Egipte, when the angell
fmote the Egiptians: but the mercye of God and his
truth wherof that bloude was a token and remembraunce
to fturre vppe their faythes wyth all. For though God
make a promyffe, yet it faueth none finallye but them
that longe for it and praye God with a ftronge fayth
to fulfill it for his mercye and truthe onlye and knowl-

ege theyr vnworthyneſſe. And euen ſo oure ſacra-
men- .P. tes (yf they be truelye miniſtred) preach Chriſt
vnto vs and leade oure faythes vnto Chriſt, by whiche
faithe oure ſynnes are done awaye and not by the
deade or worke of the ſacrament. For as it was impoſſible that the bloude off calues ſhuld put awaye ſynne:
euen ſo is it impoſſible that the water of the ryuer ſhuld
waſh oure hartes. Neuertheleſſe the ſacramentes cleſe
vs and abſolue vs of oure ſynnes as the preaſtes doo,
in preachinge of repentaunce and faith, for which cauſe
ether other of them were ordened, but yf they preach
not, whether it be the preaſt or the ſacrament, ſo pro-
fitte they not.

And yf a man allege Chriſt Iohan in the .iii. chapter
ſayeng: Excepte a man be borne agayne of water and
the holye goſte he can not ſe the kingdome of God,
and will therfore that the holy goſt is preſent in the
water and therfore the verye deade or worke doth put
awaye ſynne: then I will ſend him vnto Paule which
axeth his Galathians whether they receaued the holy
goſte by the deade of the lawe or by preachinge of
faith, and there concludeth that the holy goſt accōpany-
eth the preaching of faith, ād with the worde of faith,
entreth the harte ād purgeth it, which thou mayſt
also vnderſtonde by ſaynt Paule ſayenge: ye are borne
.P. a new out of the water thorowe the worde. So
now if baptim preach me the waſſhing in chriſtes
bloude, ſo doth the holy goſt accompany it and that
deade of preachinge thorow ſayth doth put awaye my
ſynnes. For the holy goſt is no dome god nor no god
that goeth a mummige. Yf a man ſaye of the ſacrament of Chriſtes bodye ād bloude that it is a ſacrifice
as well for the dead as for the quycke and therfore the
very deed it ſelf iuſtifieth and putteth away ſynne. I
anſwere that a ſacrifice is the ſleynge off the body of a
beeſt or a man: wherfore yf it be a ſacrifice, then is
chriſtes body there ſlayne ād his bloude there ſhed:
but that is not ſo. And therfore it is properly no
ſacrifice but a ſacrament and a memoriall of that euerlaſtinge ſacrifice once for all which he offered apon the
croſſe now apon a .xv. hundred yeres a go and preach-

eth only vnto them that are alyue. And as for them
that be dead, it is as profitable vnto them as is a can-
dell in a lantrene without light vnto them that walke
by the waye in a darke night, and as the gofpell fong
5 in laten is vnto them that vnderftond none at all, and
as a fermon preached to him that is dead and hereth
it not. It preacheth vnto them that are a lyue only,
for they that be dead, yf they dyed in the faith which
that facrament preacheth, they .P. be faffe and are
10 paft all ieopardye. For when they were alyue their
hartes loued the lawe off God and therfore fynned not,
and were fory that their membres fynned and euer
moued to fynne, and therfore thorow faith it was forgeuen them. And now their fynnefull membres be
15 dead, fo that they can now fynne no more, wherfore
it is vnto them that be dead nether facrament nor
facrifice: But vnder the pretence of their foule health
it is a fervaunt vnto oure fpiritualtyes holy couetouf-
neffe and an extorcyonar and a bylder of Abayes,
20 Colleges, Chauntryes and cathedrall chirches with falfe
gotē good, a pickpurfe, a pollar, ād a bottomleffe bagge.
  Some man wold happely faye, that the prayers of
the maffe helpe moch: not the lyuinge only, but alfo
the dead. Of the hote fire of their farvent prayer
25 which confumeth fafter then all the world is able to
bringe facrifice, I haue fayde fufficiently in other places.
Howe be it it is not poffible to bringe me in beleffe
that the prayer which helpeth hir awne mafter vnto
no vertue, fhuld purcheffe me the forgeueneffe of my
30 fynnes. If I fawe that their prayers had obtayned
thē grace to lyue foch a liffe as goddes worde did not
rebuke, then coud I fone be borne in hande that what
foeuer they axed off .P. God their prayers fhuld not
be in vayne. But now what good can he wyfh me in
35 his prayers that envieth me Chrifte the fode and the
liffe of my foule? What good can he wifh me whofe
herte cleaveth a fundre for payne when I am taught
to repent of my euell?
  Forthermore becaufe that fewe knowe the vfe of
40 the olde teftament, and the mofte parte thinke it
nothinge neceffarye but to make allegoryes, which

they fayne euery mā after hys awne brayne at all wyle
advēture without any certayne rule: therfore (though I
haue spoken off them in another place) yet left the
boke come not to all mennes handes that shall reade
this, I will speake off them here also a worde or twayne.

We had nede to take hede euery where that we be not
begyled with false allegories, whether they be drawne out
of the new testament, or the olde, ether out of any other
storye or off the creatures of the worlde, but namely in
this boke. Here a man had nede to put on all his
spectacles and to arme him selfe agenst inuisible spretes.

First allegories proue nothinge (and by allegories vnderstonde examples or similitudes borowed of straunge
matters and of another thinge than that thou entreatest
off) As thou- .P. gh circumcysyon be a figure of baptim, yet thou canst not proue baptim by circumcysion.

For this argumēt were verye feble, the Israelites
were circūcysed therfore we must be baptised. And
in like maner though the offering of Isaac were a
figure or ensample off the resurrection, yet is this
argument nought, Abraham wold haue offered Isaac,
but God delyuered him from deth, therfore we shall
ryse agayne, and so forth in all other.

But the very vse of allegories is to declare and open
a texte that it maye be the better perceaved and
vnderstonde. As when I haue a cleare texte of Christ
and of the apostles, that I must be baptysed, then I
maye borowe an ensample of circumcysion to expresse
the nature power and frute or effecte of baptim. For
as circumcysion was vnto them a comen bagge syg-
nifienge that they were all sodiars off God to warre
his warre and separatinge them from all other nacyons
disobedient vnto God: euen so baptim is oure comen
bagge and sure ernest and perpetuall memoriall that
we pertayne vnto Christ and are separated from all
that are not christes. And as circumcision was a
token certifyenge them that they were receaved vnto
the fauoure off God and theyr .P. synnes forgeven them:
euen so baptim certefyeth vs that we are wasshed in
the bloude of christ ād receaued to fauoure for his
sake. and as circumcysion signifyed vnto thē the cut-

tynge awaye of theyr awne luſtes and ſleynge of their
fre will, as they call it, to folowe the will of god even
ſo baptim ſignyfyeth vnto vs repentaunce and the mor-
tefyinge of oure vnruly mēbres and body of ſynne, to
walke in a newe lyffe and ſo forth.

And likewyſe though that the ſavinge of Noe and
of them that were with him in the ſhyppe, thorow
water, is a figure, that is to ſaye an enſample and like-
neſſe of baptim, as Peter maketh it .1. Petri 3. yet I
can not proue baptim therwith, ſaue deſcribe it only.
for as the ſheyppe ſaued thē in the water thorow faith,
in that they beleved god and as the other that wold
not beleve Noe peryſhed: even ſo baptim ſaveth vs
thorow the worde of faith which it preacheth when
all the world of the vnbelevinge peryſh. And Paule
.1. Corin. 10. maketh the ſee ād the cloude a figure of
baptim, by which and a thouſand mo I might declare it
but not proue it. Paule alſo in the ſayde place maketh
the rocke out of which Moſes brought water vnto the
childerne of Iſrael a figure or enſample of chriſt not to
proue chriſt (for that were impoſſi- .P. ble) but to
deſcribe chriſt only: even as chriſt hī ſilf Iohānis .3
boroweth a ſimilitude or figure of the braſen ſerpent to
lead Nichodemus frō his erthy imaginacyon in to the
ſpirituall vnderſtondinge of chriſt ſayenge: As Moſes
lyſted vpp a ſerpent in the wilderneſſe, ſo muſt the
ſonne of mań be lifted vpp, that none that beleue in
him peryſh but haue everlaſtinge liffe. by which ſimilitude the vertue of chriſtes deth is better deſcribed
then thou coudeſt declare it with a thouſande wordes.
for as thoſe murmurars agenſt god as ſone as they
repented were healed of their deadly woundes thorow
lokynge on the braſen ſerpent only without medicyne
or any other helpe, yee ād without any other reaſon but
that god hath ſayed it ſhuld be ſo, and not to murmoure
agayne, but to leue their murmuringe: even ſo all that
repent ād beleue in chriſt are ſaved from euerlaſtinge
deth, of pure grace without and before their good
workes, and not to ſynne agayne, but to fight agaynſt
ſynne ād henceforth to ſynne no moare.

Even ſo with the ceremonyes of this boke thou canſt

prove nothinge faue defcribe and declare only the puttyng awaye. of oure fynnes thorow the deth of chrift. for chrift is Aaron and Aarons fonnes and all that offer the facrifyce to purge fynne, And chrift is all maner .P. offering that is offered: he is the oxe, the fhepe, the gote, the kyd and lambe: he is the oxe that is burnt without the hoft and the fcapegote that caryed all the fynne of the people awaye in to the wilderneffe. for as they purged the people frō their worldly vnclenneffes thorow bloud of the facrifices, even fo doth chrift purge vs from the vnclenneffes of everlaftinge deth with his awne bloude. and as their worldly fynnes coude no otherwyfe be purged then by bloude of facrifyce, even fo can oure fynnes be no otherwyfe forgeven then thorow the bloude of chrift. All the deades in the world, faue the bloude of chrift, can purchafe no forgeveneffe of fynnes: for oure deades do but helpe oure neyghboure and mortefye the flefh ād helpe that we fynne no moare, but and if we haue fynned, it muft be frely forgeven thorow the bloude of chrift or remayne ever.

And in lyke maner of the lepers thou canft prove nothinge: thou canft never coniure out confeffiō thenfe, how be it thou haft an handfome example there to open the bindinge and lowfinge of oure preaftes with the kaye of goddes word. for as they made no man a lepre even fo oures haue no power to commaunde any man to be in fynne or to go to purgatory or hell. And therefore (in as moch as bindinge .P. and lowfinge is one power) As thofe preaftes healed no man, euen fo oures can not of their invifeble and domme power dryve any mannes fynnes awaye or delyver hym from hell or fayned purgatorye. how be it if they preached gods word purely which is the authorite that chrift gaue them, then they fhuld binde ād lowfe, kylle and make alyue agayne, make vncleane and cleane agayne, and fend to hell ād fett thence agayne, fo mighty is gods word. for if they preached the lawe of god, they fhuld bind the confciences of fynners with the bondes of the paynes of hell and bringe them vnto repētaunce. And then if they preached

them the mercye that is in chrift, they fhuld
lowfe them and quiet their raginge confciences and
certefie them of the fauoure of god and that their
fynnes be forgeven.

Fynallye beware of allegoryes, for there is not a
moare handfome or apte a thinge to be gile withall
then an allegorye, nor a more fotle and peftilent
thinge in the world to perfuade a falfe mater then
an allegorye. And contrary wyfe there is not a better, vehementer or myghtyer thinge to make a man
vnderftond with all then an allegory. For allegoryes
make a man qwick witted and prynte wyf- .P. dome
in him and maketh it to abyde, where bare wordes go
but in at the one eare and out at the other. As this
with foch like fayenges: put falt to all youre facrifices,
in fteade of this fentence, do all youre deades with difcrecion, greteth and biteth (yf it be vnderftond) moare
thē playne wordes. And when I faye in fteade off thefe
wordes boft not youre felf of youre good deades, eate not
the bloude nor the fatt of youre facrifice, there is as great
differēce betwene them as there is diftaunce betwene
heauen ād erth. For the liffe and beutye of all good
deades is of God and we are but the caren leane, we
are onlye the inftrument wherby god worketh only,
but the power is his. As god created Paule a newe,
poured hys wifdome in to him gaue him mighte and
promyfed him that his grace fhulde neuer fayle him
&c. and all without defervinges, excepte that nurteringe* the fayntes and makinge them curfe and rayle on
Chrift be meritorious. Now as it is death
to eate the bloude or fatte of any facrifice, is it not (thinke ye) damnable
to robbe god of his honoure and
to glorifye my felf with his
honoure?

* Probably a misprint for *murtheringe*, i. e., murdering; *nurtering* is given in Daye's folio of 1573.

¶ The
THYRDE BO=
ke of Moses. Cal=
led Leuiti=
cus.

¶ THE THIRDE BOKE

OF MOSES, CALLED LEUITICUS.

¶ The firſte Chapter.

1 AND the Lorde called Moſes, And ſpake vnto him oute off the tabernacle of witneſſe ſay-
2 enge, Speake vnto the childern of Iſrael, and ſaye vnto them. Who ſo- euer of you ſhall bringe a gifte vnto the Lorde, ſhall bringe it of the catell: euen of the oxen and of the ſhepe.

ℳ.C.S. The order of burnt-offringes, whether it be of ſmal or great catell or foules.

3 Yf he brynge a burntoffrynge of the oxen he ſhall offre a male without blimeſh, and ſhal brynge him to the dore of the tabernacle of witneſſe, that he maye be
4 accepted before the Lorde. And let him put his hande apon the heed of the burntſacrifice, and fauoure ſhalbe
5 geuen him to make an attonemēt for hym, ād let him kyll the oxe before the Lorde. And let the preaſtes Aarons ſonnes brynge the bloude and let them ſprinckell it rounde aboute apon the alter that is before the dore
6 of the tabernacle of witneſſe. And let the burntoff-
7 rynges be ſtrypped and hewed in peces. And thē let the ſonnes of Aaron the preaſt put fire apō the alter
8 and put wodd apon the fire, and let them laye the peces with the heed and the fatte, apon the wod that
9 is on the fire in the alter. .P. But the inwardes ād the legges they ſhall waſh in water, and the preaſt ſhall burne altogither apon the alter, that it be a burntſac-

V. 2 Homo qui obtulerit 3 ad placādū ſibi dominū 4 caput hoſtiæ & acceptabilis erit, atque in expiationē eius proficiēs. 6 detractaque pelle hoſtiæ 7 ſtrue lignorū ante cōpoſita 8 & cuncta quæ adhærēt iecori

rifice, and an offerynge of a fwete odoure vnto the Lorde.

10 Yf he will offer a burntfacrifice of the fhepe whether it be of the lambes or of the gootes: he fhall offer a 11 male without blimefh. And let him kyll it on the north fyde of the alter, before the Lorde. And let the preaftes Aarons fonnes fprinkle the bloude of it, 12 rounde aboute apon the alter. And let it be cut in peces: euen with his heed and his fatte, and let the preaft putte them apon the wodd that lyeth apon the 13 fire in the alter. But let him wafh the inwardes and the legges with water, and than bringe altogether and burne it apon the alter: that is a burntoffrynge and a facrifice of fwete fauoure vnto the Lorde.

14 Yf he will offer a burntoffrynge of the foules he fhall offer eyther of the turtyll doues or of the ionge 15 pigeons. And the preaft fhall brynge it vnto the alter, and wrynge the necke a fundre of it, and burne it on the alter, and let the bloude runne out apon the fydes 16 of the alter, ãd plucke awaye his croppe ãd his fethers, ãd caft thẽ befyde the alter on the eaft parte vppõ the 17 hepe of affhes, ãd breke his winges but [Fo. III.] plucke thẽ not a fundre. And thẽ let the preaft burne it vpõ the alter, euẽ apõ the wodd that lyeth apõ the fire, a burntfacrifice ãd an offerynge of a fwete fauoure vnto the Lorde.

V. 9 inteftinis 12 diuidentque membra, caput & omnia quæ adh. iecori 13 Et oblata omnia adol. facerdos 15 capite, ac rupto vulneris loco, 17 & nõ fecabit, neque ferro diuidet eã

L. 10 von lemmern odder zygen eyn brando. 13 Vnd der priefter foles alles opffern 15 forn den hals abftechen 17 fpalten, aber nicht abbrechen

M. M. N. 9 This *fwete odoure* is: the facryfyce of fayth & of pure affeccyon, in whych God is as delited, as a man is delited in the good fauoure of meates, as it is fayd of Noe, Gen. viii, d.

❧ The seconde Chapter.

1 YF any soule will offer a meatoffrynge vnto the Lorde, his offerynge shalbe fine floure, and he shall poure thereto oyle ād
2 put frankencens theron and shall bringe it vnto Aarons sonnes the preastes. And one of them shall take thereout his handfull of the floure, and of the oyle with all the frankencēs, ād burne it for a memoriall apō the alter: an offryng of a swete sauoure vnto the
3 Lord. And the rēnaunt of the meatofferynge shalbe Aarons ād his sonnes, as a thinge most holye of the sacrifices of the Lorde.

M.C.S. The order of meatoffrynges, of swete cakes, of fyne flower, of franckencens. &ce. with oute leuen, & with oute hony, but not with oute salt.

4 Yf any mā bringe a meatoffrynge that is bakē in the ouē, let him brynge swete cakes of fine floure mingled with oyle, ād vnleuended wafers anoynted with oyle.
5 Yf thy meatoffrynge be baken in the fryenge pan, then
6 it shalbe of swete floure mingled with oyle. And thou shalt mynce it small, ād poure oyle thereon: ād so is it a meatoffrynge.
7 Yf thy meatofferynge be a thynge broyled vppon the greadyerne, of floure myngled with oyle it shalbe.
8 And thou shalt brynge the .P. meatoffryng that is made of these thinges vnto the Lorde, and shalt delyuer it vnto the preast, and he shall brynge it vnto the
9 altare and shall heue vppe parte of the meatoffrynge for a memoriall, and shall burne it apon the alter: an
10 offerynge of a swete sauoure vnto the Lorde. And that which is left of the meatofferynge shalbe Aarons and his sonnes, as a thynge that is most holye of the offerynges off the Lorde.
11 All the meatoffrynges which ye shall brynge vnto

V. 2 ad filios A. sacerdotis 4 coctum in clibano 6 & fundes super eam oleum. 7 Si autem de craticula 9 tollet memoriale de sacrificio
L. 2 Semel mehl 4 gebacken ym offen 7 so ists eyn speysopffer.
M. M. N. 2 This *swete sauoure* figureth the prayers of the meake & faithfull, as it is interpretate in Apoc. viii, a the which prayers do withstand the furie of the Lorde.

the Lorde, ſhalbe made without leuē. For ye ſhall nether burne leuen nor honye in any offerynge of the
12 Lorde: Notwithſtondinge ye ſhall bryng the firſtlynges of them vnto the Lorde: But they ſhall not come apon the alter to make a ſwete ſauoure.

13 All thy meatofferynges thou ſhalt ſalt with ſalt: nether ſhalt thou ſoffre the ſalt of the couenaunt of thy God to be lackynge from thy meatofferynge: but apon all thyne offerynges thou ſhalt brynge ſalt.

14 Yf thou offer a meatofferynge of the firſtripe frutes vnto the Lorde, then take of that which is yet grene and drye it by the fire ād beat it ſmall, and ſo offer the meat-
15 offerynge of thy firſtrype frutes. And than poure oyle there to, and put frankencens thereon: and ſo it is a
16 [Fo. IIII.] meatoffrynge. And the preaſt ſhall burne parte of the beten corne and parte of that oyle, with all the frākencens: for a remembraunce. That is an offerynge vnto the Lorde.

☾ The thyrde Chapter

1 F any man brynge a peaceofferynge of the oxen: whether it be male or female, he ſhall brynge ſuch as is without
2 blemyſh, before the Lorde, and let him

M.C.S. The order of peaceoffringes, whyche were offered for the kepynge of peace, made

𝔐. 14 then take that
V. 12 Primitias tantum eorum 13 de ſacrificio tuo. 14 munus primitiarū ... de ſpicis adhuc virentibus .. confringes in morem farris 16 farris fracti [The Latin has nothing to repreſent Tyndale's: "That is an offerynge vnto the Lorde."]

L. 15 weyr. drauff legen, ſo iſts eyn ſpeyſsopffer. iii, 1 Iſt aber ſeyn opffer ein tödopffer von rindern

𝔐. 𝔐. N. 13 All offringes muſt be *ſalted with ſalt*, whiche ſignyfieth that all our good workes muſt be directed after the doctryne of the Apoſtles & prophetes, for then ſhall they be acceptable in the ſyghte of the Lorde, yf they ſauer of the ſalt therof, & elles not.

L. 𝔐. N. 1 *Todopffer* ſoll hie nicht eyn *todtopffer* heyſsen das nicht lebet, ſondern das da todtet vnd wurget vnnd des dings eyn end macht, vollend aus richt, Denn es bedeut das opffer, da S. Paulus Ro. 12. vnd Petrus 1. Pet. 2. von leren, das wir nach dem glauben, ſollen vnſern leyb vnd ſeyne luſte vollend todten vnd aufferbeytten, dz frid werd zwiſchen geyſt vnnd fleyſch, vnd weret, wie die andern die leben lang.

put his hande apon the heed of his offer- *of oxen, shepe, lambes and gootes.*
ynge, and kyll it before the dore of the
tabernacle of witnesse. And Aarons sonnes the preastes,
shall sprinkle the bloude apon the alter rounde aboute.
3 And they shall offre of the peaceofferynge to be a sacrifice vnto the Lord: the fatt that couereth the in-
4 wardes and all the fatt that is apon the inwardes: and
the two kydneys with the fatt that lyeth apon the
loynes: and the kall that ys on the lyuer, they shall
5 take awaye with the kydneyes. And Aarons sonnes
shall burne them apon the alter with the burntsacrifice
which is apon the wodd on the fire. That is a sacrifice
of a swete sauoure vnto the Lorde.
6 Yf a man brynge a peaceoffrynge vnto the Lorde
from of the flocke: whether it be male, or female,
7 it shalbe without blemysh. Yf he offre a lambe, he
8 shall brynge it before the Lord. P. and put his hande
apon his offrynges heede, and kyll it in the doore off
the tabernacle off wytnesse, and Aarons sonnes shall
sprinkle the bloude thereof rounde aboute the alter.
9 And of the peafeoffringe they shall brynge a sacrifyce vnto the Lorde: the fatt there of ãd the rompe
altogether, which they shall take off harde by the
backe bone: and the fatt that couereth the inwardes
10 and all the fatt that is apon the inwardes and the .ii
kydneyes with the fatt that lyeth apon them and apon
the loynes, and the kall that is apon the lyuer he
11 shall take awaye with the kydneyes. And the preast
shall burne them apon the alter to fede the Lordes
offrynge withall.

V. 9 offerent de pacificorum hostia sacrificium domino 10 operit ventrem atque vniuersa vitalia, & vtrumque ren. c. adipe qui
est iuxta ilia 11 in pabulũ ignis et oblationis dom.

L. 6 Ist aber seyn fridopffer (also v. 9) 11 zur speyse des opffers
dem HERRN.

M. M. N. 4 By the takyng awaye of the fat, the inwardes,
the .ii. kydneys & the kalle is signifyed vnto us, that yf we wylbe
a swete sacrifice vnto the Lorde we must cut of all concupisceces
& naughty desyres of the flesshe, and the euell vse of all our mẽ-
bres, and must subdue & mortyfye our affectiõs, & offre thẽ to
God, by the mortificacyon of the crosse, as sayth the Prophete
Ps. xxv, a.

12 Yf the offrynge be a goote, he shall brynge it be-
13 fore the Lorde and put his hande apon the head of it
and kyll it before the tabernacle of witnesse, and the
sonnes of Aaron shall sprinkle the bloude thereof apon
14 the alter rounde aboute. And he shall brynge thereof
his offrynge vnto the Lordes sacrifyce: the fatt that
couereth the inwardes and all the fatt that is apō the
15 inwardes and the .ii. kydneyes and the fatt that lyeth
apon them and apon the loynes, and the kall that is
apō the lyuer he shall take awaye with the kydneyes.
16 And the preast shall burne them apō the alter to sede
the Lordes sacrifyce [Fo. V.] wyth all ād to make a
swete sauoure. And thus shal all the fatt be the Lordes,
17 and it shalbe a lawe forever amonge youre generacions
after you in youre dwellynge places: that ye eate
nether fatt nor bloude.

¶ The .IIII. Chapter.

1,2 AND the Lorde talked with Moses saynge: speake vnto the children of Israel ād saye: when a soule synneth thorow igno- raunce and hath done any of those thinges which the Lorde hath forbydden in his commaundmentes to be
3 done: Yf the preast that is anoynted synne and make the people to doo amysse, he shall brynge for his synne which he hath done: an oxe wythout blemysh vnto
4 the Lorde for a synneoffrynge. And he shall brynge the oxe vn to the dore of the tabernacle of wytnesse before the Lorde, and shall put his hande apon the oxes heade and kyll him before the Lorde.
5 And the preast that is anoynted shall take of the

M.C.S. The offryng made for synnes done of ignoraunce.

M. 1 Lorde spake vnto Moses 4 vpon the oxe heade
V. 13 altar. circumitū, 14 tollentque ex ea in pastū ignis dominici ad. qui operit ventrē, & qui tegit vniv. vital., 15 duos ren. cum reticulo quod est super eos iuxta ilia 16 in alimoniā ignis & suavissimi od. iiii, 2 et de vniuersis mādatis domini . . vt non fierent 3 delinquere faciens
L. 16 zur speysz des opffers zum sussen geruch.

oxes bloude and brynge it in to the tabernacle of wit-
6 neſſe and ſhall dyppe his fynger in the bloude and
ſprinkle thereof .vii. tymes before the Lorde: euen be-
7 fore the hangynge of the holy place. And he ſhall
put ſome of the bloude apon the hornes of the alter of
ſwete cens before the Lorde which is in the .*P*. tabernacle of witneſſe, and ſhall poure all the bloude of the
oxe apon the botome of the alter of burntofferynges
which is by the dore of the tabernacle of witneſſe.
8 And he ſhall take awaye all the fatt of the oxe that
is the ſynne-offerynge: the fatt that couereth the in-
9 wardes and all the fatt that is aboute them, and the
ii. kydneyes with the fatt that lyeth apon thē and
apon the loynes, and the kall apon the lyuer let them
10 take awaye alſo with the kydneyes: as it was taken
from the oxe of the peaceoffrynge and let the preaſt
11 burne them apon the altare of burntofferynges. But
the ſkynne of the oxe and all his fleſh with his heede,
12 his legges, his inwardes with his donge, ſhall he carye
altogither out of the hoſte vnto a clene place: euen
where the aſſhes are poured out, and burne hī on wodd
with fyre: euen apon the heape of aſſhes.
13 Yf the hole comynalte of the childern comynalte,
of Iſrael ſynne thorow ygnoraunce and the *commūity,*
congregation.
thynge be hyd from their eyes: ſo that they *v. 21.*
haue commytted any of theſe thinges which the Lorde
hath forbidden to be done in his commaundmentes
14 ād haue offended, ād the ſynne which they haue ſynned
be afterwarde knowne, than ſhal they offre an oxe for
a ſynneofferynge ād ſhall brynge him before the taber-
15 nacle of wit- [Fo. VI.] neſſe, and the elders of the
multitude ſhall put their handes apon his heed before
16 the Lorde And the preaſt that is anoynted ſhall
brynge of his bloude in to the tabernacle of witneſſe,

𝔐. 5 of the oxe bloude
𝔙. 6 cōtra velum ſanctuarii 7 thym. gratiſſimi domino 8 tam eum qui vitalia operit, quam omnia quæ intrinſecus ſunt 11 omnes carnes 12 & reliquo corpore ... cin. effundi ſolent .. quæ in loco effuſorū ciner. cremabuntur. 13 omnis turba Iſr. ignorauerit & per imperitiā fecerit 15 ſeniores populi
𝔏. 9 fett das ynnwendigſt iſt 13 eyn gantze gemeyne ynn Iſrael

17 and shall dyppe his finger in the bloude, and sprinkle it seuen tymes before the Lorde: euen before the uayle.
18 And shall put of the bloude apon the hornes of the alter whiche is before the Lorde in the tabernacle of witnesse, and shall poure all the bloude apon the botome of the alter of burntoffrynges which is by the
19 dore of the tabernacle of witnesse, and shall take all
20 his fatt from him and burne it apon the altare, and shall do with his oxe as he dyd wyth the synneoffryngeoxe. And the preast shal make an attonement
21 for them, ãd so it shalbe forgeuen them. And he shall brynge the oxe without the hoste, ãd burne him as he burned the first, so is this the synneofferynge of the comynalte.
22 When a Lorde synneth and committeth thorow ignoraunce any of these thynges whiche the Lorde his God hath forbydden to be done in his commaund-
23 mentes and hath so offended: when his synne is shewed vnto him which he hath synned, he shall brynge for
24 hys offerynge an he goote without blemysh and laye his hande apon the heed of it, and kyll it in .P. the place where the burntofferynges are kylled before the
25 Lorde: this is a synneoffrynge. Thã let the preast take of the bloude of the synneoffrynge with his finger, and put it apon the hornes of the burntofferyngalter, and poure his bloude apon the botome of the burntofferyngealter and burne all his fatt apon the alter as he
26 doth the fatt of the peaceofferynges.

And the preast shall make an attonement for him as concernynge his synne, and so it shalbe forgeuen him.

27 Yf one of the comẽ people of the londe synne thorowe ignoraunce and committe any off the thinges which the Lorde hath forbidden, in his commaundementes
28 to be done, and so hath trespased, when his synne

V. 20 sic faciēs & de hoc vitulo quomodo fecit & prius & rog. pro eis fac., propitius erit eis dom. 21 quia est pro peccato multitud. (v. 24) 22 quod domini lege prohibetur. 25 & reliquum fundēs (v. 30) 26 sicut in vict. pacific. fieri solet (v. 31) 27 de populo terræ
L. 18 alles ander blut 24 Das sey seyn sundopffer 25 vnd das ander blut

whiche he hath fynned is come to his knowlege, he
fhall bringe for his offerynge, a fhe goote without blem-
29 ifh for his fynne which he hath fynned, and laye his
hande apon the heed of the fynneofferynge ād flee it
30 in the place of burntoffrynges. And the preaſt fhall
take of the bloude with his finger ād put it apō the
hornes of the burntoffryngealter and poure all the
31 bloude apō the botome of the alter, ād fhall take
awaye all his fatt as the fatt of the peaceoffrynges is
takē awaye. And the preaſt fhal burne it apō the
alter for a fwete fauoure vnto the Lorde, and [Fo. VII.]
the preaſt fhall make an attonemēt for him ād it fhalbe
forgeuen him.
32 Yf he bringe a fhepe ād offer it for a fynneofferynge, he fhall bringe a yewe without blemifh and
33 laye his hande apon the heed of the fynneofferynge
and flee it in the place where the burntoffrynges are
34 flayne. And the preaſt fhal take of the bloude of
the fynneofferynge with his finger, ād put it apō the
hornes of the burntoffryngealter, ād fhall poure all
the bloude thereof vnto the botome of the alter.
35 And he fhall take awaye all the fatt thereof, as the
fatte of the fhepe of the peaceoffringes was takē a
waye. And the preaſt fhall burne it apō the alter
for the lordes facrifice, and the preaſt fhal make an
attonemēt for his fynne, and it fhalbe forgeuen him.

⁌ The ,V. Chapter.

1 **W**HE a foule hath fynned ād herde   𝕸.𝕰.𝖅. *Of*
    the voyce of curfynge ād is a   *oothes. The*
    witneffe: whether he hath fene   *cleanfynge of*
    or knowne of it yf he haue not   *hym that toucheth vn-*
2 vttered it, he fhall bere his fynne. Ether   *cleane thynges. The pur-*

   𝕸. 32 a lambe ... bringe a female
   F. 35 adeps arietis, qui immolatur pro pacificis. v, 1 aut ipfe
vidit, aut confcius eſt
   𝕷. 35 lam des tödopffers. v, 1 eyn fluch horet

when a mā toucheth any vnclene thinge: whether it be the caryon of an vnclene beeſt or of vnclene catell or vnclene worme, worme and is not warre of it, he is alſo vnclene and hath offended.

worme, any creeping thing

gacyon of an othe and of ſynne done by ignoraunce. [vi, 1.] The offringes for ſynnes which are done wyllyngly.

3 Ether when he toucheth any vnclenneſſe of mā (whatſoeuer vnclenneſſe it be that a man is defyled with all) and is not warre of it and after- warde cometh to the knowledge of it, he

warre, aware

.P.

4 is a treſpaſer. Ether when a ſoule ſweareth: ſo that he pronounceth with his lippes to do euell or to do good (what ſoeuer it be that a man pronounceth with an othe) and the thinge be out of his mynde and afterwarde cometh to the knowledge of it, than he hath offended in one of theſe.

5 Than when he hath ſynned in one of theſe thinges,
6 he ſhall confeſſe that wherein that he hath ſynned, and ſhall bringe his treſpaceofferynge vnto the Lorde for his ſynne which he hath ſynned. A female from the flocke, whether it be an yewe or a ſhe goote, for a ſynneofferynge. And the preaſt ſhall make an attonement
7 for him for his ſynne. But yf he be not able to brynge a ſhepe, then let him brynge for his treſpace which he hath ſynned, two turtyll doues or two yonge pygeons vnto the Lorde one for a ſynneoffrynge and another
8 for a burntofferynge. And he ſhall brynge them vnto the preaſt, which ſhall offer the ſynneoffrynge firſt and wringe the necke a ſundre of it, but plucke it not clene
9 of. And let him ſprinkle of the bloude of the ſynneofferynge apon the ſyde of the alter, and let the reſte of the bloude blede apon the botome of the alter, and
10 than it is a ſynneofferynge. And let him offer the ſe-

𝔐. 5 that wherin he hath 6 whether it be a lambe
𝒱. 2 immundum, ſiue quod occiſū a beſtia eſt, aut per ſe mortuum, aut quodlibet aliud reptile . . . rea eſt & deliquit. 3 poſtea, ſubiacebit delicto. 4 iuramento & ſermone 5 agat pœnitentiam 6 agnam ſiue capram 8 retorq. caput eius ad pennulas, ita vt collo adhæreat, & nō penitus abrumpatur. 9 faciet diſtillare ad fundamentum eius

𝑳. 4 wie denn eym menſchen eyn ſchwur entfaren mag 6 die da tragen haben 8 vnd yhr fornen den hals abſtechen 9 ausblutten

[Fo. VIII.] conde for a burntoffrynge as the maner is: ad fo fhall the preaft make an atonement for him for the fynne which he hath fynned, and it fhal be forgeuen him.

11 And yet yf he be not able to brynge .ii. turtyll doues or two yonge pigeons, then let hym brynge his offerynge for his fynne: the tenth parte of an Epha of fine floure for a fynneofferynge, but put none oyle thereto nether put ony frankencens thereon, for it is a fynne-
12 offeringe. And let him brynge it to the preaft, and the preaft fhall take his handfull of it and burne it apon the alter for a remembraunce to be a facryfice
13 for the Lorde: that is a fynneoffrynge. And let the preaft make an atonement for him for his fynne (what foeuer of thefe he hath fynned) and it fhalbe forgeuen. And the remnaûte fhalbe the preaftes, as it is in the meateofferynge.

14 And the Lorde comyned with Mofes *comyned,*
15 fayenge: when a foule trefpaceth ad fyn- *communed, i. e. converfed,*
neth thorow ignoraunce in any of the holy *fpoke*
thinges of the Lorde, he fhall brynge for his trefpace vnto the Lord, a ram without blymefh out of the flocke valowed at two fycles after the holy fycle, for a trefpace-
16 offerynge. And he fhall make amendes for the harme that he hath done in the holy thynge, and put the fifte parte moare .P. there to and geue it vnto the preaft. And the preaft fhall make an attonemet for him with the ram of the trefpaceofferynge, and it fhalbe forgeuē hym.

17 When a foule fynneth and committeth any of thefe thinges which are forbiddē to be done by the cōmaundmentes of the Lorde: though he wift it *
18 not, he hath yet offended and is in fynne, ad fhall

M. 15 fycles after the fycle of the fanctuary 16 fyfte parte more to. [The following 7 verses in Tyndale are transferred in Matthew's Bible to ch. vii.]

V. 11 manus eius duos offere turt. 12 in monimentum eius qui obtulit 13 hab. in munere. 17 & peccati rea, intellexerit iniquitatem fuam

L. 12 zum gedechtnis, vnd antzunden 13 Vnd fol des priefters feyn 15 feckel des heyligthums·

brīge a ram without blymeſh out of the flocke that is eſtemed to be worthe a ſynneofferynge, vnto the preaſt. And the preaſt ſhall make an attonement for him for the ignoraunce whiche he dyd and was
19 not ware, and it ſhalbe forgeuen him. This is a treſpaceofferynge, for he treſpaced agaynſt the Lorde.

VI,1,2 And the Lorde talked with Moſes ſayenge: when a ſoule ſynneth ād treſpaceth agaynſt the Lorde and denyed vnto his neyghboure that which was taken him to kepe, or that was put vnder his hande, or that which he hath violently taken awaye, or that whiche he hath
3 deceaued his neyghboure off wyth ſotylte, or hath founde that whiche was loſte and denyeth it, and ſwereth falſely, in what ſoeuer thinge it be that a man doth and
4 ſynneth therein, Then when he hath ſynned or treſpaced, he ſhall reſtore agayne that he toke violently awaye, [Fo. IX.] or the wronge whiche he dyd, or that whiche was delyuered him to kepe, or the loſt thinge
5 which he ſounde, or what ſoeuer it be aboute which he hath ſworne falſely, ∗ he ſhall reſtore it agayne in the whole ſūme and ſhal adde the fifte parte moare thereto and geue it vnto him to whome it pertayneth, the ſame daye that he offereth for his treſ-
6 pace, and ſhall brynge for his treſpace offerynge vnto the Lorde, a ram without blymeſh out of the flocke, that is eſtemed worth a treſpaceofferynge vnto the preaſt.

Vnto my neybour pertayneth ſatiſſaccio̅, but vnto god repētaunce: and the̅ the ſacrifice of chriſtes bloude is a ful ſatiſfaccion, ād attonemēt ād apeaſinge of al wrath.

7 And the preaſt ſhall make an atonemēt for him before the Lorde, ād it ſhall be forgeuē hi̅ in what ſoeuer thinge it be that a mā doth ād treſpaceth therein.

V. 19 quia per errorem deliquit in domino. vi, 2 fidei eius creditum .. aut calumniam fecerit 3 & inficians inſuper pẹierauerit 5 voluit obtinere, integra & quintam 7 pro ſingulis quæ faciendo peccavit.
L. 18 eyn ſhuldopffers werd iſt (cf. vi. 5) 19 das er dem HERRN verfallen iſt. vi, 2 zu trawer hand 3 mit eym falſchen eyde
M. M. N. 24 Vnto my neybour pertayneth ſatiſſaccyon, but vnto god repētaunce & then the ſacrifice of Chriſtes bloude is a full ſatiſſaccio̅ & attonement & apeaſyng of all wrath.

⁋ The .VI. Chapter.

8 ND the Lorde fpake vnto Mofes
9 faynge. Commaunde Aaron and his fonnes faynge: this is the lawe of the burntoffrynge. The burntofferynge fhalbe apon the herth of the alter all nyghte vnto the mornynge, and the fire of the alter fhall burne there-
10 in. And the preaft fhall put on his lynen albe and his lynen breches apon his flefh, and take awaye the affhes whiche the fire of the burntfacrifice in the altare hath
11 made, and put them befyde the alter, ād thē put off his raymēt ād put on other .P. and carye the affhes out without the hofte vnto a clene place.
12 The fire that is apon the alter fhall burne therein and not goo out. And the preaft fhall put wodd on the fire euery morninge ād put the burntfacrifice apon it, and he fhall burne thereon the fatt of the peace-
13 offerynges. The fire fhall euer burne apon the alter and neuer goo out.
14 This is the lawe of the meatoffrynge: Aarons fonnes
15 fhall bringe it before the Lorde, vnto the alter: and one of them fhall take hys handfull of the floure of the meatoffrynge ād of the oyle with all the frankencens whiche ys thereon and fhall burne it vnto a remē-braunce apon the alter to be a fwete fauoure of the
16 memoriall of it vnto the Lorde. And the reft thereof, Aaron ād his fonnes fhall eate: vnleuended it fhalbe eaten in the holy place: euē in the courte of the tab-
17 ernacle of witneffe they fhall eate it. Their parte whiche I haue geuen them of my facrifice, fhall not be

M.C.S. The offringes for fynnes which are done wyllyngly. The lawe of the burntoff-rynges. The fyre muft abyde euer-more vpon the aulter. The offrynges of Aaron and hys fonnes.

V. 9 Cremabitur in altari ... ignis, ex eodem altari 10 cineres, quos voräs ignis exuffit 11 mūdiffimo vfque ad fauillā cōfumi fa-ciet. 12 ignis autem .. femper ardebit 13 ignis .. qui nunquam deficiet 14 lex facrificii & libamentorum .. coram ... coram
L. 9 brennen auff dem altar .. alleyn des altars feuer 12, 13 brennen vnd nymmer verleffchen (*bis*) 15 Es fol eyner Heben 17 backen yhr teyl, das ich yhn geben hab

baken with leuen, for it is moſt holye, as is the ſynne-
18 offerynge, and treſpaceoffrynge. All the males amonge
the childern of Aaron, ſhall eate of it: and it ſhalbe a
dutye for euer vnto youre generacyons of the ſacrifices
of the Lorde, nether ſhal any man twytche   *twytche, twych* [often], *touch*.
it, but he that is halowed.
19 [Fo. X.] And the Lorde ſpake vnto Moſes ſayenge:
20 this is the offrynge of Aaron ãd of his ſonnes which
he ſhall offer vnto the Lorde in the daye when they are
anoynted: the tenth parte of an Epha of floure, which is
a dayly meatofferinge perpetually: halfe in the morninge
21 and halfe at nighte: ãd in the fryenge pan it ſhalbe made
with oyle. And whẽ it is fryed, thou ſhalt brynge it in as
a baken meatofferynge mynſed ſmall, and ſhalt offer it for
22 a ſwete ſauoure vnto the Lorde. And that preaſt of his
ſonnes that is anoynted in his ſteade, ſhall offer it: ãd it
ſhall be the lordes dutye for euer, and it   *dutye, due*
23 ſhal be burnt altogether. For all the meatoffrynges of
the preaſtes ſhalbe burnt altogether, ãd ſhal not be eaten.
24, 25 And the Lorde talked with Moſes ſayenge: ſpeake
vnto Aaron and vnto his ſonnes and ſaye. This is the
lawe of the ſynneoffrynge, In the place where the
burntofferynge is kylled, ſhall the ſynneofferynge be
26 kylled alſo before the Lorde, for it is moſt holy. The
preaſt that offereth it ſhall eate it in the holye place:
27 evẽ in the courte of the tabernacle of witneſſe. No
man ſhall touche the fleſh thereof, ſaue he that is halowed. And yf any rayment be ſprynckled therewyth,
28 it ſhalbe waſſhed in an holy place, and the erthẽ pott
that it is ſoddẽ in .P. ſhalbe broken. Yf it be ſodden
in braſſe, then the pott ſhalbe ſcoured and plunged in
29 the water. All the males amonge the childern of
30 Aarõ ſhall eate therof, for it is moſt holy. Notwith-

M. 28 ſcoured and ryneſed 29 amonge the Preaſtes ſhall eate
V. 17 ideo autem non fermentabitur, quia pars eius in domini offertur incenſum. 18 Legitimum ac ſempiternum 21 Offeret autem eam calidam in odorem 23 Omne enim ſacrificium ſacerd. 28 defricabitur, & lauabitur aqua. 29 veſcetur de carnibus eius
L. 18 Das ſey ewigs recht 21 gebacken dar bringen vnd geſtuckt 27 eyn kleyd beſprenget, der ſoll ſich waſſchen 28 mit waſſer ſpulen
M. M. N. 27 There ſhall none touche it, but he that is halowed, that is, but he that is dedicated, ordeyned and appoynted to mynyſter before the Lorde, as it is Agge. ii, c.

ſtōdinge no ſynneofferynge that hath his bloude brought in to the tabernacle of witneſſe to reconcyle with all in the holy place, ſhalbe eaten: but ſhalbe burnt in the fire.

❡ The .VII. Chapter.

1 THIS is the lawe of the treſpaceofferynge which is moſt holy. 2 In the place where the burntoffrynge is kylled, the treſpaceoffrynge ſhalbe kylled alſo: ād his bloude ſhalbe ſprīkled rounde aboute apon the alter. 3 And all the fatt thereof ſhalbe offered: the rompe and the fatt that couered the 4 inwardes, and the .ii. kydneyes with the fatt that lyeth on them and apon the loynes: and the kall on 5 the lyuer ſhalbe taken awaye with the kydneyes, And the preaſt ſhall burne them apon the altare, to be an offerynge vnto the Lorde: this is a treſpace offerynge. 6 All the males amonge the preaſtes ſhal eate there-7 of in the holy place, for it is moſt holy. As the ſynneofferynge is, ſo is the treſpaceofferynge, one lawe 8 ſerueth for both: and it ſhall be the preaſtes that reconcyleth therwith. [Fo. XI.] And the preaſt that offered a mans burntofferynge, ſhall haue the ſkyn of 9 the burntofferynge which he hath offered. And all the meatofferynges that are baken in the ouen, ād all that is dreſſed apon the gredyerne ād in the fryenge 10 pan, ſhalbe the preaſtes that offereth them. And all the meatofferynges that are myngled with oyle or drye, ſhall pertayne vnto all the ſonnes of Aaron, and one ſhall haue as moche as another.

M.C.S. Treſpaceoffrynges. Synne offrynges and peaceoffrynges. The fatte and the bloude maye not be eaten.

V. 2 per gyrum altaris fundetur 5 incēſum eſt domini pro delicto. 7 ad ſacerdotem .. pertinebit 10 mēſura æqua per ſingulos diuidetur.

L. 5 altar antzunden zum opffer 10 mit ole gemenget odder treuge

M. M. N. 1 *Treſpace offringe* that is, an offring for a treſpace. Treſpace after the order of the ſcrypture ſignifyeth ſomtyme all the lyffe paſt which we haue lyued in infidelyte, being ignoraunt of the veritie, not only in doyng opē ſynnes, but alſo when we haue walked in oure awne rightweſnes, as in the Pſalme xviii, d. & .ii. Paral. xxviii, c.

11 This is the lawe of the peaceoffringes whiche shalbe
12 offered vnto the Lorde. Yf he offer to geue thanckes, he shall brynge vnto his thanckofferynge: swete cakes myngled with oyle and swete wafers anoynted with oyle,
13 and cakes myngled with oyle of fine floure fryed, ãd he shall brynge his offerynge apon cakes made of leuended bred vnto the thanckoffrynge of his peaceofferynges,
14 ãd of them all he shall offer one to be an heueoffrynge vnto the Lorde, ãd it shalbe the preastes that sprynkleth
15 the bloude of the peaceofferynges. And the flesche of the thankofferynge of his peaceofferynges shalbe eaten the same daye that it is offred, and there shall none of it be layde vpp vntyll the mornynge.
16 Yf it be a vowe or a fre willofferynge that he bryngeth, the same daye that he offereth it, .P. it shalbe eaten,
17 and that which remayneth may be eaten on the morowe:
18 but as moche of the offered flesch as remaneth vnto the thirde daye shalbe burned with fire For yf any of the flesch of the peaceoffrynges be eaten the thirde daye then shall he that offered it optayne no fauour, nether shall it be rekened vnto him: but shalbe an abhomynacion, and the soule that eateth of it shall beare the synne thereof.
19 The flesch that twycheth any vnclene thinge shall not be eaten, but burnt with fire: and all that be clene in their flesch, maye eate flesch.
20 Yf any soule eate of the flesch of the peaceofferynges, that pertayne vnto the Lorde and hys vnclennesse yet apon him, the same soule shall perisshe from amonge
21 his people. Moreouer yf a soule twych any vnclene thinge, whether it be the vnclennesse of man or of any vnclene beest or any abhominacion that is vnclene: ãd thẽ eate of the flesch of the peaceoffrynges whiche per-

V. 14 ex quibus vnus pro primitiis offertur domino 18 irrita fiet eius oblatio, nec proderit offerenti . . anima tali se edulio cont., præuaricationis rea erit.

L. 18 Es wirt yhm auch nicht zu gerechnet werden, sondern es wirt verworffen seyn . . ist eyner missethat schuldig. 21 was sonst greulich ist

M. M. N. 16 By *vowes* are vnderstand the gyftes which are acoustomed to be offred and geuen to God by any outwarde ceremonye, as it was to rounde their heares, or to dryncke no wyne. etc. Num. vi, a.

tayne vnto the Lord, that foule fhall periffh from his people.

22, 23 And the Lorde fpake vnto Mofes faynge: fpeake vnto the childern of Ifrael ād faye. Ye fhall eate no
24 maner fatt of oxen, fhepe or gootes: neuerthelater the fatt of the beeft that dyeth alone ād the fatt of that which is torne with wilde beeftes, maye be occupide, occupide in all maner [Fo. XII.] vfes: but *employed, ufed*
25 ye fhal in no wife eate of it. For whofoeuer eateth the fatt of the beeft of which mē bring an offring vnto the Lorde, that foule that eateth it fhall periffh frō
26 his people. Moreouer ye fhall eate no maner of bloud, wherefoeuer ye dwell, whether it be of foule or of
27 beeft. What fouer foule it be that eateth any maner of bloude the fame foule fhal periffhe frō his people.

28, 29 And the Lorde talked with Mofes fayenge: fpeake vnto the childrē of Ifrael ād faye He that offereth his peaceofferynge vnto the Lord, fhall bringe his gifte
30 vnto the Lord of his peaceoffrynges: his owne handes fhal bringe the offrynge of the Lorde: euē the fatt apō the breft he fhall bringe with the breft to waue it a
31 waueoffrynge before the Lorde. And the preaft fhall burne the fatt apon the alter, ād the breft fhalbe Aarōs
32 ād his fonnes. And the right fhulder they fhall geue vnto the preaft, to be an heueoffrynge, of their peace-
33 offringes. And the fame that offreth the bloud of the peaceoffringes ād the fatt, amōg the fōnes of Aarō,
34 fhall haue the right fhulder vnto his parte, for the wauebreft ād the heuefhulder I haue takē of the chil- dern of Ifrael, euen of their peace offringes, ād haue geuē it vnto Aarō the preft and vnto his fonnes: to be a dutie for euer of .P. the childern of Ifrael.

35 This is the anoyntinge of Aaron ād of the facryfices of the Lorde, in the daye when they were offered to

V. 21 interibit de populis fuis,(peribit vv. 25, 27.) 25 adipem, qui offeri debet in incenfum domini 30 tenebit manibus adipem . . . cumque ambo oblata domino 32 armus quoque dexter . . cedet in primitias facerd. 35 in ceremoniis domini

L. 30 mit feyner hand hertzu bringen 32 zur Hebe von yhren tödopffern. 34 zum ewigen recht. 35 vberantwort worden priefter zu feyn

36 be preaftes vnto the Lorde, whiche the Lorde commaunded to be geuen them in the daye when he anoynted them, of the childern of Ifrael, and to be a dutie for euer amonge their generacions. *dutie, law,*
37 This is the lawe of burntoffrynges, of *ftatute.* meatoffrynges, of fynneoffrynges, of trefpaceoffrynges,
38 of fulloffrynges, of peaceoffrynges, which the Lorde commaunded Mofes in the mount of Sinai, in the daye when he commaunded the childern of Ifrael to offer their offrynges vnto the Lorde in the wildernefſe of Sinai.

The .VIII. Chapter.

1 AND the Lorde fpake vnto Mofes
2 faynge: take Aaron and his fonnes with hĩ, and the veftures and the anoyntinge oyle, and an oxe for a fynneofferynge and two
3 rammes ãd a bafkett of fwete bred: ãd gather all the comentye together vnto the dore of the
4 tabernacle of witnefſe. And Mofes dyd as the Lorde commaunded him, and the people gathered them felues togither vnto the doore of the tabernacle of witnefſe.
5 And Mofes fayde vnto the people: this is the thinge which the Lorde commaunded to do.
6 [Fo. XIII.] And Mofes broughte Aaron and his
7 fonnes, and wafshed them with water, and put apon him the albe and gyrde him with a girdel and put apon him the tunycle and put the Ephod thereon, and gyrded him with the broderd girdel of the Ephod,

comentye, community, congregation

M.C.S. *The anoyntynge and confecracyon of Aaron and his onnes.*

Hence the *pope fett holowenge of chirches, alters, font, belles ãd fo forthe, and the anoyntinge of bifshopes preaftes, and foch like.*

V. 2 caniftrũ cũ azymis 6 Cumque lauiffet eos
L. 36 zum ewigen recht 37 fulleopffer .. tödopffer. viii, 6 wufch fie mit waffer.

8 and bounde it vnto him therewith. And he put the breſtlappe thereon, ād put in the breſtlappe lighte ād
9 perfectneſſe. And he put the myter apon his heed ād put apō the myter euē apō the forefrōt of it, the golden plate of the holy croune, as the Lorde commaunded Moſes.
10 And Moſes toke the anoyntynge oyle and anoynted the habitacion and all that was therein and ſanctified
11 them, and ſprynkled thereof apon the alter .vii. tymes and anoynted the alter and all his veſſels, and the lauer
12 with hys fote, to ſanctifie them. And he poured of the anoyntynge oyle apon Aarons heed and anoynted him
13 to ſanctifie him. And he broughte Aarons ſonnes and put albes apon them, and gyrde them with gyrdels, ād put bonettes apō their heedes: as the Lorde cōmaunded Moſes
14 And the ſynneoffrynge was brought. And Aaron and his ſonnes put their handes apon the heed of the
15 oxe of the ſynneoffryng. And when it was ſlayne, Moſes toke of the bloude, and put it apon the hornes of the alter rounde .P. aboute with his finger and purified it, ād poured the bloud vnto the botome of the
16 alter ād ſanctified it ād reconcyled it. And he toke all the fatt that was apon the inwardes ād the kal that was on the lyuer ād the two kydneyes with their fatt
17 ād burned it apō the alter. But the oxe, the hide, his fleſh ād his donge, he burnt with fire without the hoſte, as the Lorde commaunded Moſes.
18 And he broughte the ram of the burntofferynge, and Aaron ād his ſonnes put their handes apon the
19 heed of the ram, and it was kylled. And Moſes ſprink-
20 led the bloud apō the alter roūde aboute, ād cutt the ram in peces ād burnt the heed, the peces ād the fatte,
21 ād waſſhed the inwardes ād the legges in water, and burnt the ram euery whitt apō the alter. That was a

𝔐. 8 Vrim and Thumim
𝒱. 8 doctrina & veritas. 9 laminā auream cōſecratam in ſanctificatione 15 quo expiato & ſanctificato
𝔏. 8 Liecht vnd Vollickeyt. 15 entfūndiget den altar .. das er yhn verſunet. 20 zehyeb den widder yn ſtuck
𝔐. 𝔐. N. 8 Loke in Exo. xxviii, c. & Num. xxvii. d.

burntfacrifice of a fwete fauoure ād an offrynge vnto the Lorde, as the Lorde cōmaunded Mofes.

22 And he broughte the other ram that was the full-offerynge, and Aaron and his fonnes put their hādes
23 apō the heed of the ram: And when it was flayne, Mofes toke of the bloude of it, and put it apon the typpe of Aarons ryght eare and apon the thombe of his right hande, and apon the great too of his right fote.
24 Then were Aarons fonnes broughte, ād Mo- [Fo. XIIII.] fes put of the bloude on the typpe of the right eare of them, and apon the thombes of theire righte handes, and apon the great tooes of their righte fete, and fprinkled the bloud apō the alter rounde aboute.
25 And he toke the fatt ād the rompe ād all the fatt that was apon the inwardes, ād the kall of the lyuer, ād the .ii. kydneyes with their fatt ād their righte fhul-
26 der. And out of the bafket of fwete bred that was before the Lorde, he toke one fwete cake of oyled bred ād one wafer, ād put thē on the fatt ād apon the righte
27 fhulder, ād put altogether apō Aarons handes ād apō his fonnes handes, ād waued it a waueofferynge before
28 the Lorde. And thā Mofes toke thē from of their handes agayne ād burnt thē apō the alter, euen apon the burnt-offrynge: These are the fulloffrynges of a fwete fauoure ād a facrifice vnto the Lorde.
29 And Mofes toke the brefte and waued it a waueof-frynge before the Lorde, of the ram of the ful offrynges: ād it was Mofes parte, as the Lorde commaunded Mofes.
30 And Mofes toke of the anoynting oyle ād of the bloude whiche was apon the alter, and fprinkled it apō Aarō ād apon his veftimētes ād apō his fōnes ād on their veftimētes with hī ād fanctified Aarō ād his vefturs ād his fōnes .*P*. and his fonnes veftures alfo.
31 Then Mofes fayde vnto Aaron and his fonnes: boyle the flefh in the doore of the tabernacle of witneffe,

V. 24 reliquum fudit fuper altare 27 qui poftquam leuauerunt ea 28 eo quod confecrationis effet oblatio
L. 22 widder des fulleopffers 24 gos das blut

and there eate it with the bred that is in the baſket
of fullofferynges, as the Lorde commaunded ſayenge.
32 Aaron and his ſonnes ſhall eate it: ād that which
remayneth of the fleſh and of the brede, burne with
fire.
33 And ſe that ye departe not from the doore of the
tabernacle of witneſſe ſeuen dayes longe: vntill the
dayes of youre fullofferynges be at an ende. For .vii
34 dayes muſt youre hādes be filled, as they were this
daye: euē ſo the Lorde hath commaūded to do, to
35 reconcyle you with all. Se therfore that ye abyde
in the dore of the tabernacle of witneſſe daye and
nyghte ſeuen dayes longe: and kepe the watch of the
Lorde that ye dye not: for ſo I am commaunded.
36 And Aaron and his ſonnes dyd all thynges which the
Lorde commaunded by the hande of Moſes.

¶ The .IX. Chapter.

1 AND the .viii. daye Moſes called
Aaron and his ſonnes and the
2 elders of Iſrael, and ſayde vnto
Aaron: take a calfe for a ſynne
offrynge, and a ram for a burntoffrynge:
both without blemiſh, and brynge them
3 before the Lorde. And vnto the childern
of Iſrael he ſpa- [Fo. XV.] ke ſayenge:
take ye an he goote for a ſynneofferynge,
and a calfe and a lambe bothe two of a
yere olde, and without blemyſh for a
4 burntſacrifice, and an oxe and a ram for peaceoffrynges,
to offer before the Lorde, and a meateofferyng myngled
with oyle, for to daye the Lorde will appere vnto you.

*M.C.S. The
fyrſt offringes
of Aaron, for
hym ſelfe and
for the people.
Aaron bleſſeth
the people. The
glorye of the
Lorde is
ſhewed. The
fyre com-
mynge from
aboue conſum-
eth the ſacri-
fice.*

V. 31 panes quoque conſecrationis edite 33 complebitur tēpus
conſecrationis veſtræ. 34 ſicut impræſentiarum factum eſt, vt ritus
ſacrificii compleretur. ix, 4 immolate eos coram domino in ſacrificio ſingulorum
L. 33 bis an den tag, da die tage ewrs fullopffers aus find
M. M. N. 36 Loke in the .iiii. of the kinges in the .xix. ch. b.

5 And they brought that which Moſes commaunded vnto the tabernacle of witneſſe, ād all the people came
6 and ſtode before the Lorde. And Moſes ſayde, this is the thynge which the Lorde commaunded that ye ſhulde do: ād then the glorye of the Lorde ſhall appere
7 vnto you. And Moſes ſayde vnto Aaron: go vnto the alter and offer thy ſynneofferynge, and make an attonement for the and for the people: and then offer the offerynge of the people and reconcyle them alſo, as the Lorde cōmaunded Moſes.
8 And Aaron went vnto the alter, and ſlewe the calfe
9 that was his ſynneoffrynge. And the ſonnes of Aaron broughte the bloude vnto him, and he dypte his finger in the bloude and put it apon the hornes of the alter, and poured the bloude vnto the botome of the alter.
10 And the fatt and the two kydneyes with the kall of the lyuer of the ſynneoffrynge, he burnt vppon the
11 alter, as the Lorde commaunded Moſes: .₸. but the fleſh and the hyde, he burnt with fyre without the hoſte.
12 After warde he ſlewe the burntofferynge, ād Aarons ſonnes brought the bloude vnto him, and he ſprinkled it
13 rounde aboute apon the alter. And they brought the burntofferynge vnto him in peces and the heed alſo,
14 and he burnt it apon the alter, and dyd waſſhe the inwardes and the legges, and burnt them alſo apon the burntofferynge in the alter.
15 And than he broughte the peoples offerynge and toke the goote that was the peoples ſynneofferynge, and ſlewe it and offered it for a ſynofferynge: as he dyd the firſt.
16 And then broughte the burntofferynge and offered it
17 as the maner was, and broughte the meatofferynge and fylled his hande thereof, and burnt it apon the alter, beſydes the burntſacrifyce in the mornynge.
18 Then he ſlewe the oxe and the ram that were the

𝒱. 7 et deprecare pro te & pro populo. cumque mactaueris hoſtiam populi, ora pro eo, ſicut præcepit dominus. 15 expiatoque altari 17 abſque ceremoniis hol. matutini.
𝕷. 7 deyn ſundopffer vnd deyn brandopffer . . verſüne dich vnd das volck 13 zu yhm zuſtucket vnd den kopff 17 auſſer des morgens brandopffer.

peoples peaseofferynges, and Aarons sonnes broughte the bloude vnto him, and he sprinkled it apon the alter
19 rounde aboute, and toke the fatt of the oxe and of the ram: the rōpe and the fatt that couereth the inwardes
20 and the kydneyes and the kall of the lyuer: and put them apon the brestes and burnt it apon the alter:
21 but the brestes and the righte shulders Aaron waued before the Lorde, as the Lorde cō- [Fo. XVI.] maunded Moses.
22 And Aaron lifte vpp his hande ouer the people and blessed thē, and came doune from offerynge of synofferynges, burntofferynges and
23 peaseofferynges. Then Moses and Aaron wēt into the tabernacle of witnesse and came out agayne and blessed the people, and the glorye of the Lorde apered vnto
24 all the people. And there came a fyre out from before the Lorde, and consumed apon the alter: the burntofferynge and the fatt. And all the people sawe it and showted, and fell on their faces.

Of soch places the bisshopes toke their domme blessynge with .ii. fingers: But numery vi. thou maist read the goodly prayer of his blessynge.

☙ The .X. Chapter

1 AND Nadab and Abihu the sonnes of Aaron toke ether of them his censor ād put fyre there-in and put cens apō, and broughte straunge fyre be-fore the Lorde: which he cōmaunded thē not and there
2 went a fyre out frō the Lorde

M.C.S. *Nadab and Abihu are slayne. Israel mourneth for them. The Preastes are forbydden wyne. The resydew of the sacrifice the Preastes eate.*

Hereof ye se the frute of a mans good entent with out Gods word. As we maye

V. 24 turbæ, laudauerunt dominū x, 1 ignem alienum
L. 22 steyg herab vom werck 24 frolocketen sie. x, 1 frembd feur
M. M. N. 1 Herof ye se the frute of a mans good entent wythout Goddes word. As we maye do no lesse, so doeth thys ensample teache that we may do no moare then is commaunded.

| | *do nolesse, so doeth this ensample teach that we maye do no moare than is cōmaunded.* | and cōsumed thē, and they dyed before the Lorde. Then Moses sayde vnto Aarō this is it that the Lorde spake sayynge: I will be sanctifyed in them that come nye me, ād before all the people I wilbe glorifyed. And Aaron helde his peace. | *God is sanctified when we obey him ād mortify oure wyll to doo his.* |

3

4 And Moses called Misael and Elesaphā the sonnes of Vsiel the vncle of Aaron, and sayde vnto thē: goo to and carye youre brethrē from the holy place out
5 of the hoste. And they went to them and caryed them in their albes out of the hoste, as Moses bad.

6 .P. And Moses sayde vnto Aaron and vnto Eleazar and Ithamar his eldest sonnes: vncouer not youre heed nether rent youre clothes, lest ye dye and wrath come apon all the people lett youre brethren the hole house of Israel, bewepe the burnynge which the Lorde hath
7 burnt. But goo ye not out from the dore of the tabernacle of wytnesse, lest ye dye: for the anoyntynge oyle of the Lorde is apon you. And they dyd as Moses bad.

8 And the Lorde spake vnto Aaron sa-
9 ynge: drynke no wyne nor stronge drynke, nether thou nor thi sonnes with the: when ye go in to the tabernacle of witnesse, lest ye dye. And let it be a lawe foreuer vnto
10 youre childern after you: that ye maye put difference betwene holy and vnholy,
11 and betwene vnclene and clene, and that ye maye teach the childern of Israel: all the ordynaunces which the Lorde hath cōmaunded them by the handes of Moses.

Oure prelates be dronke wyth desyre of honoure and haue brought the world oute of their wittes to satisfie their lustes, and liue not sobirly to teach vs what christ commaunded by the handes of the apostels..

12 And Moses sayde vnto Aaron and vnto Eleazar ād

V. 3 tacuit Aaron. 5 tulerunt eos sicut iacebant ... vt sibi fuerat imperatum. 6 incendium, quod dominus suscitauit 10 vt habeatis scientiam discernendi

L. 3 schwyg stille. 6 brand .. gethan hat 10 das yhr kund vnterscheyden

M. M. N. 3 God is sanctified when we obey hym, and mortyfye oure wyll to do his. 4 Loke in Gen. xiii, b. 9 *For euer*, it is here taken for a tyme that hath an ende, and not euer lasting as it is also in Gen. xiii, d & Ex. xii, c.

Ithamar his sonnes that were lefte: take the meatofferynge that remayneth of the sacrifyces of the Lorde, and eate it without leuen besyde the alter, for it is
13 most holy: eate it therfore in the holy place, becaufe it is thy dutye and thi sonnes dutye of the sacrifyce of the Lorde: for so I am com- dutye [often], due
14 maunded. And the [Fo. XVII.] wauebreft and heueshulder eate in a clene place: both thou and thy sonnes and thy doughters with the. For it is thy dutye and thy sonnes dutye with the, of the peace-
15 offerynges off the childern of Israel. For the heueshulder ād the wauebreft whiche they brynge with the sacrifices of the fatt, to waue it before the Lorde, shalbe thyne and thy sonnes with the, and be a lawe for euer, as the Lorde hath commaunded.
16 And Moses soughte for the goote that was the synneofferynge, and se, it was burnt. And he was angrye with Eleazar and Ithamar the sonnes of Aaron,
17 which were lefte alyue sayenge: wherefore haue ye not eaten the synneofferynge in the holy place, seynge it is most holye: and for as moch as it is geuen you to bere the synne of the people, and make agrement for them
18 before the Lorde? Beholde, the bloude of it was not brought in within the holy place therfore shulde ye haue eaten it in the holy place as I commaunded.
19 And Aaron sayde vnto Moses: behold, this daye haue they offered their synneoffrynge and their burntoffrynge before the Lorde, and it is chaunced me after thys maner. Yf I shulde eate of the synneofferynge to *The offeringes must haue bene eaten in gladnesse: but Aaron coude not but morne for his sonnes.*
20 daye, wolde the Lorde be content with all? And when Moses herde that, he was content.

V. 17 portetis iniquitatem multitudinis & rogetis pro ea 18 sicut præceptum est mihi? 19 mihi autem accidit quod vides .. aut placere domino in cerem. mente lugubri? 20 recepit satisfactionem.

L. 17 missethat der gemeyne tragen ... sie versunet 19 es ist myr gangen, wie es da ist .. vnd gutter ding seyn 20 lies ers yhm gefallen.

M. M. N. 19 The offringes must haue bene eatē in gladnesse, but Aaron coulde not but morne for hys sonnes.

.¶. The .XI. Chapter.

AND the Lorde ſpake vnto Moſes and Aaron ſayenge: ſpeake vnto the childrē of Iſrael and ſaye, theſe are the beeſtes whiche ye ſhall eate amonge all the beeſtes that are on the erth: what ſoeuer hath hoffe and dyuydeth it in to two clawes ād cheweth cud among the beeſtes, that ſhall ye eate. Neuertheleſſe, theſe ſhall ye not eate of them that chewe cud and haue hoffes. The camel, for he cheweth cud but he deuydeth not the hoffe in to two clawes therfore he ſhall be vnclene vnto you. And the Conye, for he cheweth the cud but deuydeth not the hoffe in to two clawes, therfore he is vnclene to you. And the hare, for he likewiſe cheweth the cud, but deuydeth not the hoffe in to two clawes, he is therfore vnclene to you. And the ſwyne, for though he deuyde the hoffe in to two clawes, yet he cheweth not the cud ād therfore is vnclene to you, Of their fleſh ſee that ye eate not ād their carkaſſes ſe that ye twych not for they are vnclene to you.

Theſe ſhall ye eate of all that are in the waters: what ſoeuer hath finnes and ſkales in the waters, ſees and ryuers, that ſhall ye eate And all that haue not finnes ād ſkales in the ſees ād ryuers of all that moue and lyue in the waters, [Fo. XVIII.] ſhall ye abhorre. Se that ye eate not of their fleſh, ād alſo that ye abhorre their carkaſes: for all that haue no finnes nor ſcales in the waters, ſhalbe abhominacion vnto you.

Theſe are the foules which ye ſhall abhorre and which ſhall not be eaten, for they are an abhominacion. The egle, the gooſhauke, the cormoraunte, the kyte, the vultur and all his kynd and all kynde of

M.C.S. Of beaſtes which be cleane & which vncleane.

V. 5 Chirogryllius 7 Et ſus . . . ruminat. 8 horum carnibus 9 tam in mari quam in fluminibus & ſtagnis 11 morticina vitabitis. 13 Aquilam, & gryphē, & haliæetum 14 miluū . .
L. 5 die Canynchen 7 Vnd eyn ſchweyn 9 ynn waſſern, ym mehr vnd bechen

16 rauens, the eftrich, the nightcrowe, the cocow, the
17 fparowhauke, and al the kynde: the litle oule, the
18 ftorcke, the great oule the backe, the pellicane,
19 the pye, the heron, the Iaye with the kynde, the
20 lappwynge ād the fwalowe. And all foules that crepe ād goo apō all .iiii. fhalbe an abhominacion vnto you.
21 Yet thefe maye ye eate of all the foules that moue and goo apon .iiii. fete: euen thofe that haue no knees aboue vppon their fete to lepe with all apon the erthe,
22 euen thefe of them ye maye eate: the arbe and all his kynde: the Soleam with all his kynde: the Hargol and all the kynde, ād the Hagab ād all his kynd.
23 Al other foules that moue ād haue .iiii. fete, fhalbe
24 abhominacion vnto you. In foch ye fhalbe vnclene whofoeuer touch the carkeffe of thē fhalbe vnclene
25 vnto the euen, ād whofoeuer bereth the carkeffe of thē, fhal wafh his clothes ād fhalbe .Ṗ. vnclene vntyll euen.
26 Amonge all maner beeftes, they that haue hoffes and deuyde them not in to two clawes or that chewe not the cud, fhalbe vnclene vnto you: and all that
27 twicheth them fhalbe vnclene. And all that goeth apon his handes amonge all maner beeftes that goo on all foure, are vnclene vnto you: and as many as twych their carkeffes, fhalbe vnclene vntyll the euen.
28 And he that beareth the carkeffe of them, fhall waffhe his clothes ād be vnclene vntyll the euen, for foch are vnclene vnto you.

𝔐. 22 Selaam .. kynde, the Hagab 27 foure fete
𝔳̄. 16 larum, & accipitrem 17 bubonem et mergulum et ibin 18 cygnum et onocrotalum, et porphyrionem, 19 herodionem, charadrion .. vpupam .. vefpertilionem. 21 longiora retro crura 22 brucus .. attacus .. ophiomachus, ac locufta 25 & fi neceffe fuerit vt portet
𝔏. 21 das keyne knye oben an den beynen hat, da mit es auff erden hupffe 27 auf tappen geht
𝔐. 𝔐. N 22 *Arbe, Selaā, Hargol, Hagab* are kyndes of beaftes that crepe or fcraul on the grounde which the Hebrues them felues do not now a dayes know.
𝔏. 𝔐. N. 22 Dife vier thier find ynn vnfern landen nicht, wie wol gemeyniglich *Arbe* vnnd *Hagab*, fur Hewfchrecken gehaltē werden, die auch vierfuffige vogel find, aber es ift gewiffer, dife Ebreifche namen zu brauchen, wie wyr mit *alleluia* vnd andern frembder fprach namen thun.

29 And thefe are alfo unclene to you amonge the thinges that crepe apon the erth: the wefell the
30 moufe, the tode and all his kynde, the hedgehogge,
31 ftellio, the licerte, the fnayle and the moule. Thefe are vnclene to you amonge all that moue, and all that twych them when they be dead, fhalbe vnclene
32 vntyll the euen. And what foeuer any of the dead carkeffes of them fall apon, fhalbe vnclene: what foeuer veffel of wodd it be, or rayment, or fkynne, or bagge or what foeuer thinge it be that any worke is wroughte with all. And they fhalbe plunged in the water and be vnclene vntill the euē, and then they fhalbe clene agayne.

33 All maner of erthen veffel where in to any of them falleth, is vnclene with all that therein [Fo. XIX.] is:
34 and ye fhall breake it. All maner meate that is eaten, yf any foch water come apon it, it fhall be vnclene. And all maner drynke that is drōke in all maner foch veffels, fhalbe vnclene.

35 And whether it be ouen or kettel, it fhalbe broken. For they are vnclene and fhalbe vnclene vnto you:
36 Neuerthelater, yet the fountaynes ād welles and pondes of water, fhalbe clene ftyll. But whofoeuer twycheth their carkeffes, fhalbe vnclene.

37 Yf the dead carkeffe of any foch fall apō any feed
38 vfed to fowe, yt fhall yet be clene ftyll: but ād yf any water be poured apō the feed ād afterward the dead carkeffe of them fall thereō, then it fhalbe vnclene vnto you.

39 Yf any beeft of whiche ye eate dye, he that twitcheth the dead carkeffe fhalbe vnclene vntyll the euen.
40 And he that eateth of any foche dead carkeffe, fhall waffhe his clothes and remayne vnclene vntyll the euen. And he alfo that beareth the carkeffe of it, fhall waffhe his clothes and be vnclene vntyll euen.

V. 29 mus & crocodilus 30 migale, & chamæleon, & ftellio & lacerta 32 pelles & cilicia 34 fufa fuerit fuper eum 36 & omnis aquarum congregatio
L. 35 es fey ofen odder keffel

41 All that fcrauleth vpon the erth, is an abhominacyon and fhall not be eaten. *fcrauleth, crawleth, creepeth* v. 42
42 And what foeuer goeth apon the breſt ād what foeuer goeth apon .iiii. or moo fete amonge all that fcrauleth apon the erth, of that fe ye eate not: for they are abhomynable. Make not youre foules
43 .P. abhominable. Make not youre foules abhomynable with no thinge that crepeth, nether make youre foules vnclene with them: that ye fhulde be defiled thereby.
44 For I am the Lorde youre God, be fanctified therfore that ye maye be holy, for I am holy: and defile not youre foules with any maner thinge that crepeth apon
45 the erth. For I am the Lorde that brought you out of the londe off Egipte to be youre God: be holy therfore, for I am holy.
46 This is the lawe of beeſt and foule and off all maner thinge that lyueth ād moueth in the water
47 ād of all thinges that crepe apō the erth, that ye may put differēce betwene vnclene ād clene, ād betwene the beeſtes that are eatē and the beeſtes that are not eaten.

❧ The .XII. Chapter.

1 AND the Lorde fpake vnto Mofes and fayde: fpeake vnto the
2 childern of Ifrael ād faye: whē a womā hath conceaued ād *M.C.S. A lawe howe we men ſhulde be purged after their delyuerance.* hath borne a man childe, fhe fhalbe vnclene .vii. dayes: euen in like maner as when fhe is put aparte in tyme
3 of hir naturall difeafe. And in the .viii. daye the flefh

M. 42 *omits* Make not youre foules abhominable
V. 42 quadrupes graditur, & multos habet pedes 43 Nolite cōtaminare animas 47 differētias noveritis
L. 41 was auff erden fchleicht (42, 44) 42 auff vier odder mehr fuſſen 43 feelen vervnreyṇigen
M. M. N. 2 Some call it the monethes dyfeafe, fome the floures.

4 of the childes forefkynne fhalbe cut awaye. And fhe fhall cōtynue in the bloude of hir purifienge .xxxiii dayes, fhe fhal [Fo. XX.] twytch no halowed thinge nor come in to the fanctuary, vntyll the tyme of hir
5 purifienge be out. Yf fhe bere a maydechilde, then fhe fhalbe vnclene two wekes as when fhe hath hir naturall difeafe. And fhe fhall contynue in the bloude of hir purifienge .Lxvi. dayes.
6 And when the dayes of hir purifienge are out: whether it be a fonne or a doughter, fhe fhall brynge a lambe of one yere olde for a burntoffrynge and a yonge pigeon or a turtill doue for a fynneoffrynge vnto the dore of the tabernacle of witneffe vnto the
7 preaft: which fhall offer them before the Lorde and make an attonement for her, and fo fhe fhalbe purged of hir yffue of bloude. This is the lawe of her that hath borne a childe, whether it be male or female.
8 But and yf fhe be not able to bringe a fhepe, then let her brynge two turtyls or two yonge pigeons: the one for the burntofferynge, and the other for the fynneofferynge. And the preaft fhall make an attonement for her, ād fhe fhalbe clene.

❡ The .XIII. Chapter.

1
2 AND the Lord fpake vnto Mofes ād ūto Aarō faynge: whē there apeareth a ryfinge in any mās flefh ether a fcabbe or a gliftrīge .P. whyte: as though the

M.C.S. The Preaftes are appoynted to iudge who are the Lepers.

V. 7 mundabitur a profluuio fanguinis fui 8 Quod fi non inuenerit manus eius, nec pot. offerre agnum . . . orabitque pro ea facerdos. xiii, 2 diuerfus color fiue puftula
L. 4 tage yhrer reynigung aus find 5 da heym bleyben ynn dem blut yhrer reynigung. 6 aus find 7 reyn von yhrem blutgang 8 Vermag aber yhre hand nicht eyn fchaff. . verfünen. xiii, 2 eytter weys (4, 19, 23, 39).

XIII. 3–8.   **called Leuiticus.**   331

plage of leprofye were in the ſkynne of his fleſh, then let him be brought vnto Aaron the preaſt or vnto one of hys ſonnes
3 the preaſtes, and let the preaſt loke on the ſore that is in the ſkynne of his fleſhe. Yf the heer in the ſore be turned vnto whyte, and the ſore alſo ſeme to be lower than the ſkynne of his fleſhe, then it is ſuerly a leprofye, and let the preaſt loke on him and make hym vnclene.

4 Yf there be but a white plecke in the ſkynne of his fleſhe and ſeme not to be lower than the other ſkynne nor the heer thereof is turned unto white: then let the
5 preaſt ſhitt him vpp ſeuen dayes. And let the preaſt loke apon him the .vii. daye: yf the ſore ſeme to him to abyde ſtyll and to go no further in the ſkyne, then let the preaſt ſhutt him vppe yet .vii. dayes moo.
6 And let the preaſt loke on him agayne the .vii. daye. Then yf the ſore be waxed blackeſh and is not growen abrode in the ſkynne, let the preaſt make him clene, for it is but a ſkyrſe. And let him waſſhe his clothes, and then he is
7 clene   But and yf the ſcabbe growe in the ſkynne after
8 that he is ſene of the preaſt agayne. Yf the preaſt ſe that the ſcabbe be growen abrode in the ſkynne, let him make vnclene: for it is ſuerly a leprofye.

This chapter maketh not for cöfeſſion in the eare, but is an exäple of excommunicacion off open ſinners As theſe preſtes make vncleane äd ſende out of company, euen ſo ours binde äd excommunicat out of the cögregaciö: and as theſe make cleane, ſo doo ours lowſſe, and abſolue. Now thē that ſinne ſecretly thei binde with preachige gods word äd yf thei repēt, with preachinge thei lowſe thē agayne.

M.   3 iudge hym vnclene.
V.   3 humiliorem cute & carne reliqua . . . et ad arbitrium eius ſeparabitur. 7 & redditus munditiæ . . adducetur ad eum, 8 & immunditiæ condēnabitur.
   L.   3 vrteylen 4 verſchlieſſen ſieben tage 6 mal geſchwungen
   M. M. N.   2 The lepre ſignifyeth properly mannes doctrine, whyche ſpreadeth abroade lyke a canker: & to be ſhort all inſeccyon of vngodlynes, therfore muſt the Leuytes geue dylygent hede therto: for a lytell leuen ſoureth the whole loumpe of doughe.
   L. M. N.   4 Hie iſts offinbar das Moſes *auſſatz* heyſt allerley grind vnd blattern odder mal, da auſſatz aus werden kan oder dem auſzſatz gleych iſt. Auſſatz aber bedeut eygentlich, menſchen lere auſſer der lere Gottlichs wort, die ſelbe bluet vnnd grunet fur den leuten vnd friſſet vmb ſich, darumb den prieſtern hie mit fleys auffzuſehen gepotten wirt.

9 [Fo. XXI.] Yf the plage of leprosye be in a man, let
10 hī be broughte vnto the preaſt, and let the preaſt ſe
him. Yf the ryſinge apeare white in the ſkynne ād
haue alſo made the heer white, ād there be rawe fleſh
11 in the ſore alſo: then it is an olde leproſye in the
ſkynne of his fleſh. And the preaſt ſhall make him
vnclene, ād ſhall not ſhutte him vp for he is vnclene.
12 Yf a leproſye breake out in the ſkynne and couer all
the ſkynne from the heed to the fote ouer all where-
13 ſoeuer the preaſt loketh, then let the preaſt loke apon
him. Yf the leproſye haue couered all his fleſh, let
him make the diſeaſe clene: for in as moch as he is
14 altogether white he is therfore cleane. But and yf
there be rawe fleſh on him when he is ſene, then he
15 ſhalbe vncleane. Therfore when the preaſt ſeeth the
rawe fleſh, let him make him vnclene. For in as moch
as his fleſh is rawe, he is vnclene and it is ſuerly a true
16 leproſye. But and yf the rawe fleſh departe agayne
and chaunge vnto white, then let him come to the
17 preaſt and let the preaſt ſe him: Yf the ſore be
chaunged vnto white, let the preaſt make the diſeaſe
cleane, ād then he is cleane.
18 When there is a byele in the ſkynne byele [often],
19 of any mans fleſh and is helede and after boil
in the place of the byele there appeare a whyte ryſyng
ether .P. a ſhynynge white ſomwhat redyſh, let him
20 be ſene of the preaſt. Yf when the preaſt ſeeth hī it
appeare lower than the other ſkynne and the heer
thereof be chaunged vnto white, let the preaſt make
hī vncleane: for it is a very leproſye, that is broken
21 out in the place of the byele. But and yf when the

M. 11 iudge him vnclene 13 iudge the diſeaſe 15 iudge
17 iudge 20 iudge
V. 11 inolita cuti. 12 quicquid ſub aſpectu oculorum cadit
15 ſacerd. iudicio polluetur, & inter immundos reputabitur
18 Caro autem et cutis
L. 10 rho fleyſch ym geſchwyr
M. M. N. 13 *Couered all his fleſh*, etc. Here is that called
a leper which yet is none in dede, but ſemyth to be one: whereas
the rotneſſe of humoures brekyng forth into the vtter partes all
the body ouer, is called a leper, and yet muſt it be iudged to be
cleane.

preast loketh on it there be no white heeres therein nether the fcabbe lower than the other fkynne and be fomewhat blackefh, then the preaft fhall fhutt him
22 aparte .vii. dayes. Yf it fprede abrode in the meane feafon, then let the preaft make him vnclene: for it is
23 a leprofye. But ad yf the gliftringe white abyde ftyll in one place and go no further, then it is but the prynte of the byele, and the preaft fhal make him cleane.
24 When the fkynne of any mās flefh is burnt with fire that it be rawe and there apere in the burnynge a gliftringe white that is fomwhat redyfh or altogether
25 white, let the preaft loke apon it. Yf the heer in that brightneffe be chaunged to white and it alfo appeare lower than the other fkynne, than it is a leprofye that is broken out in the place of the burnynge. And the preaft fhall make him vncleane, for it is a leprofye. But
26 and yf (when the preaft loketh on it) he fe that there is no white heer in the bryghteneffe and that it is no lower than the other [Fo. XXII.] fkynne and that it is alfo blackefh, then let the preaft fhutt him upp feuen
27 dayes. And yf (when the preaft loketh on him the feuenth daye) it be growen abrode in the fkynne, lett
28 him make him vncleane: for it is a leprofye. But and yf that bryghtneffe abyde ftyll in one place and goo no further in the fkynne ād be blackefh, than it is but a ryfyng in the place of the burnynge, and the preaft fhall make hym cleane: for it is but the prynte of the burnynge only.
29 Whē ether man or woman hath a breakinge
30 out apon the heed or the beerde, let the preaft fe it. And yf it apeare lower than the other fkynne and there be therein golden heeres ād thyn, let the preaft make him vncleane, for it is a breaking out
31 of leprofye apō the heed or berde. yf (whē the

M. 22 iudge 23 iudge 25 out of the place .. iudge 27 iudge 30 iudge
V. 23 vlceris eft cicatrix 28 quia cicatrix eft combufturæ. 30 capillus flauus
L. 23 die narbe von der drufs 28 gefchwyr des brandmals 30 har daffelbs gulden vnd dunne

preaſt loketh on the breakīge out) he ſe that it is no lower thā the other ſkynne ād that there are blacke
32 heeres therein let hī ſhutt hī vp .vii. dayes. And let the preaſt loke on the diſeaſe the ſeuenth daye: ād yf the breakynge oute be gone no forther nether be any golden heeres therein nether the ſcabbe be lower than
33 the other ſkynne, then lett him be ſhauen, but lett hym not ſhaue the ſcabbe, and let the preaſt ſhutt him vpp
34 ſeuen .℣. dayes moo. And let the preaſt loke on the breakynge out the .vii. daye agayne: Yf the breakynge out be gone no further in the ſkynne nor moare lower thē the other ſkynne, then lett the preaſte make him cleane, and let him waſſhe his clothes and then he is
35 cleane. Yf the breakynge out growe in the ſkynne
36 after that he is once made cleane, let the preaſt ſee him. Yf it be growne abrode in dede in the ſkynne, let the preaſt ſeke no further for ony golden heeres, for
37 he is vncleane. But and yf he ſe that the ſcabbe ſtonde ſtyll and that there is blacke heer growne vpp there in, thē the ſcabbe is healed and he is cleane: and the preaſt ſhall make him cleane.
38 Yf there be founde in the ſkynne of the fleſh of man
39 or woman a gliſterynge white, let the preaſt ſe it. Yf there appeare in their fleſh a gliſterynge white ſomwhat blackeſh, thē it is but frekels growē vpp in the ſkynne: ād he is cleane
40 Yf a mans heer fall of his heed, thē he is heedbaulde
41 and cleane. yf his heer fall before in his foreheade,
42 then he is foreheadbalde and cleane. yf there be in the baulde head or baulde forehead a redyſh white ſcabbe, then there is leproſye ſpronge vpp in his baulde
43 head or baulde foreheade. And let the preaſt ſe it: and yf the ryſynge of the ſore be reddyſhwhite in his baul- [Fo. XXIII.] de heade or foreheade after the
44 maner of a leproſye in the ſkynne of the fleſh, then he is a leper and vncleane: ād the preaſt ſhall make him vncleane, for the plage of his heede.

𝔐. 34 iudge 35 iudged 37 iudge 44 iudge
℣. 37 hom. ſanatum eſſe, & confid. eum pronuntiet mundum. 43 cōdemnabit eum .. lepræ
𝕷. 31 nicht falb 44 ſolchs mals halben auff ſeym heubt

45 And the leper in whome the plage is, fhall haue his clothes rent and his heade bare ad his mouth moffeld, and fhalbe called vncleane.

46 And as longe as the dyfeafe lefteth apon him, he fhalbe vncleane: for he is vncleane, and fhall therfore dwell alone, ad even without the hoft fhall his habitacion be.

47 When the plage of leprofye is in a cloth: whether it be
48 lynen or wollen, yee and whether it be in the warpe or wolfe of the lynen or of the wollen: ether wolfe [often], in a fkynne or any thinge made of fkynne, *woof*

49 yf the difeafe be pale or fomwhat redyfh in the cloth or fkynne: whether it be in the warpe or the wolfe or any thinge that is made of fkynne, the it is a very leprofye
50 and muft be fhewed vnto the preaft. And whe the preaft feeth the plage, lett him fhutt it vpp .vii. dayes,
51 and let him loke on the plage the feuenth daye. yf it be increafed in the cloth: whether it be in the warpe or wolfe or in a fkynne or in anythynge that is made of fkynne, then the plage is a fretynge lep-   fretynge
52 rofye and it is vncleane: And that cloth [often], *eaten away;* cf. fhalbe burnt, ether warpe or wolfe, freten, v. 53, whether it be wollen or lynen or any and xiv, 44, thynge that is made of fkynne where in *freffen.* the plage is, for it is a fretyn- .P. ge leprofye, and fhalbe burnt in the fyre.

53 Yf the preaft fe that the plage hath freten no further in the cloth: ether in the warpe or wolfe or in what
54 foeuer thynge of fkynne it be, then let the preaft comaunde the to waffhe the thynge wherein the plage is,
55 and let him fhutt it vpp .vii. dayes moo. And let the preaft loke on it agayne after that the plage is waffhed: Yf the plage haue not chaunged his fafcion though it be fpred no further abrode, it is yet vncleane.

And fe that ye burne it in the fyre, for it is frete inwarde: whether in parte or in all together.

𝔐. 55 freat
𝒱. 45 contam. ac fordidum fe clamabit.
𝐋. 45 vnreyn genennet werden 51 freffend mal
𝔐. 𝔐. N. 47 Of the leprofye of clothes which was vfed amonge the Iewes, let the iudge. This is euydet that we in oure tyme foffer ouer many leprofyes in clothes.

56 But and yf the preaſt ſe that it is ſomwhat blackyſh after that it is waſſhed, let him rent it out of the clothe, or out of the ſkynne or out of the warpe or wolfe.
57 But and yf it apeare any moare in the cloth ether in the warpe or in the wolfe or in anythynge made of ſkynne, than it is a waxynge plage. And ſe that ye
58 burne that with fyre, where in the plage is. Moreouer the cloth ether warpe or wolfe or what ſoeuer thinge of ſkynne it be which thou haſt waſſhed and the plage be departed from it, ſhalbe waſſhed once agayne: and then it is cleane.
59 This is the lawe of the plage of leproſye in a cloth whether it be wollē or lynen: eyther whether it be in the warpe or wolfe or in any thynge made of ſkynnes, to make it cleane or vncleane.

[Fo. XXIIII.] .XIIII. Chapter.

1 AND the Lorde ſpake vnto Moſes
2 ſaynge: this is the lawe of a leper when he ſhalbe clēſed. he ſhalbe broughte vnto the
3 preaſt, and the preaſt ſhall goo out without the hoſte and loke apō him. Yf the plage of leproſye be healed
4 in the leper, thē ſhall the preaſt commaunde that there be brought for hī that ſhalbe clenſed .ii. lyuynge byrdes that are cleane, ād cipreſſe wodd, and a pece of purple
5 cloth and yſope. And the preaſt ſhall cōmaunde that one of the byrdes be kylled ouer an erthē veſſell of
6 runnynge water. And the preaſt ſhall take the lyuynge byrde and the cypreſſe wodd and the purple ād the yſope, ād ſhall dyppe thē and the lyuynge byrde in the bloude of the ſlayne byrde and in the rēnynge
7 water and ſprinkle it apon him that muſt be clenſed

M.C.S. The cleanſynge of the leper, and of the houſe that he is in.

M. 59 iudge. xiiii, 4 cedar wodd 5 in an erthen 6 cedar
V. 58 pura ſunt, ſecundo, & munda erunt. xiiii, 4 præcipiet ei qui purificatur .. paſſeres .. lignum cedrinum (vv. 49, 50, 51, 52) 5 in vaſe fictile ſuper aquas viuentes
L. 4 cedern holtz (throughout the chapter) 6 tuncken am lebendigen waſſer

of his leprofye .vii. tymes and clenfe him, and fhall
8 let the lyuynge byrde goo fre in to the feldes.

And he that is clēfed fhall waffhe his clothes and fhaue
off all his heer ād waffhe himfelfe in water, and thē he
is cleane. And after that he fhall come in to the
9 hofte, but fhall tarye without his tēt .vii. dayes. Whē
the feuenth daye is come, he fhall fhaue off al his heer
both apō his heade ād his berde ād on his browes:
ād euē all the heer that is on him, fhalbe fhauen off.
And he fhall waffhe his clothes and his flefh in water,
and then he fhalbe cleane.

10 .P. And when the .viii. daye is come, let him take
ii. lambes without blemyfh and a yewelambe of a
yere olde without blemyfh, and .iii. tenthdeales of fyne
floure for a meatofferynge myngled with oyle, and a
11 logge of oyle. Than let the preaft that maketh him
cleane, brynge the man that is made cleane with thofe
thynges before the Lorde vnto the dore of the taber-
12 nacle of witneffe. And lett the preaft take one of
the lābes and offer him for a trefpaceofferynge, and
the logge of oyle: and waue them before the Lorde.
13 And than let him flee the lambe in the place where
the fynofferynge and the burntofferynge are flayne:
euē in the holy place. for as the fynofferynge is, euē
fo is the trefpace offerynge the preaftes: for it is moft
holy.

14 Than lett the preaft take of the bloude of the trefpaceofferynge, and put it apō the typpe of the right
eare of him that is clenfed, and apon the thombe of
his righte hande and apon the greate too of his righte
15 fote. Then let the preaft take of the logge of oyle
16 and poure it in to the palme of his lefte hande, ād
dippe his righte finger in the oyle that is in the
palme of his lefte hand, ād let him fprinkle it with
17 his fynger .vii. tymes before the Lorde. And of the

V. 7 vt in agrum auolet 10 et feorfum olei fextariū.
L. 7 frey feld 10 Log oles 15 aus dem Log nemen
M. M. N. 15 *A logge of oyle* is a certayn meafure contayn-
yng .vi. egges, in Grec *Sextarius.*
L. M. N. 10 *Log* ift eyn kleyn maslyn auff Ebreifch alfo ge-
nennet, aber noch vngewis wie gros es fey.

rest of the oyle that is in his hande, shall the preast put apon the typpe of the righte eare of him that [Fo. XXV.] is clensed, and apon the thombe of his righte hande, and apon the great too of his righte fote: euē
18 apon the bloude of the trespaceofferynge. And the remnaunte of the oyle that is in the preastes hande, he shall poure apon the heede off hym that is clensed: and so shall the preaste make an attonement for him before the Lorde,
19 Then let the preast offer the synneofferynge, ād make an attonement for him that is clensed for his
20 vnclēnesse. And thā let the burntoffrynge be slayne, ād let the preast put both the burntofferynge and the meateoffrynge apō the alter; ād make an attonement for him, ād thā he shalbe cleane.
21 Yf he be poore ād can not gett so moch, thā let him bringe one lambe for a trespaceoffrynge to waue it and to make an attonement for him, ād a tenth deale of fine floure myngled with oyle for a meatoff-
22 rynge ād a logge of oyle, ād two turtyll doues or two yonge pygeons which he is able to gett ād let the one be a synneoffrynge and the other a burntoffryng.
23 And let him brynge them the .viii. daye for his clensynge vnto the preast to the dore of the tabernacle of witnesse before the Lorde.
24 And let the preast take the lambe that is the tres-
25 paceoffrynge and the logge of oyle, ād wa- .P. ue them before the Lorde. And whē the lambe of the trespaceoffrynge is kylled, the preast shall take of the bloude of

V. 19 faciet sacrificium
L. 21 mit seyner hand nicht so viel erwirbt 22 mit seyner hand erwerben kan
L. M. N. 21 Gleych wie der ausfatz bedeut falsch lere, falschen glauben, vnnd falsch heyligs leben, sonderlich das auff eygen werck vnnd nicht auff lauter Gottis gnade Also bedeut diss reynigen wie man ketzerey vnnd solch falsch lere vertreyben sol. Nemlich dz die prediger sollen dz ole yn der hand haben vnd mit dem finger handeln, dz ist sie sollen das Gottis wort von der gnaden ym leben beweysen vnd ynn geyst krafft predigen, damit die leut gehorchen vnd mit der hand fassen vnd folgen das dis sprengen fur dem herrn vnnd das salben der leut nichts anders ist, Denn das Euangelion fur Gott predigen vnd die leut also vom yrthum furen. Denn fewr vertilget keyn ketzerey sondern alleyn Gottis wortt ym geyst gefurt.

the trefpaceoffrynge, and put it apon the typpe of his righte eare that is clenfed, and apon the thombe of
26 his righte hande, and apon the greate too of hys righte fote. And the preaft fhall poure of the oyle in to his
27 righte hande, and fhall fprinkle with his finger of the oyle that is in his lefte hande .vii. tymes before the Lord.
28 And the preaft fhall put of the oyle that is in his hande (apon the typpe of the righte eare of hī that is clenfed, and apō the thombe of his righte hande and apon the great too of his righte fote: euen in the place where the bloude of the trefpaceofferynge was put,
29 And the refte of the oyle that is in his hande, he fhall poure apon the heede of him that is clenfed: to make
30 an attonemēt for him before the Lorde. And he fhall offer one of the turtyll doues or of the yonge pigeons,
31 foch as he can gett: the one for a fynneofferynge and the other for a burntoffrynge apō the alter. And fo fhall the preaft make an attonemēt for him that is
32 clenfed before the Lorde. This is the lawe of him that hath the plage of leprofye, whofe hand is not able to gett that which pertayneth to hys clenfynge.
33 [Fo. XXVI.] And the Lorde fpake vnto Mofes ād
34 Aarō faynge: when ye be come vnto the lond of Canaan which I geue you to poffeffe: yf I put the plage of leprofye in any houffe of the lande of youre poffef-
35 fion, let him that oweth the houfe go ād tell the preaft faynge, me thinke that there is as it were a
36 leprofy in the houffe. And the preaft fhall cōmaunde them to ryd all thinge out of the houffe, before the preafte goo in to fe the plage: that he make not all that is in the houffe vncleane, and then the preaft fhall goo in and fe the houffe.
37 Yf the preaft fe that the plage is in the walles of the houffe ād that there be holowe ftrakes pale or

M. 28 put on the oyle
V. 29 vt placet pro eo dominum 35 Quafi plaga lepræ videtur mihi effe in domo mea.
M. M. N. 37 The lepre of the howfes is any thynge ther to pertaynynge, wherby the dweller might take harme in helth of body, in hurtyng of hys goodes or otherwyfe as yf it ftoode in an euel ayre etc.

rede which seme to be lower than the other partes of
38 the wall, then let the preast go out at the housse dores
39 ãd shett vp the housse for .vii. dayes. And let the
preast come againe the seuenth daye ãd se it: yf the
40 plage be encreased in the walles of the housse, let the
preast cõmaunde thē to take awaye the stones in which
the plage is, ãd let thē cast thē in a foule place with-
41 out the citie, ãd scrape the house within rounde aboute,
ãd poure oute the dust without the citie in a foule
42 place. And let them take other stones and put them
in the places of those stones, and other morter: ãd
playster the housse with all.

43 .¶. Yf now the plage come agayne ãd breake out
in the housse, after that they haue taken awaye the
stones and scraped the housse, and after that the
44 housse is playsterd anew: let the preast come and se
it. And yf then he perceaue that the plage hath eatē
further in the housse, then it is a fretynge leprosye that
45 is in the housse ãd it is vncleane. Then they shall
breake doune the housse: both stones, tymbre ãd all
the morter of the housse, and carye it out of the citye
46 vnto a foule place. Moreouer he that goeth in to the
housse all the whyle that it is shett vp, shalbe vncleane
47 vntyll nighte. And he that slepeth in the housse shall
wasshe his clothes, and he also that eateth in the housse
shall wasshe his clothes.

48 But and yf the preast come and se that the plage
hath sprede no further in the housse after that it is new
playstered, thē let him make it cleane for the plage is
49 healed. And let hym take to clense the housse with
all: two birdes, cypresse wodd, ãd purple clothe ãd
50 ysope. And let him kyll one of the birdes ouer an
51 erthen vessel of runnynge water, ãd take the cipresse
wodd, the ysope, the purple ãd the lyuynge byrde, ãd
dyppe them in the bloude of the slayne byrde and in
the runninge water, and sprinkle apon the housse seuen

𝔐. 49 cedar wodd 50 byrdes in 51 cedar wodd
𝔙. 42 & luto alio liniri domum. 51 in sanguine pass. . . in aquis viuentibus
𝔏. 41 ringsumb schaben 42 das haus bewerffen 44 ein fressender ausfatz 50 ynn eym erden gefefs an eym lebendigen waffer.

52 tymes, and clenfe the houffe with [Fo. XXVII.] the bloude of the byrde, and with the runninge water, ād with the lyuyng byrde, ād with the cypreffe wodd, ād
53 the yfope ād the purple clothe And he fhall lett the lyuynge bird flee oute off the towne in to the wylde feldes, and fo make an attone- ment for the houffe, and it fhalbe cleane.

wylde, open,
cf. wyde xvii, 5

54 This is the lawe of all maner plage of leprofye and
55 breakynge out, and of the leprofye off clothe and
56 houffe: and of ryfynges, fcabbes and glyfterynge white,
57 to teache when a thinge is vncleane or cleane. This is the lawe off leprofye.

¶ The .XV. Chapter.

1 AND the Lorde fpake vnto Mofes
2 and Aaron fayenge, fpeake vnto the children of Ifrael and faye vnto them: euery mā that hath a runnynge yffue in his flefh, is vncleane

M.C.S. The maner of purging the vnclennes bothe of men and wemen.

3 by the reafon of his yffue. And hereby fhall it be knowne when he is vncleane. Yf his flefhe runne, or yf his flefh congele by the reafon off his yffue, than he
4 is vncleane. Euery couche whereon he lyeth ād euery thinge whereon he fytteth fhalbe vncleane
5 He that twitcheth his couch, fhall waffh his clothes ād bath him felfe with water, ād be vncleane vntyll the euen.
6 He that fytteth on that whereon he fatt, fhall .P. waffh his clothes and bathe him felfe with water and
7 be vncleane vntill the euenynge And he that twicheth his flefh fhall waffhe his clothes and bathe him felfe in

M. 52 cedar wodd
V. 53 orabit pro domo & iure mūdabitur. 54 lepræ et percuffuræ, xv, 2 patitur fluxū feminis 3 cū per fingula momenta adhæferit carni eius, atque cōcreuerit fœdus humor.
L. 56 beulen, gretz vnd eytter weys. xv, 2 feym fleyfch eyn flus fleuffet 3 eyttert odder wund gefreffen wirt

8 water and be vncleane vnto the euen. Yf any foch
fpytt apon him that is cleane, he muſt waſſhe his
clothes and bathe him felfe in water and be vncleane
vntill euen.

9 And what foeuer fadell that he rydeth apō ſhalbe
10 vncleane. And whofoeuer twicheth any thinge that
was vnder him, ſhalbe vncleane vnto the euē. And
he that beareth any foch thinges ſhall waſſh his clothes
and bathe hī felf in water ād be vncleane vnto the
11 euē, ād whofoeuer he twicheth (yf he haue not firſt
waſhed his handes in water) muſt waſſhe his clothes,
ād bathe him felfe in water, ād be vncleane vn to the
12 euenynge. And yf he twych a veſſell off erth, it ſhalbe
broken: and all veſſels of wodd ſhalbe renfed in the
water.

13 When he that hath an yſſue is clenfed of his yſſue,
let him numbre .vii. dayes after he is cleane, ād waſſhe
his clothes, and bathe his fleſhe in runnynge water,
14 ād then he is cleane. And the .viii. daye let him take
two turtill doues or two yonge pigeons, and come before the Lorde vnto the dore of the tabernacle of wit-
15 neſſe ād geue them vnto the preaſt. And the preaſt
[Fo. XXVIII.] ſhall offer them: the one for a fynneofferynge, and the other for a burntofferynge: and
make an attonement for him before the Lord, as cō-
cernynge his yſſue.

16 Yf any mans feed departe frō him in his flepe, he
ſhall waſh his fleſh in water ād be vncleane vntill euē.
17 And all the clothes or furres whereon furres, *ſkins*
foch feed chaunceth ſhalbe waſhed with water ād be
18 vncleane vnto the euē. And yf a womā lye with foche
a whone, they ſhall waſh thē felues with water and be
vncleane vntyll euen.

19 Whē a womās naturall courfe of bloud rūneth, ſhe
ſhalbe put aparte .vii. dayes: ād whofoeuer twycheth
20 her ſhalbe vncleane vnto the euē. And all that ſhe

℥. 12 rynefed in water.
𝒱. 11 quē tetigerit qui talis eſt 15 rogabitque pro eo ... vt
emūdetur a fluxu feminis fui. 18 Mulier cū qua coierit
𝕷. 18 Eyn weyb, ... follen fie fich mit waſſer baden 19 fieben
tage befeyt gethan

lyeth apō as longe as ſhe is put aparte ſhalbe vnclene.
21 And whoſoeuer twicheth hir couch ſhall waſh his clothes and bathe hī ſelfe with water ād be vncleane vnto the
22 euē. And whoſoeuer twicheth any thinge that ſhe ſatt apō, ſhall waſſh his clothes ād waſhe him ſelfe alſo
23 in water, ād be vncleane vnto the euē: ſo that whether he twich her couche or any thīge whereō ſhe hath ſetē,
24 he ſhalbe vnclene ūto the euē. ād yf a mā lye with her in the meane tyme, he ſhalbe put aparte as well as ſhe ād ſhalbe vncleane .vii. dayes, ād all his couch wherein he ſlepeth ſhalbe vncleane.
25 .¶. When a womans bloude runneth longe tyme: whether out of the tyme of hyr naturall courſe: as longe as hir vnclenneſſe runneth, ſhe ſhalbe vncleanẹ
26 after the maner as when ſhe is put aparte. All hir couches whereon ſhe lyeth (as lōge as hir yſſue laſteth) ſhalbe vnto her as hir couch when ſhe is put a parte. And what ſoeuer ſhe ſytteth apon, ſhalbe vncleane, as
27 is hir vnclenneſſe whē ſhe is put a parte. And whoſoeuer twicheth them, ſhalbe vncleane, ād ſhall waſſhe his clothes ād bathe him ſelfe in water ād be vncleane vnto euen.
28 And when ſhe is clenſed of hyr iſſue, let hyr counte
29 hir ſeuen dayes after that ſhe is cleane. And the .viii day let her take two turtils or two yonge pigeons and brynge them vnto the preaſt vnto the dore of the tab-
30 ernacle of witneſſe. And the preaſt ſhall offer the one for a ſynneoffrynge, and the other for a burntofferynge: and ſo make an attonement for her before the Lorde. as concernynge hir vncleane yſſue.
31 Make the childern of Iſrael to kepe them ſelues frō their vnclēneſſe, that they dye'not in their vnclēneſſe: whē they haue defiled my habitacion that is amonge them.

𝔐. 20 And all ẏ ſhe lyeth or ſytteth vpō as longe as ſhe 24 aparte was well 25 longe tyme: out of 28 But yf ſhe be cleane of hir yſſue

𝒱. 25 non in tempore menſtr. vel quæ poſt menſtr. ſanguin. fluere non ceſſat 30 rogabitque pro ea . . & pro fluxu immunditiæ eius.

𝓛. 20 bey ſeyt gethan iſt 25 nicht allein zur gewonlicher zeyt, fonder auch vber die gew. zeyt. 30 verſunen für dem HERRN vber dem flus yhrer vnreynickeyt.

32 This is the lawe of him that hath a runninge fore,
and of him whofe feed runneth from [Fo. XXIX.] him
33 in his flepe and is defiled therewith, and of her that
hath an yffue of bloude as longe as fhe is put a parte,
and of whofoeuer hath a runnynge fore whether it be
man or woman, and of him that flepeth with her that
is vncleane.

The .XVI. Chapter.

1 AND the Lorde fpake vnto Mo- *M.C.S. What
fes after the deeth of the two Aarō muft do
or he enterinto
fonnes of Aaron, when they the holy place.
had offered before the Lorde The cleanfyng
of the fanc-
2 and dyed: And he fayde vnto Mofes: tuary or holy
fpeake vnto Aaron thy brother that he place. Of
the feafte of
go not at all tymes in to the holy cleanfyng.
place, that is whithin the vayle that Aaron cōfeff-
eth the fynnes
hangeth before the mercyfeate which is of the chyl-
apon the arcke that he dye not. For dren of Ifrael
ouer the lyue
By the cloud I will appeare in a clowde goote & put-
vnderftonde
the fmoke off vpon the mercyfeate. teth thē vpon
hys heed.
3 the cence. But of this maner fhall
Aaron goo in in to the holy place: with a yonge oxe
for a fynneofferynge, and a ram for a burntoffrynge.
4 And he fhall put the holy lynen albe apon him, ād
fhall haue a lynen breche vppon his flefh, and fhall
gyrde him wyth a lynen gyrdell, and put the lynen
mytre apon his heede: for they are holy raymentes.
And he fhall waffhe his flefh with water, and put them
5 on. And he fhall take of the multitude of the childern

M. 3 with a bullock
V. 32 Ifta eft lex eius qui pat. fluxū fem., & qui poll. coitu,
33 & quæ men. temp. feparatur, vel quæ iugi fluit fang., & hom.
qui dormier. cum ea. xvi, 2 fuper oraculum 3 nifi hæc ante fecerit 4 cū lotus fuerit
L. 33 vnd wer eyn flus hat, es fey man odder weyb
M. M. N. 2 By the cloud vnderftāde the fmoke of the cenfe.

of Ifrael two gootes for a fynneoffrynge and a ram for a burntofferynge.

6 .P. And Aaron fhall offer the oxe for his fynneoffrynge and make an attonement for him ād for his
7 houffe. And he fhall take the two gootes and prefent them before the Lorde in the dore of the tabernacle
8 of witneffe. And Aarō caft lottes ouer the .ii. gootes: one lotte for the Lorde, ād another for a fcapegoote.
9 And Aaron fhall bringe the goote apō which the Lordes
10 lotte fell, and offer him for a fynneofferynge. But the goote on which the lotte fell to fcape, he fhall fett alyue before the Lorde to recōcyle with ād to let him
11 goo fre in to the wilderneffe. And Aaron fhall bringe the oxe of his fynoffrynge, ād reconcyle for him felfe ād for his houfholde, and kyll him.

12 And thā he fhall take a cenfer full of burninge coles out of the alter that is before the Lorde, and his handfull of fwete cens beten fmall and bringe them
13 within the vayle and put the cens apon the fire before the Lorde: that the cloude of the cens maye couer the mercyfeate that is apon the witneffe, that he dye not.
14 And he fhall take of the bloude of the oxe ād fprinkle it with his finger before the mercyfeate eaftwarde: euen vii. tymes.

15 Then fhall he kyll the goote that is the peoples fynneofferynge, and brynge hys bloude within the vayle, and doo with his bloude as [Fo. XXX.] he dyd with the bloude of the oxe, and let him fprinkle it toward the mercyfeate and before the mercyfeate:
16 ād reconcyle the holy place frō the vnclenneffe of the childern of Ifrael, and from their trefpaces ād all there fynnes. And fo let him doo alfo vnto the tabernacle of witneffe that dwelleth with them, euē among their vnclenneffes.

𝕸. 6 bullock 11 bullock 14 bullock 15 bullock
V. 8 capro emiffario 11 His rite celebratis 12 thuribulo quod de prunis altaris impleuerit 14 contra propitiatorium ad orientem. 15 Cumque mactauerit hircum .. vituli, vt afpergat eregione oraculi 16 quod fixum eſt inter eos
L. 8 dem freybock 12 eyn pfannen von glut 14 gegen dem Gnadenſtuel fprengen fornen an 16 von yhrer vbertrettung, ynn allen yren funden ... bey yhn iſt, vnter yhrer vnreynickeyt.

17 And there ſhalbe no bodye in the tabernacle of witneſſe, when he goeth in to make an attonement in the holy place, vntyll he come out agayne. And he ſhall make an attonement for him ſelfe and for his
18 houſholde, ãd for all the multitude of Iſrael. Then he ſhall goo out vnto the alter that ſtondeth before the Lorde, and reconcyle it, and ſhall take of the bloude of the oxe and of the bloude of the goote, and put it
19 apon the hornes of the altare rounde aboute, and ſprynckle of the bloude apon it with his finger ſeuen tymes, and clenſe it, and halowe it frõ the vnclenneſſes of the childern of Iſrael.
20 And whẽ he hath made an ende of recõcylinge the holy place and the tabernacle of witneſſe ãd the alter,
21 let him bringe the lyue goote ãd let Aarõ put both his handes apon the heede of the lyue goote, and con-feſſe ouer him all the myſdeades of the childern of Iſraell, .P. and all their treſpaces, and all their ſynnes: and let him put them apõ the heed of the goote ãd ſende him awaye by the handes of one that
22 is acoynted in the wyldernesse. And the   acoynted, *ac-*
goote ſhall bere apon him all their myſ- *quainted*
deades vnto the wilderneſſe, and he ſhall let the goote goo fre in the wilderneſſe.
23 And let Aaron goo in to the tabernacle of wytneſſe and put off the lynẽ clothes which he put on when he
24 wẽt in in to the holy place, ãd leaue them there. And let him waſſhe his fleſh with water in the holy place, and put on his owne rayment, and then come out and offer his burntofferynge and the burntofferynge of the people, and make an atonemẽt for him ſelfe ãd for the
25 people, and the ſatt of the ſynofferynge let him burne
26 apon the alter. And let him that caryed forth the ſcapegoote, waſſhe his clothes and bathe hys fleſh in water, and then come in to the hoſte agayne.

𝔐. 18 bullock 21 Iſraell, and their treſpaces
𝔙. 18 domino eſt, oret pro ſe, et ſumptum 21 omnes iniquitates ... vniuerſa delicta atque peccata ... per hominem paratum
𝔏. 21 alle yhre vbertretung, ynn yhren ſunden .. eyn man der furhanden iſt

27 And the oxe of the synofferynge and the goote of the synofferynge (whose bloude was brought in to make an atonemēt in the holy place) let one carye out without the hoste and burne with fyre: both their skynnes,
28 their flesh ād their donge. And let him that burneth them, wasshe his clothes ād bathe his flesh in water, and thē come in to the hoste agayne.
29 [Fo. XXXI.] And it shalbe an ordynaunce for euer vnto you. And euē in the tenth daye of the seuenth moneth, ye shall humble youre soules and shall doo no worke at all: whether it be one of youre selues or a
30 straunger that sogeorneth amonge you. for that daye shall an attonemēt be made for you to clense you from all youre synnes before the Lorde, and ye shalbe cleane.
31 It shal be a sabbath of rest vnto you, and ye shall humble youre soules, and it shalbe an ordynaunce for euer.
32 And the preast that is anoynted and whose hande was fylled to mynistre in his fathers steade, shall make the attonemēt and shall put on the holy lynē vesti-
33 mētes, and reconcyle the holy sanctuary and the tabernacle of witnesse ād the alter, and shall make an attonemēt also for the preastes and for all the people
34 of the congregacion. And this shalbe an euerlastynge ordynaunce vnto you to make an atonement for the childern of Israel for all their synnes once a yere: and it was done euē as the Lorde commaunded Moses.

𝕸. 27 bullock
𝖁. 30 In hac die expiatio erit vestri atque mundatio 31 religione perpetua 32 manus initiatæ
𝕷. 31 Ein ewig recht sey das.
𝕸. 𝕸. N. 29 *Humble youre soules:* Looke in the .xxiii. chapter, e. 34 *Euerlastinge:* Loke in Genesis .xiii. d.

❡ The .XVII. Chapter.

1,2 AND the Lorde talked with Moses faynge: speake vnto Aarō and vnto his sonnes and vnto all the childern of Ifrael ād saye .P. vnto them, this is the thynge
3 which the Lorde charged faynge: whatfoeuer he be of the houffe of Ifrael that kylleth an oxe, lambe or goote in the hofte or out of
4 the hofte and bryngeth thē not vnto the dore of the tabernacle of witneffe, to offer an offerynge vnto the Lorde before the dwellynge place of the Lorde, bloude fhalbe imputed vnto that man, as though he had fhed bloude, and that man fhall peryfh from amonge his people.

M.C.S. All facrifyce muft be brought to the dore of the tabernacle. To deuels may they not offer. Bloude and all karen is forbydden them.

5 Wherfore let the childern of Ifrael brynge their offerynges they offer in the wyde felde, vnto the Lorde: euen vnto the dore of the tabernacle of witneffe and vnto the preaft, and offer thē for peafeoffer-
6 ynges vnto the Lorde. And the preaft fhall fprinkle the bloude apon the alter of the Lorde in the dore of the tabernacle of wytneffe, and burne the fatt to
7 be a fwete fauoure vnto the Lorde. And let them no moare offer their offerynges vnto deuyls, after whom they goo a whoorynge. And this fhalbe an ordynaūce for euer vnto you thorow out youre generacyons.
8 And thou fhalt faye vnto them: what foeuer man it be of the houffe of Ifrael or of the ftraungers that fogeorne amonge you that offereth a burntofferynge
9 or any other offerynge and bryngeth it not vnto the

M. 5 offerynges ẏ they offer .. the peace offerynges
V. 4 fanguinis reus erit 5 hoftias fuas quas occidunt in agro 7 dæmonibus, cum quibus fornicati funt.
L. 4 des bluts fchuldig feyn 5 yhre tödopffer dem Herrn opffern 7 vnd mit nichte yhre opffere hyn fort ... mit den fie huren
M. M. N. 7 He offreth vnto deuelles, that offereth vnto any other thinge thē only to God, or that doth hys offeringes after any other maner then God willeth him to do, & the fame goeth a whorehuntynge after the deuell as in Pfal. lxxii, d.

dore of the taber- [Fo. XXXII.] nacle of wytneffe to offer vnto the Lorde, that felow fhall peryfh from amonge his people.

10 And what foeuer man it be of the houffe of Ifrael or of the ftraungers that foiourne amonge you that eateth any maner of bloude, I will fet my face agaynft that foule that eateth bloude, and will deftroy him
11 from amonge his people. for the life of the flefh is in the bloude, and I haue geuen it vnto you apon the alter, to make an attonement for youre foules, for bloude
12 fhall make an attonemēt for the foule. And therfore I fayde vnto the childern of Ifrael: fe that no foule of you eate bloude, nor yet any ftraunger that foiourneth amonge you.
13 Whatfoeuer man it be of the childern of Ifrael or of the ftraungers that foiurne amonge you that honteth and catcheth any beeft or foule that maye be eatē, he fhall poure out the bloude ād couer it with erthe.
14 for the life of all flefh is in the bloude, therefore I fayde vnto the childern of Ifrael, ye fhall eate the bloude of no maner of flefh. for the life of all flefh is in his bloude,
15 and whofoeuer therfore eateth it fhall peryfh. And what foeuer foule it be that eateth that which dyed alone or that which was torne with wylde beeftes: whether it be one of youre felues or a ftraunger, he fhall waffhe his .P. clothes ād bathe him felfe in water, ād fhalbe vncleane vnto the euē, ād thā is he cleane.
16 But ād yf he waffhe them not nor waffhe his flefh he fhall beare his fynne.

V. 10 obfirmabo faciem meam contra animam illius 11 dedi illum vobis, vt fuper altare meum expietis pro animabus veftris .. pro animæ piaculo 13 fi venatione atque aucupio 14 anima enim omnis carnis in fanguine eft.

L. 10 widder den will ich meyn antlitz fetzen 11 denn des leybs feel ift ym blut, vnd ich habs euch zum alltar geben 13 fehet auff der iaget 14 denn alles fleyfch lebt ym blut .. Denn alles fleyfch leben ift ynn feym blut.

❡ The .XVIII. Chapter.

1,2 AND the Lorde talked with Moses faynge: fpeake vnto the childern of Ifrael, ād faye vnto them, I am the Lorde youre
3 God Wherfore after the doynges of the land of Egipte wherein ye dwelt, fe that ye doo not: nether after the doynges of the lande of Canaan, whether I will bringe you, nether walke ye in their ordi-
4 naunces, but doo after my iudgemētes, and kepe myne ordynaunces, to walke therein: for I am the
5 Lorde youre God. Kepe therfore myne ordinaunces, ād my iudgemētes whiche yf a man doo he fhall lyue thereby: for I am the Lorde.

6 Se that ye goo to none of youre nygheft kynred for to vncouer their fecrettes, for I am the Lorde.
7 The fecrettes of thy father and thy mother, fe thou vnheale not: fhe is thy mother, therfore
8 fhalt thou not difcouer hir fecrettes. The fecrettes of thy fathers wife fhalt thou not difcouer, for they are thy fathers fecrettes.

9 Thou fhalt not difcouer the preuyte of thy fyfter, the doughter of thy father or of thy mother: whe-
[Fo. XXXIII.] ther fhe be borne at home or without.
10 Thou fhalt not difcouer the fecrettes of thy fonnes doughter or thy doughters doughter, for that is
11 thyne awne preuyte: Thou fhalt not difcouer the fecrettes of thy fathers wyues doughter, which fhe bare to thy father, for fhe is thy fufter: thou fhalt
12 therfore not difcouer hir fecrettes. Thou fhalt not vncouer the fecrettes of thy fathers fyfter, for fhe
13 is thy fathers nexte kyn. Thou fhalt not dyfcouer

M.C.S. What degrees of kynred may marye to geather & what not.

vnheale, *un-cover* [often]
difcouer, *un-cover* [often]

𝔐. 12 nexte kynfwoman
𝒱. 3 iuxta cōfuetudinem terræ Æg., ... iuxta morem regionis chan. 6 ad proximam fanguinis fui ... turpitudinem 12 turp. fororis patris .. quia caro eft patris tui.
𝔏. 3 nach den wercken [*bis*] 6 nehiften blutfreundyn thun, yhr fcham zu bloffen 12 deyns vaters nehifte blutfreundyn.

the fecrettes off thy mothers fyfter, for fhe is thy mothers nexte kyn.

14 Thou fhalt not open the fecrettes of thy fathers brother: that is thou fhalt not goo in to his wife,
15 for fhe is thyne awnte. Thou fhalt not difcouer the fecrettes of thy doughter in lawe fhe is thy fonnes
16 wyfe: therfore vncouer not hir fecrettes. Thou fhalt not vnheale the fecrettes of thy brothers wife, for
17 that is thy brothers preuyte. Thou fhalt not difcouer the preuytes of the wife ād hir doughter alfo, nether fhalt thou take hir fonnes doughter or hir doughters doughter to vncouer their fecrettes: they are hir nexte
18 kyn, it were therfore wikydneffe. Thou fhalt not take a wife and hir fifter thereto, to vexe hir that thou wold-
19 eft open hir fecrettes as longe as fhe lyueth. Thou fhalt not goo vnto a woman to open hir fecrettes, as
.P. longe as fhe is put aparte for hir vnclenneffe.

20 Thou fhalt not lye with thy neghbours wife, to
21 defyle thi felfe with her. Thou fhalt not geue of thi feed to offer it vnto Moloch, that thou defile not the name of thi God, for I am the Lorde.

22 Thou fhalt not lye with mankynde as with wo-
23 mankynde, for that is abominacion. Thou fhalt lye with no maner of beefte to defile thy felfe there-

M. 13 nextekynfwoman 14 Thou fhalt not vncouer
V. 13 caro fit matris tuæ. 14 quæ tibi affinitate coniungitur. 15 ignominiā eius. *Et vxorem fratris fui nullus accipiat.* 17 Turpitud.,... ignominiam eius .. quia caro illius funt, & talis coitus incæftus eft. 18 in pellicatum illius .. adhuc illa viuente. 19 reuelabis fœditatem eius. 20 nec feminis commiftione maculaberis. 21 vt confecretur idolo
L. 13 deyner mutter nehifte blutfreundyn. 17 vnd ift eyn lafter. 18 weyb nemen fampt yhrer fchwefter . . . weyl fie noch lebt. 20 fie zu befamen 21 dem Molech verbrant werde
M. M. N. 21 *Thy feede*, that is thy generacion, thy fonnes, thy daughters etc.—*Moloch* loke in the .xx. chap. of Leu. 1, a.
L. M. N. 21 *Molech* war eyn abgott, dem fie yhr eygen kinder zu dienft verbrantten, wie Manaffe thet der konig Iuda, vnd meyneten Gott damit zu dienen wie Abraham thet da er Ifaac feynen fon opffert, Aber weyl das Gott nicht befolhen hatte, wie er Abraham thet, war es vnrecht, darumb fpricht hie Gott, das feyn name da durch entheyligt werde, Denn es gefchach vnter Gottis namē vnd war doch teuffelifch, wie auch itzt kloftergelubd vnd ander menfchen auff fetze viel leutt verderben, vnter gottlichem namen als fey es Gottis dienft.

with, nether shall any woman stonde before a beest to lye doune thereto, for that is abhominacion.

24 Defile not youre selues in any of these thinges, for with all these thinges are these nacions defiled whiche 25 I cast out before you: and the lande is defiled, and I will visett the wykednesse thereof apon it. and the 26 lande shal spewe out hir inhabiters. Kepe ye therfore myne ordinaunces and iudgementes, and se that ye commytt none of these abominacions: nether any of you nor ony straunger that soiourneth 27 amonge you (for all these abhominacions haue the men of the lande done whiche were there before 28 you, and the lande is defiled) lest that the lande spewe you out when ye haue defiled it, as it spewed 29 out the nacions that were there before you. For whosoeuer shall cōmytt any of these abhominacions, the same soules that [Fo. XXXIIII.] commytt them 30 shall perish from amonge their people. Therfore se that ye kepe myne ordinaunces, that ye commytt none of these abhominable customes which were commytted before you: that ye defile not youre selues therewith for I am the Lorde youre God.

☙ The .XIX. Chapter.

1 AND the Lorde spake vnto Moses
2 sayenge: speake vnto all the multitude of the childern of Israel, and saye vnto them. Be holy for I the Lorde youre God am 3 holye. Se that ye feare: euery man his father and his mother, ād that ye kepe my Sabbathes, for I am the Lorde youre 4 God. Ye shall not turne vnto ydolls nor make you goddes of metall: I am the Lorde youre God.

M.C.S. A repetycion of certayne lawes pertayning to the .x. commaundemētes. A consyderacion for the poore. How we ought to iudge rightcousty. How we ought not to be auenged. Wytchcraft is forbydden.

V. 23 non succumbet iumento ... quia scelus est.
L. 23 thier zu schaffen haben

5 When ye offre youre peaceofferynges vnto the Lorde, ye ſhall offer them that ye maye be accepted.
6 And it ſhalbe eaten the ſame daye ye offer it and on the morowe, but what ſoeuer is lefte on the
7 thirde daye ſhalbe burnt in the fire. Yf it be eaten the thirde daye, it ſhalbe vncleane ād not accepted.
8 And he that eateth it ſhall bere his ſynne: becauſe he hath defiled the halowed thinges of the Lorde, ād that ſoule ſhall periſh from amonge his people.
9 .¶. When ye repe doune the rype corne of youre lande, ye ſhal not repe doune the vtmoſt borders of youre feldes, nether ſhalt thou gather that which is
10 left behynd in thy harueſt. Thou ſhalt not pluck in all thy vyneyarde clene, nether gather in the grapes that are *ouerſcaped. But thou ſhalt leaue them for the pore ād ſtraunger. *ouerſcaped, overlooked I am the Lord youre God.
11 Ye ſhall not ſteale nether lye, nether deale falſely
12 one with another. Ye ſhal not ſwere by my name falſelye: that thou defileſt not the name of thy God, I am the Lorde.
13 Thou ſhalt not begile thy neyghboure with cauellaciōs, nether robbe him violently, nether ſhall the workmans laboure abide with the vntyll the mornynge. *cauellacions, overreaching, fraud*
14 Thou ſhalt not curſe the deaffe, nether put a ſtomblinge blocke before the blynd: but ſhalt feare thy God. I am the Lorde.
15 Ye ſhall doo no vnrightuouſnes in iudgement. Thou ſhalt not fauoure the poore nor honoure the mightye, but ſhalt iudge thy neghboure rightuouſly.
16 Thou ſhalt not go vp ād doune a * preuy accuſer amōge thy people, nether *Yes for God ād with his awne cōfeſſiō*

V. 7 prophanus erit & impietatis reus 9 vſque ad folum 13 Non facies calumniam 15 Non facies quod iniquum eſt, nec iniuſte iudicabis. Non conſyderes perſonam pauperis, nec honores vultū potentis. 16 criminator nec ſuſurro in populis.

L. 9 an den enden vmbher abſchneyden 16 keynen verleumbder vnter deynem volck

M. M. N. 10 Here ſhuld we lerne to make a prouiſyon for the poore.

ſhalt thou helpe to ſhed the bloude of thy neyghboure: I am the Lorde.

ſhalt thou ac-
cuſe him, to
ſtabliſhe the
holye fathers
kingdome,

17 Thou ſhalt not hate thy brother in thyne hart [Fo. XXXV.] but ſhalt in any wyſe rebuke thy neghbour: that thou bere not ſynne for his ſake.

18 Thou ſhalt not avenge thy ſelfe nor bere hate in thy mynde againſt the childern of thi people, but ſhalt loue thy neghboure euē as thy ſelf I am the Lorde.

19 Kepe myne ordinaunces. Let none of thy catell gendre with a cōtrary kynde, nether ſowe thy felde with myngled ſeed, nether ſhalt thou put on ony garment of lynen and wollen

20 Yf a man haue to doo with a woman that is bonde and hath bene medled with al of another man which nether is boughte nor fredome geuen her, there ſhalbe a payne apon it: but they ſhall not dye,

payne, pun-
iſhment

21 becauſe ſhe was not made fre. And he ſhall brynge for his treſpaceofferynge vnto the Lorde: euen vnto the dore off the tabernacle of witneſſe, a ram for a treſpaceoffrynge. And the preaſt ſhall make an attonement for him with the ram of the treſpace-
22 offerynge before the Lord, for his ſynne which he hath done: and it ſhalbe forgeuen him, as concerninge the ſynne which he hath done.

V. 16 . . . ſtabis contra ſanguinem 18 iniuriæ ciuium tuorum 19 ex duobus texta 20 ancilla etiam nobilis . . vapulabunt ambo
 L. 19 wolle vnd leyn gemenget 20 vnd von eym andern verrucket
 M. M. N. 19 Catell maye not gēdre with a cōtrarykinde agaynſt the order of nature: moche leſſe reaſonable creatures made to the ymage of God as mē & wemē. ¶ The felde maye not be ſowen wyth mixt ſeede, that is, oure dedes & wordes maye not be myngled with ypocreſy. Nether maye our garmētes be made of lynē & wollē, that is we maye not myngle falſe doctrine wyth true, or ſhew a carnall and worldly lyfe vnder pretence of relygion.
 L. M. N. 20 *Verruckt:* dis geſetz redet vō ſolchē weyb, das zuuor von yemand beſchlaffen vnd doch nicht zur ehe genomen iſt, wie es ſeyn ſolt nach dem geſetz am. 21 capitel ym andern buch, vileicht, das ſie yhr herr dem nicht hat wollen geben, vnd als nu gleych eyner witwyn iſt vnd zum andern mal beſchlaffen wirt, wilchs denn widder ehebruch noch hurerey iſt, vnd doch ſund, die ſtrefflich iſt.

23 And when ye come to the lande ād haue plāted all maner of trees where of mē eate, ye ſhal holde them vncircumciſed as concerning their frute: euē thre yere ſhal they be vncircūcyſed vnto you ād
24 ſhall not be eatē of, ād the fourth .P. yere all the frute of thē ſhalbe holy ād acceptable to the Lorde.
25 And the fifth yere maye ye eate of the frute of thē, ād gather in the encreaſe of them: I am the Lorde youre God.
26 Ye ſhall eate nothinge with the bloude, ye ſhall vſe no witchcrafte, nor obſerue diſmall *diſmall, evil, unlucky; xx, 6, 27*
27 dayes, ye ſhall not rounde the lockes of youre heedes, nether ſhalt thou marre the tuftes of thy beerde.
28 Ye ſhall not rent youre fleſh for any ſoules ſake, nor printe any markes apon you: I am the Lorde.
29 Thou ſhalt not pollute thi doughter, that thou woldeſt maintene her to be an whoore: leſt the lāde fall to
30 whoredome, ād waxe ful of wekedneſſe. ¶ Se that ye kepe my Sabbathes and feare my ſanctuary: I am the Lorde.
31 Turne not to thē that worke with ſprites, nether regarde thē that obſerue diſemall dayes: that ye be not defiled by thē, for I am the Lorde youre God.
32 Thou ſhalt ryſe vp before the hoorehed, ād reuerence the face of the old mā ād *hoorehed, hoary head*
33 dread thy god, for I am the Lorde. Yf a ſtraunger ſoiourne by the in youre lande, ſe that ye vexe him
34 not: But let the ſtraunger that dwelleth with you, be as one of youre ſelues, and loue him as thi ſelfe, for ye were ſtraungers in the lande of [Fo. XXXVI.] Egipte. I am the Lorde youre God.
35 Ye ſhall do no vnrightuouſnes in iudgemēt nether
36 in meteyerde, weyght or meaſure. But ye ſhal haue

V. 23 ligna pomifera, auferetis præputia 26 augurabimini, nec obſ. ſomnia. 29 impl. piaculo. 31 declinetis ad magos, nec ab ariolis aliquid ſciſcitemini 33 Si habitauerit aduena . . & moratus fuerit
L. 23 beuwme pflantzt. . . vorhaut befchneytten 26 vogel geſchrey achten noch tage welen. 28 buchſtaben . . pfetzen 31 warſagern . . . zeychen deutern

true balăces, true weightes, A true Epha ād a true hin. I am the Lorde youre god which broughte you
37 out of the land of Egipte, that ye fhulde obserue all myne ordinaunces and iudgementes and that ye fhulde kepe them: I am the Lorde.

¶ The .XX. Chapter.

1
2 AND the Lorde talked with Mofes faynge: tell the childern of Ifrael, whofoeuer he be of the childern of Ifrael or of the ftraungers that dwel in Ifrael, that geueth of his feed vnto Moloch he fhall dye for it: the people off the lande fhall ftone hī with ftones.
3 And I will fett my face apon that felowe, and will deftroye him from amonge his people: becaufe he hath geuen of his feed vnto Moloch, for to defile my fanctuary and to polute myne holy name.
4 And though that the people of the lande hyde their eyes from that felowe, when he geueth of his feed vnto Moloch,
5 fo that they kyll him not: yet I will put my face apon that man and apon his houffholde, and will deftroy him and all that goo a whooringe with him and cōmytt hoordome with Moloch from amonge their people.

M.C.S. They that geue of their feede to Moloch fhall dye therfore. Other goodly lawes necefsarye to be vfed in cōmen wealthes.

If we tranfgreffe gods commaundemētes we may happelye efcape worldlye iudges, but we cā not avoid the firfe wrath of god, but it wil furely find vs out.

M. 5 and vpon hys generacion
V. 36 iuftus modius, æquufque fextarius. xx, 4 Quod fi negligens populus terræ, & quafi paruipendens imperium meum, dimiferit hominem 5 et cognationem eius
L. 36 recht Epha, recht Hin. xx, 4 durch die finger fehen wurd, dem menfchen
M. M. N. 2 *Moloch*, vnder this name moloch is forbidden almaner of ydolatrie, fpecially the exercifynge of children therto for that is abhominable before the Lorde. Moloch was an Idolle of the children of Ammon, whofe Image was holowe hauyng in it feuē clofettes, one was to offer therin fyne floure, another for turtell dowues, the thyrd for a fhepe, the fourth for a Ram, the fyfth for a calffe, the fyxt for an oxe, And for hym that wolde offre his fonne was opened the feuēth clofet. And the face of this Idoll was lyke the face of a calffe, his handes made playne ready to receaue of them that ftode by.

6 ¶. Yf any foule turne vnto them that worke with fpirites or makers of dyfemall dayes and goo a whoorynge after them, I wil put my face apon that foule
7 and will deftroye him from amonge his people. Sanctifie youre felues therfore and be holye, for I am the
8 Lorde youre God. And fe that ye kepe myne ordinaunces and doo them. For I am the Lorde which fanctifie you.

9 Whofoeuer curfeth his father or mother, fhall dye for it, his bloude on his heed, becaufe he hath curfed his father or mother.
10 He that breaketh wedlocke with another mans wife fhall dye for it: becaufe he hath broke wedlocke with his neghbours wife, and fo fhall fhe likewife.
11 Yf a man lye with his fathers wife ad vncouer his fathers fecrettes, they fhall both dye for it, their bloude be apon their heedes.
12 Yf a man lye with his doughter in lawe thei fhall dye both of them: they haue wrought abhominacion, their bloude vpon their heedes.
13 Yf a man lye with the mankynde after the maner as with womā kynd, they haue both cōmitted an abhominacion and fhall dye for it. Their bloude be apon their heed.
14 Yf a man take a wife ād hir mother thereto, it is wekedneffe. Mē fhall burne with fire both [Fo. XXXVII.] him and them, that there be no wekedneffe amonge you.
15 Yf a man lye with a beeft he fhall dye, and ye fhall flee the beeft.
16 Yf a womā go vnto a beeft ād lye doune thereto: thou fhalt kyll the womā ād the beeft alfo they fhal dye, ād their bloud be apō their hedes

𝔐. 6 him to enchaūters or expounders of tokens 9 his bloud on his head 13 with mankynde .. heades.
𝒱. 6 Anima quæ declin. ad magos & ariolos 9 fanguis eius fit fuper eum. 11 dormierit cum nouerca fua 15 iumento & pecore 16 Mulier qui fuccubuerit
𝑳. 6 warfagern vnd zeychen deuttern 11 feyns vaters weyb fchlefft

17 Yf a mā take his fyfter his fathers doughter or his mothers doughter, ād fe hir fecrettes, and fhe fe his fecrettes alfo: it is a weked thinge.

Therfore let them perifh in the fyghte of their people, he hath fene his fyfters fecretneffe, he fhall therfore bere his fynne.

18 Yf a man lye with a woman in tyme of hyr naturall difeafe and vnheale hir fecrettes and vncouer hir fountayne, ād fhe alfo open the fountayne of hir bloude, they fhall both perifhe from amonge their people.

19 Thou fhalt not vncouer the fecrettes of thy mothers fyfter nor of thy fathers fyfters, for he that doth fo, vncouereth his nexte kyn: ād thei fhall bere their myfdoynge.

20 Yf a mā lye with his vncles wife, he hath vncoured his vncles fecrettes: they fhall bere their fynne, and fhall dye childleffe. *Thei fhall dye immediatly ād not tary the byrth, as Iuda wold haue burnt Thamar being great with childe.*

21 Yf a mā take his brothers wife, it is an vnclene thinge, he hath vncouered his brothers fecrettes, they fhalbe childleffe therfore.

22 .P. Se that ye kepe therfore all myne ordinaunces and all my iudgementes, and that ye doo them: that the londe whether I brynge you to dwell therein, fpewe

23 you not oute. And fe that ye walke not in the maners of the nacyons whiche I caft oute before you: For they commytted all thefe thinges, and I abhorred them.

24 But I haue fayde vnto you that ye fhall enioye their londe, and that I will geue it vnto you to poffeffe it: euē a londe that floweth with milke and honye. I am the Lord youre God, whiche haue feparated you from

25 other nacions: that ye fhulde put difference betwene cleane beeftes and vncleane, and betwene vncleane foules and them that are cleane. Make not youre foules therfore abhominable with beeftes ād foules,

𝔐. 18 vncouer her fecrettes and open 19 father fyfter

𝔙. 17 turpitudinem fuam mutuo reuelauerint 19 ignom. carnis fuæ 20 vxore patrui, vel anunculi fui, & reu. ignom. cognationis fuæ . . abfque liberis morientur.

𝔐. 𝔐. 𝔑. 20, 21 They fhall dye immediatly & not tary the byrth as Iuda wolde haue burnt Thamar being great wyth chylde. Gen. xxviii, f.

and with all maner thinge that crepeth apon the grounde, which I haue feparated vnto you to holde
26 them vncleane. Be holy vnto me, for I the Lorde am holy and haue feuered you from other nacyons: that ye fhulde be myne.
27 Yf there be mā or womā that worketh with a fprite or a maker of dyfemall dayes, thei fhall dye for it. Mē fhall ftone them with ftones, ād their bloude fhalbe apon them.

ℂ The .XXI. Chapter.

[Fo. XXXVIII.] XXI. Chapter.

1 AND the Lorde fayde vnto Mofes: fpeake vnto the preaftes the fonnes of Aaron and faye vnto them. A preaft fhall defile him felfe at the deth of none of
2 his people, but apon his kyn that is nye vnto him: as his mother, father, fonne,
3 doughter and brother: and on his fyfter as lōge as fhe is a mayde ād dwelleth nye him and was neuer geuen to man:
4 on her he maye defile him felfe. But he fhall not make him felfe vncleane vpon a ruelar of his people to polute him felfe with all.
5 They fhall make thē no baldneffe apon their heedes or fhaue off the lockes of their beerdes, nor make any markes
6 in their flefh. Thei fhalbe holy vnto their God, ād not polute the name of

M.C.S. The preaſt is forbyddē to be at the death of any of his people, a fewe of his kynne except. Preaſtes may not be ſhauē nether on the head nor yet of the bearde. The preaſtes wyfe muſt be a mayde. The preaſtes daughter may not be an harlott.

Of the hethē preaſtes therfore toke our prelates the enſample of their balde pates.

M. 27 or that expoundeth tokens
V. 27 pythonicus, vel diuinationis fuerit fpiritus xxi, 2 nifi tantum in confanguineis, ac propinquis 6 Incenfum enim domini
L. 27 warfager oder zeychen deutter
M. M. N. 1 The preaftes be warned that they fhall not come at the cōmē waylynges & lamētacyons of the deed left they fhuld therby be the moare vnapte to do their facryfyces wherunto they were properly appoynted, and left they fhulde by theire wepyng geue an occafion to deftroye the beleue of the refurreccion of the dead.

their god, for the facrifices of the Lorde ād the bred of their God thei do offer: therfore they muſt be holy.

7 Thei fhall take no wife that is an whoore, or poluted, or put frō hir huſbonde: for a preaſt is holy 8 vnto his God. Sanctifie him therfore, for he offereth vp the bred of God: he ſhal therfore be holy vnto the, for I the Lorde whiche ſanctifie you, am holy.   *By bred vnderſtonde all fode, fleſh, frute, or whatſoeuer it be.*

9 Yf a preaſtes doughter fall to playe the whore, ſhe poluteth hir father: therfore ſhe ſhall be burnt with fire.

10 He that is the hye preaſt among his brethern .P. vppon whoſe heed the anoyntynge oyle was poured and whoſe hande was fylled to put on the veſtimētes, ſhall not vncouer his heed nor rent his clothes, 11 nether ſhall goo to any deed body nor make him 12 ſelfe vncleane: no not on his father or mother, nether ſhall goo out of the ſanctuarye, that he polute not the holy place of his God. for the croune of the anoyntynge oyle of God, is apon him. I am the Lorde.   *The anoyntynge was the coronacion both of kynges ād of preſtes alſo*

13 He ſhall take a mayden vnto his wife: 14 but no wedowe nor deuorſed nor poluted whoore.

But he ſhall take a mayden of his awne people to 15 wife, that he defyle not his feed apō his people. for I am the Lorde which ſanctifye him.

16, 17 And the Lorde ſpake vnto Moſes faynge, ſpeake vnto Aaron and faye: No man of thi feed in their generacions that hath any deformyte apon him, ſhall preſe for to offer the bred of his God. 18 ffor none that hath any blemyſh ſhall come nere: whether he be blynde, lame, ſnot   *preſe, approach, v. 21.*   *The pope forbideth all ſoch lyke wiſe tyll they haue payd for diſpenſaciōs.*

Ṁ. 17 preace 18 any myſſhapē mēbre
Ṽ. 7 marito: quia conſecratus eſt deo ſuo, 8 & panes propoſ. offert. 10 veſtituſque eſt ſanctis veſtibus 12 oleum ſanctæ vnctionis .. ſuper eum 14 repudiatam, & ſordidam, atque meretricem 15 ſtirpem generis ſui vulgo gentis ſuæ 18 torto naſo
Ł. 10 vnd ſeyne hand gefullet iſt, das er anzogen wurde mit den kleydern 12 die kron des ſalboles 15 nicht ſeynen ſamen entheylige vnter ſeym volck 18 vngeheurem gelied

19 nofed, or that hath any monſtrous mēbre, or broken
20 foted, or broken handed, or croke backed, or perleyed, or gogeleyed, or maunge or ſkaulde, or hath his ſtones broken.
21 No man that is deformed of the feed of Aaron the preaſt, ſhall come nye to offer the facrifyces of the Lorde. Yf he haue a deformyte, he ſhall not preſe to offer the bred of his God.
22 [Fo. XXXIX.] Notwithſtondynge he ſhall eate of the bred of his God: euen as well of the moſt holy,
23 as of the holy: but ſhall not goo in vnto the vayle nor come nye the alter, becauſe he is deformed that he polute not my ſanctuary, for I am the Lorde
24 that ſanctifye them. And Moſes tolde it vnto Aaron and to his ſonnes, and vnto all the childern of Iſrael.

⁋ The .XXII. Chapter.

1 AND the Lorde comened with Moſes faynge: byd Aaron and
2 his ſonnes that they abſteyne from the halowed thynges of the childern of Iſrael which they haue halowed vnto me, that they polute not myne holy name: for I am the Lorde.
3 Saye vnto them: whoſoeuer he be of all youre feed amonge youre generacion after you, that goeth vnto the halowed thinges which the childern of Iſrael ſhall haue halowed vnto the Lorde, his vnclennes ſhalbe apon him: and that ſoule ſhal peryſh from out of my ſyghte. I am the Lorde.

M.C.S. What maner perſones ought to abſtayne from eatyng the thynges that were offred. How, what, & when they ſhulde be offerd.

𝔐. 21 preace
𝒱. 20 ſi lippus, ſi albuginem 24 Iſrael cuncta quæ fuerāt ſibi imperata. xxii, 2 & non cōtaminent nomen ſanctificatorum mihi, quæ ipſi offerunt. 3 in quo eſt immunditia
𝑳. 20 fell auffem auge .. ſchehl 21 nicht erzu thun zu opffern ... nicht nahen

4 None of the feed of Aaron that is a leper or that hath a runnynge fore, fhall eate of the halowed thinges vntill he be cleane. And whofoeuer twytcheth any vncleane foule or man whofe feed runneth frō him by nyghte, 5 or whofoeuer twitcheth any worme that is vncleane to him, or man that is vncleane to him, what- foeuer vnclenneffe he hath: 6 the fame foule that hath twyched any foch thynge, fhalbe vncleane vntill euen, and fhall not eate of the halowed thynges vntill he haue waffhed his flefh with 7 water. And than when the fonne is doune he fhalbe cleane ād fhall afterward eate of the halowed thynges: 8 for they are his fode. Off a beeft that dyeth alone or is rent with wylde beaftes, he fhall not eate, to defyle 9 him felfe therwith: I am the Lorde. But let them kepe therfore myne ordynaunce, left they lade fynne apō them and dye therein when they haue defyled them felues: for I am the Lorde which fanctifye them.
10 There fhall no ftraunger eate of the halowed thinges, nether a geft of the preaftes, or an hyred 11 feruaunte. But yf the preaft bye any foule with money he maye eate of it, and he alfo that is borne in his houffe maye eate of his bred.
12 Yf the preaftes doughter be maryed vnto a ftraunger, fhe maye not eate of the halowed heueoffer-13 ynges. Notwithftondynge yf the preaftes doughter be a wedowe or deuorfed and haue no childe but is returned vnto hir fathers houffe agayne, fhe fhall eate of hir fathers bred as wel as fhe dyd in hyr youth. But therefhall no ftraunger eate there of.
14 Yf a man eate of the halowed thynges vn-wyttingly, he fhall put the fyfte parte there vnto, and 15 make good vnto the preaft the halowed thynge. And

worme, any creeping thing

𝕸. 6 that hath any foch thynge
𝒱. 4 patiens fluxum feminis 5 & quodlibet immundum 9 non fubiaceant peccato 12 cuilibet ex populo nupta 13 ficut puella confueuerat
𝕷. 5 gewurm... das yhm vnreyn.. menfchen der yhm vnreyn ift, vnd alles was yhn vervnreynigt 7 feyn futter. 9 fund auff fich laden 12 nicht von der Hebe der heylickeyt 13 wie andere dyrnen.

let the preaſtes ſee, that they defyle not the halowed thynges of the childern of Iſrael which they haue
16 offered vnto the Lorde, leſt they lade them ſelues with myſdoynge and treſpace in eatynge their halowed thinges: for I am the Lorde which halowe them.

17, 18 And the Lorde ſpake vnto Moſes ſaynge: ſpeake vnto Aaron and his ſonnes and vnto all the childern of Iſrael and ſaye vnto them, what ſoeuer he be of the houſſe of Iſrael or ſtraunger in Iſrael that will offer his offerynge: what ſoeuer vowe or frewillofferynge it be which they will offer vnto the Lorde for a
19 burntofferynge to reconcyle them ſelues, it muſt be a male without blemyſh of the oxen, ſhepe or gootes.
20 let them offer nothynge that is deformed for they ſhall gett no fauoure there with.
21 Yf a man will offer a peaſeoffrynge vnto the Lorde and ſeparate a vowe or a frewill offerynge of the oxen or the flocke, it muſt be without deformyte, that it maye be accepted. There maye be no blemyſh
22 therein: whether it be blīde, brokē, wounded or haue a wen, or be maunge or ſcabbed. ſe that ye offre no ſoch vnto the Lorde, nor put an offerynge of any ſoch apon the alter vnto the Lorde.
23 .℣. An oxe or a ſhepe that hath any membre out of proporcion, mayſt thou offer for a frewillofferynge: but
24 in a vowe it ſhal not be accepted. Thou ſhalt not offer vnto the Lorde that which hath his ſtones brooſed brokē, plucked out or cutt awaye, nether ſhalt make
25 any ſoch in youre lande, nether of a ſtraungers hande ſhall ye offer an offerynge to youre God of any ſoch. For they marre all in that they haue deformytes in them, and therfore can not be accepted for you.

26, 27 And the Lorde ſpake vnto Moſes ſaynge: when an oxe, a ſhepe or a goote is brought forth, it ſhalbe ſeuē dayes vnder the damme. And from the .viii

꜕. 24 that which is brooſed, broken, plucked
℣. 18 domini, 19 vt auferatur per vos 23 Bouem & ouem aure & cauda amputatis 25 non offeretis panes deo . . quia corrupta & maculata ſunt omnia, non fuſcipietis ea. 27 ſub vbere matris
ℒ. 21 tödopffer 23 vngehewre gelied oder keyn ſchwantz

daye forth, it shalbe accepted vnto a gifte in the sacri-
28 fice of the Lorde. And whether it be oxe or shepe, ye shall not kyll it, and hir yonge: both in one daye.

29 When ye will offre a thankofferynge vnto the Lorde, ye shall so offre it that ye maye be accepted.

30 And the same daye it must be eatē vp, so that ye leaue none of it vntill the morowe. For I am the

31 Lorde, kepe now my commaundementes and do them, for I am the Lorde.

32 And polute not my holy name, that I maye be halowed amonge the childern of Israel. For I am

33 the Lorde which halowe you, and broughte you out of the londe of Egipte, to be youre [Fo. XLI.] God: for I am the Lorde.

¶ The .XXIII. Chapter.

1 AND the Lorde spake vnto Moses
2 saynge: speake vnto the childern of Israel, and saye vnto them. These are the feastes off the Lorde which ye shal call holy
3 feastes. Sixe dayes ye shall worke, ād the seuenth is the Sabbath of rest an holy feast: so that ye maye do no worke therein, for it is the Sabbath of the Lorde, wheresoeuer ye dwell.

M.C.S. Of the holy dayes, as the Sabboth, Ester, whytsontyde, the feast of the fyrst frutes. The feast of cleansyng. The feast of trompettes. The feast of the tabernacles.

4 These are the feastes of the Lorde whiche ye shall
5 proclayme holy in their ceasons. The .xiiii. daye of
6 the first moneth at euē is the Lordes Passeouer, And the .xv. daye of the same moneth is the feast of swete bred vnto the Lorde: .vii. dayes ye must eate vnleuended bred.

7 The first daye shalbe an holy feaste vnto you, so

V. 3 sabbathi requies 5 phase domini 6 azymorum domini
L. 3 feyr des Sabbaths
M. M. N. 29 *A thankofferynge*, that is, an offeryng of thanckes geuynge. Thankes geuynge is when the benefytes of God are recyted, wherby the fayth to Godward is strēgthened the more fastly to loke for the thyng that we desyre of God. Eph. v, a. 1 Tim. iii, a. & b.

8 that ye maye do no laborious worke therein But ye fhall offer facrifices vnto the Lorde .vii. dayes, and the feuenth daye alfo fhalbe an holy feaft, fo that ye maye doo no laborious worke therein.

9, 10 And the Lorde fpake vnto Mofes fayenge: fpeake vnto the childern of Ifraell and faye vnto them: when ye be come in to the lande whiche I geue vnto you and repe doune youre harueft, ye fhall brynge a fhefe 11 of the firft frutes of youre harueft vnto the preaft, and he fhall wa- .P. ue the fhefe before the Lorde to be accepted for you: and euen the morow after the Sab- 12 bath the preafte fhall waue it. And ye fhall offer the daye when he waueth the fhefe, a lābe without blemyfh 13 of a yere old for a burntofferynge vnto the Lorde: and the meatoffrynge thereof, two tenth deales of fine floure mengled with oyle to be a facrifice vnto the Lorde of a fwete fauoure: and the drinkofferinge thereto, the 14 fourth deale of an hin of wyne. And ye fhall eate nether bred, nor parched corne, nor furmentye of new corne: vntyll the felfe fame daye that ye haue broughte an offrynge vnto youre God. And this fhalbe a lawe for euer vnto youre childern after you, where foeuer ye dwell.

15 And ye fhall counte from the morowe after the Sabbath: euen from the daye that ye broughte the 16 fheffe of the waueoffrynge, vii. wekes complete: euen vnto the morow after the .vii. weke ye fhall numbre L. dayes. And thē ye fhal bringe a newe meatoffrynge 17 vnto the Lorde. And ye fhall brynge out of youre habitacions two waueloaues made of two tenthdeales off fine floure leuended and baken, for firft frutes vnto 18 the Lorde. And ye fhall bringe with the bred feuen lambes without deformyte of one yere of age, and one yonge oxe, and .ii. rambes, [Fo. XLII.] which fhall

V. 8 dies autem feptimus erit celebrior & fanctior 10 manipulos fpicarum 11 eleuabit fafciculum 14 ex ea deo veftro. 17 panes primitiarum
L. 10 garben der erftling ewr erndten
M. M. N. 10 The *fyrftfrutes* & *tythes* were the fygnes of the faith knowleagynge to haue receaued their goodes & catell of the Lorde, as it is fayde Ex. xxii, d. and .xxiii, c.

ſerue for burntoffrynges vnto the Lorde, with meatoffringes and drinkoffringes longinge to the ſame, to be a ſacrifice of a ſwete ſauoure vnto the Lorde.

19 And ye ſhall offer an he goote for a ſynneofferinge: and two lambes of one yere old for peaceoffringes,
20 And the preaſt ſhall waue thē with the bred of the firſt frutes before the Lorde, and with the two lambes. And they ſhalbe holy vnto the Lorde, and be the
21 preaſtes. And ye ſhall make a proclamaciō the ſame daye that it be an holy feaſt vnto you, and ye ſhall do no laborious worke therein: And it ſhalbe a lawe for euer thorowe out all youre habitacions vnto youre childern after you,
22 When ye repe doune youre harueſt, thou ſhalt not make cleane ryddaunce off thy felde, nether ſhalt thou make any aftergatheringe of thy harueſt: but ſhalt leue them vnto the poore and the ſtraunger. I am the Lorde youre God.
23, 24 And the Lorde ſpake vnto Moſes ſaynge: ſpeake vnto the childern of Iſrael ād ſaye. The firſt daye of the ſeuenth moneth ſhalbe a reſt of remembraunce vnto
25 you, to blowe hornes in an holy feaſt it ſhalbe, and ye ſhall do no laborious worke therein, and ye ſhall offer ſacrifice vnto the Lorde.
26, 27 ℙ. And the Lorde ſpake vnto Moſes ſayenge: alſo the tenth daye of the ſelfe ſeuēth moneth, is a daye of an attonement, and ſhalbe an holy feaſt vnto you, ād ye ſhall humble youre ſoules and offer ſacrifice vnto
28 the Lorde. Moreouer ye ſhall do no worke the ſame daye, for it is a daye of attonement to make an at-
29 tonemēt for you before the Lord your God. For what ſoeuer ſoule it be that humbleth not him ſelfe that daye, he ſhalbe deſtroyde from amonge his peo-
30 ple. And what ſoeuer ſoule do any maner worke that daye, the ſame I will deſtroye from amonge his peo-

𝒱. 20 cedēt in vſum eius. 22 vſque ad ſolum 27 dies expiat. erit celeberrimus . . . affligetiſque animas
𝑳. 22 nicht gar auff dem feld eynſchneytten 27 ſeelen demutigen [3 times cf. vv. 29, 32.]
ℳ. ℳ. 𝒩. 27 *To humble the ſoule* is, to chaſtyce the bodye by abſtynence & affliction, as is ſayde Eſaie, lviii. a.

31 ple. Se that ye do no maner worke therfore. And it
ſhalbe a lawe for euer vnto youre generacions after
32 you in all youre dwellynges. A ſabbath of reſte it
ſhalbe vnto you, and ye ſhall humble youre ſoules.
The .ix. daye of the moneth at euen and ſo forth
from euē to euen agayne, ye ſhall kepe your Sabbath.
33, 34 And the Lorde ſpake vnto Moſes ſayenge: ſpeake
vnto the childern of Iſrael ād ſaye: the .xv. daye of
the ſame ſeuenth moneth ſhalbe the feaſt of tabernacles
35 vii. dayes ūto the Lorde. The firſt daye ſhalbe an
holy feaſt, ſo that ye ſhall do no laborious worke there-
36 in. Seuen dayes ye ſhall offer ſacrifice vnto the Lorde,
and the .viii. daye ſhalbe an holy feaſt vnto you
[Fo. XLIII.] ād ye ſhall offer ſacrifice vnto the Lorde.
It is the ende of the feaſt, and ye ſhall do no laborious
worke therein.
37 Theſe are the feaſtes of the Lorde whiche ye ſhall
proclayme holy feaſtes, for to offer ſacrifice vnto the
Lorde, burntofferynges, meatofferynges, and drink-
38 offrynges euery daye: beſyde the ſabbathes of the
Lorde, ād beſyde youre giftes, and all youre vowes,
and all your frewillofferynges whiche ye ſhall geue
vnto the Lorde.
39 Moreouer in the .xv. daye of the ſeuenth moneth
after that ye haue gathered in the frutes of the lande,
ye ſhall kepe holy daye vnto the Lorde .vii: dayes
longe. The firſt daye ſhall be a daye of reſt, and the
40 viii. daye ſhalbe a daye of reſt. And ye ſhall take you
the firſt daye, the frutes of goodly trees and the
braunches off palme trees and the bowes of thicke

V. 32 & affligetis animas veſtras 35 dies primus vocabitur
celeberrimus atque ſanctiſſimus 36 & ſeptem diebus offeretis
holocauſta domino. dies quoque octavus erit celeberr. atque
ſanct. et offer. holocauſtum .. cœtus atque collectæ 37 libamen-
ta iuxta ritum vniuſcuiuſque diei. 40 fructus arboris pulcherrimæ
L 36 es iſt der ſteur tag
M. M. N. 32 *Sabbothes, feſtes & newe mones* ſygnifie the
Ioye & gladnes of the conſcièce the renewyng of mā and the reſt
wherin we reſt from oure awne woorckes, not doynge oure wylles
but godes, which woorcketh in vs thorou hys Goſpell & glad
tidynges whyle we erneſtly beleue it. Ezech. xx, b.
L. M. N. 36 *Steuer:* Das iſt die collect odder ſamlung, da man
zuſammen trug vnd gab den armen als ynn ein gemeynen beuttel.

trees, ād wylowes of the broke, and shall reioyse be-
41 fore the Lorde .vii. dayes. And ye shall kepe it holy
daye vnto the Lorde .vii. dayes in the yere. And it
shalbe a lawe for euer vnto youre childern after you,
42 that ye kepe that feast in the seuenth moneth. And
ye shall dwell in bothes seuen dayes: euen all that are
43 Israelites borne, shall dwell in bothes, that youre childern after you maye knowe howe that I made .P. the
childern of Israel dwell in bothes, when I broughte them
out of the lande of Egipte: for I am the Lorde youre
44 God. And Moses told all the feastes of the Lorde
vnto the childern of Israel.

⁋ The .XXIIII. Chapter.

1 AND the Lorde spake vnto Moses
2 saynge: commaunde the childern of Israel that they bringe
vnto the, pure oyle olyue betē
for lightes to poure in to the lampes all-
3 waye, without the vayle of testimonye
within the tabernacle of witnesse. And
Aaron shall dresse them both euen and
morninge before the Lorde alwayes. And
it shalbe a lawe for euer amōge youre childern after
4 you. And he shal dresse the lampes apon the pure
candelsticke before the Lorde perpetually.

5 And thou shalt take fine floure ād bake .xii. wastels
thereof, two tenthdeales shall euery wastell
6 be. And make two rowes of them, sixe on
7 a rowe apon the pure table before the Lorde, and put
pure frankencens vppon the rowes. And it shalbe bred
8 of remembraunce, ād an offerynge to the Lorde. Euery

M.C.S. The oyle for the lampes and lyghtes of the bredde of re-membraunce or shewbrede. He that curs-eth must be stoned. He that kylleth shalbe kylled etc.

wastell, fine bread, cake

    M. 3 vayle of wytnesse
    V. 3 velum testimonii in tabernaculo fœderis . . cultu rituque perpetuo 7 panis in monimentum oblationis domini.
    L. 2 bawm ole 3 furhang des zeugnis ynn der hutten des zeugnis. 7 Denckbrot zum opffer dem HERRN
    M. M. N. 5 *Wastels.* The shewe bredes or the halowed loues.

Sabbath he shall put them in rowes before the Lorde euermore, geuen off the childern of Israel, that it be
9 an euerlastynge couenaunte. And they shal- [Fo. XLIIII.] be Aarons and his sonnes, and they shall eate them in the holy place. For they are most holy vnto him of the offerynges of the Lorde, and shalbe a dutye for euer. *dutye, law, statute*

10 And the sonne of an Israelitish wife whose father was an Egiptian, went out amonge the childern of Israel. And this sonne off the Israelitish wife and a
11 man of Israel, strooue togither in the hoste. And the Israelitish womans sonne blasphemed the name and cursed, and they broughte him vnto Moses.

And his mothers name was Selamyth, the doughter
12 off Dybri off the trybe of Dan: and they putt him in warde, that Moses shulde declare vnto them what the Lorde sayde thereto.

13, 14 And the Lorde spake vnto Moses sayenge, bringe him that cursed without the hoste, and let all that herde him, put their handes apō his heed, and let all the mul-
15 titude stone him. And speake vnto the children of Israel sayenge: Whosoeuer curseth his God, shall bere
16 his synne: And he that blasphemeth the name of the Lorde, shall dye for it: all the multitude shall stone him to deeth. And the straunger as well as the Israelite yf he curse the name, shall dye for it.

17, 18 .℘. He that kylleth any man, shall dye for it: but he that kylleth a beest shall paye for it, beest for beest.
19 Yf a man mayme his neyghboure as he hath done, so
20 shall it be done to him agayne: broke for broke, broke, eye for eye and toth for toth: euen *breach, fracture*

ℳ. 14 hym that blasphemed
𝒱. 11 nomen domini 12 donec nossent quid iuberet dominus. 16 nomen domini 17 percuss. & occiderit 18 animam pro anima
ℒ. 11 nennet den namen 12 bis yhn aus gelegt wurd durch den mund des HERRN. 15 soll seyne sund tragen 16 den namen nennet 18 Seele vmb Seele.
ℳ. ℳ. N. 11 Hebrue *schem* that is, name that is blessed aboue all names. 15 *Curseth:* he curseth God & blasphemeth the name of God, that despyseth and defyeth godes ordynaunces statutes & commaundemētes, or that magnifyeth mennes tradicions and lawes aboue Godes, or setteth as moch therby, as by the preceptes of the most mercyfle God.

as he hath maymed a man, fo fhall he be maymed
21 agayne. So nowe he that kylleth a beeft, fhall paye
for it: but he that kylleth a man, fhall dye for it.
22 Ye fhall haue one maner of lawe amonge you: euē for
the ftraunger as wel as for one of youre felues, for I
am the Lorde youre God.
23 And Mofes tolde the childern of Ifrael, that they
fhulde bringe him that had curfed, out of the hofte,
and ftone him with ftones. And the childern of Ifrael
dyd as the Lorde cōmaunded Mofes.

☙ The .XXV. Chapter.

1 AND the Lorde fpake vnto Mofes in mount Sinai fayenge, fpeake
2 vnto the childern of Ifrael and faye vnto thē. When ye be come in to the lande whiche I geue you,
3 let the londe reft a Sabbath vnto the Lorde. Sixe yeres thou fhalt fowe thi felde, and sixe yere thou fhalt
4 cut thi vynes and gather in thy frutes. But the feuenth yere fhall be a Sabbath of [Fo. XLV.] reft vnto the londe. The Lordes Sabbath it fhalbe, ād thou fhalt nether fowe thi felde, nor cut thy vynes.
5 The corne that groweth by it felfe thou fhalt not repe, nether gather the grapes that growe without thy dreffynge: but it fhalbe a Sabbath of reft vnto the
6 londe. Neuertheleffe the Sabbath of the londe fhalbe meate for you: euen for the and thy feruaunte and for thy mayde and for thy hyred feruaunte and for the
7 ftraunger that dwelleth with the: and for thi catell and for the beeftes that are in thy londe, fhall all the encreafe thereof be meate.

M.C.S. The Saboth of the vii. yeres and of the yere of iubelie, otherwyfe called thefyftyeyere.

V. 21 Qui perc. iumentum, reddet aliud. Qui perc. hominem, punietur. 23 lapidibus oppreſſerunt. xxv, 2 fabbathizet fabbathum domino. 4 fabbathum erit terræ requietionis domini .. vineam non putabis.
L. 3 weynberg befchneyttift 4 weynb. befchn. folt. 7 alles getreyde foll fpeyfe feyn.

8 Then numbre feuen wekes of yeres, that is, feuen tymes feuen yere: and the fpace of the feuen wekes of
9 yeres will be vnto the .xlix. yere. And then thou fhalt make an horne blowe: euen in the tenth daye of the feuenth moneth, which is the daye of attonement. And then fhall ye make the horne blowe, euen thorowe out
10 all youre lande. And ye fhal halowe the fiftith yere, and proclayme libertie thorowe out the lande vnto all the inhabiters thereof, It fhalbe a yere of hornes blowynge vnto you and ye fhall returne: euery man vnto his poffeffion and euery man vnto
11 his kynred agayne. *This horne in ebrue is called iobel, ād of this toke the pope an occafiō to make eueri .l. yere a iubelye, fo that he contrafaiteth god in eueri point ād wyl not be one ace behinde him.* A yere of hornes blowynge fhall that fiftieth yere be vnto you. Ye fhall not fowe nether re- .P. pe the corne that groweth by it felfe, nor gather the grapes that growe without thi laboure
12 For it is a yere of hornes blowinge and fhalbe holy vnto you: how be it, yet ye fhall eate of the encreafe of the
13 felde. And in this yere of hornes blowinge ye fhall returne, euery man vnto his poffeffion agayne.
14 When thou felleft oughte vnto thy neyghboure or byeft off thy neyghboures hande, ye fhall not oppreffe
15 one another: but accordynge to the numbre of yeres after the trompett yere, thou fhalt bye of thy neyghboure, and accordynge vnto the numbre off frute-

M. 10 a yere of iubilee 11 a yere of iubilee 12 a yere of iubelye 13 a yere of iubelye 15 iubelye yere
V. 9 clanges buccina 10 ipfe eft enim iubileus. 12 ob fanctificationem iubilei, fed ftatim oblata comedetis .14 cōtriftes fratrem tuum
L. 8 die zeyt der fieben iar Sabbath 9 hall der pofaunen 10 denn es ift das Halliar [and so throughout the chapter] 14 bruder fchinden
M. M. N. 8 *Wekes of yeres:* A weke is fometyme taken for the nombre of .vii. dayes as before. xxiii, c. fometyme for the nombre of feuen yeres, as here & in Daniel .ix, f. g. 10 *Iubelye* of this Hebrewe woorde iobell, which in Englyfhe fygnifieth a trumpet. A yere of fynguler myrth and ioye and of moché reft, wher in their corne and all their frutes cam forth wythout fowynge, tyllynge or any other laboures. 15 By this *iubelye* is fygnified the reftorynge of all thinge vnto his perfeccion, which fhal be after the generall iudgemente in that floryffhynge worlde, when the chofen fhal be admytted in to lybertye frō all wretchednes, pouertye, anguyfhe & oppreffion, when all fhalbe fully reftored againe in Chrift, that thorow the fynne of the fyrft man was taken awaye.

16 yeres, he shall sell vnto the. Accordinge vnto the multitude of yeres, thou shalt encrease the price thereof and accordinge to the fewnesse of yeres, thou shalt mynish the price: for the numbre of frute he shall sell
17 vnto the. And see that no mā oppresse his neyghboure, but feare thi God.
18 For I am the Lorde youre God. Wherfore do after myne ordinaunces and kepe my lawes ād doo them,
19 that ye maye dwell in the lande in saftie. And the lande shall geue her frute, and ye shall eate youre fille and dwell therein in saftie.
20 Yf ye shall saye, what shall we eate the seue- [Fo. XLVI.] nth yere in as moche as we shall not sowe nor
21 gether in oure encrease. ‘I wyll sende my blessynge apon you in the sixte yere, and it shall brynge forth
22 frute for thre yeres: and ye shall sowe the eyghte yere and eate of olde frute vntill the .ix. yere, and euen vntyll hir frutes come, ye shall eate of olde stoare.
23 Wherfore the londe shall not be solde for euer, becaufe that the lande is myne, and ye but straungers and so-
24 iourners with me: and ye shall thorowe oute all the lande of youre possession, let the londe go home fre agayne.
25 When thy brother is waxed poore and hath solde awaye of his possession: yf any off his kyn come to redeme it, he shall by out that whiche his brother solde.
26 And though he haue no man to redeme it for him, yet yf hys hande can get sufficyent to bye it oute agayne,
27 then let him counte how longe it hath bene solde, and delyuer the rest vnto him to whome he solde it, ād so
28 he shall returne vnto his possession agayne. But and yf his hande cā not get sufficiēt to restore it to him agayne, then that whiche is solde shall remayne in the hande of him that hath boughte it, vntyll the horneyere: and in the horne yere it shall come out, and he shall .ℙ. returne vnto his possession agayne.

𝔐. 28 the yere of iubelye [*bis*], so vv. 30, 31, 33, 40, 50, 52, 54.
𝒱. 16 tempus enim frugum 17 Nolite affligere contribules vestros 19 nullius impetum formidantes. 23 & vos aduenæ & coloni mei 27 sicque recipiet possessionem suam. 28 non inuenerit manus eius
𝕷. 18 ym land sicher wonen mugt

29 Yf a man fell a dwellynge houfe in a walled cytie, he maye bye it out agayne any tyme withī a hole yere after it is folde: and that fhalbe the fpace in which he 30 maye redeme it agayne. But and yf it be not bought out agayne within the fpace of a full yere, then the houffe in the walled cytie fhalbe ftablifhed for euer vnto him that boughte it and to his fucceffoures after 31 hī and fhall not goo out in the trompet yere. But the houffes in villagies which haue no walles rounde aboute them, fhalbe counted like vnto the feldes of the cuntre, and maye be boughte out agayne at any feafon, and fhall goo out fre in the trompett yere.

32 Notwithftondynge the cityes of the leuytes and the houffes in the cities of their poffeffiōs the leuytes maye 33 redeme at all ceafons. And yf a man purchace ought of the leuytes: whether it be houfe or citie that they poffeffe, the bargayne fhall goo out in the trōpet yere. for the houffes of the cyties of the leuites, are 34 their poffeffions amonge the childern of Ifrael. But the feldes that lye rounde aboute their cyties, fhall not be bought: for they are their poffeffions for euer.

35 Yf thi brother be waxed poore ād fallē in decaye with the, receaue him as a ftraunger or [Fo. XLVII.] 36 a foiourner, and let him lyue by the. And thou fhalt take none vfurye of him, nor yet vantage. But fhalt feare thi God, that thi brother maye lyue with the. 37 Thou fhalt not lende him thi money apon vfurye, nor 38 lende him of thy fode to haue avantage by it for I am the Lorde youre God which broughte you out of the lande of Egipte, to geue you the lande of Canaan and to be youre God.

39 Yf thi brother that dwelleth by the waxe poore and fell him felfe vnto the, thou fhalt not let him laboure 40 as a bondferuaunte doeth: but as an hyred feruaunte and as a foiourner he fhalbe with the, and fhall ferue 41 the vnto the trompetyere, and then fhall he departe

V. 29 intra vrbis muros, hab. licentiam redimendi 31 villa . . quæ muros non habet, agrorum iure vendetur. 35 & infirmus manu 37 frugum fuperabundantiam non exiges. 40 mercennarius & colonus

L. 35 frembdlingen oder hausgnofs 37 deyn fpeyfe auff vberfatz austhun.

frō the: both he and his childern with him, and ſhall returne vnto his awne kynred agayne and vnto the
42 poſſeſſions of his fathers. for they are my ſeruauntes which I brought out of the lande of Egipte, and ſhall
43 not be folde as bondmen. Se therfore that thou reigne not ouer him cruelly, but feare thi God.

44 Yf thou wilt haue bondſeruauntes and maydens, thou ſhalt bye them of the heythen that are rounde
45 aboute you, and of the childern of the ſtraungers that are ſoiorners amonge you, ād of their generaciōs that
46 are with you, which they begate in youre lāde. And ye ſhall poſſeſſe .P. them and geue them vnto youre childern after you, to poſſeſſe them for euer: and they ſhalbe youre bond men: But ouer youre brethern the childern of Iſrael, ye ſhall not reigne one ouer another cruelly.

47 When a ſtraunger and a ſoiourner waxeth rych by the ād thi brother that dwelleth by him waxeth poore and ſell him ſelfe vnto the ſtraunger that dwelleth by
48 the or to any of the ſtraungers kyn: after that he is folde he maye be redemed agayne. one of his brethren
49 maye bye him out: whether it be his vncle or his vncles ſonne, or any that is nye of kynne vnto him of his kynred: ether yf his hande can get ſo moch he
50 maye be looſed. And he ſhall reken with him that boughte him, from the yere that he was folde in vnto the trompet yere, and the pryce of his byenge ſhalbe acordynge vnto the numbre of yeres, and he ſhalbe
51 with him as a hyred ſeruaunte. Yf there be yet many yeres behynde, acordynge vnto them he ſhall geue agayne for his delyueraunce, of the money that he was
52 folde for. Yf there remayne but few yeres vnto the trompet yere, he ſhall ſo counte with him, and acordynge vnto his yeres geue him agayne for his redemp-
53 cion, and ſhalbe with him yere by yere as an hyred ſeruaunte, [Fo. XLVIII.] and the other ſhall not reygne

V. 43 affligas eum per potentiā 46 fratres .. ne opprimatis per potentiam 47 inualuerit apud vos manus 53 non affliget eum violēter in cōſpectu tuo
L. 43 mit der ſtrenge vber ſie hirſchen 50 vnd ſol ſeyn tagelon der gantzen zeyt mit eyn rechen [*bis*].

54 cruelly ouer him in thi fyghte. Yf he be not bought
fre in the meane tyme, then he fhall goo out in the
55 trompet yere and his childern with him. for the childern of Ifrael are my feruauntes which I broughte out
of the lande of Egipte. I am the Lorde youre God.
XXVI, 1 Ye fhall make you no ydolles, nor grauen
ymage, nether rere you vpp any piler, nether ye fhall
fett vp any ymage of ftone in youre lande to bowe
youre felues there to: for I am the Lorde youre God.
2 kepe my fabbathes and feare my fanctuary. for I am
the Lorde.

¶ The .XXVI. Chapter.

3 IF ye fhall walke in myne ordynaunces and kepe my com-
maundmentes and do them,
4 then I will fende you rayne
in the ryght ceafon ād youre londe fhall
yelde her encreafe and the trees of the
5 felde fhall geue their frute. And the
threfhynge fhall reach vnto wyne harueft, and the wyneharueft fhall reach
vnto fowyng tyme, and ye fhall eate
youre bred in plenteoufnes and fhall
6 dwell in youre lande peafably. And I
wil fende peace in youre londe, that
ye fhall .T. flepe, and no man fhal
make you afrayde. And I will ryd euell

*M.C.S.*Im-
ages are for-
bydden. Blef-
ed are they
that kepe thofe
thynges that
God byddeth
and moft
curfed are
they that kepe
them not. [*In
Matthew's Bi-
ble this chap-
ter begins
with xxvi, 1
as in the Au-
thorized Ver-
fion, while
Tyndale con-
nects xxvi,1,2
with ch.xxv.]

V. 2 pauete ad fanctuarium meum. 4 terra gignet germē fuum,
& pomis arbores replebuntur. 5 abfque pauore
L. 4 bewme auff dem felde 5 ficher ynn ewrm land
M. M. N. 2 *Feare my fanctuary:* To feare the fanctuarie, is
dylygently to performe the true worfhyppyng & feruyce of God,
to leue of nothynge, to obferue and kepe the purenes both of
bodye & mynde, verely & not ypocritelike to beleue that he knoweth, beholdeth, doeth & ruleth all thynges: to bewarre of offend-
ynge hym and with all feare and dylygence to walke in the pathes
of his lawes.

beeftes out of youre londe, and there fhall no fwerde goo thorowe out youre lande.

7 And ye fhall chace youre enemyes, and they fhall
8 fall before you vppon the fwerde. And fiue of you fhall chace an hundred, and an hundred of you fhall put .x. thoufande to flighte, and youre enemyes
9 fhall fall before you apon the fwerde. And I wil turne vnto you and encreafe you and multiplye
10 you, and fett vpp my teftament with you. And ye fhall eate olde ftore, ād caft out the olde for
11 plentuoufnes of the newe. I will make my dwellynge place amonge you, and my foule fhall not loothe you.

12 And I will walke amonge you and wilbe youre
13 God, and ye fhalbe my people. For I am the Lorde youre God whiche broughte you out off the lande of the Egiptians, that ye fhulde not be their bondemen, and I brake the bowes of youre yockes, and made you go vp righte.

14 But and yf ye will not harken vnto me, nor will
15 do all thefe my commaundementes, or yf *Note well.* ye fhall defpyfe myne ordinaunces ether yf youre foules refufe my lawes, fo that ye wil not do all my commaundmentes: but fhall breake myne appoyntment:
16 then I will do this agayne vn- [Fo. XLIX.] to you: I will vifet you with vexations, fwellynge and feuers, that fhall make youre eyes dafell and with forowes of herte. And ye fhall fowe youre feed in vayne, for
17 youre enemyes fhall eate it. And I will fet my face agenfte you and ye fhal fall before youre enemyes, and they that hate you fhal raigne ouer you, ād ye fhal flee whē no man foloweth you.

18 And yf ye will not yet for all this herken vnto me,

V. 9 firmabo pactum meum 13 cōfregi catenas ceruicū veftrarū 14 omnia mandata mea 15 fed fpreu. leges meas, & iudicia mea cont. vt non fac. ea quæ a me conftituta funt, & ad irritum perduc. pactum meum 16 velociter in egeftate & ardore, qui conficiat ocul. veft. & confumat animas veftras.

L. 8 Ewr funffe ... iagen ... iagen 9 bund ... auffrichten 11 feele .. nicht verwerffen 15 meynen bund laffen anftehen 16 fchwulft vnd fiber 17 fliehen .. niemant iaget.

than will I punifh you feuen tymes more *God beginneth*
19 for youre fynnes, and will breake the *ād augment-*
pride off youre ftrength. For I will make *moare ād*
the heauē ouer you as harde as yerne, and *moare as the*
20 youre londe as hard as braffe. And fo *their hertes*
youre laboure fhalbe fpent in vayne. For *agēfte him.*
youre londe fhall not geue hir encreafe, nether the
trees of the londe fhall geue their frutes.
21 And yf ye walke contrary vnto me and will not
herken vnto me, I will bringe feuen tymes moo plages
22 apon you acordinge to youre fynnes. I will fende in
wylde beeftes apon you, which fhall robbe you of youre
childern and deftroye youre catell, and make you fo
fewe in numbre that youre hye wayes fhall growe
vnto a wildernefle.
23 And yf ye will not be lerned yet for all this
24 but fhall walke contrarye vnto me, then will I
alfo walke contrarye vnto you and will punifh .P.
25 you yet feuen tymes for youre fynnes. I will fende
a fwerde apon you, that fhall avenge my teftament
with you. And when ye are fled vnto youre cities,
I will fende the peftelence amonge you, ye fhall
be delyuered in to the handes of youre enemyes.
26 And when I haue broken the ftaffe of youre bred:
that .x. wyues fhall bake youre bred in one ouen
and men fhall delyuer you youre bred agayne by
weyghte, thā fhal ye eate and fhall not be fatiffied.
27 And yf ye will not yet for all this harken vnto me,
28 but fhall walke contrarye vnto me, then I will walke
contrary vnto you alfo wrathfully and will alfo chaf-
29 tice you feuen tymes for youre fynnes: fo that ye fhall

𝒱. 18 addam correptiones veftr. 19 fuperbiam duritiæ 23 Quod
fi nec fic 25 gladium vltorem fœderis mei. 28 & ego incedam aduerfus vos in furore contrario
𝐋. 19 hoffart ewr ftercke 20 ewr muhe vnd erbeyt 25 ein
rachfchwerd
𝔐. 𝔐. 𝔑. 18 God begineth & augmenteth his plages moare
and moare as the people harden their hertes agenfte him. 21 *Seuen
tymes:* by that nombre vnderftande all tymes, as in this chapter, c.
26 *To breake the ftaffe of their breade*, is, to breake the ftrēgth
therof and to mynifhe hyt fo that they fhuld not haue ynowghe
to lyue by.

eate the flesh of youre sonnes and the flesh of youre
30 doughters. And I will destroye youre alters bylt
apon hye hylles, and ouerthrowe youre images, and
cast youre carkasses apon the bodies of youre ydolles,
31 and my soule shall abhorre you. And I will make
youre cities desolate, and bringe youre sanctuaries
vnto nought, and will not smell the sauoures of youre
swete odoures.
32 And I will bringe the londe vnto a wildernesse: so
that youre enemyes which dwell there in shall wondre
33 at it. And I will strawe you amonge the heethen, and
will drawe out a swerde after you, and youre lande
34 shalbe wast, and [Fo. L.] youre cities desolate. Then
the lande shall reioyse in hir Sabbathes, as longe as
it lyeth voyde and ye in youre enemies londe: euen
then shall the londe kepe holye daye and reioyse in
35 hir Sabbathes. And as longe as it lyeth voyde it
shall rest, for that it coude not reste in youre Sabbathes,
when ye dwelt therein.
36 And vppon them that are left alyue of you, I
will sende a seyntnesse in to their hertes in the londe
of their enemies: so that the sounde of a leef that
falleth, shall chace them and they shall flee as though
thei fled a swerde, and shall fall no man solowinge
37 them. And they shall fall one uppon another, as it
were before a swerde euen no man solowinge them,
and ye shall haue no power to stonde before youre
38 enemyes: And ye shall perish amonge the hethen, ād
the londe of youre enemyes shall eate you vpp.
39 And thei that are left of you, shall pyne awaye in
their vnrightuousnes, euen in their enemies londe, and
also in the mysdeades of their fathers shall they con-
40 sume. And they shall confesse their misdedes and the
misdeades of their fathers in their trespases which thei

V. 30 Cadetis inter ruinas idol. vestrorum, & abhominabitur
vos anima mea 35 sabbathizabit, & req. in sabbathis . . . solitudinis
suæ 36 terrebit eos sonitus folii volantis 37 quasi bella fugiētes
39 tabescent in iniquit.,. . . affligentur: 40 donec confiteantur
L. 30 ewre hohen altar . . ewre leychnam . . gotzen leychnam
31 ewre kirchen eynreyssen 36 eyn seyg hertz machen . . . eyn
rausschend blat iagen 39 verwesen ynn der seynde land

haue trefpafed againft me, and for that alfo that they
41 haue walked contrary vnto me. Therfore I alfo will
walke contrary vnto them, and will brynge them in
to the londe of their enemyes.

.P. And then at the leeft waye their vncircumcyfed
hertes fhall be tamed, ād then they fhall make an
attonement for their mifdedes.

42 And I wil remembre my bonde with *Mercy is neuer*
Iacob and my teftamēt with Ifaac, and *denyed vnto him that re-*
my teftament with Abraham, and will *penteth.*
thinke on the londe.

43 For the londe fhall be lefte of them and fhall haue
pleafure in hir Sabbathes, while fhe lyeth waft without them, and they fhall make an attonement for
their mifdeades, becaufe they defpyfed my lawes and
44 their foules refufed myne ordinaunces. And yet for
all that when thei be in the londe of their enemyes,
I will not fo caft them awaye nor my foule fhall not
fo abhorre them, that I will vtterlye deftroye thē ād
breake myne appoyntment with them: for I am the
45 Lorde their God. I will therfore remēbre vnto thē
the firft couenaunt made when I broughte them out
of the lond of Egipte in the fighte of the hethen to
be their God: for I am the Lorde.

46 Thefe are the ordinaunces, iudgemētes, ād lawes
which the Lorde made betwene him ād the childern
of Ifrael in mount Sinai by the hāde of Mofes.

⁋ The .XXVII. Chapter.

M. 44 lande of their enemye
V. 41 donec erubefcat incircūcifa 43 Ipfi vero rogabunt pro
peccatis fuis 44 non penitus abieci eos 45 record. fœd. mei prift.
L. 41 vnbefchnyttens hertz 46 fatzung vnd rechte vnd gefetze
M. M. N. 42 Mercy is never denyed vnto him that repenteth

XXVII. Chapter. [Fo. LI.]

AND the Lorde fpake vnto Mofes fayuge: fpeake vnto the children of Ifrael and faye vnto them: Yf any man will geue a fynguler vowe vnto the Lorde acordynge to the value of his foule, then fhall the male from xx. yere vnto .Lx. be fet at fyftie fycles of fyluer, after the fycle of the fanctuary, and the female at .xxx fycles. And from .v. yeres to .xx. the male fhalbe fet at .xx. fycles, and the female at .x. fycles. And from a moneth vnto .v. yere, the male fhalbe fet at .v. fycles of fyluer, and the female at thre. And the man that is .Lx. and aboue, fhalbe valowed at .xv. ficles, ãd the woman at .x. Yf he be to pore fo to be fet, thẽ let him come before the preaft: and let the preaft value him, acordynge as the hande of him that vowed is able to gete.

Yf it be of the beeftes of which men bringe an offeringe vnto the Lorde: all that any man geueth of foch vnto the Lorde, fhalbe holy.

He maye not alter it nor chaunge it: a good for a bad or a bad for a goode. Yf he chaunge beeft for beeft, then both the fame beeft and it alfo where with it was chaunged fhall be holy. Yf it be any maner of vncleane beeft of which men maye not offer vnto the Lorde, let him brynge the beeft before the preaft and let the preaft value it. And whether it be good or bad .P. as the preaft fetteth it, fo fhall it be. And yf he will bye it agayne, let him geue the fyfte part moare to that it was fet at.

V. 2 & fpofpŏderit deo animam fuam, 3 fub æftimatione dabit pretium. 8 & viderit eũ poffe reddere, tantũ dabit. 12 malum fit, ftatuet pretium.
L. 2 befonder glubde 3 fchetzen auff [throughout] 8 priefter fol yhn fchetzen, Er fol yhn aber fchetzen nach dem feyne hand, des der gelobd hat, erwerben kan.

14 Yf any man dedicate his houffe, it fhalbe holy vnto the Lorde. And the preaft fhall fet it. whether it be good or bad, and as the preaft hath fet it, fo it fhalbe.
15 Yf he that fanctifyed it will redeme his houffe, let him geue the fyfte parte of the money that it was iudged at thereto, and it fhalbe his.
16 Yf a man halowe a pece of his enhereted londe vnto the Lorde, it fhalbe fet acordynge to that it beareth. Yf it bere an homer of barlye, it fhall be fet at fyftie
17 ficles of fyluer. yf he halowe his felde immediatly from the trompet yere, it fhalbe worth acordynge as it
18 is eftemed. But and if he halowe his felde after the trōpetyere, the preaft fhall rekē the price with him acordynge to the yeres that remayne vnto the trōpet yere, ād there after it fhalbe lower fett.
19 Yf he that fanctifyed the felde will redeme it agayne, let him put the fyfte parte of the pryce that it was fet
20 at, there vnto and it fhalbe his yf he will not it fhalbe
21 redemed nomoare. But when the felde goeth out in the trompet yere, it fhalbe holy vnto the Lorde: euen as a thinge dedycated, ād it fhall be the preaftes poffeffion.
22 Yf a man fanctifie vnto the Lorde a felde. [Fo. LII.] which he hath boughte and is not of his enheritaunce,
23 then the preaft fhall reken with him what it is worth vnto the trompet yere, and he fhall geue the price that it is fet at the fame daye, and it fhalbe holy vnto the
24 Lorde. But in the trompet yere, the felde fhall returne vnto him of whome he boughte it, whofe enheritaunce of londe it was.
25 And all fettinge fhalbe acordinge to the holy fycle. One fycle maketh .xx. Geras.

𝔐. 17 yere of iubely 21 yere of iubelye 23 yere of iubelye 24 yere of iubelye
𝒱. 14 confyderabit eam facerdos ... & iuxta pret. quod ab eo fuerit conftitutum, venundabitur 18 poft aliquantulum temporis 21 & poffeffio cōfecrata ad ius pertinet facerdotum. 24 in fortem poffeffionis fuæ. 25 viginti obolos
𝔏. 21 wie eyn verbannet acker, vnd fol des priefters erbgut feyn.
𝔐. 𝔐. 𝔑. 16 To *halow* & to *fanctifie* are bothe one, what fanctyfieng is loke Gen. iii, a. 25 *Holy fycle* or *fycle of the fanctuarye:* they be both one.

26 But the firstborne of the beestes that pertayne vnto the Lorde, maye no mā sanctifie: whether it be oxe or
27 shepe, for they are the Lordes allredy. Yf it be an vncleane beest, then let him redeme it as it is sett at, and geue the fifte parte moare thereto. Yf it be not redemed, thē let it be solde as it is rated.
28 Notwithstondinge no dedicated thinge that a man dedicateth vnto the Lorde, of all his goode, whether it be man or beest or lande off his enheritaunce, shalbe solde or redemed: for all dedicate thīges are most holy vnto the Lorde.
29 No dedicate thinge therfore that is dedicate of mā, may be redemed, but must nedes dye
30 All thefe tithes of the londe, whether it be of the corne of the felde or frute of the trees, shalbe holy vnto
31 the Lorde. Yf any man will redeme oughte of his tithes, let him adde the fifte .℣. parte moare thereto.
32 And the tithes of oxen and shepe and of all that goeth vnder the herdemans kepinge, shalbe holye tithes
33 vnto the Lorde. Men shal not loke yf it be good or bad nor shall chaunge it. Yf any man chaunge it then both it and that it was chaunged with all, shalbe holy and maye not be redemed.
34 Thefe are the commaundmentes whiche the Lorde gaue Mofes in charge to geue vnto the childern of Ifrael in mount Sinai.

⁋ The ende of the thyrde boke
of Mofes.

℣. 29 Et omnis confecratio .. morte morietur. 32 fub paftoris virga tranfeunt
𝕷. 28 keyn verbantes verkeuffen ... verbannet ... verbante 29 verbanten .. todts fterben. 32 was vnter der rutten gehet

¶ A prologe in to the fourth boke of Moses, called Nu‑ meri.

P. W T

¶ A Prologe in to the fourth boke of Moses, called Numeri.

IN the seconde ād thirde boke they receaved ẏ lawe. And in this .iiii. they begynne to worke and to practyse. Of which practisynge ye se many good ensamples of vnbe-
5 leffe & what frewill doth, when she taketh in hand to kepe the lawe of her awne power with out help of fayth in the promyses of god: how she leueth her masters carkesses by the way in the wildernesse and bringeth them not in to the londe of rest. Why coude they not
10 entre in? Because of their vnbeleffe Hebre. iii. For had they beleved, so had they bene vnder grace, and their old synnes had bene forgeuen thē, ād power shulde haue bene geuē them to haue fulfilled the lawe thenceforth & they shuld haue bene kepte from all temptaciōs
15 that had bene to stronge for them. For it is wrytten Iohan .i. He gaue them power to be the sonnes of god, thorow belevynge in his name. Nowe to be the sonne of god is to loue god and his commaundmentes and to walke in his waye after the ensample of his
20 sonne Christ. But these people toke vppon them to worke without faith as thou seyste in the .xiiii. of this boke, where they wold fight and also did, without the worde of promysse: euē when they were warned that they shuld not. And in ẏ .xvi. agayne they wolde
25 please god .P. with their holye faithlesse workes (for where gods worde is not there can be no faith) but ẏ fyre of god consumed their holy workes, as it did Nadab and Abihu Leui. x. And frō these vnbeleuers turne thyne eyes vnto the pharesyes which before the com-
30 ynge of Christ in his flesh, had layde the fundacion of frewill after the same ensample. Wher on thei bilt

holy workes after their awne imaginacion with out
faith of the worde, fo fervently that for the greate zele
of them they flew the kinge of all holy workes and the
lorde of frewill which only thorow his grace maketh
the will fre and lowfeth her from bondage of fynne,
and geueth her loue and luft vnto the lawes of god,
and power to fulfyll them. And fo thorowe their holye
workes done by the power of frewill, they excluded
them felues out of the holy reft of forgeueneffe of
fynnes by faith in the bloude of Chrift.

And then loke on oure ypocrites which in like
maner folowinge the doctryne of Ariftotle and other
hethen paganes, haue agenfte all the fcripture fett vpp
frewill agayne, vnto whofe power they afcribe the
kepynge of ỹ cōmaundmētes of god. For they haue
fet vp wilfull povertye of a nother maner then any is
cōmaunded of god. And the chaftite of matrimony
vtterlye defyed, they haue fet vp a nother wilfull
chaftite not required of god, whiche they fwere, vowe
& profeffe to geue god, .P. whether he will geue it
them or no, and compell all their difciples there vnto,
fayenge that it is in the power of euery mans frewill
to obferue it, contrarye to Christ and his apoftle Paule.

And the obedience of god and man excluded they
haue vowed a nother wilfull obedience condemned of
all the fcripture whiche they will yet geue God whether
he will or wyll not.

And what is become of their wilfull pouertye? hath
it not robbed the whole worlde & brought all vnder
them? Can there be ether kynge or emperoure or of
what foeuer degre it be, excepte he will hold of them
ād be fworne vnto them to be their fervaunte, to go
and come at their lufte and to defende their quarels
be they falfe or true? Their wilfull pouertye hath all
readye eaten vpp the whole worlde & is yet ftill gredyar
then euer it was in fo moche that ten worldes mo were
not ynough to fatiffye the hongre thereof.

Moreouer befydes dayly corruptinge of other mens
wyues and open whoredome, vnto what abominacions
to fylthye to be fpokē off hath their voluntarye chaftite
broughte them?

And as for their wilfull obediēce what is it but ẏ
difobediēce & the diffiaūce both of all ẏ lawes of god
& mā: in fo moch ẏ yf any price begīne to execute any
law of mā vppō thē, .P. they curfe him vnto the botom
5 of hell & proclayme him no right kinge & that his
lordes ought no lenger to obaye him, and interdite his
comen people as they were hethē turkes or faracenes.
And yf any man preache them gods lawe, him they
make an heretike and burne him to affhes. And in
10 fteade of gods lawe and mans, they haue fette vpp one
off their awne imaginacion which they obferue with
difpenfacions.

And yet in thefe workes they haue fo greate confidence that they not onlye trufte to be faued therby,
15 and to be hyer in heauen then they that be faued
thorow chrift: but alfo promeffe to all other forgeueneffe of their fynnes thorow the merites of the fame.
Wherin they reft and teach other to reft alfo, ex-
cludynge the whole worlde from the refte of forgeueneffe
20 of fynnes thorowe faith in Chriftes bloude.

And now feynge that faith only letteth a mā in
ūto reft & vnbeleffe excludeth hī, what is the caufe of
this vnbeleffe? verely no fynne ẏ the world feyth, but
a pope holyneffe & a rightuoufnes of theire awne im-
25 aginacion as Paule fayeth Roma. x. They be ignoraūte
of ẏ rightuoufnes wherwith god iuftifieth & haue fet
vp a rightuoufnes of their awne makīge thorow which
they be disobediēt vnto ẏ rightuoufnes of god. And
Chrift rebuketh not the pharifeys for groffe fynnes
30 whiche .P. the worlde fawe, but for thofe holye deades
whiche fo blered the eyes of the worlde that they were
takē as goddes: euē for long prayers, for faftynge, for
tythīge fo diligētly that they lefte not fo moch as their
herbes vntithed, for their clenneffe in waffhynge be-
35 fore meate and for waffhynge of cuppes, diffhes, and all
maner veffels, for buyldinge the prophetes fepulchres,
and for kepinge the holy daye, and for turnynge the
hethen vnto the fayth, and for gevynge of almes. For
vnto foch holy deades they afcribed rightuoufnes and
40 therfore when the rightuoufneffe of god was preached
vnto them they coude not but perfecute it, the devell

was so stronge in thē. Which thinge Christ well descri-
beth Luce. xi. sayenge that after the devell is cast out
he cometh agayne and syndeth his house swepte and
made gaye and then taketh seuen worse then him selfe
and dwelleth therein, and so is the ende of that man
worse then the beginnynge. That is, when they be a
litle clensed from grosse synnes whiche the worlde seyth
and then made gaye in their awne syght with the
rightuousnes of tradicions, then cometh seuen, that is
to saye the hole power of ẏ devell, for seuē with ẏ
hebrues signifieth a multitude without nūbre & the
extremyte of a thinge & is a speach borowed (I suppose)
out of leuiticus where is so oft mencion made of seuē.
Where I wolde saye: I will punish the .P. that all the
world shall take an ensample of the, there the Iewe
wold saye, I will circumcyse the or baptise the .vii. tymes.
And so here by seuen is ment all the devels of hell &
all ẏ might & power of the devell. For vnto what
further blindnesse coude al the deuels in hell bringe
thē, then to make them beleue ẏ they were iustified
thorow their awne good workes. For whē they once
beleued ẏ they were purged frō their synnes & made
rightuousse thorowe their awne holye workes, what
rowme was there lefte for ẏ rightuousnes ẏ is in christes
bloudeshedinge? And therfore whē they be fallen in
to this blindnesse they cā not but hate & persecute the
light. And the more cleare & evidently their deades
be rebuked ẏ furiousser & maliciousser blind are thei
vntill they breake out in to opē blasphemye & synnynge
agenst ẏ holy gost, which is ẏ malicious persecutīge
of the cleare trouth so manifestly proued that they cā
not once hijsh agenst it. As the pharesyes persecuted
Christ becàuse he rebuked their holy deades. And
when he proued his doctrine with ẏ scripture & miracles,
yet though they coude not improue him nor reason
agenst him they tought ẏ the scripture must haue some
other meaninge becaùse his interpretacion vndermyned
their fundacion & plucked vpp by the rootes the sectes
which they had plāted, & they ascribed also his miracles to the deuell. And in like .P. maner though oure
ypocrites can not denye but this is scripture, yet be-

caufe there can be no nother fens gathered thereof, but
that ouerthroweth their byldynges, therfore they euer
thinke that it hath fome other meanynge than as the
wordes founde and that no man vnderftondeth it or
5 vnderftode it fens the tyme of the Apoftles. Or yf
they thynke that fome that wrote vppon it fens the
apoftles vnderftode it: they yet thynke that we in like
maner as we vnderftonde not the texte it felfe, fo we
vnderftande not the meanynge of the wordes of that
10 doctoure.

For when thou layeft the iuftifyinge of holy workes
and denyeft the iuftifyinge of fayth, howe canft thou
vnderftond faynt Paule, Peter, Iohan and the Actes
of the apoftles or any fcripture at all, feynge the iufti-
15 fyinge of faith is almoft all that they entende to proue.

Fynally, concernynge vowes whereof thou readeft
chaptre .xxx. there maye be many queftyons, where-
unto I anfwere fhortly that we ought to put falt to
all oure offerynges: that is, we ought to miniftre
20 knowledge in all ovre workes and to do nothinge
whereof we coude not geue a reafon out off gods
wordes. We be now in the daye light, and all the
fecretes of God and all his counfell and will is opened
vnto vs, and he ẏ was promyfed fhuld come and
25 bleffe vs, is .P. come all readye and hath fhed his
bloud for vs and hath bleffed vs with all maner bleffynges and hath obtayned all grace for vs, and in him
we haue all. Wherfore god henceforth will receaue
no moare facrifices of beeftes of vs as thou readeft
30 Hebre. x. Yf thou burne vnto god the bloud or fatt
of beeftes, to obtayne forgeueneffe of fynnes therby or
that god fhuld the better heare thy requeft, then thou
doeft wronge vnto the bloude of chrift, and chrift vnto
the is dead in vaine. For in him god hath promyfed
35 not forgeueneffe of fynnes only, but alfo what foeuer
we axe to kepe vs from fynne and temptacion with
all. And what yf thou burne frankencens vnto him,
what yf thou burne a cādle, what yf thou burne thi
chaftite or virginite vnto him for the fame purpoffe,
40 doeft thou not like rebuke vnto chriftes bloude?

Moreouer yf thou offer gold fyluer or any other good

for the fame entent, is there any difference? And euen fo if thou go in pilgrymage or faftift or goeft wolward or fpricleft thy felfe with holy water or els what foeuer dead it is, or obferueft what foeuer cere-monye it be for like meanynge, then it is like abhominacion. We muft therfore bringe the falt of the knowledge of gods worde with all oure facrifices, or els we fhall make no fwete fauoure vnto God thereof. Thou wilt axe me, fhall I vowe nothynge at all? yes, gods .P. commaundement whiche thou haft vowed in thy baptyme. For what entent? verely for the loue of Chrift whiche hath bought the with his bloude & made the fonne & heyre of god with him, ẏ thou fhuldeft wayte on his will & cōmaundmentes and puryfye thy mēbres acordinge to ẏ fame doctryne that hath puryfyed thyne harte, for if the knowlege of gods worde haue not puryfyed thyne harte, fo that thou confenteft vnto the lawe of god that it is right-uouffe & good and foroweft, that thy membres moue the vnto the contrarye, fo haft thou no parte with Chrifte.

For yf thou repent not of thy fynne, fo it is impoffible that thou fhuldeft beleue that Chrifte had delyuered the from the daunger therof. Yf thou beleue not that Chrifte hathe delyuered the, fo is it impoffible that thou fhuldeft loue goddes commaundementes. Yf thou loue not the commaundementes, fo is Chriftes fprete not in the whiche is the ernefte off forgeueneffe of fynne and of faluacion.

For fcripture teacheth, firft repentaunce then fayth in Chrift, that for his fake fynne is forgeuen to them that repent: then good workes, whiche are nothynge faue the commaundement of god only. And the commaundemētes are nothinge els faue the helpinge of oure neyghboures at their neade & the tamyinge of oure mēbres that they myghte .P. be pure alfo as the harte is pure thorow hate of vice and loue of vertue as gods worde teacheth vs which workes muft procede out of faith: ẏ is, I muft do them for the loue which I haue to god for that greate mercye which he hath fhewed me in chrift, or els I do them not in ẏ fight of god. And that I faynte not in the payne of the fleyinge of the fynne that is in my flefh, myne helpe is the promeffe of the affiftence of the power of god and ẏ comforte of the rewarde to come which rewarde I afcribe vnto the goodneffe, mercye ād truth of the promifer that hath chofe me, called me, taught me and geuen me the erneft therof, ād not vnto the merites of my doenges or foferiges. For all that I do & foffre is but ẏ waye to the rewarde ād not the deferuinge thereof. As if the kinges grace fhuld promeffe me to defend me at whome in myne awne royalme yet the waye thyther is thorow the fee wherin I might happlye foffre no litle trouble. And yet for all that, yf I might lyue in reft when I come thither, I wold think & fo wold other faye, that my paynes were well rewarded: which reward & benefyte I wold not proudlye afcribe vnto the merites of my paynes takynge by the waye: but vnto the goodneffe, mercyfulneffe and conftaunt truth of the kinges grace whofe gifte it is and to whome ẏ prayfe ād thanke thereof belongeth of duetye and right. So now a rewarde is a gift geuē .P. frelye of the goodneffe of the geuer and not of the deferuinges of the receauer. Thus it appeareth, that if I vowe what foeuer it be, for any other purpoffe then to tame my membres and to be an enfample of vertue ād edefyenge vnto my neyghboure, my facrifice is vnfauery and cleane without falt and my lāpe without oyle and I one of the folyfh virginis and fhalbe fhutt out from the feaft of the bruydegrome when I thinke my felf moft fure to entre in.

Yf I vowe voluntary pouerty, this muft be my purpoffe, that I will be content with a competent lyuinge which cometh vnto me ether by fucceffion of myne elders or which I gette truly with my laboure in miniftringe and doynge feruice vnto the comen welth in one office or in a nother or in one occupatyon or other, becaufe that riches and honoure fhall not corrupte my mynde and drawe myne harte from god, and to geue an enfample of vertue and edefyinge vnto other and ẏ my neyghboure may haue a lyuinge by

me as well as I, if I make a cloke of diſſimulacion of
my vowe, laynge a net of fayned beggerye to catch
ſuperfluous aboundaunce of ryches and hye degre ād
authorite & thorow the eſtimacion of falſe holineſſe
to fede and maītayne my ſlowthfull ydleneſſe with ẏ
ſweate, laboure, lādes, & rentes of other mē (after
ẏ enſample of oure ſpiritualtye) robbinge thē .P. of
their faythes and god of his honoure turnynge vnto
myne ypocriſye that confidence, which ſhuld be geuē
vnto ẏ promyſes of god only, am I not a wilye fox &
a raueninge wolfe in a lābes ſkynne & a paynted
ſepulchre fayre without ād filthye with in? In like
maner though I ſeke no worldlye promocyon therebye,
yet if I do it to be iuſtifyed therwith ād to gett an hyer
place in heauen, thinkynge that I do it of myne awne
naturall ſtrength & of the naturall power of my frewill
& ẏ euery man hath might euen ſo to doo and that
they do it not is their faute & negligēce and ſo with
the proude phareſye in cōparyſon of my ſelf deſpiſe
the ſinfull publicanes: what other thinge do I then
eate ẏ bloude & ſatt of my ſacrifice devowringe ẏ my
ſelf which ſhuld be offered vnto god alone and his
chriſte. And ſhortly what ſoeuer a man doeth of his
naturall giftes, of his naturall witte, wiſdom, vnderſtondinge, reaſon, will, & good entent before he be
otherwyſe & cleane cōtrary taught of goddes ſprete
& haue receaued other witt and vnderſtondinge, reaſon ād will, is fleſh, worldlye and wrought ī abomi-
nable blīdneſſe, with which a man can but ſeke him
ſelf, his awne profyte, glory & honoure, euē in very
ſpirituall matters. As if I were alone in a wildernesse
where no man were to ſeke profite or prayſe of yet
if I wold ſeke heuē of god there, I coude of myne
awne naturall gyftes ſeke it no no- .P. ther wayes then
for the merites and deſeruinges of my good workes
and to entre therin by a nother waye then by ẏ dore
chriſt, which were very thefte, for chriſt is lord ouer
all and what ſo euer any man wil haue of god, he muſt
haue it geuen him frelye for chriſtes ſake. Now to
haue heauen for myne awne deſeruinge, is myne awne
prayſe and not chriſtes. For I can not haue it by

fauoure & grace in chrift and by myne awne merites alfo: For fregeuinge and deferuinge can not ftôd to gether.

Yf thou wilt vowe of thy goodes vnto god thou muſt put falt vnto this facrifice: that is thou muſt miniſtre knowlege in this deade as Peter teacheth. 2 pet. i. Thou muſt put oyle of gods worde in thy lāpe & do it accordinge to knowlege, if thou wayte for the comynge of the bridegrome to entre in with him in to his reſt. Thou wilt hăge it aboute the image to moue men to deuocyon. Deuocyon is a feruent loue vnto gods cōmaūdmentes and a defyre to be with god and with his euerlaſtinge promyfes. Now fhall the fight of foch riches as are fhewed at faynt thomas fhryne or at walfingham moue a man to loue the cōmaundmētes of god better and to defyre to be loofed from his flefh and to be with god, or fhall it not rather make his poore herte figh because he hath no foch at home and to wyfh parte of it in a nother place?

.P. The preaſt fhall haue it in gods ſtead. Shall the preaſt haue it? Yf the preaſt be bought with chriſtes bloude, thē he is chriſtes feruaūte & not his awne & ought therefore to feade chriſtes flocke with chriſtes doctryne & to miniſtre chriſtes facramētes vnto thē purely for very loue & not for felthy lucres fake or to be lord ouer thē as Peter teacheth 1 pet. v. & paule Actes .xx. Befyde this chriſt is oures ād is a gifte geuen vs, & we be heyres of chriſt & of all that is chriſtes Wherfore the preaſtes doctryne is oures & we heires of it, it is ẏ fode of oure foules. Therfore if he miniſtre it not truly ād frely vnto vs with out fellinge, he is a thefe & a foule murtherar: ād euen fo is he if he take vppon him to fede vs & haue not wherewith. And for a like conclufyon becaufe we alfo with all that we haue be chriſtes, therfore is the preaſt heyre with vs alfo of all that we haue receaued of god, wherfore in as moch as ẏ preaſt wayteth on ẏ worde of god ād is oure feruaunte therin, therfore of right we are his dettars & owe him a fufficyent lyuinge of oure goodes, ād euen therto a wiffe of oure doughters owe we vnto him if he requyre her. And now when we haue appoynted him

a sufficiēt liuinge, whether in tythes rentes or in yere-
lye wages, he ought to be cōtent & to require no more
nor yet to receaue any more, but to be an enſample
of ſoberneſſe & of diſpyſinge worldly thinges vnto the
en- .P. ſample of his paryſheonars.

Wilt thou vowe to offre vnto ẏ poore people? that
is pleaſaunte in ẏ ſight of god, for they be lefte here
to do oure almes apō in chriſtes ſtead & they be ẏ
right heyres of all oure abundaūce & ouerplus. Moreouer we muſt haue a ſcole to teach goddes worde ī
(though it neded not to be ſo coſtely) & therfore it is
lawfull to vowe vnto the buyldynge or mayntenaūce
therof & vnto helpinge of all good werkes. And we
ought to vowe to paye cuſtome, tolle, rent & all maner
dutyes and what ſoeuer we owe: for that is gods
commaundmēt.

Yf thou wilt vowe pilgrimage, thou muſt put ſalt
therto in like maner if it ſhalbe accepted, if thou vowe
to go ād viſet the poore or to here gods worde or
what ſoeuer edifieth thy ſoule vnto loue & good worke
after knowlege or what ſoeuer god cōmaūdeth, it is
well done and a ſacrifyce that fauoreth well ye will
happlye ſaye, that ye will go to this or ẏ place becauſe
god hath choſen one place more then a nother and
will heare youre peticyon more in one place then a
nother. As for youre prayer it muſt be accordīge to
goddes worde. Ye may not deſyer god to take vēgeaunce on him whō goddes worde teacheth you to
pytye & to praye for. And as for ẏ other gloſe, ẏ god
will heare you more ī one place thē in a nother, I ſuppoſe it ſal infatuatum, ſalt vnſauerye, for if it were wiſdome how coude .P. we excuſe the deeth of ſteuē Acts
vii. which dyed for ẏ article that god dwelleth not in
tēples made with hādes we that beleue in god are ẏ
temple of god ſayth paule, if a man loue god & kepe
his worde he is the tēple of god & hath god preſently
dwellinge in him, as witneſſeth chriſt Iohan .xiiii. ſayēge: If a mā loue me he will kepe my worde, & thē my
father will loue him & we will come vnto him and
dwell with him. And in the .xv. he ſayth: if ye abyde
in me and my wordes alſo abyde in you, then axe what

ye will & ye fhall haue it. If thou beleue in chrift &
haft the promyfes which god hath made the in thyne
harte, thē go on pilgrymage vnto thyne awne harte ād
there praye & god will heare ẏ for his mercy and
5 truthes fake and for his fonne chriftes fake and not for
a few ftones fakes. What careth god for the temple?
The very beeftes in that they haue liffe in them be
moch better then an hepe of ftonnes couched to
gether.

10 To fpeake of chaftite, it is a gifte not geuen vnto
all perfones teftifyeth both chrift and alfo his apoftle
Paule, wherfore all perfones maye not vowe it. Moreouer there be caufes wherfore many perfones maye better lyue chaft at one tyme then at a nother. Many
15 maye lyue chaft at twentye and thirtye for certayne
colde difeafes folowinge them, which at .xl. when their
helth is come can not do fo. Many be occupyed with
wylde .P. phantafyes in their youth ẏ they care not for
mariage which fame when they be waxē fad fhalbe
20 greatly defyroufe, yt is a daungerous thynge to make
fynne where none is ād to forfwere ẏ benefyte of god
& to bynde thy felf vnder payne of dānacyon of thy
foule that thou woldeft not vfe the remeadye that god
hath created if nead requyred. ¶ A nother thinge
25 is this, beware that thou gett the not a falfe fayned
chaftite made with ẏ vngodly perfwafions of faynte Hierō
or of Ouide in his fylthye boke of the remedye agenft
loue, left when thorow foch imaginacyons thou haft
vtterlye defpyfed, defyed ād abhorred all woman
30 kynde, thou come in to foch cafe thorow the fierce
wrath of god, ẏ thou canft nether lyue chaft nor
fynde in thy harte to marye ād fo be cōpelled to
faule into the abhominacion of the pope agenft nature
and kynde.

35 Moreouer god is a wyfe father & knoweth all ẏ infirmityes of his children & alfo mercyfull, ād therfore
hath created a remedye without fynne ād geuen therto his fauoure and bleffinge.

Let vs not be wyfer then god with oure ymagina-
40 cyōs nor tēpte him, for as godly chaftite is not euery
mās gyfte: euen fo he ẏ hath it to daye hath not

power to continue it at his awne pleafure, nether hath
god promyfed to geue it him ftill & to cure his infirm-
ytyes with out his naturall remeadye no more then he
hath promyfed to flake his hongre .P. with out meate
or thirft with out drinke.

Wherfore other let all thinges byde fre as wife god
hath created them & nother vowe that which god
requyreth not nor forfwere that which god permitteth
the with his fauoure and bleffinge alfo: or els if thou
wilt neades vowe, then vowe godly & vnder a cōdityon,
ẏ thou wilt contynue chaft, fo longe as god geueth the
ẏ gyfte ād as longe as nether thyne awne neceffyte
nether cheryte toward thy neighboure nor ẏ authorite
of thē vnder whofe power thou arte dryue ẏ vnto the
contrarye.

The purpoffe of thy vowe muft be falted alfo with
ẏ wifdom of god. Thou mayeft not vowe to be iuftefyed
therbye or to make fatiffaction for thy fynnes or to
wynne heauē nor an hyer place: for then dideft thou
wrōge vnto the bloude of chrift & thy vowe were
playne Idolatrye & abhominable in ẏ fight of god.
Thy vowe muft be only vnto ẏ furtheraunce of ẏ commaūdmētes of god, which are as I haue fayde nothinge
but ẏ taminge of thy mēbres & the feruice of thy neyghboure: that is if thou thyncke thy backe to weake for
the burthen of wedlocke & ẏ thou canft not rule thy
wiff, children feruaūtes and make prouifion for thē
godlye & with out ouermoch bufyenge and vnquyet-
ynge thy felf ād drounynge thy felf in worldly bufy-
neffe vnchriftenlye or that thou canft ferue thy
neyghboure in fome office better beynge chaft then
maryed. And then .P. thy vowe is good & lawfull.
And euē fo muft thou vowe abftinēce of meates &
drynkes fo far forth as it is profitable vnto thy neyghbours & vnto ẏ tamīge of thy flefh: But thou mayft
vowe nether of them vnto ẏ fleynge of thy bodye. As
Paule cōmaūdeth tymothe to drincke wyne & no moare
water becaufe of his difeafes. Thou wilt faye ẏ timo-
thy had not happlye forfworne wyne. I thinke the
fame and that the apoftles forfware not wedlocke
though many of them lyued chaft nother yet any

meate or drincke, though they abſteyned from thē, &
that it were good for vs to folow their enſample. How
be it though I vowe & ſwere ād thynke on none ex-
ceptyon, yet is the breakynge of gods cōmaūdmētes
5 except & all chaunces that hāge of god. As if I ſwere
to be in a certayne place at a certayne houre to make
a louedaye with out exception, yet if the kinge in the
meane tyme commaunde me a nother waye, I muſt
goo by gods commaūdment ād yet breake not myne
10 othe. And in like caſe if my father and mother be
ſeke and requyre my preſence, or if my wiff, children
or houſhold be viſited that my aſſiſtence be requyred,
or if my neyghbours houſe be a fyre at the ſame houre
and a thouſand ſoch chaunces: in which all I breake
15 myne oth and am not forſworne and ſo forth. Read
gods word diligently and with a good herte and it
ſhall teach the all thynges.

The four
the boke of Mofes called

Numeri.

I. Chapter. [Fo. II.]

¶ THE .IIII. BOKE
OF MOSES, CALLED NUMERI.

1 AND the Lorde fpake vnto Mo- *M.C.S. All*
fes in the wilderneffe of Sinai, *that are apte*
in the tabernacle of witneffe, *for batell are*
the fyrſt daye of the feconde *nombred. The*
moneth, ād in the feconde yere after they *trybe of Leuy*
were come out of y̆ londe of Egipte fay- *is appoynted*
2 enge: take ye the fumme of al the multi- *to myniſtre to*
tude of the childern of Ifrael, in their kynredes and *the taberna-*
houſholdes of their fathers and numbre thē by name *cle.*
3 all that are males, polle by polle, frō .xx. yere &
aboue: euen all y̆ are able to goo forthe in to warre
in Ifraell, thou & Aarō ſhall nūbre thē in their armies,
4 & with you ſhalbe of euery trybe a heed man in the
houſe of his father.
5 And thefe are the names of y̆ mē y̆ ſhall ſtōde with
6 you: in Rubē, Elizur y̆ fonne of Sedeur: In Simeō,
7 Selumiel y̆ fonne of Suri Sadai: In y̆ tribe of Iuda,
8 Naheſſon y̆ fonne of Aminadab: In Iſachar, Nathaneel
9 y̆ fonne of Zuar: In Sebulō, Eliab y̆ fonne of Helō.
10 Amōge y̆ childern of Iofeph: In Ephraī, Elifama y̆
fonne of Amihud: In Manaſſe, Gamaliel y̆ fōne of Peda
11, 12 zur: In Bē Iamin, Abidan the fonne of Gedeoni: In
13 Dan, Ahiefer the fonne of Ammi Sadai: In Aſſer,
14 Pagiel the fonne of Ochran: In Gad, Eliafaph the fōne
15 of Deguel: In Naphtaly, Ahira the fonne of Enan.

M. 5 ſtande ... of Ruben 6 of Simeon 7 of .. of Iuda 8 of
Iſachar 9 of Zabulon 10 of Ephraim .. of Manaſſe 11 of Ben Ia-
min 12 of Dan 13 of Aſer 15 of Nephthali
V. 1 tabernaculo fœderis 2 quicquid fexus eſt mafculini ...
3 omnium virorum fortium 13 Phegiel filius Ochran.
L. 2 heufer, bey der zal der namen ... von heubt zu heubt
M. M. N. 13 or Phegiel

16 .¶. These were councelers of the congregacion and lordes in the trybes of their fathers & captaynes ouer
17 thousandes in Israel. And Moses and Aaron toke
18 these men aboue named and gathered all the congregacion together, the fyrst daye of the seconde moneth, and rekened them after their byrth & kinredes and houses of their fathers by name frō .xx. yere & aboue
19 hed by hed: as the Lorde cōmaunded Moses, euē so he numbred them in ẏ wildernesse of Sinai.
20 And the childern of Ruben Israels eldest sonne in their generacions, kynredes ād houses of their fathers, whē they were numbred euery man by name, all that were males frō .xx. yere and aboue, as many
21 as were able to goo forth in warre: were numbred in the trybe off Ruben, .xlvi. thousande and fiue hundred.
22 Among the childern of Simeon: their generaciō in their kynredes and housses of their fathers (when euery mans name was tolde) of all the males from .xx yeres and aboue, whatsoeuer was mete for the warre:
23 were numbred in the trybe of Simeon .Lix. thousande and .iii. hundred.
24 Amonge the childern of Gad: their generacion in their kynredes and housholdes of their fathers, when thei were tolde by name, frō .xx. yere and aboue, all
25 that were mete for the warre: were numbred in the tribe of Gad .xlv. [Fo. III.] thousande, sixe hundred and fyftie.
26 Amonge the childern of Iuda: their generacion in their kinredes and housses of their fathers (by the numbre of names) from .xx. yere and aboue, all that
27 were able to warre, were tolde in the trybe of Iuda Lxxiiii. thousande and sixe hundred.
28 Amonge the childern of Isachar: their generacion,

V. 18 recēsentes eos 19 Numeratique sunt in deserto Sinai. 20 de Ruben . . procedentiū ad bellum 24 omnes qui ad bella procederent 26 poterant ad bella procedere (so of Iuda, Issachar, Zabulon, Ephraim, Manasse, Benjamin, Dan, Aser and Nephtali, and 45.)

L. 16 die namhafftigen der gemeyne . . heubter vnd fursten 20 Ruben . . . yns heer zu zihen tuchte 24 Gad . . tuchtig war 26 Iuda . . yns heer zu zihen tuchte (so vv. 20, 24, 28, 30, 32, 34, 36, 38.)

M. M. N. 20 Of Ruben 22 Of Simeon 24 Of Gad 26 Of Iuda 28 Of Isachar

in their kinredes and houfes of their fathers (when
their names were counted) from .xx. yere ād aboue,
29 what foeuer was apte for warre: were numbred in ẙ
trybe of Ifachar .Liiii. thoufande and .iiii. hundred.

30 Among the childern of Sebulon: their generacion,
in their kynredes and houfes of their fathers (after the
numbre of names) from .xx. yere and aboue, whofo-
31 euer was mete for the warre: were counted in ẙ trybe
of Sebulō .Lvii. thoufande and .iiii. hundred.

32 Amonge the childern of Iofeph: fyrft amōge the
childern of Ephraim: their generacion, in their kynredes and houffes of theyre fathers (when the names
of all that were apte to the warre were tolde) from .xx
33 yeres and aboue: were in numbre in the trybe off
Ephraim, .xl. thoufande and fyxe hundred.

34 Amonge the childern of Manaffe: their generacion,
in their kynredes and houfes of their fathers (when
the names of all ẙ were apte to warre were tolde) from
35 xx. and aboue .Ῥ. were numbred in the tribe of Manaffe .xxxii. thoufand and two hundred.

36 Amonge the childern of Ben Iamin: their generacion, in their kynredes and houffes of their fathers
(by the tale of names) from twentye yere   tale, *number*,
and aboue of all that were mete for warre,   cf. German
                                                           Zahl
37 were numbred in the trybe off Ben Iamin .xxxv. thoufande and .iiii. hundred.

38 Amonge the childern of Dan: their generacion in
theyr kynreddes and houffes off their fathers (in the
fumme of names) off all that was apte to warre from
39 twentye yere and aboue, were numbred in the trybe
of Dan .Lxii. thoufande and .vii. hundred.

40 Amonge the childern of Afer: their generacyon, in
their kynredes & houfes of their fathers (when thei
were fummed by name) from .xx. yeres & aboue, all
41 that were apte to warre were numbred in the tribe
of Afer .xli. thoufande and .v. hundred.

42 Amōge the childern of Nepthali: their generacion,

L. 40 Affer ... yns heer zihen mochte (fo vv. 42, 45.)
ff. ff. N. 30 Of Zabulon 32 Of Iofeph 34 Of Manaffes 36 Of
Bē Iamin. 38 Of Dan 40 Of Afer 42 Of Nephtali

in their kynredes & houſſes of their fathers (when their names were tolde) from .xx. yeres ād aboue, what ſo-
43 euer was mete to warre: were numbred in the trybe of Nephtali .Liii. thouſande and .iiii. hundred.

44 Theſe are the numbres which Moſes ād Aarō numbred with ẏ .xii. princes of Iſrael: of euery houſſe of
45 their fathers a man. And all the numbres of the childern of Iſrael, in [Fo. IIII.] the houſſes of their fathers, from twentye yere and aboue, what ſoeuer was
46 mete for the warre in Iſraell, drewe vnto the ſumme
47 of ſyxe hundred thouſande, fyue hundred and .L. But the leuites in the tribe off their fathers were not numbred amonge them.

48, 49 And the Lorde ſpake vnto Moſes ſayenge: only ſe that thou numbre not the trybe of Leui, nether take the ſumme of them amonge the childern of Iſrael.
50 But thou ſhalt appoynte the leuites vnto the habitaciō of witneſſe, and to all the apparell thereof and vnto all that longeth thereto. For they ſhall bere the tabernacle and all the ordinaunce thereof, and they ſhall miniſtre it and ſhall *longeth, belongeth, vi, 15*
51 pitche their tentes rounde aboute it. And when the tabernacle goeth forth the leuites ſhall take it doune: and when the tabernacle is pitched, they ſhall ſett it vpp: for yf any ſtraunger come nere, he ſhall dye.
52 And the childern of Iſrael ſhall pitch their tentes, euery man in his owne companye and euery mā by his awne ſtandert thorow out all their hoſtes.
53 But the leuites ſhall pitche rounde aboute the habitacion of witneſſe, that there fall no wrath vpon the congregacion of the childrē of Iſrael, and the leuites
54 ſhall wayte apon the habitacion of witneſſe. And the childern of Iſrael dyd acordinge to all that the Lord commaunded Moſes.

M. 43 thrye and fyſtye 46 ſyxe hundred and thre thouſande
V. 46 ſexcēta tria millia virorum quingenti quinquaginta. 50 vaſa eius, & quicquid ad ceremonias pertinet. 52 per turmas & cuneos atque exercitū ſuum. 53 ne fiat indignatio . . & excubabunt in cuſtodiis tabern.
L. 50 wonung des zeugnis 53 Leuiten der hutt wartten an der wonung des zeugnis.

¶. ℂ The .II. Chapter.

1 AND the Lorde spake vnto Moses and Aaron sayenge: The
2 childern of Israel shall pitch: euery man by his owne standert with the armes of their fathers houses, a waye, *away* a waye from the presence of the tabernacle of witnesse,
3 On the east syde towarde the rysynge of ⟨the⟩ sonne, shall they of the standert of the hoste of Iuda pitch with their armes: And Nahesson the sonne of Aminadab shalbe captaine ouer the
4 sonnes of Iuda. And his hoste and the numbre of them
5 Lxxiiii. thousande and .vi. hundred. And nexte vnto him shall the trybe of Isachar pitche and Nathaneel the
6 sonne of Zuar captayne ouer ⟨the⟩ childrē of Isachar: his hoste and the numbre of them .Liiii. thousande and
7 iiii. hundred. And than the trybe of Zabulon: with Eliab the sonne of Helon, captayne ouer the childern
8 of Zabulon, and his hoste in the numbre of them: .Lvii
9 thousande and .iiii. hundred. So that all they that perteyne vnto the host of Iuda, are an hundred thousande Lxxxvi. thousande ād .iiii. hundred in their companies: and these shall goo in the forefront, wen they iurney.
10 And on the southsyde, the standert of the hoste of Ruben shall lye with their companyes and the captayne ouer the sonnes of Ruben, Elizur the sonne of Sedeur,
11 and his hoste and the numbre of them .xlvi. thousande,
12 [Fo. V.] and .v. hundred. And fast by him shall ⟨the⟩ trybe of Simeon pitche, and the capteyne ouer ⟨the⟩ sonnes

M.C.S. The order of the pytchyng of the tentes rounde aboute the tabernacle of wytnesse. The heades and chefe Lordes of the kynredes of Israel are named.

𝒱. 2 per turmas, signa atque vexilla 3 Iudas . . per turmas exercitus sui 4 summa pugnantium 5 Issachar 6 numerus pugnatorum 7 Zabulon 8 exercitus pugnatorum 10 Ruben 11 & cūctus exercitus pugnatorum

ℒ. 2 panir vnd zeychen nach yhrer veter haus 9 Iuda . . . heer, (and so throughout the chapter)

M. M. N. 3 On the east syde the cōpanye of Iuda, Isachar & Zabulon. 10 On the southsyde the companye of Ruben, Simeō & Gad.

13 of Simeon. Selumiel the fonne of zuri Sadai, & his hofte and the nūbre of them .Lix. thoufande and .iii. hundred
14 And the trybe of Gad alfo: And the captayne ouer the
15 fonnes of Gad, Eliafaph the fonne of Deguel and his hofte and the numbre of them .xlv. thoufande .vi. hun-
16 dred and .L. So that all $\cancel{y}$ numbre that pertayne vnto the hofte of Ruben, are an hundred thoufande .Li thoufande .iiii. hundred & fyftie, with their companyes, and they fhall be the feconde in the iourney
17 And the tabernacle of witneffe with the hofte of the leuites, fhall goo in the myddes of $\cancel{y}$ hoftes: as they lye in their tētes, euen fo fhall they procede in the iurney, euery man in his quarter aboute their ftandertes.
18 On the weft fyde, the ftandarte and the hofte of Ephraim fhall lye with their companies. And the captayne ouer the fonnes of Ephraim, Elifama the
19 fonne of Amihud: & his hofte and the numbre of them
20 xl. thoufande & .v. hundred. And faft faft by, *clofe to* by him, the trybe of Manaffe, and the captayne ouer the fonnes of Manaffe, Gamaleel $\cancel{y}$ fonne of Peda zur
21 and his hofte and the numbre of them .xxxii. thoufande
22 and .ii. hundred. And the trybe of Ben Iamin alfo: and the captayne ouer the fonnes of Ben Iamin, Abidan
23 the fonne of Gedeoni, ād his hofte and the numbre of
24 thē .P. xxxv. thoufande and .iiii. hundred. All the nūbre that perteyned vnto the hofte of Ephraim, were an hundred thoufand .viii. thoufande and an hundred in their hoftes: and they fhalbe the thryde in the iurneye
25 And the ftandert and the hofte of Dan fhall lye on the north fyde with their companyes: & the captayne ouer $\cancel{y}$ childrē of Dan, Ahiezer the fonne of Ammi
26 Sadai: and his hofte and the nūbre of them .Lxii. thou-

V. 12 Simeon 13 & cunctus exercitus pugnat. (so 15, 19, 21, 23, 26, 28, 30) 16 Omnes qui recēfiti funt 17 Leuabitur autē tabernac. teftim. per officia leuitarum & turmas eorum. quomodo erigetur, ita et deponetur. 24 caftris Ephraim ... per turmas fuas
L. 18 Gezelt vnd panier Ephraim
M. M. N. 17 The leuytes with the tabernacle in the myddes. 18 On the weft fyde the cōpany of Ephraim Manaffe and Ben Iamin 25 On the north fyde the company of Dan, Affer and Nephthali.

27 fande & .vii. hundred. And faſt by him ſhall the trybe of Aſſer pitche: and the captayne ouer the ſones of
28 Aſſer, Pagiel the ſonne of Ochran: & his hoſte & the
29 nūbre of them .xli. thouſande & .v. hundred. And the trybe of Naphtali alſo, and the captayne ouer ẏ chil-
30 dern of Naphtali: Ahira the ſonne of Enan: & his hoſte and the nūbre of them .Liii. thouſande & .iiii. hūdred
31 So ẏ the hole nūbre of all that perteyned vnto ẏ hoſte of Dan, was an hūdred thouſande .Lvii. thouſande & vi. hūdred. And they ſhalbe the laſt in ẏ iurney with their ſtādertes.
32 Theſe are ẏ ſūmes of ẏ childern of Yſrael in the houſſes of their fathers: euen all the nūbres of the hoſtes with their cōpanies .vi. hūdred thouſande .iii. thou-
33 ſande .v. hūdred and fyftie. And yet ẏ leuites were not nūbred amōge the childern of Yſrael, as the Lorde
34 commaunded Moſes. And ẏ childern of Yſrael dyd acordynge to all that the Lorde cōmaūded Moſes, & ſo they pitched with their ſtan- [Fo. VI.] dertes, and ſo they iurneyd: euery man in his kynred, and in the houſſholde of his father.

⁋ The .III. Chapter.

1 THESE are the generacions of Aaron and Moſes, when the Lorde ſpake vnto Moſes in
2 Mount Sinai, and theſe are the names of the ſonnes of Aaron: Nadab the eldeſt ſonne, and Abihu Eleazar and
3 Ithamar. Theſe are the names of the ſonnes of Aaron which were preaſtes anoynted and their handes fylled to myn-

M.C.S. The Leuites are not nombred to go to batell, but to myniſtre to the holy place or ſanctuary. They muſt alſo pitch their tentes next to the habyta-cyon.

V. 31 caſtris Dan, fuerunt 32 per domos cognatlonum ſuarum & turmas diuiſi exercitus 34 Caſtrametati ſunt per turmas ſuas, & profecti per familias ac domos patrum ſuorum. iii, 3 vncti ſunt, & quorū repletæ & conſecratæ manus vt ſacerdotio fungerentur.
L. 34 lagerten ſich vnter yhre panier, vnd zogen aus, eyn iglicher ynn ſeynem geſchlecht nach yhrer veter haus. iii, 3 zu prieſter gefalbet .. hende gefullet zum prieſterthum.

4 iſtre but Nadab and Abihu dyed before the Lorde, as they broughte ſtraunge fyre before the Lorde in the wyldernesse of Sinai, and had no childern. And Eleazar and Ithamar myniſtred in the ſyght of Aaron their father.

5, 6 And the Lorde ſpake vnto Moſes ſaynge brynge the trybe of leui, and ſet them before Aaron the preaſt,
7 and let them ſerue him ād wayte apon him, & apon all the multitude, before the tabernacle of witneſſe, to doo
8 the ſeruyce of the habitacion. And they ſhall wayte apō all ẏ apparell of ẏ tabernacle of witneſſe & apon ẏ childern of Yſrael, to doo ẏ ſeruyce of the habitaciō.
9 And thou ſhalt geue the leuites vnto Aaron & his ſonnes, for they are geuen vnto him of ẏ childern of
10 Yſrael. And thou ſhalt appoīte Aarō & his ſonnes to wayte on their preaſtes office: & the ſtraūger ẏ cometh nye, ſhall dye for it.

11, 12 And ẏ Lorde ſpake vnto Moſes ſaynge: beholde, I haue takē the leuites frō amonge ẏ .P. childern of Yſrael, for all the firſtborne that openeth the matryce amonge the childern of Yſrael, ſo that the leuites ſhall
13 be myne: becauſe all the firſt borne are myne: for ẏ ſame daye that I ſmote all the fyrſtborne in the lande of Egipte, I halowed vnto me all the firſtborne in Yſrael, both man and beeſt, and myne they ſhall be: for I am the Lorde.

14 And the Lorde ſpake vnto Moſes in the wildernesse
15 of Sinai ſayenge: Numbre the childern of Leui in ẏ houſſes of their fathers and Kynredes, all ẏ are males
16 from a moneth olde and aboue. And Moſes numbred them at the worde of the Lorde, as he was cōmaūded.
17 And theſe are ẏ names of ẏ childrē of Leui: Gerſon,
18 Cahath, & Merari. And ẏ ſe are the   ẏ ſe, *theſe* names of the childern of Gerſon in their kynredes:

V 6 vt miniſtrēt ei 7 & excubēt & obſeruēt 10 ſuper cultū ſacerdotii. Externus qui ad miniſtrandum acceſſerit

L. 4 hatten keyne ſone. 7 gemeyne hutt wartten 8 hutt der kinder Iſrael zu dienen am dienſt der wonung.

M. M. N. 12 Leuyte ſomtyme ſygnifyeth only a mynyſter or ſeruaunt, as here and Eſa. lxvi, g.

19 Libni and Semei. And the sônes of Cahath in their kynredes were Amram. Iezehar. Hebron and Vſiel.
20 And the ſonnes of Merari in their kynredes were Maheli and Muſi. Theſe are the kynredes of Leui in the houſſes of their fathers.
21 And of Gerſon came the kynred of ẏ Libnites and the Semeites, which are the kynredes of the Gerſonites.
22 And ẏ ſumme of them (when all the males were tolde) from a moneth olde and aboue, were .vii. thouſande and fyue hundred. *tolde, numbered*
23 And the kynredes of the Gerſonites pitched behynde
24 the habitacion weſt warde. And the captayne of the moſt awnciēt [Fo. VII.] houſſe amonge ẏ Gerſonites,
25 was Eliaſaph the ſonne of Lael. And the office of the childern of Gerſon in the tabernacle of witneſſe was the habitacion and the tente with the coueringe theroff and the hangynge of the dore of the tabernacle of
26 witneſſe, and the hangynges of the courte, and the curtayne of the dore of the courte: which courte went rounde aboute the dwellynge, and the alter, and the cordes ẏ perteyned vnto all the ſeruyce therof
27 And of Cahath came the kynred of ẏ Amramites and the kynred of the Iezeharites & of the Hebronites and of the Vſielites: And theſe are the kynredes of ẏ
28 Cahathites. And the numbre of all the males from a moneth olde and aboue, was .viii. thouſande and ſixe
29 hundred: which wayted on ẏ holy place. And the kynred of the childern of Cahath, pitched on ẏ ſouth
30 ſyde of ẏ dwellynge And ẏ captayne in ẏ moſt auncyent houſſe of the kynredes of the Cahathites, was
31 Elizaphan the ſonne of Vſiel, and their office was: the arcke, the table, the candelſticke, and the alter and the holy veſſels to minyſtre with and the vayle with

𝔐. 25 was to kepe the habitacyon 31 was to kepe the arcke
𝔙. 21 De Gerſon fuere familiæ duæ 25 Et habebunt excubias in tab. fœderis 26 quicquid ad ritum altaris pertinet 28 habebunt excubias ſanctuarii 30 Oziel 31 & cuſtodient arcam
𝔏. 25 vnd ſie ſollen warten 31 Heyligthums, daran ſie dienen, vnd des tuchs
𝔐. 𝔐. N. 21 The Gerſonites pitch on the weſt ſyde. 27 The Cahathites are aſſygned to the ſouthſyde.

32 all that ſerued there to. And Eleazar ẏ ſonne of Aaron the preaſt, was captayne ouer all the captaynes of the Leuites, and had the ouer ſyghte of them that wayted vppon the holythynges.

33 And of Merari came the kynredes of the Mahelites and of the Muſites: and theſe .P. are the kynredes
34 of the Merarites. And the nūbre of them (when all the males frō a moneth olde ād aboue was tolde) drewe vnto .vi. thouſande & .ii. hundred.   drewe vnto,
35 And ẏ captayne of the moſt auncient *amounted to* houſſe amonge the kynredes of the Merarites, was Zuriel the ſonne of Abihail which pitched on the north
36 ſyde of the dwellynge. And the office of the ſonnes of Merari was: the bordes of ẏ dwellynge & the barres, pilers with the ſokettes thereof, and all the inſtrumētes
37 there of & all that ſerued thereto: & the pilers of the courte rounde aboute and their ſokettes, with their
38 pynnes & cordes. But on ẏ fore front of ẏ habitaciō ād before the tabernacle of witneſſe eaſt warde, ſhall Moſes and Aaron & his ſonnes pytch and wayte on the ſanctuary in the ſteade of ẏ childern of Yſrael. And the
39 ſtraunger ẏ cometh nye, ſhall dye for it. And the hole ſumme of the leuites which Moſes & Aaron nūbred, at ẏ cōmaūdmēt of ẏ Lorde thorow out their kynredes euen, of all ẏ males of a moneth olde & aboue, was xxii. thouſande.

40 And the Lorde ſayde vnto Moſes: Numbre all ẏ firſt borne that are males amōge the childern of Yſrael, frō a moneth olde & aboue and take ẏ numbre of their
41 names. And thou ſhalt appoynte ẏ leuites to me the Lorde, for all the firſtborne amōge ẏ childern of Yſrael and the catell of ẏ leuites for the firſtborne of the
42 childern of Yſrael. And Moſes nūbred [Fo. VIII.] as ẏ Lorde cōmaūded him, all the firſtborne of ẏ chil-

   M̃.   36 was to kepe ẏ bordes
   V. 32 erit ſuper excubitores cuſtodiæ ſanctuarii. 36 Erunt ſub cuſtodia eorum tabulæ 38 habentes cuſtod. ſanctuarii in medio filiorum Iſrael. 42 Recenſuit Moyſes
   L.   32 Eleaſar . . . vber die verordnet ſind zu wartten
   M̃. M̃. N.   33 The Merarites aſſygned on the north ſyde. 38 Moſes & Aaron & their ſonnes on the eaſt ſide. 39 kynredes, euen

43 dern of Yfrael. And all the firftborne males, in ў fumme of names, from a moneth olde and aboue, were numbred .xxii. thoufande .ii. hundred and .Lxxiii.

44, 45 And the Lorde fpake vnto Mofes fayenge: take the leuites for all the fyrftborne of the childern of Ifrael, ād the catell of the leuites for their catell: & the
46 leuites fhalbe myne whiche am the Lorde. And for the redemynge of the two hundred and .Lxxiii. whiche are moo than the leuites in the firftborne of the chil-
47 dren of Ifrael, take .v. fycles of euery pece, after the
48 fycle of ў holy place .xx. geras the fycle. And geue ў money wherewith the odde numbre of them is re-
49 demed, vnto Aaron ād his fonnes. And Mofes toke the redempciō money of the ouerplus that were moo
50 then the leuites, amonge the firftborne of the childern of Ifrael: & it came to a thoufande .iii. hundred &
51 Lxv. fycles, of the holye fycle. And he gaue that redempcionmoney vnto Aaron & his fonnes at the worde of the Lorde, euen as the Lorde commaunded Mofes.

¶ The .IIII. Chapter.

1 AND ў Lord fpake vnto Mofes &
2 Aarō & bade thē take ў fumme of ў childern of Cahath frō amonge ў fonnes of leui, in their kynredes and houffes of their fathers,

M.C.S. The offyces of the Leuytes, euery one after the flocke that he came of.

3 from .xxx. yere and aboue vntill fyftie, all that were able to warre, for to doo the worke in .P. the tabernacle
4, 5 of witneffe: euen in the moft holy place. And when

M. iiii, 4 witneffe. [Tyndale omits the following clause] This fhalbe the office of the chyldrē of Kahath in the tabernacle of witneffe which is mooft holy.
V. 47 viginti obolos. iiii, 3 qui ingrediūtur vt ftent & miniftrēt 4 Hic eft cultus filiorū Caath
L. 46 vberlengen erften gepurten ... vber der Leuiten zal 48 daffelb gelt, das vberleng ift vber yhre zal 49 Lofegelt das vberlenge war. iiii, 3 alle die yns heer tugen, das fie thun die werck ynn der hutten des zeugnis

ỹ hoſte remoueth, Aaron ãd his ſonnes ſhall come and take doune the vayle and couer the arcke of witneſſe
6 there with, and ſhall put there on a coueryṅge of taxus ſkynnes, and ſhall ſprede a cloth ỹ is altogether of Iacyncte aboue all, and put the ſtaues thereof in.
7 And apon the ſhewe table, they ſhall ſprede a cloth of Iacyncte, and put thereō, the diſhes, ſpones, flat peces and pottes to poure with, and the dayly bred
8 ſhal be thereon: and they ſhall ſpred apon them a coueryṅge of purple, and couer the ſame with a coueryṅge of taxus ſkynnes, and put the ſtaues thereof in.
9 And they ſhall take a cloth of Iacyncte & couer the candelſticke of light and hir lãpes and hir ſnoffers and fyre pannes and all hir oyle veſſels which they
10 occupye aboute it, & ſhall put apon her and on all hir inſtrumentes, a coueryṅge of taxus ſkynnes, and put
11 it apon ſtaues. And apon the golden alter they ſhall ſprede a cloth of Iacyncte, and put on hir ſtaues.
12 And they ſhall take all the thiges which they occupye to minyſtre with in ỹ holy place, & put a cloth of Iacyncte apon them and couer them with a coueryṅge of taxus ſkynnes and put them on ſtaues.
13 And they ſhall take a waye the aſſhes out of the alter,
14 and ſprede a ſcarlet cloth thereon: & put aboute it, the fyre pannes, the fleſh hokes, the ſho- [Fo. IX.] uels, the baſens, and all that belongeth vnto the alter, and they ſhall ſprede apon it a coueryṅg of taxus ſkynnes and put on the ſtaues of it
15 And when Aaron and his ſonnes haue made an ende of coueryṅge the ſanctuary ãd all the thinges of the ſanctuarye, agenſt that the hoſte remoue, then the ſonnes of Cahath ſhall come in for to bere,

V. 6 velamine hyacinthinarum pellium . . . pallium totum hyacinthinum 7 hyac. pallio. . . panes ſemper in ea erunt 8 pallium coccineum . . velamento hyac. pellium 10 operimentum hyac. pellium, & inducent 11 inuoluent hyac. veſtimento & ext. deſuper oper. hyac. pellium 12 ſanctuario inuoluent hyac. pallio . . oper. hyac. pellium 13 altare . . . purpureo veſtimento 14 ſimul vel. hyac. pellium

L. 6 dachs fellen [ſo throughout the chapter where Tyndale renders *taxus ſkynnes*] 7 ſchawtiſch auch eyn gel kleyd [ſo throughout the chapter where Tyndale renders *Iacyncte*]

and fo let them not twich the fanctuary left they
dye. And this ys the charge of the fonnes of Ca-
16 hath in the tabernacle of witneffe. And Eleazar
the fonne of Aaron the preaft, fhall haue the charge
to prepare oyle for the lightes and fwete cens, & the
dayly meatofferynge and the anoyntinge oyle, and
the ouerfyghte of all the dwellynge and of all that
therein is: both ouer the fanctuary & ouer all that pertayneth thereto.
17 And the Lorde fpake vnto Mofes & Aaron fayenge:
18 deftroye not the trybe of the kynredes of the Cahathites,
19 from amonge the leuites. But thus doo vnto them that
they maye lyve and not dye, whē they goo vnto ẙ
moft holy place. Aaron and his fonnés fhall goo in
and put them, euery man vnto his feruyce and vnto
20 his burthen. But let them not goo in to fe when they
couer the fanctuarye, left they dye.
21, 22 And the Lorde fpake vnto Mofes fayenge Take
the fumme of the childern of Gerfon, in the houfes of
23 their fathers ād in their kyn- .℞. redes: from .xxx. yere
and aboue, vntyll .L. all that are able to goo forth in
warre, for to doo feruyce in the tabernacle of witneffe.
24 And this is the feruyce of the kynred of the Gerfonites,
25 to ferue and to beare. They fhall bere the curtaynes
of the dwellynge and the roffe of ẙ tabernacle of witneffe and his couerynge ād the coueryng of taxus
fkynnes that is an hye aboue apon it, and an hye, *on high*
the hangynge of the dore of the tabernacle of witneffe:
26 and the hanginge of the courte and the hangynge of
the gate of the courte that is rounde aboute the dwellynge and the altare, and the cordes of them, and all
the inftrumentes that ferue vnto them and all that is

℣. 15 filii Caath vt portent inuoluta .. onera filior. Caa. in tabernaculo fœderis, 16 fuper quos erit Eleazar . . facrificium quod femper offertur 18 Nolite perdere 20 Alii nulla curiofitate videāt quæ funt in fanctuario priufquam inuoluantur 22 Tolle fummam etiam fil. Gerfon. 23 Numera omnes qui ingred. et miniftr. in tab. fœderis. 25 & tectum fœd. operimentum aliud ... velamen hyac.
ℒ. 16 das tegliche fpeyfopffer 18 nicht verderben vnter den Leuiten 20 zu fchawen vnbedacht das Heyligthum 22 Gerfon 23 zum heer tuchtig

27 made for them. And at the mouth of Aaron and his ſonnes, ſhall all the ſeruyce of the childern of the Gerſonites be done, in all their charges and in all their ſeruyce, and ye ſhall appoynte them vnto al their charges
28 that they ſhall wayte apō. And this is the ſeruyce of the kynred of the children of the Gerſonites in ẏ tabernacle of witneſſe, and their wayte ſhalbe in the honde of Ithamar the ſonne of Aaron the preaſt.

<small>wayte, *watch*, *ſervice, charge* cf. Germ. *Hut*</small>

29 And thou ſhalt numbre the ſonnes of Merari in their
30 kynredes and in the houſes of their fathers, from .xxx yeres and aboue vnto .L. All that is able to goo forth in warre, to doo the ſeruyce of the tabernacle of witneſſe.
31 And this is the charge that they muſt way- [Fo. X.] te vppon in all that they muſt ſerue in the tabernacle of witneſſe: The bordes of the dwellynge, and the
32 barres, pylers, and ſokettes thereof, and the pylers of the courte rounde aboute, and their ſokettes, pynnes and cordes with all that pertayneth and ſerueth vnto them. And by name ye ſhall reken the thynges that
33 they muſt wayte apon to bere. Thys is the ſeruyce ot the kynreddes of the ſonnes of Merari in all theyr ſeruyce in the tabernacle of witneſſe by the hande of Ithamar the ſonne of Aaron the preaſt.
34 And Moſes and Aaron and the princes of the multitude numbred the ſonnes of the Cahathites in their
35 kynredes and houſſes of theire fathers, from .xxx. yere and aboue vnto fyſtie, all that were able to goo forth in the hoſte and to do ſeruyce in the tabernacle of witneſſe.
36 And the numbre of them in their kynredes were two
37 thouſande, ſeuen hundred and .L. Theſe are the numbres of the kynredes of the Cahathites, of all that dyd ſeruyce in the tabernacle of witneſſe, whyche Moſes and

V. 27 et ſcient ſinguli cui debeant oneri mancipari. 28 eruntque ſub manu Ithamar 29 Merari . . . recenſebis 30 omnes qui ingred. ad officium miniſterii ſui & cultū fœd. teſtimonii. 31 Hæc ſunt onera eorū 31 Portabunt 32 ad numerum accipient 35 omnes qui ingred. ad min. tab. fœd.

L. 29 Merari 30 alle die yns heer tugen 32 ſeyn teyl der laſt am gered zu warten 34 Kahathither 35 alle die yns heer tuchten

Aaron dyd numbre at the commaundment of the Lorde of by the hāde of Mofes.

38 And the fonnes of Gerfon were numbred in their
39 kynredes and in the houffes of their fathers, from .xxx. yere vp vnto fyftye, .P. all that were able to goo forth in the hofte for to doo feruyce in the tabernacle of wit-
40 neffe. And the numbre of them in their kynredes, and in the houffes of their fathers, was two thoufande, fixe
41 hundred and .xxx. This is the numbre of the kynredes of the fonnes of Gerfon, of all that dyd feruyce in the tabernacle of witneffe, which Mofes and Aaron dyd numbre at the commaundement of the Lorde.
42 And the kynredes of the fonnes of Merari were numbred in their kynredes and in the houfes of their
43 fathers, from .xxx. yere vp vnto fyftie. all that were able to goo forth with the hofte, to doo feruice in ẏ
44 tabernacle of witneffe. And the numbre of them was in theyr kynredes, thre thoufande and two hundred.
45 This is the numbre of the kynredes of ẏ fonnes of Merari, whiche Mofes and Aaron numbred at the byddynge of the Lorde, by ẏ hande of Mofes.
46 The whole fumme which Mofes, Aaron and the lordes of Ifraell numbred amonge the leuites in their
47 kynredes and houfholdes of their fathers, from .xxx. yere vpp vnto .L. euery man to doo his office and feruyce and to bere his burthen in the tabernacle of wit-
48 neffe: was .viii. thoufande, fyue hundred ād .Lxxx
49 which they numbred at the commaundement of the Lorde by the honde of Mofes euery man vnto his feruyce and burthen: as [Fo. XI.] the Lorde commaunded Mofes.

V. 38 Gerfon 39 omnes qui ingred. vt min. in tab. fœd. 41 populus Gerfonitarum 42 Merari 43 omnes qui ingred. ad explēdos ritus tab. fœd. 47 ingredientes ad minifterium tabernaculi & onera portanda
L. 38 Gerfon 39 alle die yns heer tuchten 42 Merari 43 alle die yns heer tuchten 49 zu feynem ampt vnd laft

❡ The . fyfte Chapter.

1 AND the Lorde ſpake vnto Moſes
2 ſayenge: commaunde the childern of Iſrael that they put
out of the hoſte, all the lepers
and all that haue yſſues and all that are
3 defyled apon the deed, whether they be
males or females ye ſhall put them out
of the hoſte, that they defyle not the tentes
4 amöge which I dwell. And the childern
of Iſrael dyd ſo, and put them out of the hoſte: euen as the
Lorde cömaunded Moſes, ſo dyd the childern of Iſrael.
5, 6 And the Lorde ſpake vnto Moſes ſayenge: ſpeake
vnto the childern of Iſrael: whether it be man or
woman, whē they haue ſynned any maner of ſynne
which a man doeth wherewith a man treſpaſeth agenſt
the Lorde, ſo that the ſoule hath done amyſſe:
7 then they ſhall knowlege their ſynnes
which they haue done, and reſtore a gayne
the hurte that they haue done in the hole,
and put the fyfte parte of it moare there-
8 to, and geue it vnto him whom he hath
treſpaſed agenſte. But and yf he that
maketh the amendes haue no man to
doo it to, then the amendes that is
made ſhalbe the Lordes and the preaſtes,
beſyde the ram of the attonementoffer-
ynge where with he maketh an attonemēt
9 for hymſelfe .P. And all heueofferynges
of all the halowed thinges which the childern of

M.C.S. Who they be that ought to be caſt out of the hoſte. The knowlegynge of ſynne. The cleanſyng of ſynne done of ignoraunce. The laweofthe fyrſt frutes & of gelouſye.

knowlege, acknowledge, confeſs

in the hole, in the whole, i. e. the principal

Yf ye haue falſe gotten goodes & no mā to reſtore it vnto, then bringe it vnto ƿ pope ād he will diſpēce with it.

M. 3 amöge which ye dwell.
V. 2 leproſum, & qui femine fluit 3 cum habitauerint vobiſ-
cum. 8 excepto ariete 9 Omnes quoque primitiæ
L. 2 alle die eytter fluſſe haben 3 darynnen ich vnter yhnen
wone 6 hat die ſeel eyn ſchuld auff yhr 7 verſunen mit der ſumma
8 prieſter, ausgenomen den widder
M. M. N. 6 This text is to be vnderſtāded of ſoche treſpaces,
wherwith we hurt oure neybours in worldly goodes (as they cal
thē) & therfore muſt the hurt be reſtored and the fyſth parte
moare therto: If the partye remayned not to whom the reſtitucyon was due, ner any of his leafull heares, then muſt it be the
preaſtes wages, whiche at that tyme had no nother lyuehode.

v. 10-19.   called Numeri.   417

Israel brynge vnto the preaste, shalbe the preastes, and
10 euery mans halowed thinges shalbe his awne, but what
soeuer any man geueth the preast, it shalbe the preastes.
11, 12   And the Lorde spake vnto Moses sayenge: speake
vnto the childern of Israell and saye vnto them.
Yf any mans wyfe goo a syde and trespase agaynst
13 hym, so that another man lye with her fleshely and
the thynge be hydd from the eyes of hir husbonde and
is not come to lighte that she is defyled (for there is
no witnesse agenst her) in as moche as she was not taken
14 with the maner, and the sprete of geloufye with the man-
cometh apon him and he is geloufe ouer er, *in the act*
his wife and she defyled, Or happely the sprete of
geloufye cometh apon him, and he is geloufe ouer hys
15 wyfe ād she yet vndefyled. Thē let hyr husbonde
bringe her vnto the preaste and brynge an offerynge
for her: the tenthe parte of an Epha of barlye meele,
but shall poure none oyle there vnto, nor put frankencens thereon: for it is an offerynge of geloufye, and an
offerynge that maketh remembraunce of synne.
16   And let the preast brynge her and sett her before the
17 Lorde, and let him take holy water in an erthen veffell
& of the dust that is in ý flore of the habytacyon, and
18 put it in to the [Fo. XII.] water. And the preast shall
set the wyfe before the Lorde and vncouer wyfe, *woman*
hir heed, and put the memoryall of the vv. 22, 25, 31
offerynge in hyr handes whiche is the & xxv, 6
geloufye offerynge, and ý preast shall haue bytter and
19 curfynge water in his hande, and he shall   coniure, *ad-*
coniure her and shall saye vnto her. Yf *jure*

V. 13 hoc maritus deprehendere nō quiuerit, sed latet adul-
terium ... inuenta in stupro 14 polluta est, vel falsa sufpicione
appetitur 15 sacrificium zelotypiæ est, & oblatio inuestigans adul-
terium. 18 sacrif. recordationis, & oblationem zelotypiæ ... aquas
amarissimas, in quibus cum execratione maledicta congessit.
L. 14 eyffergeyst entzundet yhn 15 eyn eyffer opffer vnd eyn
rüge opffer, das missethat rüget. 18 bitter verflucht waffer
M. M. N. 14 The hole lawe of geloufie semeth to be a feare
& a certen nourtour of wyues that they shulde be obediēt to their
husbādes, chaste, manerly & faythfull, and foche as geue no oc-
casiō to be sufpect: & therto serued thys lawe whyle it kept thē
vnder & gaue thē no licēs to rēne at large wherby they might
haue come in some sufpect & so haue come to thys greate shame
before the congregacyon.

no man haue lyen wyth the nether hafte gone afyde, and defyled thy felfe behynde thy hufbonde, then haue thou no harme of this bytter curfynge water.

20 But and yf thou haft gone afyde behynde thyne hufbonde and art defyled and fome other man hath 21 lyen with the befyde thyne hufbonde (and let the preafte coniure her with the coniuracyon of the curfe and faye vnto her,) the Lorde make the a curfe and a coniuracyon amonge thy people: fo that the Lorde 22 make thy thye rotte, and thy bely fwell and thys bytter curfynge water goo in to the bowels of the, that thy bely fwell and thy thye rotte, and the wyfe fhall faye Amen Amen.

23 And the preaft fhall wrytte this curfe in a byll and 24 waffhe it out in the bytter water. And when the curf-
25 ynge water ys yn her that it is bytter, then let the preaft take the geloufyofferynge out of the wyfes hande, and waue it before the Lorde, and brynge it vnto the 26 altare: and he fhall take an hande- .P. full off the memoryall offerynge and burne it apon the alter, and 27 then make her dryncke the water and when he hath made her dryncke the water. Yf fhe be defyled and haue trefpafed agenft her hufbond, then fhall the curf- ynge water goo in to her and be fo bitter, ẏ hir bely fhall fwell and hir thye fhall rotte, & fhe fhalbe a curfe 28 amonge hir people. And yf fhe be not defyled but is cleane, then fhe fhall haue no harme, but that fhe maye conceaue.

29 This is the lawe of geloufye, when a wyfe goeth a 30 fyde behynde hyr hufbonde ād is defyled, or when the

𝒱. 19 fi nō polluta es deferto mariti thoro .. amariffimæ, in quas maledicta congeffi 20 altero viro, 21 his maledictionibus fubiacebis .. tumens vterus tuus difrumpatur. 23 congeffit 24 & dabit ei bibere. Quas cum exhauferit, 25 tollet facerdos 26 & fic potū det mulieri 27 mulier in maledictionem & in exemplū omni populo.

𝑳. 21 fetze dich zum fluch vnd zum fchwur .. bauch berften laffe 22 deyn bauch berfte 24 das yhr bitter wirt 27 ynn fie gehen vnd fie verbittern .. berften 31 weyb foll feyn miffethat tragen.

𝓜. 𝓜. N. 22 Amen is an Hebrew word & fygnifyeth euen fo be it, or be it faft and fewer, approuynge & alowing the fentēce going before: and when it is doubled it augmenteth the confyr- macyon, as in many pfalms & Iohn .v. & .vi.

ſpirite of geloufye cometh apon a man, ſo that he is gelouſe ouer his wife: then he ſhall bringe her before the Lorde, and the preaſt ſhall miniſtre all this lawe
31 vnto her, & the man ſhalbe giltleſſe, & the wyfe ſhall bere hir ſynne.

⁋ The .VI. Chapter.

1 AND the Lorde ſpake vnto Mo-   𝔐.𝕰.𝕾. *The*
2 ſes ſaynge: ſpeake vnto ẏ   *lawe of them that toke vp-*
childrē of Iſrael & ſaye vnto   *pon them ab-*
them: when ether man or   *ſtynence. The maner of bleſſ-*
appoynteth, woman appoynteth to vowe   *yng the people.*
reſolveth   a vowe of abſtinence for to abſtene vnto
3 the Lorde, he ſhall abſtene from wyne and ſtronge drynke, and ſhall dryncke no vynegre of wyne or of ſtronge drynke, nor ſhal drynke what ſoeuer is preſſed out of grapes: & ſhal eate no freſh grapes nether yet
4 dry- [Fo. XIII.] ed, as lōge as his abſtinēce ēdureth. Moreouer he ſhall eate nothyng ẏ is made of the vyne tre, no not ſo moch as ẏ cornels or the   cornels, ker-
huſke of the grape.   nels
5 And as longe as the vowe of his abſtinēce endureth, there ſhall no raſure nor ſheres come apon his heed, vntill his dayes be out which he faſteth vnto the Lorde, and he ſhalbe holy and ſhall let the lockes of his heer
6 growe. As longe as he abſteneth vnto the Lorde he

    V. 2 vt ſanctificentur, & ſe voluerint domino conſecrare 3 a vino, & omni quod inebriare poteſt
    L. 2 eyn zucht gelubd, das er dem herrn zuchtet 3 weyns vnd ſtarcks getrencks
    𝔐. 𝔐. N. 2 Here it appereth what a *vowe* is after the olde teſtament, whyche was a fygure of the vowe that a Chriſtē man ought to do, geuyng & dedicatinge hymſelfe to God: as it is ſpoken Roma. xii. a.
    L. 𝔐. N. 2 Auff Ebreiſch heyſt diſe zucht *Neſer* vnd der ſie helt heyſt *Naſir*, wilchem nach auch vnſer herr Iheſus Chriſtus *Naſarenus* heyſt, vnd er der rechte Naſir iſt, weyl wir aber keyn deutſch wort drauff haben muſſen wyrs die weyl zucht vnd Naſir nennen. Denn auff deutſch ſagen wyr von ſolchen leuiten. Er zuchtet alſo theur etc.

7 ſhall come at no deed bodye: he ſhall not make him
ſelfe vncleane at the deeth of his father, mother,
brother or ſyſter. for the abſtinẽce of his God is
8 apon his heed. And therfore as longe as his abſtynence laſteth, he ſhalbe holy vnto the Lorde.

9 And yf it fortune that any man by chaunce dye
ſodenly before him, and defyle the heed of his abſtinẽce, then muſt he ſhaue his heed the daye of his
clẽſynge: euen the ſeuenth daye he ſhall ſhaue it.
10 And the eyght daye he ſhall brynge .ii. turtels or .ii
yonge pigeons to the preaſt, vnto ẏ dore of ẏ taber-
11 nacle of witneſſe And ẏ preaſt ſhall offer the one for
a ſynofferynge and the other for a burntofferynge &
make an atonement for him, as concernynge that
he ſynned apon the deed, and ſhall alſo halowe his
12 heed the ſame daye and he ſhall abſtene vnto the
Lorde the tyme of his abſtinencye, and ſhall brynge
a lambe of an yere olde for a treſpace offerynge: but
the dayes ẏ .Ṗ. were before are loſt, becauſe his abſti-
13 nence was defyled. ⁌ This is the lawe of the abſteyner, when the tyme of his abſtinẽce is   is out, *com-
out. he ſhalbe broughte vnto ẏ dore of *pleted*
14 ẏ tabernacle of witneſſe & he ſhall brynge his offerynge
vnto ẏ Lord: an he lãbe of a yere olde with out blemyſh for a burntofferynge & a ſhe lambe of a yere olde
without blemyſh for a ſynofferynge, a ram without
15 blemyſh alſo for a peaſeofferynge, & a baſket of ſwete
breed of fyne floure myngled with oyle & wafers of
ſwete bred anoyntyd with oyle with meatofferynges
ãd drynkofferynges that longe thereto.
16 And the preaſt ſhall brynge him before ẏ Lorde &
17 offer his ſynofferynge & his burntofferynge, & ſhall
offer ẏ ram for a peaſeofferynge vnto ẏ Lorde with

V. 7 cõſecratio dei ſui 9 in eadem die .. & rurſum ſeptima.
11 ſuper mortuo
L. 7 Denn die zucht ſeyns Gottis 9 das iſt am ſiebenden tage
11 an eym todten 14 tödopffer (17, 18.)
M. M. N. 7 To haue *the abſtynence of God* vpon his heed is,
to ſhew a token of refuſing the care of bodely thynges by that he
ſetteth not by the hayre of hys heed, or by the trymmynge of hys
buſſhe or bearde, which thĩg the world ſo greatly eſteameth.

the basket of swete brede, ād the preast shall offer also
18 his meat offerynge & his drynckofferynge. And ỹ
abſteyner shall shaue his heed in ỹ dore of ỹ tabernacle
of witnesse ād shall take the heer of his sober heed &
put it in ỹ fyre which is vnder the peaseofferynge.
19 Then the preast shall take the sodden shulder of ỹ
ram ād one swete cake out of ỹ basket & one swete
wafer also ād put them in the hāde of the abſteyner
20 after he hath shauē his abſtinēce of, & the preast shall
waue them vnto the Lorde, which offerynge shalbe
holy vnto the preast with ỹ wauebreſt and heue
shulder: & then the abſteyner maye drynke wyne.
21 This is the lawe of the abſtey- [Fo. XIIII.] ner which
hath vowed his offerynge vnto ỹ Lorde for his abſtynence, besydes that his hāde can gete And acordyng
to the vowe which he vowed, euen so he muſt doo in
the lawe of his abſtinence.
22, 23 And the Lorde talked with Moſes ſayenge: ſpeake
vnto Aaron and his ſonnes ſayēge: of this wiſe ye ſhall
bleſſe the childern of Yſrael ſaynge vnto them.
24 The lorde bleſſe the and kepe the.
25 The lorde make his face shyne apon
the & be mercyfull vnto the.
26 The lorde lifte vpp his countenaunce
27 apō the, and geue the peace For ye
shall put my name apon the childern of
Yſrael, that I maye bleſſe them.

Here of ye ſe that Aarŏ, when he lift vpp his hande and bleſſed the people, was not dumme as oure biſhopes be.

V. 18 radetur Nazaræus 20 Suſceptaque rurſum ab eo... ſa-
cerdotis erunt, ſicut pectuſculum quod ſeparari iuſſum eſt, & fe-
mur. 21 exceptis his quæ inuenerit manus eius 25 Oſtendat dom.
faciem, 26 Conuertat dom. vultū ſuum ad te

L. 18 Vnd ſoll dem zuchter... beſcheren 19 nach dem er
ſeyn zucht beſchoren hat 20 zu der Webebruſt vnd der Hebe-
ſchuldern 21 auſſer dem das ſeyne hand erwerben kan 25 erleuchte
ſeyn angeſicht 26 hebe ſeyne angeſicht auff dich

M. M. N. 25 *To make his face to shijne* is to geue a token of
his louyng kyndenes.

❡ The .VII. Chapter.

M.C.S. The offryng of the Lordes and heades of Israell when the tabernacle was sett vp.

1 AND when Moses had full sett vp the habitacion and anoynted it ād sanctifyed it and all the apparell thereof, and had anoynted & sanctifyed ẏ alter also and all the vessels there of:
2 then the pry̆nces of Ysrael heedes ouer the housses of their fathers which were the lordes
3 of the trybes that stode ād numbred, offered ād broughte their giftes before the Lorde sixe couered charettes and .xii. oxen: two and two a charet and an oxe euery man, and they broughte them before the habitacion.
4, 5 .P. And the Lorde spake vnto Moses saynge take it of them and let them be to do the seruyce of ẏ tabernacle of witnesse, and geue them vnto the leuites,
6 euery man acordynge vnto his office And Moses toke the charettes ād the oxen, & gaue them vnto the leuites:
7 .ii. charettes and .iiii. oxen he gaue vnto the sonnes
8 of Gerson acordynge vnto their office. And .iiii. charettes and eyght oxen he gaue vnto ẏ sonnes of Merari acordynge vnto their offices, vnder the handes of
9 Ithamar the sonne of Aaron the preast. But vnto the sonnes of Cahath he gaue none, for the office that perteyned to them was holy, & therfore they must bere vppon shulders.
10 And the princes offered vnto the dedycatynge of the alter in the daye ẏ it was anoynted, and brought
11 their giftes before the alter And the Lorde sayde vnto Moses: let the prices brynge their offerynges, euery daye one prynce, vnto the dedicatynge of the alter.

V. 2 principes Israel & capita familiarum, quæ erant per singulas tribus præfecti eorum qui numerati fuerant 3 duo duces 7 iuxta id quod habebant necessarium. 8 Merari secundum officia & cultum suum, 9 Caath non dedit plaustra & boues: quia in sanctuario seruiunt 10 obtulerunt duces

L. 2 die heubtleut Israel, die die vbirsten waren ynn yhrer veter hause. Denn sie waren die heubtleut vnter den geschlechten vnd stunden vber den getzeleten. 3 zween heubtleut 7 nach yhrem ampt 8 nach yhrem ampt 9 gab er nicht, darumb das sie eyn heylig ampt auff yhn hatten 10 Vnd die heubtleut

12 He that offered his offerynge ẏ firſt daye, was Naheſſon the ſonne of Aminadab of the trybe of Iuda.
13 And his offerynge was: a ſyluer charger, of an hundred and .xxx. ſicles weight: and a ſyluer boule of .Lxx. ſicles of the holy ſicle, both of them full of fyne whetē
14 floure myngled with oyle for a meat offerynge: & a
15 ſpone of .x. ſicles of golde full of cens: & an oxe, a ram
16 ād a lambe of a yere olde for burnt offerynges, and an
17 he goote for a ſynnofferyn- [Fo. XV.] ge: and for peaſe offerynges .ii. oxen .v. rammes .v. he gootes and .v. lambes of a yere olde. and this was the gifte of Naheſſon the ſonne of Aminadab.

18 The ſeconde daye, dyd Nathaneel offer, ẏ ſonne of
19 Zuar, captayne ouer Yſachar. And his offerynge which he broughte was: a ſyluer charger of an hundred & .xxx. ſicles weyght, and a ſyluern boule of .Lxx. ſicles, of ẏ holy ſicle: [* and both full of fyne floure
20 myngled with oyle for a meatofferynge:] and a golden
21 ſpone of .x. ſicles full of cens: and an oxe, a ram and a lambe of a yere olde for burntofferynges: [22 see foot
23 note**] ād for peaſeofferynges .ii. oxen .v. rammes v. he gootes and .v. lambes of one yere olde. And this was ẏ offerynge of Nathaneel the ſonne of Zuar.

24 The thyrde daye, Eliab the ſonne of Helon the chefeſt amonge the childern of Zabulon, brought his
25 offerynge. And his offerynge was, a ſyluer charger of an hundred and .xxx. ſicles weyghte, and a ſyluern boule of .Lxx. ſicles of the holy ſicle, & both full of fyne floure myngled with oyle for a meat offerynge:
26, 27 and a golden ſpone of .x. ſicles full of cēs: and an oxe and a ram and a lambe of a yere olde for burntof-
28, 29 ferynges, and an he goote for a ſynofferynge: and for peaſeofferynges .ii. oxen .v. rammes .v. he gootes

℟. 15 & an bullock 19 and both full of fyne floure myngled with oyle for a meatofferynge: 21 a bullock
℟. ℟. N. 12 The offerynge of Naheſſon. 18 The offrynge of Nathanael. 24 The offrynge of Eliab.

---

* The passage in brackets, omitted by Tyndale, has been supplied from *Matthew's Bible.*
** Tyndale and Matthew omit v. 22, which by analogy of v. 16 may be supplied thus: and an he goote for a synofferynge.

and .v. lambes of one yere olde. And this was the offerynge of Eliab the fonne of Helon.

30 The fourt daye, Elizur the fonne of Sedeur, chefe lorde amonge the childern of Ru- .P. ben, broughte his
31 offerynge. And his gifte was: a fyluer charger of an hundred and .xxx. ficles weyghte, and a fyluern boule of .Lxx. ficles of the holy ficle, & both full of fyne
32 floure myngled with oyle for a meatofferynge: and a
33 golden fpone of .x. ficles full of cens: and an oxe, a
34 ram & a lambe of a yere olde for burntofferynges, and
35 an he goote for a fynofferynge: and for peafeofferynges ii. oxen .v. rammes .v. he gootes and .v. lambes of one yere olde. And this was the offerynge of Elizur the fonne of Sedeur.

36 The fyfth daye, Selumiel ẏ fonne of Zuri Sadai, chefe lorde amonge the childern of Simeon, offered.
37 whofe gifte was: a fyluer charger of an hundred & .xxx ficles weyghte: and a fyluer boule of .Lxx. ficles of the holy ficle: ād both full of fyne floure myngled with oyle
38 for a meatofferynge: & a golden fpone of .x. ficles full
39 of cens. And an oxe, a ram ād a lābe of a yere olde
40 for burntofferynges, ād an he goote for a fynofferynge:
41 & for peafeofferīges .ii. oxen .v. rāmes .v. he gootes ād .v. lābes of a yere olde. And this was the offerynge of Selumiel the fonne of Zuri Sadai.

42 The fixte daye, Eliafaph ẏ fonne of Deguel the chefe lorde amonge the childern of Gad, offered.
43 whofe gifte was: a fyluer charger of an hundred and xxx. ficles weyghte: and a fyluern boule of .Lxx. ficles of the holy [Fo. XVI.] ficle: & both full of fyne floure
44 myngled with oyle for a meatofferynge: and a golden
45 fpone of .x. ficles full of cens. And an oxe, a ram ād a
46 lambe of a yere olde for burntofferynges, & an he goote
47 for a fynofferynge: And for peafeofferynges .ii. oxen .v rammes .v. he gootes and .v. lābes of one yere olde. And this was the offerynge of Eliafaph the fonne of Deguel.

𝔐. 33 a bullock 39 a bullock
𝔐. 𝔐. N. 30 The offrynge of Elizur. 36 The offrynge of Selumiel. 42 The offrynge of Eliafaph.

48   The feuenth daye, Elifama the fonne of Amiud, ẏ
49 chefe lorde of ẏ childern of Ephraim, offered. And his
gifte was a fyluern charger of an hundred and .xxx. ficles
weyght: ād a fyluern boule of .Lxx. ficles of the holy
ficle: ād both full of fyne floure myngled with oyle for
50 a meatofferynge: and a golden fpone of .x. ficles, full of
51 cens. And an oxe, a ram and a lambe of a yere olde
52 for burntofferynges, ād an he goote for a fynofferynge:
53 and for peafeofferynges .ii. oxen .v. rammes .v. he
gootes & .v. lambes of a yere olde. And this was ẏ
offerynge of Elifama the fonne of Amiud.
54   The .viii. daye, offered Gamaliel the fonne of Peda-
55 zur, the chefe lorde of the children of Manaffe. And
his gifte was: a fylueren charger of ān hundred and
xxx. ficles weyght: and a fyluern boule of .Lxx. ficles
of the holy ficle: ād both full of fyne floure myngled
56 with oyle for a meatofferynge: & a golden fpone of .x
57 fycles, full of cēs. And an oxe, a ram .P. and a lambe
58 of a yere olde for burntofferynges, and an he goote for
59 a fynofferynge: and for peafeofferynges .ii. oxen .v
rammes, fyue he gootes and fyue lābes of a yere olde.
And this was the offerynge of Gamaliel the fonne of
Peda zur.
60   The .ix. daye, Abidan ẏ fonne of Gedeoni ẏ chefe
61 lord amōge ẏ childern of Ben Iamin offered. And his
gifte was: a fyluern charger of an hundred and .xxx
ficles weyght: & a fyluern boule of .Lxx. ficles of the
holy ficle, and both full of fyne floure myngled with
62 oyle for a meatofferynge: and a golden fpone of .x. ficles,
63 full of cens. and an oxe, a ram and a lambe of one
64 yere olde for burntofferynges: & an he goote for a
65 fynofferynge: and for peafeofferynges .ii. oxen .v. rammes
v. he gootes & .v. lambes of one yere olde. And this
was the offerynge of Abidan the fonne of Gedeoni.
66   The .x. daye, Ahiefer the fonne of Ammi Sadai,
67 chefe lorde amōge ẏ childern of Dan offered. And his

ℳ. 51 a bullock 57 a bullock 63 a bullock
ℳ. ℳ. N. 48 The offerynge of Elifama. 54 The offerynge
of Gamaliel. 60 The offryng of Abidan. 66 The offryng of
Ahiezer.

gifte was: a fyluern charger of an hundred and .xxx fycles weyght: a fyluern boule of feuentye ficles of the holy fycle: and both full of fyne floure myngled
68 with oyle for a meatofferynge: and a golden fpone of .x
69 ficles full of cens: and an oxe, a rà and a lambe of a
70 yere olde for burntofferynges, and an he goote for
71 a fynofferynge: and for peafeofferynges .ii. oxen .v rammes, fyue he gootes and fyue làbes of a yere olde. And [Fo. XVII.] this was the offrynge of Ahiefer the fonne of Ammi Sadai.

72 The .xi. daye, Pagiel the fonne of Ochran the chefe
73 Lorde amonge the childern of Affer offered: And his gifte was: a fyluerē charger of an hundred and .xxx fycles weyghte: a fylueren boule of .Lxx. fycles of the holye fycle and both full of fyne floure myngled with
74 oyle for a meateoffrynge: and a golden fpone of .x. fycles,
75 full of cens. And an oxe, a ram and a lambe of one
76 yere olde for burntofferinges: and an he goote for a
77 fynneofferynge: ād for peaceofferynges: two oxen, fyue rammes .v. he gootes and .v. lambes of one yere olde. And this was the offerynge of Pagiel ÿ fonne of Ochran.

78 The .xii. daye, Ahira the fonne of Enan, chefe lorde
79 amonge the childern of Nephtali offered. And his gifte was: a fylueren charger of an hundred and .xxx fycles weyghte: a fylueren boule of .Lxx. fycles of the holye fycle, both full of fyne floure myngled with oyle
80 for a meatofferynge: and a golden fpone of twentye
81 fycles, full of cens. And an oxe, a ram and a lambe
82 of one yere olde for burntofferynges: and an he goote
83 for a fynneofferinge: and for peaceofferynges, two oxen v. rāmes .v. he gootes and .v. lambes of one yere olde. And this was the offerynge of Ahira, the fonne of Enan.

84 Of this maner was the dedicacyon of the .℣. alter, when it was anoynted: vnto the whiche was broughte of

ℳ. 69 a bullock 75 a bullock 81 a bullock
℣. 72 Phegiel
ℳ. ℳ. N. 72 The offryng of Pagiell, or Phegiell. 78 The offryng of Ahira.

the prynces of Ifrael .xii. chargers of fyluer .xii. fyluern
85 boules and .xii. fpones of golde: euery charger contaynynge an hundred and .xxx. fycles of fyluer, and euery boule .Lxx. fo that all the fyluer of all the veffels, was two thoufande and .iiii. hundred fycles of the
86 holy fycle. And the .xii. golden fpones which were full of cens, contayned ten fycles a pece of the holy fycle: fo that all the golde of the fpones, was an hundred and .xx. fycles.
87 All the oxen that were broughte for the burntoffrynges were .xii. and the rāmes .xii. & the lābes .xii of a yere olde a pece, with the meateofferynges: with
88 he gootes for fynne offrynges. And all the oxē of the peaceofferynges were .xxiiii. the rammes .Lx. the gootes Lx. and lambes of a yere olde a pece .Lx. & this was the dedicacion of the alter, after ẏ it was anoynted.
89 And when Mofes was gone in to the tabernacle of witneffe to fpeke with hī, he harde the voyce of one fpeakinge vnto him from of the mercyfeate that was apon the arcke of witneffe: euen from betwene the two cherubyns he fpake vnto him.

⁋ The .VIII. Chapter.

[Fo. XVIII.] VIII. Chapter.

1
2 AND the Lorde fpake vnto Mofes faynge: fpeake vnto Aaron and faye vnto hym: when thou putteft on the lampes fe that they lighte all feuen apon the forefront
3 of the candelfticke. And Aaron dyd euen

M.C.S. The difpoficion and order of the lampes. The forme of the candelftyck. The cleanfyng and

V. 84 principibus 88 altaris quando vnctum 89 vt confuleret oraculum .. vnde & loquebatur ei. viii, 2 lucernas, – candelabrum in auftrali parte erigatur. Hoc igitur præcipe vt lucernæ contra boream eregione refpiciant ad menfam panum propofitionis: .. contra eam partem quam candelabrum refpicit, lucere debebunt.

L. 84 heubtleut 88 nachdem er gefalbet wart. 89 von dannen wart mit yhm geredt.

so, and put the lampes apon the forefrōt of the candelsticke, as the Lorde com- *offryng of the Leuytes. The age of the same.*
4 maunded Moses, and the worke of the candelsticke was of stiffe golde: both the shaft and the floures thereof. And accord- *stiffe, solid, beaten*
inge vnto the visyon whiche the Lorde had shewed Moses, euen so he made the candelsticke.

5, 6 And the Lorde spake vnto Moses sayenge: take the leuites from amonge the childern of Israel, and
7 clense them. And this doo vnto them when thou clensest them, sprinckle water of purifyenge apon them and make a rasure to runne alonge apon all the flesshe of them, and let them wasshe their clothes, and then
8 they shall be cleane. And let them take a bollocke and his meatofferynge, fyne floure myngled with oyle: & another bollocke shalt thou take to be a synneofferynge.

9 Than brynge the leuites before the tabernacle of witnesse and gather the hole multitude of the chyldern
10 of Israel together. And bringe the leuites before the Lorde, and let the childern of Israel put their handes
11 apon the leuites. And let Aaron heue the leuites before the LORDE, for an heueoffe- .P. rynge geuen of the childern of Israel, ād thē let them be appoynted to wayte apon the seruyce of the Lorde.

12 And let the leuites put their handes vpō the heedes of the bollockes, and then offer them: the one for a synneofferynge and the other for a burntofferynge vnto the Lorde, to make an attonement for the leuites.
13 And make the leuites stonde before Aaron & hys sonnes, and heue them to be a heueofferynge vnto the
14 Lorde. And thou shalt separate the leuites, from amonge the childern of Israel, that they be myne:
15 and after that let them goo and do the seruice of the

V. 4 iuxta exemplum 7 iuxta hunc ritum .. aqua lustrationis, et radant omnes pilos carnis 9 omni multitudine 11 vt seruiant in ministerio eius

L. 4 nach dem geficht 9 gantze gemeyne 11 auf das sie dienen mugen an dem ampt des Herrn.

L. M. N. 7 *Entfund Wasser:* Entsunden ist so viel als absoluiren oder los sprechen, daher das wasser damit sie absoluirt wurden von sunden heyst entsund wasser.

tabernacle of witnesse. Clenfe them and waue them,
16 for they are geuen vnto me from amonge the childrē of Ifrael: for I haue taken them vnto me for all ye firstborne that opē any matrice amöge the childern of Ifrael.
17 For all the fyrstborne among the childern of Ifrael are myne both man and beeft: becaufe the fame tyme that I fmote the fyrstborne in the lande of Egipte, I fanctyfyde
18 them for my felfe: and I haue taken the Leuites for all the fyrstborne amonge the childern of Ifrael, and haue
19 geuen them vnto Aaron and his fonnes from amonge the childern of Ifrael, to doo the feruyce of the childern of Ifrael in the tabernacle of witneffe and to make an attonement for the chyldern of Ifraell, that there be no plage amonge the childern [Fo. XIX.] of Yfraell, yf they come nye vnto the fanctuarye
20 And Mofes and Aaron and all the congregacion of the childern of Ifrael dyd vnto the leuites acordynge
21 vnto all that ye Lorde commaunded Mofes. And the leuites purifyed them felues, and waffhed their clothes. And Aaron waued them before ye Lorde, and made
22 an attonement for them to clenfe them. And after that they went in to doo their feruyce in the tabernacle of wytneffe, before Aaron and his fonnes. And acordinge as the Lorde had commaunded Mofes as concernynge the leuites, euen fo they dyd vnto them.
23, 24 And the Lorde fpake vnto Mofes fayenge: this fhalbe the maner of the leuites: from .xxv. yere vppwarde they fhall goo in to wayte vppon the feruyce in
25 the tabernacle of witneffe, and at fyftye they fhall ceaffe waytynge apon the feruyce thereof, and fhall laboure
26 no moare: but fhall miniftre vnto their bretheren in the tabernacle of witneffe, and there wayte, but fhall doo no moare feruyce.

And fe that thou doo after this maner vnto the leuites in their waytynge tymes.

⁋ The .IX. Chapter.

V. 15 ingrediantur 16 accepi eos. 17 Ex die quo 19 dono Aaron 22 vt purificati ingrederentur 25 annum ætatis impleuerint

L. 15 hyneyn gehen 16 vnd hab fie myr genomen 19 zum gefchencke Aaron 22 Darnach giengen fie hyneyn

.P. .IX. Chapter.

M.C.S. The ester or passeouer offringe of the cleane and vncleane. A cloude couerynge the tabernacle leadeth the hoste.

1 AND the Lorde spake vnto Moses in the wildernesse of Sinai, in the fyrste moneth of the seconde yere, after they were come out of the londe of Egipte sayeng:
2 let ẏ childern of Israel offer Passeouer in
3 his season: euen the .xiiii. daye of this moneth at euen they shall kepe it in his season, accordynge to all the ordinaunces & maners thereof.
4 And Moses bade the childern of Ysrael that they
5 shulde offer Passeouer, & they offered Passeouer the xiiii. daye of the first moneth at euen in the wildernesse of Sinai: and dyd acordinge to all that the Lorde commaunded Moses.
6 And it chaunced that certayne men whyche were defyled with a deed corse that they myghte not offer Passeouer the same daye, came before Moses and Aaron
7 the same daye, and sayde: we are defyled apon a deed corse, wherfore are we kepte backe that we maye not offer an offerynge vnto the Lorde in the due season,
8 amonge the childern of Israell? And Moses sayde vnto them: tary, that I maye heare what the Lorde wille
9 commaunde you. And the Lord spake vnto Moses
10 sayenge: speake vnto the childern of Israell and saye. Yf any man amonge you or youre childern after you be vncleane by the reason of a corse or is in the waye ferre of, then lett hym offer Passeouer vnto ẏ Lorde:
11 the .xiiii. [Fo. XX.] daye of the seconde moneth at euen, and eate it with swete bred and soure herbes,
12 ãd let them leaue none of it vnto the mornynge nor breake any boone of it. And acordynge to all the ordinaunce of the Passeouer let them offer it.
13 But yf a man be cleane and not let in a iurney, and

V. 5 Qui fecerunt tempore suo 7 quare fraudamur vt non valeamus 11 lactucis agrestibus

yet was negligent to offer Paſſeouer, the ſame ſoule ſhall periſh from his people, becauſe he brought not an offerynge vnto the Lorde in his due ſeaſon: and 14 he ſhall bere his ſynne. And when a ſtraunger dwelleth amonge you and will offer Paſſeouer vnto the Lorde, accordynge to the ordinaunce of Paſſeouer and maner thereof ſhall he offre it. And ye ſhall haue one lawe both for the ſtraunger and for him that was borne at home in the lande.

15 And the ſame daye that the habitaciō was reered vpp, a cloude couered it an hye apon the tabernacle of witneſſe: and at euen there was apon the habitacyon, as it were the ſymilitude of fyre vntyll the 16 mornynge. And ſo it was allwaye, that the cloude couered it by daye, and the ſymylitude of fyre by 17 nyghte. And when the cloude was taken vpp from of the tabernacle, then the childern of Iſrael iurneyed: and where the cloude abode there the childern of 18 Iſrael pitched their tentes. At the mouthe of the Lorde the childern of Iſraell iurneyed, and at the mouthe of . Ṗ. the Lorde they pitched. And as longe as the cloude abode apon the habitacion, they laye 19 ſtyll, and when the cloude taryed ſtill apon the habitacion longe tyme, the childern of Iſraell wayted apon the Lorde and iurneyed not.

20 Yf it chaunced that the cloude abode any ſpace of tyme apon the habitacion, then they kepte their tentes at the mouth of the Lorde: and they iurneyed 21 alſo at the commaundement of the Lorde. And yf it happened that the cloude was apon the habitacion from euen vnto mornynge and was taken vpp in ẏ

𝒱. 15 quaſi ſpecies ignis 19 in excubiis domini v. 23.
𝕷. 15 ein geſtalt des fewrs v. 16. 19 wartten . . . auff die hutt des Herrn v. 23.
𝔐. 𝔐. 𝔑. 13 In lyke māner is it with vs in oure *ſpirituall eſter* or *paſſeouer*, who ſoeuer doth not reuerently beleue the redēpcyon of mankynde whyche was thoroulye ſyniſhed in offrynge the true lābe chriſt and amendeth not his life, nor turneth frō vyce to vertue in the tyme of this mortal life ſhall not belöge vnto the glory of the reſurreccion, which ſhall be geuen vnto the true worſhippers of chriſt: but ſhall be roted oute frō the companye of the ſaynctes.

mornynge, then they iurneyed. Whether it was by daye or by nyghte that ẏ cloude was taken vpp, they
22 iurneyed. But when ẏ cloude taryed two dayes or a moneth or a longe feafon apon the habitacion, as longe as it taried thereon, the childern of Ifrael kepte their tentes and iurneyed not. And as foone as the cloude was taken vpp, they iurneyed.
23 At the mouth of the Lorde they refted, and at the commaundment of the Lorde they iurneyed. And thus they kepte the wayte of the Lorde, at the commaundement of the Lorde by the hande of Mofes.

The .X. Chapter.

1 AND the Lorde fpake vnto Mofes
2 fayenge: Make the two trompettes of harde fyluer, that thou mayſt vfe thē to call the congregacion together, and when [Fo. XXI.]
3 the hofte fhall iurney. when they blowe with them, all the multitude fhall reforte to the, vnto the dore of the tabernacle of
4 witneffe. Yf but one trumpet blowe only, then the princes which are heedes ouer the thoufandes of
5 Yfrael fhall come vnto the. And when ye trompe the firſt tyme, the hoftes that lye
6 on the eaſt partes fhall goo forwarde. And when ye trōpe the feconde tyme, then the hoftes that lye on ẏ fouth fyde fhall take their iurney: for they fhall trompe
7 when they take their iurneyes. And in gatherynge

M.C.S. The trompettes of fyluer and the vfe therof. The Ifraeliites depart from Sinai. The captaynes of the hofte are nombred. Hobab refufeth to go with Mofes.

trompe, to sound a trumpet

M. 2 beaten fyluer
V. 4 principes, & capita multitudinis 6 & iuxta hunc modum reliqui facient vlulantibus tubis in profectionem.
L. 4 vbirſten vber die taufent ynn Ifrael.
M. M. N. 22 *Two dayes etc.,* after the grekes certayne dayes, a fewe or fome dayes. x, 4 *To blowe with one trumpet* is, to fhew the worde of helth fynglye after the vnytye of the faith.

the congregacion together, ye shall blowe and not
8 trompe. And the sonnes of Aaron the preastes shall blowe the trompettes and shall haue them and it shalbe a lawe vnto you for euer & amonge youre childern after you.
9 And when ye shall goo to warre in youre londe agenst youre enymies that vexe you, ye shall trompe with the trompettes and ye shalbe remēbred before the
10 Lorde youre God and saued from youre enymies. Also when ye be mery in youre sest dayes and *Hēce oure* in the firstdayes of youre monethes, ye *belles were sett.* shall blowe the trompettes ouer youre burnt sacrifices and peaseofferynges, that it maye be a remēbraūce of you before youre God. I am the lorde youre God.
11 And it came to passe the .xx. daye of the seconde moneth in ẏ seconde yere, that the cloude was take
12 vpp from of the habitacion of .P. witnesse. And the childern of Israel toke their iurney out of the deserte of Sinai, and the cloude rested in ẏ wildernesse of Parā.
13 And ẏ first toke their iurney at the mouth of the Lorde,
14 by the honde of Moses: euen the standerte of ẏ hoste of Iuda remoued first with their armies, whose captayne
15 was Nahesson ẏ sonne of Aminadab. And ouer the hoste of ẏ trybe of the childern of Isachar, was Nathaneel
16 the sonne of zuar. And ouer the hoste of ẏ trybe of the childern of Zabulon, was Eliab the sonne of Helon.
17 And the habitacion was taken doune: and the sonnes of Gerson and Merari went forth bearynge the habitacion
18 Then the standert of the hoste of Ruben went forth with their armies, whose captayne was Elizur the
19 sonne of Sedeur. And ouer the hoste of the trybe of

𝔐. 13 they first
𝒱. 7 simplex tubarum clangor erit, & non concise vlulabunt. 10 canetis tubis 13 Moueruntque castra primi
𝕷. 7 blasen vnd nicht drometen.
𝔐. 𝔐. N. 7 *Blowe and not trompe:* The cōmen people must they teache playnely, and with oute curiositye. 9 *Trompe with the trompettes:* In tyme of warre must they trumpe with trumpetes: which sygnifyeth when moste neade is at hande then must saithe prayer and lystyng vp of the mynde to God be chesely exercysed.

ỹ childern of Simeon, was Selumiel the ſonne [of
20 Suri ſaddai. And ouer the hoſte of the tribe of the
chyldren of Gad was Eliaſaph the ſonne]* of Deguel.
21 Then the Cahathites went forwarde and bare the
holy thinges, and the other dyd ſet vp the habitacion agenſt they came.

22 Then the ſtandert of the hoſte of the childern of
Ephraim went forth with their armies, whoſe captayne
23 was Eliſama the ſonne of Amiud. And ouer the hoſte
of the trybe of the ſonnes of Manaſſe, was Samaleel the
24 ſonne of Peda zur. And ouer the hoſte of the trybe of
the ſonnes of Ben Iamin, was Abi- [Fo. XXII.] dan the
ſonne of Gedeoni.

25 And hynmoſt of all the hoſte came the ſtandert of
the hoſte of the childern of Dan with their armies:
whoſe captayne was, Ahiezar the ſonne of Ammi Sadai.
26 And ouer the hoſte of the trybe of the childern of
27 Aſſer, was Pagiel the ſonne of Ochran. And ouer the
hoſte of the trybe of the childern of Naphtali, was
28 Ahira the ſonne of Enan, of this maner were the
iurneyes of the childern of Iſrael, with their armies
when they remoued.

29 And Moſes ſayde vnto Hobab the ſonne of Raguel
the Madianyte, Moſes father lawe: we goo vnto the
place of which the Lorde ſayde I will geue it you.
Goo with us ãd we will doo the good, for the Lorde
30 hath promyſed goode vnto Iſrael. And he ſayde vnto

 𝔐. 19 Salamiel ỹ ſonne of Suri ſaddai. And ouer the hoſte
of the tribe of the chyldren of Gad was Eliaſaph the ſonne of
23 Gamaliel 29 father in lawe
 𝒱. 21 Tamdiu tabernaculum portabatur, donec venirent ad
erectionis locum.
 𝔏. 21 vnd richteten auff die wonung bis ſie hyneyn kamen.
29 das beſte bey dyr thun
 𝔐. 𝔐. N. 26 *Pagiel:* or phegiell. 29 *Hobab* is the ſame
which before is called Iethro euē as Salamō is called ī ſome places
Idida, & as Oſias is alſo called Azarias. He was the ſonne of
Raguell & father to zephora Moſes wyfe: all be it that in the
ſecond of exod. Raguell be called her father, not becauſe he
was ſo in deade but becauſe he was her fathers father: which
maner of ſpeakyng is not a ſewe tymes vſed in the ſcrypture.

---

* The paſſage in brackets omitted by Tyndale, has been ſupplied from *Matthew's Bible.*

him: I will not: but will goo to myne awne londe and
31 to my kynred. And Moſes ſayde oh nay, leaue us not, for thou knoweſt where is beſt for us to pitche in the
32 wilderneſſe: and thou ſhalt be oure eyes And yf thou goo with us, loke what goodneſſe the Lorde ſheweth apon us, the ſame we will ſhewe apon the
33 And they departed from the mount of the Lorde iii. dayes iurney, and the arcke of the teſtament of the Lorde went before .Ṗ. them in the .iii. dayes iurney
34 to ſerche out a reſtynge place for them. And the cloude of the Lorde was ouer them by daye, when they went out of the tentes.
35 And when the arcke went forth, Moſes ſayde Ryſe vp Lorde and lat thine enemies be ſcatered, and let
36 them that hate the flee before the. And when the arcke reſted, he ſayde returne Lorde, vnto the many thouſandes of Yſrael.

⁋ The .XI. Chapter.

1 AND the people waxed vnpacient, and it diſpleaſed the eares of the Lorde. And when the Lorde herde it he was wroth, and the fyre of the Lorde burnt amonge them and conſumed the vttermoſt of
2 the hoſte. And the people cried vnto Moſes, & he made interceſſion vnto the
3 Lorde and the fyre qwenched. And they called ẏ name of the place Tabera be-

M.C.S. The people murmureth & is puny∫hedwith fyre. They loothe māna. The murmuryng and waueryng fayth of Moſes. The Lorde dyuydeth the burden of Moſes to ſeuentye

M. 1 complayned
V. 32 quicquid optimum fuerit 36 ad multitudinem exercitus Iſrael. xi, 2 abſorptus eſt ignis.
L. 30 meyn land zu meyner freuntſchafft 36 zu der menge der tauſent Iſrael. xi, 2 verſchwand das feur
M. M. N. 31 *Eyes:* or gyde. xi, 1 *Complained:* Or waxed diſcontent, ſome tyme dyd wekedly. 3 *Thaberah* ſignyfyeth, kyndlyng inflamyng or fyryng.

cause the fyre of the Lorde burnt amonge them.

of the auncyentes, and they prophesye. Eldad and Medad do also prophesye in the hoste. It rayneth quayles. The flesh raueners are punnyshed.

4 And the rascall people that was amonge them fell a lustynge, And the childern of Ysrael also went to and wepte and sayde: who
5 shall geue us flesh to eate? we remembre the fysh which we shulde eate in Egipte for noughte, and of the Cucumbers and melouns, lekes, onyouns
6 and garleke. But now oure soules ar dryed a waye, for oure eyes loke on nothynge els, saue apon Manna.
7 The Manna was as it had bene corian-
8 der seed, and to see to lyke Bedellion. And ẏ people went aboute and gathered it, & groūde it in milles, or bett it in morters and boke it in pannes and made cakes of it. And the tast of it was like vnto
9 the tast of an oylecake And when the dewe fell aboute ẏ hoste in the nyghte, the Manna fell therewithe.
10 And when Moses herde the people wepe in their housholdes euery man in the dore of his tent, then the wrath of the Lorde waxed whote exced-
11 yngly: and it greued Moses also. And Moses sayde vnto the Lorde: wherfore dealest thou so cruelly with thi seruaunte? wherfore doo I not fynde fauoure in thi syghte, seynge that thou puttest the
12 weyght of this people apon me? haue I conceyued all this people, or haue I begote them, that thou shuldest saye vnto me, carye them in thi bosome (as a nurse beareth the suckynge childe) vnto the londe which
13 thou swarest vnto their fathers? where shulde I haue flesh to geue vnto all this people? For they wepe vnto me sayenge: geue us flesh that we maye eate.
14 I am not able to bere all this people alone, for it is
15 to heuy for me. Wherfore yf thou deale thus with

rascall people, *rabble*, cf. French, *racaille* and *racler*, to scrape together

[Fo. XXIII.]

boke, *baked*

whote, *hot*

v. 33

𝔐. 8 baked ... kakes
𝒱. 6 Anima n. arida 10 Moyſi intoleranda res viſa eſt 12 nutrix infantulum 14 grauis eſt mihi.
ℒ. 6 vnſer ſeele verdorret 10 verdros Moſen auch 14 es iſt myr zu ſchweer

me, kyll me, I praye the, yf I haue founde fauoure in thi fyght and let me not fe my wrechidneffe.

16 And the Lorde fayde vnto Mofes: gather vnto me Lxx. of the elders of Yfrael, which thou knoweft that they are the elders of ỹ pe- .P. ple and officers ouer them, and brynge them vnto the tabernacle of witneffe,
17 and let them ftonde there with the. And I wyll come doune and talke with the there, and take of ỹ fpirite which is apon the and put apon them, ãd they fhall bere with the in the burthen of the people, and fo fhalt thou not beare alone.
18 And faye vnto ỹ people: halowe youre felues agenft to morow, that ye maye eate flefh for ye *whyned, wept* cf. German *weinen* haue whyned in the eares of the Lorde faynge: who fhall geue vs flefh to eate, for we were happie when we were in Egipte? therefore the Lorde
19 will geue you flefh, and ye fhall eate: Ye fhall not eate one daye only ether .ii. or .v. dayes, ether .x. or .xx
20 dayes: but euen a moneth longe, ãd vntill it come out at the noftrels of you, that ye be ready to perbrake: becaufe that ye haue caft ỹ Lorde a fyde which is amonge you, and haue wepte before him faynge: why came we out of Egipte.
21 And Mofes fayde: fixe hundred .thoufande fotemen are there of the people, amonge which I am. And thou haft fayde: I will geue them flefh and they fhall
22 eate a moneth lõge. Shall the fhepe ãd the oxen be flayne for them to fynde them, ether fhall all the fyfh of the fee be gathered together to ferue
23 them? And the Lorde fayde vnto Mofes: is the lordes hande waxed fhorte? Thou fhalt fe whe-

𝔐. 17 put apon the and apon them
𝔙. 15 ne tantis afficiar malis. 18 Sanctificamini: cras comedetis 20 exeat per nares veftras, & vertatur in naufeam 22 boum multitudo 23 manus dom. inualida eft?
𝔏. 15 das ich nicht meynen iamer fehen muffe. 18 heyliget euch auff morgen 20 euch zur nafen ausgehe, vnd auch eyn ekel fey 23 hand.. verkürtzt?
𝔐. 𝔐. N. 17 I wyll come doune: loke Gene. ix, a. *Take of ỹ fpirite:* That is I wyll enfpyre them with the fame fpryte. 20 *Noftrels:* Or mouthes.

[Fo. XXIIII.] ther my worde fhall come to paffe vnto the or not.

24 And mofes went out and tolde the people the fayenge of the Lorde, and gathered the .Lxx. elders of the people, and fett them rounde aboute the taber-
25 nacle. And the Lorde came doune in a cloude and fpake vnto him, ād toke of the fprete that was apon him, ād put it apon the .Lxx. elders. And as the fpirite refted apon them, they prophecied and did
26 nought els. But there remayned .ii. of y̅ mē in the hofte: the one called Eldad, ād the other Medad. And the fpirite refted apon them for they were of them that were written, but they wēt not out vnto the tabernacle: and they prophecied in the hofte.
27 And there ran a younge man & tolde Mofes and fayed: Eldad ād Medad do prophecye in the hofte.
28 And Iofua the fonne of Nū the feruaunte of Mofes which he had chofen out, anfwered and fayed: mafter
29 Mofes, forbyd them. And Mofes fayed vnto him: enuyeft thou for my fake? wolde God that all the Lordes people coude prophecye, and that the Lorde wolde put his fpirite apon them.
30 And then both Mofes and the elders of Ifrael, gat them in to the hofte.
31 And there went forth a wynde frō y̅ lorde and brought quayles from the fee and let them fall aboute the hofte, euen a dayes iurney rounde aboute on euery fyde of the hofte, and .ii. cubetes hye
32 apon the erth. And the people ftode vpp all that nyghte and on the morowe, ād gathered quayles. And

The pope wold that none of the lordes people coud prophecie & that none had his fpirite.

.P.

𝔐. 32 ftode vp all that daye & all that nyghte
𝒱. 31 volabantque in aere duobus cubitis altitudine fuper terram 32 & ficcauerunt eas
𝕷. 29 wolt Gott
𝔐. 𝔐. N. 23 *fhall come to paffe* etc: After the greke & the chalde: Some, of what value it fhalbe. 25 *Did nought els:* To prophecye is other to preache the worde to the people, as it is i. corin. xiiii. a. or to fhewe the wōderful workes of God, or to fhewe thinges to come: but to prophecye & do nought elles is here to rule the people of God accordyng to the fpyryte & to gouerne theyr fubiectes with iudgement, Iuftyce and truthe.

he that gathered the left, gathered .x. homers full. And they kylled them rounde aboute the hofte

33 And whyle the flefh was yet betwene their teeth, yer it was chewed vpp, the wrath of the yer, *ere, before* Lorde waxed whote apon the people, and the Lorde flewe of the people an exceadynge myghtie flaughter.

34 And they called the name of the place, the graues of luft: becaufe they buried the people that lufted there.

35 And the people toke their iurney from the graues of luft vnto hazeroth, and bode at hazeroth.

⁋ The .XII. Chapter.

1 AND Mir Iam and Aaron fpake ageſt Mofes, becaufe of his wife of inde which he had taken: for he had taken to wyfe one of India. And they fayed: doth ẏ Lorde fpeake ŏly thorow Mofes? doth he not fpeake alfo by us? And the Lorde herde it. But Mofes was a very meke man aboue all the men of the erthe. And ẏ Lorde fpake attonce vnto Mofes vnto Aaron & Mir Iam: come out ye .iii vnto the tabernacle of witneffe: and they came out all thre.

M.C.S. Aaron and Mir Iam grudge agaynft Mofes. Miriam was ftrycken with the leper and healed at the prayer of Mofes.

5 And the Lorde came doune in the piler of the cloude and ſtode in the dore of the taber- [Fo. XXV.] nacle and called Aaron ād Mir Iam. And they went out

6 both of them. And he fayed: heare my wordes. Yf there be a prophet of the Lordes amonge you, I will fhewe my felfe vnto him in a vifion and will fpeake

---

M. 34 place kibrath hathauah 35 kibrafh hathauah
V. 33 nec defecerat huiufcemodi cibus. xii, 1 vxorem eius Æthiopiffam 2 nonne & nobis fimiliter eft loquutus? 6 in vifione apparebo
L. 33 ehe es auff war. xii, 1 der morynnen ... darumb das er eyne morynne zum weybe 6 ynn eym geficht
M. M. N. 35 *Kibrath hathauah:* That is the graues of luft. xii, 5 *came doune:* Loke Gene. xii, a.

7 vnto him in a dreame: But my servaunte Moses is not
8 so, which is faythfull in all myne housse. Vnto him I
speake mouth to mouth and he seeth the syght and
the facyon of the Lorde, ād not thorow rydels. Wherfore thē were ye not afrayed to speake agenst my servaunte Moses?
9 And the Lorde was angrye with them and went his
10 waye, and the cloude departed from the tabernacle.
And beholde, Myr-Iam was become leprous, as it were
snowe And when Aaron looked apon Mir Iam and
11 sawe that she was leprous, he sayed vnto Moses: Oh
I beseche the my lorde, put not the synne apon vs
12 which we haue solishly commytted and synned. Oh,
let her not be as one that came deed oute of his mothers
wombe: for halfe hyr fleshe is eaten awaye.
13 And Moses cryed vnto the Lorde sayenge: Oh god,
14 heale her. And the Lorde sayed vnto Moses: Yf hir
father had spitte in hyr face, sholde she not be ashamed
15 vii. dayes? let her be shut out of the hoste .vii. dayes,
& after that let her be receyued in agayne. And Mir
Iam was shett out of the hoste .vii. dayes: ād the people remoued not, till she was .P. broughte in agayne.
16 And afterwarde they remoued from Hazeroth, and
pitched in ȳ wildernesse of Pharan.

V. 8 ore enim ad os loquor 9 abiit 10 apparuit candens lepra quasi nix. 12 quasi mortua, & vt abortiuū ... medium carnis eius devoratum est a lepra. 14 reuocabitur. 15 reuocata est Maria.

L. 8 Mundlich rede ich mit yhm 9 wand sich weg 10 war .. ausfetzig 12 wie eyn todes, das von seyner mutter leybe kompt 14 widder auff nemen 15 auffgenomen wart.

𝔐. 𝔐. N. 8 *Mouth to mouth*, that is I speake not to hym ī dreames but by manifest tokens and vysyble sygnes & vndoute-fully geue I hym knowledge of my mynde: here is no bodely mouth meant. 14 *To spytte in her face* is, to punnyshe her & cause her to se her offēce. The Lorde is a father & punnyssheth his chosē not to dāme thē but to correct & feare thē, & to dryue thē to ernest repētaunce. After .viii. dayes was she receaued agayne into the hoste, so after repentaunce had must we be receaued in to the congregacion.

⁋ The .XIII. Chapter.

1,2 AND the Lorde fpake vnto Mofes fayenge: Sende men out to ferche the londe of Canaan, which I geue vnto the childern of Ifrael: of euery trybe of their fathers a man and let them all be foche as are rue- 3 lars amonge them. And Mofes at the commaundement of the Lorde fent forth out of the wilderneffe of Pharan: foche men as were all heedes 4 amonge the childern of Ifrael, whofe names are thefe.

M.C.T. Certen are fend to fearche the land of Canaan: which bryng with thẽ a cloufter of grapes for a figne of fertylytye and fruitfulnes.

5 In the trybe of Ruben, Sammua ᵹ fonne of Zacur: In 6 the trybe of Symeon, Saphat the fonne of Hori. In the 7 trybe of Iuda Caleph the fonne of Iephune. In the trybe 8 of Ifachar, Igeal the fonne of Iofeph. In the trybe of 9 Ephraim, Hofea the fonne of Nun. In the trybe of 10 Ben Iamin, Palti the fonne of Raphu. In the trybe 11 of Zabulon, Gadiel the fonne of Sodi. In the trybe of Iofeph: In the trybe of Manaffe, Gaddi the fonne of 12 Sufi. In the trybe of Dan, Amiel the fonne of Gemali. 13 In the trybe of Affer, Sethur the fonne of Micheel. 14 In the trybe of Nephtali, Nahebi the fonne of Vaphfi. 15, 16 In the trybe of Gad, Guel the fonne of Machi. Thefe are the names of the men whiche Mofes fent to [Fo. XXVI.] fpie out the londe. And Mofes called the name of Hofea the fonne of Nun, Iofua.

17 And Mofes fent them forth to fpie out the lande of Canaan, and fayed vnto them: get you fouthwarde and 18 goo vpp in to the hye contre, and fe the londe what maner thynge it is ãd the people that dwelleth therein: whether they be ftronge or weke, ether fewe or many, 19 and what the londe is that they dwell in whether it

M. 11 Iofeph: that was of Manaffe, Gaddi
V. 2 confyderent terram 4 principes 18 cumque veneritis ad montes 19 confiderate
L. 2 Canaan erkunden 18 auff das gepirge 19 befehet
M. M. N. 16 *Hofea:* Hofea or ofee fygnifieth fauyng or fauiour. Iofua or Iehofua fignifyeth the faluaciõ of the Lorde.

be good or bad, and what maner of cities they dwell
20 in: whether they dwell in tentes or walled townes, ād
what maner of londe it is: whether it be fatt or leane,
& whether there be trees therein or not. And be of
a good corage, and brynge of the frutes of the londe.
And it was aboute the tyme that grapes are firſt rype.
21 And they went vp and ſerched out the lande from
the wildernesse of Zin vnto Rehob as men goo to He-
22 math, and they aſcended vnto the ſouth and came vnto
Hebron, where Ahiman was and Seſai and Thalmani
the ſonnes of Enacke. Hebron was bylt .vii. yere be-
23 fore Zoan in Egipte. And they came vnto the ryuer of
Eſcol and they cutte doune there a braunch with one
clouſter of grapes & bare it apō a ſtaffe betwene twayne,
& alſo of the pomgranates & of the ſygges of the place.
24 The ryuer was called Eſcol, becauſe of the clouſter of
grapes whiche the childern of Iſrael cutt doune there.
25 .℗. And they turned backe agayne from ſerchinge the
26 londe, at .xl. dayes ende. And thei went and came to
Moſes and Aaron & vnto all the multitude of the childern of Iſrael, vnto the wildernesse of Pharan: euen vnto
Cades, and broughte them worde and alſo vnto all the
congregacion, and ſhewed them the frute of the lande.
27 And they tolde him ſayenge: we came vnto the londe
wether thou ſendedſt vs, & ſurely it is a lōde that floweth
28 with milke & honye & here is of the frute of it Neuertheleſſe the people be ſtronge ỹ dwell in the londe, and
the cities are walled and exceadinge greate, and more-

ℳ. 24 Nehel Eſcol
𝒱. 20 vrbes quales, muratæ, an abſque muris 22 explorauerunt
terram 24 ad torrentem botri 25 qui appellatus eſt Nehel eſchol,
id eſt Torrens botri, eo quod botrum portaſſent 27 Pharan quod
eſt in Cades. 28 vt ex his fructibus cognoſci poteſt
ℒ. 20 mit mauren verwaret ſind odder nicht 22 erkundeten
24 bach Eſcol 25 der ort heyſt bach Eſcol .. daſelbs abſchnytten.
27 Paran gen Kades 28 vnd dis iſt yhre frucht
ℳ. ℳ. 𝒩. 22 *Enacke:* Loke ludi. i, d. *Zoan:* Otherwyſe
Tanis, after the Chalde. 24 *Nehel Eſcol* ſygnifyeth by interpretacion the ryuer of the grape or as ſome wyll the valeye of the
clouſter. 27 *Floweth with mylcke & honye* that is, full of good
paſtures, herbes, bees, catell, vynes, trees, pleaſaunt woodes ſo
that vnder heuē ther was not a moare choſen peace of grounde
for aboundance and plenteouſnes.
ℒ. ℳ. 𝒩. 24 *Eſcol* heyſt eyn drauben, daraus wirt der name
draubenbach.

29 ouer we fawe the childrē of Enack there. The amaleckes dwel in the fouth cuntre, and the Hethites, Iebufites and the Amorites dwell in the moūtaynes, and the Cananites dwell by the fee ād alonge by the cofte of Iordayne.
30 And Caleb ftylled the murmure of the people agenft Mofes fayenge: let vs goo vp and conquere it, for we
31 be able to ouercome it. But the men that went vpp with him, fayde: We be not able to goo vpp agenft
32 the people, for they are ftronger than we: And they broughte vpp an euell reporte of the londe which they had ferched, vnto the childern of Ifrael fayenge. The londe which we haue gone thorowe to ferche it out, is a londe that eateth vpp the inhabiters thereof, and the people that we fawe in it are men of ftature. [Fo. XXVII.]
33 And there we fawe alfo geantes, the childrē of Enack which are of the geaūtes. And we femed in oure fyght as it were grefhoppers and fo we dyd in their fighte.

¶ The .XIIII. Chapter.

1 AND the multitude cryed out, & the people wepte thorow out
2 that nyght, & all the childern of Yfrael murmured agenft Mofes & Aaron. And the hole congregacion fayed vnto them: wolde god that we had dyed in the lond of Egipte, ether we wolde that we had dyed in thys
3 wildernesse. Wherfore hath the Lorde broughte vs vnto this londe to fall apon the fwerde, that both oure wyues, & alfo oure childrē fhulde be a praye? is it not

M.C.S. The people difpearyng of cōmyng to the land promyfed, do murmur agaynft God, and woold haue ftoned Caleb and Iofue. The fearchers of the land dye. Amalech kylleth the Ifraelites.

V. 31 Caleb compefcens murmur populi 33 terra quam luftrauimus, deuorat 34 quibus comparati... videbamur. xiiii, 3 ducantur captiui.
L. 31 Caleb aber ftillet das volck 32 land da durch wyr gangen find zu erkunden 34 fur vnfern augen... auch ynn yhren augen. xiiii, 3 vnfer kinder eyn raub werden
M. M. N. 32 *Eateth up etc.* that is, fuffereth them not to lyue, but with battell & vyolēce of geauntes confumeth them.

4 better that we returne vnto Egipte agayne? And they fayde one to another: let vs make a captayne and returne vnto Egipte agayne.

5 And Mofes & Aaron fell on their faces before all the congregacion of the multitude of the childern of Yfrael.

6 And Iofua the fonne of Nun, and Caleb the fonne of Iephune which were of them that ferched the londe

7 rent their clothes and fpake vnto all the companye of the childern of Yfrael faynge: The londe which we

8 walked thorowe to ferche it, is a very good lande. Yf the Lorde haue luft to vs, he will bring vs in to this londe & geue it vs, which is a *luft to, delight in*

9 lond y̆ floweth with mylke & hony. But in any wife rebell not agenft .Ṗ. the Lorde, Moreouer feare ye not the people of the londe, for they are but bred for vs. Their fhylde is departed from them, & the Lorde is with vs: feare them not therfore.

10 And all the whole multitude bade ftone them with ftones. But the glorie of the Lorde appered in the tabernacle of witneffe, vnto all the childern of Ifrael.

11 And the Lorde fayed vnto Mofes: Howe longe fhall thys people rayle apon me, and how longe will it be, yer they beleue me, for all my fignes whiche I haue

12 fhewed amonge them? I will fmyte them with the peftilence & deftroy thē, and will make of the a greatter nacion and a mightier then they.

13 And Mofes fayed vnto the Lorde: then the Egiptians fhall heare it, for thou broughteft this people with thy mighte *The Pope wolde not fo haue prayed if thei had been aboute*

14 from amonge them. And it wilbe tolde *to ftone him.* to the inhabiters of this lande alfo, for they haue herde likewife, that thou the Lorde art amōge this people,

V. 4 Conftituamus nobis ducem 6 qui et ipfi luftrauerunt
12 gentem magnam et fortiorem
L. 4 heuptman auffwerfen 6 die auch das land erkundet hatten
12 groffern vnd mechtigern volck
𝔐. 𝔐. N. 6 *Rent their clothes*, loke Gene. xxxvii, f. 11 *To rayle apon the Lorde*, to prouoke him, to refyft withftand or ftryue agaynft hym: all foche maners of fpeache where foeuer ye fynde them, do fygnifye no thyng elles: but not to beleue his wordes, as in the Pfal. v, c. & .ix. f.

ād ẏ thou art ſene face to face, & ẏ thy cloude ſtondeth
ouer them & that thou goeſt before them by daye tyme
15 in a piler of cloude, & in a piler of fyre by nyght. Yf
thou ſhalt kill all this people as thei were but one mā
then the nacions which haue herde the fame of the,
16 will ſpeake ſayenge: becauſe ẏ Lorde was not able to
bringe in this people in to ẏ londe which he ſwore vnto
them, therfore he ſlewe them in the wilderneſſe.
17 [Fo. XXVIII.] So now lat the power of my Lord
18 be greate, acordynge as thou haſt ſpoken ſayenge: the
Lorde is longe yer he be angrye, ād full of mercy, and
ſuffereth ſynne and treſpace, and leaueth no man innocent,
and viſiteth the vnryghtuouſneſſe of the fathers vppon
19 ẏ childern, euē vpō ẏ thirde & fourth generacion. be
mercyfull I beſeche ẏ therfore, vnto ẏ ſynne of this
people acordinge vnto thi greate mercy, & acordinge
as thou haſt forgeuē this people from Egipte euen vnto
this place.
20 And the Lorde ſayed: I haue forgeuē it, acordynge
21 to thy requeſt. But as trulye as I lyue, all the erth
22 ſhalbe fylled with my glorye. For of all thoſe mē
whiche haue ſene my glorye & my miracles which I dyd
in Egipte & in ẏ wilderneſſe, & yet haue tempted me
now this .x. tymes & haue not herkened vnto my voyce,
23 there ſhall not one ſe the lond whiche I ſware vnto
their fathers, nether ſhall any of thē that rayled apō
24 me, ſe it. But my ſervaūte Caleb. becauſe there is another maner ſprite with hī, & becauſe he hath folowed
me vnto the vttmoſt: him I will bringe in to the lond
which he hath walked in, & his ſeed ſhall conquere it,
25 & alſo the Amalechites ād Cananites which dwell in
the lowe contrees Tomorowe turne you and gete you in
to the wilderneſſe: euen the waye towarde the red ſee.
26 .P. And the Lorde ſpake vnto Moſes ād Aaron ſayenge:

V. 24 terram hanc quam circumiuit
L. 24 dareyn er kommen iſt
M. M. N. 21 *The erth ſhalbe fylled with my glory:* That he
wyl haue the erth fylled with his glorye is, that he wyll be magny-
fyed, preached ſpoken of honoured and prayſed thorou oute the
erth. Ps. xvii, d.

27 how longe ſhall this euell multitude murmure agenſt
me? I haue herde ẏ murmurynges of ẏ childern of
28 Yſrael whyche they murmure agenſte me. Tell them,
ẏ the Lorde ſayeth. As truely as I lyue, I wil do vnto
29 you euen as ye haue ſpoken in myne eares. Youre
carkaſſes ſhall lye in this wilderneſſe, nether ſhall any
of theſe numbres which were numbred from .xx. yere
& aboue of you which haue murmured agenſt me
30 come in to the londe ouer which I lifted myne hande
to make you dwell therein, ſaue Caleb the ſonne of
Iephune, and Ioſua the ſonne of Nun.

31 And youre childern whiche ye ſayed ſhuld be a
praye, thē I will bringe in, & they ſhall knowe the
32 londe which ye haue refuſed, and youre carkeſſes ſhall
33 lye in this wilderneſſe And youre childern ſhall wādre
in this wilderneſſe .xl. yeres & ſuffre for youre whoredome vntill your carkaſſes be waſted in the wilderneſſe,
34 after the numbre of the dayes in which ye ſerched out
ẏ londe .xl. dayes, & euery daye a yere: ſo that they
ſhall bere your vnrightuouſnes .xl. yere, & ye ſhall fele
35 my vengeaunce I the Lorde haue ſayed ẏ I will do it
vnto all this euell congregacion ẏ are gathered together
agenſt me: euen in thys wilderneſſe ye ſhalbe conſumed,
and here ye ſhall dye.

36 [Fo. XXIX.] And the men which Moſes ſent to
ſerche the londe, and which (when they came agayne)
made all the people to murmure agenſt it in that they
37 broughte vpp a ſlaunder apon ẏ londe: dyed for their
bryngenge vp that euell ſlaunder apon it, and were
38 plaged before the Lorde. But Ioſua the ſonne of Nun
and Caleb the ſonne of Iephune which were of ẏ mē
39 that went to ſerche the londe, lyued ſtill. And Moſes

V. 29 iacebunt cadauera veſtra. 33 Filii .. vagi ... conſuman-
tur cadauera patrum 34 et ſcietis vltionem meam 35 deficiet &
morietur. 37 mortui ſunt et percuſſi
L. 29 Ewre leiber .. verfallen 32 yhr ſampt ewern leiben ..
verfallen 33 kinder ſollen hirten ſeyn 35 ſollen ſie alle werden ..
ſterben. 36 alſo ſtorben vnd worden geplagt
M. M. N. 30 *I lyfted etc.* Loke Exod. vi, b. 33 *Whoredome*
for infydelytye or Idolatrye as in .iiii. Regū. ix, c. & Sapiē.
xiiii, b.

tolde thefe fayenges vnto all the childern of Yfrael, and the people toke great forowe.

40 And they rofe vp yerlee in the mornynge & gatt them vpp in to the toppe of the mountayne fayenge: lo we be here, ad will goo vpp vnto the place of which the Lorde fayed, for we haue fynned. *Blinde reafō which yerwhile wolde not let them beleue in Gods worde, teacheth them now to truft in their awne workes.*
41 And Mofes fayed: wherfore will ye goo on this maner beyonde the worde of the
42 Lorde? it will not come well to paffe goo not vpp for the Lorde is not amonge you that ye be not flayne be-
43 fore youre enemyes. For the Amalechytes and the Cananites are there before you, & ye will fall apon the fwerde: becaufe ye are turned a waye from ỹ Lorde, and therfore the Lorde wyll not be with you.
44 But they were blynded to goo vpp in to ỹ hylltoppe: Neuer the lather, the arke of the teftament of the Lorde and Mofes *blynded, darkened as to the mind,* cf. Latin *contenebratus*
45 departed not out of the hofte. Then the Amalekytes ad the Cananites which dwelt in that hill, came .P. doune and fmote them and hewed thē: euen vnto Horma.

¶ The .XV. Chapter.

1 AND the Lorde fpake vnto Mo-
2 fes fayēge: fpeake vnto the childern of Ifrael & faye vnto them: when ye be come in to ỹ londe of youre habitacion which I geue
3 vnto you, and will offre an offerynge apon

M.C.S. The drynckofferinges of thē that enter i to the lāde. The punyfhment of hym that fynneth

V. 42 ne corruatis 44 contenebrati 45 percutiens eos atque concidens, perfecutus xv, 2 terram habitationis

L. 42 gefchlahen werdet 44 verblendet 45 fchlugen vnd zufchmiffen xv, 2 land ewr wonung

M. M. N. 40 fq. Blinde reafon which yer while wolde not let them beleue in Gods worde, teacheth them now to truft in their awne workes.

the fyre vnto the Lorde, whether it be a burntofferynge or a fpeciall vowe or frewill offerynge or yf it be in youre principall feftes to make a fwete fauoure vnto the Lorde, of the oxen or of the flocke.

of arrogāce or pryde. The man is ftooned that gethered ftyckes on the Saboth. Gardes muſt be made vpō the quarters of theyr garmentes.

deale, part, portion, cf. German *Theil*

4 Then, let him that offereth his offerynge vnto the Lorde, brynge alfo a meatofferynge of a tenth deale of floure myn-
5 gled with the fourth parte of an hin of oyle, and the fourth parte of an hin of wine for a drynkofferynge and offer with ẏ burntofferynge or any other
6 offerynge when it is a lambe. And vnto a rā thou fhalt offer a meatofferynge of .ii. tenth deales of floure,
7 myngled with ẏ thyrde parte of an hin of oyle, and to a drynkofferynge thou fhalt offer the thyrde parte of an hin of wyne, to be a fwete fauoure vnto the Lorde.
8 When thou offerift an oxe to a burntofferynge or in any fpeciall vowe or peafeofferinge vnto the Lorde,
9 then thou fhalt brynge vnto an oxe, a meatofferynge of .iii. tenth deales [Fo. XXX.] of floure myngled with
10 half an hin of oyle. And thou fhalt brynge for a drynkofferynge halfe an hin of wyne, that is an offer-
11 ynge of a fwete fauoure vnto the Lorde. This is the maner that fhalbe done vnto one oxe, one ram a
12 lambe or a kyd. And acordynge to the numbre of foche offerynges, thou fhalt encreafe ẏ meatofferynges and the drynkofferynges
13 All that are of youre felues fhall do thefe thinges after this maner, when he offereth an offerynge of fwete
14 fauoure vnto the Lorde And yf there be a ftraunger with you or be amonge you in youre generacions, and will offer an offerynge of a fwete fauoure vnto ẏ Lorde:
15 euen as ye do, fo he fhall doo. One ordynaunce fhall

V. 4 quartam partem hin: 5 & vinum ... eiufdem menfuræ [cf. the Hebrew and Latin vv. 10–24] .. Per agnos fingulos 6 & arietes 8 pacificas victimas

L. 4 vierden teyls (cf. *deale*) 8 zum befonderen gelübdopffer .. tödtopffer 14 der fol thun, wie fie thun

ſerue both for you of the congregacion, and alſo for the ſtraunger. And it ſhalbe an ordynaunce for euer amonge youre childern after you, that the ſtraunger
16 and ye ſhalbe lyke before the Lorde. One lawe and one maner ſhall ſerue, both for you and for ẏ ſtraunger that dwelleth with you.

17, 18 And the Lorde ſpake vnto Moſes ſayenge: ſpeake vnto the childern of Iſrael ād ſaye vnto them: when ye be come in to the londe whether I will brynge you,
19 then whē ye will eate of the bred of the londe, ye
20 ſhall geue an heue offerynge vnto the Lorde. Ye ſhall geue a cake of the firſt of youre dowe vnto an heue offerynge: as ye do the heue offerynge of the barne,
21 euen ſo ye ſhall heue it .ℙ. Of the firſt of youre dowe ye muſt geue vnto the Lorde an heue offerynge, thorow out youre generacions.

22 Yf ye ouerſe youre ſelues and obſerue   ouerſe youre not all theſe commaundmētes which the ſelues, *err*
23 Lorde hath ſpoken vnto Moſes, & all that *through ignoraunce or in-* the Lorde hath commaunded you by ẏ *aduertence,* cf. hāde of Moſes, from the firſt daye for- Germ. *überſe-* warde that the Lorde commaunded amonge youre *hen, verſehen*
24 generacion: when oughte is commytted ignorantly before the eyes of the congregacion, then all the multitude ſhall offer a calfe for a burntofferynge to be a ſwete ſauoure vnto the Lorde, & the meatofferynge and the drynkofferynge there to, acordynge to the maner: and an he goote for a ſynof-   maner, *cuſ-*
25 ferynge. And the preaſt ſhall make an *tom, uſage as preſcribed by* atonement for all the multitude of ẏ chil- *law*

𝒱. 23 a die qua cœpit iubere & vltra 24 oblitaque fuerit facere multitudo .. vt ceremoniæ poſtulant

𝑳. 15 Der gantzen gemeyn ſey eyn ſatzung ... eyne ewige ſatzung ſoll das ſeyn ewrn nachkomen das fur dem Herrn der frembling ſey, wie yhr 23 von dem tage an da er anfieng zu gepieten 24 die gemeyne etwas vnwiſſent thet... wie es recht iſt 25 Vnd der prieſter

𝔐. 𝔐. N. 15 This cōmaundement was a fore token of gethering the gentyles & the hebrues in to one church of Chriſte, Iohan. x, c. wherin there is no dyfference betwene the Hebrue or Iewe and the grecyan, ryche and poore, cytezen and ſtraunger or forener.

dern of Israel, ād it shalbe forgeuen thē for it was ignoraunce. And they shall brynge their giftes vnto the offerynge of the Lorde, and their synofferynge
26 before the Lorde for their ignoraunce. And it shalbe forgeuen vnto all the multitude of the childern of Israel, & vnto the straunger that dwelleth amōge you: for the ignorauncye perteyneth vnto all the people.
27 Yf any one soule synne thorow ignoraunce he shall brynge a she goote of a yere olde for a synneofferynge.
28 And the preast shall make an atonement for the soule that synned ignorauntly with the synofferynge before the [Fo. XXXI.] Lorde and reconsyle him, and it
29 shalbe forgeuen him. And both thou that art borne one of the childern of Israel and the straunger that dwelleth amonge you shall haue both one lawe, yf ye synne thorow ignorauncye.
30 And the soule that doth ought presumptuously, whether he be an Israelite or a straūger, the same hath despysed the Lorde. And that soule shalbe de-
31 stroyed from amonge his people, becaufe he hath despised the worde of the Lorde & hath brokē his cōmaūdmentes, ẏ soule therfore shall perysh ād his synne shalbe apon him.
32 And whyle the childern of Ysrael were in the wildernesse, they founde a man gatherynge stickes vppon
33 the Sabath daye. And they ẏ founde him gatherynge stickes, brought him vnto Moses and Aaron and vnto
34 all ẏ congregacion: ād they put him in warde, for it was not declared what shulde be done vnto him.
35 And the Lorde sayed vnto Moses: ẏ mā shall dye. let all the multitude stone him with stones without

V. 25 nihilominus 26 quoniam culpa est omnis populi per ignorantiam. 29 Tam indigenis quam aduenis vna lex erit omnium qui peccauerint ignorantes. 30 Anima vero quæ per superbiam .. quon. aduersus dominum rebellis fuit 34 nescientes quid super eo facere deberent. 35 Morte moriatur

L. 26 das gantze volck ist ynn solcher vnwissenheyt. 29 Vnd es soll eyn gesetz seyn 30 eyn seele aus hoffart ... der hat den Herrn geschmecht 34 Denn es war nicht ausgedruckt, was man mit yhm thun solte 35 des todts sterben

M. M. N. 32 Necessytye droue him not to gether styckes & therfore was he woorthye this cruell death, for as moche as he dispysed to heare the woorde of the Lorde wher vnto he was so straytlye cōmaunded to geue eare on the saboth daye.

36 the hoste. And all ỷ multitude broughte him with out the hoste ād stoned him with stones, and he dyed as the Lorde commaunded Moses.

37, 38 And the Lorde spake vnto Moses sayenge: speake vnto the childern of Ysrael and byd them, that they make them gardes apon the quarters of their garmētes thorow out their generacions, ād let them make the gardes .P. of ribandes of
39 Iacyncte And the garde shall be vnto you to loke apon it, that ye remembre all the commaundmentes of the Lorde and doo them: that ye seke not a waye after youre awne hertes and after youre awne eyes, for to goo a whooringe after them:
40 but that ye remembre and doo all my commaundmentes and be holy vnto youre
41 God, for I am ỷ Lorde youre God, which broughte you out of ỷ londe of Egipte, to be youre God. I am the Lorde God.

gardes, fringes quarters, corners

Iacyncte, blue

Gods signes were to put men in remēbraunce of his worde, that they shuld not seke a waye to please God after their awne imaginacion.

⁌ The .XVI. Chapter.

1 AND Corah the sonne of Iezehar the sonne of Cahath the sonne of Leui: & Dathan & Abiram the sonne of Eliab, and On the sonne of Peleth, the sonne of Ruben:
2 stode vpp before Moses, with other of the childern of Israel .ii. hundred and fystie, heedes of the congregacion, and councelers, and men

M.C.S. The rebelliō & resystaunce of Corah, Dathan & Abiram. The erth opened and swalowed them vp.

M. 41 Egipte, for to be youre God
V. 38 fimbrias per angulos . . . vittas hyacinthinas 40 sintque sancti deo suo. xvi, 2 contra Moysen . . . viri proceres synagogæ, & qui tempore concilii per nomina vocabantur.
L. 38 lepplin machen an den fittichen . . . gelle schnurlin 40 heylig seyn ewrem Gott. xvi, 2 fur Mose . . heubtleut der gemeyne, radtsherrn vnd berumpt leut
M. M. N. 38 Soche *gardes* shulde the christen haue depely fixed in their hertes, consydering what they are bounde to the Lorde, of what god what a seruyce they haue takē vpō thē: that they myght with al dyligēce & cyrcumspectiō fullfyl that, which they haue promised etc. xvi, 1 Some wryte Koreh the sonne of Izachar. Some wryte Abirom.

3 of fame, and they gathered thē felues together agenſt Moſes and Aaron & ſayed vnto them: ye haue done ynough. For all the multitude are holy euery one of them, and the Lorde is amonge them. Why therfore heue ye youre ſelues vpp aboue the con- *heue, lift* gregacion of the Lorde.

4, 5 When Moſes herde it, he fell apon his face and ſpake vnto Corah and vnto all his companye ſayenge: tomorow the Lorde will ſhewe who is his and who is holy, and will take them vnto him, and whom ſo euer he [Fo. XXXII.] hath choſen, he will cauſe to come
6 to him. This doo: take fyrepannes, thou Corah and
7 all thi companye, and do fyre therein ād put cēs thereto before the Lorde tomorowe: And then whom ſoeuer the Lorde doeth choſe, the ſame is holy. Ye make ynough to doo ye childern of Leui.

8 And Moſes ſayed vnto Corah: heare ye childern of
9 leui, Semeth it but a ſmall thynge vnto you, that ẏ God of Iſrael hath ſeparated you frō the multitude of Iſrael to brynge you to him, to doo the ſeruyce of the dwellynge place of the Lorde, and to ſtonde before the
10 people to minyſtre vnto them? he hath taken the to him and all thi brethern the ſonnes of leui with the,
11 and ye ſeke the office of ẏ preaſt alſo. For which cauſe both thou and all thi companye are gathered together agenſt the Lorde: for what is Aaron, that ye ſhulde murmure agenſt him.

12 And Moſes ſent to call Dathan ād Abiram the ſonnes of Eliab, and they anſwered: we will not come.
13 Semeth it a ſmall thynge vnto the that thou haſt broughte us out of a londe that floweth with mylke and honye, to kyll us in ẏ wilderneſſe. But that thou
14 ſhuldeſt reygne ouer us alſo? More ouer thou haſt broughte us vnto no londe that floweth with mylke and honye, nether haſt geuen us poſſeſſions of feldes or

V. 5 quos elegerit appropinquabūt ei. 10 vt vobis etiam ſacerdotium vendicetis 14 Reuera induxiſti nos in terram ..
L. 5 Wilchen er erwelet der ſol ſich zu yhm nahen 10 vnd yhr fucht nu auch das prieſterthum 14 wie feyn haſtu vns bracht ynn eyn land

of vynes. Ether wilt thou pull out the eyes of thefe men? we wyll .P. not come.

15 And Mofes waxed very angrye and fayed vnto the Lorde: Turne not vnto their offerynges. I haue not taken fo moch as an affe from them, ne- *Can oure prel-*
16 ther haue vexed any of them. Then *ates fo faye?* Mofes fayed vnto Corah: Be thou ãd all thy companye before the Lorde: both thou, they and Aaron to
17 morowe. And take euery man his cenfer and put cens in them, & come before the Lorde euery man with hys cenfer: two hundred and fyftie cenfers, and Aaron with
18 his cenfer. And they toke euery man his cenfer and put fyre in them & layed cens thereon, and ftode in the dore of the tabernacle of witneffe, and Mofes &
19 Aaron alfo. And Corah gathered all the congregacyon agenft them vnto the dore of the tabernacle of witneffe.

And the glorye of the Lorde appered vnto all the
20 congregacion. And the Lorde fpake vnto Mofes and
21 Aaron fayenge: feparate youre felues from this con-
22 gregacion, that I maye confume them atonce. And they fell apon their faces and fayed: O moft myghtie God of the fpirites of all flefhe, one mã hath fynned,
23 and wylt thou be wroth with all the multitude? And
24 the Lorde fpake vnto Mofes fayenge: fpeake vnto the congregacion and faye: Gett you awaye from aboute the dwellynge of Corah, Dathan & Abiram.
25 And Mofes rofe vpp and went vnto Da- [Fo. XXXIII.] than & Abirã, & the elders of Ifrael folowed
26 him. And he fpake vnto the congregacyon fayenge: departe from the tentes of thefe weked men and twyche nothinge of theres: left ye peryfhe in all there fynnes.
27 And they gate them from the dwellynge of Corah,

V. 14 an & oculos noftros vis eruere? 15 Ne refpicias 16 & Aaron die craftino feparatim. 22 Fortiffime deus fpirituum vniverfæ carnis... ira tua defæuiet? 26 ne inuoluamini in peccatis eorum.
L. 14 Wiltu den leutten auch die augen aus brechen? 15 wende dich nicht 16 morgen... du, fie auch vnd Aaron 22 Gott Gott der geyfter alles fleyfchs.. vber die gantze gemeyne wueten? 26 das yhr nicht villeicht vmbkompt ynn yrgent yhrer funden eyne.

Dathan and Abiram, on euery fide. And Dathan and Abiram came out & ftode in ẙ dore of there tētes with their wyues, their fonnes and their childern.

28 And Mofes fayed: Hereby ye fhall knowe that the Lorde hath fent me to doo all thefe workes, and that
29 I haue not done them of myne awne mynde: Yf thefe men dye the comon deth of all men or yf they be vifyted after the vifitacion of all men, then the Lorde
30 hath not fent me. But and yf the Lorde make a new thinge, and the erth open hir mouthe and fwalowe them and all that pertayne vnto them, fo that they goo doune quycke in to hell: then ye fhall vnderftōd, that thefe mē haue rayled apon the Lorde.

31 And as foone as he had made an ende of fpeakynge all thefe wordes, the grounde cloue afunder that was
32 vnder them, and ẙ erth opened hir mouthe and fwalowed them and their houffes and all the mē that
33 were with Corah and all their goodes. And they and all that pertayned vnto them, went doune alyue vnto hell, and the erthe clofed apon them, and they
34 peryfhed from amonge the .Ꝑ. congregacyon. And all Ifrael that were aboute them, fledde at the crye of them.

For they fayed: The erthe myghte happelye fwalowe
35 vs alfo. And there came oute a fyre from the Lorde and confumed the two hundred and fyftye men that offred cens.
36, 37 And the Lorde fpake vnto Mofes fayenge: Speake vnto Eleazer the fonne of Aaron the preafte and let him take vppe the cenfers oute of the burnynge
38 and fcater the fyre here and there, for the cenfers of thefe fynners are halowed in theyr deethes: and

---

V̄. 27 a tentoriis eorū per circumitum ... & liberis, omnique frequentia. 28 & non ex proprio ea corde protulerim. 30 fcietis quod blafphemauerint dominum. 33 defcenderuntque viui in infernum operti humo 34 fugit a clamore pereuntium 37 quoniam fanctificata funt 38 in mortibus peccatorum

L. 27 traten an die thur yhrer hutten mit yhren weyben vnd fonen vnd kindern 28 vnd nicht von meynem hertzen 30 erkennen, das dife leut den Herrn geleftert haben 33 vnd furen hyn vntern lebendig ynn die helle 34 floh fur yhrem gefchrey

M. M. N. 29 *Vifited:* That is pūnyfhed with the punnyfhement. 30 *To go doune quycke or a lyue into hell* is, to peryfh by foudayne deeth and to be ouerwhelmed with the erth.

let them be beten in to thyne plates thyne, *thin* and faftened apon the altare. For they offred thē before the Lorde, and therfore they are holye and they fhalbe a fygne vnto the childern of Ifrael.

39 And Eleazar the preaft toke the brafen cenfers which they that were burnt had offered, and bet them
40 and faftened them vppon the altare, to be a remembraunce vnto the childern of Ifrael, that no ftraunger whiche is not of the feed of Aaron, come nere to offer cens before the Lorde, that he be not made like vnto Corah and his companye: as the Lorde fayed vnto him by the hande of Mofes.

41 And on the morowe all the multitude of the childern of Ifraell murmured agenfte Mofes and Aaron fayenge: ye haue kylled [Fo. XXXIIII.] the people of
42 the Lorde. And when the multitude was gathered agenfte Mofes and Aaron, they loked towarde the tabernacle of witneffe. And beholde, the cloude had couered it and the glorye of the Lorde appeared.
43 And Mofes and Aaron went before the tabernacle of
44 witneffe. And the Lorde fpake vnto Mofes fayenge:
45 Gett you from this congregacyon, that I maye confume them quyckelye. And they fell apon theyr faces.
46 And Mofes fayde vnto Aaron: take a cenfer and put fyre therein out of the alter, and poure on cens, and goo quyckly vnto the cōgregacion and make an attonement for thē. For there is wrath gone oute from the
47 Lorde, and there is a plage begone. And Aaron toke

V. 38 eo quod oblatum fit . . . et fanctificata fint . . pro figno & monimēto 42 Cumque oriretur feditio & tumultus increfceret 43 Moyfes & Aaron fugerūt . . Quod poftquam ingreffi funt, operuit nubes, & apparuit gloria domini. 44 Dixitque dominus 45 etiam nunc delebo eos. 46 et plaga defæuit. 47 Quod cum feciffet Aaron

L. 38 denn folche pfannen der funder find geheyligt, durch yhre feele . . . denn fie find geopffert fur dem Herrn vnd geheyliget, vnd follen den kindern Ifrael zum zeychen feyn. 42 gemeyne verfamlet widder Mofe vnd Aaron, wandten fie fich zu der hutten des zeugnis. Vnd fihe, da bedecket es die wolcken, vnd die herlickeyt des Herrn erfcheyn 45 ich will fie bald freffen 47 Vnd Aaron nam. . .

M. M. N. 38 The cenfers were *halowed in theyr deathes* becaufe that by them was geuen an enfample vnto other to feare.

as Moſes commaunded him, and ran vnto the congregacion: and beholde, the plage was begone amonge
the people, and he put on cens, and made an attone-
48 ment for the people. And he ſtode betwene the deed,
49 and them that were alyue, and the plage ceaſed. And
the numbre of them that dyed in the plage, were
xiiii. thouſande and ſeuen hundred: beſyde them that
50 dyed aboute the buſynes of Corah. And Aaron went
agayne vnto Moſes vnto the dore off the tabernacle of
witneſſe, and the plage ceaſed.

❧ The .XVII. Chapter.

.P. XVII. Chapter.

1
2 AND the Lorde ſpake vnto Moſes ſayenge: ſpeake vnto the
childern of Iſrael and take
of them, for euery pryncypall
houſſe a rod, of their princes ouer the houſſes of their
fathers: euen .xii. roddes, and wryte euery mans name
3 apon his rod. And wryte Aarons name apon the ſtaffe
of Leui: for euery heedman ouer the houſſes of their
4 fathers ſhall haue a rod. And put thē in the taber-
5 nacle of witneſſe where I wyll mete you. And his
rod whom I choſe, ſhall bloſſome: So I wyll make ceaſe
from me the grudgynges of the children of Iſrael which
they grudge agenſt you.
6 And Moſes ſpake vnto the childern off Iſrael, and

*M.C.S. Aa-
rons rodde
buddeth and
beareth bloſ-
ſomes.*

V. 48 & ſtans inter mortuos ac viuentes 50 poſtquam quieuit
interitus. xvii, 4 coram teſtimonio vbi loquar ad te. 5 et cohibebo
a me querimonias filiorum Iſrael, quibus contra vos murmurant.
L. 47 vnd die plage iſt angangen vnter 48 vnd ſtund zwiſchen
den todten vnd lebendigen 50 vnd der plage wart geweret.
xvii, 4 fur dem zeugnis da ich euch zeuge 5 das ich das murren
der kinder Iſrael, das ſie widder euch murren, ſtille.
M. M. N. 48 Aaron is heare a fygure of Chriſt which is the
medyatoure betwene God and the churche which reſtraineth the
iuſt vengeaunce of God for the ſynnes of the worlde, which helpeth the choſen whē they be in ieopardye.

all the prynces gaue him for euery prynce ouer their
fathers houffes, a rod: euen .xii. roddes, and the rod
7 of Aaron was amonge the rodes. And Mofes put ẏ
roddes before the Lorde in the tabernacle of witneffe.
8 And on the morowe, Mofes went in to the tabernacle:
and beholde, the rod of Aaron of the houffe of Leui
9 was budded & bare blofomes and almondes. And
Mofes broughte out all the ftaues from before the
Lorde, vnto all the childern of Ifrael, & thei loked
apon them, and toke euery man his ftaffe.
10 And the Lorde fayed vnto Mofes: brynge Aarons
rod agayne before the witneffe to be kepte for a token
vnto the childern of re- [Fo. XXXV.] bellyon, that
their murmurynges maye ceaffe fro me, that they
11 dye not. And Mofes dyd as the Lorde commaunded
12 him. And the childern of Ifrael fpake vnto Mofes
fayenge: beholde, we are deftroyed and all come to
13 nought: for whofoeuer cometh nye the dwellynge of
the Lord, dyeth. Shall we vtterly confume awaye?

☛ The .XVIII. Chapter.

1 **A**ND the Lorde fayed vnto Aaron: *M.C.S. The offyce of the Leuites. The tythes and fyrft frutes muft be geuen them. Aarons herytage.*
Thou and thy fonnes and thy
fathers houffe with the, fhall
bere the faute of that whiche
faute, *fault,* is done amyffe in the holy
iniquity. place.
And thou and thy fonnes with the, fhall beare the

V. 6 et dederunt ei omnes principes virgas per fingulas tribus
fueruntque virgæ duodecim abfque virga Aaron. 10 in fignum re
bellium filiorum 12 Ecce cōfumpti fumus, omnes periimus 13 num
vfque ad internecionem cuncti delendi fumus?
L. 6 gaben yhm zwelff ftecken, eyn iglicher heubtman eynen
ftecken nach dem haus yhrer veter, Vnd der ftecke Aaron war
auch vnter yhren ftecken. 10 zum zeichen den widderfpenftigen
kindern 12 Sihe, wyr nemen ab vnd komen vmb, werden all vnd
komen vmb 13 Sollen wyr denn allerding abnemen?
M. M. N. 1 *Holy place:* Vnderftāde yf ye take not heade
that it be not touched.

faute of that whiche is done amyſſe in youre preaſt-
2 hode. And thy brethern alſo ẏ tribe of leui, ẏ trybe
of thy father take with the, and let them be yoyned
vnto the and miniſtre vnto the.

And thou and thy ſonnes with the ſhall miniſtre
3 before the tabernacle of witneſſe. And let them wayte
apon the and apon all the tabernacle: only let them
not come nye the holy veſſels & the alter, that both
4 they ād ye alſo dye not. And let them be by the and
wayte on the tabernacle of witneſſe, and on all the
ſeruyce of the tabernacle, and let no ſtraunger come
nye vnto you.

5 Wayte therfore apon the holye place and .P. apon
the alter, ẏ there fall no moare wrath apon the childern
6 of Iſrael: beholde, I haue taken youre brethern the
leuites from amonge [the] childern of Iſrael, to be
youres, as giftes geuen vnto the Lorde to doo the
7 ſeruyce of the tabernacle of witneſſe. And ſe that
both thou and thy ſonnes with the take hede vnto
youre preaſtes office, in all thinges that pertayne
vnto the alter and within the vayle. And ſe that
ye ſerue, for I haue geuē youre preaſtes office vnto
you for a gifte to do ſeruyce: & the ſtraunger that
cometh nye, ſhall dye.

8 And the Lorde ſpake vnto Aaron: beholde, I haue
geuen the the kepynge of myne heueofferynges in all
the halowed thynges of the childern of Iſrael. And
vnto the I haue geuen them vnto anoyntynge ād to
9 thy ſonnes: to be a dutye for euer. This   dutye, *due*,
ſhall be thyne of moſt holy ſacrifyces: All noun
their giftes, thorow out all their meatofferynges ſynne-

    M. 6 from amonge the chyldren
    V. 1 peccata ſacerd. 2 fratres tuos de tribu Leui, ſceptro patris
tui ſume tecum . . in tabernaculo teſtimonii. 3 Excubabuntque
Leuitæ ad præcepta tua . . . ne & illi moriantur, vt vos pereatis
ſimul. 4 Alienigena non miſcebitur vobis. 5 ne oriatur indignatio
7 per ſacerdotes adminiſtrabuntur. 8 dedi tibi cuſtodiam primitiarum mearum. 9 & cedit in ſancta ſanctorum
    L. 1 miſſethat ewrs prieſterthums 2 deyne bruder des ſtams
Leui deyne vatters . . . fur der hutten des zeugnis 4 Vnd keyn
frembder ſol ſich zu euch nahen 5 das furt nicht mehr eyn wueten
kome 7 denn ewr prieſterthum gebe ich euch eyn zum ampt fur
eyn gabe 8 meyne Hebeopffer 9 das aller heyligſt ſeyn.

offrynges and trefpaceoffrynges whiche they bringe vnto me: They fhalbe moft holy vnto the ãd vnto
10 thy fonnes. And ye fhall eate it in the moft holye place: all that are males fhall eate of it: for it fhalbe holye vnto the.
11 And this fhalbe thyne: the heueofferynge of their giftes, thorow out all the waueofferynges of the childern of Ifrael, for I haue geuen them vnto the and thy fonnes, [Fo. XXXVI.] and thy doughters with the, to be a dutye for euer: and all that are cleane in thy
12 houfe, fhall eate of it, all the fatt of the oyle, of the wyne and of the corne: their firftfrutes which they geue
13 vnto the Lorde that haue I geuen vnto the. The firft frutes of all that is in their londes whiche they brynge vnto the Lorde, fhalbe thyne: and all that are cleane in thyne houffe, fhall eate off it.
14, 15 All dedicate thinges in Ifrael, fhalbe thine. All that breaketh the matrice of all flefh that men bringe vnto the Lorde, bothe of man and beeft, fhalbe thyne. Neuerthelater the firftborne of man fhalbe redemed, and the firftborne of vncleane beeftes fhalbe redemed.
16 And their redemptions fhalbe at a moneth olde, valowed at .v. fycles of fyluer, of the holy fycle. A fycle
17 maketh twentye Geras. But the firftborne of oxen, fhepe & gootes fhall not be redemed. For they are holy, and thou fhalt fprinkle their bloud apon the alter, and fhalt burne their fatt to be a facrifyce of a fwete fauoure vnto the Lorde.
18 And the flefh of them fhalbe thyne, as the waue
19 breft and all the right fhulder is thyne. All the holy heueofferynges whiche the childern of Ifrael heue vnto ẏ Lorde, I geue the & thy fonnes & thi doughters with the to be a dutye for euer. And it fhalbe a

V 10 mares tantum edent ex eo, quia confecratum eft tibi 13 Vniuerfa frugum initia, quæ gignit humus 14 Omne quod ex voto 15 ita duntaxat 16 obolos 17 quia fanctificata funt domino 19 Omnes primitias fanctuarii ...

L. 10 Am allerheyligften ort foltu es effen ... Was menlich ift ... denn es fol dyr heylig feyn. 13 Die erfte frucht, alles das ynn yhrem land 14 Alles verbannete ynn Ifrael 15 doch das du die erfte menfchen frucht 16 Gera. 17 denn fie find heylig 19 Alle Hebopffer die die kinder Ifrael heyligen ...

salted couenaunte for euer, before the Lorde: vnto the and to thy seed with the.

20 ¶. And the Lorde spake vnto Aaron: thou shalt haue none enheritaunce in their lande, nor parte amonge them. For I am thy parte and thy enheritaunce
21 among the childern of Israel. And beholde I haue geuen the childern of Leui, the tenth in Israel to enherite, for the seruyce whiche they serue in the taber-
22 nacle of witnesse, that the childrē of Israel henceforth come not nye the tabernacle of witnesse, and beare
23 synne and dye. And the leuites shall do the seruyce in the tabernacle of witnesse and beare their synne, and it shalbe a lawe for euer vnto youre childern after you: But amonge the childern of Israel they shall en-
24 heret none enheritaunce. For the tithes of the childern of Israel whiche they heve vnto the Lorde, I haue geuen the Leuites to enherett. Wherfore I haue sayed vnto them: Amonge the chyldern off Israell ye shall enherett none enheritaunce. *Oures, will haue tithes & landes & rētes & kingdomes & emperies and all.*

25, 26 And the Lorde spake vnto Moses sayenge: speake vnto the leuites and saye vnto thē: when ye take of the childern of Israel the tithes whiche I haue geuen you of them to youre enheritaunce, ye shall take an heueoffrynge of that same for the Lorde: euen the
27 tenth of that tythe. And it shalbe rekened vnto you for youre heueofferynge, euen as though ye gaue corne out of the barne or a fullofferynge from the wynepresse.
28 [Fo. XXXVII.] And of this maner ye shall heue an heueofferynge vnto ẏ Lorde, of all youre tithes which ye receaue of the childern of Israel, & ye shall geue

V. 19 Pactum salis est 21 in possessionem pro ministerio 22 nec cōmittant peccatū mortiferū 24 decimarum oblatione contenti, quas in vsus eorum & necessaria separaui.

L. 19 eyn vnuerwesenlich bund 21 alle zehenden geben ynn Israel zum erbgut 22 das hynfurt .. nicht nahen .. sund auff sich zu laden vnd sterben.

M. M. N. 19 *Salted couenaūt* for a fyrm suer and stable couenaunt.

L. M. N. 19 Im Ebreischen heysst es eyn saltzbund, das wie das saltz erhelt das fleysch vnuerweslich, also soll auch diser bund vnuerrucklich seyn. So redet die schrifft auch .2. Paralip. 13. Gott hatt das reych Dauid geben vnd seynen mit eym saltzbund.

there of the Lordes heueofferinge vnto Aaron the
29 preaſt Of all youre giftes, ye ſhall take out the Lordes
heueofferynge: euen the fatt of all their halowed
thynges.
30 And thou ſhalt ſaye vnto them: when ye haue take
a waye the fatt of it from it, it ſhalbe counted vnto
31 the leuites, as ẏ encreaſe of corne and wyne And ye
ſhall eate it in all places both ye and youre houſholdes,
for it is youre rewarde for youre ſeruyce in the taber-
32 nacle of witneſſe. And ye ſhall beare no ſynne by ẏ
reaſon of it, when ye haue taken from it the fatt of it:
nether ſhall ye vnhalowe ẏ halowed thynges of the
childern of Iſrael, and ſo ſhall ye not dye.

☙ The .XIX. Chapter.

1 AND the Lorde ſpake vnto Moſes
2 and Aaron ſayenge: this is the
ordynaunce of the lawe which
ẏ Lorde cōmaūdeth ſayenge:
ſpeake vnto ẏ childern of Iſrael and let
them take the a redd cowe with out ſpot
wherein is no blemyſh,& which neuer bare
3 yocke apō her. And ye ſhall geue her
vnto Eleazer the preaſt, and he ſhall brynge her with
out the hoſte and cauſe her to be ſlayne before him.
4 And Eleazar ẏ preaſt ſhall take of hir bloude vppon
his fynger, and ſprynkle it ſtreght .P. towarde the tab-
5 ernacle of witneſſe .vii. tymes And he ſhall cauſe the

*M.C.S. Of
the redde
cowe. The
lawe of him
that dyeth in
the taberna-
cle: and of
hym alſo
that toucheth
any vncleane
thyng.*

V. 29 Omnia quæ offeretis ex decimis, & in donaria domini
ſeparabitis 30 reputabitur vobis 32 ne polluatis oblationes filiorum
Iſrael, & moriamini. xix, 2 religio victimæ . . . vaccam ruſam
ætatis integræ 3 in conſpectu omnium
L. 30 ſo ſols den leuiten gerechnet werden 32 vnd nicht ent-
weyhen das geheyligete der kinder Iſrael, vnd nicht ſterben.
xix, 2 Diſe weyſe ſol eyn geſetz ſeyn . . . eyn rodlichte kue . . .
auff die noch nie keyn ioch komen iſt 3 daſelbs fur yhm 4 ſtracks
gegen die hutten

cowe to be burnt in his fyghte: both fkyn, flefh and
6 bloude, with the doūge alfo. And let the preaft take
cipreffe wodd, and Ifope and purple cloth, and caft
7 it apon the cowe as fhe burneth. And let the preaft
wafh his clothes and bathe his flefh in water, and then
come in to the hofte, and ỹ preaft fhalbe vncleane
vnto the euen.

8 And he that burneth her, fhall wafh his clothes in
water & bathe his flefh alfo in water, ād be vncleane
9 vntill euen. And one that is cleane, fhall goo and
take vpp the affhes of the cowe, and put them without
the hofte in a cleane place, where they fhall be kepte to
make fprynklynge water for the multitude *Hēce came*
of the childern of Ifrael: for it is a fynoffer- *holy water*
10 ynge And let him that gathereth the affhes of the
cowe, wafh his clothes, and remayne vncleane vntill
euen. And this fhalbe vnto the childern of Ifrael ād
vnto the ftraunger ỹ dwelleth amonge them, a maner
for euer.

11 He that twycheth any deed perfone, fhalbe vn-
12 cleane .vii. dayes. And he fhall purifye him felfe with
the affhes the thyrde daye ād then he fhalbe cleane
the feuenth daye. And yf he purifye not himfelfe the
thyrde daye, thē the feuenth daye, he fhall not be
13 cleane. Whofoeuer twicheth any perfone ỹ dyeth &
fprynkleth not him felfe, defyleth the dwellynge of
[Fo. XXXVIII.] the Lorde: ād therfore that foule
fhalbe roted out of Ifrael, becaufe he hath not fpryn-

𝔐. 6 Cedar wood 13 whofoeuer toucheth
𝒱. 5 comburetque eam cunctis videntibus 6 in flammam, quæ
... vorat 7 corpore fuo 9 in loco puriffimo ... quia pro peccato vacca combufta eft. 10 fanctum iure perpetuo. 13 Omnis
qui ... et peribit ex Ifrael ... et manebit fpurcitia eius fuper eum.
𝔏. 5 kue fur yhm verbrennen 6 auff die brennende kue 7 feyn
leyb (v. 8) 9 an eyne reyne ftette ... denn es ift eyn fundopfer.
10 eyn ewigs recht 13 folche feele fol ausgerotet werden
𝔐. 𝔐. 𝔑. 10 *For euer* loke gene. xiii, d. 13 As they were
defyled with the touchyng of the deed, fo are the foules of the
chriften defyled when they commyt deedly fynne: which is
cleanfed with chriftes facryfyce and merytes onely: and that
cleāfyng obtayned by the paffyon and deth of Chrift oure Lorde
who foeuer contēneth his foule fhall be rooted oute frō among
the chofen.

kled the fprynklynge water vppon him. he fhalbe vncleane, and his vnclenneffe fhall remayne vppon him.

14 This is the lawe of the man that dyeth in a tent: all that come in to the tent and all ẙ is in the tent, fhalbe
15 vncleane .vii. dayes. And all the veffels that be opē which haue no lyd nor couerynge apon them, are vn-
16 cleane. And who foeuer twicheth one that is flayne with a fwerde in the feldes, or a deed perfone, or a bone of a deed man, or a graue: fhall be vncleane .vii dayes.
17 And they fhall take for an vncleane perfone, of the burnt affhes of the fynofferynge, & put runnynge water
18 thereto in to a veffell. And a cleane perfone fhall take Ifope and dyppe it in the water, and fprynkle it apon ẙ tent and apon all the veffells and on the foules that were there, and apon him that twyched a bone or a
19 flayne perfone or a deed body or a graue. And the cleane perfone fhall fprynkle apon the vncleane the thyrde daye and the feuenth daye. And the feuenth daye he fhall purifie him felfe and waffhe his clothes and bathe him felfe in water, and fhalbe cleane at euen.
20 Yf any be vncleane and fprynkle not himfelfe, the fame foule fhalbe deftroyed frō amōge the congregacion: for he hath defyled .P. the holy place of the Lorde. And he that fprynkleth ẙ fprynklynge water, fhall waffh his clothes.
21 And he that twicheth the fprynklynge water, fhal-
22 be vncleane vntill euē. And whatfoeuer ẙ vncleane perfone twicheth, fhalbe vncleane. And the foule that twicheth it, fhalbe uncleane vntill the euen.

M. 20 holy place of ẙ Lorde, & is not fprynkled with fprinklyng water therfore is he vncleane. And this fhalbe a perpetual lawe vnto thē.

V. 16 aut per fe mortui 17 cineribus combuftionis atque peccati 18 & homines huiufcemodi contagione pollutos 20 Si quis hoc ritu non fuerit expiatus ... de medio ecclefiæ 22 et anima quæ horum quippiam tetigerit

L. 16 oder eyn todten 17 nemen der affchen difes verbranten fundopffers 18 vnd alle feelen die drynnen find. Alfo auch denen der eyns todten beyn, odder erfchlagenen, odder todten, odder grab angeruret hat 20 Wilcher aber vnreyn feyn wirt vnd fich nicht entfundigen wil 22 Vnd wilche feel er anruren wirt

❡ The .XX. Chapter.

1 AND the whole multitude of ẏ childern of Israel, came in to the deserte of Sin in the first moneth, & the people dwelt at cades. And there dyed Mir Iam, &
2 was buried there. More ouer there was no water for the multitude, wherfore they gathered thē selues together agēst Moses
3 and agēst Aaron. And the people chode with Moses and spake sayenge: wold God that we had peryshed when oure brethern
4 peryshed before ẏ Lorde. Why haue ye brought the congregacion of the Lorde vnto this wildernesse, that
5 both we & oure catell shulde dye here? Wherfore brought ye us out of Egipte, to brynge us in to this vngracious place, which is no place of seed nor of sygges nor vynes nor of pomgranates, nether is there any water to drynke?

6 And Moses and Aaron went from the congregacion vnto the dore of the tabernacle of witnesse, and fell apon their faces. And ẏ glorye of the Lorde appered
7 vnto them. And [Fo. XXXIX.] the Lorde spake vnto
8 Moses sayenge: take ẏ staffe, and gather thou and thi brother Aarō the congregacion together, and saye vnto the rocke before their eyes, that he geue forth his water. And thou shalt brynge thē water out of the rocke and shalt geue the company drynke, and their beesse also.

M.C.S. Mir Iam dyeth. The people murmur. They haue water euen oute of the rocke. Edom denyeth the Israelites passage thorow his reaulme. The death of Aaron in whose roume Eleasar succedeth.

V. 3 & versi in seditionem ... Vtinam periissemus inter fratres nostros 4 ecclesiam domini 6 Ingressusque Moyses & Aaron dimissa multitudine in tabernaculum fœderis ... — *clamaueruntque ad dominum, atque dixerunt, Domine deus audi clamorem huius populi, & aperi eis thesaurū tuum fontē aquæ viuæ, vt satiati cesset murmuratio eorum* . . 8 loquimini ad petram

L. 2 haddert mit Mose .. Ach das wyr vmbkomen weren da vnser bruder vmbkamen 4 gemeyne des Herrn 6 von der gemeyne zur thur der hutten des zeugnis 8 redet mit dem fels

9 And Moſes toke the ſtaffe from before ẏ Lorde, as
10 he commaunded him. And Moſes and Aaron gathered
the congregacion together before the rocke, ād he
ſayed vnto thē heare ye rebellyons, muſt we ſett you
11 water out of this rocke? And Moſes lifte vp his hāde
with his ſtaffe and ſmote the rocke .ii. tymes, and the
water came out abundantly, & the multitude dranke
and their beeſſe alſo.

12 And the Lorde ſpake vnto Moſes & Aaron: Becauſe
ye beleued me not, to ſanctifye me in the eyes of the
childern of Iſrael, therfore ye ſhall not brynge this congregacion in to the londe which I haue geuen them.

13 This is the water of ſtryffe, becauſe the childern of
Iſrael ſtroüe with the Lorde, & he was ſanctifyed
apon them.

14 And Moſes ſent meſſengers from cades vnto the
kynge of Edome. Thus ſayeth thi brother Iſrael:
Thou knoweſt all the trauell ẏ hath happened us,
15 how oure fathers wēt doune in to Egipte, and how we
haue dwelt in Egipte a longe tyme, and how the
16 Egiptians vexed both us and oure fathers. Then .P.
we cryed vnto the Lorde and he herde oure voyces,
and ſent an angell and hath ſett us out of Egipte.
And beholde, we are in Cades a citie harde by the
17 borders of thi contre let us goo a good a good felow-
felowſhipe thorow thi contre we wyll not ſhipe, *peace-*
goo thorow the feldes nor thorow the *ably* cf. xxii, 6
vyneyardes, nether will we drynke of the water of the
fountaynes: but we will goo by the hye waye and nether turne vnto ẏ ryghte hande nor to ẏ leſte, vntill
we be paſt thi contre.

18 And Edom anſwered him: Se thou come not by me,
19 leſt I come out agēſt the with the ſwerde And the

V. 10 Audite rebelles et increduli 13 aqua cōtradictionis
14 omnem laborem 16 Cades, quæ eſt in extremis finibus tuis
17 via publica 18 alioquin armatus occurram tibi.

L. 10 Horet yhr widderſpenſtigen 13 das hadder waſſer 14 alle
die muhe 16 Kades ynn der ſtadt an deynen grentzen 17 die land
ſtraſſe 18 dyr mit dem ſchwerdt entgegen zihen

M. M. N. 12 *To ſanctifye* here is, to ſhewe and declare to be
holy as in Math. vi, b.

childern of Ifrael fayed vnto him: we will goo by the beeten waye: & yf ether we or oure catell drynke of thi water, we will paye for it, we wyll doo nomoare but 20 paffe thorow by fote only. And he fayed: ye fhall not goo thorow. And Edom came out agenft him with 21 moch people and with a mightie power. And thus Edom denyed to geue Ifrael paffage thorow his contre. And Ifrael turned a waye from him.

22 And the childern of Ifrael remoued frō Cades and went vnto mount Hor with all the congregacion. 23 And the Lorde fpake vnto Mofes and Aaron in mount Hor, harde vppon the coftes of the londe harde vppon, 24 of Edom fayenge: let Aaron be put vnto *near to* his people, for he fhall not come in to the londe which I haue [Fo. XL.] geuen vnto the childern of Ifrael: becaufe ye difhobeyed my mouth at the water of ftryffę 25 Take Aaron and Eleazer his fonne, & brynge them 26 vpp in to mount Hor, and ftryppe Aaron out of his veftimentes and put them apon Eleazer his fonne, ād let Aaron be put vnto his people and dye there.

27 And Mofes dyd as the Lorde commaunded: and they went vpp in to mount Hor in the fyghte of all the 28 multitude. And Mofes toke off Aarons clothes and put them apon Eleazer his fonne, and Aaron dyed there in the toppe of the mount. And Mofes & 29 Eleazer came doune out of the mount. And all ỹ houffe of Ifrael morned for Aarō .xxx. dayes

℣. 19 Per tritam gradiemur viam ... dabimus quod iuftum eft 20 cum infinita multitudine, & manu forti 22 Hor, qui eft in finibus terræ Edom 23 vbi 24 eo quod incredulus fuerit ori meo 25 Tolle Aaron & filium eius cum eo 26 nudaueris patrem vefte fua .. Aaron colligetur, & morietur ibi. 28 defcendit cum Eleazaro. 30 per cunctas familias fuas.

℣. 19 auff der gebeenten ftrafs .. fo wollen wyrs betzalen 20 mit mechtigem volck vnd ftarcker hand. 22 Hor am gepirge 23 Hor am gepirge an den grentzen des lands der Edomiter 24 darumb das yhr meynem mund widderfpenftig geweft feyd 25 Nym Aar. vnd feynen fon Eleafar 26 Aaron fol fich dafelbs famlen vnd fterben. 28 Mofe aber vnd El. ftygen erab vom berge 29 Aaron dahyn war ... das gantze haus Ifrael.

The .XXI. Chapter.

Hence couetousnes sett monethes myndes and hath encreased the with yeres myndes ād seuen yeres mides ye as longe as the wife liueth she must once in the yere offer somewhat for her olde husbond.

1 AND when kynge Arad the cananite which dwelt in the south parties, harde tell that Ifrael came by the waye that the fpies had founde out: he came and foughte with Ifrael and toke fome of them prefoners. 2 Then Ifrael vowed a vowe vnto the Lorde and fayed: Yf thou wilt geue this people in to oure hādes, we will deftroye their cities. 3 And the Lorde herde ȳ voyce of Ifrael, ād delyuered them the Cananites And they deftroyed both them and their cities, and called the place Horma.

M.C.S. Ifrael vanquefſheth kyng Arad. The fyerye ferpentes ſtynge them: but when they loke at the brafen ferpent which the Lord commaunded Mofes to lyft vp, they are healed. The kynges, Sehon and Og are ouercome in batell.

4 .P. Then they departed from mount hor towarde the redd fe: to compaffe the londe of Edō. And the 5 foules of the people faynted by the waye. And the people fpake agenft God and agenft Mofes: wherfore haft thou brought us out of Egipte, for to dye in the wildernefſe for here is nether bred nor water, and oure foules lotheth this lyghte bred.

6 Then the Lorde fent fyrie ferpentes amōge the people, which ftonge them: fo that moch people dyed 7 in Ifrael. And the people came to Mofes and fayed: we haue fynned, for we haue fpoken agenft the Lorde

V. 1 et victor exiftens, duxit ex eo prædam. 3 quem ille interfecit fubuerfis vrbibus eius: & vocauit nomen loci illius, Horma, id eft anathema. 4 Et tædere cœpit populum itineris ac laboris 5 anima noftra iam naufeat fuper cibo ifto leuiffimo 6 ad quorum plagas & mortes

L. 1 vnd furet etlich gefangen 3 Vnd hies die ftett Harma. 4 dem volck wart die feele vnluftig auff dem wege 5 vnfer feele ekelt vber difer lofen fpeyfe. 6 die biffen das volck

M. M. N. 5 *Lyghte bread:* Or that is fo lytell woorth. 6 The plage of ferpentes

L. M. N. 3 *Harma* heyft eyn bann

and agenst the make intercession to the Lorde, that he take awaye the serpentes from us And Moses
8 made intercession for the people. And the Lorde sayed vnto Moses: make the a serpent ād hāge it vpp for a sygne, and lett as many as are bytten loke apon
9 it and they shall lyue. And Moses made a serpent of brasse ād sett it vpp for a sygne And when the serpentes had bytten any man, he went and behelde the serpent of brasse and recouered.

10 . And the childern of Israel remoued and pitched in
11 Oboth. And they departed from Oboth and laye at Egebarim in the wildernesse which is before Moab on
12 the east syde. And they remoued thence, and pitched
13 apon the ryuer of zarad. And they departed thence and pitched on the other syde of Arnō, which ryuer is in the wildernesse, and cometh out of [Fo. XLI.] the costes of the Amorites: for Arnon is the border of Moab, betwene Moab and the Amorites.
14 Wherfore it is spoken in the boke of the warre of the Lorde: goo with a violence, both on the
15 ryuer of Arnon and on the ryuers heed, whiche shoteth doune to dwell at Ar, and leneth vppon the costes of Moab.

16 And from thence they came to Bear, whiche is the well whereof the Lorde spake vnto Moses: gather the
17 people together, that I maye geue them water. Then Israel sange this songe: Aryse vpp well, synge thereto:
18 The well whiche the rulers dygged and the captaynes of the people with the helpe of the lawegeuer and with their staues.

V. 9 quem cum percussi aspicerent, sanabantur. 13 & prominet in finibus Amorrhæi ... diuidēs Moabitas & Amorrhæos. 14 Sicut fecit in mari rubro, sic faciet in torrētibus Arnon. 15 Scopuli torrentium inclinati sunt, vt requiescerent in Ar, & recumberent in finibus Moabitarum. 16 Ex eo loco apparuit puteus 17 Ascendat puteus. Concinebant 18 in datore legis, & in baculis suis.

L. 9 vnd bleyb leben 13 vnd eraus fleusst an der grentze der Amoriter .. zwidsschen Moab vnd den Amoritern 14 Vnd far mit vngestum beyde an den bechen Arnon 15 vnd der beche quellen, wilcher neygt sich hyn, das er wone zu Ar, vnd lehnet sich an, das er der Moabiter grentze wirt. 16 Vnd von dannen zogen sie zum brunnen. 17 sungen eyns vmbs ander vber dem brun. 18 durch den lerer vnd yhre stebe.

M. M. N. 14 Some thinck it to be the boke of iudges.

19 And from this wildernesse they went to Matana, and from Matana to Nahaliel, and from Nahaliel to Bamoth,
20 and from Bamoth to the valay that is in the felde of Moab in the toppe of Pisga which boweth towarde the wildernesse.
21 And Israel sent messengers vnto Sihō, kynge of the
22 Amorites sayenge: let vs goo thorow thy londe. we will not turne in to thy feldes nor in to thy vyneyardes, nether drynke of the water of the welles: but we will goo alonge by the comon waye, vntill we be past thy
23 contre. And Sihō wolde geue Israel no licence to passe thorow his contre, but gathered all his people together & went out agēst .P. Israel in to the wildernesse. And he came to Iaheza and foughte with Israel.
24 And Israel smote him with the edge of the swerde and conquered his londe, from Arnon vnto Iabock: euen vnto the childern of Ammon. For the borders
25 of the childern of Ammon, are stronge. And Israel toke all these cities & dwelt in all ẏ cities of ẏ Amorites: in Esbon and in all the townes that longe there
26 to. For Esbon was the citie of Sihon the kinge of the Amorites which Sihon had fought before with the kinge of the Moabites, ād had taken all his londe out of his hande, euen vnto Arnon.
27 Wherfore it is a prouerbe: goo to Hesbō and let the
28 citie of Sihon be bylt ād made redye for there is a fyre gone out of Hesbon & a flame frō the citie of Sihō ād hath cōsumed Ar of 'the Moabites and the men of
29 the hylles of Arnon. Wo be to the Moab: o people of Chemos ye are forloren. His sonnes are put to flighte & his doughters brought captyue vnto Sihon kinge of the Amorites.

forloren, *lost,* cf. German *verloren*

𝔐. 20 Phasgah which boweth toward Iesimon. 29 Chamos ẏ are vndone
𝒱. 22 via regia 24 A quo percussus est in ore gladii 25 in Hesebon scilicet, & viculis eius. 28 & habitatores excelsorum Arnon.
𝕷. 22 die landstrasse 24 Israel aber schlug yhn mit der scherff des schwerds 25 Hesbon mit allen yhren tochtern 28 vnd die burger der höhe Arnon
𝔐. 𝔐. N. 20 *Phasgah:* After the commen translacyon. Chald. a hylle. *Iesimon:* Grec. wyldernesse. 29 *Chamos* is the name of a certen image.

30 There lighte is out from Hesbon vnto Dibon and we made a wildernesse euen vnto Nopha whiche reacheth vnto Mediba.
31 And thus Israell dwelt in the londe of the Amorites.
32 And Moses sent to serche oute Iaezer, & they toke the townes belongynge thereto ād conquered the Amorites that were there.
33 [Fo. XLII.] And then they turned and went vppe to warde Bason. And Og the kynge of Bason came out agenst them, both he and all his people, to warre at
34 Edrei. And the Lorde sayed vnto Moses: feare him not, for I haue delyuered him in to thy handes with all his people and his lande. And thou shalt do with him as thou dydest with Sihon the kynge of the
35 Amorites which dwelt at Hesbon. And they smote him and his sonnes and all hys people, vntyll there was nothinge left him. And they conquered his lande.
XXII, 1 And ỹ children of Israel remoued and pitched in the feldes of Moab, on the other syde of Iordane, by Iericho.

❡ The .XXII. Chapter.

2 AND Balac the sonne of Ziphor sawe all that Israel had done
3 to the Amorites, and the Moabites were sore afrayed of the people, becaufe they were many, and ab-
4 horred the childern of Israel: And Moab

M.C.S. Kyng Balac sendeth for Balam to thyntent that he shulde curse Israel: but Balam can do nothynge

V. 30 Iugum ipsorum disperiit ab Hesebon vsque Dibon 32 cuius ceperunt viculos, & possederunt habitatores. 35 vsque ad internecionem xxii, 1 vbi trans Iordanem Iericho sita est. 2 Israel Amorrhæo 3 & impetum eius ferre non possent

L. 30 yhr herlickeyt ist zu nicht worden von Hesbon bis gen Dibon 32 vnd gewonnen yhre töchter, vnd namen die Amoriter eyn die drynnen waren. 35 bis das keyner vberblieb. xxii, 1 iensid dem Iordan bey Iericho. 2 den Amoritern 3 grawet fur

L. M. N. 32 *Tochter:* das ist die dorffer vnd flecken vmb die stad her ligend.

XXII. 5-12.   *called Numeri.*   471

ſayed vnto the elders of Madian, now this *agaynſt the* / *wyll of the* / *Lorde. Ba-* / *lams aſſe* / *ſpeaketh to* / *him in the* / *waye.*
companye hath lickte vpp all that are
rounde aboute vs, as an oxe lycketh vp
the graſſe of the felde. And Balac the
ſonne of Ziphor was kinge of the Moabites at that tyme.

5 And he ſent meſſangers vnto Balam the ſonne of Beor, the interpreter whiche dwelt vppon the ryuer of the lande of the childern .P. of his folke, to call him ſayenge: beholde, there is a people come out of Egipte which couereth the face of the erthe and lye euen harde
6 by me. Come nowe a felaſhippe and curſe me this peo- ple. For they are to myghtie for me, ſo perauenture I myghte be able to ſmyte them and to dryue them oute of the londe. For I wote that whome thou bleſſ- eſt ſhalbe bleſſed, and whome thou curſeſt ſhalbe curſed.
7 And the elders of Moab went with the elders of Madian, and the rewarde of the ſothe ſayenge in their handes. And they came vnto Balam and tolde him
8 the wordes of Balac. And he ſayed vnto them: tary here all nyghte and I will bringe you worde, euen as the Lorde ſhall ſaye vnto me. And the lordes of Moab abode with Balam.
9 And god came vnto Balam and ſayed: what men
10 are theſe which are with the? And Balam ſayed vnto god: Balac the ſonne of Ziphor kynge of Moab hath
11 ſent vnto me ſayenge: beholde, there is a people come out of Egipte and couereth the face of the erthe: come now therfore and curſe me them, that ſo peraduenture I maye be able to ouercome them in batell, and to
12 dryue thē out. And god ſayed vnto Balam: thou ſhalt not goo with them, nether curſe the people, for they are bleſſed.

M.   5 lyeth euen harde
V.   4 delebit hic populus 5 Balaam filium Beor ariolum . . . terræ filiorum Ammon . . . ſedens contra me 6 de terra mea. 7 omnia verba Balac 9 Quid ſibi volunt 10 Reſpondit, Balac
L.   4 Nu wirt diſer hauffe auff nagen 5 Bileam dem ſon Beor, der eyn ausleger war 6 vnd ligt gegen myr .. denn es iſt myr zu mechtig 8 ſo wil ich euch widder ſagen 9 Wer ſind die leut? 10 Bileam ſprach zu Gott

13 [Fo. XLIII.] And Balam rofe vp in the mornynge &
fayed vnto the lordes of Balac: gett you vnto youre
lande, for the Lorde will not fuffre me to goo with you.
14 And the lordes of Moab rofe vpp and went vnto Balac
15 and fayed Balam wolde not come with vs. And Balac
fent agayne a greatter companye of lordes ād more
16 honorable than they. And they came to Balam and
tolde him: Thus fayeth Balac the fonne of Ziphor:
17 oh, let nothynge lett the to come vnto me, for I will
greatly promote the vnto great honoure, ād will doo
whatfoeuer thou fayeft vnto me, come therfore I praye
the, curfe me this people.
18 And Balam anfwered and fayed vnto the feruauntes
of Balac: Yf Balac wolde geue me his houffull of fyluer
and golde, I can goo no further than the worde of the
19 Lorde my god, to do leffe or moare. Neuertheleffe
tarye ye here all nyghte: that I maye wete, what
20 the Lorde will faye vnto me once moare. And God
came to Balam by nyghte and fayed vnto him: Yf
the men come to fett the, ryfe vppe and goo with
them: but what I faye vnto the, that onlye thou
fhalt doo.
21 And Balam rofe vppe early and fadelde his affe and
22 went with the lordes of Moab, But God was angrye becaufe he went.

And the angell of the Lorde ftode in the waye
agenfte hym. And he ryd vppon hys .P. affe and two
23 feruauntes with him. And when the affe fawe the
angell of the Lorde ftonde in the waye and his fwerde
drawen in his hande, fhe turned a fyde oute of the waye
and went out in to the felde. And Balam fmote the
affe, to turne her in to the waye.
24 And the angell of the Lorde went and ftode in a

𝔐. 20 God came vnto Balam by nyghte
𝒱. 13 quia prohibuit me dominus 15 Rurfum ille 16 Ne cunc-
teris venire ad me 17 et quicquid volueris dabo 18 non potero
immutare 21 afina . . . cum eis. 22 contra Balaam
𝑳. 13 denn der Herr wils nicht geftatten das ich mit euch
zihe 15 Da fandte Balak 17 Lieber were dich nicht zu myr zu
zihen 18 doch nicht vbergehen das wort des Herrn 21 efelyn . .
mit den furften der Moabiter. 22 das er hinzoch . . . das er yhm
widder ftunde

path betwene the vyneyardes, where was a wall on the
25 one fyde and another on the other. When the affe fawe
the angell of the Lorde, fhe wrenfhed   wrenfhed,
vnto the walle and thruft Balams fote vnto *pufhed, thruft*
26 the wall, and he fmote her agayne. And the angell
of ў Lorde went forder and ftode in a narowe place,
where was no waye to turne, ether to the right hande
27 or to the lyfte. And when the affe fawe the angell of
the Lorde, fhe fell downe vnder Balam: & Balam was
wroth & fmote the affe with a ftaffe.

28 And the Lorde opened the mouthe of the affe, and
fhe fayed vnto Balam: what haue I done vnto the,
29 that thou fmyteft me this .iii. tymes? And Balam
fayde vnto the Affe: becaufe thou haft mocked me?
I wolde that I had a fwerde in myne hande, that I
30 myghte now kyll the. And the affe fayed vnto Balam: am not I thyne affe whiche thou haft rydden vppon fence thou waft borne vnto this daye? Was I
euer wont to do fo vnto [Fo.XLIIII.] the? And he
fayed, nay.
31 And the lorde opened the eyes of Balam that he
fawe the angell of the Lorde ftondinge in the waye,
with his fwerde drawen in his honde. And he bowed
32 him felfe and fell flatt on his face. And ў angell of ў
Lord fayed vnto him: Wherfore fmyteft thou thyne
affe this .iii. tymes? beholde, I came oute to refyft the,
33 for the waye is contrarye vnto me: and the affe fawe
me and avoyded me thre tymes: or elfe (had fhe not
turned fro me) I had fuerly flayne the and faued her
alyue.
34 And Balam fayed vnto the angell of ў Lorde: I
haue fynned: for I wift not that thou ftodeft in the
waye agenft me. Now therfore yf it difpleafe thyne
35 eyes, I will turne agayne. And the angell fayde vnto

M. 28 fmyteft me thus .iii. tymes 33 thus .iii. tymes?
V. 27 concidit fub pedibus fedentis... fufte latera eius. 29 Quia
commeruifti & illufifti mihi 30 cui femper 31 pronus in terram.
32 quia peruerfa eft via tua, mihique contraria.
L. 27 auff yhre knie vnter dem Bileam 29 Das du meyn ge-
fpottet haft 30 zu deyner zeyt 32 denn der weg ift myr entgegen
33 auch itzt erwurget... haben.

Balam, goo with the men: but in any wife, what I faye vnto the, that faye. And Balam went with the lordes of Balac.

36 And when Balac herde that Balā was come he went out agenſt him vnto a cytie off Moab that ſtode in the border of Arnŏ, whiche was the vttmoſt parte of his
37 contre. And Balac ſayed vnto Balam: dyd I not ſende for the, to call the? wherfore cameſt thou not vnto me? thinkeſt thou that I am not able to promote the vnto
38 honoure? And Balam ſayed vnto Balac: Loo I am come vnto the. But I can ſaye nothynge at all .P. ſaue what God putteth in my mouthe that muſt I ſpeake.
39 And Balam went with Balac, and they came vnto the
40 cytie of Huzoth. And Balac offered oxen and ſhepe, & ſent for Balam and for the lordes that were with hym.

❡ The .XXIII. Chapter.

41 AND on the mornynge Balac toke Balam and brought him vpp in to the hye place of Baall, ād thēce he ſawe vnto the vtt- XXIII, 1 moſt parte of the people. And Balam ſayed vnto Balac: bylde me here ſeven alters and prouyde here ſeuē oxen
2 and ſeuen rammes. And Balac dyd as Balam ſayed. And Balac and Balam offered on euery alter an oxe and a ram.

M.C.S. Balam bleſſeth the people, where he was required to curſe thē and propheſyeth that they ſhalbe a greate people.

M. 39 came vnto the large cytie. xxiii, 1 ſeuen bullockes 2 alter a bullock

V. 35 caue ne aliud quam 36 Quod cum audiſſet Balac, egreſſus eſt in occurſum eius in oppido Moabitarum, quod ſitum eſt in extremis finibus Arnon. 37 cur non ſtatim . . . an quia mercedem aduētui tuo reddere nequeo? 39 vrbem quæ in extremis regni eius finibus erat. 40 miſit ad Balaam . . . munera.

L. 35 aber nichts anders denn was ich 36 die da ligt an der grentze 39 vnd kamen in die gaſſenſtadt 40 ſandte nach Bileam

M. M. N. 39 The large cytie: Ebre. of places or of ſtreates. Some full of people in the ſtreates.

3 And Balam fayed vnto Balac: ftonde by the facrifyce, whyle I goo to wete whether the Lorde will come ād mete me: & what foeuer he fheweth me, I will tell the, and he went forthwith.

4 And god came vnto Balam, and Balam fayed vnto him: I haue prepared .vii. alters, and haue offered apō
5 euery alter, an oxe & a ram. And ẙ Lorde put a fayenge in Balās mouth & fayed: goo agayne to Balac
6 & faye on this wyfe. And he went agayne vnto him and loo, he ftode by his facrifice, both he ād all the
7 lordes of Moab. And he began hys parable and fayed: Balac the kinge of [Fo. XLV.] Moab hath fett me fro Mefopotamia out of the mountaynes of the eafte fayenge: come & curfe me Iacob, come and defye me
8 Ifrael. How fhall I curfe whom God *The pope cā* curfeth not and how fhall I defye whom *tell howe.*
9 the Lorde defyeth not? from the toppe of ẙ rockes I fe him and from the hylles I beholde him: loo, ẙ people fhall dwell by him felfe and fhall not be rekened
10 amōge other nacions. Who can tell the duft of Iacob & the numbre of the fourth parte of Ifrael. I praye God that my foule, maye dye the deeth of the righteous, ād that my laft ende maye be like his.

11 And Balac fayed vnto Balam, what haft thou done vnto me? I fett ẙ to curfe myne enemyes: and be-
12 holde, thou bleffeft them. And he anfwered and fayed: muft I not kepe that and fpeake it, which the Lorde
13 hath put in my mouthe? And Balac fayed vnto him: Come I praye the with me vnto another place, whence thou fhalt fe them, and fhalt fe but ẙ vtmofte parte of them ād fhalt not fe them all and curfe me them there.

M. 4 alter, a bullock
V. 3 Sta paulifper... donec 7 propera et deteftare Ifrael. 10 & noffe numerum ftirpis Ifrael? 12 Num aliud poffum loqui nifi quod iufferit dominus? 13 vnde partem Ifrael videas, & totum videre non poffis

L. 7 kom fchilt Ifrael 10 die zahl des vierden teyls Ifrael? 12 Mus ich nicht das halten vnd reden, das myr der Herr ynn den mund gibt?

M. M. N. 9 *To dwell by him felfe* is, to lyue in lybertye with oute trouble and oute of the fubieccion of other people as in Deutero. xxxiii, d. *Rekened:* After the chald. deftroyed.

14 And he brought him in to a playne felde where men myght fe farre, euen to the toppe of Pifga, and bylt .vii. alters and offered an oxe and a rā on euery
15 alter. And he fayed vnto Balac: ſtonde here by thi
16 ſacrifyce whyle I goo yonder. And the Lorde mett Balam and put wordes in his mouth and ſayed: goo
17 agayne vnto Balac ād thus ſaye. And when .¶. he came to him: beholde, he ſtode by his ſacrifyce and the lordes of Moab with him And Balac ſayed vnto him: what fayeth ẏ Lorde?
18 And he toke vp his parable and ſayed: ryſe vpp Balac and heare, and herken vnto me thou fonne of
19 Ziphor The Lorde is not a mā, that he can lye, nether the fonne of a mā that he can repent: fhulde he ſaye and not doo, or fhulde he fpeake and not make it
20 good? beholde, I haue begon to bleffe and haue bleffed,
21 and can not goo backe there fro. He beheld no wikedneffe in Iacob nor fawe Idolatrye in Ifrael: The Lorde his God is with him, and the trompe of a kynge amonge
22 thē. God that broughte them out of Egipte, is as the
23 ſtrength of an vnycorne vnto them, for there is no forcerer, in Iacob, nor fothſayer in Ifrael. When the tyme cometh, it wylbe fayed of Iacob & of Ifrael, what
24 God hath wrought Beholde, ẏ people fhall ryfe vp as

V. 14 locum ſublimem ſuper verticem montis Phaſga 19 vt mutetur 21 Non eſt idolum in Iacob, nec videtur ſimulachrum in Ifrael. Dominus deus eius cum eo eſt, & clangor victoriæ regis in illo. 23 Non eſt augurium in Iacob, nec diuinatio in Ifrael.

L. 14 eyn freyen platz auff der hohe Piſga 19 das yhn etwas gerewe 21 keyn muhe in Iacob noch keyn erbeyt ynn Ifrael, der Herr feyn Gott iſt bey yhm vnd das drometen des konigs vnter yhm 23 keyn zeuberey ynn Iacob vnd keyn warſager ynn Ifrael . . . was Gott thut

M. M. N. 21 *He behelde no wikedneſſe:* Ther is no people wythoute fynne nether yet Ifrael, but God loketh not on hit, he waxeth not angrye in the ende, he auengeth it not accordynge as it deſerueth, but amendeth it by his grace. *Triumphe of a kynge:* Chal. habitacion dwellyng place or courte.

L. M. N. 21 *Muhe vnd erbeyt* heyſt die ſchrifft die groffen gutten werck on glawben gethan Pſal. 10. Vnter ſeyner zungē iſt muhe vnd erbeyt, Denn folch lere vnd werck macht boſe fchwere gewiſſen die der glaube leicht vnd frolich macht.—*Drometen des konigs*, das iſt, die leyplichen drometen gottis yhres konigs, der ſie zu machen befolen hatt, darumb, ſie vnvber windlich waren ym ſtreyt. Bedeut aber das Euangelion in der Chriſtenheyt.

a lyoneffe and heue vpp hym felfe as a lion, & fhall not lye downe agayne, vntill he haue eaten of the praye and dronke of the bloude of them that are flayne.

25 And Balac fayed vnto Balam: nether curfe them 26 nor bleffe thẽ. And Balam anfwered ãd fayed vnto Balac: tolde not I the fayẽge, all that the Lorde 27 byddeth me, ỹ I muft doo? And Balac fayed vnto Balam: come I praye the, I will brynge the yet vnto another place: fo perauenture it fhall pleafe God, that 28 [Fo. XLVI.] thou mayft curfe thẽ there. And Balac broughte Balam vnto the toppe of Peor, that boweth 29 towarde the wilderneffe. And Balam fayed vnto Balac: make me here .vii. alters, & prepare me here .vii. bol- 30 lockes and .vii. rãmes And Balac dyd as Balam had fayed, and offered a bollocke and a ram on euery alter.

⁌ The .XXIIII. Chapter.

1 WHEN Balam fawe that it pleafed ỹ Lorde that he fhulde bleffe Ifrael, he went not as he dyd twyfe before to fett fothfay- enge, but fett his face towarde ỹ wilder- 2 neffe, and lyfte vpp his eyes and loked apon Ifrael as he laye with his trybes, and 3 the fpirite of God came apon him. And he toke vp his parable and fayed: Balã the fonne of Beor hath fayed, and the 4 man whofe eye is open hath fayed: he hath fayed which heareth the wordes of God and feeth the vifions of the allmightie, which falleth downe & his eyes are opened.

M.C.S. Balam prophe- fieth of the kyngdome of Ifrael and of the comyng of Chrift. Balac is angrie with Balam. The deftruccion of the Amelick- ites and of the Kenytes.

V. 4 qui vifionem omnipotentis intuitus eft, qui cadit & fic aperiuntur oculi eius

L. 24 eyn iunger lewe. xxiiii, 4 der des almechtigen geficht fahe, der da nydder fiel

L. M. N. 1 Hyraus merckt man, das Bileam droben altzeyt fey zu zeuberey gangen vnter Gottis namen. Aber der Herr ift yhm ymer begegenet vnd hat die zeuberey gehyndert, das er hat muffen das recht gottis wort faffen an ftatt der zeuberey.

5 How goodly are the tentes of Iacob and thine ha-
6 bitacions Ifrael, euen as the brode valeyes and as gardens by the ryuers fyde, as the tentes which the Lorde hath pitched & as ciperstrees apon the water.
7 The water fhall flowe out of his boket and his feed fhall be many waters, and his kynge fhalbe hyer then
8 Agag, And his kyngdome .P. fhalbe exalted. God that broughte him out of Egipte is as the ftrenght of an vnycorne vnto him, and he fhall eate the nacions that are his enemies and breake their bones and perfe
9 them thorow with his arowes. He couched him felfe and laye doune as a lion and as a lyoneffe, who fhall ftere him vp? bleffed is he that bleffeth the, ād curfed is he that curfeth the.

10 And Balac was wroth with balam and fmote his handes together, and fayed vnto him: I fent for the to curfe myne enemyes: & beholde, thou haft bleffed
11 them this thre tymes, and now gett the quyckly vnto thi place. I thoughte that I wolde promote the vnto honoure, but the Lorde hath kepte the backe from
12 worfhepe. And Balam fayed vnto Balac: tolde I not
13 thi meffēgers which thou fenteft vnto me fayenge: Yf balac wolde geue me his houfe ful of fyluer ād golde, I can not paffe the mouth of the Lorde, to doo ether good or bad of myne awne mynde. What the Lorde
14 fayeth, that muft I fpeake. And now beholde, I goo vnto my people: come let me fhewe the, what this people fhall doo to thi folke in the later dayes.
15 And he began his parable ād fayed: Balam the fonne of Beor hath fayed, and ẏ man that hath his eye

M. 5 thyne habitacion. 8 Egypt his ftrenght is as the ftrenght

V. 6 cedri 7 in aquas multas. 8 Deuorabunt gentes hoftes illius ... et perforabunt fagittis. 13 non potero præterire 14 quid populus tuus populo huic faciat extremo tempore

L. 6 cedern 7 eyn grofs waffer 8 Seyne freydigkeyt ift wie eyns Eynhorns ... pfeylen zu fchmettern 9 wie eyn iunger lewe 13 fo kund ich doch fur des Herrn wort nicht vber 14 was dis volck mit deynem volck thun folle

M. M. N. 5 By all thefe fimilitudes wolde Balam declare the felycitye of the people of Ifrael which came of God. as ye haue in the Pfal. cxi, & Iere. xvii, b.

16 open hath fayed, & he hath fayed that heareth the
wordes of God & hath the knowlege of the moſt hye
and beholdeth ẏ [Fo. XLVII.] viſion of the allmightie,
17 and when he falleth downe hath his eyes opened. I
ſe him but not now, I beholde him but not nye. There
ſhall come a ſtarre of Iacob and ryſe a cepter of Iſrael,
which ſhall ſmyte ẏ cooſtes of Moab and vndermyne
18 all the childern of Seth. And Edom ſhalbe his poſſeſſion, and ẏ poſſeſſion of Seir ſhalbe their enimyes, and
19 Iſrael ſhall doo manfully. And out of Iacob ſhall
come he that ſhall deſtroye the remnaūt of the cities.
20 And he loked on Amaleck and began his parable
and ſayed: Amaleck is the firſt of the nacions, but his
21 latter ende ſhall peryſh utterly. And he loked on the
Kenites, and toke his parable and ſayed: ſtronge is thi
22 dwellynge place and put thi neſt apon a rocke, Neuer
thelater thou ſhalt be a burnynge to Kain, vntill Aſſur
23 take ẏ priſoner. And he toke his parable & ſayed:
24 Alas, who ſhall lyue when God doeth this? The
ſhippes ſhall come out of the coſte of Cittim and ſubdue Aſſur and ſubdue Eber, and he him ſelfe ſhall
25 peryſh at the laſt. And Balam roſe vp and went and
dwelt in his place: and Balac alſo went his waye.

M. 24 Chittim
V. 17 conſurget virga de Iſrael ... duces Moab, vaſtabitque
omnes filios Seth. 18 Iſrael vero fortiter aget. 19 qui dominetur, et
perdat 22 & fueris electus de ſtirpe Cin 24 Venient in trieribus de
Italia ... vaſtabuntque Hebræos & ad extremum etiam ipſi peri-
bunt. 25 Balac quoque via qua venerat, rediit.
L. 17 eyn ſcepter aus Iſrael auff komen, vnd wirt zu ſchmet-
tern die vberſten der Moabiter vnd vberweldigen alle kinder Seth.
18 Iſrael aber wirt redlich thatten thun. 19 der hirſcher komen,
vnd vmb bringen 22 aber du wirſt eyn antzundung werden Kain
24 Er aber wirt auch gar vmbkomen 25 vnd Balak zoch ſeynen
weg.
M. M. N. 24 *Chittim:* Chalde & the cōmen tranſl. Italy.—
Eber: That is the Hebrues or thoſe that are be yonde the floude
of Euphrates.
L. M. N. 17 Diſer ſtern is Dauid, wilcher ſolche leut vnd
lender vnter ſich bracht hat, Denn Bileam redet nichts vō Chriſto,
ſondern nur vom leyblichē reych des volcks Iſrael, wie wol da
durch Chriſtus allenthalben bedeut iſt. 20 Amalek war der erſte
vnter den heyden den die kinder Iſrael anfochten Exod. 17. aber
durch Saul vertilget. 1. Re. 15.—23, 24 Diſer ſpruch iſt auff die
Romer biſher gedeutte, Aber der text laut, als ſey der gros Alex-
ander damit bedeut.

The XXV. Chapter.

1 AND Israel dwelt in Sittim, and
2 the people began to commytt
whoredome with the dough-
ters of Moab, which called the
people vnto ẏ sacrifyce of their goddes. And the people ate and worshipped
3 their goddes, and Israel coupled him selfe
vnto Baal Peor. Then ẏ Lorde was angrie
with Israel, and sayed vnto Moses: take
all ẏ heedes of the people, and hange them vp vnto
ẏ Lorde agenst the sonne, that the wrath of the Lorde
5 maye turne awaye from Israel. And Moses sayed vnto
the iudges of Israel: goo and slee those men that ioyned
thē selues vnto Baal Peor.

6 And beholde, one of the childern of Israel came and
broughte vnto his brethern, a Madianitish wife euen in
the sighte of Moses & in the sighte of all the multitude
of ẏ childern of Israel, as they were wepynge in the
7 dore of the tabernacle of witnesse. And when Phineas
the sonne of Eleazer the sonne of Aarō the preast sawe
it, he rose vp out of the companye and toke a wepon
8 in his hande, and wēt after the man of Israel in to the
horehousse, & thrust them thorow: both the man of
Israel and also the woman euen thorow the belye of
hir. And the plage ceased from the childern of Israel.
9 And there dyed in the plage .xxiiii. thousande.

M.C.S. The *people cōmitteth fornication with the daughters of Moab. Phinehes kylleth Zamri and Cosbi. God commaundeth to kyll the Madianites.*

V. 2 At illi comederunt & adorauerunt deos earum. 3 Initiatusque est Israel Beelphegor 4 et suspende eos contra solem in patibulis: vt auertatur furor meus ab Israel. 6 intrauit coram fratribus suis ad scortum Mad. 7 et arrepto pugione 8 in lupanar . . . in locis genitalibus.

L. 2 zu huren mit der Moab. töchter . . . als vnd bettet yhr gotter an . . . vnterwarff sich dem Baal Peor. 4 henge sie dem Herrn an die sonne, auff das der grymmige zorn . . . gewand werde. 6 lies Mose zu sehen 7 eyn messer yn seyne hand 8 ynn das hurhaus . . . durch yhren bauch.

M. M. N. 4 *To hang agaynst the sonne* is, to be put to execucion openly before all people. 8 *Thorow* etc. After the chald. The Grec & the cōmen transl. throwe the shamelie or syltye membres. Some reade, euen in the stewes.

10, 11 And the Lorde fpake vnto Mofes fayenge: Phineas the fonne of Eleazer the fonne of Aaron the preaft, hath turned myne anger awaye from the childern of Ifrael, becaufe he was gelous for my fake amonge them, that I had not cōfumed the childern of Ifrael in my
12 [Fo. XLVIII.] geloufye. Wherfore faye: beholde, I
13 geue vnto him my couenaunte of peafe, and he fhall haue it and his feed after him, euen the couenaunte of the preaftis office for euer, becaufe he was gelous for his Gods fake and made an atonement for the childern of Ifrael.
14 The name of the Ifraelite which was fmytten with the Madianitifh wife, was Simri the fonne of Salu, a lorde of an aunciēt houffe amonge the Simeonites.
15 And the name of the Madianitifh wife, was Cofbi the doughter of Zur and heed ouer the people of an auncient houffe in Madian.
16, 17 And the Lorde fpake vnto Mofes fayenge: vexe
18 the Madianites and fmyte them, for they haue troubled you with their wiles with the which they haue begyled you, thorow Peor and thorow their fyfter Cosby ẏ doughter of a lorde in Madian, which was flayne in ẏ daye of the plage for Peors fake.

ℂ The .XXVI. Chapter.

1 ND after the plage, ẏ Lorde fpake vnto Mofes and vnto
2 Eleazer fayenge: take the number of all the multitude of the childern of Ifrael from .xx. yere ād aboue thorow out their fathers houffes, all that

M.C.S. The chyldrē of Ifraell are nombred a gayne when they fhulde entre in to the lande of Canaan.

𝔐. 15 Zur a heed
𝒱. 11 quia zelo meo . . . in zelo meo. 12 pacem fœderis mei 13 zelatus eft 14 dux de cognatione, & tribu Simeonis. 15 principis nobiliffimi 17 Hoftes vos fentiant Madianitæ 18 per idolum Phogor . . . pro facrilegio Phogor.
𝔏. 11 feynen eyffer . . . in meynem eyffer 12 meynen bund des frydes 14 eyn heubtman des haus des vatters der Simeon. 15 eyn vberfter der leut war eyns gefchlechts 17 thut den Midianitern leyd

3 are able to goo to warre in Israel. And Moses & Eleazer the preast tolde them in the seldes .P. of Moab, by Iordane fast by Iericho, from .xx. yere and aboue, as the Lorde commaunded Moses. And the childern of Israel that came out of Egipte were.

5 Ruben the eldest sonne of Israel. The childern of Ruben were, Hanoch, of whome cometh the kynred of the Hanochites: & of Palu, cometh the kynred of
6 the Paluites: And of Hesron, cometh the kynred of the Hesronites: and of Carmi, cometh the kynred of the
7 Carmites. These are the kynredes of the Rubenites, which were in numbre .xliii. thousande .vii. hūdred
8, 9 and .xxx. And the sonnes of Palu were Eliab. And the sonnes of Eliab were: Nemuel, Dathan and Abiram.

This is that Dathan and Abiram councelers in the cōgregacion, which stroue agēst Moses and Aaron in the companye of Corah, when they stroue agenst the
10 Lorde. And the erth opened hir mouth ād swalowed thē and Corah also, when the multitude dyed, what tyme the fyre consumed .ii. hundred and siftie men, and
11 they became a signe: Notwithstondynge, the childern of Corah dyed not.

12 And the childern of Simeon in their kynredes were: Nemuel, of whom cometh ẏ kynred of the Nemuelites: Iamin, of whom cometh the kynred of the Iaminytes: Iachin,
13 of whom cometh the kynred of the Iachinites: Serah, of whom cometh the kynred of the Serahites: Saul, of whom cometh the kyn- [Fo. XLIX.] red of the Saulites.
14 These are the kynredes of the Simeonites: in numbre xxii. thousande and .ii. hundred.
15 And the childern of Gad in their kynredes were: Zephon, of whom cometh the kynred of the Zephonites: and of Haggi, cometh the kynred of the Haggites: and

V. 3 Locuti sunt itaque Moyses, & Eleazar 4 sicut dominus imperauerat, quorum iste est numerus 9 in seditione Core 10 morientibus plurimis . . . et factum est grande miraculum
L. 3 Vnd Mose redet mit yhn 4 wie der Herr Mose gepotten hatte vnd den kindern Israel, die aus Egypten zogen waren. 9 in der rotten Korah 10 da die rotte starb 12 vnd waren zum zeychen
M. M. N. 5 The kynred of Ruben. 12 The kynred of Simeon. 15 The kynred of Gad.

16 of Suni, cometh the kynred of the Sunites: and of
17 Aſeni, cometh the kynred of the Aſenites: and of Eri cometh the kynred of the Erites: and of Arod cometh the kynred of the Arodites: and of Ariel cometh the
18 kynred of the Arielites. Theſe are the kynredes of the children of Gad, in numbre .xl. thouſande and .v. hundred.
19 The childern of Iuda: Er and Onă, whiche dyed in
20 the londe of Canaan. But the childern of Iuda in their kynred were: Sela of whom cometh the kynred of the Selamites: and of Phares cometh the kynred of ẙ Phareſites: and of Serah cometh the kynred of the
21 Serahites. And the childern of Phares were Heſron, of whom cometh the kynred of the Heſronites: and of
22 Hamul cometh ẙ kynred of the Hamulites. Theſe are the kynredes of Iuda, in numbre .Lxxvi. thouſande and .v. hundred.
23 And the childern of Iſachar in their kynredes were: Tola, of whŏ cometh ẙ kynred of the Tolaites : & Phuva,
24 of whŏ cometh ẙ kinred of the Phuuaites: and of Iaſub cometh .Ƥ. the kynred of the Iaſubites: and of Symron
25 cometh the kynred of the Simronites. Theſe are ẙ kynredes of Iſachar in numbre .Lxiiii. thouſande and iii. hundred.
26 The childern of Zabulon in their kynredes were: Sered, of whom cometh the kynred of the Seredites: and Elon, of whom cometh the kynred of the Elonites: and of Iaheliel, cometh the kynred of the Iehalelites.
27 Theſe are the kynredes of Zabulon: in numbre .Lx thouſand & .v. hundred.
28 The childern of Ioſeph in their kinredes were:
29 Manaſſe ăd Ephraim. The childern of Manaſſe: Machir, of whom cometh the kynred of the Machirites. And Machir begat Gilead, of whom cometh the kinred
30 off the Gileadites. And theſe are the childern of Gilead: Hieſer, of whom cometh the kynred of the Hieſerites: and of Helech cometh the kynred of the Helechites:

ℳ. 23 Thola ... Tholaites
ℳ. ℳ. N. 19 The kynred of Iuda. 23 The kynred of Iſachar. 26 The kynred of Zabulon. 28 The kynred of Ioſeph.

31 and of Afriel ẏ kinred of the Afrielites: and of Sichem
32 cometh the kinred of the Sichimites: & of Simida cometh the kinred of the Simidites: & of Hepher
33 cometh the kinred of the Hepherites. And Zelaphead the fonne of Hepher had no fonnes but doughters And ẏ names of ẏ doughters of Zelaphead were: Mahela,
34 Noa, Hagla, Milcha ād Thirza. Thefe are the kinredes of Manaffe, in numbre .Lii. thoufande and feuen hundred.
35 Thefe are the childern of Ephraim in the- [Fo. L.] ir kinredes: Suthelah, of whom cometh the kinred of the Suthelahites: and Becher, of whom cometh the kinred of the Becherites: & of Thaha cometh the kynred
36 of the Thahanites. And thefe are the childern of Suthelah: Eran, of whom cometh the kynred of the
37 Eranites. Thefe are the kynredes of the childern of Ephraim in numbre .xxxii. thoufande & .v. hundred. And thefe are the childern of Iofeph in their kinredes.
38 Thefe are the childern of Ben Iamin in their kinredes: Bela, of whom cometh the kinred of the Belaites: and of Afbel cometh the kinred of the Afbelites: and
39 of Ahiram, the kinred of the Ahiramites: and of Supha the kinred of the Suphamites: and of Hupham the kin-
40 red of the Huphamites. And the childern of Bela were Ard and Naamā fro whence come the kinredes of the
41 Ardites and of the Naamites. Thefe are the childern of Ben Iamin in their kinreddes, and in numbre .xlv thoufande and fyxe hundred.
42 Thefe are the childern of Dan in their kynreddes: Suham, of whom cometh the kynred of the Suhamites. Thefe are the kynreddes of Dan in their generacyons.
43 And all the kynreddes of the Suhamites were in numbre .Lxiiii. thoufande ād .iiii. hundred.
44 The childern of Affer in their kynredes .P. were: Iemna, of whom cometh the kynred of the Iemnites: ād Ifui, of whom cometh the kinred of the Ifuites: & of
45 Bria cometh the kinred of Briites. And the childern

M. M. N. 35 The kynred of Ephraim. 38 The kynred of Ben Iamin. 42 The kynred of Dan. 44 The kynred of Afer.

of bria were Heber, of whom cometh ẏ kynred of the Heberites: and of Malchiel came the kynred of the Mal-
46 chielites. And ẏ doughter of Affer was called Sarah.
47 Thefe are the kinredes of Affer in numbre .Liii. thoufande and .iiii. hundred.
48 The childern of Nephtali in their kynreddes were: Iaheziel, of whom came the kynred of the Iahezielites: and Guni, of whom came the kynred of the Gunites:
49 & of Iezer, came the kynred of the Iezerites: and of
50 Silem the kynred of Silemites. Thefe are the kinredes of Naphtali in their generaciōs in numbre .xlv. thou-
51 fande and .iiii. hundred. Thefe are the numbres of the childern of Ifrael: fixe hundred thoufande, & a thou-fande .vii. hundred and .xxx.
52, 53 And the Lorde fpake vnto Mofes fayenge: vnto thefe the londe fhalbe deuyded to enherett, acordinge
54 to the numbre of names: to many thou fhalt geue ẏ moare enheritaunce & to fewe ẏ leffe: to euery tribe fhall ẏ enheritaūce be geuē acordinge to ẏ numbre
55 therof. Notwithftondinge, ẏ londe fhalbe deuyded by
56 lott, & acordinge to ẏ names of ẏ tribes of their fathers, thei fhall enherett: & acordinge to their lott thou fhalt deuyde their lond, both [Fo. LI.] to the many and to the fewe.
57 Thefe are the fummes of ẏ leuites in their kinredes: of Gerfon, came the kynred of ẏ Gerfonites: and of Cahath came the kinred of the Cahathites: and of
58 Merari came the kinred of the Merarites. Thefe are the kynredes of Leui: the kinred of the Libnites, the kynred of the Hebronites, the kynred of the Mahelites, the kynred of the Mufites, the kynred of the Karahites.
59 Kahath begate Amram, and Amrams wife was called Iochebed a doughter of leui, which was borne him in Egipte. And fhe bare vnto Amram, Aaron,

V. 54 fingulis ficut nunc recenfiti funt tradetur poffeffio: 55 ita duntaxat vt fors terram tribubus diuidat & familiis.
L. 54 iglichen fol man geben nach yhrer zal, 55 Doch man fol das land durchs los teylen, nach den namen der ftemme yhrer veter follen fie erb nemen

ℳ. ℳ. N. 48 The kynred of Nephthali. 57 The nombre of the Leuites.

60 Moses and Mir Iam their syster. And vnto Aaron were
61 borne, Nadab, Abihu, Eleazer and Ithamar. But Nadab and Abihu dyed, as they offered straunge fyre
62 before the Lorde. And the numbre of them was xxiii. thousande, of all the males from a moneth olde and aboue For they were not numbred amonge ẏ children of Israel, becaufe there was no enheritaunce geuen them amonge the childern off Israel.

63 These are the numbres of the childern of Israel which Moses and Eleazer the preast numbred in the
64 feldes of Moab, fast by Iordane nye to Iericho. And amonge these there was not a man of the numbre of the children of Israel which Moses and Aaron tolde in
65 the wildernesse of Sinai. For the Lor- .P. de sayed vnto them, that they shulde dye in ẏ wildernesse & that there shulde not be lefte a man of them: saue Caleb the sonne of Iephune & Iosua the sonne of Nun.

¶ The .XXVII. Chaptre

1 AND the doughters of Zelaphead the sonne of Heber the sonne of Gilead, the sonne of Machir the sonne of Manasse, of the kinredes of Manasse the sonne of Ioseph (whose names were Mahela, Noa, Hagla,
2 Melcha and Thirza) came & stode before Moses and Eleazer the preast ād before the lordes & all the multitude in the
3 dore of the tabernacle of witnesse sayenge: oure father dyed in the wildernesse, & was not amonge the companye of them that gathered them selues together agenst the Lorde in the congregation of Corah: But

M.C.S. The lawe of the herytage of the daughters of Zelaphead. The land of promesse is shewed vnto Moses: in whose steade is appoynted Iosue.

V. 62 nec eis cum cæteris data possessio est. 65 Prædixerat enim dominus. xxvii, 3 nec fuit in seditione quæ concitata est contra dominum sub Core ... hic nõ habuit mares filios ... inter cognatos patris nostri.
L. 62 denn man gab yhn keyn erbe vnter den K. Israel. xxvii, 3 vnd war nicht mit vnter der gemeyne die sich widder den Herrn auflehnten ynn der rotten K.

4 dyed in his awne fynne, and had no fonnes. Wherfore fhulde the name of oure fathers be taken awaye from amonge hys kynred, becaufe he had no fonne? Geue vnto vs a poffeffyon amonge the brethern of oure father.
5 And Mofes broughte their caufe before the Lorde.
6, 7 And ẙ Lorde fpake vnto Mofes fayenge: The doughters of Zelaphead fpeke righte: thou fhalt geue them a poffeffion to en- [Fo. LII.] herett amonge their fathers brethern, & fhalt turne the enheritaunce of their fa-
8 ther vnto them. And fpeake vnto the childern of Ifrael fayenge: Yf a man dye and haue no fonne ye
9 fhall turne his enheritaunce vnto his doughter. Yf he haue no doughter, ye fhall geue his enheritaunce vnto
10 his brethern. Yf he haue no brethern, ye fhall geue
11 his enheritaunce vnto his fathers brethern. Yf he haue no fathers brethern, ye fhall geue his enheritaunce vnto him that is nexte to him of his kinred, & let him poffeffe it. And this fhalbe vnto the childern of Ifrael an ordynaunce, and a lawe, as the Lorde hath commaūded Mofes.
12 And the Lorde fayed vnto Mofes: get ẙ vpp in to this mount Aabrim, and beholde, the londe which
13 I haue geuen vnto the children of Ifrael. And whē thou haft fene it, thou fhalt be gathered vnto thy people alfo, as Aaron thy brother was gathered vnto
14 his people. For ye were difobedient vnto my mouthe in the deferte of Zin in ẙ ftryfe of the congregacion, that ye fanctified me not in the water before their eyes. That is the water of ftryfe in cades in the wildernefle

𝔐. 12 Abarim
𝒱. 4 Retulitque Moyfes caufam earum ad iudicium domini. 6 Iuftam rem poftulant filiæ Salphaad . . . & ei in hæreditate fuccedant. 8 ad filiam eius tranfibit hæreditas. 10 dabitis hæred. fratribus patris eius. 11 dabitur hær. his qui ei proximi funt. 12 daturus fum 14 quia offendiftis me . . . fuper aquas.
𝔏. 5 Mofe bracht yhr recht fur den Herrn 7 die t. Zel. haben recht geredt . . . vnd folt yhrs vaters erbe yhn zu wenden. 8 fo folt yhr feyn erbe feyner tochter zu wenden 10 feynen vettern geben 11 feynen nehiften freunden die yn anhören ynn feynem gefchlecht 12 geben werde 14 wie yhr meynem wort vngehorfam gewefen feit . . . durch das waffer

15 of Zin. And Moſes ſpake vnto the Lorde
16 ſayenge: let the Lorde God of the ſpirites
of all fleſh, ſett a man ouer the congrega-
17 cion, which maye goo in & out before them,
and to lede them in and oute that the congregacion
of the Lorde be not as a flocke of ſhepe without a
ſheparde.

O faithfull & mercifull Moſes ful onlike oure Balams.

18 And y̔ Lorde ſayed vnto Moſes: take Ioſua the
ſonne of Nun in whom there is ſpirite, and put thyne
19 handes apon him, and ſet him before Eleazer the preaſt
and before all the congregacion and geue him a charge
20 in their ſyghte. And put of thi prayſe apon him that
all the companye of y̔ childern of Iſrael maye heare.
21 And he ſhall ſtonde before Eleazar y̔ preaſt which ſhall
axe councell for him after y̔ maner of the
* lighte before y̔ Lorde: And at the mouth
of Eleazer ſhall both he and all the childern of Iſrael with him and all the congregacion, goo in and out.

22 And Moſes dyd as the Lorde com-
23 maūded him, and he toke Ioſua and ſette
him before Eleazer the preaſt and be-

There was of likelyhod a bryght ſtonne in the ephod, wherei the hie preaſt loked & ſawe the will of God in tymes of neade, as thou mayſt ſe in the ſtory of Dauid:

M̃. 21 After the iudgemēt of Vrim
V̄. 16 dominus deus ſpirituum omnis carnis 17 ſicut oues
abſque paſtore. 18 in quo eſt ſpiritus 20 & partem gloriæ tuæ, vt
audiat eum 21 Eleazar ſacerdos conſulet dominum.
L. 16 der Herr der Gott vber die geyſter alles fleyſchs 17 wie
die ſchaff on hirten. 18 ynn dem der geyſt iſt 19 vnd gepeut yhm
fur yhren augen 20 vnd lobe yhn mit deynem lobe, das yhm
gehorche 21 der ſol fur yhn radt fragē, durch die weyſe des
Liechts fur dem Herrn
M̃. M̃. N. 17 *To go in and oute before them* is to gouerne,
teache, counfort, leade, & defende them etc. 21 *After the Iudgement of Vrim*, that is, after the iudgemēt of the light, loke Exodi.
xxviii, e. It is very lyke that in the Ephod was ſome bryght ſtone,
wherin the hye preſte loked & ſawe the wyll of God, as it appereth in the ſtorye of Dauid
L. M̃. N. 20 *Vnd lobe yhn:* das iſt, lobe du yhn vnd ſage viel
guttis von yhm, damit du yhn ehrlich vnd angenehm machiſt fur
dem volck, das leget St Pau. aus Rom. 3 da er ſpricht Gottis gerechtickeyt die Chriſtus iſt ſind bezeuget, von dem geſetz vnd
propheten. 21 *Des liechts:* das iſt das liecht auff der bruſt des
hohen prieſters. Exo. 28. daher ſagen etlich, wenn Gott habe
auffs prieſters frage geantwortet dz hat ſollen, ia, ſeyn, ſo habe
das liecht glentz von ſich geben.

fore all the congregacion, & * put his *This was*
handes apon him & geue him a charge, *the maner of*
as the Lorde commaunded thorow the *the Ebrues to*
hande of Mofes. *make their of-*
ficers & of
this maner did the apoftle make deakons, preaftes & bifhopes,
with oute any other ceremony as thou feift i thactes, ād mayft
gather of paul to Timothe:

⁋ The .XXVIII. Chaptre

1 AND the Lorde fpake vnto Mo- *M.C.S. What*
2 fes fayenge: geue ẙ childern *muft be offered*
 of Ifrael a charge and faye *on euery feaft*
 daye.
 vnto them, that they take hede to offer
 vnto me ẙ offryng of my * bred in the *Bred is here*
 facrifyce of fwete fauoure, in his due fea- *borowed &*
3 fon. And faye vnto thē. This is ẙ offer- *takē for all*
 ynge which ye fhall offer vnto ẙ Lorde *maner of fode*
 generally:
 ii. lābes [Fo. LIII.] of a yeare olde with out fpot daye
4 by daye to be a burntofferynge perpetually. One
 lambe thou fhalt offer in the mornynge, and ẙ other
5 at euen, And thereto ẙ tēth parte of an Epha of floure
 for a meatofferynge myngled with beten oyle, the
6 fourth parte of an hin: which is a dayly offerynge ordened in the mount Sinai vnto a fwete fauoure in the
7 facrifyce of ẙ Lorde. And the drynkofferynge of the
 fame: the fourth parte of an hin vnto one lambe, &
 poure the drynkofferynge in the holy place, to be good
8 drynke vnto the Lorde. And ẙ other lambe thou fhalt
 offer at euen, with the meatofferynge and the drynkofferynge after ẙ maner of the mornynge: a facrifyce of
 a fwete fauoure vnto the Lorde.

M. 2 offer vnto the offeryng.
V. 23 replicauit quæ mandauerat dominus. xxviii, 3 quotidie
in holocauftum fempiternum (v. 10, 15) 4 ad vefperum 6 holocauftum iuge eft 8 ad vefperam
L. 23 vnd gepot yhm wie der Herr mit Mofe geredt hatte.
xxviii, 3 zum teglichen brandopffer 4 zwiffchen abents (v. 8) 6 das
ift eyn teglich brandopffer (v. 10) 7 yns Heyligtum goffen werden
zur gabe dem Herrn.

9 And on the Sabbath daye .ii. lambes of a yere olde a pece and with out ſpot, and two têthdeales of floure for a meatofferynge myngled with oyle, and the drynk-
10 offerynge thereto. This is the burntofferynge of euery Sabbath, beſydes the dayly burntofferynge and his drynkofferynge.
11 And in the firſt daye of youre monethes, ye ſhall offer a burntofferynge vnto the Lorde: two yonge bollockes, and a ram, and .vii. lambes of a yere olde
12 without ſpott, and .iii. têthdeales of floure for a meatofferynge mingled with oyle vnto one bollocke, and ii. têth deales of floure for a meatofferynge myngled
13 with oyle vnto one rā. And euer moare, .ƥ. a têth deale of floure myngled with oyle, for a meatofferinge vnto one lābe. That is a burntofferynge of a ſwete
14 ſauoure in the ſacrifyce of the Lorde. And their drynkofferynges ſhalbe halfe an hin of wyne vnto one bollocke, ād the thyrde parte of an hin of wyne vnto a ram and the fourth parte of an hin vnto a lambe. This is the burntofferynge of euery moneth
15 thorow out all the monethes of the yere: & one he goote for a ſynofferynge vnto the Lorde, which ſhalbe offered with the dayly burntofferynge and his drynkofferynge.
16 And the .xiiii. daye of the firſt moneth ſhalbe Paſſe-
17 ouer vnto the Lorde. And ẏ .xv. daye of the ſame moneth ſhalbe a feaſt, in which .vii. dayes men muſt
18 eate vnleuêded bred The firſt daye ſhalbe an holy feaſt, ſo that ye ſhall do no maner of laboryous worke
19 therein. And ye ſhall offer a burntofferynge vnto the Lorde .ii. bollockes, one ram, and .vii. lambes of a yere
20 olde without ſpott, and their meatofferynge of floure myngled with oyle .iii. tenthdeales vnto a bollocke,
21 and .ii. tenthdeales vnto a ram, and euermoare one

𝔐. 19 two younge bullockes
𝔙. 13 holocauſtum ſuauiſſimi odoris atque incenſi eſt domino. 14 per omnes menſes, qui ſibi anno vertente ſuccedunt. 16 phaſe domini erit 18 dies prima venerabilis & ſancta erit
𝔏. 13 Das iſt das brandopffer des ſuſſen geruchs eyn opffer dem Herrn. 14 eyns iglichen monden ym iar. 16 Oſtern dem Herrn 18 Der erſte tag heyſt heylig

tenthdeale vnto a lambe, thorow out the .vii. lambes:
22 & an hegoote for a synofferynge to make an atone-
23 ment for you. And ye shall offer these, besyde the
burntofferynge in ẏ mornynge that is allway offered.
24 And after this maner ye shall offer thorow out the .vii
dayes, the fode of the sacrifice of swete sauoure vnto
the Lor- [Fo. LIIII.] de. And it shalbe done besyde
25 the dayly burntofferynge and his drynkofferynge. And
the seuenth daye shalbe an holy feast vnto you, so that
ye shall doo no laboryous worke therein.
26 And the daye of youre first frutes when ye brynge
a new meatofferynge vnto the Lorde in youre wekes,
shalbe an holy feast vnto you: so that ye shall doo no
27 laboryous worke therein. And ye shall offer a burntofferynge of a swete sauoure vnto the Lorde .ii. younge
bollockes, and a ram, and .vii. lambes of a yere olde
28 a pece, with their meatofferynges of floure myngled
with oyle .iii. tenthdeales vnto a bollocke .ii. tenthdeales
29 to a ram, ãd euermoare one tenthdeale vnto a lambe
30 thorow out the .vii. lambes, ãd an he goote to make an
31 atonement for you. And this ye shall doo besydes the
dayly burntofferynge, and his meatofferynge: & they
shalbe without spot, with their drynkofferynges.

¶ The .XXIX. Chapter.

1 AND ẏ first daye of ẏ .vii. moneth shalbe an holy feast vnto you, ãd ye shall doo no laboryous worke therein. It shalbe a *M.C.S. What must be offred the .viii. first dayes of the seuenth mone.*
2 daye of trompetblowynge vnto you. And ye shall

V. 22 & hircum pro peccato vnum, vt expietur pro vobis 23 matutinum quod semper 24 Ita facietis per singulos dies septem dierum in somitem ignis 25 Dies quoque septimus celeberrimus & sanctus erit vobis 26 quando offeretis nouas fruges 29 hircum quoque vnum 30 qui mactatur pro expiatione 31 cum libationibus suis. xxix, 1 quia dies clangoris est & tubarum.
L. 22 das man euch versune 23 wilchs eyn teglich brandopffer ist 24 Nach diser weyse 27 heylig heyssen. xxix, 1 Es ist ewr drometen tag

offer a burntofferynge of a fwete fauoure vnto ẏ Lorde:
one younge bollocke & one rā & .vii. lābes of a yere
³ olde a pece that are pure. And their meatofferinges
of floure .Ṗ. myngled with oyle: .iii. tenthdeales vnto
⁴ the bollocke, and .ii. vnto the ram, and one tenthdeale
⁵ vnto one lambe thorow the .vii. lambes And an he
goote for a fynofferynge to make an atonement for
⁶ you, befyde the burntofferynge of the moneth and his
meatofferynge and befyde the dayly burntofferynge
and his meatofferynge, and the drynkofferynges of the
fame: acordynge vnto the maner of them for a fauoure
of fwetneffe in the facrifice of ẏ Lorde.

⁷ And the tenth daye of that fame feuenth moneth
fhalbe an holy feaft vnto you, and ye fhall humble
youre foules and fhall doo no maner worke therein.
⁸ And ye fhall offer a burntofferynge vnto the Lorde
of a fwete fauoure: one bollocke, and a ram, and .vii
⁹ lambes of a yere olde a pece, without faute & their
meatofferynges of floure myngled with oyle: iii. tenth-
¹⁰ deales to a bollocke, ād .ii. to a rā and all waye a
tenthdeale vnto a lambe, thorow out the .vii. lambes
¹¹ And one he goote for a fynofferynge, befyde ẏ fynofferynge of atonement and the dayly burntofferynge, and
ẏ meate and drynkofferynges that longe to the fame.

¹² And the .xv. daye of the feuenth moneth fhalbe
holy daye & ye fhall doo no laboryous worke therein,
and ye fhall kepe a feaft vnto ẏ Lorde of .vii. dayes
¹³ longe. And ye fhall offer a burntofferynge of a fwete
fauoure vnto the [Fo. LV.] Lorde: .xiii. bollockes .ii
rammes and .xiiii. lābes which are yerelynges and pure,
¹⁴ with oyle .iii. tenthdeales vnto euery one of the .xiii
¹⁵ bollockes .ii. tēthdeales to ether of the rammes, and
¹⁶ one tenthdeale vnto eche of the .xiiii. lambes. And
one he goote vnto a fynofferynge, befyde ẏ dayly burntofferynge with his meate and drynkofferynges.

V. 6 præter holocauftum calendarum ... holocauftum fempiternum (vv. 11, 16, 19, 22, 25, 28, 31, 34, 38) cum libatjonibus
folitis. 7 fancta atque venerabilis (v. 12), et affligetis animas veftras
L. 6 on das brandopffer des monden ... nach yhrem rechten
7 foll .. heylig heyffen, vnd folt ewre feelen demutigen 11 tegliche
brandopffer (vv. 16, 19, 22, 25, 28, 31, 34, 38) 12 heylig heyffen

17 And the feconde daye .xii. yonnge bollockes .ii
18 rammes & .xiiii. yerlynge lambes without fpot: & their meatofferynges and drynkofferynges vnto the bollockes, rammes and lambes, acordynge to the numbre of them
19 & after the maner And an he goote for a fynofferynge, befyde the dayly burntofferynge ād his meate and drynkofferynges.
20 And the thyrde daye .xi. bollockes .ii. rammes &
21 xiiii. yerelynge lambes without fpot: & their meate and drynkofferynges vnto the bollockes, rammes & lambes, after the numbre of thē & acordynge to the maner.
22 And an he goote for a fynofferynge, befyde the dayly burntofferynge & his meate and drynkofferynges.
23 And the fourth daye .x. bollockes .ii. rammes & .xiiii.
24 lābes, yerelynges & pure: ād their meate & drynkofferynges vnto the bollockes rāmes & lābes, acordynge
25 to their nūbre and after the maner. And an hegoote for a fynofferynge, befyde the dayly burntofferynge ād his meate and drynkofferynges.
26 .P. And the fyfte daye .ix. bollockes .ii. rāmes and xiiii. lambes of one yere olde a pece without fpott.
27 And their meat and drynkofferynges vnto the bollockes, rāmes and lambes, acordynge to the numbre
28 of them and after the maner. And an hegoote for a fynofferynge, befyde the dayly burntofferynge and his meate and drynkofferynges.
29 And the fyxte daye .viii. bollockes .ii. rammes ād
30 xiiii. yerelynge lambes without fpot And their meate and drynkofferynges vnto the bollockes, rammes and
31 lambes, acordynge to the maner. And an hegoote for a fynofferynge, befyde the dayly burntofferynge and his meate and drynkofferynges.
32 And the feuenth daye .vii. bollockes .ii. rāmes and
33 xiiii. lambes that are yerelynges & pure. And their meate and drynkofferynges vnto the bollockes, rammes and lābes, acordynge to their numbre & to the maner.

M. 23 yerelynges pure 24 accordyng to the nombre of them 32 .xiii. lambes
V. 18 rite celebrabitis (vv. 21, 24, 27, 30, 33, 37)
L. 18 nach dem recht (vv. 21, 24, 27, 30, 33, 37)

34 And an hegoote for a fynofferynge, befyde ẏ dayly burntofferynge and his meate and drynkofferynges.
35 And the eyght daye fhalbe the concluſion of ẏ feaſte vnto you, & ye fhall doo
36 no maner laboryous worke therein. And ye fhall offer a burntofferynge of a fwete fauoure vnto the Lorde: one bollocke, one rā & .vii
37 yerelynge lābes without fpott. And the meate & drynkofferynges vnto the bollocke, rā and lābes, acordynge to their nūbres & acordynge to ẏ ma- [Fo. LVI.]
38 ner. And an he goote for a fynofferynge befyde the dayly burntofferynge and his meate & drynkofferynges.
39 Thefe thinges ye fhall doo vnto the Lorde in youre feaſtes: befyde youre vowes and frewyll offerynges, in youre burntofferinges meatofferynges, drynkofferynges
40 and peafe offerynges. And Mofes tolde the childern of Ifrael, acordynge to all that the Lorde commaunded him.

Out of fock come oure octaues ād feaſtes of eight dayes longe.

❡ The .XXX. Chapter.

1 AND Mofes fpake vnto the heedes of the trybes of ẏ childern of Ifrael fayēge: this is the thynge which the Lorde com-
2 maundeth. Yf a man vowe a vowe vnto the Lorde or fwere an othe ād bynde his foule, he fhall not goo backe with his worde: but fhal fulfyll all ẏ proceadeth out of his mouth
3 Yf a damfell vowe a vowe vnto ẏ

M.C.S. Of vowes when they ſhalbe kept and when not.

Hēce was fett the exāple of oure vowes of chaſtite, obediens and willfull pouertie: oure offerynges ād oure pilgremage.

V. 39 præter vota & oblationes fpontaneas xxx, 2 ad principes tribuum ... Iſte eſt fermo
L. 39 ausgenomen was yhr gelobd vnd freywillig gebt xxx, 2 vbirſten der ſtemme .. Das iſts ..
M. M. N. 2 *If a man vowe etc.* This vowe here is that which a man voweth for a certayne fpace, whether it be to faſt or to chaſtyce the bodye, or any other thyng, as it is fayd Leui. vii, d.
L. M. N. 35 *Am achten tage, folt yhr ſteur thun:* Diſe ſteuer war das man fur die armen zu hauff trug eyn gemeyn gutt von allerley was Gott geben hatte.

Lorde & binde herselfe beynge in hir fathers housse
4 and vnmaried: Yf hir father heare hir vowe & bonde
which she hath made vppon hir soule, & holde his
pease thereto: then all hir vowes & bodes which she
5 hath made vppō hir soule shall stonde in effecte. But
& yf hir father forbyd her the same daye that he heareth it, none of hir vowes nor bondes which she hath
made vppon hir soule shalbe of value, ād the Lorde
shall forgeue her, becaufe hir father forbade her.

6 Yf she had an husbonde when she vowed .P. or pro-
nounsed oughte out of hir lippes wherewith she bonde
7 hir soule, and hir husbonde herde it and helde his peace
thereat the same daye he herde it: Then hir vowes and
hir bondes wherewith she bounde hir soule, shal stonde
8 in effecte. But ād yf hir husbonde forbade her the
same daye that he herde it, than hath he made hir
vowe which she had vppō her of none effecte, and
that also whiche she pronounfed with hir lippes wherewith she bounde hir soule, and the Lorde shall forgeue
her.

9 The vowe of a wedowe and of her that is deuorsed,
& all that they haue bound their soules with all, shall
stonde in effecte with them.

10 Yf she vowed in her husbandes housse or bounde her
11 soule with an oth, and her husbande herde it and helde
his peace and forbade her not: then all her vowes and
bondes wherewith she bound her soule, shall stōde.
12 But yf her husbande disanulled them ẏ same daye that
he herde them, then nothing that proceded out of her
lippes in vowes ād boundes wherewith she bounde her

V. 3 non faciet irritum verbum suum 4 voti rea erit 6 statim
vt audierit ... irrita erunt, nec obnoxia tenebitur sponsioni 9 propitius erit ei dominus. 10 Vidua & repudiata quicquid vouerint,
reddent. 11 Vxor in domo 12 si audierit vir

L. 3 soll seyn wort nicht schwechen 5 so gilt alle yhr gelubd
vnd alle yhr verbundnis, des sie sich vber yhr seele verbunden hat.
6 des Tags wenn ers horet ... Vnd der Herr wirt yhr gnedig
seyn (v. 13) 10 verstossene 11 gesinde 12 hausherr ... so gilt all
dasselb gelubd vnd alles wes es sich verbunden hat vber seyn seele

L. M. N. 3 *Seyn seele:* das ist, wenn sie sich verbunden zu
fasten odder sonst wz zu thun mit yhrem leybe Got zu dienst das
seele hie heysse, so viel, als der lebendige leyb wie die schrifft allenthalben braucht.

ſoule ſhall ſtonde in effecte: for her huſbande hath lowſed them, and the Lorde ſhall forgeue her.

13 All vowes and othes that binde to humble the ſoule,
14 maye her huſbande ſtabliſh or breake. But yf her huſbande hold his peace from one daye vnto another, then he ſtabliſheth [Fo. LVII.] all her vowes and boundes whiche ſhe had vppon her, becauſe he helde his peace
15 the ſame daye that he herde them. And yf he afterwarde breake them, he ſhall beare her ſynne him ſelf.
16 Theſe are the ordinaunces which ẏ Lorde commaunded Moſes, betwene a man and his wife, and betwene the father and his doughter, beyenge a damſell in hir fathers houſſe.

☜ The .XXXI. Chapter.

1
2 AND the Lorde ſpake vnto Moſes ſayenge: auenge the childern of Iſrael of the Madianites, and afterwarde be gathered
3 vnto thy people. And Moſes ſpake vnto harneſſe, *arm*, the folke ſayenge: Harneſſe vv. 20, 21, cf. ſome of you vnto warre, and vv. 17, 26, 30, 32 let them goo apon the Madianites and auenge the Lorde of the Madianitis. Ye ſhall ſende vnto the warre
4 a thouſande of euery trybe thorow out all the trybes
5 of Iſrael. And there were taken oute of the thouſandes of Iſrael .xii. thouſande prepared vnto warre, of euery

M.E.S. The Madianytes & Balā are ſlayne. The praye was brought to Moſes & equallye deuyded. A preſent geuē of Iſrael becauſe none of their men were ſlayne.

V. 13 ſinautem extemplo contradixerit ... quia maritus contradixit, & dominus ei propitius erit. 14 affligat animam ſuam: in arbitrio viri erit ſiue faciat, ſiue non faciat. 15 quod ſi audiens vir tacuerit 16 ſin autem contrad. ... portabit ipſe iniquitatem eius. xxxi, 2 Vlciſcere prius ... & ſic colligeris 3 Statimque Moyſes, Armate, inquit ... qui poſſint vltionem domini expetere 5 Dederuntque

L. 13 Machts aber der hausherr des tags los ... denn der hausherr hats los gemacht 14 hausherr krefftigen odder ſchwechen 15 Wenn er dazu ſchweygt ... ſo bekrefftiget er 16 Wirt ers aber ſchwechen ... ſo ſol er die miſſetat tragen. xxxi, 2 darnach dich ſamleſt 3 mit dem volck ... Ruſtet 5 Vnd ſie namen an

6 trybe a thoufande. And Mofes fent them a thoufande of euery trybe, with Phineas the fonne of Eleazer the preafte to warre, and the holye veffels & the trompettes to blowewith in his honde.
7 And they warred agenft the Madianites, as the Lorde commaunded Mofes, ād .P. flewe all the males.
8 And they flewe the kynges of Madian among other that were flayne: Eui, Rekem, Zur, Hur and Reba: fyue kynges of Madian. And they flewe Balā the
9 fonne of Beor with the fwerde. And the children of Ifrael toke all the wemen of Madian prefoners and their childern, and fpoyled all their catell, their fub-
10 ftance and their goodes. And they burnt all their cities wherein they dwelt, and all their caftels with
11 fyre. And they toke all the fpoyle and all they coude
12 catche, both of men and beeftes. And they broughte the captyues and that which they had taken and all the fpoyle vnto Mofes and Eleazer the preaft ād vnto the companye of the childern of Ifrael: euen vnto the hofte, in ȳ feldes of Moab by Iordane nye to Iericho.
13 And Mofes and Eleazer the preaft and all the lordes of the congregacion went out of the hofte agenft them.
14 And Mofes was angrie with the officers of the hofte, with ȳ captaynes ouer thoufandes and ouer hundredes,
15 which came from warre and batayle, and fayde vnto
16 them: Haue ye faued the wemen alyue? beholde, thefe caufed the childern of Ifrael thorow Balam, to commytt trefpace agēft ȳ Lorde, by ȳ reafon of Peor, & their folowed a plage amōge ȳ congregacion of the Lorde.
17 Nowe therfore flee all the men childern and the wemen
18 that haue lyen [Fo. LVIII.] with men flefhlye: But all the wemen children that haue not lyen with men, kepe

V. 6 vafaque fancta, & tubas ad clangendum 9 & cunctam fupellectilem. quicquid habere potuerant depopulati funt. 12 ad omnem multitudinem 14 principibus, exercitus 15 Cur fœminas referuaftis? 16 fuper peccato Phogor 17 quæ nouerunt viros in coitu, iugulate 18 referuate vobis

L. 6 den heyligen gezeug vnd die Hall drometen 9 namen gefangen ... all yhr habe, vnd alle yhre gutter 14 heubtleut ... die aus dem heer vnd ftreyt kamen 15 habt yhr allerley weyber leben laffen? 16 vber dem Peor 17 So erwurget ... die man erkand vnd bey gelegen haben 18 laft fur euch leben

19 alyue for youre felues. And lodge without the hofte vii. dayes all that haue killed any perfone & all that haue twiched any dead body, & purifye both youre
20 felues & youre prefoners the .iii. daye & the .vii. And fprinkle all youre raymentes & all that is made of fkynnes, & all worke of gootes heer, ād all thynges made of wodd.
21 And Eleazer the preaft fayed vnto all ẏ mē of warre which went out to batayle: this is the ordinaunce of
22 the lawe which the Lorde commaunded Mofes: Gold,
23 fyluer, braffe, yeron, tyn & leed, & all that maye abyde ẏ fyre, ye fhall make it goo thorow the fyre, ād then it is cleane. Neuerthelater, it fhalbe fprinkled with fprinklinge water. And all ẏ foffereth not the fyre,
24 ye fhall make goo thorow the water. And wafh youre clothes the feuenth daye, & then ye are cleane. And after warde come in to the hofte.
25, 26 And the Lorde fpake vnto Mofes fayenge: take the fumme of the praye that was taken, both of the wemē & of catell, thou & Eleazer the preaft and the
27 auncient heedes of ẏ congregacion. And deuyde it in to two parties, betwene them that toke the warre vppō thē and went out to batayle and all the congregacion.
28 And take a porcion vnto the Lorde of the men of warre whiche went oute to .P. batayle one of fyue hundred, of the wemen and of the oxen and of the affes and of the
29 fhepe: and ye fhall take it of their halfe and geue it vnto Eleazer the preaft, an heueofferynge vnto the
30 Lorde. And of the halfe of ẏ childern of Ifrael, take one of fyftye, of ẏ wemen, of the oxen, of the affes and of the fhepe, and of all maner of beeftes, & geue them vnto the leuites which wayte apon ẏ habitacion of the Lorde.
31 And Mofes and Eleazer the preaft did as the Lorde

V. 19 luftrabitur 20 expiabitur. 23 igne purgabitur ... aqua expiationis fanctificabitur 26 principes vulgi 27 omnem reliquam multitudinem 28 vnam animam 29 quia primitiæ domini funt. 30 qui excubant in cuftodiis (v. 47)
L. 19 entfundiget (v. 20) 23 mit dem Sprenge waffer entfundiget 26 die vbirften veter der gemeyne 27 der gemeyne 28 eyn feele 29 zur Hebe dem Herrn. 30 die der hut warten (v. 47)

32 commaunded Moſes. And ẏ botye and the praye
which the men of warre had caught, was .vi. hundred
33 thouſande & .Lxxv. thouſande ſhepe: ād .Lxxii. thou-
34, 35 ſande oxen: & .Lxi. thouſande aſſes: & .xxxii. thouſande wemen that had lyen by no man.

36   And the halfe which was the parte of thē that wēt
out to warre, was .iii. hundred thouſande and .xxxvii
37 thouſande and fyue hundred ſhepe: And the Lordes
38 parte of the ſhepe was .vi. hundred and .Lxxv. And
the oxen were .xxxvi. thouſande, of which the Lordes
39 parte was .Lxxii. And the aſſes were .xxx. thouſande
and fyue hundred, of whiche the Lordes parte was
40 Lxi. And the wemen were .xvi. thouſande, of which
41 the Lordes parte was .xxxii. foules. And Moſes gaue
that ſumme which was the Lordes heueofferynge vnto
Eleazer the preaſt: as the Lorde cōmaunded Moſes.

42   [Fo. LIX.] And the other halfe of the childern of
Iſrael whiche Moſes ſeperated from the men of warre
43 (that is to wete, the halfe that pertayned vnto the
congregacion) was .iii. hundred thouſande and .xxxvii
44 thouſande and fyue hundred ſhepe: and .xxxvi. thou-
45 ſande oxen: and .xxx. thouſande aſſes and fyue hūdred:
46, 47 and .xvi. thouſande wemen. And Moſes toke of this
halfe that pertayned vnto the childern of Iſrael: one
of euery fyftie, both of the wemen & of the catell, and
gaue them vnto the leuites which wayted vppon the
habitacion of the Lorde, as the Lorde commaunded
Moſes.

48   And the officers of thouſandes of the hoſte, the
captaynes ouer the thouſandes and the captaynes ouer
49 the hundreds came forth & ſayed vnto Moſes: Thy
ſervauntes haue taken the ſumme of the men of warre,
which were vnder oure hande, & there lacked not one
50 man of them. We haue therfore broughte a preſent
vnto the Lorde what euery man founde of Iewels of

V. 37 in partem domini ſupputatæ ſunt 40 ceſſerunt in partem
domini 41 numerum primitiarum domini 43 reliquæ multitudini
L. 32 der vbrigen ausbeutte 41 ſolch Hebe 43 der gemeyne
zuſtendig
𝔐. 𝔐. N. 43 *vnto the congregacion:* which was not at the warre.

golde, cheyns, bracelettes, ringes, earynges & spangels, to make an attonement for oure soules before the Lorde.

51 And Moses & Eleazer toke the golde off them:
52 Iewels of all maner facions. And all the golde of the heueoffrynge of the Lord, of the captaynes ouer thousandes & hundreds was .xvi. thousand .vii. hundred &
53 L. sycles, .P. which ẏ mē of warre had spoyled, euery
54 man for him selfe. And Moses & Eleazer ẏ preast toke the golde of the captaynes ouer the thousandes & ouer the hundreds, & brought it in to the tabernacle of witnesse: to be a memoriall vnto ẏ childern of Israel, before ẏ Lorde.

The .XXXII. Chapter.

1 THE children of Rubē & the childern of Gad, had an exceadinge greate multitude of catell. And whē they sawe the lōde of Iaeser & the lōde of Gilead ẏ
2 it was an apte place for catell, they came & spake vnto Moses & Eleazer ẏ preast & vnto ẏ lordes of ẏ cōgregaciō sayenge.
3 The lōde of Ataroth Dibo & Beon,
4 whiche contre ẏ Lorde smote before the congregacion of Israel: is a londe for catell and we

M.C.X. To Ruben and Gad and to halfe the trybe of Manasses, is promesed the possession beyounde Iordan eastward: yf they bryng their brethren into the lande of promesse.

M. 3 Ataroth & Dibō & Iazer, and Nemrah & Hesbon & Elealeh & Sabam & Nebo & Beon

V. 50 vt depreceris pro nobis dominum. 53 Vnusquisque enim quod in præda rapuerat, suum erat. xxxii, 1 pecora multa, & erat illis in iumentis infinita substantia . . . aptas animalibus alendis terras 3 Ataroth, & Dibon, & Iazer, & Nemra, & Hesebon, & Eleale, & Sabam, & Nebo, & Beon 4 regionis vberrimæ . . . iumenta plurima

L. 50 vnser seelen versunet werden fur dem Herrn 53 denn die kriegs leutt hatten geraubt eyn iglicher fur sich xxxii, 1 hatten viel vnd seer eyn gros viech . . bequeme stet 3 Atroth, Dibon, Iaeser, Nimra, Hesbon, Eleale, Sebam, Nebo vnd Beon 4 ist bequeme . . . haben viech.

5 thy fervauntes haue catell wherfore (fayed they) yf we haue founde grace in thy fyghte, let this londe be geuen vnto thy fervauntes to poffeffe, and bringe vs not ouer Iordane.

6 And Mofes fayed vnto the childrē of Gad and of Ruben: fhall youre brethern goo to warre and ye
7 tarye here? Wherfore difcorage ye the hertes of the children of Ifrael for to goo ouer in to the londe which
8 the Lorde hath geuē them? This dyd youre fathers, whē I fent them from Cades bernea to fe the londe.
9 And they went vp euen vnto the ryuer of Efcol & fawe the londe, & difcoraged the hertes of the childern of Ifrael, that they fhulde [Fo. LX.] not goo in to the londe whiche the Lorde had geuen them.
10 And the Lorde was wroth the fame tyme and fware
11 fayenge: None of the men that came out of Egipte frō twentye yere olde and aboue, fhall fe the londe whiche I fwore vnto Abraham, Ifaac and Iacob, becaufe they
12 haue not continually folowed me: faue Caleb the fonne of Iephune the Kenefite, & Iofua the fonne of Nun, for
13 they haue folowed me continually. And the Lorde was angrie with Ifrael, and made them wandre in the wilderneffe .xl. yere, vntill all the generacion that had done euell in the fyghte of the Lorde were confumed.
14 And beholde, ye are ryfen vp in youre fathers ftede, the encreafe of fynfull men, to augmente the ferfe
15 wrath of the Lorde to Ifrael warde. For yf ye turne awaye from after him, he wyll yet agayne leue the people in the wilderneffe, fo fhall ye deftroy all this folke.   folke, *people*
16 And they went nere him ād fayed: we will bylde fhepefoldes here for oure fhepe and for oure catell, and

M. 14 fteade, to ỹ encreafe ... & to augmēte
V. 5 in poffeffionem, nec facias 7 Cur fubuertitis mentes (v. 9) 9 vallem Botri 12 ifti impleuerunt voluntatem meam. 14 incrementa, & alumni hominum peccatorum 15 et vos caufa eritis necis omnium. 16 vrbes munitas
L. 5 fo wollen wyr nicht vber den Iordan zihen. 7 macht ... hertz wendig (v. 9) 11 follen ia ... nicht fehen ... das fie myr nicht gentzlich nach gefolgt haben (cf. v. 12).

17 cities for oure childern: But we oure felues will go
ready armed before ẏ childern of Ifrael, vntill we haue
broughte them vnto their place. And oure childrē
fhall dwell in the ftronge cities, becaufe of the inhabi-
18 ters of the londe. And we will not returne vnto oure
houffes, vntill the childern off .P. Ifrael haue enhereted:
19 euery man his enheritaunce. For we will not enheret
with them on yonder fyde Iordane forwarde, becaufe
oure enheritaunce is fallen to vs on this fyde Iordane
eaftwarde.

20 And Mofes fayed vnto them: Yf ye will do this
thinge, that ye will go all harneffed before the Lorde
21 to warre, and will go all of you in harneffe ouer Iordane before ẏ Lorde, vntill he haue caft out his ene-
22 myes before him, & vntill the londe be fubdued before
ẏ Lorde: then ye fhall returne & be without finne
agenft the Lorde & agenft Ifrael, & this lōde fhalbe
23 youre poffeffion before the Lorde. But & yf ye will
not do fo, beholde, ye fynne agenft the Lorde: ād be
24 fure youre fynne will fynde you out. Bilde youre
cities for youre childern & foldes for youre fhepe, &
fe ye do ẏ ye haue fpoken.

25 And the childern of Gad & of Ruben fpake vnto
Mofes fayenge: thy fervauntes will do as my lorde
26 commaundeth. Oure childrē oure wiues fubftāce &
all oure catell fhall remayne here in the cities of Gilead.
27 But we thi fervauntes will goo all harneffed for the
warre vnto batayle before the Lorde, as my lorde hath
fayed.

28 And Mofes cōmaūded Eleazer ẏ preaft & Iofua ẏ
fonne of Nun & the aunciēt hedes of the tribes of the
29 childern of Ifrael, & fayed vnto them: Yf the childern
of Gad and Ru- [Fo. LXI.] ben will goo with you ouer

ſ͡ϻ. 17 fenced cyties
V. 17 nos autem ipfi armati & accincti ... ad loca fua ...
propter habitatorum infidias. 18 in domos noftras 20 expediti
... ad pugnam 21 et omnis vir bellator armatus 22 inculpabiles
23 nulli dubium eft quin peccetis 27 omnes expediti

L. 17 an yhren ort 21 ruftet zum ftreyt ... wer vnter euch
gerüft ift (cf. vv. 27, 29, 30, 32) 22 vnfchuldig 23 vnd werdet ewr
funden ynnen werden, wenn fie euch finden wirt.

Iordane, all prepared to fyghte before the Lorde: then when the lande is fubdued vnto you, geue them the
30 londe of Gilead to poffeffe, but & yf they will not goo ouer with you in harneffe, then they fhall haue their poffeffions amonge you in ẏ londe of Canaan.
31 And the childern of Gad & Ruben anfwered fayenge: that which ẏ Lorde hath fayed vnto thi feruautes
32 we will doo We wil goo harneffed before the Lorde in to the londe of Canaan, & the poffeffion of oure enheritaunce fhalbe on this fyde the Iordane.
33 And Mofes gaue vnto ẏ childern of Gad and of Ruben & vnto halfe the trybe of Manaffe the fonne of Iofeph, the kyngdome of Sihon kynge of the Amorites, and the kyngdome of Og kynge of Bafan, the lande that longed vnto the cities thereof in the coftes
34 of the contre rounde aboute. And the childern of Gad
35 bylt Dibō, atharoth, Aroer, Atroth, Sophan, Iaefer,
36 Iegabeha, Bethnimra & Betharan ftronge cities, and
37 they bylt foldes for their fhepe. And the childern of
38 Ruben bylt Hefebon, Elalea, Kiriathaim, Nebo, Baal Meon and turned their names, and Sibama alfo: & gaue names vnto the cities which they bylt.
39 And the childern of Machir the fonne of Manaffe went to Gilead and toke it, and put out the Amorites
40 ẏ were therein. And Mo- .Ⅰ. fes gaue Gilead vnto
41 Machir the fonne of Manaffe & he dwelt therein. And Iair the fonne of Manaffe wēt & toke ẏ fmall townes
42 thereof, & called thē the townes of Iair. And Nobah went & toke kenath with the townes longinge thereto, & called it Nobah after his awne name.

𝔐. 36 Betharan fencend cyties [fenced]
𝒱. 29 omnes armati 30 armati (v. 32) 32 trans Iordanem. 36 vrbes munitas 41 Auoth iair, id eft villas Iair.
𝑳. 32 diffeyt des Iordans 36 verfchloffen ftedte 41 Hauoth 42 mit yhren tochtern

❧ The .XXXIII. Chapter

1 **T**HESE are the iurneyes of the childern of Israel which went out of the lande of Egipte with their armies vnder Mo-
2 ses ād Aaron. And Moses wrote their goenge out by their iurneyes at ẏ cō-maundment of the Lorde: euen these
3 are ẏ iurneyes of their goenge out. The childern of Israel departed from Rahēses the .xv. daye of the first moneth, on ẏ morowe after Passeouer & went out with
4 an hye hande in the syghte of all Egipte, while the Egiptians buried all their firstborne which the Lorde had smoten amonge thē. And vppō their goddes also
5 the Lorde dyd execucion. And ẏ childern of Israel remoued from Rahemses and pitched in Sucoth.
6 And they departed frō Sucoth & pitched their tentes
7 in Ethā, which is in the edge of ẏ wyldernesse. And they remoued frō Ethā ād turned vnto the entrynge of Hiroth which is before baall Zephon, & pitched be-
8 fore Migdol. And they departed frō before Hiroth & went thorow the myddes of the see in to the wilder- [Fo. LXII.]
9 nesse, & wēt .iii. dayes iurney in ẏ wil- dernesse of Ethā, & pitched in Marah. And they remoued frō Marah & wēt vnto Elim where were .xii fountaynes ād .Lxx. datetrees and they pitched there.
10 And they remoued from Elim & laye fast by the
11 red see. And they remoued frō the red see & laye in
12 ẏ wildernesse of Sin. And they toke their iurney out of ẏ wildernesse of Sin, & sett vpp their tentes in Daphka.
13 And they departed from Daphka, and laye in Alus.
14 And they remoued from Alus, & laye at Raphedim,

M.C.S. The iourneys and departynges frō place to place of Israel are nombred. They are cōmaunded to kyll the Canaanites.

M. 4 smyttē 9 .Lxx. paulmetrees
V. 3 altera die phase . . . in manu excelsa 4 nam & in diis eorum exercuerat vltionem 9 & palmæ septuaginta
L. 2 beschreyb yhren auszug 3 des andern tags der ostern, durch eyn hohe hand

15 where was no water for the people to drynke. And they departed from Raphedim, and pitched in the wildernesse of Sinai
16 And they remoued from the deserte of Sinai, &
17 lodged at the graues of lust. And they departed from
18 the sepulchres of lust, ād laye at Haseroth. And they
19 departed from Hazeroth, & pitched in Rithma. And departed frō Rithma and pitched at Rimon Parez.
20 And they departed from Rimon Parez, & pitched in
21 Libna. And they remoued from Libna, & pitched at
22 Rissa And they iurneyed frō Rissa ād pitched at Ke-
23 helatha. And they went frō Kehelatha, & pitched in
24 moūt Sapher And they remoued from mount Sapher,
25 and laye in Harada. And they remoued from Harada, and pitched in Makeheloth.
26 And they remoued from Makeheloth, & laye at
27 Tahath, ād they departed frō Tahath & pitched at
28 Tharath And they remoued frō .P. Tharath, and
29 pitched in Mithca. And they went from Mithca, and
30 lodged in Hasmona. And they departed from Has-
31 mona, and laye at Moseroth. And they departed from Moseroth, and pitched amonge the childern of
32 Iaecon. And they remoued from the childern of Iae-
33 con, ād laye at Hor gidgad. And they went from Hor
34 gidgad, and pitched in Iathbatha. And they remoued
35 from Iathbatha, and laye at Abrona. And they departed
36 from Abrona, and laye at Ezeon gaber. And they remoued from Ezeon gaber, and pitched in the wildernesse of Zin, which is Cades.
37 And they remoued from Cades, & pitched in mount
38 Hor, in ẏ edge of the londe of Moab. And Aaron the preast went vpp in to mount Hor at the commaūdment of ẏ Lorde & dyed there, euen in the fortieth yere after the childern of Israel were come out of ẏ londe of

M. 31 pytched in Bane Iakan. 32 And they remoued from Bane Iakan, and laye at Hor gadgad. Hor gadgad 37 land of Edom
V. 16 ad Sepulchra concupiscentiæ. 17 Sep. concup. 31 castrametati sunt in Bene-iaacan. 32 Profectique de Bene-iaacan venerunt in montem Gadgad.
L. 16 lustgreber (v. 17) 31 lagerten sich ynn Bne Iaekon, Von Bne Iaekon zogen sie aus vnd lagerten sich in Hor gidgad

39 Egipte, & in the firſt daye of the fyfte moneth. And Aaron was an hundred ād .xxxiii. yere olde when he dyed in mount Hor

40 And kinge Erad the canaanite which dwelt in ẏ ſouth of ẏ lond of canaā, herd ẏ the childern of Iſrael were come.

41 And they departed frō mount Hor, & pitched in
42 Zalmona. And they departed from Zalmona, & pitched
43 in Phimon, & they departed from Phimon, & pitched in
44 Oboth. And they departed frō Oboth, & pitched in Igim
45 [Fo. LXIII.] Abarim in the borders of Moab. And they
46 departed from Igim, and pitched in Dibon Gad. And they remoued from Dibon Gad, and laye in Almon Dibla-
47 thama. And they remoued from Almon Diblathama, ād
48 pitched in ẏ mountaynes of Abarim before Nibo. And they departed from the mountaynes of Abarim, & pitched in the feldes of Moab faſt by Iordane nye to
49 Iericho. And they pitched apon Iordayne, from Beth Haieſmoth vnto ẏ playne of Sitim in ẏ feldes of Moab

50 And the Lorde ſpake vnto Moſes in the feldes of Moab
51 by Iordayne nye vnto Iericho, ſayēge: ſpeake vnto the childern of Iſrael and ſaye vnto them: when ye are
52 come ouer Iordane in to the londe of Canaan, ſe that ye dryue out all the inhabiters of the londe before you, & deſtroy their Ymaginacions & all their Ymages of Metall, ād plucke downe all their alters bylt on hilles:
53 And poſſeſſe ẏ londe & dwell therein, for I haue geuen you
54 the londe to enioye it. And ye ſhall deuyde the enher-itaunce of the londe by lott amonge youre kynreddes, ād geue to the moo the moare enheritaunce, & to the fewer the leſſe enheritaunce. And youre enheritaunce ſhalbe in ẏ trybes of youre fathers, in ẏ place where euery mans lott falleth.

𝔐. 44 Iehabarim 46 Iehabarim 49 Abelſatim 52 deſtroye their chappelles

𝔙. 52 confringite titulos, & ſtatuas comminuete, atque omnia excelſa vaſtate

𝕷. 52 vertreyben fur ewrem angeſicht, vnd alle yhre ſeulen vnd alle yhre gegoſſene bilder vmbringen vnd alle yhre höhe vertilgen

𝔐. 𝔐. N. 52 *Chapelles:* After the Chald. Ra. Salo. and Ra. Abr. graued pauing ſtones.

55 But and yf ye will not dryue out the inhabiters of
ẏ londe before you, then thefe which ye let remayne
of thē, fhalbe thornes in youre .P. eyes and dartes in
youre fydes, & fhall vexe you in the lōde wherein ye
56 dwell. More ouer it will come to paffe, ẏ I fhall doo
vnto you as I thought to doo vnto them.

❡ The .XXXIIII. Chapter.

1, 2 AND the Lorde fpake vnto Mofes fayenge: cōmaūde the childern of Ifrael and faye vnto them: when ye come in to the londe of Canaan, this is the londe that fhall fall vnto youre enheritaunce, the londe of
3 Canaan with all hir coftes. And youre fouth quarter fhalbe from the wilderneffe of Zin alonge by the cofte of Edom, fo that youre fouth quarter fhalbe from the
4 fyde of the falte fee eaftwarde, & fhall fet a compaffe frō the fouth vpp to Acrabim, & reach to Zinna. And it fhall goo out on ẏ fouth fide of Cades Bernea, & goo out alfo at Hazar Adar, and goo alōge to Azmon.
5 And fhall fet a cōpaffe from Azmon vnto the ryuer of Egipte, and fhall goo out at the fee.
6 And youre weft quarter fhall be the greate fee, which cofte fhalbe youre weft cofte.
7, 8 And this fhalbe youre north quarter: ye fhall compaffe from the great fee vnto moūt Hor. And from

M.C.S. The Cooftes and borders of the land of promeffe. Certein are affygned to deuyde the lande.

𝔐. 55 thofe which
𝒱. 55 claui in oculis, & lanceæ in lateribus, et aduerfabuntur vobis xxxiiii, 2 forte ceciderit 3 mare falfiffimum 4 per afcenfum fcorpionis... ad villam nomine Adar 5 ad torrentem Ægypti, & magni maris litore finietur. 6 a mari magno incipiet, & ipfo fine claudetur. 7 montem altiffimum
𝔏. 55 zu dornen werden in ewern augen vnd zu ftachel ynn ewern feytten, vnd werden euch drengen 56 So wirts denn gehen, das ich euch gleich thun werde xxxiiii, 2 euch zum erbteyl fellet 3 ecke .. faltz meers 4 Hazor Adar 5 den bach Egypti
𝔐. 𝔐. 𝔑. 55 *Thornes in youre eyes* that is, they fhall be youre rodde fcourge and vndoars.

mount Hor, ye ſhall compaſſe & goo vnto Hemath, 9 and the ende of ẏ coſte ſhalbe at Zedada, & the coſte ſhall reach out to Ziphron and goo out at Hazor Enan. And this ſhalbe youre north quarter.

10 [Fo. LXIIII.] And ye ſhall compaſſe youre eaſt 11 quarter frō Hazar Enan to Sepham   And the coſte ſhall goo downe from Sepham to Ribla on the eaſt ſyde of Ain.   And then deſcende and goo out at the ſyde 12 of the ſee of Chinereth eaſtwarde.   And then goo downe alonge by Iordayne, and leue at the ſalte ſee. And this ſhall be youre lõde with all the coſtes thereof rounde aboute.

13 And Moſes commaunded the childern of Iſrael, ſayẽge: this is the lõde which ye ſhall enherett by lotte, and which the Lorde cõmaũded to geue vnto 14 ix. trybes and an halfe: for the trybe of the childern of Rubeṅ haue receaued, in the houſſholdes of their fathers, and the trybe of the childern of Gad in their fathers houſſholdes, & halfe the trybe of Manaſſe, haue 15 receaued their enheritaunce, that is to wete .ii. trybes and an halfe haue receaued their enheritaunce on ẏ other ſyde of Iordayne by Iericho eaſtwarde, towarde the ſonne ryſynge.

16, 17 And the Lorde ſpake to Moſes ſayenge: Theſe are the names of ẏ men, which ſhall deuyde you the londe to enherett.   Eleazer ẏ preaſt, ãd Ioſua the 18 ſonne of Nun.   And ye ſhall take alſo a lorde of euery 19 trybe to deuyde the londe, whoſe names are theſe: In 20 the trybe of Iuda, Caleb ẏ ſonne of Iephune.   And in ẏ trybe of ẏ childern of Simeon, Demuel ẏ ſõne of 21 Amiud, ãd in ẏ tribe of Bē Iamin, Eli- .Ƥ. dad the 22 ſonne of Ciſlon.   And in the trybe of ẏ childern of 23 Dan, the lorde Bucki the ſonne of Iagli.   And amonge the childern of Ioſeph: in the trybe of the childern of 24 Manaſſe, the lorde Haniel the ſonne of Ephod.   And

ℳ. 20 Semuel the ſonne of Amiud.
Ʋ. 9 villam Enan (v. 10). 11 Reblatha contra fontem Daphnim 15 trans Iordanem contra Iericho ad orientalem plagam.
ℒ. 9 Hazor Enan (v. 10) 15 diſſeyt des Iordans gegen Iericho gegen dem morgen.

in the trybe of the childern of Ephraim, ẏ lorde Cemuel
25 the fonne of Siphtan. And in the trybe of the fonnes
of Zabulon, ẏ lorde Elizaphan the fonne of Parnac.
26 And in the trybe of the childern of Ifachar, the lorde
27 Palthiel ẏ fonne of Afan. And in the trybe of the
fonnes of Affer, the lorde Ahihud ẏ fonne of Selomi.
28 And in the trybe of the childern of Naphtali, the lorde
29 Peda El the fonne of Ammihud. Thefe are they which
the Lorde commaūded to deuyde the enheritaūce vnto
the childern of Ifrael, in the londe of Canaan.

The .XXXV. Chapter.

1 AND the Lorde fpake vnto Mofes in ẏ feldes of Moab by Ior-
2 dayne Iericho fayenge: com-maunde the childern of Ifrael,
that they geue vnto the leuites of the en-heritaūce of their poffeffion: cities to dwell
in. And ye fhall geue alfo vnto the cities of ẏ leuites, fuburbes rounde aboute them.
3 The cities fhalbe for them to dwell in, and ẏ fuburbes for their catell, poffeffion and
all maner beftes of theirs.

M.C.S. Vnto the Leuites muft be geuen Cytyes and fuburbes. The Cyties of ref-uge or fanctu-aryes. The lawe of man-quellyng. For one mannes wytneffe fhall no man be condempned.

4 And the fuburbes of the cities which ye fhall geue
vnto the leuites, fhall reach from the wall of ẏ citie
outwarde, a thoufande cu- [Fo. LXV.] bites rounde
5 aboute. And ye fhall meafure without the citie, and
make the vtmoft border of the eaftfyde: two thoufande
cubites, And the vtmoft border of the fouth fyde: two
thoufande cubetes, And the vtmoft border of the weft
fyde: two thoufande cubetes: and the vtmoft border
of the north fyde: two thoufande cubetes alfo: and the

ℳ. 1 Iordan ouer againft Iericho
𝒱. 3 et fuburbana earum per circūitum ... fint pecoribus ac
iumentis, 4 quæ a muris ciuitatum forinfecus per circumitum ...
tendentur. 5 æquali termino finietur. eruntque vrbes in medio, &
foris fuburbana
ℒ. 3 allerley thier haben 5 an der ecken (3 times)

citie fhalbe in the myddes. And thefe fhall be the fuburbes of their cities.

6 And amonge the cities which ye fhall geue vnto the leuites, there fhall be fixe cities of fraunches which ye fhall geue to that intent that he which killeth, maye flye thyder. And to them ye fhall adde .xlii. cities mo: fo that all the cities which ye fhall geue the leuites fhalbe .xlviii. with their fuburbes.

fraunches, franchise, i.e. a fanctuary facuring to the criminal freedom from arreft, cf. vv. 27, 32

8 And of the cities which ye fhall geue oute of the poffeffyons of the childern of Ifrael, ye fhall geue many out of their poffeffions that haue moche and fewe out of their poffeffiōs that haue litle: fo that euery tribe fhall geue of his cities vnto the leuites, acordinge to the enheritaunce which he enhereteth.

9, 10 And the Lorde fpake vnto Mofes fayenge: fpeake vnto the childern of Ifrael and faye vnto them: when ye be come ouer Iordayne in to the londe of Canaan,
11 ye fhall bylde cities whiche fhalbe preuyleged townes for you: that he whiche fleeth a man vnwares, maye flye thi-
12 ther. And the cities fhalbe to .P. flee from the executer of bloude, that he whyche kylled dye not, vntill he
13 ftonde before the congregacion in iudgement. And of thefe .vi. fre cities which ye fhall geue
14 .iii. ye fhall geue on this fyde Iordayne
15 and .iii. in ye londe of Canaan. And thefe fixe fre cities fhalbe for the childern of Ifrael & for the ftraunger & for him that dwelleth amonge you, ye all thei which kill any perfone vnwares, maye flee thither.

The righte vfe of fanctuaryes.

16 Yf any man fmyte another with a wepō of yerne that he dye, than he is a murtherer, & fhall dye for it.

V. 6 fex erunt in fugitiuorum auxilia feparata 11 decernite quæ vrbes effe debeant in præfidia fugit. qui nolentes, fanguinem fuderint 12 cognatus occifi . . . & caufa illius iudicetur. 14 trans Iordanem 16 reus erit homicidii, & ipfe morietur.

L. 6 fechs frey ftedte geben 12 blut recher, das der nicht fterben muffe, der eyn todfchlag than hat, bis das er fur der gemeyne zu gericht geftanden fey.

M. M. N. 11 The ryght vfe of fanctuaries.

17 Yf he fmyte him with a throwinge ftone that he dye therwith, then he fhall dye: For he is a murtherer and fhalbe flayne therfore.

18 Yf he fmyte him with a handwepon of wodd that he dye therwith, then he fhall dye: for he is a murtherer and fhalbe flayne therfore.

19 The iudge of bloude fhall flee the murtherer, as
20 fone as he fyndeth him: Yf he thruft him of hate or
21 hourle at him with layenge of wayte that he dye or fmyte him with his hande of enuye that he dye, he that fmote him fhall dye, for he is a murtherer. The iuftice of bloude fhall flee him as foone as he fyndeth him.

22 But and yf he puffhed him by chaunce & not of hate or caft at him with any maner of [Fo. LXVI.]
23 thynge and not of layenge of wayte: or caft any maner of ftone at him that he dye therwith, and fawe him not: And he caft it apon him and he dyed, but was
24 not his enemye, nether foughte him ony harme: Then the cōgregacion fhall iudge betwene the fleer ād the
25 executer of bloude in foche cafes. And the congregacion fhall delyuer the fleer out of the hande of the iudge of bloude, and fhall reftore him agayne vnto the fraunchefed cytye, whother he was fleed. And he fhall byde there vnto the dethe off the hye preafte whiche was anoynted with holy oyle.

26 But and yf he came without the borders of his
27 preuyleged citie whether he was fled, yf the bloudvenger fynde him without the borders of his fre towne, he
28 fhall flee the murtherer and be giltleffe, becaufe he fhulde haue bidden in his fre towne vntyll the deth of the hye preafte, and after the deth of the hye preafte, he fhall returne agayne vnto the londe of his poffeffyon.

𝔐. 19 the iuftice of bloude 26 yf the añeger of bloud
𝒱. 17 Si lapidem iecerit, & ictus occubuerit: fimiliter punietur. 18 percufforis fanguine vindicabitur. 19 Propinquus occifi, homic. interficiet: ftatim vt apprehenderit eum, interficiet. 21 inimicus ... cognatus occifi ftatim vt inuenerit eū, iugulabit. 23 & inimicitiis quicquam horum fecerit 24 inter percufforem & propinquum fanguinis quæftio ventilata 25 liberabitur innocens de vltoris manu 26 quæ exulibus deputatæ funt
𝓛. 25 frey ftad (cf. vv. 26, 27, 28) 28 widder zum land feynes erbguts komen

29 And this shalbe an ordinaunce and a lawe vnto you, amonge youre childern after you in all youre habitacions.
30 Whosoeuer sleeth, shalbe slaine at ẏ mouthe of witnesses. For one witnesse shall not answere agenste one
31 persone to put him to deeth. Moreouer ye shall take none amendes for the lyfe of the murtherer whiche is
32 worthy to dye: But he shall be put to deeth. Also ye shall take none atonement for him ẏ is fled to a fre citie, that he shulde come agayne and dwell in the londe before the deeth of the hye preast.
33 And se that ye polute not the londe which ye are in, for bloude defyleth the londe. And the londe can none other wyse be clensed of ẏ bloude that is shed
34 therein, but by the bloude of it that shed it. Defyle not therfore the londe which ye inhabitt, & in the myddes of which I also dwell, for I am ẏ Lorde which dwell amonge the childern of Israel.

⁋ The .XXXVI. Chapter.

1 AND the auncyēt heedes of the childern of Gilead the sonne of Machir ẏ sonne of Manasse of the kynred of ẏ childern of Ioseph, came forth and spake before Moses and the prynces which were auncię̄t heedes
2 amōge the childern of Israel & sayed: The Lorde commaunded my lorde to geue ẏ lande to enherette by lotte to the childern of Israel. And then my lord commaunded in ẏ

M.C.S. An order for the maryage of the daughters of Zelaphead. One of the trybes may not marye wyth another: but euery one must take hym a wyfe of hys awne trybe.

M. 33 bloude of hym 34 I also dwell amonge the chyldren of Israel.
V. 30 Homicida sub testibus punietur 34 Atque ita emūdabitur vestra possessio   xxxvi, 2 Tibi domino nostro præcepit dominus, vt terram sorte diuideres filiis Israel & vt filiabus
L. 32 Vnd yhr solt keyne versunung nehmen 33 wenn wer blut schuldig ist, der schendet das land.   xxxvi, 2 Lieber herr
M. M. N. 30 For one mannes wytnesse ought no man to be condemned.

name of the Lorde to geue the enheritaunce of Zela-
3 phead oure brother vnto his doughters. Now when
any of the sonnes of the trybes of Israel take them to
wyues, then shall their enheritaunce be taken from
the enheritaunce of oure fathers, and shall be put vnto
the enheritaunce of the trybe in which they [Fo.
LXVII.] are and shalbe taken from the lott of oure
4 enheritaunce. And when the fre yere cometh vnto
the childern of Israel, then shall their enheritaunce be
put vnto the enheritaunce of the trybe where they are
in, and so shall their enheritaunce be taken awaye
from the enheritaunce of the trybe of oure fathers.
5 And Moses commaunded the childern of Israel at
the mouth of the Lorde sayenge: the trybe of ẏ chil-
6 dern of Ioseph haue sayed well. This therefore doeth
the Lorde commaūde the doughters of Zelaphead sayenge: let them be wyues to whom they thē silse thynke
best, but in the kynred of the trybe of their fathers
7 shall they marye, that the enheritaunce of the children
of Israel roole not from trybe to trybe. But that the
childern of Israel maye abyde, euery man in the enherit-
8 aunce of the trybe of his fathers And euery doughter
that possesseth any enheritaunce amonge the trybes of the
childern of Israel, shalbe wife vnto one of the kynred of
the trybe of hir father, that the childern of Israel maye
enioy euery man the enheritaunce of his father, &
9 that the enheritaunce goo not from one trybe to
another: but that the trybes of the childern of Israel,
maye abyde euery man in his awne enheritaunce.
10 And as the Lorde commaunded Moses euen so dyd
11 the doughters of Zelaphead: Mahela, Thirza, Hagla,

𝔐. 4 And when the yere of iubelye .. wherin they are
𝔙. 3 quas si alterius tribus homines vxores acceperint ... de
nostra hæreditate minuetur 4 iubileus, id est quinquagesimus
annus remissionis aduenerit, confundatur sortium distributio, &
aliorum possessio ad alios transeat. 5 Respondit Moyses filiis Israel,
& domino præcipiente ait, Recte ... locuta est 7 ne commisceatur
possessio filiorum Israel de tribu in tribum. Omnes enim 9 nec
sibi misceantur tribus, sed ita maneant 10 vt a domino separatæ sunt.
𝔏. 5 hat recht geredt. 7 vnd nicht eyn erbteyl von eym stam
falle auff den andern 9 sondern eyn iglicher hange an seynem
erbe

Milca and Noa, .P. ād were maried vnto their fathers
12 brothers fonnes, of the kynred of the childern of Manaſſe the ſonne of Ioſeph: ād ſo they had their enheritaunce in the trybe of the kynred of their father.

13 Theſe are the commaundmentes & lawes which the Lorde commaunded thorow Moſes, vnto the childern of Iſrael in the feldes of Moab apon Iordayne nye vnto Iericho.

⁋ The ende of the .iiii. boke of Moſes.

V. 11 filiis patrui ſui 12 et poſſeſſio quæ illis fuerat attributa, manſit 13 per manum Moyſi
L. 11 den kindern yhrer vettern 12 Alſo bleyb yhr erbteyl.

A PRO
LOGE IN TO THE
fyfte boke of Moses, cal-
led Deuteronomye.

THIS is a boke worthye to be rede in daye and nyghte and neuer to be oute of handes. For it is the moſt excellent of all the bokes of Moſes   It is eaſye alſo and light and a very pure goſpell that is to wete, a preachinge of fayth and loue: deducinge the loue to God oute of faith, and the loue of a mans neyghboure oute of the loue of God. Herin alſo thou mayſt lerne right meditacion or contemplacyon, which is nothing els ſaue the callynge to mynde and a repeatyng in the hert of the glorioufe ād wonderfull deades of God, and of his terreble handelinge off his enemyes and mercyfull entreating of them that come when he calleth them which thinge this boke doth and almoſt nothinge els.

In the .iiii. firſt chaptres he reherſeth the benefites of God done vnto thē, to prouoke thē to loue, ād his mightie deades done aboue all naturall power ād beyonde all naturall capacite of faith, that they might beleue God ād truſt in him and in his ſtrength.   And thyrdlye he reherſeth the firce plages of God vppon hys enemyes and on them which thorowe impacientie and vnbeleffe fell from him: partelye to tame .P. and abate the appetites of the fleſhe whiche alwaye fyght agenſt the ſpirite, and partely to bridle the wilde raginge luſtes of thē in whom was no ſpirite: that though they had no power to do good of loue, yet at the leſt waye they ſhulde abſteyne from outwarde euell for feare of wrath and cruell vengeaunce whiche ſhuld fall vppon them and ſhortly finde them oute, yf they caſt vpp goddes nurter and runne at ryotte beyonde his lawes and ordinaunces.   Moreouer he chargeth them to put nought to nor take oughte awaye from goddes wordes, but to be diligent onlye to kepe them in remēbraunce and in the harte and to teache theire childern, for feare of forgettinge. And to beware ether of makynge imagerye or of bowinge them felues vnto images fayenge: Ye fawe no image when God fpake vnto you, but herde avoyce onlye and that voyce kepe and therunto cleaue, for it is youre liffe and it fhall faue you. And finally yf (as the frayltie of al flefh is) they fhall haue fallen from God and he haue brought them in to troble, aduerfyte, ād cōbraunce ād all neceffite: yet yf they repent and turne, he promyfeth them that God fhall remēbre his mercie ād receave thē to grace agayne

In the fifte he repeteth the .x. commaūdmētes and that they myght fe a caufe to do them .P. of loue, he biddeth them remembre that they were bounde in Egipte and how God delyuered them with a mightie hande and a ftretchedout arme, to ferue him and to kepe his commaundmentes: as Paule fayeth that we are bought with Chriftes bloude ād therfore are his fervauntes ād not oure awne, ād ought to feke his will and honoure onlye ād to loue ād ferue one another for his fake.

In the fixte he fetteth out the fountayne off all commaundmentes: that is, that they beleue how that there is but one God that doeth all, and therfore ought onlye to be loued with all the herte, all the foule and all the myghte. For loue only is the fulfillinge of the commaundementes, as Paule alfo fayeth vnto, the Romaynes and Galathians likewife. He warneth thē alfo that they forgett not the commaundmentes, but teach thē their childern ād to fhew their childern alfo how God delyuered thē out of the bondage of the Egiptiās to ferue him and his commaundmētes, that the childern myght fe a caufe to worke of loue, likewife.

The feuēth is all together of faith: he remoueth all occafiōs that might withdrawe them from the fayth, and pulleth them alfo from all confidence in them felues, and fturreth thē vp to truft in god boldlye and onlye.

.P. Of the eyght chaptre thou feyft how that the caufe of all temptation is, that a mā might fe his awne herte. For whē I am brought in to that extremite that I muft ether fuffre or forfake god, then I fhall feale how moch I beleue and truft in him, and how moch I loue him. In like maner, yf my brother do me euel for my good, then yf I loue him when there is no caufe in him, I fe that my loue was of god, ād euē fo yf I then hate him, I feale and perceaue that my loue was but wordly, And finallye he fturreth thē to the fayth ād loue of god, ād dryveth them frō all confidence of theire awne felves.

In the nynth alfo he moueth thē vnto faith and to put their truft in god, and draweth thē from confidence of them felues by rehearfinge all the wekedneffe which they had wrought from the firft daye he knew them vnto that fame daye. And in the end he repeteth how he coniured god in horeb ād ouercame him with prayer, where thou mayeft lerne the right maner to praye.

In the tenth he rekeneth vpp the pith of all lawes and the kepinge of the lawe in the harte: which is to feare god loue him ād ferue him with all their harte foule and mighte ād kepe his commaundmentes of loue. And he fheweth a reafon why they fhuld that doo: euen .P. becaufe god is lord of heuen and erth ād hath alfo done all for them of his awne goodneffe without their defervinge. And then out of the loue vnto god he bringeth the love vnto a mans neyghboure fayenge: god is lorde aboue all lordes and loveth all his feruauntes indifferently, as well the poore and feble and the ftraunger, as the rich and mightye, ād therfore wil that we loue the poore and the ftraunger. And he addeth a caufe, for ye were ftraungers and god deliuered you and hath brought you vnto a londe where ye be at home. Loue the ftraunger therfore for his fake.

In the .xi. he exhorteth them to loue and feare god, and reherfeth the terrible dedes off god vppon his enemies, and on them that rebelled agenft him. And he teftifyeth vnto thē both what will folow yf they loue and feare god, and whate alfo yf they defpife him ād breake his commaundment.

In the .xii. he cōmaundeth to put out of the waye all that might be an occafion to hurte the fayth and forbiddeth to do ought after their awne mindes, or to altre the worde of god.

In the .xiii. he forbiddeth to herken vnto ought faue vnto gods worde: no though he which coūfeleth cōtrarye fhuld come with miracles, as Paule doth vnto the Galathians.

.¶. In the .xiiii. the beeftes are forbiddē, partely for the vnclenneffe of thē, ād partely to caufe hate betwene the hethē ād thē, that they haue no cōuerfatiō to gether, in that one abhorreth whatt the other eateth. Vnto this xv. chaptre all pertayne vnto faith and loue cheflye. And in this .xv. he beginneth to entreate moare fpeciallye of thinges pertayninge vnto the comen welth ād equite ād exhorteth vnto the loue of a mans neyghboure. And in the .xvi. amonge other he forgetteth not the fame. And in the .xvii. he entreateth of right and equite chefly, in fo moche that when he loketh vnto faithe and vnto the, punyfhment of ydolatres, he yet endeth in a lawe of loue and equite: forbiddinge to condemne any man vnder leffe *then twoo witneffes at the left and commaundeth to bringe the trefpacers vnto the open gate of the citye where all men goo in and out, that all men might heare the caufe and fe that he had but right. But the pope hath founde a better waye, even to appoffe him with out any accufare ād that fecretlye, that no man knowe whether he haue right or no, ether hare his articles or anfwere: for feare left the people fhuld ferch whether it were fo or no.

In the .xviii. he forbiddeth all falfe and develifh craftes that hurte true fayth. Moreouer .¶. becaufe the people coude not heare the voyce of the lawe fpokē to thē in fire, he promifeth thē a nother prophete to brīge thē better tydinges which was fpokē of chrift oure fauiour.

The .xix. ād fo forth vnto the ende of the .xxvii. is almoft al to gether of love vnto oure neyboures ād of lawes of equite ād honeftye with now ād then a refpecte vnto fayth.

---

* The original has: them.

The .xxviii. is a terreble chaptre ād to be trēbled at: A chriftē mans harte might wel bleed for forow at the readinge of it, for feare of the wrath that is like to come vpō us accordinge vnto all the curfes which thou there readeft.

For acordinge vnto thefe curfes hath god delt with all nacions, after they were fallē in to the abhominacions of blindneffe.

The .xxix. is like terreble with a godly leffō in the ende that we fhuld leue ferchīge of goddes fecrettes ād geue diligēce to walke accordinge to that he hath opened vnto us. For the kepīge of the cōmaūdmētes of god teacheth wifdome as thou mayēfte fe in the fame chapter, where Mofes fayeth, kepe the cōmaūdmētes, that ye maye vnderftōd whate ye ought to do. But to ferch goddes fecretes blīdeth a mā as it is wel proved by the fwarmes of oure fophifters, whofe wife bokes are now whē we loke ī the fcripture, foūde but ful of folifhneffe.

THE FYFTE

BOKE OF MOSES. CAL= led Deuteronomye.*

* *This title page does not form part of the Lenox copy of the Pentateuch of 1530; the copy recently added to the Astor Library is also without it. The subjoined entries, in the latter, made by an English hand, and signed D., are given as curiosa.*

On the Fly Leaf: "According to the various readings of Bp. Wilson's Bible by his Editor, these four last books of Moses are translated by Matthews. D."
"A. D. 1433 seems to be on a piece of parchment bound in with them. Is this the year of binding and Translin? D."
In the margin of Fo. I. Deuteronomye: "This, accordg. to Bp. Wilson's Editor, is Matthews, Transln. D."

The first Chapter of Deuteronomye. [Fo. I.]

1 **T**HESE be the wordes which Moses spake vnto all Israel, on the other syde Iordayne in the wildernesse and in the feldes by the red see, betwene Pharā ād Tophel,
2 Laban, Hazeroth and Disahab .xii. dayes iurney from Horeb vnto Cades bernea, by
3 the waye that leadeth vnto mount Seir. And it fortuned the first daye of the .xi. moneth in the fortieth yere, that Moses spake vnto the childern of Israel acordinge vnto all that the Lorde had geuen him in
4 commaundment vnto them, after that he had smote Sihon the kynge of the Amorites which dwelt in Hesbon, and Og kinge of Basan which dwelt at Astaroth in Edrei.
5 On the other syde Iordayne in the londe of Moab,
6 Moses begane to declare this lawe saynge: the Lorde oure God spake vnto vs in Horeb sayenge: Ye haue
7 dwelt longe ynough in this mount: departe therfore and take youre iurney and goo vnto the hilles of the Amorites and vnto all places nye there vnto: both feldes, hilles and dales: and vnto the south and vnto the sees syde in the londe of Canaan, and vnto libanon:
8 euen vnto the greate ryuer Eu- .P. phrates. Beholde, I haue set the londe before you: goo in therfore and

M.C.S. A briefe rehersall of thynges done before, from the pytchynge at mounte Horeb vntyll they came to Cades barne.

M. 2 .xi. dayes .. barne 4 Sehon .. Edrai.
V. 1 trans Iordanem (v. 5.) .. Aseroth vbi auri est plurimum. 4 habitauit .. mansit 5 explanare legem 6 in hoc monte 7 & iuxta litus maris .. vque ad flumen magnum Euphraten. 8 En, inquit tradidi vobis
L. 1 iensyd (v. 5) 5 aus zulegen dis gesetz 6 an disem berge 7 gegen den ansurt des meeris .. bis an das grosse wasser Phrath, 8 Sihe da ich hab das land fur euch geben (v. 21)
M. M. N. 6 Horeb and Sinai are both one.

possesse the londe which the Lord sware vnto youre fathers Abraham, Isaac and Iacob, to geue vnto them and their seed after them.

9 And I sayde vnto yov the same seafon: I am not
10 able to bere you myselfe alone. For the Lorde youre God hath multiplyed you: so that ye are this daye
11 as the starres of heauen in numbre (the Lorde god of youre fathers make you a thousande tymes so many moo as ye are, and blesse you as he hath   *moo, more*
12 promysed you) how (sayde I) can I myselfe alone, beare the combraunce, charge and stryffe that is amonge you:
13 brynge therfore men of wisdome and of vnderstondinge and expert knowne amonge youre trybes, that I maye make them ruelars ouer you.

14 And ye answered me and sayed: that which thou
15 hast spoken is good to be done. And then I toke the heedes of youre trybes, men of wysdome and that were expert, and made them ruelers ouer you: captaynes ouer thousandes and ouer hundredes ouer fyftye and ouer ten, and officers amonge youre trybes.

16 And I charged youre Iudges the same   *Iudges*. tyme sayenge: heare youre brethern and iudge [Fo. II.] righteously betwene euery man and his brother
17 and the straunger that is with him. Se that ye knowe no man in Iudgement: but heare the small as well as the greate and be afrayed of no man, for the lawe is Gods. And the cause that is to harde for you, brynge
18 vnto me and I will heare it. And I commaunded you the same seafon, all the thinges which ye shulde doo.

19 And then we departed from Horeb and walked thorow all that greate and terreble wildernesse as ye

---

𝔐. 17 for the iudgement is Gods
𝒱. 10 solus suftinere vos ... ficut stellæ cæli, plurimi. 12 negotia vestra ... & pondus ac iurgia. 13 & quorum conuersatio fit probata 14 quam vis facere. 15 ac decanos, qui docerent vos fingula 16 Præcepique eis, dicens, Audite illos, & quod iustum est iudicate: fiue ciuis fit ille, fiue peregrinus. 17 Nulla erit diftantia personarum
𝔏. 9 nicht alleyn ertragen 10 wie die menge der stern am hymel 12 muhe. last. hadder 14 das du es thun wilt. 16 richtet recht zwisschen yderman vnd seynem bruder vnd dem frembdlingen 17 niemants person euch schewen
𝔐. 𝔐. N. 16 Iudges.

haue fene alonge by the waye that ledeth vnto the hilles of the Amorites, as the Lorde oure God com-
20 maunded us, and came to Cades bernea. And there I fayed vnto you: Ye are come vnto the hilles of the Amorites, which the Lorde oure God doth geue vnto
21 us. Beholde the Lorde thi God hath fett the londe before the, goo vpp and conquere it, as the Lorde God of thy fathers fayeth vnto the: feare not, nether be difcoraged.
22 And then ye came vnto me euery one and fayed: Let us fende men before us, to ferche us out the londe and to brynge us worde agayne, both what waye we fhall goo vpp by, and vnto what cities we fhall come.
23 And the fayenge pleaffed me well .P. and I toke .xii
24 men of you, of euery trybe one. And they departed and went vp in to the hye contre and came vnto the
25 ryuer Efcoll, and ferched it out, and toke of the frute of the londe in their hondes and brought it doune vnto us and brought us worde agayne and fayde: it is a good lande which the Lorde oure God doeth geue us.
26 Notwithftondinge ye wolde not confente to goo vpp, but were difhobedient vnto the mouth of the
27 Lorde youre God, ãd murmured in youre tentes and fayde: becaufe the Lorde hateth us, therfore he hath brought us out of the londe of Egipte, to delyuer us in to the handes of the Amorites and to deftroye us.
28 How fhall we goo vpp? Oure brethern haue difcoraged oure hartes fayenge: the people is greater and taller than we, ãd the cities are greatte and walled euen vpp to heauen, and moreouer we haue fene the fonnes of the Enakimes there.

𝔐. 20 barne
𝒱. 20 daturus eft vobis. 21 dabit . . nec quicquam paueas. 24 Vallem botri 25 attulerunt ad nos, atque dixerunt 28 Quo afcendemus ? nuntii terruerunt
𝑳. 20 geben wirt 22 furcht dich nicht vnd fchew 23 Das gefiel myr wol 25 fagten vns widder 28 Wo follen wyr hynauff ?
𝔐. 𝔐. 𝔑. 21 *Before the:* That is, at the commaundement. 26 *But were dyfobedyent:* The people beyng vnfaithfull wolde not go vnto the land promefed. 27 *Hateth vs:* God is fayd to hate a man whõ he putteth him forth of hys hert, & geueth him not of his grace. Pfal. v, b and .xxx, b.

29 And I fayed vnto you: dreade not nor be afrayed
30 of the: The Lorde youre God which goeth before you, he fhall fyghte for you, acordynge to all that he dyd
31 vnto you in Egipte before youre eies ād in the wildernefſe: as thou haſt ſene how that the Lorde thy God bare the as a man fhulde beare his fonne, thorow [Fo. III.] out all the waye which ye haue gone, vntill ye
32 came vnto this place. And yet for all this fayenge ye dyd not beleue the Lorde youre God which goeth the
33 waye before you, to ferche you out a place to pitche youre tentes in, in fyre by nyght, that ye myghte fe what waye to go and in a cloude by daye.

34 And the Lorde herde the voyce of youre wordes
35 and was wroth and fwore fayenge, there fhall not one of thefe men of this frowarde generacion fe that good
36 londe which I fware to geue vnto youre fathers, faue Caleb the fonne of Iephune, he fhall fe it, and to him I will geue the londe which he hath walked in ād to his childern, becaufe he hath contynually folowed the
37 Lorde. Likewife the Lorde was angrye with me for youre fakes fayenge: thou alfo fhalt not go in thither.
38 But Iofua the fōne of Nun which ſtondeth before the, he fhall go in thither. Bolde him therfore   bolde, *verb*,
39 for he fhall deuyde it vnto Ifrael. More- *to encourage* ouer youre childern which ye fayed fhulde be a praye, and youre fonnes which knowe nether good nor bad this daye, they fhall goo in thither ād vnto them I will
40 geue it, ād they fhall enioye it. But as for you, turne backe and take youre iurneye in to the wildernefſe: euen the waye to the reed fee.

41 Than ye anfwered and fayed vnto me: We .P. haue fynned agenſt the Lorde: we will goo vp and fyghte, acordinge to all that the Lorde oure God cōmaunded

ᜟ. 38 Boldē
V. 30 qui ductor eſt veſter 32 Et nec ſic quidem credidiſtis 33 metatus eſt locum 35 ſub iuramento pollicitus ſum 36 quia ſecutus eſt dominum. 37 Nec miranda indignatio in populum 38 forte terram diuidet 39 qui hodie
L. 30 zeucht fur euch hyn 32 Aber das gallt nichts bey euch ... hettet gegleubt 33 euch die ſtette zu weyfen 36 volliglich ... gefolget hat 39 die heuts tags

us. And whē ye had gyrde on euery man his wepons
42 of warre and were ready to goo vp in to the hilles, the
Lorde fayed vnto me: faye vnto thē, fe that ye go not
vp and that ye fighte not, for I am not amōge you:
left ye be plaged before youre enemies.

43 *Here thou feift the verey image of the papiftes. For thei like wife where Gods wordēis, there they beleue not ād where it is not there they be bold.*

* And whē I told you ye wold not
heare: but difobeyed the mouth of the
Lorde, and went prefumptoufly vp in to
the hilles.

44 Thē the Amorites which dwelt in thofe
hilles, came out agenft you and chafed you
as bees doo, and hewed you in Seir, euē
45 vnto Horma. And ye came agayne and
wepte before the Lorde: but the Lorde wolde not
46 heare youre voyce nor geue you audience. And fo ye
abode in Cades alōge feafon, acordinge vnto the tymᴇ
that ye there dwelt.

The .II. Chapter.

1 THEN we turned and toke oure
iurney in to the wildernefle,
euen the waye to the red fee
as the Lord cōmaunded me.
And we compaffed the mountayns of Seir
2 a lōge tyme Thē the Lorde fpake vnto
3 me faienge: Ye haue cōpaffed this mountayns lōge ynough, turne you northwarde.
4 And warne the people fay- [Fo. IIII.]
enge: Ye fhall goo thorow the coftes of youre brethern

M.C.S. A reherfall of that which was done from the tyme that they departed from Cades barne, vnto the battell agaynft the kynges Sehon & Og.

M. 46 *omits:* acordinge vnto the tyme that ye there dwelt.
V. 41 inftructi armis 42 ne cadatis 43 tumentes fuperbia
44 ficut folent apes perfequi: & cecidit de Seir vfque Horma.
ii, 1 circumiuimus
L. 41 Da yhr euch nu ruftet eyn iglicher mit feynem harnfch
42 gefchlagen werdet 43 wart vermeffen 44 wie die byenen thun,
vnd fchlugen euch zu Seir bis gen Harma, ii, 1 vmbzogen
M. M. N. 43 *Ye wold not heare:* Here thou feyft the verye
Image of vs that lyue ī this moft perloufe tyme, for euen we lykewyfe, where goddes worde is, here beleue we not: and where it
is not, there be we bolde.

the childern of Esau which dwell in Seir, and they shalbe afrayed of you: But take good hede vnto youre
5 selues that ye prouoke thē not, for I wil not geue you of their lōde, no not so moch as a fote breadeth: because I haue geuē mount Seir vnto Esau to possesse.
6 Ye shall bye meate of thē for money to eate, and ye
7 shall bye water of thē for money to drīke. For the Lorde thy God hath blessed the in all the workes of thine hāde, ād knew the as thou wēteft thorow this greate wildernesse. Moreouer the Lorde thi God hath bene with the this .xl. yeres, so that thou hast lacked nothinge.
8 And whē we were departed from oure brethern the childern of Esau which dwelt in Seir by the felde waye from Elath ād Ezion Gaber, we turned ād went the
9 waye to the wildernesse of Moab. Thē the Lorde sayed vnto me se that thou vexe not the Moabites, nether prouoke thē to batayle for I will not geue the of their lōde to possesse: becaufe I haue geuē Ar vnto the chil-
10 dern of loth to possesse. The Emimes dwelt there in in tymes past, a people greate, many ād tal, as the Ena-
11 kimes: which also were takē for geantes as the Enakimes: And the Moabites called thē Emymes.
12 In like maner the Horimes dwelt in Seir before time which .⁋. the childern of Esau cast out, ād destroyed thē before them and dwelt there in their stede: as Israel dyd in the londe of his possessiō which the Lorde gaue them
13 Now ryse vpp (sayed I) ād get you ouer the ryuer
14 Zared: ād we went ouer the ryuer Zared. The space

ℳ. 11 Emims. 12 Horims
𝒱. 5 ne moueamini contra eos 8 de Asion-gaber, venimus ad iter 9 Non pugnes . . . nec ineas aduersus eos prælium . . . filiis Lot 13 venimus ad eum.
𝕷. 5 nicht reytzet, denn ich werd euch yhres lands nicht eynen fuss breyt geben 6 das yhr esset . . . trincket 8 Ezeongaber, wandten wyr vns vnd giengen 9 nicht beleydigen noch sie reytzen zum streyt
ℳ. ℳ. N. 10 *Emims:* Emym a kynd of Geauntes so called becaufe they were terrible & cruell for Emym sygnifyeth terryblenesse. *Enakyms* loke Iudic. i, d. 12 *Horims* a kynde of Geauntes and sygnifyeth noble, becaufe that of pryde they called thē selues nobles or gentels.

in which we came from Cades bernea vntill we were come ouer the ryuer Zared was .xxxviii. yeres: vntill all the generacion of the men of warre were wasted
15 out of the host as the Lorde sware vnto thē. For in dede the hande of the Lorde was agēst thē, to destroye them out of the host, till they were consumed.

16 And as soone as all the men of warre were consumed
17 and deed from amonge the people, then the Lorde
18 spake vnto me sayenge. Thou shalt goo thorow Ar
19 the coste of Moab this daye, and shalt come nye vnto the childern of Ammon: se that thou vexe them not, nor yet prouoke them. For I will not geue the of the londe of the childern of Ammon to possesse, becuase I haue geuen it vnto the childern of loth to possesse.
20 That also was taken for a londe of geauntes and geauntes dwelt therin in olde tyme, and the Ammonites called
21 them Zamzumyms. A people that was great, many and taule, as the Enakyms. But the [Fo. V.] Lorde destroyed them before the Ammonites, and they cast
22 them out and they dwelt there ī their steade: as he dyd for the childern of Esau which dwell in Seir: euē as he destroyed the horyms before them, ād they cast them out and dwell in their steade vnto this daye.

23 And the Avims which dwelt in Hazarim euē vnto Aza, the Caphthoryms which came out of Caphthor destroyed them and dwelt in their rowmes.

24 Ryse vp, take youre yourney and goo ouer the ryuer Arnon. Beholde, I haue geuen in to thy hād Sihō the Amorite kynge of Hesbō, ād his londe. Goo to and
25 conquere and prouoke hī to batayle. This daye I will begynne to send the feare and dreade of the vppon all

M. 14 barne 20 Zamzumims 21 Enakims 24 Sehon
V. 14 donec consumeretur 15 vt interirent de castrorum medio. 18 vrbem nomine Ar 20 reputata est 22 quam possident vsque in præsens. 24 incipe possidere
L. 14 eyn ende nemen 15 vmbkemen . . . bis das yhr eyn ende wurde. 20 geschetzt 22 besitzen, das sie da an yhrer stat woneten, bis auff disen tag. 24 heb an zu eintzunem
M. M. N. 20 *Zāsumims:* Zamzumim a kynde of geauntes and sygnysyeth myscheuouse. They were tyrauntes, cruell theues & pollars. 24 *Sehon & his lande before the:* Or at thy cōmaundement

nacions that are vnder al portes of heauen: so that whē they heare speake of the, they shall tremble and quake for seare of the.

26 Then I sent messengers out of the wildernesse of kedemoth vnto Syhon kynge of Hesbon, with wordes
27 of peace saynge: Let me goo thorow thy londe. I will goo allweyes alonge by the hye waye and will nether turne vnto the righte hande nor to the left.
28 Sell me meate for money for to eate, and geue me drinke for money for to drynke: I will goo thorowe
29 by fote only (as the childern of Esau dyd vnto me whi- .P. che dwell in Seir and the Moabites whiche dwell in Ar) vntyll I be come ouer Iordayne, in to the londe which the Lorde oure God geueth vs.

30 But Sihon the kinge of Hesbon wolde not let vs passe by him, for the Lord thy God had hardened his sprite and made his herte tough becaufe he wold delyuer him into thy hondes as it is come to passe this daye.

31 And the Lorde sayed vnto me: beholde, I haue begonne to set Sihon and his londe before the: goo to
32 and conquere, that thou mayst possesse his londe. Then both Sihon and all his people came out agenst vs
33 vnto batayle at Iahab. And the Lorde set him before vs, and we smote hym and his sonnes and all hys people.

34 And we toke all his cities the same seafon, and destroyed all the cities with men, wemen, and childern
35 ād let nothinge remayne, saue the catell only we

𝔐. 26 wildernesse of the easte .. Sehon 29 Iordan 30 Sehon 32 Sehon . . . Iahaza

V. 25 sub omni cælo: vt . . . paueāt, & in morem parturentium contremiscant, & dolore teneantur. 27 publica grad. via 28 Tantum est vt nobis concedas transitum 29 ad Iordanem 30 indurauerat dominus deus tuus spiritum eius, & obfirmauerat cor illius . . . ficut nunc vides. 32 incipe possidere eam.

L. 25 vnter allen hymeln, das wenn sie von dyr horen, toben vnd sich engsten fur deyner zukunfft. 28 Ich wil nur zu fuss durch hyn gehen 29 vber den Iordan 30 verhertet seynen mut vnd verstockt yhm seyn hertz . . . wie es ist itzt am tage. 31 eyn zu nemen zu besitzen seyn land 34 alle seyne stedte vnd verbanten alle stedte

𝔐. 𝔐. N. 32 *Iahaza:* Otherwyse Iasa.

caught vnto oure selues and the spoyle of the cities
36 which we toke, from Aroer vppon the brynke off the
riuer off Arnon, and the citie in the ryuer, vnto Gilead:
there was not one citye to stronge for vs. The Lorde
37 oure God delyuered all vnto vs: only vnto the londe
of the childern of Ammon ye came not, nor vnto all
the coste of the riuer Iabock [Fo. VI.] ner vnto the
cities in the mountaynes, nor vnto what soeuer the
Lorde oure God forbade vs.

❡ The .III. Chapter.

1 THEN we turned and went vpp the waye to Basan. And Og the kinge of Basan came out agenst vs: both he and all his
2 people to batayle at Edrey. And the Lorde sayed vnto me: feare him not, for I haue delyuered him and all his people ād his lande in to thy hande ād thou shalt deale with hī as thou dealest with Sihon kynge of the
3 Amorites which dwelt at Hesbon. And so the Lorde oure God delyuered in to oure handes, Og also the kynge off Basan and al his folke, And we smote him vntyll noughte was left him.

4 And we toke all his cities the same ceason (for there was not a citie whiche we toke not from them) euen iii. score cities, all the region of Argob, the kyngdome of Og in Basan.

5 All these cities were made stronge with hye walles, gates and barres, besyde vnwalled townes a greate

M.C.S. A rehersall of thynges that chaunsed from the vyctorye of the .ii. kynges Sehon & Og, vnto the Institucion of Iosue in Moses steade.

𝔐. 36 Galaad. iii, 1 Edrai 2 Sehon
𝔙. 35 Absque iumentis 36 torrentis Arnon, & oppido, quod in valle . . Non fuit vicus & ciuitas 37 Absque terra . . . torrenti Ieboc iii, 2 traditus est 3 percussimusque eos vsque ad internecionem 4 vno tempore. 5 absque oppidis innumeris
𝔏. 36 des bachs Arnon 37 on zu dem land . . . bach Iabok iii, 2 ich hab . . . geben 3 schlugen bis das yhm nichts vberbleyb.
𝔐. 𝔐. N. 5 *Vnwalled townes:* As thoroufares and vyllages.

6 maynye. And we vtterly deſtroyed them, as we played with Sihon kynge off Heſbon: bringing to nought al the cities with men, wemen and childern.
7 But all the catell and the ſpoyle of the cities, we caughte for .P. oure ſelues.
8 And thus we toke the ſame ceaſon, the lōde out of the hande of two kynges of the Amorites on the other ſyde Iordayne, from the ryuer of Arnon vnto mount
9 Hermon (which Hermon the Sidons call Sirion, but
10 the Amorites call it Senyr) all the cities in the playne ād all Gilead and all Baſan vnto Salcha and Edrei,
11 cities of the kingdome of Og in Baſan. For only Og kynge of Baſan remayned of the remnaūt of the geauntes: beholde, his yernen bed is yet at Rabath amonge the childern off Ammō .ix. cubettes longe ād, .iiii. cubetes brode, of the cubettes of a man.
12 · And when we had conquered this londe the ſame tyme, I gaue from Aroer which is apon the riuer of Arnon, and halfe mount Gilead and the cities thereof
13 vnto the Rubenites, and Gadites. And the reſt of Gilead and all Baſan the kingdome of Og, I gaue vnto the halfe trybe of Manaſſe: all the regiō of Argob with all
14 Baſan was called the londe of geauntes. Iair the ſonne of Manaſſe toke all the region of Argob vnto the coſtes of Geſuri ād Maachati, and called the townes of Baſan after his owne name: the townes of Iair vnto thys daye.
15,16 And I gaue half Gilead vnto Machir. And vnto Ruben ād Gad, I gaue from Gile- [Fo. VII.] ad vnto the ryuer of Arnon ād half the valey ād the coſte, euē vnto the ryuer Iabock which is the border of the chil-
17 dern of Ammon, and the feldes ad Iordayne with the

ℳ. 6 Sehon 10 Galaad .. Salecha .. Edrai 12 Galad 13 Galaad 14 & called them after his owne name: Baſan Hauoth Iair vnto this daye. 15 Galaad 16 Galaad
𝒱. 8 trans Iordanem 11 Et monſtratur lectus 14 Baſan, Auoth-Iair, id eſt Villas Iair
𝕃. 6 vnd verbanneten (bis) 8 ienſyd dem Iordan 11 alhie zu Rabath
ℳ. ℳ. N. 14 *Hauoth Iair:* That is ſuburbes or vyllages belongyng to Iair.

coste, from Cenereth even vnto the see in the felde which is the salt see vnder the sprynges off Pisga eastwarde.

18 And I commaunded you the same tyme (ye Ruben ād Gad) sayeng: the Lorde your God hath geuen you this londe to enioye it: se that ye go harnessed before youre brethern the childern of Israel, all that are mē
19 of warre amonge you. Youre wyues only youre childern ād youre catell (for I wote that ye haue moch catell) shall abyde in youre cities which I haue geuen
20 you, vntyll the Lorde haue geuē rest vnto your brethern as well as vnto you, and vntyll they also haue conquered the londe which the Lorde youre God hath geuen them beyond Iordayne: and then returne agayne euery mā vnto his possession which I haue geuē you.
21 And I warned Iosua the same tyme sayeng thyne eyes haue sene all that the Lorde youre God hath done vnto these two kynges, euē so the Lorde will doo
22 vnto all kyngdomes whither thou goest. Feare them not, for the Lorde youre God he it is that fighteth for you.
23 And I besoughte the Lorde the same tyme .P. say-
24 enge: O lorde Iehoua, thou hast begonne to shewe thy servaunte thy greatnesse and thy mightie hande for there is no God in heauen nor in erth that can do
25 after thy workes and after thy power: let me goo ouer ād se the good londe that is beyonde Iordayne, that goodly
26 hye contre and Libanon. But the Lorde was angrie with me for youre sakes and wolde not heare me, but sayed

𝔐. 17 Ceneroth .. Phasgah 24 O lorde God
𝒱. 17 & planitiem solitudinis . . . ad mare deserti, quod est falsissimum ad radices montis Phasga 20 trans Iordanem 21 quæ fecit dominus deus vester duobus his regibus: sic faciet omnibus regnis ad quæ transiturus es. 24 comparari fortitudini tuæ. 25 montem istum egregium
𝐋. 17 vnden am berge Pisga 20 iensyd dem Iordan 24 der es deynen wercken vnd deyner macht kunde nach thun? 25 dis gutte gepirge . . .
𝔐. 𝔐. N. 17 *Vnder ý springes of Phasgah:* Some the hyll fote. Heb. Esdoth which signifyeth spriges, although some wyll that it be the name of a towne.

vnto me, be content, and speake henceforth no moare
27 vnto me of this matter, Get the vp in to the toppe
of Pisga ãd lifte vpp thine eyes west, north, south ãd
easte, ãd beholde it with thyne eyes for thou shalt not
28 goo ouer this Iordayne. Moreouer, charge Iosua and
corage him and bolde him. For he shall go ouer before
his people, and he shall deuyde the londe which thou
29 shalt se vnto them. And so we abode in the valaye
besyde Beth Peor.

corage, verb, to encourage,   *bolde, verb, to encourage*

⁋ The .IIII. Chapter.

1 AND now herken Israel vnto the ordinaunces ãd lawes which I teache you, for to doo them, that ye maye lyue ãd goo ãd conquere the londe which the Lorde God of youre fathers geueth you. Ye 2 shall put nothinge vnto the worde which I commaunde you nether doo ought there from, that ye maye kepe [Fo. VIII.] the commaundmentes off the Lorde youre
3 God which I commaunde you. Youre eyes haue sene what the Lorde dyd vnto Baal Peor: for al the men that folowed Baal Peor, the Lorde youre God hath

M.C.S. An exhortacyon to geue dylygent heede vnto the lawe, & that they shulde not take awaye or adde any thyng therto. Images may not be worshypped nor yet made. The .iii. Cytyes of refuge.

No: ner yet corrupt it with false gloses to cõfirme Aristotle: but rebuke Aristotles false leruinge therewith.

M. 27 Phasgah
V. 26 Sufficit tibi, nequaquam vltra loquaris de hac re ad me.
27 et oculos tuos circunfer... & aspice. 28 corrobora... conforta 29 contra phanum Phogor. iiii, 1 doceo te... daturus est
2 verbum quod vobis loquor.. custodite 3 contra Beel-phegor, quomodo contriuerit.

L. 26 Las gnug seyn, sage myr dauon nicht mehr 29 Also blieben wyr ym tal gegen dem haus Peor. iiii, 1 euch lere.. gibt 2 nichts dazu thun, das ich euch gepiete... auff das yhr behaltet 3 vber dem Baal Peor

M. M. N. 2 *To put to the woord and to take awaye therfro* is, to Iudge & thynck otherwyse of the wyll of god then is shewed vs in the scrypture, as in Deut. xii, d. Prouer. xxx, a.

4 deſtroyed from amōge you: But ye that claue vnto the Lorde youre God, are alyue euery one of you this
5 daye. Beholde, I haue taught you ordinaunces and lawes, ſoche as the Lorde my God commaūded me, that ye ſhulde do euē ſo in the londe whether ye goo to poſſeſſe it
6 Kepe them therfore and doo them, for that is youre wiſdome and vnderſtandynge in the ſyghte of the nacyons: whiche when they haue herde all theſe ordinaunces, ſhall ſaye:
O what a wyſe and vnderſtondynge people is this
7 greate nacion. For what nacyon is ſo greate that hath Goddes ſo nye vnto hym: as the Lorde oure God is nye vnto vs, in all thinges, when we call vnto hym?
8 Yee, and what nacyon is ſo greate that hath ordinaunces and lawes ſo ryghtuouſſe, as all thys lawe which I ſett before you this daye.
9 Take hede to thy ſelfe therfore only ād kepe thy ſoule diligently, that thou forgett not the thinges which thyne eyes haue ſene and that they departe not out of thyne harte, all the dayes of thine life: but *Teach youre* teach them thy ſon- .P. nes, ād thy ſonnes *childern.*
10 ſonnes. The daye that I ſtode before the Lorde youre god in Horeb, whē he ſayed vnto me, gather me the people together, that I maye make them heare my wordes that they maye lerne to ſere me as longe as thei lyue vppon the erth and that they maye teache
11 their childern: ye came ād ſtode alſo vnder the hyll ād the hyll burnt with fire: euen vnto the myddes of heauē, ād there was darckneſſe, clowdes ād myſt.

𝔐. 9 thy lyfe
𝒱. 4 adhæretis 5 Scitis... ſic facietis ea in terra quā poſſeſſuri eſtis 6 ſapientia, & intellectus coram populis... gens magna. 7 natio tam grandis... deos appropinquantes ſibi 8 alia gens ſic inclyta... ceremonias, iuſtaque iudicia, & vniuerſam legem... proponam hodie ante oculos veſtros? 9 cunctis diebus vitæ tuæ. 11 ad radices montis... tenebræ, et nubes, & caligo.
𝔏. 4 anhienget 5 Sihe.. das yhr alſo 6 weyſzheyt vnd verſtand fur allen volckern... vnd eyn trefflich volck 7 Gotter alſo nahe ſich thun.. ſo offt wir yhn an ruffen? 8 furlege? 9 alle deyn leben lang 11 vnden an dem berge... finſternis, wolcken vnd tunckel.
𝔐. 𝔐. N. 9 Teache your chyldrē.

12 And the Lorde spake vnto you out of the fire ād ye
herde the voyce of the wordes: But sawe
no ymage, saue herde a voyce only, *The voice is all to gether: vnto that image ought men to bowe there hertes.*
13 And he declared vnto you his coue-
naunt, which he commaunded you to doo,
euen .x. verses and wrote them in two
14 tables of stone. And the Lorde commaunded me the
same seasen to teache you ordynaunces and lawes, for
to doo them in the londe whether ye goo to possesse it
15 Take hede vnto youre selues diligently as pertayninge vnto youre soules, for ye sawe no maner of ymage
the daye when the Lorde spake vnto you in Horeb out
16 of the fire: lest ye marre youre selues and make you
grauen ymages after what soeuer likenesse it be: whe-
17 ther after the likenesse of mā or womā or any maner
beest that is on the erth or of any maner sether- [Fo.
18 IX.] red foule that fleth in the ayre, or of any maner
worme that crepeth on the erth or of any maner fysh
19 that is in the water beneth the erth: Ye and leste thou
lyste vpp thyne eyes vnto heuen, and when thou seyst
the sonne and the mone and the starres and what soeuer is
contayned in heauen, shuldest be disceaued and shuldest bow thi selfe vnto them ād serue the thinges which
the Lorde thy God hath distributed vnto all nacions
that are vnder al quarters of heauen.
20 For the Lorde toke you and broughte you out of
the yernen fornace of Egipte, to be vnto him a people
21 of enheritaunce, as it is come to passe this daye. For-
thermoare, the Lorde was angrye with me for youre
sakes and sware, that I shulde not goo ouer Iordane
and that I shulde not goo vnto that good londe, which

V. 12 formam penitus non vidistis. 16 sculptam similitudinem, aut imaginem 19 omnia astra cæli, & errore deceptus .. quæ creauit .. in ministerium cunctis gentibus 21 propter sermones vestros ... terram optimam quam daturus est vobis.

L. 13 nemlich die zehen wort 19 das gantze heer des hymels (corrected into: yrgent eyn heer des hymels) 21 vmb ewres thuns willen

M. M. N. 12 *The voyce of the wordes:* The voyce is al to gether: vnto that ymage ought men to bowe there hertes. 20 *Yron fornace:* By the yron fornace is vnderstande anguysh & greate sorowe & carefulnes of hert .iii. Reg. viii, f. & Ierem. xi, a.

22 the Lorde thy God geueth te to enherytaunce. For I muſt dye in this londe, and ſhall not goo ouer Iordane: But ye ſhall goo ouer and conquere that good londe
23 Take hede vnto youre ſelues therfore, that ye forgett not the appoyntment of the Lorde youre God which he made with you, and that ye make you no grauen ymage of whatſoeuer it be that
24 the Lorde thi God hath for-bidden the. For the Lorde thi God is a cõſuminge fyre, and a geloufe God.

[margin: appoyntment, covenant] .P.

25 Yf after thou haſt gotten childern and childerns childern and haſt dwelt longe in the londe, ye ſhall marre youre ſelues and make grauen ymages after the likneſſe of what ſo euer it be, and ſhall worke wekedneſſe in the ſyghte of the Lorde thy God, to prouoke him.
26 I call heauen and erth to recorde vnto you this daye, that ye ſhall ſhortely pereſſh from of the londe whether ye goo ouer Iordayne to poſſeſſe it: Ye ſhall not prolonge
27 youre dayes therin, but ſhall ſhortly be deſtroyed. And the Lorde ſhall ſcater you amonge nacions, and ye ſhalbe lefte few in numbre amonge the people whother the
28 Lorde ſhall brynge you: and there ye ſhall ſerue goddes which are the workes of mans hande, wod and ſtone which nether ſe nor heare not eate nor ſmell.
29 Neuer the later ye ſhall ſeke the Lorde youre God euen there, and ſhalt fynde him yf thou ſeke him with
30 all thine herte and with all thy ſoule. In thi tribulacion and when all theſe thinges are come apon the, euen in the later dayes, thou ſhalt turne vnto the Lorde

V. 22 Ecce morior ... terram egregiam. 23 quæ fieri dominus prohibuit. 24 deus æmulator. 25 patrantes malum ... ad iracundiam prouocetis 27 et remanebitis pauci 29 & tota tribulatione animæ tuæ. 30 Poſtquam te inuenerint omnia quæ prædicta ſunt, nouiſſimo autem tempore reuerteris

L. 22 ſondern ... gutt land 23 wie der Herr deyn Got gepotten hat 27 eyn geringe pobel vberig ſeyn

M. M. N. 24 *Conſuminge fyre:* Becauſe God proueth his by afflyccion, therfore is he called a conſumyng fyre. Hebr. xii, g. & becauſe he confumeth the vnfaithfull remedyleſſe, for ther is nothing that can refyſt his anger toward thẽ. And he is called geloufe becauſe he can not ſuffer that any ſhuld fall from hym.

thy God, and ſhalt herken vn- [Fo. X.] to his voyce.
31 For the Lorde thy God is a pitiefull God: he will not
forſake the nether deſtroye the, nor forgett the appoyntmēt made with thy fathers which he ſware vnto them.
32 For axe I praye the of the dayes that are paſt which were before the, ſence the daye that God created man vppon the erth and from the one ſyde of heauen vnto the other whether any thinge hath bene lyke vnto this greate thinge or whether any ſoche thinge hath bene
33 herde as it is, that a nacion hath herde the voyce of God ſpeakinge out of fyre as thou haſt herde, and yet
34 lyued? ether whether God aſſayed to goo and take him a people from amonge nacions, thorow temptacions and ſygnes and wonders and thorow warre and with a mightie hande and a ſtretched out arme and wyth myghtye terreble ſightes, acordynge vnto all that the Lorde youre God dyd vnto you in Egipte before youre eyes.
35 Vnto the it was ſhewed, that thou myghteſt knowe, how that the Lorde he is God and that there is none but he.
36 Out of heauen he made the heare his voyce to nurter the, and vppon erth he ſhewed *nurter, verb, to bring up, educate* .T. the his greate fyre, and thou hardeſt
37 his wordes out of the fyre. And becauſe he loued thy fathers, therfore he choſe their ſeed after them and broughte the out with his preſence and with his
38 myghtye power of Egipte: to thruſt out nations greater ād myghtyer then thou before the, to bringe the in and to geue the their londe to enheritaunce: as it is come to paſſe this daye.
39 Vnderſtonde therfore this daye and turne it to thine herte, that the Lorde he is God in heauen aboue

V. 31 nec omnino delebit 34 ſi fecit deus ... de medio nationum ... & horribiles viſiones ... oculis tuis: 35 vt ſcires 36 vt doceret te 37 Eduxitque te præcedens in virtute ſua magna ex Ægypto 38. in introitu tuo: & introduceret te
L. 34 Oder ob Got verſucht habe ... durch groſſe geſichte 36 dz er dich zuchtiget 37 ausgefurt mit ſeym angeſicht durch groſſe krafft aus Egypten

and vppon the erth beneth there is no moo: *moo, besides,*
40 kepe therfore his ordynaunces, and his *else* commaundmentes which I commaunde the this daye, that it maye goo well with the and with thi childern after the and that thou mayst prolonge thy dayes vppon the erth which the Lorde thi God geueth the for euer.

41 Then Moses seuered .iii. cities on the other syde
42 Iordane towarde the sonne rysynge, that he shulde fle thiter which had kylled his neyghboure vnwares and hated him not in tyme past and therfore shulde fle vnto
43 one of the same cities and lyue: Bezer in the wildernesse euen in the playne contre amonge the Rubenites: and Ramoth in Gilead amonge the Gaddites and Solan in Basan amonge the Manassites.

44 [Fo. XI.] This is the lawe which Moses set before
45 the childern of Israel, and these are the witnesse, ordinaunces and statutes which Moses tolde the childern
46 of Israel after they came out of Egipte, on the other syde Iordayne in the valey besyde Beth Peor in the londe of Sihō kinge of the Amorites which dwelt at Hesbon, whom Moses and the childern of Israel smote
47 after they were come out of Egipte, ād conquered his lande and the lande of Og kinge of Basan .ii. kynges of the Amorites on the other syde Iordayne towarde
48 the sonne rysynge: from Aroar vppon the bancke of the ryuer Arnon, vnto mount Sion which is called
49 Hermon ād all the feldes on the other syde Iordayne eastwarde: euen vnto the see in the selde vnder the springes of Pisga.

M. 40 geueth the thy lyfe longe 43 Galaad 45 witnesses 46 Sehon 49 Phasgah
V. 40 Custodi . . : vt bene sit tibi . . quam dom. deus tuus daturus est tibi. 42 nec sibi fuerit inimicus ante vnum & alterum diem, & ad harum aliq. vrbium possit euadere 44 proposuit 46 trans (vv. 47, 49) Iordanem in valle contra phanum Phogor . . . quem percussit Moyses. Filii quoque Israel egressi ex Ægypto 48 qui est & Hermon 49 & vsque ad radices montis Phasga.
L. 40 das du haltest . . . so wirt dyrs . . . wolgehn . . . gibt deyn leben lang. 42 nicht seynd gewesen ist, der sol ynn der stedte eyne fliehen 45 fur legt 46 iensid (vv. 47, 49) dem Iordan ym tal gegen dem haus Peor . . den Mose vnd die kinder Israel schlugen, da sie aus Egypten zogen waren 49 vnden am berge Pisga.

The .V. Chapter.

1 AND Moses called vnto all Israell and sayed vnto them: Heare Israel the ordynaunces and lawes which I speke in thyne eares this daye, and lerne them and take 2 hede that ye doo them. The Lorde oure God made an appoyntment with us in Horeb. 3 The Lorde made not this bonde with oure fathers, but with us: we are they, which are .Ṗ. al heare a lyue 4 this daye. The Lord talked with you face to face in 5 the moūt out of the fyre. And I stode betwene the Lorde and you the same tyme, to shewe you the sayenge of the Lorde. For ye were afrayed of the fyre and therfore went not vpp in to the mount and he sayed.

6 I am the Lorde thy God which brought the out of 7 the lōde of Egipte the housse of bōdage. Thou shalt haue therefore none other goddes in my presence. 8 Thou shalt make the no grauen Image *Image* off any maner lykenesse that is in heauen aboue, or in the erth beneth, or in the water beneth the erth. 9 Thou shalt nether bowe thy self vnto them nor serue them, for I the Lorde thy God, am a gelouse God, visettinge the wikednesse of the fathers vppon the childern, euen in the thyrde and the fourth generacion, 10 amonge them that hate me: and shew mercye apon thousandes amonge them that loue me and kepe my commaundmentes.

M.C.S. The .x commaundementes of the lawe. No Image maye be made.

𝔐. 8 in erth benethe
𝒱. 1 Vocauitque ... discite ea, & opere complete. 4 locutus est nobis 5 Ego sequester & medius fui ... vt annuntiarem 7 in conspectu meo. 8 in aquis 9 deus æmulator .. generationem
𝔏. 1 rieff 4 mit vns 5 ansagete 7 fur myr 8 keyn bildnis ... ym wasser 9 eyn eyfferiger Gott ... gelied
𝔐. 𝔐. 𝔑. 4 *Face to face* the Chaldees woorde to worde, that is to saye, with so manyfest woordes and sygnes that it cannot be denyed but that it was god. 8 *Images.*

11 Thou ſhalt not take the name of the Lorde thy God in vayne: for the Lorde will not holde him giltleſſe, that taketh his name in vayne.

12 Kepe the Sabbath daye that thou ſancti- [Fo. XII.] fie it, as the Lorde thy God hath commaunded the.
13 Syxe dayes thou ſhalt laboure and doo all that thou
14 haſt to doo, but the ſeuenth daye is the Sabbath of the Lorde thy God: thou ſhalt doo no maner worke, nether thou nor thy ſonne nor thy doughter nor thy ſeruaunte nor thy mayde nor thine oxe nor thyne aſſe nor any of thi catell nor the ſtraunger that is within thy cytye, that thy ſeruaunte and thy mayde maye reſt as well
15 as thou. * And remembre that thou waſt a ſeruaunte in the londe of Egypte and how that the Lorde God, brought the out thence with a myghtye hande and a ſtretched out arme. For which cauſe the Lorde thy God commaundeth the to kepe the Sabbath daye. *God ſheweth a cauſe why we oughte to kepe his commaundmentes the pope doth not.*

16 Honoure thi father and thi mother, as the Lord thi God hath cōmaūded the: that thou mayſt prolonge thi dayes, and that it maye go well with the on the londe, which the Lorde thi God geueth the.

17 Thou ſhalt not flee.
18 Thou ſhalt not breake wedlocke.
19 Thou ſhalt not ſteale.
20 Thou ſhalt not beare falſe witneſſe agenſt thy neghboure,
21 Thou ſhalt not luſte after thi neghbours .P. wife: thou ſhalt not couet thi neyghbours houſſe, felde, ſeruaunte, mayde, oxe, aſſe nor ought that is thi neghbours.
22 Theſe wordes the Lorde ſpake vnto al youre multitude in the mount out of the fyre, cloude and darckneſſe, with a loude voyce and added nomoare there

---

V. 11 Non vſurpabis nomen ... fruſtra .. qui ſuper re vana nomen eius aſſumpſerit. 14 Septimus dies ſabbathi eſt, id eſt requies 18 mœchaberis. 22 multitudinem veſtrã in monte de medio ignis
L. 11 Du ſolt den namen ... nicht vergeblich furen, denn der HERR wirt den nicht vnſchuldig halten, der ſeynen namen vergeblich furet. 18 ehebrechen. 22 gemeyne auff dem berge ...

to, and wrote them in .ii. tables of ſtone and delyuered them vnto me.

23 But as ſoone as ye herde the voyce out off the darckneſſe and ſawe the hill burne with fyre, ye came vnto me all the heedes of youre tribes and youre 24 elders: and ye ſayed: beholde, the Lorde oure God hath ſhewed us his glorye and his greatneſſe, and we haue herde his voyce out of the fyre, and we haue ſene this daye that God maye talke with a man and he 25 yet lyue. And now wherfore ſhulde we dye that this greate fyre ſhulde conſume us: Yf we ſhulde heare the voyce of the Lorde oure God any moare, we ſhulde 26 dye. For what is any fleſh that he ſhulde heare the voyce of the lyuynge God ſpeakynge out of the fyre as 27 we haue done and ſhulde yet lyue: Goo thou ãd heare all that the Lorde oure God ſayeth, and tell thou vnto us all that the Lorde oure God ſayeth vnto the, and we will heare it and doo it.

28 [Fo. XIII.] And the Lorde herde the voyce of youre wordes when ye ſpake vnto me, and he ſayed vnto me: I haue herde the voyce of the wordes of this people which they haue ſpokē vnto the they haue well ſayed all that they haue ſayed.

29 Oh that they had ſoche an herte with them to feare me ãd kepe all my commaundmentes alwaye, that it myghte goo well with them and with their childern 30 for euer. Goo ãd ſaye vnto them: gett you in to 31 youre tentes agayne, but ſtonde thou here before me and I will tell the all the commaundmentes, ordinaunces ãd lawes which thou ſhalt teache thē, that they may doo them in the londe whiche I geue them to poſſeſſe.

32 Take hede therfore that ye do as the *walke* Lorde youre God hath commaunded you, *ſtrayght*

V. 22 in duabus tabulis 23 de medio 24 maieſtatem & magnitudinem ſuam . . . , & probauimus hodie 26 Quid eſt omnis caro 27 Tu magis accede 29 Quis det talem eos habere mentem 30 Reuertimini 31 hic ſta mecum . . in poſſeſſionem.

L. 22 auff zwo ſteynern taffeln 24 herlickeyt vnd ſeyne groſſe 26 Denn was iſt alles fleyſch 30 Gehet heym 31 hie fur myr

M. M. N. 32 Walke ſtraight.

and turne not afyde: ether to the righte hande or to
33 the lefte: but walke in all the wayes which the Lorde
youre God hath cōmaunded you, that ye maye lyve
and that it maye goo well with you ād that ye maye
prolonge youre dayes in the lond which ye fhall poffeffe.

¶ The .VI. Chapter

1 THESE are the commaundmentes, ordinaunces and lawes which the Lorde youre God commaunded to teach you, that ye might doo them in the londe whother ye goo to 2 pof- .P. feffe it: that thou mighteft feare the Lorde thy God, to kepe all his ordinaunces and his commaundmentes which I commaunde the, both thou and thy fonne and thy fonnes fonne all dayes off 3 thy lyfe, that thy dayes maye be prolonged. Heare therfore Ifrael and take hede that thou doo thereafter, that it maye goo well with the and that ye maye encreafe myghtely: euē as the Lord God of thy fathers hath promyfed the, a lōde that floweth with mylk ād hony 4, 5 Heare Ifrael, the Lorde thy God is Lorde only and thou fhalt loue the Lorde thy God with all thyne harte, with all thy foule and with all thy myght. 6 And thefe wordes which I commaunde 7 the this daye, fhalbe in thine herte ād thou fhalt whett them on thy childern, and fhalt talke of them when thou art at home in thyne houffe and as

M.C.S. The lawe muft be erneftly prynted in their hartes and to kepe it in memorye they muft wryte it on the dores and pooftes of their houfes, And teache it vnto their chylderne.

It is herefy with vs for a laye mā to loke of gods worde or to reade it.

whett on, to fharpen, difcipline, ftimulate

V. 33 fed per viam quam ... ambulabitis ... & protelentur dies veftri in terra poffeffionis veftræ. vi, 1 vt docerem vos 2 tibi & filiis ac nepotibus tuis . . . vt prolongentur dies tui. 3 ficut pollicitus eft . . . terram lacte & melle manantem. 5 fortitudine tua. 7 & narrabis ea . . & meditaberis fedens . . .

L. 33 fondern wandelt ynn allen wegen. vi, 2 du vnd deyne kinder vnd deyns kinds kinder 3 dyr geredt hat 7 fcherffen

M. M. N. 2 To feare God is to honoure him in putting thy confydence in him, and in hauyng a good and rightwes conuerfacion in hys fyght. 7 *Whett them on thy children* that is, exercyfe thy chyldren in them & put thē in vre with them.

thou walkeſt by the waye, and when thou lyeſt doune and
8 when thou ryſeſt vpp: and thou ſhalt bynde them for a
fygne vppon thyne hande. And they ſhalbe papers
9 off remembraunce betwene thyne eyes, and ſhalt write
them vppon the poſtes of thy houſſe ād vppon thy
gates.

10 And when the Lorde thy God hath brought the in
to the lond which he ſware vnto thy fathers Abraham,
Iſaac and Iacob, to geue the with greate and goodly
11 cities which thou byl- [Fo. XIIII.] deſt not, and houſſes
full of all maner goodes which thou filledeſt not, and
welles dygged which thou dyggedeſt not, ād vynes
and olyue trees which thou plantedeſt not, ād whē
12 thou haſt eaten, and art full: Then beware leſt thou
forget the Lorde which broughte the out off the lande
of Egipte the houſſe of bondage.

13 But feare the Lorde thy God and ſerue hym, and
14 ſwere by his name, and ſe that ye walke not after
ſtraunge goddes of the Goddes off the nacyons whiche
15 are aboute you. For the Lorde thy God is a geloufe
God among you leſt the wrath of the Lorde thy God
waxe hotte vppon the and deſtroye the from the erth.

16 Ye ſhall not tempte the Lorde youre God as ye
17 dyd at Maſa. But ſe that ye kepe the commaundmentes of the Lorde youre God, his witneſſes and his
18 ordinaunces which he hath commaunded the, and ſe
thou doo that which is right and good in *Right in goddes ſight is that he commaundeth*
the ſyghte of the Lorde: that thou mayſt
proſpere and that thou mayſt goo ād cōquere that good lāde which the Lorde ſware vnto thy
19 fathers, and that the Lorde maye caſt out all thine
enemies before the as he hath ſayed.

V. 8 & mouebuntur inter oculos tuos 11 quas non extruxiſti 13 & illi ſoli 15 de ſuperficie terræ. 16 Non tentabis .. in loco tentationis. 18 in conſpectu domini

L. 8 eyn denckmal fur deynen augen 11 ausgehawen brunne 15 von der erden 17 ſondern 18 fur den augen des HERRN

M. M. N. 13 *Swere by his name:* Loke beneth in the .x. chapter d. 15 *Gelouſe* loke Exod. xx, a and the chapter next afore this. 16 *Maſa:* or Maſah. 18 Right ī goddes ſyght is that which he commaundeth.

20 When thy sonne axeth the in tyme to *Teach youre*
come sayenge: What meaneth the witness- *childern.*
es, ordina-. P. unces and lawes which the Lorde oure God
21 hath commaunded you? Then thou shalt saye vnto thy
sonne: We were bondmen vnto Pharao in Egipte, but
the Lorde brought vs out of Egipte with a mightie hande.
22 And the Lorde shewed signes and won- *The outwarde*
dres both greate ād evell vppon Egipte, *deade is right-*
uousnesse vnto
Pharao and vppon all his housholde, before *the avoidinge*
23 oure eyes and broughte vs from thence: to *of punishmēt,*
threteninges
brynge vs in ād to geue vs the londe *ād curses ād*
24 which he sware vnto oure fathers. And *to opteine tem-*
porall bless-
therfore cōmaunded vs to do all these *iges: but vnto*
ordinaunces ād for to feare the Lord *the life to*
come thou
welth, *pros-* oure God, for oure welth *must haue the*
perity, happi- alwayes and that he might *rightuous-*
nes *nesse of faith*
saue vs, as it is come to passe *ād there by*
25 this daye. Moreouer it shalbe rightuous- *receaue for-*
nes vnto vs before the Lorde oure God, *geuenesse of*
sinnes ād
yf we take hede to kepe all these cō- *promise of en-*
maundmētes as he hath commaund- *heritaunce ād*
power to
ed vs, *worke of loue.*

V. 20 cras 22 fecitque signa... contra Pharaonem .. in conspectu nostro 24 omnia legitima hæc .. vt bene sit nobis cunctis diebus vitæ nostræ 25 Eritque nostri misericors

L. 20 heut odder morgen 22 Vnd der HERR thet grosse vnd bose zeychen vnd wunder ... fur vnsern augen 24 allen disen sitten ... auff das vns wol gehe all vnser lebtage 25 vnd es wirt vns zur gerechtickeyt gedeyen fur dem HERRN

M. M. N. 20 Teach youre chyldern. 25 *Righteousnes vnto vs,* etc: The outwarde deade is righteousnesse vnto the auoydinge of punnishemēt, threteninges & curses & to optayne tēporall blessynges: but vnto the life to come thou must haue the ryghteousnesse of faith & thereby receaue forgeuenesse of sinnes & promise of enheritaunce & power to worke of loue.

The .VII. Chapter.

1 THE the Lorde thy God hath brought the in to the lond whither thou goest to poffeffe it, and hath caft out manye nacions before the: the Hethites, the Girgofites, the Amorites, the Cananites, the Pherefites, the Heuites and the Iebufites: vii nacions moo in numbre ād mightier than 2 thou: ād whē the Lorde thy God hath fett them before the that thou ſhuldeſt ſmyte them ſe that thou vtterly deſtroye them and make no couenaunt [Fo. XV.] with 3 them nor haue compaſſion on them. Alſo thou ſhalt make no mariages with them, nether geue thy doughter vnto his ſonne nor take his 4 doughter vnto thy ſonne. For they will make youre ſonnes departe fro me and ſerue ſtraunge Goddes, and then will the wrath off the Lorde waxe whote vppon you ād deſtroye you ſhortely.

5 But thus ye ſhall deale with them: ouerthrowe their alters, breake doune their pilers, cut doune their groves 6 ād burne their ymages with fyre. For thou art an holy nacion vnto the Lorde thy God the Lorde thy God hath choſen the to be a feuerall people vnto him ſilf of all nacions that are vppon the erth.

7 It was not becauſe of the multitude of you aboue all nacions, that the Lorde had luſt vnto you and choſe you. For ye

M.C.S. The Iſraelites may make no couenaũt or appoyntment with the Gentyles. They muſt deſtroye their Idolles. Them that keape the cōmaundementes doth God loue and bleſſe, and the contrary hateth & puniſheth. Idolatrers muſt be ſlayne.

feuerall, *ſeparate*

Gods awne goodneſſe ād his awne trueth cauſeth hī to worke.

M. 1 Gergeſites 2 not haue compaſſyon
V. 1 et deleuerit 2 tradideritque eas 4 quia ſeducet filium tuum 5 ſubuertite, & confringite ſtatuas 6 populus peculiaris 7 vobis iunctus eſt dominus
L. 1 vnd aus wortzelt 2 Vnd wenn ſie . . . fur dyr gibt . . . noch yhn gonſt erzeygeſt 5 yhr feulen zu brechen 7 Nicht hat euch der HERR vmbfangen vnd euch erwelet [*corrected* into: nicht hat der HERR luſt zu euch gehabt]
M. M. N. 7 Gods awne goodneſſe & his awne trueth cauſeth him to worke.

8 were feweſt of all nacions: But becauſe the Lorde loued you and becauſe he wolde kepe the othe which he had ſworne vnto youre fathers, therfore he brought you out of Egipte with a mightie hande ād delyuered you out of the houſſe of bondage: euē frō the hande of Pharao kinge of Egipte.

9 Vnderſtonde therfore, that the Lorde thy God he is God and that a true God, which kepeth poyntment and mercy vnto them that loue him and kepe his commaundmentes, euen .Ƿ. thorowe out a thouſande gen-
10 eracions and rewardeth them that hate him before his face ſo that he bringeth them to noughte, and wil not defferre the tyme vnto him that hateth hī but will rewarde *Before his face in his preſece, while he loketh on.*
11 him before his face. Kepe therfore the commaundmentes, ordinaunces and lawes which I commaunde you this daye, that ye doo them.

12 Yf ye ſhall herken vnto theſe lawes ād ſhall obſerue and do them, then ſhall the Lorde thy God kepe poyntment with the and the mercy which he ſwore
13 vnto thy fathers and will loue the, bleſſe the and multiplye the: he will bleſſe the frute of thy wombe and the frute of thi ſelde, thy corne, thy wyne and thy oyle, the frute of thyne oxen and the flockes of thy ſhepe in the londe which he ſwore vnto thy fathers to
14 geue the. Thou ſhalt be bleſſed aboue all nacions, there ſhalbe nether man nor woman vnfrutefull amonge you, nor any thinge vnfrutefull amonge youre catell.
15 Moreouer the Lorde will turne from the all maner infirmityes, and will put none off the euell dyſeaſes off Egipte (whiche thou knoweſt) apon the, but wyll ſende them vppon them that hate the.

𝔐. 13 thyne oyle
𝒱. 8 Eduxitque vos in manu forti 9 quia dominus deus tuus, ipſe eſt deus fortis & fidelis 10 ſtatim . . . & vltra non differat, protinus eis reſtituens quod merentur. 12 Si poſtquam audieris 13 oleo, & armentis, gregibus ouium 14 inter omnes populos . . . vtriuſque ſexus, tam in hominibus quam in gregibus tuis. 15 ſed cunctis hoſtibus tuis.

𝔏. 8 hat er euch ausgefuret mit mechtiger hand 10 fur ſeynem angeſicht 14 vber allen volckern 15 allen deynen heſſern

𝔐. 𝔐. N. 10 *Before his face:* Before his face in his preſence, whyle he loketh on.

16 Thou shalt bringe to nought all nacions which the Lorde thy God delyuereth the, thy- [Fo. XVI.] ne eye shall haue no pitie vppon them nether shalt thou
17 serue their goddes, for that shalbe thy decaye. Yf thou shalt saye in thine hert these nacions are moo than I,
18 how cā I cast them out? Feare thē not, but remēbre what the Lorde thy god dyd
19 vnto Pharao ād vnto all Egipte, ād the greate temptacions which thine eyes sawe, ād the signes ād wonders ād mightie hāde ād stretched out arme wherewith the Lord thy god broughte the out: euē so shall the Lorde thy God doo vnto all the nacions of which thou art afrayed.

God is as able now also to deliuer vs out of the captiuite of the pope

20 Thereto, the Lorde thy God will send hornettes amonge them vntyll they that are lefte, and hyde them
21 selues frō the, be destroyed. Se thou feare thē not for the lord thi god is amōg you a mightie god ād a
22 terrible. The Lord thy god will put out these naciōs before the a litle ād a litle: thou maist not cōsume thē at ōce left the beestes of the felde encrease vpō the.
23 And the lorde thy god shall delyuer thē vnto the ād sterre vp a mightie tēpest amōge thē, vntil thei be
24 brought to nought. And he shal deliuer their kinges in to thine hāde, ād thou shalt destroye their names frō vnder heauē. There shal no mā stonde before the,
25 vntill thou haue destroyed them. The images of their goddes thou shalt burne with fire, ād se that thou couet not .P. the syluer or golde that is on them nor take it

V. 16 Deuorabis omnes populos 17 delere eas ? 18 noli metuere sed 19 plagas maximas ... sic faciet cunctis 20 qui te fugerint, & latere non potuerint. 22 ipse confumet ... paulatim atque per partes ... pariter 23 et interficiet illos 25 Sculptilia eorum ... de quibus facta sunt

L. 16 Du wirst alle volcker fressen ... denn das wurde dyr eyn strick seyn. 19 durch grosse versuchung 20 vnd sich verbirget fur dyr 22 Er der Herr deyn Gott wirt dise leut aus wurtzelen fur dyr, eyns nach dem andern ... nicht eylend alle machen 23 wirt sie mit grosser schlacht erschlahen 25 Die bild yhrer Gotter ... das dran ist

M. M. N. 20 What hornettes are loke Exod. xxiii, d. 25 *Sylver or golde:* Whatsoeuer golde or syluer honoure or proset, calleth frō the woorde of God, belōgeth to the Images of their goddes & must be therfore abhorred: yee yf they be good worckes whē thou thynkest that thou doest thē of thyne awne strenght & not helped of God.

vnto the, left thou be fnared therewith. For it is an
26 abhominacyon vnto the Lorde thy God. Brynge not
therfore the abhominacyon to thyne houffe, left thou
be a damned thynge as it is: but vtterlye defye it and
abhorre it, for it is a thinge that muft be deftroyed.

⁋ The .VIII. Chaptre.

1 ALL the commaundmentes which *M.C.S. Mo-*
I commaunde the this daye ye *fes putteth*
fhal kepe for to do them, that *the Ifraelites*
ye maye lyue and multiplye *in remem-*
braunce of the
and goo and poffeffe the londe whiche the *afflicyons and*
benifytes that
2 Lorde fware vnto youre fathers. And *they hadde the*
thinke on all the waye which the Lorde *xl. yere which*
they were in
thy God led the this .xl. yere in the wil- *the wilder-*
derneffe, for to humble the ād to proue *neffe.*
the, to wete what was in thine herte, whether thou
3 woldeft kepe his commaundmentes or no, He humbled the and made the hongre and fed the with
man which nether thou nor thy father knewe of. to
make the know that a man muft not lyue by bred
only: but by al that procedeth out of *The word is*
the mouth of the Lorde muft a man lyue. *life*
4 Thy rayment waxed not olde vppon the, nether dyd
thy fete fwell thys .xl. yere.

V. 26 quippiam ex idolo ... ne fias anathema ... Quafi
fpurcitiam deteftaberis, & velut inquinamentum ac fordes abomi-
nationi habebis viii, 2 Et recordaberis .. vt affligeret te atque
tentaret 3 Afflixit te penuria .. vt oftenderet tibi ... in folo pane ...
in omni verbo 4 Veftimentum tuum quo operiebaris, nequaquam
vetuftate defecit

L. 25 nicht drynnen verfehift 26 fondern du folt eyn ekel vnd
grewel daran haben. viii, 2 vnd gedenckft .. demutiget vnd ver-
fucht 3 am brot alleyn, fondern an allem 4 veraltet an dyr .. ge-
fchwollen

M. M. N. 26 *Damned,* Or curfed. viii, 3 *Humbled the:* Humbled loke after .xxi. c.—The word is lyfe. 4 *Thy rayment,* etc.:
Here mayft thou fe that they fhall want nothyng that beleue the
woorde & lyue after it, but that God careth for them in all thynges
yf they cōmytt them felues wholy to his prouifyon. i. Pet. v, d.

5 Vnderſtonde therfore in thine herte, that as a man nurtereth his ſonne, euen ſo the Lorde thy God nurter-
6 eth the. Kepe therfore the com- [Fo. XVII.] maundmentes of the Lorde thy God that thou walke in
7 his wayes and that thou feare him For the Lorde thy God bringeth the in to a good lande, a londe of riuers of water, of foūtens and of ſpringes
8 that ſpringe out both in valayes and hylles: a londe of whete and of barly, of vynes, figtrees and pomgranates, a lond of olyuetrees with oyle and of
9 honye: a lande wherin thou ſhalt not eate bred in ſcarceneſſe, and where thou ſhalt lacke nothinge, a londe whoſe ſtones are yerne, and out of whoſe hylles
10 thou ſhalt dygge braſſe. When thou haſt eaten therfore and filled thy ſelfe, then bleſſe the Lord for the good lond which he hath geuen the.
11 But bewarre that thou forgett not the Lorde thy God, that thou woldeſt not kepe his cōmaundmentes, lawes and ordinaunces which I commaunde the this
12 daye: yee and when thou haſt eatē ād filled thy ſelfe
13 ād haſt bylt goodly houſſes ād dwelt therin, ād when thy beeſſe ād thy ſhepe are waxed manye ād thy ſyluer ād thy golde is multiplied ād all that thou haſt en-
14 creaſed, then bewarre leſt thine herte ryſe ād thou forgett the Lorde thy God which brought the out of the
15 londe of Egipte the houſſe of bondage, ād which led the in the wilderneſſe both greate ād terreble with ſyrye ſerpentes ād ſcor- .℗. piōs ād thurſte where was no water which brought the water out of the rocke of
16 flynt: whiche fed the in the wilderneſſe with Man where of thy fathers knewe not, for to humble the and to

𝕸. 15 and drouth
𝒱. 5 Vt recogites 6 vt cuſtodias 7 terram riuorum, aquarumque, & fontium: in cuius campis & montibus erumpunt fluuiorum abyſſi 9 abſque vlla penuria ... & rerum omnium abundantia perſrueris ... æris metalla 10 vt cū comederis 13 armenta boum, & ouium greges 14 eleuetur cor tuū 15 ſerpens flatu adurens 16 Et poſtquam ...
𝕷. 7 beche. brunnen. tieſſen ... die an den bergen vnd ynn den awen flieſſen 8 ölebewm vnd honnig ynnen wechſt. 9 ertz aus den bergen 11 So hütt dich nu 14 deyn hertz ſich nicht erhebe 15 feuer ſpeyeten

proue the, that he might doo the good at thy later ende.

17 And beware that thou faye not in thine herte, my power and the might of myne awne hāde hath done
18 me all thefe actes: But remembre the Lorde thy God, how that it is he which gaue the power to do māfully, for to make good the promeffe which he fware vnto thy fathers, as it is come to paffe this daye, *Gods power worketh and not we*
19 For yf thou fhalt forget the Lorde thy god and fhalt walke after ftraunge goddes and ferue them and worfheppe them, I teftyfye vnto you this daye, that ye
20 fhall furely peryfh. As the nacyons whiche the Lorde deftroyeth before the, euen fo ye fhall peryfhe, becaufe ye wolde not herken vnto the voyce of the Lord youre God.

❧ The .IX. Chapter.

1 HEARE Ifrael, thou goeft ouer Iordayne this daye, to goo and conquere nacions greater and mightier than thy felfe: and cities greate ād walled vp to heauen,
2 ād people greate and tall, euen the childern of the Enakims, which thou knoweft and of whom thou haft [Fo. XVIII.] herde faye who is able to ftond before the chil-
3 dern of Enack? But vnderftonde this

M.C.S. They are forbiddē to truft in their awne ftreāgth. A reherfall of certen thynges that were done after the lawe was geuen, vnto the murmuring at the Graues of Luft.

V. 16 ad extremū mifertus eft tui 18 vt impleret pactum fuum ...ficut præfens indicat dies. 19 omnino difpereas. 20 quas deleuit dominus in introitu tuo ix, 1 & ad cælū vfque muratas 2 quibus nullus poteft ex aduerfo refiftere.

L. 16 das er dyr hernach wol thett 7 difs vermugen 18 auffricht feynen bund ... wie es gehet heuts tags. ix, 1 vermauret bis yn den hymel 2 Wer kan widder die kinder Enak beftehen?

M. M. N. 17 *And beware*, etc.: By the helpe of God onely doeft thou what foeuer good is, & not by thyne awne helpe, no not by the helpe of any of the faynctes were he neuer fo holy. ix, 1 *Walled vp to heauē* is a fyguratyue fpeache, fygnyfyēg that the walles were hye and not eafye to be wōne.

daye that the Lorde thy God which goeth ouer before the a confumyng fire, he fhall deftroye them and he fhall fubdue them before the. And thou fhalt caft them out, and brynge them to noughte quyckely as the Lorde hath fayed vnto the.

4 Speake not in thyne hert, after that the Lorde thy God hath caft them out before the fayenge: for my rightuoufnes the Lorde hath brought me *where is mās* in to poffeffe this lōde. Nay, but for *rightewefneffe.* the wekedneffe of thefe nacions the Lord doth caft
5 thē out before the. It is not for thi rightuoufnes fake ād right hert that thou goeft to poffeffe their lōd: But partely for the wekedneffe of thefe naciōs, the Lord thy god doth caft thē out before the, and partly to performe that which the Lorde thy God fware vnto thi fathers, Abraham, Ifaac and Iacob.

6 Vnderftond therfore that it is not for thy rightuoufnes fake, that the Lorde thy God doth geue the this good lond to poffeffe it, for thou art a ftiffenecked
7 people. Remēbre ād forget not how thou prouokedeft the Lorde thi god in the wilderneffe: for fens the daye that thou cameft ôut of the lond of Egipte vntyll ye came vnto this place, ye haue rebelled agenft the
8 .P. Lorde. Alfo in Horeb ye angred the Lorde fo that the Lorde was wroth with you, euē to haue de-
9 ftroyed you, after that I was gone vpp in to the mount, to fett the tables of ftone, the tables of appoyntment which the Lorde made with you. And I abode in the hyll .xl. dayes ād .xl. nightes and nether ate bred nor
10 dranke water. And the Lorde delyuered me two tables of ftone writen with the finger of God, and in them was acordynge to all the wordes which the Lorde

𝔐. 3 caft thē out, and brynge them out, and brynge them to noughte 4 in to poffeffe.
𝔙. 3 ignis deuorans atque cōfumens, qui conterat eos & deleat atque difperdat ante faciē tuā velociter 6 cum duriffimæ ceruicis fis populus. 7 ad iracundiam prouocaueris... femper aduerfum dominum contendifti. 8 prouocafti eum
𝔏. 3 er wirt fie vertilgen... vnd vmbringen bald 6 fyntemal du ein halftarrig volck bift 7 erzorntift ynn der wuften 8 ynn Horeb ertzurntet
𝔐. 𝔐. N. 4 Where is mans rightwefnes?

fayed vnto you in the mount out of the fire in the daye whē the people were gathered together.

11 And whē the .xl. dayes and .xl. nyghtes were ended, the Lorde gaue me: the two tables off ſtone, the tables
12 of the teſtament, and fayed vnto me: Vpp, and get the doune quyckely from hence, for thy people which thou haſt broughte out of Egipte, haue marred them felues. *marred, hurt, injured, damaged*

They are turned attonce out of the waye, whiche I commaunded them, and haue made thē a god of metall.
13 Furthermore the Lorde fpake vnto me fayenge: I fe
14 this people how that it is a ſtiffenecked people, let me alone that I maye deſtroye them and put out the name off them from vnder heauen, and I will make off the a nacion both greater ād moo than they.

15 [Fo. XIX.] And I turned awaye and came doune from the hyll (and the hyll burnt with fire) and had
16 the two tables of the appoyntment in my handes. And when I loked and fawe that ye had fynned agenſt the Lorde youre God and had made you a calfe of metall and had turned attonce out of the waye whiche the
17 Lorde had commaunded you. Thē I toke the two tables and caſt them out of my two handes, and brake
18 thē before youre eyes. And I fell before the Lorde: euen as at the firſt tyme .xl. dayes ād .xl. nightes and nether ate bred nor dranke water ouer all youre fynnes whiche ye had fynned in doynge wekedly in the fyght
19 of the Lorde ād in prouokinge him. For I was afrayed of the wrath and fearfneſſe wherwith the Lord was angrie with you, euē for to haue deſtroyed you But the Lorde herde my peticion at that tyme alfo.

20 The Lorde was very angrie with Aaron alfo, euē for to haue deſtroyed him: But I made interceſſion
21 for Aarō alfo the fame tyme. And I toke youre fynne, the calfe which ye had made ād burnt him

V. 10 quando concio populi congregata eſt. 12 Ægypto, deferuerunt velociter viam, quam demonſtraſti eis, feceruntque fibi conflatile. 14 dimitte me 16 vitulum conflatilem 18 procidi . . . & eum ad iracundiam prouocaſtis. 20 fimiliter

L. 12 eyn gegoſſens bild 14 las ab von myr 16 eyn gegoſſen kalb 18 fiel fur . . . yhn zu erzurnen 20 zur felben zeyt

with fire ād ſtampe him and grounde   ſtampe, *verb,*
him a good, euē vnto ſmal duſt. And   *paſt tenſe*
I caſt the duſt thereof in to the broke a good, *thor-*
that deſcended out of the mount.   *oughly*

22 Alſo at Thabeera and at Maſa and at the .P. ſepul-
23 chres of luſt ye angred the Lorde, yee ād when the
Lorde ſent you from Cades Bernea ſayenge: goo vpp
and conquere the lond whiche I haue geuen you, ye
diſobeyed the mouth of the Lorde youre God, and
24 nether beleued hī nor herkened vnto his voyce. Thus
ye haue bene diſobediēt vnto the Lord, ſence the daye
that I knew you.

25 And I fell before the Lorde .xl. dayes   *Lerne to*
and .xl. nightes whiche I laye there, for *praye.*
26 the Lorde was minded to haue deſtroyed you. But I
made interceſſion vnto the Lorde and ſayed: O Lorde
Iehoua, deſtroye not thy people and thyne enheritaūce which thou haſt delyuered thorow thi greatneſſe
and which thou haſt brought out of Egipte with a
27 mightie hand. Remēbre thy ſervauntes Abraham,
Iſaac and Iacob and loke not vnto the ſtoburneſſe
28 of this people nor vnto their wekedneſſe and ſynne: left
the londe whence thou broughteſt them ſaye: Becauſe
the Lorde was not able to brynge them in to the londe
which he promyſed them and becauſe he hated them,
therfore he caried them out to deſtroye them in the
29 wilderneſſe. Moreouer they are thy people and thine
enheritaunce, whiche thou broughteſt out with thy
myghtye power and wyth thy ſtretched out arme.

M. 22 Thaberah 23 Barne
V. 22 In incendio quoque, & in tentatione, & in Sepulchris
cōcupiſcentiæ 23 & contempſiſtis imperium domini 24 ſed ſemper
fuiſtis rebelles a die qua noſſe vos cœpi. 25 quibus eum ſuppliciter
deprecabar . . . vt fuerat comminatus 26 in magnitudine tua 28
dicāt habitatores terræ . . . quam pollicitus eſt eis
L. 22 zu Thabeera vnd zu Maſſa vnd bey den Luſtgrebern
24 denn yhr ſeyt vngehorſam dem Herrn geweſt, ſo lang ich euch
kand habe. 25 die ich da lag, Denn der Herr ſprach 28 das land
ſage . . . das er yhnen geredet hatte
M. M. N. 25 Lerne to praye.

[Fo. XX.] ¶ The .X. Chapte.

1 IN the fame ceafon the Lord fayed vnto me hewe the two tables of ftone like vnto the firft and come vp vnto me in to the
2 mount ād make the an Arke of wod, and I will wryte in the table, the wordes that were in the firft tables which thou brakeft,
3 ād thou fhalt put thē in the arcke. And I made an arke of fethī wod ād hewed two tables of ftone like vnto the firft, ād went vp in to the mountayne and the ii. tables in myne hande.
4 And he wrote in the tables, acording to the firft writinge (the .x. verfes whiche the Lorde fpake vnto you in the mount out of the fire in the daye when the
5 people were gathered) ād gaue thē vnto me. And I departed ād came doune frō the hyll and put the tables in the arcke which I had made: ād there they remayned, as the Lorde commaunded me
6 And the childern of Ifrael toke their iurney from Beroth Bē Iakē to Mofera, where Aarō dyed ād where he was buried, ād Eleazer his fonne became preaft ī
7 his fteade. And frō thēce they departed vnto Gudgod: ād frō Gudgod to Iathbath, a lōd of riuers of water.
8 And the fame ceafon the Lorde feparated the trybe of Leui to beare the arcke of the appoyntment .P. of the Lorde and to ftonde before the Lorde, ād to min-

M.C.S. A repeticyon of fome of the Iourneys of the Ifraelites. The renuyng of the tables. An exhortacyon to geue heede to the Lawe.

𝔐. 2 in the tables 4 mount of the fire ... people gethered together 6 Beroth of the childrē of Iakan 7 Gadgad (bis)
𝒱. 2 in his quas ante cōfregifti 3 habens eas in manibus. 4 quādo populus cōgregatus eft 5 quæ hucufque ibi funt 6 Beroth filiorū Iacan 7 in terra aquarū atque torrentiū. 8 arcam fœderis domini ... ac benediceret in nomine illius
𝔏. 2 die auff den erften waren, die du zu brochen haft 4 zur zeyt der verfamlung 5 das die dafelbs weren 7 eyn land da beche find. 8 die lade des bunds des Herrn ... vnd feynen namen zu loben

𝔐. 𝔐. N. 7 *Gadgad:* Or Gadgadah: Iathbath: or Iatebath.

istre vnto him and to blesse in his name vnto this
9 daye. Wherfore the Leuites haue no parte nor enheritaunce with their brethern. The Lorde he is their enheritaunce, as the Lorde thy God hath promyfed them.

10 And I taried in the mount, euē as at the firſt tyme xl. dayes and .xl. nyghtes and the Lorde herkened vnto me at that tyme alſo, ſo that the Lorde wolde
11 not deſtroye the. And the Lorde ſayed vnto me: vpp ād goo forth in the iurney before the people and let them goo in ād conquere the lond which I ſware vnto their fathers to geue vnto them.

12 And now Iſrael what is it that the Lord thi God requyreth of the, but to feare the Lord thi God and to walke in all his wayes and to loue him and to ſerue the Lorde thy God with all thyne herte and with all thy
13 ſoule, that thou kepe the commaundmentes of the Lorde ād his ordinaunces which I commaunde the this
14 daye, for thy welth. Beholde, heauen and the heauen of heauens is the Lordes thy god, and the erth with all that there- *welth, happinefs, welfare, cſ. weal*
15 in is: only the Lorde had a luſt vnto thy fathers to loue them, and therfore choſe you theire ſeed after them off all nacyons, as it is come to paſſe this daye.

16 [Fo. XXI.] Circumcyſe therfore the foreſkynne of
17 youre hartes, and be no longer ſtiffnecked. For the Lorde youre God, he is God of goddes and lorde of lordes, a greate God, a myghtye and a terreble which
18 regardeth no mans perſon nor taketh giftes: but doeth right vnto the fatherleſſe and wedowe and loueth the
19 ſtraunger, to geue him ſode and rayment. Loue therfore the ſtraunger, for ye were ſtraungers youre ſelues in the londe of Egipte.

V. 9 non habuit Leui ... ſicut promiſit ei 11 poſſideat terram 15 & tamen patribus tuis cōglutinatus eſt dominus, ... id eſt vos 17 dominus dominantium
L. 9 die Leuiten ... yhnen geredt hat. 11 das land eynnemen 15 Noch hat er alleyn zu deynen vetern luſt gehabt 17 keyn perſon achtet

20 Thou shalt feare the Lorde thi God and serue him
21 and cleaue vnto him ād swere by his name, for he is
thi prayse ād he is thi God that hath done these greate
and terreble thinges for the, which thine eyes haue
22 sene. Thi fathers went doune in to Egipte with .Lxx
soules, ād now the Lorde thi God hath made the as
the starres of heauen in multitude.

⁋ The .XI. Chapter.

1 LOUE the Lorde thi God and kepe his obseruaunces, his ordinaunces, his lawes and his commaundmentes alwaye. 2 And call to mynde this daye that which youre childern haue nether knowen nor sene: euen the nurture of the Lorde youre God, his greatnesse, his myghtye hande 3 and his stretched out arme: his miracles and his actes which he dyd amonge .P. the Egiptiās, euen vnto Pharao the kinge 4 off Egipte and vnto all his lōde: ād what he dyd vnto the host of the Egiptiās, vnto their horses ād charettes, how he brought the water of the red see vppon thē as they chased you, and how the Lorde hath brought them to nought vnto

M.C.S. An exhortacion to regarde the Lawe, and how they ought to haue it in their hertes alwayes and before theire eyes, and to talck of hit when they ryse, when they sytt doune and when they walke by the waye &c.

V. 20 & ei soli seruies: ipsi adhærebis, iurabisque in nomine illius. xi, 1 obserua præcepta eius 2 Cognoscite hodie ... disciplinam domini 4 omnique exercitui .. et deleuerit

L. 20 yhm soltu dienen, yhm soltu anhangen, vnd bey seynem namen schweren 21 bey dyr. xi, 1 vnd seyne hut 2 erkennet... nemlich die zuchtigung 4 an der macht der Egypter ... da sie euch nach iagten .. vmbracht

M. M. N. 20 *Swere by his name:* To sweare that which is true in a cause of sayth ether to the honoure of God or profet of thy neyghboure is leafull. And then wyll Moses that the othe be made by the name of God: by which he meaneth, that yf we must neades sweare, we refer the othe to God onely although thou sweare by a boke or other thyng: as paull dyd by his conscience. Roma. ix. a.

5 this daye: ād what he dyd vnto you in the wildernesse,
6 vntill ye came vnto this place: ād what he dyd vnto Dathan and Abiram the sonnes of Eliab the sonne of Ruben, how the erth opened hir mouth ād swalowed thē with their housholdes and their tentes, ād all their substāce that was in their possessiō, in the myddes of Israel.
7 For youre eyes haue sene all the greate deades of
8 the Lorde which he dyd. Kepe therfore al the cōmaundmentes which I cōmaunde the this daye that ye maye be stronge ād goo and conquere the londe
9 whother ye go to possesse it, ād that ye maye prolonge youre dayes in the londe which the Lorde sware vnto youre fathers to geue vnto them ād to their seed, a londe that floweth with mylke and honye.
10 For the londe whother thou goest to possesse it, is not as the londe of Egipte whence thou camest out, where thou sowedest thi seed and wateredest it with
11 thi laboure as a garden of herbes: but the londe whither ye goo ouer [Fo. XXII.] to possesse it, is a londe of hilles and valeyes and drynketh water of the rayne of
12 heauē, and a londe which the Lorde thi God careth for. The eyes of the Lord thi God are always apō it, from the begynnynge of the yere vnto the later ende of the yere.
13 Yf thou shalt herken therfore vnto my commaundementes which I commaunde you this daye, that ye loue the Lorde youre God and serue him with all youre
14 hertes and with all youre soules: then he will geue rayne vnto youre londe in due season, both the fyrst rayne and the later, and thou shalt gather in thy corne,

V. 6 in medio Israelis. 10 vbi iacto semine in hortorum morem aquæ ducuntur irriguæ 12 semper inuisit

L. 6 yhrem gesind .. mitten vnter dem gantzen Israel. 8 gesterckt werdet 10 da du deynen samen sehist vnd trenckest es zu sussen, wie eyn kol garten, 12 nach wilchem land der Herr ... fraget ... ymer dar drynen 14 so wil ich ... regen geben

M. M. N. 6 *Abiram:* Or Abirom. 10 *Waterdest*, etc: By this is meant that water was wonte to be brought ouer all Egypt oute of the ryuer Nilus by laboure becaufe they wanted rayne. 14 *Rayne & the later:* That is after the Hebre. the rayne in october which is after heruest, & in spring tyme.

15 thy wyne and thyne oyle. And he will sende graffe in thy feldes for thy catell: and thou shalt eate and fyll thy selfe.

16 But bewarre that youre hertes disceaue you not that ye turne asyde and serue straunge goddes and worshepe
17 them, and thē the wrath of the Lorde waxe hote vpon you ād shott vp the heauen that there be no rayne and that youre londe yeld not hir frute, and that ye peresh quickly from of the good lōde which the Lorde geueth you.

18 Putt vp therfore these my wordes in youre hertes and in youre soules, and bynde them for a sygne vnto youre handes, and lett .℗. them be as papers of re-
19 membraunce betwene youre eyes, and teach them youre childern: so that thou ✷ talke of them when thou sytteſt in thyne houſſe, and when thou walkeſt by the waye, and when *Talke of rob-ynkod saye oure prelates*
20 thou lyeſt doune and when thou ryſeſt vpp: yee and write them vppon the doreposſtes of thine houſſe and
21 vppon thi gates, that youre dayes may be multiplyed ād the dayes of youre childern apon the erth which the Lorde sware vnto youre fathers to geue them, as longe as the dayes of heauē laſt vpon the erth.

22 For yf ye shall kepe all these cōmaundmentes which I cōmaunde you, so that ye doo thē and loue the Lorde youre God and walke in all his wayes and cleaue vnto
23 him. Then will the Lorde caſt out all these nacions
24 both greatter and myghtyer then youre selues. All the places where on the soles of youre fete shall treade, shalbe youres: euen from the wilderneſſe and from

𝔐. 23 all these nacions & ye shall conquere thē which are both greatter

𝕍. 17 iratusque dominus claudat cælum .. de terra optima ... daturus eſt 18 & suspendite ea pro signa in manibus, & ... collocate. 19 vt illa meditētur 21 quamdiu cælum immineret terræ. 23 poſſidebitis 24 Omnis locus quem calcauerit

𝕷. 15 vnd wil ... gras geben 16 das sich ewr hertz nicht vberreden laſſe 18 bindet sie zum zeichen auff ewre hand, das sie eyn denckmal fur ewren augen seyen. 19 leret sie ... das du dauon rediſt 21 so lange die tage von hymel auff erden weren. 24 Alle ortter darauff ewr fuſs solen trit

Libanon and from the ryuer Euphrates, euen vnto the
25 vttemoſt ſee ſhall youre coſtes be. There ſhall no man
be able to ſtonde before you: the Lorde youre God ſhal
caſt the feare and dreade of you vppō all londes whether ye ſhall come, as he hath ſayed vnto you.

26 Beholde, I ſett before you this daye a ble- [Fo.
27 XXIII.] ſſynge and a curſe: a bleſſynge: yf ye herkē
vnto the commaundmentes of the Lorde youre God
28 which I cōmaūde you this daye: And a curſe: yf ye will
not herkē vnto the cōmaundmentes of the Lord youre
God: but turne out of the waye which I commaūde
you this daye to goo after ſtraunge goddes which ye
haue not knowen.

29 When the Lorde thi God hath brought the in to
the londe whother thou goeſt to poſſeſſe it, then put
the bleſſinge vppon mount Griſim and the curſe vppon
30 mount Ebal, which are on the other ſyde Iordane on
the backe ſide of the waye towarde the goynge doune
of the ſonne in the lōde of the Cananites which dwell
in the feldes ouer agenſt Gilgal beſyde moregroue.
31 Fo ye ſhall goo ouer to goo and poſſeſſe the londe
which the Lorde youre God geueth you, and ſhall con-
32 quere it ād dwell there in. Take hede therfore that
ye doo al the cōmaundmentes and lawes, which I ſett
before you this daye.

M. 29 Garizim 30 agenſt Galgal beſyde the groue of Moreh.
V. 24 a flumine magno Euphrate vſque ad mare occidentale
25 ſuper omnem terram quā calcaturi eſtis 28 quam ego nunc
oſtendo vobis 30 poſt viam quæ vergit ad ſolis occubitum . . .
Galgalam, quæ eſt iuxta vallem tendentem & intrantem procul.
32 Videte ergo
L. 24 bis ans letzte meer 25 darynnen yhr reyſet 29 den ſegen geben 30 der ſtraſſen nach von der ſonnen nyddergang . . .
blachen felt wonen gegen Gilgal vber, bey dem hayn More 32 So
behaltet nu

XII. 1-9.   called Deuteronomye.   563

The .XII. Chapter.

1 HESE are the ordinaunces and *M.C.S. Idol-*
lawes which ye shall obserue *atrye must the*
to doo in the londe which the *stroye and flee*
Lorde God of thy fathers geueth *fro. They must*
the to possesse it, as longe as ye lyue vppon *They must one-*
2 the .P. erth. Se that ye destroye all places *ly do that*
where the nacyons which ye conquere *God com-*
serue their goddes, vppon hye mountaynes *maundeth.*
3 and on hye hilles and vnder euery grene tree. Ouerthrowe their alters and breake their pylers and burne
their groues with fyre and hewdowne the ymages off
theyr goddes, and brynge the names of them to noughte
out of that place.
4, 5 Se ye doo not so vnto the Lorde youre God but
ye shall enquere the place which the Lorde youre God
shall haue chosen out of all youre trybes to put his
name there and there to dwell. And thyther thou
6 shalt come, and thyther ye shall brynge youre burnt-
sacryfices and youre offerynges, youre tithes and heueofferynges off youre handes, youre vowes and frewillofferynges and thy fyrst borne off youre oxen and off
7 youre shepe. And there ye shall eate before the
Lorde youre God, and ye shall reioyse in all that ye
laye youre handes on: both ye and youre housholdes,
becaufe the Lord thy God hath blessed the.
8 Ye shall doo after nothinge that we doo   *
here this daye, euery man what semeth hi good in his
9 awne eyes. For ye are not yet come to rest nor vnto the

M. 6 and the fyrst borne
V. 1 daturus est 2 omnia loca .. mōtes excelsos, & colles ....
lignum frondosum. 3 Dissipate aras .. & idola comminuite: dis-
perdite nomina eorum de locis illis. 5 ad locum ... venietis 6 et
offeretis in loco illo 7 miseritis manum vos & domus 8 Non facietis
ibi quæ nos hic facimus hodie
L. 1 geben hat 2 auff hohen bergen, auff hugelln odder vnter
grünen b. 3 brecht ab .. die gotzen yhrer Gotter .. aus dem selben
ort. 5 solt yhr forschen vnd dahyn komen 7 essen vnd frolich seyn
8 der keyns thun

enheritaunce which the Lorde [Fo. XXIIII.] youre God
10 geueth you. But ye ſhal goo ouer Iordayne ād dwell
in the lōde which the Lorde youre God geueth you to
enheret, ād he ſhal geue you reſt frō al youre enemies
rounde aboute: and ye ſhall dwell in ſafetie.

11 Therfore when the Lorde youre God hath choſen a
place to make his name dwell there, thither ye ſhall
brynge all that I commaunde you, youre burntſacry-
fices and youre offerynges, youre tithes and the heueofferynges of youre handes and all youre godly vowes
which ye vowe vnto the Lorde.

12 And ye ſhall reioyſe before the Lorde youre God,
both ye, youre ſonnes and youre doughters, youre ſeruauntes and youre maydes and the leuite that is within
youre gates for he hath nether parte nor enheritaunce
with you.

13 Take hede that thou offer not thi burntofferynges
14 in what foeuer place thou ſeyſt: but in the place which
the Lorde ſhall haue choſen amonge one of thy trybes,
there thou ſhalt offer thi burntofferynges and there
15 thou ſhalt doo all that I commaunde the. Not with-
ſtondynge thou mayſt kyll ād eate fleſh in al thi cities,
what foeuer thi foule luſteth after acordinge to the
bleſſinge of the Lorde thi God which he hath geuen
the both the .℗. * vncleane and the cleane *Vncleane as*
mayſt thou eate, euen as the roo and the *pertayninge*
vn to ſacrifice
16 hert: only eate not the bloude, but poure *as beeſtes that*
it apon the erth as water. *had deformi-*
ties: but not
17 Thou mayſt not eate within thi gates *of the vncleane*
the tythe of thi corne, of thy wyne and *that was for-*
of thi oyle, ether the firſtborne of thine *biddē*

V. 9 daturus eſt (v. 10) 10 et abſque vllo timore habitetis 11 &
quicquid præcipuū eſt in muneribus quæ vouiſtis 12 Ibi epulabi-
mini 13 holocauſta 14 offeres hoſtias 15 Si autem comedere volueris, ... dedit tibi in vrbibus tuis: ſiue immundū fuerit, hoc eſt ma-
culatū, & debile: ſiue mūdum, hoc eſt integrū & ſine macula,
quod offerri licet

L. 10 vnd werdet ſicher wonen. 11 brandopffer, ewr ander
opffer 15 beyde reyn vnd vnreyn mugens eſſen

M. M. N. 15 *Vncleane:* Vncleane as pertayninge vnto ſacrifyce, as beaſtes that had deformyties: but not of the vncleane
that was forbidden.

oxen or of thy sḥepe, nether any of thi vowes which
thou voweſt, nor thi frewilofferinges or heueofferynges
18 of thyne handes: but thou muſt eate them before the
Lorde thi God, in the place which the Lorde thi God
hath choſen: both thou thi ſonne and thi doughter, thi
ſeruaunte and thy mayde ād the leuite that is within
thi gates: ād thou ſhalt reioyſe before the Lorde thi
19 God, in al that thou putteſt thine hande to. And be
warre that thou forſake not the leuite as lōge as thou
lyueſt vppon the erth.

20   Yf (when the Lorde thi God hath enlarged thi coſtes
as he hath promyſed the) thou ſaye: I will eate fleſh,
becauſe thi ſoule longeth to eate fleſh: then thou ſhalt
21 eate fleſh, whatſoeuer thi ſoule luſteth. Yf the place
which the Lorde thi God hath choſen to put his name
there be to ferre from the, then thou mayſt kylle of thi
oxen and of thi ſhepe which the Lorde hath geuen the
as I haue commaunded the and thou mayſt eate in thine
awne citie what [Fo. XXV.] ſoeuer thi ſoule luſteth.
22 Neuer the later, as the roo and the herte is eaten, euen
ſo thou ſhalt eate it: the vncleane and the cleane in-
23 differently thou ſhalt eate. But be ſtrong that thou
eate not the bloude. For the bloude, that is the lyfe:

V. 18 Leuites, qui manent (manet, *Complut.*) 20 ſicut locutus
eſt tibi, et volueris veſci carnibus ... 21 locus autem
  𝕷. 18 ſoltu ſolchs eſſen laſſen 20 weyl deyne ſeele fleyſch zu
eſſen geluſtet, ſo iſs fleyſch nach aller luſt deyner ſeele 22 wie man
eyn rehe odder hirs iſſet, ... beyde reyn odder vnreyn mugens
zu gleych eſſen
  𝕸. 𝕸. N. 22 *Eate not the bloude:* By that they ſhulde eate
no bloude is ſygnifyed that they ſhulde abhorre from bloude
ſhedyng, & māquellyng.
  𝕷. 𝕸. N. 21 *So opffere:* Wie ſollen ſie opffern vnd doch nicht
opffern, an iglichem ort? Item, wie ſollen ſie von den zehenden
eſſen &c. ſo fie doch ſolchs den leuiten vnd prieſtern geben
muſten? Antwort, am 14. ca. hernach legt er das aus nemlich
alſo, wenn die ſtett zu fern war, ſo ſolten ſie die zehendē, vnd
alles was, zu opffern war frey eſſen odder verkeuffen vnd zu gelde
machen, vnd dasſelb an den ort bringen, vnd anders ſo viel
keuffen vnd opffern, vnd den prieſtern geben. Drumb mus hie
das wortlin opffern heyſſen, ſo viel als das opffer eſſen, oder mit
gelde gedencken zu uergleychen. Vnd eſſen von den zehenden
odder gelubden ſo viel, als eſſen laſſen, nemlich die prieſter.
Doch iſt mit ſolchen wortten daneben angezeigt, das alles volck
fur Got prieſter ſeyen, wie er ſagt Exo. 19.

24 and thou mayſt not eate the life with the fleſh: thou maiſt not eate it: but muſt power it vppō the erth as
25 water. Se thou eate it not therfore that it maye goo well with the and with thy childern after the, when thou ſhalt haue done that whyche is ryghte in the ſyghte off the Lorde.
26 But thy holye thinges which thou haſt and thy vowes, thou ſhalt take and go vnto the place which
27 the Lorde hath choſen, and thou ſhalt offer thy burnt-offrynges, both fleſh ād bloude apon the alter of the Lorde thy God, and the bloude of thine offrynges thou ſhalt poure out vppon the alter of the Lorde thy God,
28 and ſhalt eate the fleſh. Take hede and heare all theſe wordes which I commaunde the that it maye goo well with the and with thy children after the for euer, whē thou doeſt that whiche is good and right in the ſighte of the Lorde thy God.
29 When the Lorde thy God hath deſtroyed the nacions before the, whother thou goeſt to conquere them, and when thou haſt conque- .¶. red them, and dwelt
30 in their landes: Bewarre that thou be not taken in a ſnare after thē, after that they be deſtroyed before the, and that thou axenot after their goddes ſaynge: how dyd theſe nacyons ſerue their goddes, that I maye doo
31 ſo likewyſe? Nay, thou ſhalt not doo ſo vnto the Lorde thy God: for all abhominacyons which the Lorde hated dyd they vnto their goddes. For they burnt both their ſonnes ād their doughters with fire vnto their
32 goddes. But what ſoeuer I commaunde you that take hede ye do: ād put nought thereto, nor take ought there from.

Put noughte to ner take ought awaye.

V. 23 ſanguis enim eorum pro anima eſt, & idcirco non debes 27 offeres oblationes tuas 28 bonum eſt & placitum 29 diſperdiderit .. poſſidendas, & poſſederis 30 caue ne imiteris eas .. Sicut coluerunt .. ita & ego colam. 32 hoc tātum facito domino.

L. 23 alleyn faſſe ... denn das blut iſt der ſeelen, Darumb ſoltu die ſeele nicht mit dem fleyſch eſſen 26 heyligſt etwas das deyn iſt 28 recht vnd geſellig 30 das du nicht ynn den ſtrick felleſt yhnen nach .. nicht frageſt noch .. Wi diſe volcker haben .. gedienet, alſo wil ich auch thun

M. M. N. 32 Put noughte to nor take ought awaye.

XIII. 1-6. called Deuteronomye. 567

⁋ The .XIII. Chapter.

1 F there aryſe amonge you a prophett or a dreamer of dreames and geue the a ſygne or a wondre, 2 and that ſygne or wonder which he hath ſayed come to paſſe, and then ſaye: lat vs goo after ſtraunge Goddes which thou 3 haſt not knowen, and let vs ſerue them: herken not vnto the wordes of that prophete or dreamer of dreames. For the Lorde thy God tēpteth you, to wete whether ye loue the Lord youre God with all youre hertes ād with al youre ſoules. 4 For ye muſt walke after the Lorde youre God ād feare him and kepe his cōmaū-[Fo. XXVI.] dmentes and herken vnto his voyce and ſerue him and cleaue vnto 5 him. And that prophete or dreamer of dreames ſhall dye for it, becauſe he hath ſpokē to turne you awaye frō the Lorde youre God which broughte you out of the londe of Egipte ād delyuered you out of the houſſe of bondage, to thruſt the out of the waye whiche the Lorde thy God commaunded the to walke in: and ſo thou ſhalt put euell awaye from the.

6 Yf thy brother the ſonne of thy mother or thyne awne ſonne or thy doughter or the wife that lieth in thy boſome or thy frende which is as thyne awne ſoule vnto the, entyce the ſecretly ſayenge: let vs goo and ſerue ſtraunge goddes which thou haſt not knowē nor

M.C.S. The falſſe prophete muſt be put to death. God proueth oure fayth by falſſe myracles.

God geueth vs his worde ād cōfirmeth it with miracles to proue who hath a true herte. we muſt take hede to the ſcripture, leſt falſe prophetes or falſe miracles deceaue vs.

V. 2 & euenerit quod locutus eſt 3 tentat 4 adhærebitis. 5 fictor ſomniorum ... quia locutus eſt vt vos auerteret ... vt errare te faceret de via ... & auferes malum 6 vxor quæ eſt in ſinu tuo, aut amicus quē diligis vt animam tuam
L. 3 verſucht euch 4 Denn .. anhangen. 5 den boſen 6 weyb ynn deynen armen
M. M. N. 3 *For the Lorde thy God tēpteth you, etc:* God geueth vs his worde & confirmeth it with myracles to proue who hath a true herte. We muſt take hede to the ſcripture, leſt falſe prophetes or falſe myracles deceaue vs

7 yet thy fathers, of the goddes of the people whiche are rounde aboute the, whether thei be nye vnto the or farre of from the, from the one ende of the lande vnto
8 the other: Se thou confente not vnto him nor herken vnto him: no let not thyne eye pitye him nor haue
9 compaffyon on hym, nor kepe him fecrett, but caufe him to be flayne: Thine hande fhalbe firft apon hym to
10 kyll him: and then the handes off all the people. And thou fhalt ftone hym with ftones that he dye, becaufe he hath gone .P. aboute to thruft the awaye from the Lord thy God which brought the out of Egipte the
11 houffe of bondage. And all Ifrael fhall heare and feare åd fhall doo no moare any foche wekedneffe as this is, amonge them.

12 Yf thou fhalt heare faye of one of thy cities which
13 the Lorde thy God hath geuen the to dwell in, that certen beyng the childern of Beliall are gone out from amonge you and haue moued the enhabiters of their citie fayeng: lat vs goo and ferue ftraunge Goddes
14 whiche ye haue not knowen. Then feke and make ferche and enquere diligently. Yf it be true and the thinge of a fuertie that foch abhominacion is wrought
15 among you: then thou fhalt fmyte the dwellers of that citie with the edge of the fwerde, and deftroye it mercyleffe and all that is therin, and euen the very
16 catell thereof with the edge of the fwerde. And gather all the fpoyle of it in to the myddes of the ftreates there-

M. 15 deftroye hit 16 fpoyle of hit

V. 7 ab initio vfque ad finem terræ 9 fed ftatim interficies. fit primum manus tua fuper eum, & poft te omnis populus mittat manum. 10 quia voluit te abftrahere 11 & nequaquam vltra faciat quippiam huius rei fimile. 13 et auerterunt habitatores 14 quære folicite, & diligenter ... certum effe quod dicitur 15 ore gladii, & delebis eam, omniaque quæ in illa funt vfque ad pecora 16 quicquid etiam fupellectilis

L. 7 von eym end der erden bis an das ander 10 Denn er fuchte dich auszuftoffen 11 nicht mehr folchs vbel furneme 14 fo foltu wol fuchen, forfchen vnd fragen ... die warheyt das gewis alfo ift 16 raub

M. M. N. 13 *Belial:* Belial by interpretacion fygnifieth malyce, or as fome wyll wyckedneffe, wherfore all myfcheuoufe, wycked and curfed mē that caft the youcke of God of their neckes & wil not obeye God, are called the chyldren of Belial or men of Belial. Iudicū. xix, f. and Regum. i, c.

of, and burne with fire: both the citie and all the spoyle
thereof euery whitte vnto the Lord thy God. And it
shalbe an hepe for euer and shall not be bylt agayne.
17 And se that their cleaue nought of the damned thinge
in thine hande, that the Lorde maye turne frō his fearse
wrath and shewe the mercye ād haue compassion on the
and multiplye the, as he hath sworne vnto [Fo. XXVII.]
18 thy fathers: when thou hast herkened vnto the voyce
of the Lorde thy God, to kepe all his cōmaundmentes
which I cōmaunde the thys daye so that thou doo
that which is right in the eyes of the Lorde thy God.

⁋ The .XIIII. Chapter.

1 YE are the childern of the Lorde youre God, cut not youre selues nor make you any baldnes betwene the eyes for any mās 2 deeth. For thou art an holy people vnto the Lord thy God, ād the Lorde hath chosen the to be a feuerall people vnto him selfe, of all the nacyons that are vppon the erth.

M.C.S. The maners of the gentyles may not befolowed. What beastes are cleane to be eaten & what not.

3, 4 Ye shall eate no maner of abhominacyon. These
are the beestes which ye shall eate of: oxen, shepe and
5 gootes, hert, roo and bugle, hertgoote, vnicorne, origen
6 and Camelion. And all beestes that cleaue the hoffe
and flytte it in to two clawes and chewe the cud, them
7 ye shal eate. Neuertheleffe, these ye shall not eate of

M. 5 bugle wyldegoote, vnicorne
V. 17 de illo anathemate . . . & misereatur tui, multiplicetque
te xiiii, 1 nec facietis caluitiū 2 populum peculiarem 3 immunda
4 Hoc est animal 5 bubalum, tragelaphum, pygargum, orygem,
camelopardalum.
L. 17 von dem grym feyns zorns . . . vnd gebe dyr barmhertzickeyt vnd erbarme sich deyner. xiiii, 1 kalh zwisschen
ewren augen 3 grewel 4 Dis ist aber das viech 5 Hirs, Rehe,
Hemps, Steynbock, Eynhorn, Vrochs, vnd Elend
M. M. N. 1 *Chyldren of the Lorde:* They are here called
the chyldren of the Lorde, becaufe a boue al other people of the
worlde they were Indued with the gyftes and benifites of the
Lorde Psal. xxviii, a.

them that chew cud ād of thē that deuyde and cleaue the hoffe: the camell, the hare ād the conye. For they chew cud, but deuyde not the hoffe: ād ther-
8 fore are vncleane vnto you: ād alfo the fwyne, for though he deuyde the hoffe, yet he cheweth not cud, ād therfor is vncleane vn- .P. to you: Ye fhall not eate of the flefh of thē nor twich the deed carkaffes of them.

9 Thefe ye fhall eate off all that are in the waters: All that haue fynnes and fcales.

10 And what foeuer hath not finnes and fcales, of that ye may not eate, for that is vncleane vnto you.

11, 12 Of all cleane byrdes ye fhall eate, but thefe are they of which ye maye not eate: the egle, the gofhauke,
13 the cormerant, the ixion, the vultur, the kyte and hyr
14, 15 kynde, and all kynde off rauens, the Eftrich, the nyghtcrowe, the kuckoo, the fparowhauke and all hir
16, 17 kynde, the litle oule, the greate oule, the backe, the
18 bytture, the pye the ftorke, the heron, the Iaye in his
19 kynde, the lapwynge, the fwalowe: And all crepynge foules are vncleane vnto you and maye not be eaten
20 of: but of all cleane foules ye maye well eate.

21 Ye fhall eate of nothinge that dyeth alone: But thou mayeft geue it vnto the ftraunger that is in thy citie that he eate it, or mayft fell it vnto an Aliēt. For thou art an holy people vnto the Lorde thy God. Thou fhalt not feth a kyd in his mothers mylke.

22 Thou fhalt tyeth all the encreafe of thy feed that cometh out of the felde yere by yere.

23 And thou fhalt eate before the Lorde thy [Fo. XXVIII.] God in the place whiche he hath chofen to make his name dwell there the tyth off thy corne, of thy wyne and of thyne oyle, and the firftborne of thine

V. 7 chirogryllium 10 quia immunda funt. 12 Immundas ne comedatis 21 Peregrino ... da .. aut vende ei ... Non coques hœdum in lacte matris fuæ. 22 feparabis 23 & comedes
L. 10 denn es ift euch vnreyn. 11 Alle reyne vogel effet 21 dem frembdlingen ynn deynem thor magftus geben .. eym frembden Du folt das bocklin nicht kochen, weyl es noch feyn mutter feuget 22 abfondern 23 vnd folts effen
M. M. N. 21 Sethe a kyd: Loke exod. xxiii, c.

oxen and of thy flocke that thou mayſt lerne to feare the Lorde thy God allwaye.

24 Yf the waye be to longe for the, ſo that thou art not able to carie it, becauſe the place is to farre from the whiche the Lorde thy God hath choſen to ſet his name there (for the Lorde thy God hath bleſſed the)
25 then make it in money and take the money in thyne hande, and goo vnto the place which the Lorde thy
26 God hath choſen, and beſtowe that moneye on what ſoeuer thy ſoule luſteth after: on oxen ſhepe, wyne and good drynke, and on what ſoeuer thy ſoule deſyreth, and eate there before the Lorde thy God and be mery:
27 both thou and thyne houſholde and the Leuite that is in thy cytye. Se thou forſake not the Leuite, for he hath nether parte nor enheritaunce with the.

28 At the ende of thre yere, thou ſhalt brynge forth all the tithes of thine encreaſe the ſame yere and laye
29 it vpp within thyne awne cytye, and the Leuite ſhall come becauſe he hath nether parte nor enheritaunce with the, and the ſtraunger and the fatherleſſe and the wedo- .℣. we which are whithin thy citie and ſhall eate and fyll them ſelues: that the Lorde thy God maye bleſſe the in all the workes of thine hond which thou doeſt.

𝔐. 26 luſteth after: of oxen
℣. 23 omni tempore. 24 elegerit... tibique benedixerit 25 vendes omnia, & in pretium rediges 26 & emes ex eadem pecunia quicquid tibi placuerit... & epulaberis 27 intra portas tuas (v. 29.) 28 ſeparabis... & repones intra ianuas tuas.
𝕷. 23 deyn leben lang. 25 ſo gibs vmb gelt 26 vnd ſey frolich 27 ynn deynem thor (vv. 28, 29) 28 auszihen... vnd ſolts laſſen

The .XV. Chapter.

1 AT the ende of seuen yere thou
2 shalt make a fre yere. And
this is the maner off the fre
yere, whosoeuer lendeth ought
with his hande vnto his neyghboure, maye
not axe agayne that which he hath lent,
of his neyghboure or of his brother: be-
3 cause it is called the lordes fre yere, yet
of a straunger thou maist call it home
agayne. But that which thou hast with
4 thy brother thyne hande shall remytt, and that in any
wyse, that there be no begger amonge you. For the
Lorde shall blesse the lande whiche the Lorde thy God
5 geueth the, an heritaunce to possesse it: so that thou
herken vnto the voyce of the Lorde thy God, to obserue
ãd doo all these commaundmentes which I commaunde
6 you this daye: ye and then the Lorde thy God shall
blesse the as he hath promysed the, and thou shalt
lende vnto many nacyons, and shalt borowe of no
man, and shalt raygne ouer many nacyons, but none
shal reygne ouer the.
7 [Fo. XXIX.] When one of thi brethern amonge you
is waxed poore in any of thi cities within thi lõde which
the Lorde thi God geueth the, se that thou harden not
thine hert nor shetto thyne hande from thi poore bro-
8 ther: But open thyne hand vnto him and lende him
9 sufficient for his nede which he hath. And beware that

M.C.S. The forgeuenes of detles in the seuenth yere. If the Israelites obey God they are promysed that they shall not suffre pouertye. How and after what maner we ought to lende.

M. 2 aske agayne 4 enheritaūce
V. 1 remissionem 2 quæ hoc ordine celebrabitur. Cui debetur aliquid ab amico vel proximo ac fratre suo, repetere non poterit 3 exiges: ciuem & propinquum repetendi non habebis potestatem. 4 omnino indigens, & mendicus ... vt 5 Si tamen ... quæ iussit, & quæ ... præcipio 5 vt pollicitus est. 7 Si vnus ... ad paupertatem deuenerit 8 quo eum indigere perspexeris.
L. 1 Freyiar 2 Also sols aber zugehen .. eynmanen (v. 3) ... denn es heyst 4 Es sol aller dinge keyn ... denn 5 alleyn

there be not a poynte of Belial in thine hert, that thou
woldeſt ſaye. The ſeuenth yere, the yere of fredome is
at honde, and therſore it greue the to loke on thy poore
brother and geueſt him nought and he then crye vnto
10 the Lorde agenſt the and it be ſynne vnto the: But
geue him, and let it not greue thine hert to geue. Becauſe that for that thinge, the Lorde thy God ſhall
bleſſe the in all thi workes and in all that thou putteſt
11 thine hande to. For the londe ſhall neuer be without
poore. Wherſore I cōmaunde the ſayenge: open thine
hande vnto thi brother that is neady ād poore in thy
lande.
12 Yf thi brother an Hebrue ſell him ſelf to the or an
Hebruas, he ſhall ſerue the ſyxe yere and the ſeuenth
13 yere thou ſhalt lett him go fre from the. And when
thou ſendeſt hym out fre from the, thou ſhalt not let
14 him goo awaye emptye: but ſhalt geue him of thy ſhepe
and of thi corne and of thy wyne, and geue him off .*P*
that where with the Lorde thi God hath bleſſed the.
15 And remembre that thou waſt a ſeruaunte in the londe
of Egipte, and the Lorde thi God delyuered the thence:
wherfore I commaunde the this thinge to daye.
16 But and yf he ſaye vnto the, I will not goo awaye
from the, becauſe he loueth the and thine houſſe and
17 is well at eaſe with the. Then take a naule a naule, *an awl*
and nayle his eare too the doore there with ād let him
be thi ſeruaunte foreuer and vnto thi mayde ſeruaunte
18 thou ſhalt doo likewiſe. And let it not greue thine

V. 9 ſubrepat tibi impia cogitatio, & dicas in corde tuo ... &
auertas oculos tuos (18) .. clamet contra te 10 nec ages quippiam
callide in eius neceſſitatibus ſubleuandis ... ad quæ manum miſeris. 12 Hebræus aut Hebræa 14 ſed dabis viaticum 15 & liberauerit
te 17 & perforabis aurem eius

L. 9 eyn Belial tuck ſey, das da ſprech ... vnd ſiheſt deynen
... vnfreuntlich an 10 ſondern du ſolt yhm geben vnd deyn hertz
nicht verdriſſen laſſen, das du yhm gibſt 12 Ebreer odder Ebreeryn
17 bore yhm durch ſeyn ohr an der thur 18 Vnd las dichs nicht
ſchwer duncken

M. M. N. 9 *A poynte of Belial in thine herte:* A poynt of
Belial here for the wycked and frowarde councell of Belial.
17 *Then take a naule and nayle, etc:* The entent of this lawe is
to cauſe thē to abhorre bōdage wherunto this open ſhame ſhulde
dryue them for God wyll not that the loue of any man ſhulde be
dearer vnto hym then lybertye.

eyes to lett him goo out from the, for he hath bene worthe a double hired feruaunte to the in his feruyce vi. yeres. And the Lorde thi God fhall bleffe the in all that thou doeft.

19 All the firftborne that come of thine oxen and of thi fhepe that are males, thou fhalt halowe vnto the Lorde thi God. Thou fhalt do no feruyce with the firftborne
20 of thi fhepe: but fhalt eate thē before the Lorde thi God yere by yere in the place which the Lorde hath chofen both thou and thine houffholde.
21 Yf there be any deformyte there in, whether it be lame or blinde or what foeuer euell fauerednesse it hath,
22 thou fhalt not offer it vnto the Lorde thi God: But fhalt eate it in thine awne citie, the vncleane and the cleane in- [Fo. XXX.] differently, as the roo and the
23 hert. Only eate not the bloude there of, but poure it vppon the grounde as water.

V. 18 quoniam iuxta mercedem mercennarii 19 deo tuo. Non operaberis in primogenito bouis, & non tondebis primogenita ouium. 21 aut in aliqua parte deforme vel debile 22 tam mundus quam immundus fimiliter vefcentur eis

L. 18 denn er hat dyr als eyn zwiffeltig tagloner 19 heyligen. Du folt nicht ackern mit dem erftling deyner ochfen, vnd nicht befcheren die erfthling deyner fchaff 21 odder fonft yrgen eyn bofen feyl 22 fondern ynn deynem thor foltu es effen (du feyft vnreyn oder reyn)

M. M. N. 22 *The vncleane and the cleane indifferētly*, etc.: Or whether thou be cleane or vncleane, & lyke wyfe in the .xii chapter b, and c. In the Hebrue it is indifferēt in al thefe places, to aplye the cleanes or vncleanes to the perfon that eateth it, or to the beaft that is eaten.

¶ The .XVI. Chapter.

1 OBSERUE the moneth of Abyb, and offer paſſeover vnto the Lorde thi God. For in the moneth of Abib, the Lorde thy God brought the out of Egipte by nyght. *M.C.S. Of Eaſter, whytſontyde, & the feaſt of tabernacles. what offycers ought to be ordeyned.*

2 Thou ſhalt therfore offer paſſeover vnto the Lorde thi God, and ſhepe and oxen in the place which the
3 Lorde ſhall choſe to make his name dwell there. Thou ſhalt eate no leueded bred there with: but ſhalt eate there with the bred of tribulaciō .vii. dayes lōge. For thou cameſt out of the lōde of Egipte in haſt, that tḧou mayſt remembre the daye when thou cameſt out of
4 the londe of Egipte, all dayes of thi life. And ſe that there be no leuended bred ſene in all thi coſtes .vii dayes longe, and that there remayne nothinge of the fleſh which thou haſt offered the fyrſt daye at euen, vntil the mornynge.

5 Thou mayſt not offer paſſeover in any of thi cities
6 which the Lord thi god geueth the: But in the place which the Lorde thi God ſhall choſe to make his name dwell in, there thou .P. ſhalt offer Paſſeouer at euen aboute the goyngdoune of the ſonne, euen in the
7 ſeaſon that thou cameſt out of Egipte. And thou ſhalt ſeth and eate in the place which the Lorde thi God hath choſen, and departe on the morowe and
8 gette the vnto thi tente. Sixe dayes thou ſhalt eate

V. 1 menſem nouarum frugum, & verni primū temporis... in iſto menſe 2 de ouibus 3 Non comedes in eo .. abſque fermento, afflictionis panem .. in pauore egreſſus 4 immolatum 5 immolare .. phaſe .. daturus eſt 7 maneque conſurgens vades
L. 1 bey der nacht 2 Vnd ſolt ... zu Oſtern opffern 3 vngefeuerts brod deyns elends 5 Oſtern opffern (v. 6) 7 vnd darnach dich wenden des morgens vnd heym gehen
M. M. N. 1 *Abib:* Abib, that is of apryll, when all thynges do ſprynge of freaſſhe Exod. xxiii, b.

fwete bred, and the feuenth daye is for the people to come together to the Lorde thi God, that thou mayſt do no worke.

9 Then reken the .vii. wekes, and begynne to rekē the .vii. wekes when the fyccle begynneth in the corne, 10 and kepe the feaſt of wekes vnto the Lorde thi God, that thou geue a frewilofferinge of thine hāde vnto the Lord thi God acordinge as the Lorde thi God hath 11 bleſſed the. And reioyſe before the Lorde thi God both thou, thi ſonne, thi doughter, thi feruaunte and thi mayde, and the leuite that is within thi gates, and the ſtraunger, the fatherleſſe ād the wedowe that are amonge you, in the place which the Lorde thi God 12 hath choſen to make his name dwel there. And remēbre that thou waſt a feruaūte in *why.* Egipte, that thou obſerue and doo theſe ordinaunces. 13 · Thou ſhalt obſerue the feaſt of tabernacles .vii. dayes longe, after that thou haſt gathered in thi corne and 14 thi wyne. And thou ſhalt reioyſe in that thi feaſt, both thou and thi ſonne, [Fo. XXXI.] thi doughter, thi feruaunte, thi mayde, the leuite, the ſtraunger, the fatherleſſe and the wedowe that are in thi cities. 15 Seuen dayes thou ſhalt kepe holy daye vnto the Lorde thi God, in the place which the Lorde ſhal choſe: for the Lorde thi God ſhall bleſſe the in all thi frutes and in all the workes of thine handes, and thou 16 ſhalt be all together gladneſſe. Thre tymes in the yere ſhall al youre males appere before the Lorde thi God in the place which he ſhal choſe: In the feaſt of

𝔐. 15 handes, & therfore ſhalt thou be glad.
𝔙. 8 collecta eſt domini 9 Sept. hebd. numerabis tibi ab ea die qua falcem in ſegetem miſeris 10 diem feſtum hebdomadarum 11 & epulaberis (v. 14) 12 cuſtodieſque ac facies quæ præcepta funt. 14 feſtiuitate tua 15 erifque in lætitia.
𝔏. 8 die ſteur 9 zelen, vnd an heben zu zehlen 11 frölich ſeyn (v. 14) 12 haltiſt vnd thuſt nach diſen ſitten. 15 das feſt halten 16 erwelet hat
𝔐. 𝔐. N. 11 *Gates:* By gates is oft tymes vnderſtande cytyes Iuriſdycyon rule and gouernaunce as in this ſame chapter beneth in d. (v. 18).

fwete bred, in the feaſt of wekes and in the booth feaſt. And they ſhal not appere before the Lorde emptie:
17 but euery mā with the gifte of his honde, acordynge to the bleſſinge of the Lorde thi God, which he hath geuen the.

The .XVII. Chapter.

18 **I**VDGES and officers thou ſhalt make the in all thi cities which the Lorde thi God geueth the thorow out thi trybes. and lett *Iudges.* thē iudge the people right-
19 eouſly. Wreſt not the lawe nor knowe any perſone nether take any rewarde: for giftes blynde the wiſe and peruerte the
20 wordes of the righteous. But in all thinge folowe righteouſneſſe, that thou mayſt lyue and enioye the londe which the Lord thi God geueth the.

M.C.S. The payne and punyſhement for Idolatrie. The doutefull ſentence muſt be referred vnto the greate Iudges. The punyſhement of a rebeller or preſumptuouſe withſtander of the lawe. The Inſtitucyon of a Kynge.

21 .¶. Thou ſhalt plante no groue of what ſoeuer trees it be, nye vnto the altare of the Lorde thi God which
22 thou ſhalt make the. Thou ſhalt fett the vpp no piler,
XVII, 1 which the Lorde thy God hateth. Thou ſhalt offer vnto the Lorde thy God no oxe or ſhepe where in is any deformyte, what ſoeuer euell fauerednefſe it be: for that is an abhominacion vnto the Lorde thi God.
2 Yf there be founde amonge you in any of thi cities

M. 16 feaſt *of tabernacles (* Margin, see below. This chapter ends in Matthew's Bible as in the Authorized Version; v. 17 of the latter is the last verse of Ch. xvi. in Tyndale).' xvii, 2 the cytyes
V. 18 Iudices & magiſtros 19 nec in alteram partem declinent. ... excæcant oculos ... mutant verba 20 Iuſte quod iuſtum eſt, perſequeris. xvii, 1 macula aut quippiā vitii
L. 18 richten mit rechtem gericht 19 Du ſolt das recht nicht beugen ... verleytten die rechten ſachen 20 Was recht iſt dem ſoltu nach iagen. xvii, 1 etwas boſes
M. M. N. 16 *Of tabernacles:* Or bothes. 18 Iudges.

which the Lord thi God geueth the man or woman that hath wrought wekedneſſe in the ſighte of the Lord thi God, that they haue gone beyonde his appoynt-
3 ment, ſo that they haue gone and ſerued ſtraūge goddes ād worſhipped thē, whether it be the ſonne or mone or
4 any thinge contayned in heauē which I forbade, and it was tolde the ād thou haſt herde of it: Then thou ſhalt enquere diligently.

And yf it be true and the thinge of a ſuertye that
5 ſoch abhomynacion is wrought in Iſrael, thē thou ſhalt bringe forth that mā or that woman whiche haue cō-mytted that weked thinge, * vnto thi gates ād ſhalt ſtone thē with ſtones ād they ſhall
6 dye. At the mouth of .ii. or .iii. witneſſes ſhal he that is worthy of deeth, dye: but at the mouth of one witneſſe he ſhall not
7 dye. And the handes of the witneſſes ſhalbe fi- [Fo. XXXII.] rſt vppon hym to kyll him, ād afterwarde the handes of all the people: ſo ſhalt thou put weked-neſſe awaye from the.

Opinly in the gates and not ſecretlye in preſon: with lawfull witneſſe and not torment-ynge them or makēge them ſwer agenſt thē ſelues or forſwere thē ſelues.

8 Yſ a matter be to harde for the in iudgemēt be-twene bloud and bloude, plee and plee, plage and plage in maters of ſtrife within thi cities: Then Ariſe and gett the vpp vnto the place which the Lorde thi
9 God hath choſen, and goo vnto the preaſtes the leuites and vnto the iudge that ſhalbe in thoſe dayes, and axe,
10 and they ſhall ſhewe the how to iudge. And ſe that

𝔐. 5 vnto the gates 9 dayes, and aſke

𝒱. 2 malum 3 omnem militiam cæli, quæ non præcepi 4 in-quiſieris diligenter 5 et lapidibus obruentur. 6 peribit qui inter-ficietur 7 vt auferas malum de medio tui (v. 12). 8 Si difficile & ambiguū ... lepram & non lepram, & iudicum intra portas tuas videris verba variari 9 qui indicabunt tibi iudicii veritatem.

𝔏. 2 vbels thut 3 yrgent eyn heer des hymels, das ich nicht gepotten habe 5 vnd ſolt ſie zu todt ſteynigen 7 das du den boſen von dyr thueſt (v. 12). 8 zwiſſchen plage vnd plage, vnd was zen-kiſche ſachen ſind ynn deynen thoren 9 die ſollen dyr das vrteyl ſprechen

𝔐. 𝔐. N. 5 *Vnto the gates:* Opēly in the gates & not ſe-cretly in preſon With lawful witneſſe and not tormentinge them or makynge thē ſwere agaynſt them ſelues or forſwere them ſelues.

thou doo acordinge to that which they of that place which the Lorde hath chofen fhew the and fe that thou obferue to doo acordinge to all that they enforme the.

11 Acordinge to the lawe which they teach the and maner of iudgement which they tell the, fe that thou doo and that thou bowe not from that which they fhewe the, nether to the right hande nor to the lyfte.

12 And that man that will doo prefumptuously, fo that he will not herken vnto the preaft that ftondeth there to myniftre vnto the Lorde thi God or vnto the iudge, fhall dye: and fo thou fhalt put awaye euell from Ifrael.

13 And all the people fhall heare and fhall feare, and fhall doo nomare prefumptuofly,

14 .¶. When thou art come vnto the lōde which the Lorde thi God geueth the and enioyeft it and dwelleft therin: Yf thou fhalt faye, I will fett a kinge ouer *kynges.* me, like vnto all the nacions that are aboute me:

15 Then thou fhalt make him kinge ouer the, whom the Lorde thi God fhal chofe. One of thi brethern muft thou make kinge ouer the, and mayft not fett a ftraunger

16 ouer the which is not of thi brethern. But in ani wyfe let hi not holde to many horffes, that he bringe not the people agayne to Egipte thorow the multitude of horffes, for as moch as the Lorde hath fayed vnto you: ye fhall

17 hence forth goo no moare agayne that waye. Alfo he fhall not haue to many wyues, left his hert turne awaye, nether fhall he gather him fyluer and golde to moch.

18 And when he is feten vppon the feate off his

𝔐. 18 And when he is fett
V. 11 iuxta legem eius, fequerisque fententiam eorum, nec declinabis 12 Qui autem fuperbierit ... ex decreto iudicis 13 vt nullus deinceps intumefcat fuperbia. 14 poffederis eam, habitauerifque in illa 15 Non poteris alterius gentis hominem regem facere, qui non fit frater tuus. 16 Cumque fuerit conftitutus ... equitatus numero fubleuatus ... vt nequaquam amplius per eandem viam reuertamini. 17 quæ alliciant animum eius
L. 10 nach allem das fie dich leren werden 11 foltu dich halten ... nicht abweycheft 12 vermeffen handeln ... ampt ftehet 14 nymeft es eyn vnd woneft drynnen 16 nicht viel roffer halte ... vmb der roffe menge willen ... fort nicht widder durch difen weg komen folt 17 das feyn hertze nicht abgewand werde
𝔐. 𝔐. N. 14 Kynges.

kingdome, he ſhall write him out this ſeconde lawe in a boke takynge a copye of the preaſtes the leuites. 19 And it ſhalbe with him and he ſhall reade there in all dayes of his lyfe that he maye lerne to feare the Lorde his God for to kepe all the wordes *
20 of this lawe ād theſe ordinaunces for to doo them: that his hert aryſe not aboue his brethern and that he turne not from the commaundment: ether to the righte hande or to the lifte: that both he ād his [Fo. XXXIII.] childern maye prolonge their dayes in his kingdome in Iſrael.

¶ The .XVIII. Chapter.

1 THE preaſtes the Leuites all the trybe off Leui ſhall haue no parte nor enheritaunce with Iſrael. The offrynges of the Lorde ād his enheritaunce 2 they ſhall eate, but ſhall haue no enheritaunce amonge their brethern: the Lorde he is their enheritaunce, as he 3 hath ſayed vnto them. And this is the dutie of the preaſtes, of the people and of them that offer, whether it be oxe or ſhepe: They muſt geue vnto the preaſt, the ſhulder and the two chekes and the 4 maw, the firſtfrutes of thy corne, wyne and oyle, and the firſt of thy ſhepeſheryng muſt thou geue 5 him. For the Lorde thy God hath choſen him out

Marginal notes:

I meruel that oure diſſigured coude make no figure of this all this while.

M.E.S. The Leuytes myght haue no poſſeſſyons. Idolatrye muſt be fledde. The prophet Chryſt is promyſed. The falſe prophet muſt be ſlayne, & how he may be knowē.

V. 18 deſcribet ſibi Deuteronomium legis huius in volumine, accipiens exemplar a ſacerdotibus Leuiticæ tribus 19 & ceremonias eius quæ in lege præcepta ſunt. 20 in ſuperbiam ſuper fratres ſuos . . . vt . . regnet ipſe & filii eius ſuper Iſrael. xviii, 1 quia 3 Hoc erit iudicium ſacerdotum
   L. 18 alle wort diſes geſetzs vnd diſe ſitten 20 auff ſeynem konigreych. xviii, 3 das recht der prieſter

of all thy trybes to ſtonde and to miniſtre in the name of the Lorde: both hī and his ſonnes for euer.

6 Yf a Leuite come out of any of thy cities or any place of Iſrael, where he is a ſegeorner, ād come with all the luſt of his herte vnto the place which the Lorde
7 hath choſen: he ſhall there miniſtre in the name of the Lorde his god as all his brethern the Leuites doo
8 whiche ſtonde there before the Lord. And they ſhall haue lyke porcyons to eate, beſyde that whiche cometh to hym of the patrimonye of hys .P. elders.

9 When thou art come in to the londe which the Lorde thy God geueth the, ſe that thou lerne not to
10 doo after the abhominacyōs of theſe nacyons. Let there not be founde amonge you that maketh his ſonne or his doughter go thorow fyre, ether   bruterar, a bruterar or a maker of diſmale dayes or *murmurer* diſmale dayes,
11 that vſeth witchcraft or a ſorcerar or a *unlucky days* charmar or that ſpeaketh with a ſpirite or a ſothſayer
12 or that talketh with them that are deed. For all that doo ſoch thinges are abhominacion vnto the Lorde: and becauſe of theſe abhominacyons the Lorde thy
13 God doeth caſt them out before the, be pure therfore
14 with the Lorde thy God. For theſe nacyons whiche thou ſhalt conquere, herken vnto makers off dyſemall dayes and bruterars.

𝔐. 5 all the trybes 10 ſonne or daughter to go thorow the fyre, or that vſeth withcraft, or a choſer oute of dayes or that regardeth the flyēg of ſoules, or a ſorcerar 11 or a charmar, or that counceleth with ſpretes, or a propheciar or that aſketh the aduyſe of the deed. 14 herken vnto choſers oute of dayes and prophecyars.

V. 6 deſyderans locum 8 ex paterna ei ſucceſſione debetur. 9 dabit . . . ne imitari velis 10 qui luſtret . . . ducens per ignem: aut qui ariolos ſciſcitetur, & obſeruet ſomnia atque auguria. nec ſit maleficus, 11 nec incātator, neque qui pythones conſulat, nec diuinos, & quærat a mortuis veritatē. 12 delebit eos in introitu tuo. 13 perfectus eris & abſque macula 14 tu autem . . aliter inſtitutus es.

𝕷. 6 vnd kompt nach aller luſt ſeyner ſeele 8 on was er hat von dem verkaufften gutt ſeyner veter. 9 geben wirt 10 odder eyn weyſſager, odder eyn tage weler, odder der auff vogel geſchrey achte, odder zeuberer, 11 odder beſchwerer, odder warſager, odder eyn zeychen deutter, odder der die todten frage. 13 on wandel

𝔐. 𝔐. N. 10 *Withcrafte:* Or arte magyke. *Choſer oute of dayes:* Some that haue regarde to tymes. 11 *Aſketh the aduyſe of the deed:* They aſke ẏ aduyſe of ẏ deed that cōiure ſprytes in the nyght thinckyng that they are ſoules departed

But the Lorde thy God permytteth not that to the.
15 The Lorde thy God will fterre vpp a prophete amonge you: euē of thy brethern like vnto me: and
16 vnto him ye fhall herken acording to all that thou defyredeft of the Lorde thy god in Horeb in the daye when the people were gathered fayenge: Let me heare the voyce of my Lorde God nomoare nor fe *Chrift is here promyfed a preacher off better tydinges then Mofes.*
17 this greate fire any moare, that I dye not. And the
18 Lorde fayed vnto me: they haue well fpoken, I will [Fo. XXXIIII.] rayfe them vpp a prophett from amonge their brethern like vnto the ād will put my wordes in to his mouth and he fhall fpeake vnto thē al that I
19 fhall commaunde him. And whofoeuer will not herken vnto the wordes which he fhall fpeake in my name, I will requyre it off him.
20 But the prophete which fhall prefume to fpeake ought in my name which I commaunded him not to fpeake, and he that fpeaketh in the name of ftraunge
21 Goddes, the fame prophete fhall dye. And yf thou faye in thine hert, howe fhall I knowe that whiche
22 the Lorde hath not fpoken? When a prophete fpeaketh in the name of the Lorde, yf the thynge folow not nor come to paffe, that is the thinge which the Lorde hath not fpoken. But the prophete hath fpoken it prefumptuoufly: be not aferde therfore of him.

𝔐. 20 commaunded not to fpeake
𝔙. 15 de gente tua & de fratribus tuis 16 quando contio congregata eft 17 Bene omnia funt locuti 19 ego vltor exiftam. 21 fi tacita cogitatione 22 hoc habebis fignum: ... fed per tumorem animi fui propheta confinxit, & idcirco
𝔏. 14 nicht alfo ftellen dem Herrn 16 am tage der verfamlung 19 von dem wil ichs fuchen. 20 vermeffen 22 mit vermeffenheyt geredt, darumb
𝔐. 𝔐. N. 15 Chrift is here promyfed a preacher of better tydynges then Mofes.
𝔏. 𝔐. N. 15 Hie wirt klerlich eyn ander predigt verheyffen denn Mofes predigt, wilche kan nicht das gefetze feyn, das gnugfam durch Mofe geben, drum mus es das Euangelion feyn, Vnd difer prophet niemant denn Ihefus Chriftus felbs der folch newe predigt auff erden hat bracht.

⁋ The .XIX. Chapter.

1 WHEN the Lorde thy God hath deſtroyed the nacyons whoſe londe the Lorde thy God geueth the, and thou haſt conquered thē and dwelleſt in their cities and in their houſſes: thou ſhalt appoynte .iii. cities in the lande whiche the Lorde thy God geueth the to .P. poſſeſſe

M.C.S. The fraunchefed townes. The punyſhement of hym that beareth falſe wytneſſe.

3 it: thou ſhalt prepare the waye and deuyde the coſtes of thy lande whiche the Lorde thy God geueth the to enheret, in to .iii. partes that whoſoeuer committeth murthur may flee thither.

4 And this is the cauſe of the ſleyer that ſhal flee thither and be ſaued: Yf he ſmyte his neghboure ignorantly and hated him

5 not in tyme paſſed: As when a man goeth vnto the wodd with his neghboure to hew wod, and as his hāde fetcheth a ſtroke with the axe, the head ſlippeth from the helue and ſmyteth his neghboure that he dye: the ſame ſhall flee vnto one off the ſame cities ād be ſaued.

The popiſ ſetuaries are of an other purpoſe. For he had leuer haue the frenſhep of the euel, thē to ſaue them that are Good.

6 Leſt the executer of bloude folowe after the ſleyer while his hert is whote and ouertake him, becauſe

---

V. 2 ſeparabis tibi 3 ſternens diligenter viam 4 Hæc erit lex homicidæ fugientis ... neſciens, & qui heri & nudiuſtertius nullum contra eum odium habuiſſe comprobatur 5 ferrumque lapſum de manubrio .. ad vnam ſupradictarum vrbium 6 dolore ſtimulatus

L. 2 ausſondern 4 Vnd das ſol die ſach ſeyn ... vnwiſſend, vnd hat vorhyn keyn haſs auff yhn gehabt 5 das eyſen ſure vom ſtiel 6 der blut recher dem todſchleger nach iage, weyl ſeyn hertz erhitzt iſt

M. M. N. 4 *If he ſmyte, etc.:* Here are ſhewed .ii. maner of māquellyng one done wyllyngly & of ſet purpoſe, the other vnwyllinglye: for euē he that kylleth with the hande maye before God be no māquellare: and agayne he that is angrye and enuyeth althoughe he kyll not wyth the hāde, cānot but be a manſlear before God: becauſe he wylleth hys neyghboure euyll. As it is ſayde .i. Iohan .iii, c.

the waye is longe, and flee him, and yet there is no caufe worthy of deeth in him, in as moch as he hated not his neghbour in tyme paffed. *As hate maketh the dead euell: fo love maketh it good.*

7 Wherfore I commaunde the fayeng: fe that thou appoynte out .iii. cities

8 And yf the Lorde thy God enlarge thy coftes as he hath fworne vnto thy fathers and geue the all the londe which he fayed he wold geue vnto

9 thy fathers (fo that thou kepe all thefe commaundmentes to doo them, which I commaunde the this daye, that thou loue the Lord thy god ād walke in his wayes euer) then thou [Fo. XXXV.] fhalt adde .iii

10 cities moo vnto thofe .iii. that innocent bloude be not fhed in thi lande which the Lorde thy God geueth the to enheret, and fo bloude come vppon the,

11 But and yf there be any man that hateth his neyghboure and layeth awayte for him and ryfeth agenft him and fmyteth him that he dye, and fleeth vnto any of

12 thefe cities. Then let the elders of his citie fende and fetche him thence and delyuer him in to the hondes

13 of the iuftice of bloude, and he fhall dye, Let thyne eye haue no pitie on him, and fo thou fhalt put awaye innocent bloude from Ifrael, and happie arte thou.

14 Thou fhalt not remoue thy neghbours marke which they of olde tyme haue fett in thyne enheritaunce that thou enheretteft in the londe which the Lorde thy God geueth the to enioye it.

15 One witneffe fhall not ryfe agenft a man in any maner trefpace or fynne, what foeuer fynne a man fynneth: But at the mouthe of two witneffes or of .iii. witneffes fhall all maters be tryed. *Yee in all mater of herefie agenft holye churche:*

16 Yf an vnrighteous witneffe ryfe vp agenft a man to

𝒱. 6 qui non eft reus mortis:.. contra eum qui occifus eft, odium... monftratur. 8 quam eis pollicitus eft 9 omni tempore ... et fupradict. trium vrbium numerum duplicabis 10 ne fis fanguinis reus. 12 de loco effugii .. proximi, cuius fanguis effufus eft 13 Non mifereberis eius .. vt bene fit tibi. 15 ftabit omne verbum.

𝔏. 6 fo doch keyn vrteyl des todts an yhm ift 7 ausfonderft. 8 geredt hat 9 deyn leben lang 10 vnd kome blut auff dich. 12 des blut rechers 13 deyn augen follen feyn nicht verfchonen (v. 21) .. das dyrs wol gehe. 15 fol alle fache beftehen. 16 eyn freueler zeuge

17 accuse him of trespace: then let both the men which stryue together stonde before the Lorde, before the preastes and the iudges .⁋. which shalbe in those dayes,
18 and let the iudges enquyre a good. And yf the witnesse be founde false and that he hath geuen false witnesse agenst his *a good, in good earnest, thoroughly*
19 brother thē shall ye do vnto hī as he had thought to do vnto his brother, and so thou shalt put euel away
20 frō the. And other shal heare ād feare ād shal hēceforth comytt no more any soch wekednesse amōg you.
21 And let thyne eye haue no compassiō, but life for life, eye for eye, toth for toth, hande for hand, and sote for sote.

⁋ The .XX. Chapter

1 WHEN thou goest out to batayle agenst thine enemyes, and seest horses and charettes and people moo then thou, be not aferde of them, for the Lorde thy God is with the whiche broughte the out of the
2 londe off Egipte. And when ye are come nye vnto batayle, let the preast come forth and speake
3 vnto the people and saye vnto them: Heare Israel, ye are come vnto batayle agenste youre enemyes, let not youre hartes faynte, nether feare nor be amased nor a dreade of them.
4 For the Lorde thy God goeth with you to fyghte for you agenste youre enemyes and to saue you.

M.C.S. Who ought to go to battel. The Lawe of Armes amonge the Israelites. The Canaanytes must they kyll.

𝒱. 18 Cumque diligentissime perscrutantes 19 & auferes malum de medio tui 20 talia audeant facere. 21 Non misereberis eius, sed . . . exiges. xx, 1 ad bellum . . . equitatus & currus, & maiorem quam tu habeas, aduersarii exercitus multitudinem 2 prælio, stabit sac. ante aciem 4 contra aduersarios dimicabit, vt eruat vos de periculo.

L. 18 wol forschen 19 das bose von dyr weg thust 20 solche bose stuck furnemen zu thun. xx, 1 ynn eyn krieg . . . ross vnd wagen des volcks das grosser sey, denn du 2 zum streyt 3 furcht euch nicht, vnd zappelt nicht

5 And let the officers speake vnto the peo‑ [Fo. XXXVI.] ple sayenge: Yf any man haue bylt a new housse and haue not * dedicate it, let him 6 goo and returne to his housse lest he dye in the batayle, and another dedicate it. And yf any man haue planted a vyneyarde and haue not made it comen *, let him goo and returne agayne vnto his house, lest he dye in the batayle and another make it comen. And 7 yf any man be betrothed vnto a wyfe and haue not taken hyr, let hym goo and returne agayne vnto his housse, lest he dye in the batayle and another take her.

Dedicat: the leuites I suppose, halowed thē as we doo oure shippes.

Comē: the iii. first yeres the frute myghte not be eatē the fourth it might be offred ād the fifte eaten ād that ys to make it comē to bringe it to the vsse of the laye people.

8 And let the officers speake further vnto the people and saye. Yf any man feare and be faynte herted, let him goo and returne vnto his housse, lest his brothers 9 hert be made faynte as well as his. And when the officers haue made an ende off speakynge vnto the people, let thē make captaynes of warre ouer them.

10 When thou comest nye vnto a citie to fight agenst 11 it, offre them peace. And yf they answere the agayne peasably, and open vnto the, then let all the people that is founde therein be tributaries vnto the and serue 12 the. But and yf they will make no peace with the, then make warre agenste the citie and besege it.

13 .P. And when the Lord thy God hath delyuered it in to thine handes, smyte all the males thereof with

V. 6 fecit eam esse communem, & de qua vesci omnibus liceat? ... & alius homo eius fungatur officio. 8 sicut ipse timore perterritus est. 9 siluerint duces exercitus ... vnusquisque suos ad bellandum cuneos præparabit. 10 offeres ei primum pacem. 11 Si receperit ... saluabitur, & seruiet tibi sub tributo. 12 sin autem fœdus inire noluerit, & cœperit contra te bellum

L. 5 die heubtleut sollen mit dem volck reden 6 noch nicht gemeyn gemacht 8 seyner brüder hertz seyg mache wie sein hertz ist. 9 die heubtleut ... sollen sie die vbirsten des heers fur das volck an die spitzen stellen. 11 Antworttet sie dyr fridelich ... dyr zinsbar vnd vnterthan seyn. 12 Wil sie aber nicht fridelich mit dyr handeln, vnd wil mit dyr kriegen

M. M. N. 5 *Dedicat:* Same note as in Tyndale. 6 *Comē.* Same note as in Tyndale.

14 the edge of the fwerde, faue the wemē and the childern and the catell and all that is in the citie and all the fpoyle thereof take vnto thy felfe and eate the fpoyle of thyne enemies which the Lord thy God geueth the.
15 Thus thou fhalt doo vnto all the cities whiche are a greate waye of from the ād not of the cities of thefe nacions.
16 But in the cities of thefe nacions which the Lorde thy God geueth the to enheret, thou fhalt faue alyue
17 nothinge that bretheth. But fhalt deftroye them with out redempcion, both the Hethites, the Amorites, the Cananites, the Pherezites, the Heuites and the Iebufites, as the Lorde thy God hath commaunded the,
18 that they teach you not to doo after all their abhominacyons whiche they doo vnto theire goddes, and fo fhulde fynne agenft the Lorde youre God
19 When thou haft befeged a citie longe tyme in makinge warre agenft it to take it. deftroye not the trees thereof, that thou woldeft thruft an axe vnto them. For thou mayft eate of thē, and therfore deftroye them not. For the trees of the feldes are no men, that they
20 myght come agenft the to befege the. Neuerthelater thofe [Fo. XXXVII.] trees which thou knoweft that mē eate not of them, thou maift deftroye and cutte them doune and make bolwerkes agenft the citie that maketh warre with the, vntyll it be ouerthrowne.

V. 14 Omnem prædam exercitui diuides .. de fpoliis 15 & non funt de his vrbibus quas in poffeffionem accepturus es. 17 fed interficies in ore gladii 19 nec fecuribus per circūitum debes vaftare regionem . . . nec poteft bellantium contra te augere numerum. 20 non funt pomifera, fed agreftia & in cæteros apta vfus, fuccide & inftrue machinas

L. 14 allen raub foltu vnter dich austeylen . . . von der ausbeut 15 vnd nicht hie von den ftedten find difer völcker. 17 fondern folt fie verbannen 19 daß du mit exten dran farift . . . Ifts doch holtz auff dem feld . . . vnd kan nicht zum bolwerg komen widder dich. 20 bolwerg draus bawen.

⁋ The .XXI. Chapter.

1 YF one be founde flayne in the land whiche the Lorde thy God geueth the to poffeffe it, and lieth in the feldes, and
2 not knowne who hath flayne him: Then let thine elders and thy iudges come forth åd meet vnto the cities that are rounde
3 aboute the flayne. And let the elders of that citie which is nexte vnto the flayne mã, take an heyffer that is not laboured
4 with nor hath drawen in the iocke, and let them bringe her vnto a valeye where is nether earinge nor fowenge, ãd ftrike of hir heed there in the valey.

M.C.S. The purgacion of hym that is founde deed & is not knowen how he was flayne. How we ought to take to wyfe her that is takē in warre. The ryght of the fyrft begotten. The punyfhment of the fonne that is dyfobedyent to hys father and mother.

5 Then let the preaftes the fonnes of Leui come forth (for the Lorde thy God hath chofen them to miniftre and to bleffe in the name off the Lorde and therfore at
6 their mouthe fhall all ftrife and plage be tryed). And all the elders of the citie that is nexte to the flayne man fhall waffhe their handes ouer the heyffer that is
7 beheded in the playne, and fhall anfwere ãd faye: oure handes haue not fhed this bloude ne- .⁋. ther haue oure
8 eyes fene it. Be mercifull Lord vnto thy people Ifrael which thou haft delyuered and put not innocent bloude vnto thy people Ifrael: and the bloude fhalbe forgeuen

V. 2 & metientur a loco cadaueris fingularum per circumitum fpatia ciuitatum 3 quæ non traxit iugum, nec terram fcidit vomere 4 vallem afperam et faxofam, quæ nunquam arata eft, nec fementem recepit 5 & ad verbum eorum omne negotium pendet: & quicquid mundum vel immundum eft, iudicetur. 7 & dicent 8 Et auferetur ab eis reatus fanguinis

L. 2 vnd von dem erfchlagenen meffen an die ftedte die vmbherliegen 3 da mit man nicht geerbeyttet hat, noch am ioch gezogen hat 4 ynn eynen kiefichten grund, der widder geerbeytet noch befeet ift 5 nach yhrem mund follen alle fach vnd alle plage gehandelt werden 7 vnd follen antwortten vnd fagen 8 So werden fie vber dem blut verfunet feyn

9 thē And fo fhalt thou put innocent bloud frō the, when thou fhalt haue done that which is right in the fyght of the Lorde. *Right in the lordes fighte, ād not in thyne*
10 When thou goeft to warre agenft thyne *imaginacion.* enemies and the Lorde thy God hath delyuered them in to thine handes and thou haft take them captyue,
11 and feift amonge the captyues a bewtifull woman and haft a fantafye vnto her that thou woldeft *fantafye, lik-*
12 haue her to thy wyfe. Then bringe her *ing, fondnefs* home to thine houffe and let her fhaue hir heed and
13 pare hir nayles ād put hir rayment that fhe was taken in from hir, and let hir remayne in thine houffe and be wepe hir father and hir mother a moneth long and after that goo in vnto her ād marie her ād let her be
14 thi wife. And yf thou haue no fauoure vnto her, then let her go whother fhe lufteth: for thou mayft not fell her for monye nor make cheuefaūce of her, *cheuefaunce,* becaufe thou haft hūbled her. *bargain*

15 Yf a man haue two wyues, one loued and a nother hated, and they haue borne him children, both the loued and alfo the hated. Yf the firftborne be the fonne of the
16 hated: then whē [Fo. XXXVIII.] he deal- *dealeth, di-* eth his goodes amonge his childern, he *videth* maye not make the fonne of the beloued firftborne before the fonne of the hated whiche is in deade the firft-
17 borne: But he fhall knowe the fonne off the hated for

V. 9 tu autem alienus eris ab innocentis cruore qui fufus eft, cum feceris quod præcepit dominus. 11 adamaueris eam 13 & poftea intrabis ad eam, dormiefque cum illa 14 non federit animo tuo ... nec opprimere per potentiam 17 fed filium odiofæ agnofcet
 L. 9 Alfo foltu das vnfchuldige blut von dyr thun, das du thueft was recht ift fur den augen d. H. 11 haft luft zu yhr ... 12 befcheren 14 wenn du aber nicht luft zu yhr haft 14 verkeuffen noch verfetzen 17 fondern ... erkennen
 M. M. N. 9 *Innocēt bloud:* The Chald. interpre. him that fhedeth innocēt bloude. 11 *Haue her to thy wyfe:* Here were they permytted to take a wife of the gentyles but fyrft to fhaue her head & cut her nayles &c. which ceremony fygnifyed that fhe fhuld be inftruct to cutt a waye the wantoneffe, & fuperfluoufe deckyng with the delycate condycions of the gentyles, left the cleane people of the Iewes fhulde in fhort fpace abhorre her, yf fhe contynued in her olde maners. 14 *Haft humbled her*, that is, afflyct vexed & greued her by takīg awaye her father contrey & goodes &c. as in the Pfal. xxxvii, b.

his firstborne, that he geue him dowble off all that he hath. For he is the first off his strength, and to him belongeth the right of the firstborneshippe.

18 Yf any man haue a sonne that is stuburne, and disobedient, that he will not herken vnto the voyce of his father and voyce of his mother, and they haue taught him nurture, but he wolde not herken vnto 19 them: Then let his father and his mother take him and brynge hym out vnto the elders of that citie and 20 vnto the gate of that same place, ād saye vnto the elders of the citie. This oure sonne is stoburne and disobedient and will not herken vnto oure voyce, he 21 is a ryoter and a dronkarde. Then let all the men of that citie stone him with stones vnto deeth. And so thou shalt put euell awaye from the, and all Israel shall heare and feare.

22 Yf a man haue commytted a trespace worthy of deeth and is put to deeth for it and hanged on tree: 23 let not his body remayne all nyghte vppon the tree, but burye hym .P. the same daye. For the curse off God is on him that is hanged. Defile not thy londe therfore, whiche the Lorde thy God geueth the to enherett.

¶ The .XXII. Chapter.

1 YF thou se thy brothers oxe or shepe goo astraye, thou shalt not with drawe thy selfe from them: But shalt brynge them 2 home agayne vnto thy brother. Yf thy

M.C.S. What thou oughtest to do when thou fyndest thy neyghboures beast goyng astraye.

M. 21 And thou shalt put
V. 17 iste est enim principium liberorum eius 19 ad portam iudicii 20 contemnit, comessationibus vacat, & luxuriæ atque conuiuiis 21 vt auferatis malum 22 morte plectendum est, & adiudicatus morti appensus fuerit in patibulo. xxii, 1 Non videbis ... & præteribis: sed reduces

L. 17 Denn der selb ist der anfang seynes vermugens 20 vnd ist eyn schwelger vnd truncken bolt 21 das bose 22 des todes wirdig ist, vnd wirt also getodt das man yhn auff eyn holtz henget. xx, 1 Wenn du ... sihest ... so soltu dich nicht entzihen.

brother be not nye vnto the or yf thou knowe him not, then bringe them vnto thine awne houffe and lett them be with the, vntyll thy brother axe after them, and
3 then delyuer him them agayne. In like maner fhalt thou doo with his affe, with his rayment and with all loft thinges of thy brother which he hath loft and thou haft founde, and thou maift not withdrawe thy felfe.

A man fhall not were wemens clothkyng or a womā manes clothyng. To weare a cote of woolle & of flaxe is also forbiddē. The punnyfhement of hym that accufeth a man vnrighteoufly: of an aduowtrer alfo & of hym that rauyfheth a mayde.

4 Yf thou fe that thy brothers affe or oxe is fallen doune by the waye, thou fhalt not withdrawe thy felfe from them: but fhalt helpe him to heue them vp agayne.

5 The woman fhall not weere that whiche pertayneth vnto the man, nether fhall a man put on womans rayment. For all that doo fo, are abhomynacyon vnto the Lorde thi God.

6 Yf thou chaunce vppon a byrds neft by the [Fo. XXXIX.] waye, in what foeuer tree it be or on the groūde, whether they be younge or egges, ād the dame fittenge vppon the younge or vppō the egges:
7 Thou fhalt not take the mother with the younge. But fhalt in any wyfe let the dame go and take the younge, that thou mayft profpere and prolonge thy dayes.

8 When thou byldeft a new houffe, thou fhalt make

M. 2 afke
V. 2 quærat ... & recipiat. 3 ne negligas quafi alienam. 4 non defpicies, fed fubleuabis cum eo. 5 apud deum 7 abire patieris
L. 2 fuche, vnd denn yhm widder gebift 3 du kanft dich nicht entzihen. 4 fondern folt yhm auff helffen. 7 folt die mutter fliegen laffen
M. M. N. 5 It is not here forbyddē but that to extue (*sic*) or auoyde Ieopardye, or to paffe the tyme merely or to begile oure enemyes a womā may were a mans harneffe or veftimentes & contrarywyfe a man womās clothes: but that they be not erneftly & cuftomablye vfed, that due honefty & dignytye may be obferued of bothe kyndes: feyng to do other wyfe is vncomely. 6 *The mother with the younge:* Thou fhalt not kil the mother, etc. This lawe will no moare but that in dealinge mercifully with beaftes we fhulde lerne mercyfulneffe vnto oure neyghboures. 8 *A new houfe:* The houfes be flat in thofe contreys.

a batelmēt vnto the roffe, that thou lade not bloude vppon thine houffe, yf any mā fall there of. *The houſſes beſtattinthoſe cōtres.*

9 Thou fhalt not fowe thy vyneyarde with dyuerfe fede: left thou halowe the fede whiche thou haft fowen with the frute off thy vyneyarde.

10 Thou fhalt not plowe with an oxe ād an affe togetherr

11 Thou fhalt not weere a garment made of woll and flax together.

12 Thou fhalt put rybandes vpō the .iiii. quarters of thy vefture wherewith thou couereft thy felfe.

13 Yf a man take a wyfe and when he hath lyen with
14 her hate her ād leye fhamefull thinges vnto hyr charge and brynge vp an euell name vppon her and faye: I toke this wyfe, and whē I came to her, I founde her
15 not a mayde: Thē let the father of the damfell and the mother .P. brynge forth the tokens of the damfels virginite, vnto the elders of the citie, euen vnto the gate.
16 And let the damfels father faye vnto the elders, I gaue my doughter vnto this man to wife and he hateth her:
17 and loo, he layeth fhamefull thinges vnto hir charge faynge, I founde not thy doughter a mayde. And yet thefe ar the tokens of my doughters virginite. And let them fprede the vefture before the elders off the citie.

V. 8 murum tecti per circūitum: ne effundatur fanguis in domo tua, & fis reus labente alio, & in præceps ruente. 9 ne & fementis quam feuifti, & quæ nafcuntur ex vinea, pariter fanctificētur. 11 contextum 12 quatuor angulos pallii tui 13 & poftea odio habuerit eam, 14 quæfieritque occafiones ... obiiciens ei nomen peffimum 15 tollent eam ... & ferent 17 imponit ei nomen peffimum ... hæc funt figna

L. 8 eyn lehnen drumb auff d. dache, auff das du nicht blut auff deyn haus ladift 9 das du nicht zur fulle heyligeft ... fampt dem eynkomen des weynbergis. 11 zu gleych gemenget. 12 an den vier fittigen deynes mantels 13 vnd wirt yhr gram, wenn er fie befchlaffen hat, 14 vnd legt yhr was fchendlichs auff 15 fie nemen, vnd fur die Eltiften der ftad yn dem thor eraus bringen 17 vnd legt eyn fchendlich ding auff fie

M. M. N. 9 *With diuerſe ſeede* for then the one fhulde hurte the other: fo the maners & dealīg of men may not be double but fingle fymple agreable in opinions & not of contrary fectes & dyuerfe doctrynes. 10 To not plowe with an oxe and an affe and not to were a garmēt of wollen & lynē do meane both one thyng, and are expounded in Leuiti. xix, d.

18 Then let the elders of that citie take that man and
19 chaſtyce him and merce him in an hundred ſycles of ſyluer and geue them vnto the father of the damſell, becauſe he hath brought vpp an euell name vppon a mayde in Iſrael. And ſhe ſhalbe his wife, and he maye
20 not put her awaye all his dayes. But and yf the thinge be of a ſuertie that the damſell be not founde a virgen,
21 let them brynge her vnto the dore of hir fathers houſſe, and let the men of that citie ſtone her with ſtones tc deeth, becauſe ſhe hath wrought folye in Iſrael, to playe the whore in hir fathers houſſe. And ſo thou ſhalt put euell awaye from the.
22 Yf a man be founde lyenge with a woman, that hath a wedded huſbonde, then let the dye etherother of the: both the man that laye with the wife and alſo the wife: ſo ſhalt thou put awaye euell from Iſrael. *etherother, both the one and the other*
23 Yf a mayde be hanfaſted vnto an huſ- bonde, and then a man finde her in the
24 towne and leye with her, then ye ſhall brynge them both out vnto the gates of that ſame citie and ſhall ſtone them with ſtones to deeth: The damſell becauſe ſhe cried not beynge in the citie: And the man, becauſe he hath humbled his neyghbours wife, and thou ſhalt put awaye evell from the. *hanfaſted, i. e. handfaſted, betrothed*
25 But yf a man finde a betrothed damſell in the felde and force her and leye with her: The the man that
26 laye with her ſhall dye alone, and vnto the damſell thou ſhalt doo no harme: becauſe there is in the damſell no cauſe of deeth. For as when a man ryſeth

𝒱. 19 quos dabit .. diffamauit nomen peſſimum ... non poterit dimittere eam 20 non eſt in puella inuenta virginitas: 21 eiicient eam ... quoniam fecit nefas in Iſrael ... & auferes malum (vv. 22, 24) 22 morietur, id eſt, adulter & adultera 23 Si puellam. deſponderit vir ... 24 quia humiliauit vxorem proximi ſui. 25 & apprehendens concubuerit cum ea, ipſe morietur ſolus 26 quoniam ſicut latro

𝑳. 19 ſeyn leben lang nicht laſſen muge. 20 Iſts aber die warheyt, das ... nicht iſt iungfraw funden 21 torheyt in Iſr. begangen hat .. das boſe (vv. 22, 24) 22 der man vnd das weyb, bey dem er geſchlaffen hat 23 yemand vertrawet iſt 24 geſchrien hat 25 auff dem felde krieget, vnd ergreyfft ſie vnd ſchlefft bey yhr ... der man alleyne ſterben 26 Sondern gleych wie yemand

agenste his neyghboure and sleyeth him, euē so is this
27 matter. For he founde her in the feldes and the betrothed damsell cried: but there was no mā to succoure
her.

28 Yf a man finde a mayde that is not betrothed ād
29 take her ād lye with her ād be founde: Then the man
that laye with her shall geue vnto the damsells father
L. sycles of syluer. And she shall be his wife, because
he hath humbled her, and he maye not put her awaye
all hys dayes.

30 No man shall take his fathers wife, nor vnheale his
fathers couerynge.

.P.   ¶ The .XXIII. Chapter

1 NONE that is gelded or hath his
preuey membres cutt of, shall
come in to the congregacion
of the Lorde. And he that is
2 borne of a comen woman shall not come
in- the congregacion of the Lorde, no in
the tenth generacyon he shall not entre in to the con-
3 gregacyon of the Lorde. The Ammonites and the
Moabites shall not come in to the cōgregacyon of the
Lorde, no not in the tenth generacion, no they shall

M.C.S. What maner of men may not be admyt in to the churche. Pollucios that happe in the night. Vsurie.

M. 2 in to the congregacyō
V. 26 animam eius: ita et puella perpessa est. 27 liberaret
eam. 28 & res ad iudicium venerit 29 cunctis diebus vitæ suæ.
30 nec reuelabit operimentum eius. xxiii, 1 eunuchus attritis vel
amputatis testiculis, & absciso veretro 2 mamzer, hoc est de scorto
natus ... vsque
L. 26 schluge seyne seele todt, so ist dis auch 27 schrey, vnd
war niemant der yhr halff. 28 vnd werden gefunden 29 nicht
lassen seyn leben lang. 30 nicht auff decken seyns vaters decke.
xxiii, 1 gebrochener noch verschnyttener 2 hurkind ... auch nach
dem zehenden gelid, sondern sol schlecht nicht
M. M. N. 29 What humble signifieth here loke Thren. v. b.
xxiii, 1 *To come into the cōgregacyon* is to haue office or mynistra-
cion, amōg the congregacion: which no deformed person myght
haue: lest his deformytye shuld be an occasyon to despyse the
offyce or admynystracion wherin he was ordeyned.

4 neuer come in to the cōgregacion of the Lorde, becaufe they met you not with bred and water in the waye when ye came out of Egipte, and becaufe they hyred agenft the Balaam the fonne of Beor the inter-
5 preter of Mefopotamia, to curfe the. Neuertheleffe the Lorde thy God wolde not herken vnto Balaam, but turned the curfe to a bleffinge vnto the, becaufe the
6 Lorde thy God loued the. Thou fhalt neuer therfore feke that which is profperoufe or good for them all thy dayes for euer.
7 Thou fhalt not abhorre an Edomite, for he is thy brother: nether fhalt thou abhorre an Egiptian, becaufe
8 thou waft a ftraunger in hys londe. The childern that are begotten of them fhall come in to the congregacyon of the Lorde in the .iii. generacion.
9 [Fo. XLI.] When thou goeft out with the hoft agenft thine enemies, kepe the frō all wekedneffe for the Lorde is amonge you.
10 Yf there be any man that is vncleane by the reafon of vnclenneffe that chaunceth hym by nyght, let him
11 goo out of the hoft and not come in agayne vntyll he haue wafhed him felfe with water before the euen: ād then whē the fonne is doune, let him come in to the hoft agayne.
12 Thou fhalt haue a place without the hoft whother
13 thou fhalt reforte to and thou fhalt haue a fharpe poynte at the ende of thy wepon: and when thou wilt eafe thy felfe, digge therewith and turne and couer that which

𝒱. 4 quia conduxerunt contra 6 Non facies cum eis pacem, nec quæris eis bona 7 nec Ægyptium 9 re mala. 10 Si fuerit inter vos ... nocturno pollutus fit fomnio 12 ad requifita naturæ 13 gerens paxillum in balteo

ℒ. 4 widder euch dingeten 6 Du folt yhn widder glück noch heyl wundfchen deyn leben lang ewiglich. 7 nicht fur grewel halten 9 fur allem bofen. 10 Wenn yemand vnter dyr ift, der nicht reyn ift, das yhm des nachts was widder faren ift 12 zur nott hynaus

𝕸. 𝕸. 𝕹. 13 *Wepon:* If foche polycies muft be hadde in fowdyars tentes to kepe thē cleane, moch moare in cyties and townes. If foche a thyng, which of it felfe is not euell, muft be fo erneftly feene to: what fyngular prouyfyō ought ther to be hadde that no opē whoredome, aduowtrye, theft, pollyng, exaccion etc. were vfed.

14 is departed from the. For the Lorde thy God walketh in thyne hoſt, to rydd the and to ſett thine enemyes before the. Let thine hoſt be pure that he ſe no vncleane thinge amonge you and turne from you.

15 Thou ſhalt not delyuer vnto his maſter the ſeruaunt
16 which is eſcaped from his maſter vnto the. Let him dwel with the, euē amonge you in what place he him ſelfe liketh beſt, in one of thi cities where it is good for him, and vexe him not.

17 There ſhalbe no whore of the doughters of Iſrael,
18 nor whorekeper of the ſonnes of Iſrael .¶. Thou ſhalt nether brynge the hyre of an whore nor the pryce of a dogge in to the houſſe of the Lorde thy God, in no maner of vowe: for euē both of them are abhominacion vnto the Lorde thy God.

The pope wil take tribute of them yet ād biſſhopes, ād abottes deſire no better tenauntes.

19 Thou ſhalt be no vſurer vnto thy brother, nether in mony nor in ſode, nor in any maner thinge that is lent
20 vppon vſerye. Vnto a ſtraūger thou maiſt lende vppon vſerye, but not vnto thy brother, that the Lorde thy God maye bleſſe the in all that thou ſetteſt thyne hande to in the londe whother thou goeſt to conquere it.

21 When thou haſt vow.ed a vowe vnto the Lorde thy God, ſe thou be not ſlacke to paye it. For he will ſurely requyre it of the, and it ſhalbe ſynne vnto the.
22 Yf thou ſhalt leue vowinge, it ſhalbe no ſynne vnto
23 the: but that which is once gone out off thy lippes, thou muſt kepe and doo, accordynge as thou haſt vowed vnto the Lorde thy god a frewiloffrynge whiche thou haſt ſpoken with thy mouth.

24 When thou comeſt in to thy neghboures vyneyarde,

V. 14 vt eruat te 16 in loco qui ei placuerit ... ne contriſtes eum. 17 ſcortator 20 ſed alieno. Fratri autem tuo abſque vſura id quod indiget, cōmodabis 23 ſicut promiſiſti domino deo tuo, & propria voluntate & ore tuo locutus es.

L. 14 das er dich erredte 16 ſolt yhn nicht ſchinden. 17 hurer 20 An dem frembden magſtu wuchern

M. M. N. 18 *The hyre*, etc. There be now many that deſyre no beter rentes.

thou mayſt eate grapes thy belyfull at thine awne pleaſure: but thou ſhalt put none in thy bagge.

25 When thou goeſt in to thy neyghbours corne, thou mayſt plucke the eares with thine hãd [Fo. XLII.] but thou mayſt not moue a ſycle vnto thy neghbours corne.

⁌ The .XXIIII. Chapter.

1 WHEN a man hath taken a wyfe and maried her, yf ſhe finde no fauoure in his eyes, becauſe he hath ſpied ſome vnclenneſſe in her. Then let him write her a bylle of devorcement and put it in hir hande 2 and ſende her out of his houſſe. Yf when ſhe is departed out of his houſſe, ſhe goo 3 and be another mans wife and the ſeconde huſbonde hate her and write her a letter of deuorcement and put it in hir hande and ſende her out of his houſſe, or yf the ſeconde man dye whiche toke her to 4 wyfe. Hir firſt man whiche ſent hir awaye maye not take her agayne to be his wyfe, in as moche as ſhe is defiled. For that is abhominacyon in the ſyght of the Lorde: that thou defile not the lõde with ſynne, which the Lorde thy God geueth the to enherett.

5 When a man taketh a newe wyfe, he ſhall not goo a warrefare nether ſhalbe charged wyth any buſyneſſe: but ſhalbe fre at home one yere and reioyſe with his wife whiche he hath taken.

M.C.S. Deuorcement is permytted. He that is newly maryed ſhall not be compelled to go to warre. The remnaunte of corne muſt be left in herueſt for the poore.

𝒱. 24 quantum tibi placuerit: foras autem ne efferas tecum. 25 falce autem non metes. xxiiii, 1 propter aliquam fœdidatem 2 Cumque egreſſa alterum maritum duxerit 3 oderit eam, .. domo ſua, .. fuerit 4 polluta eſt, & abominabilis facta .. ne peccare facias terram tuam 5 non procedet ad bellum, nec ei quippiam neceſſitatis iniungetur publice

ℒ. 24 bis du ſatt habiſt, aber du ſolt nichts ynn deyn geſeſs thun. 25 nicht drynnen hyn vnd her faren. xxiiii, 1 vmb etwa eyner vnluſt willen 4 nach dem ſie iſt vnreyn vnd eyn grewel fur dem HERRN, Auff das du das land nicht zu ſunden machiſt 5 yhm nichts aufflegen.

6 .P. No mā shall take the nether or the vpper milstone to pledge, for then he taketh a mans lyfe to pledge.
7 Yf any man be founde stealynge any of his brethern the childern of Israel, ād maketh cheuesaunce of him or selleth him, the these shall dye. And thou shalt put euell awaye from the.
8 Take hede to thy selfe as concernynge the plage of leprosye, that thou obserue diligently to doo acordinge to all that the preastes the leuites shall
9 shall obserue to doo. Remembre what the Lorde thy God dyd vnto Mir Iam by the waye, after that ye were come out off Egipte.

Do as the preastes teache you: but as I haue taughte thē and not as they fayne.

10 Yf thou lende thy brother any maner soker, thou
11 shalt not goo in to his housse to fetche a pledge: but shalt stonde without and the man to whom thou lend-
12 est, shall brynge the the pledge out at the dore. Forthermore yf it be a pore body, goo not to slepe with his pledge: but delyuer hym the pledge agayne by that
13 the sonne goo doune, and let him slepe in his owne rayment and blesse the. And it shalbe rightuousnes vnto the, before the Lorde thy God.
14 Thou shalt not defraude an hyred seruaunte that is nedye and poore, whether he be off thy [Fo. XLIII.] brethern or a straunger that is in thy lond with in thy
15 cities. Geue him his hyre the same daye, and let not the

V. 6 quia animam suam apposuit tibi. 7 Israel, & vendito eo acceperit pretium 8 sacerdotes Leuitici generis ... & imple solicite. 10 Cum repetes 11 proferet quod habuerit. 14 indigentis, & pauperis fratris tui

L. 6 denn er hat dyr die seel zu pfand gesetzt. 7 eyn seele stilet ... versetzt odder verkeufft sie 10 yrgent eyne schuld borgest 14 nicht vervorteylen das lohn des bnöttigeten vnd armen

M. M. N. 6 By the nether or vpper mylstone is signysyed any thinge which is necessarily requyred to a borower or debtour, wherof he nourysseth & sustayneth hym selfe, that may no creditoure take frō him, in especiall his crafte & occupacyō wherō he chesely liueth may he not, by enpresonnement (which some most cruelly do) kepe hym from: Lest he be compelled to paye his dett with double disprofet. One, that his milstone is idell in the meane tyme. Another, that he is constrayned to come further in dett otherwayse: or to sell his necessary goodes with out which he cannot lyue, to makepayment.

sonne goo doune thereon. For he is nedye ād therewith fufteyneth his life, left he crye agenſt the vnto the Lorde ād it be fynne vnto the.

16 The fathers ſhal not dye for the childern nor the childern for the fathers: but euery mā ſhall dye for his awne fynne.

17 Hynder not the right of the ſtraunger nor of the
18 fatherleſſe, nor take wedowes rayment to pledge. But remembre that thou waſt a feruaunte in Egipte, ād how the Lord thy God delyuered the thēce. Wherfore I cōmaūde the to doo this thinge.

19 When thou cutteſt doune thyne herueſte in the felde and haſt forgotte a ſhefe in the felde thou ſhalt not goo agayne and fett it: But it ſhalbe for the ſtraunger, the fatherleſſe and the wedowe, that the Lorde thy God maye bleſſe the in all the workes of thyne
20 hande. When thou beateſt doune thyne oylue, trees thou ſhalt not make cleane riddaunce after the: but it ſhalbe
21 for the ſtraunger, the fatherleſſe and the wedowe. And when thou gathereſt thy vyneyarde, thou ſhalt not gather cleane after the: but it ſhalbe for the ſtraunger,
22 the fatherleſſe and the wedowe. And remembre that thou waſt a .P. feruaunte in the lond of Egipte: wherfore I cōmaunde the to doo this thinge.

¶ The XXV. Chapter.

1 WHEN there is ſtrife betwene men, let thē come vnto the lawe, and let the iudges iuſtifie the rightuous and condemne the
2 trefpeafer. And yf the trefpeafer be wor-

M.C.S. The punnyſhment of offendars. The lawe of reaſyng feed to the brother that is deed.

M. 1 If there be
V. 15 fuftentat animam fuam 17 Non peruertes 20 collegeris .. non reuerteris vt colligas 21 non colliges remanentes racemos xxv. 1 & interpellauerint iudices, ... iuſtitiæ palmam dabunt: ... condemnabunt impietatis.
L. 15 erhelt feyne feele darauff 17 nicht beugen 20 abgelefen ... genaw ablefen ... 21 weinberg gelefen .. genaw aufflefen. xxv, 1 fur gericht bringen ... den gerechten rechtfertigen vnd den gotlofen verdamnen.

thy of ftrypes, then let the iudge caufe to *Meafures and* take him doune and to bete him before *weyghtes.*
his face accordynge to his trefpace, vnto a certayne
3 numbre. XL. ftripes he fhall geue him and not paffe: left yf he fhulde exceade and beate him aboue that with many ftripes, thi brother fhuld appere vngodly before thyne eyes.

4 Thou fhalt not mofell the oxe that treadeth out the corne.

5 When brethren dwell together and *It were hard to proue this* one of them dye ād haue no childe, the *a ceremonye* wyfe of the deed fhall not be geuen out vnto a ftraunger: but hir brotherlawe fhall goo in vnto her and take
6 her to wife and marie her. And the eldeft fonne which fhe beareth, fhall ftonde vp in the name of his brother which is deed, that his name be not put out in Ifrael.

7 But and yf the man will not take his fyfterlawe, then let her goo to the gate vnto the el- [Fo. XLIIII.] ders and faye: My brotherlawe refufeth to fterre vpp vnto his brother a name in Ifrael, he will not marie
8 me. Then let the elders of his citie call vnto him and comen with him. Yf he ftonde and faye: I will not take her, then let his fyfterlawe goo vnto him in the prefence of the elders and loofe his fhowe of his fote and fpytt in his face and anfwere and faye.

9 So fhall it be done vnto that man that will not
10 bylde his brothers houffe. And his name fhalbe called in Ifrael, the vnfhoed houffe.

M. 3 vngoodly 7 fyfter in lawe (v. 8)
V. 2 Pro menfura peccati, erit & plagarum modus 3 non exedant: ne fœde laceratus 6 & primogenitum ex ea filium nomine illius appellabit 7 accipere vxorem frat. fui quæ ei lege debetur ... ad portam ciuitatis, & interpellabit .. dicetque 10 Domus difcalceati.
L. 2 nach der mas vnd zal feyner miffethat 3 fo man mehr fchlege gibt, er zu viel gefchlagen werd, vnd deyn bruder fcheuflich fur deynen augen fey. 7 fchwegeryn neme, fo fol fie, feyne fchwegeryn hinauff gehen vnter das thor ... eyn namen zu erwecken. 8 Wenn er denn fteht 10 des Barfuffers haus.
M. M. N. 3 *XL. ftrypes:* Therfore had S. Paul no mo at any tyme. 2 Cor. xi, f. 6 *Which is deed:* So that he fhulde be the chylde of the brother that deed was, & not his that gatt him

11 Yf when men ftryue together, one with another, the wife of the one rūne to, for to ryd hyr hufbonde out of the handes of him that fmyteth him and put forth
12 hir hande and take him by the fecrettes: cutt of hir hande, and let not thine eye pitie her.
13 Thou fhalt not haue in thy bagge two maner
14 weyghtes, a greate and a fmall: nether fhalt thou haue in thine houfe dyuerfe meafures, a great ād a fmall.
15 But thou fhalt haue a perfect ād a iuft meafure: that thy dayes maye be lengthed in the londe whiche the
16 Lorde thy God geueth the, For all that do foche thinges ād all that doo vnright, are abhominacion vnright,*wrong* vnto the Lorde thy God.
17 .¶. Remembre what Amalech dyd vnto the by the
18 waye after thou cameft out of Egipte, he mett the by the waye and fmote the hynmoft of you, all that were ouer laboured and dragged by hynde, when thou waft
19 faynted and werye, and he feared not God. Therfore when the Lorde thy God hath geuen the reft from all thyne enemyes rounde aboute, in the londe whiche the Lorde thy God geueth the to enheret and poffeffe: fe that thou put out the name of Amalech from vnder heauen, ād forget not.

𝕸. 13 two maner of weyghtes
𝖁. 11 iurgium viri duo, & vnus contra alterum rixari cœperit 12 nec flecteris fuper eam vlla mifericordia. 15 pondus habebis iuftum & verum, & modius æqualis & verus 16 abominatur... & auerfatur omnem iniuftitiam. 19 requiem, & fubiecerit... delebis
𝕷. 11 leufft zu 12 auge fol yhr nicht verfchonen. 15 vollig vnd recht gewicht... Epha 19 austilgen.
𝕸. 𝕸. N. 11 *Put forth her hande* etc.: God wyll that a woman be moare fhame faft then ether to exercyfe the feate of a mā in feyghtynge or to touche that mēbre.

The .XXVI. Chapter.

1 WHEN thou art come in to the londe whiche the Lorde thy God geueth the to enherett and haft enioyed it and dwell- 2 eft there in: take of the firft of all the frute of the erthe, which thou haft brought in out of the lande that the Lorde thy God geueth the and put it in a maunde and goo vnto the place which the Lorde thy God fhall chofe to 3 make his name dwell there. And thou fhalt come vnto the preaft that fhalbe in thofe dayes ād faye vnto him I knowledge this daye vnto the Lorde thy God, that I am come vnto the contre whiche the Lorde fware vnto oure fathers for to geue vs.

M.C.S. The fyrſt frutes and tythes to the Leuites, fatherleſſe, wedowes, and ſtraungers.

maunde, baſket

4 [Fo. XLV.] And the preaft fhall take the maunde out of thine hande, and fet it doune before the alter of the 5 Lorde thy God. And thou fhalt anſwere ād faye before the Lorde thy God: The Sirians wolde haue deftroyed my father, and he went doune in to Egipte ād fogeorned there with a few folke and grewe there vnto a nacyon 6 greate, myghtie and full of people. And the Egiptians vexed vs ād troubled vs, and laded vs with cruell bond- 7 age. And we cried vnto the Lorde God of oure fathers,

V. 1 daturus eſt poſſidendam, & obtinueris eam 2 de cunctis frugibus tuis primitias, & pones .. vt ibi inuocetur nomen 3 Profiteor hodie coram domino 5 loqueris .. Syrus perſequebatur ... in paucissimo numero ... & infinitæ multitudinis.

L. 1 zum erbe geben wirt, vnd nympſt es eyn 2 die aus der erden komen 3 Ich verkundige heutt dem Herrn deynem Gott 5 antworten ... Die Syrer wolten meynen vater vmb bringen

M. M. N. 5 *The Siriās would haue deſtroyed etc.:* The Chaldee interpret. readeth, The Sirian went aboute to deſtroye my father meanyng (as ſome ſuppoſe) laban, of whom Gene. xxxi. The .Lxx. my father left or forſoke Siria. The comē tranſlacyon readeth, the Sirian did perſequute my father: ſignifying, as ſome interpretate, that Siria the contrey of their fathers had expelled thē and thruſt them out.

and the Lorde herde oure voyce and loked on oure
8 aduerſyte, laboure and oppreſſyon. And the Lorde
brought vs out of Egipte with a mightye hande and a
ſtretched out arme and with greate terebleneſſe and
9 with ſygnes and wonders. And he hath brought vs
in to this place and hath geuē vs this londe that floweth
10 with mylke and honye. And nowe loo, I haue brought
the firſt frutes off the londe whiche the Lorde hath
geuen me. And ſet it before the Lorde thy God and
11 worſhepe before the Lorde thy God and reioyſe ouer
all the good thinges whiche the Lorde thy God
hath geuē vnto the and vnto thyne houſſe, both
thou the Leuite and the ſtraunger that is amonge
you.

12 When thou haſt made an ende of tithynge .P. all
the tithes of thine encreaſe the thyrde yere, the yere
of tythynge: and haſt geuen it vnto the Leuite, the
ſtraunger, the fatherleſſe ād the wedowe, and they
13 haue eaten in thy gates ād ſylled them ſelues. Then
ſaye before the Lorde thy God: I haue brought the
halowed thinges out of myne houſſe: and haue geuen
them vnto the Leuite, the ſtraunger, the fatherleſſe and
the wedowe acordynge to all the commaundmentes
which thou commaundeſt me: I haue not ouerſkypped
14 thy commaundmentes, nor forgetten them. I haue
not eaten thereof in my moornynge nor taken awaye
thereof vnto any vnclenneſſe, nor ſpente thereof aboute
any deed corſe: but haue herkened vnto the uoyce of the
Lorde my God, and haue done after all that he com-
15 maūded me, loke doune from thy holy habitacyon
heauen and bleſſe thy people Iſrael and the lande which

𝒱. 7 humilitatem noſtram, & laborem atque anguſtias 8 et
eduxit nos 9 introduxit 10 Et idcirco nunc offero ... dominus
dedit mihi. 12 Quando compleueris ... vt comedant intra portas
tuas, & ſaturentur 13 non præteriui mandata tua, nec ſum oblitus
imperii tui. 14 in re funebri ... ſicut præcepiſti mihi. 15 ſanctuario
tuo, & de excelſo cælorum habitaculo
 𝓛. 7 zwang, erbeyt and leyd 8 vnd furet vns aus 9 vnd bracht
vns 10 Nu bringe ich ... das der Herr vns geben hat. 12 zuſammen bracht haſt ... das ſie eſſen ynn deynem thor vnd ſatt
werden. 14 nicht zu den todten dauon gegeben ... wie du myr
gepotten haſt. 15 heyligen wonung vom hymel

thou haſt geuen vs (as thou ſwareſt vnto oure fathers) a lond that floweth with mylke and honye.

16 This daye the Lorde thy God hath commaunded the to doo theſe ordinaunces and lawes. Kepe them therfore and doo them with all thyne hert and all thy
17 ſoule. Thou haſt ſett vpp the Lorde this daye to be thy God and to walke in hys wayes and to kepe his ordinaunces, his commaundmentes and his lawes, and
18 [Fo. XLVI.] to herken vnto his voyce. And the Lord hath ſett the vp this daye, to be a ſeuerall people vnto him (as he hath promyſed the) and that thou kepe his commaundmentes, and to
19 make the hye aboue all nacyons which he hath made, in prayſe, in name and honoure: that thou mayſt be an holy people vnto the Lord thy God, as he hath ſayed.

ſeuerall, ſep-arate

¶ The .XXVII. Chapter.

1 AND Moſes with the elders of Iſrael cōmaunded the people ſayenge: kepe all the commaundmentes which I com-
2 maunde you this daye. And when ye be come ouer Iordayne vnto the londe which the Lorde thy God geueth the, ſett vpp greate ſtones and playſter them with playſ-
3 ter, and write vpō thē all the wordes of this lawe,

M.C.S. An aultare muſt be bylded before they go ouer Iordan. The bleſſynges in the hyll Gariʒim. The Curſes in the hyll Eball.

V. 17 Dominum elegiſti hodie .. 18 populus peculiaris, ſicut locutus eſt tibi 19 & faciat te excelſiorem cunctis gentibus quas creauit in laudem, & nomen, & gloriam ſuam   xxvii, 2 dabit tibi (v. 3) .. calce leuigabis (v. 4)

L. 17 Dem Herrn haſtu heutte geredt 18 Vnd der Herr hatt dyr heut geredt ... ſeym volck des eygenthums ſeyn ſolt wie er dyr geredt hat ... vnd er dich das hohiſte mache zu lob, namen, vnd preyſs vber alle völcker. xxvii, 1 ſampt den Eltiſten 2 geben wirt (v. 3) .. kalck tunchen (v. 4)

M. M. N.   17 *Thou haſt ſett vp the Lorde etc.*: Or thou haſte cauſed to be ſayde that ẏ Lorde ſhulde be vnto the for thy God: or, as many will, he made the to ſaye, that is, he was the cauſe that thou ſhuldeſt ſaye, that the Lorde ſhulde be vnto ẏ for thy God.

when thou arte come ouer: that thou mayſt come in to the londe whiche the Lorde thy God geueth the: a londe that floweth with mylke and honye, as the Lorde God off thy fathers hath promyſed the.

4 When ye be come ouer Iordayne, ſe that ye ſet vpp theſe ſtones which I commaunde you this daye in
5 mount Eball, and playſter them with playſter. And there bylde vnto the Lord thy God, an altare of ſtones and ſe thou lifte .P. vpp no yerne uppon them:
6 But thou ſhalt make the altare of the Lorde thy God of rughſtones and offer burntoffrynges thereon vnto
7 the Lorde thy God. And thou ſhalt offer peaceoffrynges and ſhalt eate there and reioyſe before the Lorde
8 thy God. And thou ſhalt write vppon the ſtones all the wordes of this lawe, manyfeſtly and well

9 And Moſes with the preaſtes the Leuites ſpake vnto all Iſrael ſayenge: take hede ãd heare Iſrael, this daye thou art become the people of the Lorde thy God.
10 Herken therfore vnto the voyce of the Lorde thi God ãd do his cõmaundmẽtes ãd his ordinaunces which I commaunde you this daye.

11 And Moſes charged the people the ſame daye ſay-
12 enge: theſe ſhall ſtonde vppon mount Griſim to bleſſe the people, when ye are come ouer Iordayne: Symeon,
13 Leui, Iuda, Iſachar, Ioſeph and Ben Iamin. And theſe ſhall ſtonde apon mount Eball to curſe: Ruben, Gad
14 Aſſer, Zabulon, Dan and Neptaly. And the Leuites ſhall beginne ãd ſay vnto all the men of Iſrael with a loude voyce.

15 Curſed be he that maketh any carued image or image of metall (an abhominacion vnto the Lorde, the worke of the handes of the crafteſman) and putteth it in a ſecrett place: [Fo. XLVII.] And all the people ſhall anſwere and ſaye Amen.

Here of take the popes an occaſiõ to curſe .iiii tymes in the yere

M. 12 Garizim
V. 5 quos ferrum non tetigit 6 ſaxis informibus & impolitis 8 plane et lucide. 10 audies vocem eius 15 ponetque illud in abſcondito.
L. 5 dar vber keyn eyſen feret 6 gantzen ſteynen 7 todopffer 8 klar vnd wol. 10 das du der ſtym des Herrn deyns Gottis gehorſam ſeyſt 15 vnd ſetzt es verporgen

16 Curſed be he that curſeth his father or hys mother, and all the people ſhall ſaye Amen.

17 Curſed be he that remoueth his neghbours marke and all the people ſhall ſaye Amen.

18 Curſed be he that maketh the blynde goo out off his waye, and all the people ſhall ſaye Amen,

19 Curſed be he that hyndreth the right of the ſtraunger, fatherleſſe and wedowe, and all the people ſhall ſaye Amen.

20 Curſed be he that lieth with his fathers wife becauſe he hath opened his fathers coueringe, ād all the people ſhall ſaye Amen.

21 Curſed be he that lieth with any maner beeſt, and all the people ſhall ſaye Amen.

22 Curſed be he that lieth with his ſyſter whether ſhe be the doughter of his father or off his mother, and all the people ſhall ſaye Amen

23 Curſed be he that lieth with his mother in lawe, and all the people ſhall ſaye Amen.

24 Curſed be he that ſmyteth his neghboure ſecretly, and all the people ſhall ſaye Amē.

25 Curſed be he that taketh a rewarde to ſlee innocent bloude, and all the people ſhall ſaye Amen.

26 Curſed be he that mātayneth not all the wor-*P*. des of this lawe to doo them, ād all the people ſhall ſaye Amen.

V. 16 non honorat patrem 17 tranſſert 18 errare facit 19 peruertit iudicium 20 dormit cum vxore . . reuelat operimentum lectuli eius. 24 clam percuſſerit —*Maledictus qui dormit cum vxore proximi ſui. &* dicet omnis populus, Amen* . . 25 animam ſanguinis innocentis. 26 permanet in ſermonībus legis huius, nec eos opere perficit.

L. 16 ſeym vater ... flucht 17 grentze engert 18 yrren macht 19 das recht ... beuget 20 bey ſeynes vaters weyb ligt ... den flugel 24 heymlich ſchlecht 25 die ſeele des vnſchuldigen bluts 26 alle wort diſes geſetzs auffrichtet das er darnach thue

¶ The .XXVIII. Chapter

1 IF thou shalt herken diligently vnto the voyce of the Lorde thy God, to obserue and to do all his commaundmentes whiche I commaunde the this daye. The Lorde wil set the an hye aboue all nacions 2 of the erth. And all these blessynges shall come on the and ouer take the, yf thou shalt herken 3 vnto the voyce of the Lorde thy God. Blessed shalt 4 thou be in the towne and blessed in the feldes, blessed shalbe the frute of thy body, the frute of thy grounde and the frute of thy catell, the frute of thine oxen, and 5 thy flockes of shepe, blessed shall thine 6 almery be ad thy store. Blessed shalt thou be, both when thou goest out, ad blessed whē thou comest in.

M.C.S. The promyses of the blessynges vnto them that regarde the commaundementes: and the curses to the contrarye.

almery, a cupboard

7 The Lorde shall smyte thyne enemyes that ryse agenst the before thy face. They shall come out agenst 8 the one waye, and flee before the seuen wayes. The Lorde shal commaunde the blessynge to be with the in thy store housses ād in all that thou settest thine hande to, and will blesse the in the lande which the Lord thi god geueth the.

9 The Lorde shall make the an holye people [Fo. XLVIII.] vnto himselfe, as he hath sworen vnto the:

V. 1 Si autem audieris 2 & apprehendent te: si tamen .. audieris. 4 ventris ... greges armentorum .. caulæ ouium 5 reliquiæ tuæ (v. 17). 6 Benedictus eris ingrediens & egrediens. 7 in conspectu tuo. 8 Emittet dom. benedictionem super cellaria .. opera manuum tuarum .. in terra quam acceperis.

L. 1 Vnd wenn ... gehorchen wirst 2 werden vber dich komen .. dich treffen (v. 15) darumb das du ... bist gehorsam gewest. 4 fruchte deyner ochsen ... fruchte deyner schaff 5 deyn vbrigs 6 Gesegnet ... Gesegenet 8 gepieten dem segen ... keller ... fur handen nimpst

L. M. N. 5 *Deyn korb:* das ist alles was du beseyt legest zu behalten vnd alles was du brauchest.

yf thou ſhalt kepe the commaundmentes of the Lorde thy God and walke in hys wayes.

10 And all nacyons of the erthe ſhall ſe that thou arte called after the name of the Lorde, and they ſhalbe 11 aſerde off the. And the Lorde ſhall make the plenteous in goodes, in the frute of thy body, in the frute off thy catell and in the frute of thy grounde, in the londe whiche the Lorde ſware vnto thy fathers to geue the.

12 The Lorde ſhall open vnto the his good treaſure, euen the heauen, to geue rayne vnto thy londe in due ceaſon and to bleſſe all the laboures of thine hande. And thou ſhalt lende vnto many nacyös, but ſhalt not nede to borowe thy ſelfe. 13 And the Lorde ſhall ſett the before and not behinde, and thou ſhalt be aboue only and not beneth: yf that thou herken vnto the commaundmentes of the Lorde thy God which I commaunde the this daye to 14 kepe and to doo them. And ſe that thou bowe not from any of theſe wordes which I commaunde the this daye ether to the right hande or to the lefte, that thou woldeſt goo after ſtraung goddes to ſerue them.

15 But and yf thou wilt not herken vnto the voyce of the Lorde thy God to kepe and to ꝑ. doo all his commaundmentes and ordinaunces which I commaunde the this daye: then all theſe curſes ſhall come vppon 16 the and ouertake the: Curſed ſhalt thou be in the 17 towne, and cursed in the felde, curſed ſhall thyne almery 18 be and thi ſtore. Curſed ſhall be the frute of thy body ād the frute of thy lond be ād the frute of thine oxen 19 ād the flockes of thy ſhepe. And curſed ſhalt thou be when thou goeſt in, ād whē thou goeſt out.

20 And the Lorde ſhall ſende vppon the curſynge,

V. 9 ſi cuſtodieris 11 fructu terræ tuæ quam iurauit 13 in caput, et non in caudam (v. 44): & eris ſemper ſupra, & non ſubter 14 non declinaueris 15 & apprehendent te.

L. 9 darumb das du ... heltiſt 10 nach dem namen 13 zum heubt .. nicht zum ſchwantz (v. 44) vnd ... oben ſchweben vnd nicht vnten liegen 14 nicht gewichen biſt

M. M. N. 14 *Bowe not from any* etc.: To bowe vnto the ryght hāde is to adde to the woorde of God, And to bowe vnto the lefte is to take awaye, as in the prouer .iiii. d.

goynge to nought and complaynyng in all that thou fetteſt thine hande to what foeuer thou doeſt: vntyll thou be deſtroyed ād brought to nought quyckely, becauſe of the wekedneſſe of thyne invencyons in that
21 thou haſt forſaken the Lorde. And the Lorde ſhall make the peſtilence cleaue vnto the, vntyll he haue conſumed the from the londe whether thou goeſt to
22 enioye it. And the Lorde ſhall ſmyte the with ſwellynge, with feuers, heet, burnynge, wetherynge, with ſmytynge and blaſtinge. And they ſhall folowe the, vntyll thou periſhe.
23 And the heauen that is ouer thy heed ſhalbe braſſe, and the erth that is vnder the, yerne.
24 And the Lorde ſhall turne the rayne of the lāde vnto powder ād duſt: euen frō heauen they [Fo. XLIX.] ſhal come doune vpō the, vntyll thou be brought to
25 nought. And the Lorde ſhall plage the before thine enemyes: Thou ſhalt come out one waye agenſt them, and flee ſeuen wayes before them, ād ſhalt be ſcatered
26 amonge all the kingdomes of the erth. And thy carcaſſe ſhalbe meate vnto all maner foules of the ayre ād vnto the beeſtes of the erth, and no man ſhall fraye them awaye.
27 And the Lorde will ſmyte the with the botches of Egipte and the emorodes, ſcalle and maungyneſſe,
28 that thou ſhalt not be healed thereof. And the Lorde ſhall ſmyte the with madneſſe, blyndneſſe and daſynge

V. 20 famem & efuriem, & increpationem ... velociter, propter adinuentiones tuas peſſimas 21 Adiungat ... peſtilentiam 22 egeſtate, febri & frigore, ardore & æſtu, et aere corrupto ac rubigine, & perſequatur 23 terra quam calcas 24 puluerem, & de cælo .. cinis 25 Tradat te dom. corruentem 26 abigat. 27 vlcere Ægypti, & partem corporis per quam ſtercora digeruntur, ſcabie quoque & prurigine 28 furore mentis

L. 20 bald vmbringe, vmb deynes boſen thuns willen 22 ſchwulſt, fiber, hitze, brand, brunſt, durre vnd bleyche, vnd wirt dich verfolgen 24 ſtaub, vnd aſſchen fur regen .. aſſchen vom hymel 26 ſcheucht. 27 druſen Egypti, mit feygwartzen, mit grind und kretz 28 raſen des hertzen ...

L. M. N. 20 *Klagen:* das iſt wenn das volck klagt, heulet vnd ſchreyet vber die theurung vnd iamer ym land da alles ſich weg friſſet vnd vnterhenden verſchwindet, wilches geſchicht, das Gott dem land nicht ſegenet, ſondern flucht vnd ſchilt.

29 of herte. And thou shalt grope at none daye as the blynde gropeth in darkenesse, and shalt not come to the right waye.

And thou shalt suffre wronge only and be polled euermore, and no man shall *polled, plundered, robbed*
30 soker the, thou shalt be betrothed vnto a *soker, succor* wife, and another shall lye with her. Thou shalt bylde an housse and another shall dwell therein. Thou shalt plante a vyneyarde, and shalt not make it comen.
31 Thine oxe shalbe slayne before thyne eyes, ād thou shalt not eate thereof. Thine asse shalbe violently taken awaye euen before thi face, and shall not be restored the agayne. Thy shepe shalbe geuen vnto thine enemyes, ād no .P. man shall helpe the.
32 Thy sonnes ād thy doughters shall be geuē vnto another nacion, and thyne eyes shall se and dase vppon them all daye longe, but shalt haue no myghte in thyne
33 hande. The frute of thy londe and all thy laboures shall a nacyon which thou knowest not, eate, ād thou shalt but soffre violence only and be oppressed alwaye:
34 that thou shalt be cleane besyde thy selfe for the syghte of thyne eyes whiche thou shalt se.
35 The Lord shall smyte the with a myscheuous botche in the knees ād legges, so that thou cāst not be healed: euē from the sole of the fote vnto the toppe of the heed.
36 The Lorde shall brynge both the and thy kynge which thou hast sett ouer the, vnto a nacyon whiche nether thou nor thy fathers haue knowne, and there thou shalt serue straunge goddes: euen wodd ād stone.
37 And thou shalt goo to wast ād be made an ensample ād a gestyngestocke vnto al naciōs whether the Lord shall carye the. *gestyngestocke a laughingstock*
38 Thou shalt carie moch seed out in to

𝔐. 29 at none dayes ... ȝ ryght awaye 30 betrawthed
𝒱. 29 non dirigas vias tuas ... calumniam sustineas, & opprimaris violentia 30 non habites in ea ... non vindemies eam. 32 deficientibus ad conspectum eorum 33 semper calumniam sustinens, & oppressus 34 stupens ad terrorem eorum 37 eris perditus, in prouerbium ac fabulam
𝐋. 30 nicht drynnen wonen 31 nicht gemeyn machen. 32 alle werden vber yhnen 34 wansynnig 37 vnd wirst verwustet, vnd eyn sprich wort vnd sabel

the felde, and fhalt gather but litle in: for the locuftes
39 fhall deftroye it, Thou fhalt plante a vyneyarde and
dreffe it, but fhalt nether drynke off the wyne nether
gather of the grapes,[Fo. L.] for the wormes fhall eate
40 it. Thou fhalt haue olyue trees in all thy coftes, but
fhalt not be anoynted with the oyle, for thyne olyue
41 trees fhalbe rooted out. Thou fhalt get fonnes ād
doughters, but fhalt not haue them: for they fhalbe
42 caried awaye captyue. All thy trees and frute of thy
londe fhalbe marred with blaftynge.
43 The ftraungers that are amonge you fhall clyme
aboue the vpp an hye, ād thou fhalt come doune be-
44 neth alowe. He fhall lende the ād thou fhalt not lende
him, he fhalbe before ād thou behynde.
45 Moreouer all thefe curfes fhall come vppō the and
fhall folowe the and ouertake the, tyll thou be deftroyed: becaufe thou herkenedeft not vnto the voyce
of the Lorde thy God, to kepe his cōmaundmētes ād
46 ordinaunces whiche he cōmaūded the, ād they fhalbe
vppō the as miracles ād wonders ād vppon thy feed
47 for euer. And becaufe thou feruedeft not the Lorde
thy God with ioyfulneffe and with a good herte for the
48 abundaunce of all thinges, therfore thou fhalt ferue
thyne enemye whiche the Lorde fhall fende vppon the:
in hunger and thruft, in nakedneffe and in nede off all
thynge: and he fhall put a yocke off yerne vppon thyne
necke, vntyll he haue broughte .P. the to noughte.
49 And the Lorde fhall brynge a nacion vppon the
from a farre, euen from the ende off the worlde, as
50 fwyfte as an egle fleeth: a nacion whofe tonge thou

M. 38 for the grefhoppers 49 flyeth
V. 40 quia defluent, & deperibunt 41 et non frueris eis 42 rubigo 43 defcendes, & eris inferior. 46 Et erunt in te figna atque prodigia 47 in gaudio, cordifque lætitia 49 in fimilitudinem aquilæ volantis cum impetu
L. 40 ausgeriffen 43 erunder fteygen vnd ymer vnterligen 46 darumb werden zeychen vnd wunder an dyr feyn 47 mit frolichem vnd gutem hertzen 49 wie eyn Adeler fleuget
M. M. N. 42 *blaftynge:* Or grefhoppers, fome reade vermyn. 46 *as miracles and wonders:* Myracles do fometyme ftreangthen the weakneffe of the faithfull and blynde the vnfaythfull, and be vnto them a wytneffe of dānacyon.

ſhalt not vnderſtonde: a herde fauoured nacion whiche
ſhall not regarde the perſon of the olde nor haue com-
51 paſſiō on the younge. And he ſhall eate the frute of
thy londe and the frute of thy catell vntyll he haue
deſtroyed the: ſo that he ſhall leaue the nether corne,
wyne, nor oyle, nether the ēcreaſe of thyne oxen nor
the flockes of thy ſhepe: vntyll he haue brought the
52 to nought. And he ſhall kepe the in all thy cities,
vntyll thy hye ād ſtronge walles be come doune wereī
thou truſtedeſt, thorow all thy londe. And he ſhall
beſege the in all thy cities thorow out all thy land
whiche the Lorde thy God hath geuen the.

53 And thou ſhalt eate the frute of thyne awne bodye:
the fleſſh of thy ſonnes and off thy doughters which the
Lorde thy God hath geuen the, in that ſtrayteneſſe and
54 ſege wherewith thyne enemye ſhall beſege the: ſo that
it ſhall greue the man that is tender and exceadynge
delycate amonge you, to loke on his brother and vppon
his wife that lyeth in hys boſome ād on the remnaunte
55 of his childern, whiche he hath yet lefte, for ſeare of
geuynge [Fo. LI.] vnto any of them of the fleſh of hys
childern, whiche he eateth, becauſe he hath noughte
lefte him in that ſtrayteneſſe and ſege wherewith thyne
enemye ſhall beſege the in all thy cytyes.

56 Yee and the woman that is ſo tender and delycate
amonge you that ſhe dare not auenture to ſett the ſole
of hyr foote vppon the grounde for ſoftneſſe and ten-
derneſſe, ſhalbe greued to loke on the huſbonde that
leyeth in hir boſome and on hyr ſonne and on hyr
57 doughter: euen becauſe of the afterbyrthe that ys
come out from betwene hyr legges, and becauſe of hyr
childern whiche ſhe hath borne, becauſe ſhe wolde eate

M. 52 kepe the in, in all thy cities ... thorow all the lande
56 auēture

V. 50 gentem procaciſſimam, quæ non deſerat 52 conterat ...
Obſideberis 53 in anguſtia & vaſtitate qua opprimet 55 in ob-
ſidione & penuria qua vaſtauerint 56 Tenera mulier & delicata
(v. 54) ... propter mollitiem & teneritudinem nimiam, inuidebit

L. 52 engſten ... geengſtet werden 53 angſt vnd not (vv. 55,
57) 54 ein man der zuuor zertlich vnd ynn luſten .. vergonnen (cf.
v. 56 Eyn weyb, etc.) 55 engſten 57 die affterburd die zwiſſchen
yhr eygen beynen ſind ausgangen

them for nede off all thynges fecretly, in the ftrayteneffe and fege wherewith thine enemye fhall befege the in thy cities.

58 Yf thou wilt not be diligent to doo all the wordes of this lawe that are wrytten in thys boke, for to feare this glorious and fearfull name of the Lorde thy God:
59 the Lorde will fmyte both the and thy feed with wonderfull plages and with greate plages and of longe continuaunce, and with euell fekeneffes and of longe duraunce.
60 Moreouer he wyll brynge vppon the all the difeafes off Egipte whiche thou waft afrayed off, and they fhall
61 clea- .P. ue vnto the. Thereto all maner fekeneffes and all maner plages whiche are not wrytten in the boke of this lawe, wyll the Lorde brynge vppon the
62 vntyll thou be come to noughte. And ye fhalbe lefte fewe in numbre, where to fore ye were as the ftarres off heauen in multitude: becaufe thou woldeft not herkē vnto the voyce of the Lorde thy God.
63 And as the Lorde reioyfed ouer you to do you good and to multiplye you: euen fo he will reioyfe ouer you, to deftroye you and to brynge you to nought. And ye fhalbe wafted from of the lande whother thou goeft
64 to enioye it, And the Lorde fhall fcater the amonge all nacyons from the one ende of the worlde vnto the other, and there thou fhalt ferue ftraunge goddes, which nether thou nor thy fathers haue knowne: euen wod and ftone.
65 And amonge thefe nacyons thou fhalt be no fmall feafon, and yet fhalt haue no refte for the fole of thy foote. For the Lorde fhall geue the there a trēblynge
66 herte ād dafynge eyes and forowe of mynde. And thy lyfe fhall hange before the, and thou fhalt feare both daye

V. 58 nomen ... hoc eft dominum deum tuum 59 plagas magnas & perfeuerantes, infirmitates peffimas & perpetuas 60 omnes afflictiones Ægypti 64 a fummitate terræ vfque ad terminos eius 65 non quiefces ... cor pauidum, & defic. oculos, & animam confumptam mœrore 66 vita tua quafi pendens ante te.

𝔏. 58 namen den Herrn deynen Gott 59 wunderlich mit dyr vmbgehen 60 alle feuge Egypti 62 ewer wenig pubels vberbleyben 64 von eym end der welt bis ans ander 65 keyn wehre haben ... bebendes hertz .. ammacht der augen .. verfchmachte feele, 66 das deyn leben wirt fur dyr hangen

67 and nyghte ād ſhalt haue no truſt in thy lyfe. In the mornynge thou ſhalt ſaye, wolde God it were nyghte. And at nyghte thou ſhalt ſaye, [Fo. LII.] wolde God it were mornynge. For ſeare off thyne herte whiche thou ſhalt ſeare, and for the ſyghte of thyne eyes whiche thou ſhalt ſe.

68 And the Lorde ſhall brynge the in to Egipte agayne with ſhippes, by the waye which I bade the that thou ſhuldeſt ſe it nomoare. And there ye ſhalbe ſolde vnto youre enemyes, for bondmen and bondwemen: and yet no man ſhall bye you.

⁋ The .XXIX. Chapter.

M.C.S. *The people are exhorted to obſerue the cōmaundementes for the conſyderacion of benefytes receaued: which yf they breake they are threatned to be plaged.*

1 THESE are the wordes of the appoyntmēt which the Lorde commaunded Moſes to make with the childern of Iſrael in the londe of Moab, beſyde the appoyntment whiche he made with them in Horeb.

2 And Moſes called vnto all Iſrael and ſayed vnto them: Ye haue ſene all that the Lorde dyd before youre eyes in the lande of Egipte, vnto Pharao and vnto all his

3 ſeruauntes, and vnto all his londe, and the greate temptacyons whiche thyne eyes haue ſene and thoſe

4 greate myracles and wonders: and yet the Lorde hath not geuen you an herte to perceaue, nor eyes to ſe, nor eares to heare vnto this daye.

5 .P. And I haue led you .xl. yere in the wilderneſſe: and youre clothes are not waxed olde vppon you, nor are

6 thy ſhowes waxed olde vppon thy fete. Ye haue eaten

V. 67 propter cordis tui formidinem, qua terreberis 68 per viam de qua dixit tibi xxix, 2 in terra Ægypti 3 ſigna illa portentaque ingentia 4 cor intelligens 5 Adduxit vos ... attrita veſtimenta ... calceamenta ... vetuſtate conſumpta ſunt

L. 67 Wer gibt ... Wer gibt ... fur groſſer furcht .. die dich ſchrecken 68 durch den weg, dauon ich geſagt hab. xxix, 2 ynn Egypten .. 3 groſſe zeychen vnd wunder 4 eyn hertz, das verſtendig were 5 Er hat euch ... laſſen wandeln .. veraltet .. veraltet

no bred nor droncke wyne or ftrounge dryncke: that
ye myghte knowe, howe that he is the Lorde youre
God.

7 And at the laſt ye came vnto this place, ād Sihon the
kynge of Heſbon and Og kynge of Baſan came out agenſt
8 you vnto batayle, and we ſmote them and toke their
londe and gaue it an heritaunce vnto the Rubenites
9 and Gadites and to the halfe tribe of Manaſſe. Kepe
therfore the worde of this appoyntment and doo them,
that ye maye vnderſtonde all that ye ought to doo.

10 Ye ſtonde here this daye euery one of you before
the Lorde youre God: both the heedes of youre trybes,
youre elders, youre officers ād all the mē of Iſrael:
11 youre childern, youre wyues and the ſtraungere that
are in thyne hoſt, from the hewer of thy wod vnto the
12 drawer of thy water: that thou ſhuldeſt come vnder the
appoyntment of the Lorde thy God, and vnder his othe
which the Lorde thy God maketh with the this daye.
13 For to make the a people vnto him ſelfe, and that he
maye be vnto the a God, as he hath ſayed vnto the and
[Fo. LIII.] as he hath ſworne vnto thi fathers Abraham, Iſaac and Iacob.

14 Alſo I make not this bonde and this othe with you
15 only: but both with him that ſtōdeth here with us
this daye before the Lorde oure God, and alſo with
16 him that is not here with us this daye. For ye knowe
how we haue dwelt in the londe of Egipte, and how
we came thorow the myddes of the nacions which we
17 paſſed by. And ye haue ſene their abhominaciōs and
their ydolles: wod, ſtone, ſiluer and golde which they
had.

M. 9 wordes
V. 6 vt ſciretis 7 et veniſtis ... occurrentes nobis ad pugnam.
9 verba ... vt intelligatis vniuerſa quæ facitis. 10 atque doctores,
omnis populus Iſrael 11 exceptis lignorum cæſor. 12 vt tranſeas
in fœdere 15 ſed cunctis præſentibus & abſentibus. 17 abomina-
tiones & ſordes, id eſt idola eorum ... quæ colebant.

L. 6 auff das du wiſſeſt 7 Vnd da yhr kamet ... mit vns zu
ſtreytten 9 die wort ... auff das yhr klug ſeyt ynn allem das yhr
thut. 10 die vberſten ewr ſtemmen, ewr Eltiſten, ewr amptleut,
eyn yderman 12 eynhergehen 15 mit denen, die heutte nicht mit
vns ſind, 17 yhr grewel vnd yhre gotzen ... die bey yhn waren.

18 Left there be amonge you man or woman kynred or trybe that turneth awaye in his hert this daye from the Lord oure God, to goo ād ſerue the goddes of theſe nacions: and left there be amonge you ſome roote that
19 bereth gall and wormwod, ſo that when he heareth the wordes of this curſe, he bleſſe him ſelfe in his hert ſayenge: I feare it not, I will ther fore walke after the luſt of myne awne hert, that the drounken deſtroye the thurſtie.
20 And ſo the Lorde will not be mercyfull vnto him, but then the wrath of the Lorde ād his geloufye, ſmoke agenſt that man, ād al the curſes that are written in this boke light vppō him, and the Lorde doo out
21 his name frō vnder heauen, and ſeparate him vnto euell out of .P. all the trybes of Iſrael acordynge vnto all the curſes of the appoyntement that is written in the boke of this lawe.
22 So that the generacion to come of youre childern that ſhal ryſe vpp after you ād the ſtraunger that ſhall come from a ferre londe, ſaye when they ſe the plages

𝔐. 19 ſayinge. I ſhall haue peace. I will therfore worcke . . . that the donckē may peryſh with the thryſtye.

𝒱. 18 mulier, familia . . . radix germinans fel & amaritudinem. 19 iuramenti huius . . . Pax erit mihi, & ambul. in prauitate cordis mei: & aſſumat ebria ſitientem 20 quammaxime furor eius fumet . . . & deleat 21 & conſumat eum in perditionem . . in libro legis huius ac fœderis

𝔏. 18 eyn weyb, odder eyn geſind . . . galle vnd wermut trage 19 diſes fluchs dennoch ſich ſegene . . . ſpreche, Es wirt ſo boſe nicht, Ich . . . wie es meyn hertz dunckt, das die trunckne mit der durſtigen verloren werde. 20 austilgen 21 abſondern zum vbel . . . lautts aller fluche des bunds

𝔐. 𝔐. N. 19 *The dronckē man etc.:* By this is ſygnyfyed, that bothe the wycked teacher & the dyſcyple which receaueth euell doctryne ſhall peryſh together. Some reade that the droncken maye be put to the thriſye (*ſic*). Some, that dronckneſſe maye be put to thriſt.

𝔏. 𝔐. N. 19 *Es wirt ſo boſe nicht:* Das iſt der rauchloſen leut wort vnd gedancken, Ey die helle iſt nicht ſo heyſs, Es hat nicht nott, der teuffel iſt nicht ſo grewlich als man yhn malet, wilchs alle werckheyligen frech vnd turſtiglich thun, ia noch lohn ym hymel gewarten. *das die trunckene:* Das iſt, das lerer vnd iunger miteynander verloren werden, Der lerer iſt der truncken von ſeynem tollen weyn, da Eſaias von ſagt, der gehet vber vnd verfuret mit ſich die durſtigen vnd ledigen ſeelen, die da ymer lernen, vnd nymer zur warheit komen, wie Sanct Paulus ſagt.

of that londe, and the difeafes where with the Lorde
23 hath fmytten it how all the londe is burnt vpp with
bremftone and falt, that it is nether fowne nor beareth
nor any graffe groweth therein, after the ouerthrowenge
of Sodome, Gomor, Adama ād Zeboim: which the
Lorde ouerthrewe in his wrath and angre.
24 And than all nacions alfo faye: wherfore hath the
Lorde done of this facion vnto this londe? O how
25 fearfe is this greatt wrath? And men fhall faye: becaufe they lefte the teftamēt of the Lorde God of their
fathers which he made with them, whē he brought
26 them out of the lande of Egipte. And they went ād
ferued ftraunge goddes and worfhipped them: goddes
which they knewe not and which had geuen them
27 nought. And therfore the wrath off the Lorde waxed
whote vppon that londe to brynge vppon it all the
28 curfes that are written in this boke. And the Lorde
caft them out of their londe in angre, wrath and greate
furyou- [Fo. LIIII.] fneffe, and caft thē in to a ftraunge
londe, as it is come to paffe this daye.
29 The fecrettes perteyne vnto the Lorde oure God
and the thinges that are opened perteyne vnto us and
oure childern for euer, that we doo all the wordes of
this lawe.

M. 23 falt, & ẏ it is 24 And then fhall 29 The fecrettes of the
Lorde oure God are opened vnto us
V. 23 ita vt vltra non feratur . . in exemplum fubuerfionis
Sod. . . . quas fubuertit 24 quæ eft hæc ira furoris eius immenfa ?
25 Ægypti: 26 & feruierunt . . . & quibus non fuerant attributi
28 in indignatione maxima . . . ficut hodie comprobatur. 29 Ab-
fcondita, domino . . . : quæ manifefta funt, nobis
V. 23 gleych wie Sodom . . . vmbkeret find 24 Was ift das
fur fo groffer grymmiger zorn? 26 vnd find hyngangen . . . vnd
den nichts zu geteylet ift. 28 mit groffem zorn, grym vnd vngna-
den . . . wie es ftehet heuttigs tages. 29 Das geheymnis des Herrn
vnfers Gottis ift vns vnd vnfern kindern eroffnet ewiglich
M. M. N. 29 *are opened:* That is, the Lord hath opened vnto
vs his wyll before all other people.
L. M. N. 29 *Das geheymnis:* wil fo fagen, Vns Iuden hat
Got fur allen volckern auff erden, feynen willen offenbart, vnd
was er ym fynn hatt, drumb follen wir auch defte vleiffiger feyn.

The .XXX. Chapter.

1 WHEN all these wordes are come vpō the whether it be the blessinge or the cursse which I haue set before the: yet yf thou turne vnto thyne hert amonge all the nacions whother the Lorde thi God hath
2 thruste the, and come agayne vnto the Lorde thi God ād herken vnto his voyce acordinge to all that I cōmaunde the this daye: both thou and thi childern with
3 all thine hert and all thi soule: Then the Lorde thi God wil turne thi captiuite ād haue cōppassion vpō the ād goo ād sett the agayne from all the nacions, amōge which the Lorde thi God shall haue scatered the.
4 Though thou wast cast vnto the extreme partes of heauen: euen from thence will the Lorde thi God gather
5 the and from thence sett the and brynge the in to the lande which thi fathers possessed, and thou shalt enioye it. And he will shewe the kyndnesse and .P. multiplye
6 the aboue thi fathers. And the Lorde thi God will circumcyse thine hert and the hert of thi seed for to loue the Lorde thi God with all thine hert and all thi
7 soule, that thou mayst lyue. And the Lorde thi God will put al these curses vpō thine enemyes and on thē that hate the and persecute the.
8 But thou shalt turne and herken vnto the voyce of the Lorde and doo all his commaundmentes which I
9 commaunde the this daye And the Lorde thi God will make the plenteous in all the workes of thine hande and in the frute of thi bodye, in the frute of thi

M.C.S. The worde of God is not farre from thē that seke for it, but in their mouthes and hertes.

V. 1 & ductus pœnitudine cordis tui in vniuersis gentibus 2 & reuersus (vv. 8, 9, 10) fueris ad eum 3 reducet . . . te ante disperfit. 4 inde te retrahet 7 conuertet super inimicos tuos 9 & abundare . . . in sobole vteri tui

L. 2 vnd bekerist (vv. 8, 9, 10) dich zu dem Herrn deynem Got 3 deyn gesengnis wenden 7 auff deyne seynde legen 9 dich lassen vberflussig seyn

catell and frute of thi lande and in riches. For the
Lorde will turne agayne and reioyfe ouer the to doo the
10 good, as he reioyfed ouer thi fathers: Yf thou herken
vnto the voyce of the Lorde thy God, to kepe his commaundmentes and ordynaunces which are written in
the boke of this lawe, yf thou turne vnto the Lord thi
God with all thine hert and all thi foule.

11 For the commaundment which I commaunde the
this daye, is not feparated from the nether ferre of.
12 It is not in heauen, that thou neadeft to faye: who
fhall goo vpp for us in to heauen, and fett it us, that
13 we maye heare it ād doo it: Nether is it beyonde the
fee, that thou fhuldeft faye: who fhall goo ouer fee for us
and fett [Fo. LV.] it us that we maye heare it and doo
14 it: But the worde is very nye vnto the: euen in thi
mouth and in thine hert, that thou doo it.

15 Beholde I haue fett before you this daye lyfe and
16 good, deeth and euell: in that I commaunde the this
daye to loue the Lorde thi God and to walke in his
wayes and to kepe his commaundementes, his ordynaunces and his lawes: that thou mayft lyue and multiplye, and that the Lorde thy God maye bleffe the in
the londe whother thou goeft to poffeffe it.

17 But and yf thyne hert turne awaye, fo that thou
wilt not heare: but fhalt goo aftraye and worfhepe
18 ftraunge goddes and ferue them, I pronounce vnto you
this daye, that ye fhal furely perefh and that ye fhall
not prolonge youre dayes vppon the londe whother
thou paffeft ouer Iordayne to goo and poffeffe it.

19 I call to recorde this daye vnto you, heauen and
erth, that I haue fett before you lyfe and deeth, bleffynge and curfynge: but chofe lyfe, that thou and thi

𝔐. 12 for vs to heauen
𝒱. 9 in vbertate terræ tuæ, & in rerum omnium largitate.
11 non fupra te 13 vt cauferis, & dicas ... poterit transfretare
mare .. audire & facere quod præceptum eft ? 15 bonum, & econ-
trario mortem & malum: 16 vt diligas ... atque multiplicet 17
atque errore deceptus 18 prædico tibi 19 Elige ergo vitam
ℒ. 9 an der frucht deyns lands, zum gutten. 11 nicht zu wunderlich, noch zu ferne 14 faft nah 15 das bofe, 16 der ich dyr
heute gepiete 17 fondern felleft aus 19 das du das leben erweleft

20 feed maye lyue, in that thou loueſt the Lorde thi God herkeneſt vnto his voyce and cleaueſt vnto him. For he is thi life and the lengthe of thi dayes, that thou mayſt dwell vppon the erth which the Lorde ſware vnto thi fathers: Abraham, Iſaac and Iacob to .P. geue them.

❧ The .XXXI. Chapter.

1 AND Moſes went and ſpake theſe
2 wordes vnto all Iſrael and ſayed vnto them I am an hundred ād .xx. yere olde this daye, ād can nomoare goo out and in. Alſo the Lorde hath ſayed vnto me, thou ſhalt
3 not go ouer this Iordayne. The Lord youre God he will go ouer before the ād he will deſtroye theſe nacions before the, ād thou ſhalt cōquere thē. And Ioſua he ſhall goo ouer before the, as the Lorde
4 hath ſayed. And the Lorde ſhall doo vnto them, as he dyd to Sihon ād Og kynges of the Amorites ād vnto their landes which kinges he deſtroyed.
5 And when the Lorde hath delyuered them to the, ſe that ye doo vnto them acordynge vnto all the cō-
6 maundmentes which I haue cōmaunded you. Plucke vpp youre hartes and be ſtronge, dreade not nor be aferde of them: for the Lorde thi God him ſelfe will goo with the, and wil nether let the goo nor forſake the:

M.C.S. *Moſes beyng readye to dye ordereth Ioſue to rule the people in his ſteade. This boke Deuteronomye is wrytten and layde in the tabernacle beſyde the arcke The Leuites are charged to reade hit to the people.*

M. 2 an hūdred & .xx. yere this daye 4 Sehon
V. 20 et illi adhæreas (ipſe eſt enim vita . . .) xxxi, 2 præſertim cum 3 deus tuus . . omnes gentes has 4 delebitque eos. 5 ſimiliter facietis 6 Viriliter agite, & confortamini . . . nec paueatis ad conſpectum eorum
L. 20 vnd yhm anhanget, Denn das iſt deyn leben. xxxi, 3 Der Herr deyn Gott . . das du ſie eynnemeſt 6 Seyt getroſt vnd freydig
M. M. N. 2 *Go out and in:* To go in and oute is to exercyſe the offyce of a myniſtre & leader of thē: as chriſt ſayth of the miniſters aud paſtoures. Iohan. x, a.

7 And Moses called vnto Iosua and sayed vnto him in the sighte of all Israel: Be ströge and bolde, for thou must goo with this people vnto the londe which the Lorde [Fo. LVI.] hath sworne vnto their fathers to geue them, and thou shalt geue it them to enheret.
8 And the Lorde he shall goo before the ād he shall be with the, and wil not let the goo nor forsake the, feare not therfore nor be discomforted.
9 And Moses wrote this lawe and delyuered it vnto the preastes the sonnes of Leui which bare the arke of the testament of the Lorde, and vnto all the elders of Israel,
10 and commaunded them sayenge: At the ende of .vii yere, in the tyme of the fre yere, in the fest of the tab-
11 ernacles, when all Israel is come to appere before the Lorde thi God, in the place which he hath chosen: se that thou reade this lawe before all Israel in their eares
12 Gather the people together: both men, wemen and childern and the straungers that are in thi cities, that they maye heare, lerne and feare the Lorde youre God, and be diligent to kepe all the wordes of this lawe,
13 and that theyr childern which knowe nothinge maye heare and lerne to feare the Lorde youre God, as longe as ye lyue in the londe whother ye goo ouer Iordayne to possesse it.
14 And the Lorde sayed vnto Moses:
Beholde thy dayes are come, that thou .P. must dye. Call Iosua and come and stonde in the tabernacle of witnesse, that I maye geue him a charge. And Moses and Iosua went and stode in the tabernacle off witnesse.
15 And the Lorde apeared in the tabernacle: euen in the pyler off the cloude. And the piler of the cloude stode ouer the dore of the tabernacle.

V. 7 Confortare... eam forte diuides. 8 nec paueas. 13 filii ... qui nunc ignorant: vt audire possint, & timeant.. versantur 14 prope sunt dies mortis 15 dominus ibi in columna nubis quæ stetit

L. 7 vnter sie austeylen 8 mit dyr seyn ... erchrick nicht. 11 ort, den er erwelen wirt 12 fur der versamlung des volcks ... ynn deynem thor 13 kinder die nichts wissen 14 deyne zeyt.. das du sterbist.. yhm befelh thue 15 ynn der hutten

16 And the Lorde fayed vnto Mofes: beholde, thou muſt flepe with thi fathers, and this people will goo a whorynge after ſtraunge goddes off the londe whother they goo and will forſake me and breake the appoyntement which I haue made with them.
17 And then my wrath will waxe whote agenſt them, and I will forſake them and will hyde my face from them, and they ſhalbe conſumed. And when moch aduerſyte and tribulacion is come vppon them, then they will ſaye: becauſe oure God is not amonge us,
18 theſe tribulacions are come vppon us. But I wil hyde my face that ſame tyme for all the euels ſake which they ſhall haue wrought, in that they are turned vnto ſtraunge goddes.
19 Now therfore write ye this ſonge, and teach it the childern of Iſrael and put it in their mouthes that this ſonge maye be my witneſſe [Fo. LVII.] vnto
20 the childern of Iſrael. For when I haue brought them in to the londe whiche I ſware vnto their fathers that runneth with mylke ād honye, then they will eate and fyll them ſelues and waxe ſatt and turne vnto ſtraunge goddes and ſerue them and
21 rayle on me and breake my teſtament. And then when moch myſchefe and tribulacion is come vppon them, this ſonge ſhall anſwere before them, and be a witneſſe. It ſhall not be forgetten out of the mouthes of their ſeed: for I knowe their imaginacyon whiche they goo aboute euen now before I haue
22 broughte them in to the londe which I ſware. And

V. 16 irritum faciet fœdus 17 & erit in deuorationem ... omnia mala ... non eſt deus mecum, inuenerunt me 18 abſcondam, & celabo faciem 19 vt memoriter teneant & ore decantent 20 Introducam .. Cumque comederint 21 reſpondebit ei canticum .. terram quam ei pollicitus ſum.

L. 16 den bund faren laſſen (v. 20) 17 viel vngluck vnd angſt .. mich .. myr 19 legts ynn yhren mund 20 ich wil ſie .. bringen ..⁚ mich leſtern 21 ſur yhn antwortten 22 Alſo ſchreyb Moſe

M. M. N. 17 *hyde my face:* To hyde hys face is as moch as not to heare & to take a waye the tokens of hys kyndneſſe, as whē he geueth no eare to vs or oure prayers nor ſheweth vs any tokē of loue but ſetteth before oure eyes greuouſe afflyccions and euen verye death. As in Iob .xiii, d & Miche. iii, b.

Mofes wrote this fonge the fame feafon, and taught it the childern of Ifrael.

23 And the Lorde gaue Iofua the fonne off Nun a charge and fayed: be bolde and ftronge for thou fhalt brynge the childern of Ifrael in to the lond which I fware vnto them, ād I will be with the.

24 When Mofes had made an ende of wrytynge out the wordes of this lawe in a boke vnto the ende of them
25 he commaunded the Leuites which bare the arcke of
26 the teftamēt of the Lorde fayenge: take the boke off thys lawe and put it by the fyde of the arcke of the teftament of the Lorde youre God, and let it .P. be there
27 for a witneffe vnto the. For I knowe thi ftuberneffe and thi ftiffe necke: beholde, while I am yet a lyue with you this daye, ye haue bene difhobedient vnto the Lorde: ād how moch moare after my deeth.

28 Gather vnto me al the elders of youre trybes and youre officers, that I maye fpeake thefe wordes in their eares and call heauē ād erth to recorde agenft them.
29 For I am fure that after my deeth, they will vtterly marre them felues and turne from the waye which I commaunded you, and tribulacion will come vppon you in the later dayes, when ye haue wrought wekedneffe in the fight of the Lorde to prouoke him with the
30 workes of youre handes. And Mofes fpake in the eares of all the congregacion of Ifrael the wordes of this fonge, vnto the ende of them.

𝔐. 29 wickedneffe.
𝒱. 26 Tollite librum iftum .. contra te 27 femper cont. egiftis 28 atque doctores 29 inique agetis .. mala in extremo tempore
𝑳. 23 Vnd befalh Iofua .. getroft vnd frifch 24 gantz ausge-fchrieben 25 laden des zeugnis 26 zeuge fey widder dich 29 das yhrs ... verderben werdet .. vngluck begegen hernach

The .XXXII. Chapter.

1 HEARE o heauen, what I shall speake and heare o erth the wordes of my mouth. **M.C.S.** *The song of Moses. He gothe vp vnto the toppe of Abarim to see the lande of promesse.*

2 My doctrine droppe as doeth the rayne, ād my speach flowe as doeth the mesellynge, dewe, as the mesellynge vpō the herbes, *small rain, drizzle*

3 ād as the droppes vppō the grasse. For I wil call on the name of the Lorde: Magnifie the might of oure God.

4 [Fo. LVIII.] He is a rocke and perfecte are his deades, for all his wayes are with discrecion. God is faithfull and without wekednesse, both rightuous and iuste is he.

5 The frowarde and ouerthwarte generacion hath marred them selues to himward, *ouerthwarte, adj. opposite, perverse* ād are not his sonnes for their deformities sake,

6 Doest thou so rewarde the Lorde? O foolish nacyon ād vnwyse. Is not he thy father ād thyne owner? hath he not made the and ordeyned the?

7 Remembre the dayes that are past: consydre the

V. 1 cæli... Concrescat in pluuiam doctrina.. imber... stillæ 3 date magnificentiam 4 Dei perfecta sunt opera, & omnes viæ eius iudicia. 5 Peccauerunt ei, & non filii eius: in sordibus, gen. praua atque peruersa. 6 pater tuus, qui possedit 7 cogita generationes singulas

L. 4 On wandel sind die werck des Felsen 5 verkerete vnd verruckte art.. verterbet.. vmb yhrs taddels willen. 6 nerricht vnd vnweyses volck?.. bereyttet? 7 iar der vorigen geschlechten.

M. M. N. 1 *Heare O heauē:* The Prophetes coustomably, when they speake with a feruent affeccion, do speake vnto thynges that haue no lyfe, as thoughe they spake to men, as in Esai. the fyrst a. And here Moses thynkyng that the chyldren of Israel wold not ernestly heare hym, and that he shulde lose hys laboure willeth yet heuen and erth to heare him & to be his wytnesses that he recyted this song vnto them. 4 *Rock.* God is called a Rock, becaufe he & hys worde lasteth for euer, he is suer to trust to, & a perfect consort to beleuers, and their singuler defence at all times 2 Reg. xxii, a.

L. M. N. 4 *Felsen:* die Ebreisch sprach heyst Got eynen Fels, das ist, eyn trotz, trost, hord, vnd sicherung, allen die sich auff yhn verlassen vnd yhm trawen. *Gerichte:* das ist das sie yderman recht verschaffen vnd niemant vnrecht thun.

yeres from tyme to tyme. Axe thy father ād he will
shewe the, thyne elders and they wyll tell the.

8 Whē the most hyghest gaue the nacyons an enheritaunce, ād diuided the sonnes of Adam he put the borders of the nacions, fast by the multitude of the childern
of Israel.

9 For the Lordes parte is his folke, ād Israel is the
porcion of his enheritaunce.

10 He founde him in a deserte londe, in a voyde ground
ād a rorynge wildernesse. he led hī aboute and gaue
him vnderstondynge, ād kepte him as the aple of his eye.

11 As an egle that stereth vpp hyr nest and flotereth
ouer hyr younge, he stretched oute his wynges and
toke hym vpp and bare hym.P. on his shulders.

12 The Lorde alone was his guyde, and there was no
straunge God with him.

13 He sett him vpp apon an hye londe, and he ate the
encreafe of the feldes. And he gaue hī honye to sucke
out of the rocke, ād oyle out of the harde stone.

14 With butter of the kyne and mylke of the shepe,
with fatt of the lambes ād fatt rammes and he gootes
with fatt kydneyes and with whete. And of the
bloude of grapes thou drōkest wyne.

15 And Israel waxed fatt and kyked. Thou wast fatt,
thicke and smothe, And he let God goo that made hī
and despysed the rocke that saued him.

M. 9 and Iacob is the porcion 14 of kyne
V. 8 diuidebat .. constit. term. pop. iuxta numerum filiorum
Isr. 9 funiculus hæred. 10 loco horroris, & vastæ solitudinis. 11 pro-
uocans ad volandum .. volitans ... in humeris suis. 14 & hircos
cum medulla tritici 15 Incrassatus est dilectus, & recalcitrauit,
incrassatus, impinguatus, dilatatus .. 15 a deo salutari suo.
L. 8 austeylet .. der menschen kinder .. nach der zal der kinder
Israel. 9 schnur seyns erbs. 10 eynode da es heulet. 11 auffweckt
seyn nest .. schwebt .. trug yhn auff seynen flugeln. 13 vnd etzet
yhn 14 vnd böcke mit fetten nieren, vnd weytzen. 15 wart er geyl.
Du bist fett vnd dick vnd glat worden .. Gott faren lassen
M. M. N. 9 *Iacob:* Onely the faythfull, which are sygnifyed by
Iacob, are Goddes porcion: the vnbeleuers be longe not to him.
11 *Bare hym on his shulders:* To beare thē on his shoulders is
to saue & kepe thē from euell, & let thē haue the fruicyon of hys
goodnes, as in Nume. xi, c. 14 *butter of kyne etc.:* By these
thynges named, are sygnifyed aboundaūce of all good thynges as
it is sayd in Psal. Lxii, b.

16 They angred him with straūge goddes ād with abhominacions prouoked him.

17 They offered vnto feldedeuels and not to God, ād to goddes which they knewe not ād to newe goddes that came newly vpp whiche their fathers feared not. *feldedeuels, satyrs*

18 Of the rocke that begat the thou arte vnmyndefull and haſt forgott God that made the.

19 And when the Lorde ſawe it, he was angre becauſe of the prouokynge of his ſonnes and doughters.

20 [Fo. LIX.] And he ſayed: I will hyde my face from thē and will ſe what their ende ſhall be. For they are a froward generacion ād childern in whō is no ſayth.

21 They haue angred me with that whiche is no god, and prouoked me with their vanities And I agayne will angre them with thē whiche are no people, and will prouoke thē with a foeliſh nacion.

22 For fire is kyndled in my wrath, ād ſhal burne vnto the botome of heell. And ſhall conſume the erth with her encreaſe, and ſet a fire the botoms of the mountaynes.

23 I will hepe myſcheues vpon the ād will ſpēde all myne arowes at them.

24 Burnt with hungre ād conſumed with heet and with bitter peſtilence. I will alſo ſende the tethe of beeſtes vppon them and poyſon ſerpentes.

25 Without forth, the ſwerde ſhall robbe thē off theire childern: and wythin in the chamber, feare: both younge men and younge wemen and the ſuckelynges with the mē of gray heedes.

𝔙. 20 generatio enim peruerſa eſt, & infideles filii. 22 vſque ad inferni nouiſſima . . . germine 24 Conſumentur fame, & deuorabunt eos aues morſu amariſſimo . . cum furore trahentium

𝔏. 16 zu eyffer gereytzet durch frembde. 17 felt teuffeln geopffert . . . den newen die newlich komen find . . ewr veter 18 fels der dich geporn hat (cf. v. 16) 20 kinder da keyn glawb ynnen iſt. 22 bis ynn die vnterſten hell . . . gewechs 23 vngluck . . heuffen 24 verzehret werden vom fiber, vnd von bittern feuchen 25 berauben, vnd ynn den kamern

𝔐. 𝔐. N. 20 *I wyll hyde etc.:* Loke afore in the .xxxi, d.

26 I haue determened to fcater thē therowout the worlde, ād to make awaye the remēbraunce of them from amonge men.
27 Were it not that I feared the raylynge off .P. theyr enemyes, left theire aduerfaries wolde be prowde and faye: oure hye hande hath done al thefe workes and not the Lorde.
28 For it is a nacion that hath an vnhappye forcaft,
29 and hath no vnderftonge in them. I wolde they ware wyfe and vnderftode this ād wolde confider their later ende. *vnderftonge, underftanding*
30 Howe it cometh that one fhall chace a thoufande, and two putt ten thoufande off them to flyghte? excepte theire rocke had folde them, and becaufe the Lorde had delyuered them.
31 For oure rocke is not as their rocke, no though oure enemyes be iudge.
32 But their vynes are of the vynes of Sodom, and of the feldes of Gomorra. Their grapes are grapes of gall, and theire clufters be bytter.
33 Their wyne is the poyfon of dragons, ād the cruell gall of afpes.
34 Are not foch thinges layed in ftore with me, ād feeled vpp amonge my treafures?
35 Vengeaunce is myne and I will rewarde: their fete fhall flyde, when the tyme cometh. For the tyme of their deftruction is at honde, and the tyme that fhall come vppon them maketh haft.
36 For the Lorde will doo iuftice vnto hys [Fo. LX.] people, and haue compaffion on his feruauntes. For it

V. 26 dixi, Vbi nam funt? ceffare faciam ex hominibus memoriam eorum. 28 Gens abfque confilio 29 ac nouiffima prouiderent. 30 Quomodo ... deus fuus ... dominus conclufit illos? 31 Non enim eft deus nofter, vt dii eorum, & inimici 32 de fuburbanis Gom. 33 Fel drachonum ... & venenum afpidum infanabile. 34 condita ... fignata 35 retribuam eis in tempore
L. 26 Ich wil fagen, wo find fie? 28 keyn radt yn ift 30 Wie gehets zu .. yhr fels verkaufft 31 fels ... fels 32 acker Gomora .. trachen grym, Vnd wutiger ottern gall. 34 verfigelt 35 zu feyner zeyt fol yhr fufs gleytten

ſhalbe ſene that theire power ſhall fayle, and at the laſt they ſhalbe preſoned and forſaken.

37 And it ſhalbe ſayed: where are their goddes ād their rocke wherein they truſted?

38 The fatt of whoſe ſacrifices they ate and drancke the wyne of their drynckofferynges, let them ryſe vpp and helpe you and be youre protection.

39 Se now howe that I, I am he, and that there is no God but I. I can kyll and make alyue, ād what I haue ſmyten that I can heale: nether ys there that can delyuer any man oute off my honde.

40 For I will lifte vp my hande to heauē, ād will ſaye: I lyue euer.

41 Yf I whett the lyghtenynge of my ſwerde, and myne hande take in hande to doo iuſtyce, I will ſhewe vengeaunce on myne enemyes and will rewarde them that hate me.

42 I will make myne arowes dronkē with bloude, and my ſwerde ſhall eate fleſh of the bloud of the ſlayne and of the captyue and of the bare heed of the enemye.

43 Reioyſe hethen wyth hys people, for he will auenge the bloude off his ſervauntes, and wyll auenge hym off hys aduerſaryes, .P. and wilbe mercyfull vnto the londe off hys people.

M. 41 whett the edge of my ſwerde 43 Prayſe ye hethen his people

V. 36 Videbit quod infirmata ſit manus, & clauſi quoque defecerunt, reſiduique conſumpti ſunt. 37 dii eorum, in quibus 38 & in neceſſitate vos protegant. 39 percutiam & ego ſanabo 41 Si acuero vt fulgur gladium 42 Inebriabo ... & de captiuitate nudati inimicorum capitis. 43 Laudate gentes populum eius

L. 36 Vnd aus iſt auch mit dem der verſchloſſen vnd vbrig war. 37 ſels 39 was ich zu ſchlagen hab das kan ich heylen 41 Wenn ich den blitz meyns ſchwerds wetzen werde 42 ſol fleyſch freſſen, vber dem blutt ... vnd das des ſeynds heubt entbloſſet ſeyn wirt. 43 mit ſeym volck

M. M. N. 42 *Of the ſlayne:* Here recyteth he .iii. plages of the ſwerde, that many ſhalbe ſlayne, that they ſhall be leade captyue and brought in to bondage, & that their head ſhuld become bare, that is, their kyngdom and preſthode ſhulde be taken awaye frō thē.

L. M. N. 42 *Vber dem blut:* das ſind drey ſtraffen des ſchwerds, die erſt, das yhr vil erſchagen wirt, die ander das ſie gefangen gefurt werden, die drit, das yhr heubt blos ſolt werden, das iſt konigreich vnd prieſterthum ſolt von yhn genomen werden, wilche durchs har auff dem heubt bedeut wart.

44 And Moses went ād spake all the wordes of this songe in the eares of the people, both he and Iosua
45 the sonne of Nun. And when Moses had spoken all
46 these wordes vnto the ende to all Israel, then he sayed vnto them.

Sett youre hertes vnto all the wordes whiche I testifye vnto you this daye: that ye commaunde them vnto youre childern, to obserue and doo all the wordes
47 off thys lawe. For it is not a vayne worde vnto you: but it is youre lyfe, and thorow thys worde ye shall prolonge youre dayes in the lond whother ye goo ouer Iordayne to conquere it.

48 And the Lorde spake vnto Moses the selfe same daye
49 sayenge: get the vpp in to this mountayne Abarim vnto mount Nebo, which is in the londe of Moab ouer agenst Iericho.

And beholde the londe of Canaan whiche I geue vnto the childern of Israel to possesse.

50 And dye in the mount whiche thou goest vppon, and be gathered vnto thy people: As Aaron thy brother dyed in mounte Hor ād was gathered vnto his
51 people. For ye trespased agenst me amonge the childern of Israel at the waters off striffe, at Cades in the wyldernesse of Zin: becaufe ye sanctified me not a- [Fo.
52 LXI.] monge the childern of Israel. Thou shalt se the londe before the, but shall not goo thither vnto the londe which I geue the childern off Israel.

V. 46 Ponite corda ... testificor vobis ... vniuersa quæ scripta sunt in volumine legis huius 49 Abarim, id est, transitum, in montem Nebo 50 iungeris populis tuis .. appositus

L. 46 Nempt zu hertzen 50 wenn du hynauff komen bist ... versamle ... versamlet 51 an myr vergriffen 52 das land gegen dyr ... nicht hyneyn komen.

M. M. N. 46 *the wordes which I testifye:* To testifye the worde is to preache the worde & therfore is the worde called a testymonye or witnesse. Psal. cxviii, b.

The .XXXIII. Chapter.

1 THIS is the bleſſinge where with Moſes gods man bleſſed the childern of Iſrael before his deeth ſayenge: The Lord 2 came frō Sinai and ſhewed his beames from Seir vnto them, and appered glorioussy from mount Paran, and he came with thouſandes of ſayntes, and in his right 3 hande a lawe of fyre for them How loued he the people? All his ſayntes are in his honde. They yoyned thē ſelues vnto thy ſote and receaued thi wordes. 4 Moſes gaue us a lawe which is the enheritaunce of 5 the cōgregacion of Iacob. And he was in Iſrael kinge when he gathered the heedes of the people and the tribes of Iſrael to gether.

M.C.S. Moſes dying bleſſeth all the trybes of Iſrael.

6 Rubén ſhall lyue and ſhall not dye: but his people ſhalbe few in numbre.

7 This is the bleſſynge of Iuda. And he ſayed: heare Lorde the voyce of Iuda and bringe him vnto his people: let his handes fyght for him: but be thou his helpe agēſt his enemies.

8 And vnto Leui he ſayed: thy perfectneſſe .P. ād thi light be after thy mercifull mā whō thou tempteſt at

M. 2 Pharan 8 tēptedeſt at Maſah
V. 2 ortus eſt nobis 3 ſancti . . . & qui appropinquant pedibus eius, accipient de doctrina illius. 5 Erit apud rectiſſimum rex 7 adiutor illius . . . erit. 8 & doctrina tua a viro ſancto tuo
L. 2 vnd iſt yhnen auffgangen . . ſeurigs geſetz an ſie 3 heyligen ſind ynn deyner hand 5 Vnd er war in der fulle des konigs 7 ſeyne hende laſſe ſich mehren 8 Deyn Vollickeyt vnd deyn Liecht ſey nach dem man deyner barmhertzickeyt

M. M. N. 3 *All his ſayntes:* That is, let thy preaſtes offyce be happye and fortunate before God & men; by prayer, teachynge and good enſample geuynge, as it was in Moſes. 8 *Thy perfectneſſe and thy light:* This is the light & perfectneſſe, which Moſes put ī the breaſt lappe of iudgemēt Exo. xxviii, c & Num. xxvii, d. The Chald. interpr. readeth with perfectneſſe & light induedſt thou the man that was founde holye.

L. M. N. 5 *Fulle des konigs:* die fulle iſt das volck Iſrael, das Chriſti ſeyns konigs fulle iſt, wie Paulus die Chriſtenheyt nennet die fulle Chriſti Ephe. i. 8 *Vollickeyt:* Das iſt, wie Exo. 28 ſtehet das Heyligthum auff dem bruſtlatzen, wil alſo ſagen, Dein prieſterlich ampt ſey gluckſelig fur Gott vnd den menſchen, mit beten vnd leren wie es war an Moſe, der yhn von gottis gnaden geben war.

Mafa ād with whom thou ftriuedft at the waters of ftrife.
9 He that faieth vnto his father ād mother. I fawe him not ād vnto his brethern I knewe not, and to his fonne I wote not: for they haue obferued thi wordes and kepte thi tef-
10 tament. They fhall teach Iacob thi iudgementes ād Ifrael thi lawes. They fhall put cens before thi nofe and
11 whole facrifices apon thine altare. Bleffe Lorde their power and accepte the workes of their hondes: fmyte the backes of them that ryfe agēst them and of them that hate them: that they ryfe not agayne.
12 Vnto Ben Iamin he fayed: The Lordes derlynge fhall dwell in faffetye by him and kepe him felfe in the hauen by hym contynually, and fhall dwell betwene his fhulders.
13 And vnto Iofeph he fayed: bleffed of the Lorde is his londe with the goodly frutes off heauen, with dewe
14 and with fprynges that lye beneth: and with frutes of the encreafe of the fonne and wyth rype frute off the
15 monethes, and with the toppes of mountaynes that were from the begynnynge and with the dayntes of
16 hilles that laft euer and with goodly frute of the erth and off [Fo. LXII.] the fulneffe there of. And the good will of him that dwelleth in the bufh fhall come vppon the heed of Iofeph and vppon the toppe of the heed of him that was feparated frō
17 amonge his brethern his bewtye is as a firftborne oxe and his hornes as the hornes of an vnycorne. And with them he fhall pufh the nacions to gether, euen vnto the endes of the worlde. Thefe are the

M. 9 wyth whom thou ftryuedeft 11 hate them: they ryfe
V. 9 Nefcio vos . . . & nefcierunt filios fuos . . . feruauerunt, 10 iudicia tua o Iacob & legem (Heb. docebunt Iacob iudicia tua, & Ifrael legem tuam) . . . thymiama in furore tuo 12 quafi in thalamo tota die 13 rore, atque abyffo fubiacente. 15 de pomis collium 16 nazaræi 17 in ipfis ventilabit
L. 10 reuchwerg fur deyne nafe legen 12 Den gantzen tag wirt er vber yhn halten 13 vom taw, vnd von der tieffen die hunden ligt 16 Der gutte wille des der ynn dem pufch wonet . . des Nafir 17 wie eynhorners horner . . . ftoffen zu hauff
L. M. N. 13 *Edle fruchte:* Das ift vom konigreich Ifrael gefagt wilchs hoch gefegenet wart mit allem dz hymel, fonn, mond, erden, berg, tal, waffer vnd alles zeytlich gutt, trug vnd gab, dazu auch Propheten vnd heilig regentē hatte.

many thousandes of Ephraim and the thousandes off
Manasse.

18 And vnto Zabulon he sayed: Reioyse Zabulon in thi
19 goenge out, and thou Isachar in thi tentes. They shall
call the people vnto the hill, and there they shall offer
offerynges of righteousnes. For they shall sucke of the
abundaunce of the see and of treasure hyd in the sonde.
20 And vnto Gad he sayed: blessed is the rowmmaker
Gad. He dwelleth as a lion and caught the arme ād
21 also the toppe of the heed He sawe his begynnynge,
that a parte of the teachers were hyd there ād come
with the heedes of the people, and executed the righteousnes of the Lorde and his iudgementes with Israel.
22 And vnto Dan he sayed: Dan is a lions whelpe, he
shall flowe from Basan.
23 .P. And vnto Nepthali he sayed: Nepthali he shall
haue abundance of pleasure and shalbe fylled with the
blessinge of the Lorde ād shall haue his possessions in
the southwest.
24 And of Asser he sayed: Assar shalbe blessed with
childern: he shalbe acceptable vnto his brethern and
25 shall dyppe his fote in oyle: Yern and brasse shall hange
on thi showes and thine age shalbe as thi youth.
26 There is none like vnto the God of the off Israel: he
that sitteth vppon heauen shalbe thine helpe, whose

M. 17 Manasses. 21 a parte of the teacher was ... and came
26 vnto the God of Israel

V. 17 multitudines Ephraim, ... millia Manasse. 19 quasi lac
sugent 20 in latitudine Gad 21 principatum suum, quod in parte
sua doctor esset repositus 22 fluet largiter 23 abundantia perfru-
etur ... mare & meridiem 26 vt deus rectissimi .. Magnificentia
eius discurrunt nubes

L. 20 der raum macher ... der lerer hauffe verborgen lagen
23 gegen abend vnd mittag 26 Got des richtigen.

M. M. N. 19 *Sucke of the abundance etc.:* That is, they shall
haue aboundaunce of rychesse, what of marchaundyse cōmyng by
see, and of metalles of the erthe. 20 *Roummaker*, because with
warre he made roume: for he was a valyaunt warryer. 21 *Teacher:* Or (as some will) lawgeuer. *Was hyd there:* The Chald. interpre. was buryed there. 26 *There is none lyke etc.*; Why
Simeō is left oute there appeareth no cause, that is euydēt and
worthye to be beleued.

L. M. N. 20 Den segen Gad, hat der konig Iehu aufgericht
4 reg. x. da er Baal vertilget vnd das volck wider zu recht bracht
vnd schlug zween konige todt dazu auch Isabel.

27 glorie is in the cloudes, that is the dwellinge place of God from the begynnynge and from vnder the armes of the worlde: he hath caſt out thine enemies before
28 the and ſayed: deſtroye. And Iſrael ſhall dwell in ſaffetye alone. And the eyes of Iacob ſhall loke appon a londe of corne and wyne, moreouer his heauen ſhall
29 droppe with dewe. Happye art thou Iſrael, who is like vnto the? A people that art ſaued by the Lorde thy ſhilde and helper and ſwerde of thi glorye. And thyne enemyes ſhall hyde them ſelues from the, and thou ſhalt walke vppon their hye hilles.

The .XXXIIII. Chapter

1 AND Moſes went frō the feldes of Moab vpp in to mount Nebo which is the [Fo. LXIII.] toppe of Piſga, that is ouer agenſt Iericho. *M.C.S. Moſes dyeth. Iſraell wepeth. Ioſua ſuccedeth in Moſes roume.*

And the Lorde ſhewed him all the londe off Gilead
2 euen vnto Dan, and all nephtali and the londe of Ephraim and Manaſſe, ād all the londe of Iuda: euen vnto
3 the vtmoſt ſee, ād the ſouth and the region of the playne
4 of Iericho the citye of datetrees euen vnto Zoar. And the Lorde ſayed vnto him. This is the londe which I ſware vnto Abraham, Iſaac and Iacob ſayenge: I will geue it vnto thy ſeed. I haue ſhewed it the before thyne eyes: but thou ſhalt not goo ouer thither.
5 So Moſes the ſeruaunte of the Lorde dyed there in the londe of Moab at the commaundment of the Lorde.
6 And he buryed him in a valey in the londe of Moab

M. 1 Galaad 3 paulmetrees
V. 27 habitaculum eius ſurſum, & ſubter brachia ſempiterna 29 negabunt te. xxxiiii, 3 Segor. 4 Vidiſti eam oculis tuis
L. 27 wonung Gottis von anfang 29 Deyne ſeynde werden verſchmachten. xxxiiii, 3 Zoar 4 Du haſt es mit deynen augen geſehen

M. M. N. 28 *In ſafety alone:* loke Numeri. xxiii, b. vpō this worde to dwell by him ſelfe.

besyde Beeth Peor: but no man wyst of his sepulchre
7 vnto this daye. And Moses was an hundred an
xx. yere olde when he dyed, ād yet his eyes were
8 not dym nor his chekes abated. And the childern
of Israel wepte for Moses in the feldes off Moab .xxx.
dayes. And the dayes off wepynge and mornynge for
Moses were ended.

9 And Iosua the sonne of Nun was full of the spirite of
wisdome: for Moses had put his hande vppon him. And
all the childern of Israel herkened vnto him and dyd
10 as the Lorde .P. cōmaunded Moses. But there arose
not a prophett sense in Israel lyke vnto Moses, whom
11 the Lorde knewe face to face, in all the miracles and
wonders which the Lorde sent him
    to doo in the londe of Egipte vnto Pharao
    and all his seruauntes and vnto all his
12   londe: and in all the myghtye dea-
      des and greate tereble thin-
        ges which Moses dyd
          in the sight of
            all Isra-
              el

⁌ The ende of the fifth boke of Moses.

Avims, A kinde of geauntes, and the worde signifieth crooked vnright or weked.

Belial weked or wekednesse, he that hath cast the
yoke of God of his necke ād will not obeye god.

Bruterar, prophesiers or sothsayers.

Emims, a kinde of geaūtes so called be cause they
were tereble and cruell for emin signifieth tereblenesse.

Enack, a kinde of geauntes, so called happlye be-

V. 6 Moab contra Phogor 7 non caligauit oculus eus, nec
dentes illius moti sunt. 8 dies planctus lugentium 11 quæ misit
per eum ... terræ illius, 12 & cunctam manum robustam

L. 6 gegen dem hause Peor 7 seyne augen waren nicht
tunckel worden vnd seyne wangen waren nicht verfallen 8 die
tag des weynens vnd klagens 12 zu aller diser mechtiger hand
vnd grossen gesichten

caufe they ware cheynes aboute their neckes, for enack fignifieth foch a cheyne as men weer aboute their neckes.

.P. [*Recto.* No numeral]. Horims, A kinde of geauntes, ād fignifieth noble, becaufe that of pride they called thē felues nobles or gentles.

Rocke, God is called a rocke, becaufe both he ād his worde lafteth euer.

Whett thē on thy childern, that is exercyfe thy childern in thē ād put them in vre.

Zamzumims, a kinde of geaūtes, ād fignifieth myfcheuous or that be all waye imaginīge.